Exchange-Traded Funds

Exchange-Traded Funds

Conceptual and Practical Investment Approaches

Edited by A. Seddik Meziani

Published by Risk Books, a Division of Incisive Financial Publishing Ltd

Haymarket House
28–29 Haymarket
London SW1Y 4RX
Tel: +44 (0)207 484 9700
Fax: +44 (0)207 484 9797
E-mail: books@incisivemedia.com
Sites: www.riskbooks.com
www.incisivemedia.com

ISBN 978 1 906348 23 6

British Library Cataloguing in Publication Data
A catalogue record for this book is available from the British Library

Publisher: Nick Carver
Managing Editor: Jennifer Gibb
Designer: Lisa Ling

Typeset by Sunrise Setting Ltd, Torquay, UK

Printed and bound in the UK by PrintonDemand-Worldwide

Contents

List of Figures ix

List of Tables xiii

About the Editor xvii

About the Authors xix

Preface xxxiii

Acknowledgements xxxv

1 **Indexes and Indexing** 1
John A. Prestbo
Dow Jones

2 **Conceptual Approaches to Indexes for Exchange-Traded Funds** 13
David M. Blitzer
Standard & Poor's

3 **Alternatives to Cap-Weighted ETFs** 25
John M. West, Robert D. Arnott
Research Affiliates, LLC

4 **Mapping the ETF Universe** 43
Richard A. Ferri
Portfolio Solutions, LLC

5 **Legal and Regulatory Issues Related to ETFs and Certain Other Exchange-Traded Instruments** 85
Kathleen H. Moriarty
Katten Muchin Rosenman LLP

6 **Understanding ETF Structures Important in Building Portfolios** 127
Gus Sauter
Vanguard

7 **Finding the Right ETF for the Investor** 143
Greg Friedman
Barclays Global Investors

8 **ETFs: The More Efficient Way to Track an Index** 159
Thorsten Michalik, Manooj Mistry
Deutsche Bank

9 **ETF Strategies** 181
Robert Holderith
Emerging Global Advisors, LLC

10 **Creating an All-ETF Portfolio** 193
Richard D. Romey
ETF Portfolio Solutions

11 **Exchange-Traded Funds and Tactical Asset Allocation** 215
Michael E. Kitces, Kenneth R. Solow
Pinnacle Advisory Group

12 **Option Strategies Using ETFs** 239
A. Seddik Meziani
Montclair State University

13 **The Present and Future ETF Bond Market** 271
James Ross
State Street Global Advisors

14 **Sector Investment through ETFs** 303
Jane Li
FundQuest Incorporated

15 **Real Estate Investment Trust ETFs** 333
Brad Case
NAREIT

16 **Commodity ETFs** 353
John T. Hyland
United States Commodity Funds LLC

17 **Trading Strategies Using Currencies and Currency-Based Exchange Products** 401
Kevin Rich
Deutsche Bank

18 **International Equity ETFs** 427
Kirk Kinder
Picket Fence Financial

19 **Building Diversified Global Portfolios with Exchange-Traded Funds** 475
Richard A. Ciuba, Lisa Meyer, John Prestbo
Dow Jones Indexes

20 **Exchange-Traded Funds in the Middle East: Opportunities and Challenges in the GCC Countries** 495
Sulaiman T. Al-Abduljader; Imad A. Moosa
Coast Investment and Development Co, KSC;
Monash University

21 **401(k) Plans: The Unconquered Frontier for ETFs** **521**
Kevin D. Mahn
Hennion & Walsh Asset Management

22 **Use of ETFs in Managed Accounts** **539**
Ron Pruitt
Placemark Investments

23 **Accident and Genius: What History Tells Us About the Future of ETFs** **557**
Albert S. Neubert
Information Management Network

24 **Trends and Future of ETFs** **567**
Michael Jabara
Citigroup Investment Research

Index **595**

List of Figures

2.1	The equity ETF family tree	15
3.1	RAFI returns in different environments	33
3.2	RAFI US Large versus S&P 500: rolling five-year return (1967–2007)	34
3.3	Tracking error of RAFI and S&P 500	38
4.1	Index strategy map	51
4.2	Passive security selection	54
4.3	Russell 3000 index family	56
4.4	S&P 500 industry sector weights	57
4.5	Passive security selection	58
4.6	Screened index security selection	59
4.7	Quantitative security selection	62
4.8	Quantitative index security selection	63
4.9	Capitalisation weighting	67
4.10	Fundamental weighting	71
4.11	Fixed weight	75
4.12	Strategy cost comparison by index strategy box	79
4.13	iShares S&P 500 Index (IVV) index strategy box	80
4.14	WisdomTree US Large Cap Dividend (DLN) index strategy box	81
4.15	PowerShares Dynamic Large Cap Value Portfolio (PJF) index strategy box	82
7.1	Constructing methodology	149
7.2	Small-cap index performance comparison	150
7.3	Total-cost comparison for large-cap ETFs	153
7.4	Some ETFs deliver price efficiency through tighter spreads	154
7.5	Price efficiency of ETFs	155
8.1	ETF market growth, Europe	160
8.2	MSCI World ETF NAV vs. net TR index	161
8.3	Tracking error: MSCI World ETF NAV vs. net TR index (in basis points)	162
8.4	Synthetic replication-based ETF vs. traditional ETF	162
8.5	Tracking error of 10 future baskets (MSCI World), in %	163
8.6	Divergence of performance of traditional ETFs	167
8.7	Traditional ETF, tracking error (in basis points, 60-day)	167
8.8	Synthetic replication-based ETF vs. traditional ETFs (EURO STOXX 50, relative performance)	168
8.9	Creation/redemption process, traditional ETF	169

8.10	Creation/redemption process, synthetic replication ETF	170
8.11	Swap details	171
8.12	EURO STOXX 50 ETF relative performance	172
8.13	Exchange trading	175
8.14	Market price and OTC offer	175
8.15	Efficient index tracking	177
9.1	Traditional asset allocation	189
9.2	Neo asset allocation	189
9.3	Core and satellite	190
9.4	Bollinger Bands	191
9.5	Variable long short – example is net long	191
9.6	Market-neutral	192
9.7	Income portfolio	192
10.1	ETF market share growth accelerates	195
10.2	ETFs experience rapid growth	196
10.3	The cost of investment advice	197
10.4	Risk and return associated with changing asset-allocation mix	201
10.5	Asset classes	202
10.6	Risk-and-return characteristics of two different asset allocations	203
10.7	Strategic asset-allocation models	203
10.8	US dollar losses based on percentage losses	204
10.9	Example of some of the available equity ETFs by asset class	207
10.10	Example of multiple ETFs tracking the same underlying index	208
10.11	Questions to consider before managing your own portfolio	211
10.12	Questions to ask a potential financial adviser	212
11.1	Strategic portfolio	224
11.2	Tactical portfolio	224
12.1	Payoff and profit to call holder	247
12.2	Payoff and profit to call writer	251
12.3	Payoff and profit to put holder	252
12.4	Payoff and profit to put seller	253
12.5	Protective put	256
12.6	Covered call	257
12.7	Value of a straddle at expiration	261
12.8	Value of a bullish spread at expiration	263
12.9	Bear call spread	265
12.10	Put bull spread	266
12.11	Put bear spread	266
12.12	Collar	268
13.1	Treasury yield curve	276

14.1	Sector weightings changes over one year	307
14.2	Sector weightings changes over 15 years	307
14.3	Efficient frontiers comparison	321
15.1	REITs are less likely to produce investment losses	340
15.2	Risk-adjusted performance and diversification power	341
15.3	Locations of 30,000 REIT-owned properties in the US	343
15.4	Asset-class returns in high-inflation and low-inflation environments	346
15.5	REIT returns cover high inflation rates more effectively than other assets	346
15.6	Risk-adjusted performance and diversification power	347
15.7	Asset allocations in Ibbotson's optimal forward-looking portfolios	348
15.8	REIT total returns during three market downturns	349
15.9	Total-return difference between equity REITs and S&P 500	350
15.10	REIT returns and underlying property values, 1989–1993	351
16.1	Backwardation	389
16.2	Contango	389
16.3	Seasonal commodities	390
16.4	Backwardation example A	391
16.5	Backwardation example B	391
16.6	Backwardation example C	392
16.7	Contango example	393
18.1	Equity portfolio Sharpe Ratio improvement for different levels of correlation (assumed 80/20 US/international allocation)	429
18.2	Equity returns of developed markets	430
18.3	World market cap and US market cap as percentage of world market cap 2004 – present	431
18.4	Annualised change in portfolio volatility when combining US and international equities	432
18.5	Active management versus benchmark	434
18.6	EAFE regional allocation 1970–2005	436
18.7	MSCI	443
18.8	FTSE investable index universe	447
20.1	Nominal GDP (US$000)	497
20.2	GCC real GDP (US$ million)	497
20.3	GCC aggregate stock market data	499
20.4	GCC market capitalisation/nominal GDP (2007)	499
20.5	GCC market capitalisation (allocation by country, July 28, 2008)	504
20.6	Performance of selected GCC stock markets	506

20.7 US, Europe and GCC market performance 507
20.8 Efficient frontier of global portfolios (January 2001–April 2006) 515

21.1 ETF assets (in US$ millions) – growth trend 522
21.2 Number of ETFs – growth trend 522
21.3 Lifecycle funds 526
21.4 Lifestyle funds 526

22.1 2008 Q1 Unified managed accounts assets (US$ billion) 550
22.2 Russell 1000 Index cap breakdown 554
22.3 Trailing returns (April 2003 to March 2008) 555

24.1 ETF assets and number of funds 568
24.2 2008 new fund breakdown 571
24.3 ETF rankings by assets at year-end 2008 576
24.4 ETF concentration at year-end 2008 577
24.5 ETF assets by fund sponsor at year-end 2008 580
24.6 Number of ETFs by fund sponsor as of year-end 2008 581

List of Tables

3.1	Performance of top 10 stocks by capitalisation	28
3.2	1962–2008 Fundamental Index performance	32
3.3	Global evidence for the Fundamental Index concept	35
3.4	RAFI in less efficient markets	36
3.5	Fundamental Index sector performance	39
4.1	Security selection categories and a sampling of strategies	53
4.2	Sampled security weighting categories and sampled strategies	67
6.1	Total-return performance of an open-end ETF versus a UIT ETF (for periods ended September 30, 2008)	131
6.2	Five-year annualised performance (NAV) of comparable ETFs through September 30, 2008 (sorted by capture ratio)	136
6.3	Comparison of the most common ETF structures	140
7.1	Average annual fees of traditional funds and ETFs	145
7.2	ETF portfolio strategies	147
7.3	Comparison of structures	157
8.1	MSCI World future-tracking	163
8.2	Tracking errors summary	164
8.3	Withholding taxes	165
8.4	Swap example	174
9.1	Exchange-traded funds product-development timeline, 1993–2008	182
9.2	ETFs as complementary portfolio components	186
9.3	ETFs as primary or exclusive portfolio components	188
11.1	20-year returns ending 1999–2005 (87 periods)	220
11.2	Ten S&P 500 sectors and how they fit in the market cycle	229
12.1	List of options on ETFs	240
12.2	Value at expiration of the call with exercise price at US$100.00	247
12.3	Protective put	254
12.4	Long straddle	260
13.1	Performance of 80/20 hypothetical portfolios	272
13.2	Periodic table of bond returns	278

13.3	Price plus coupon equals bond total return	280
13.4	Taxable bonds versus tax-exempt municipals	284
13.5	US ETFs as of September 2008	285
13.6	Long-term bond correlations	287
13.7	Average expense ratios of fixed-income investment vehicles	289
13.8	Long-term returns of bonds versus other major asset classes	290
13.9	Three-year returns and correlations for fixed-income assets	293
13.10	International inflation-linked bonds as US dollar hedge	295
13.11	Predicted out-of-pocket healthcare costs	297
14.1	Sector classification systems	305
14.2	Changes in sector weightings	308
14.3	Sector investment (as of June 30, 2008)	310
14.4	Number of sector ETFs in study (as of June 30, 2008)	311
14.5	Number of sector open-end funds in study (as of June 30, 2008)	311
14.6	Number of sector funds in study (as of June 30, 2008)	311
14.7	Assets of sector funds (million as of 30/06/2008)	312
14.8	Historical three-year real alpha (July 1, 1993–June 30, 2008)	315
14.9	Historical real alpha in bull and bear markets (July 1, 1993–June 30, 2008)	316
14.10	Active/passive recommendation based on real alpha	317
14.11	Historical three-year exotic beta (July 1, 1993–June 30, 2008)	318
14.12	Historical exotic beta in bull and bear markets (July 1, 1993–June 30, 2008)	318
14.13	Allocation recommendation based on exotic beta	319
14.14	Correlation coefficients between asset categories (data period: 01/07/1993–30/06/2008)	321
14.15	Performance comparison of four financials ETFs (performance as of June 30, 2008)	323
14.16	Industry weightings	324
14.17	Portfolio characteristics	325
14.18	Analysis inputs	328
15.1	Correlations among asset classes, styles, and sectors	335
15.2	Risk-adjusted returns of REITs and stock market indexes	339
16.1	ETF timeline	356
16.2	Major commodity indexes	357
16.3	Ten-year correlation matrix 1997–2007	373
16.4	Hypothetical diversified portfolio total returns including crude oil exposure (1998–2007)	375
17.1	US exchange traded products – directional currency pair exposure	409
17.2	US exchange traded products – directional broad US dollar exposure	410
17.3	US exchange traded products – carry strategies	423
17.4	US exchange traded products – currencies	424

17.5	South African exchange traded products – currencies	425
17.6	German exchange traded products – currencies	425
18.1	S&P 500/EAFE correlations, 1970–2007	428
18.2	S&P 500/international small-cap correlations 1970–2007	429
18.3	Average ETF and index fund expense ratios	435
18.4	Actively managed international fund performance versus EAFE performance	437
18.5	EAFE versus slice and dice allocations	437
18.6	FTSE regional review dates	439
18.7	FTSE index qualifications	440
18.8	FTSE market capitalisation inclusion percentages	441
18.9	Global Industry Classification System	442
18.10	Global market ETF statistics	450
18.11	Percentage holdings by country	451
18.12	Top 10 holdings	451
18.13	Percentage holdings by industry	452
18.14	Broad international ETF statistics	453
18.15	Percentage holdings by country	453
18.16	Top 10 holdings	454
18.17	Percentage holdings by industry	454
18.18	MSCI developed market countries	455
18.19	Developed-markets statistics	459
18.20	Percentage holdings by country	459
18.21	Top 10 holdings	460
18.22	Percentage holdings by industry	461
18.23	Emerging-markets statistics	463
18.24	Percentage holdings by country	463
18.25	Top 10 holdings	464
18.26	Percentage holdings by industry	465
18.27	International small-cap statistics	468
18.28	Percentage by country	468
18.29	Top 10 holdings	469
18.30	Percentage holdings by industry	470
18.31	International industry ETF	471
18.32	Country/regional ETF	472
20.1	GCC economic snapshot (2008)	498
20.2	Overview of GCC stock markets (July 28, 2008)	505
20.3	GCC trading volume (February 2008)	505
20.4	Derivatives in the GCC	509
20.5	Descriptive statistics of regional ETFs (July 31, 2008)	510
20.6	Price, volume and cost of regional ETFs (as of August 15, 2008)	511
20.7	Description of ETF underlying indexes	511
21.1	401(k) assets in mutual funds	527
21.2	IRA assets in mutual funds	528

21.3 Sample ETF and index-tracking mutual fund expense ratio comparisons 529
21.4 Sample ETF and index-tracking mutual fund historical performance comparisons 530
21.5 SmartGrowth mutual funds 534
21.6 Seligman TargetFunds 535
21.7 Federated Target ETF funds 536
21.8 Wellington ETF Allocation Fund 536

22.1 Potential losses generated as a percentage of original investment via ownership of funds versus individual securities 547

23.1 A historical record of exchange-traded index portfolios 558

24.1 ETF growth 569
24.2 Top 50 ETFs ranked by assets at year-end 2008 574
24.3 Shifts in ETFs by type 578

About the Editor

A. Seddik Meziani is a professor in the Department of Economics and Finance in the School of Business (SBUS) at Montclair State University (MSU). He has extensive corporate and consulting experience. Prior to joining the faculty of MSU, Seddik worked as a senior research analyst at both Standard & Poor's and TIAA-CREF. He received a PhD in managerial economics from Rensselaer Polytechnic Institute and an MBA in finance and international business from New York University.

His teaching and scholarship is focused in the area of finance. Seddik's primary field of expertise is in the area of exchange-traded Funds (ETFs) and other index-linked products. His previous publicatios include the book *Exchange-Traded Funds as an Investment Option* (2006) and numerous publications in both academic and practitioners' journals including in seven consecutive *Institutional Investor's Investment Guides on ETFs*.

Seddik has been invited to present his research and moderate panels at numerous conferences in the US and abroad. He recently delivered the keynote address at The 2008 Art of Indexing Summit in Washington DC and moderated roundtables of industry experts at both the 2008 Annual Super Bowl of Indexing in Phoenix, AZ and 2009 Annual Global ETF Awards. Seddik has developed and presented a series of seminars involving several of his research topics to various corporate and government clients; the most recent was for a professional seminar on ETFs in London, in November 2008.

He has also made numerous local appearances to talk about various aspects of the current financial crisis, including the Estate Planning Council of Bergen County, the Township of Montclair, and several presentations for the Capital One Bank Chairman's Club.

In 2006, Seddik was awarded a lifetime membership in Beta Gamma Sigma for outstanding achievements. In 2009, he was nominated to be the SBUS faculty inductee to Phi Kappa Phi, the University Honor Society.

About the Authors

Sulaiman T. Al-Abduljader is vice president of Coast Investment and Development Company where he served as a financial consultant before heading a group of three departments, investment services, corporate finance and business development. Sulaiman is involved in the investment advisory and strategic asset allocation of Coast's portfolios and funds in excess of US$3 billion. He led various innovative projects including the development of the FTSE Coast Kuwait 40 Index, the launch of the first GCC exchange traded fund listed in the London stock exchange, the first retail capital guaranteed fund with regional exposure and the first leveraged portfolio in the region. Prior to joining Coast, Sulaiman was an instructor of finance and real estate at Gulf University for Science and Technology, and a real estate consultant for KPMG-Kuwait. He also served as a financial consultant to various local and regional shareholding companies and stock exchanges.

Robert D. Arnott is chairman of Research Affiliates. Over his 25-year career, Robert has endeavoured to bridge two disparate worlds; the theoretical academy and the practical marketplace. His success in doing so has resulted in a reputation as one of the world's most provocative and respected financial analysts. Several unconventional portfolio strategies now in wide application figure among Rob's pioneering innovations: tactical asset allocation, global tactical asset allocation, tax-advantaged equity management, and the Fundamental Index approach to indexation, among others. An intrepid entrepreneur, Rob started up and managed two important asset management firms before founding Research Affiliates. In 2002, he established Research Affiliates as a research intensive asset management firm that focuses on innovative products that add value for the global investment community. Innovations are constantly pursued, as the firm explores novel approaches to active asset allocation, optimal portfolio construction, and innovative indexation.

A widely published financial thinker, Rob has been a frequent contributor to leading financial journals and books. He has published more than 100 refereed journal articles in the *Financial Analysts Journal*, the *Journal of Portfolio Management* and the *Harvard Business Review*, to name a few. He served as editor in chief at the *Financial Analysts Journal* from 2002 through 2006, and on their advisory council for several years after he stepped down as editor in chief. In recognition of his achievements as a financial writer, Rob has received five Graham and Dodd Scrolls, awarded annually by the CFA Institute for best articles of the year. He has received two Bernstein-Fabozzi/Jacobs-Levy awards from the *Journal of Portfolio Management* and *Institutional Investor* magazine. Rob lectures frequently, has served as a visiting professor at UCLA, and has served on the product advisory board of the Chicago Board Options Exchange and two other exchanges.

Rob is the former chairman of First Quadrant, LP, where he developed quantitative asset management products. He also served as global equity strategist at Salomon Brothers (now part of Citigroup), the president of TSA Capital Management (now part of Analytic), and as a vice president at The Boston Company (now PanAgora). Rob graduated *summa cum laude* from the University of California, Santa Barbara in 1977 in economics, applied mathematics and computer science. He is the author of *The Fundamental Index® – A Better Way to Invest* (2008).

David M. Blitzer is a managing director and the chairman of the S&P Index Committee with overall responsibility for security selection for S&P's indexes and index analysis and management. Prior to becoming chairman David was chief economist for Standard & Poor's. Before joining Standard & Poor's, he was corporate economist at The McGraw-Hill Companies, S&P's parent corporation. Prior to that, he was a senior economic analyst with National Economic Research Associates, Inc. and did consulting work for various government and private sector agencies including the New Jersey Department of Environmental Protection, the National Commission on Materials Policy, and Natural Resources Defense Council.

David is the author of *Outpacing the Pros: Using Indices to Beat Wall Street's Savviest Money Managers*, (2001) and *What's the Economy Trying to Tell You? Everyone's Guide to Understanding and Profiting from the Economy*, (1997). In the year 2000, he was ranked seventh on *SmartMoney* magazine's distinguished list of "the 30 most influential people in the world of investing, and in the year 1998, David was named the nation's top economist, receiving the Blue Chip Economic Forecasting Award for most accurately predicting the country's leading economic indicators for four years in a row. A well known speaker at investing and indexing conferences, David is often quoted in the US business press, including the *New York Times, Wall Street Journal, USA Today* and various financial and industry publications. He is also frequently heard on US television and radio.

A graduate of Cornell University with a BS in engineering, David received his MA in economics from the George Washington University and his PhD in economics from Columbia University.

Brad Case is vice president, Research and Industry Association for the National Association of Real Estate Investment Trusts, a non-profit organisation based in Washington, DC. Formerly on the staff of the Federal Reserve Board of Governors, he holds a PhD in economics from Yale University, where his doctoral dissertation focused on international diversification in real estate investments. He has studied residential and commercial real estate for more than 20 years, and is a Level II candidate in the Chartered Financial Analyst (CFA) programme.

Richard A. Ciuba is senior director, Americas Sales of Dow Jones Indexes, a unit of Dow Jones & Company. Richard joined Dow Jones Indexes in 1997 just after Dow Jones began commercialising its long-standing indexes such as the Dow Jones Industrial Average. His responsibilities include business development, promotion and sales of the Dow Jones index family to the investment community throughout the US, Canada and Latin America. Richard's focus is on the sales and development of new index ideas to be used as the basis of exchange traded funds and derivatives, as well as structured, insurance and other financial products. His current research and professional interests focus on the inter-relationship among sectors and portfolio performance optimisation. Richard holds a BS in finance and economics from Drexel University and is currently pursuing advanced studies. He, his wife and two children reside in central New Jersey.

Richard A. Ferri is CEO of Portfolio Solutions, LLC, an investment management firm based in Troy, MI. Portfolio Solutions manages over

US$700 million in separate accounts for high-net-worth individuals, families, non-profit organisations, and corporate pension plans. The firm specialises in a low-cost, tax-efficient, asset allocation investment approach to building wealth. Rick has written five books on asset allocation, index funds and ETFs. His latest book, *The ETF Book* was recently published. He is also author of *Serious Money, Straight Talk about Investing for Retirement, All About Index Funds 2nd Edition, Protecting Your Wealth in Good Times and Bad* and *All About Asset Allocation*. Rick earned a Bachelor of Science degree in business administration from the University of Rhode Island and a Master of Science degree in finance from Walsh College. He also holds the designation of Chartered Financial Analyst (CFA). Prior to joining the investment community in 1988, Rick served as an officer and jet pilot in the US Marine Corps and is now retired from the Marine Corps Reserve.

Greg Friedman is head of global iShares relationships and has been with Barclays Global Investors for 15 years. Greg is responsible for the relationships with the broker-dealers, exchanges, index providers and specialists. Prior to his current job, Greg was head of product management for all the iShares listed in the US. Prior to his iShares work, Greg was the senior portfolio manager for the WEBS product, within the International Portfolio Management team. Greg received his BA from the University of California at Davis, and attended Golden Gate University School of Law.

Robert Holderith is founder and CEO of Emerging Global Advisors, a newly formed emerging markets research and ETF firm. Prior to founding EGA, he was managing director, institutional sales and investment analytics at ProShare Advisors. Before joining ProShare Advisors in 2006, Robert led a variety of product, asset management and senior sales initiatives for UBS Wealth management. As programme manager for UBS' discretionary asset management programmes, he was responsible for developing three equity model portfolios, a unique security screening system and a portfolio management trading system. In addition, Robert helped develop the firm's first ETF models and an advisory ETF Portfolio Management platform. He has been using ETF products, modelling ETF portfolios and has developed numerous ETF-based investment solutions since 2000. He is well known as an early adopter in this segment of the financial services industry.

John T. Hyland is the chief investment office of the United States Commodity Funds LLC, a US-based sponsor of commodity-based exchange traded securities. John has over 20 years of experience in the investment management profession, primarily in areas involving alternative investment categories and the development of new investment vehicles. He has been awarded Chartered Financial Analyst (CFA) designation and is a former president of the Security Analysts of San Francisco Society. John is a graduate of the University of California, Berkeley.

Michael Jabara is an associate analyst in the ETF and Closed-End Fund Research Group at Citigroup Global Markets Inc. Michael has been at Citigroup since 2005. Prior to Citigroup, he was an associate analyst for Prudential Securities Inc. Michael graduated from Villanova University and currently resides in New York City.

Kirk Kinder, CFP is the founder of Picket Fence Financial, LLC, a fee-only wealth management firm. Picket Fence Financial specialises in building portfolios exclusively with exchange traded funds. Kirk speaks frequently at industry conferences on the use of exchange traded funds, and he is a contributor to *ETFGuide.com* and the *Motley Fool*. Kirk graduated from the Coast Guard Academy in New London, Connnecticut.

Michael E. Kitces is the director of financial planning for Pinnacle Advisory Group, a private wealth management firm located in Columbia, Maryland that oversees approximately US$600 million of client assets. In addition, he is the publisher of the e-newsletter *The Kitces Report* and the blog *Nerd's Eye View* through his website kitces.com, dedicated to advancing knowledge in financial planning. Beyond his website, Michael is an active writer and editor across the industry and has been featured in publications including *Financial Planning*, the *Journal of Financial Planning*, *Journal of Retirement Planning*, *Practical Tax Strategies*, and *Leimberg Information Services*, as well as *The Wall Street Journal*, *BusinessWeek*, *CNBC PowerLunch*, *NBC Nightly News*, and more. In addition, Michael is a co-author with John Olsen of *The Annuity Advisor*, the first balanced and objective book on annuities written for attorneys, accountants, and financial planners, and is also a co-author of *Tools & Techniques of Retirement Income Planning* with Steve Leimberg and others.

Michael was recognised as one of only five financial planning practitioner "Movers and Shakers" for 2006 by *Financial Planning* magazine, and was recognised as one of 20 "Rising Stars in Wealth Management" by *Institutional Investor News* for 2007. These awards were presented to honour Michael's active work in the financial planning community, serving as a member of the Editorial Review Board for the *Journal of Financial Planning*, a moderator for the discussion boards on *Financial-Planning.com*, a commentator on annuity, retirement distribution, and retirement planning issues for *Leimberg Information Services, Inc*, and for his work as an active member of the Financial Planning Association at the local and National level. Michael is also a co-founder of NexGen, a community of the next generation of financial planners that aims to ensure the transference of wisdom, tradition, and integrity, from the pioneers of financial planning to the next generation of the profession.

Jingying (Jane) Li is manager of FundQuest's investment management and research team and a member of the Investment Committee. She joined the firm in 2000, and is the portfolio manager for the FundQuest Large Core Equity separate account strategy. She also performs research on mutual funds, exchange traded funds and alternative investments. Jane produces quantitative research studies for FundQuest and has published several white papers featuring her analysis. Previously, Jane was a financial services representative for MetLife Financial Services (1999). Prior to this, she was a credit analyst and portfolio manager for the Agricultural Bank of China (1992–1997). Jane has 13 years of industry and investment management experience. She received her BA in economics from Fudan University, an MA in economics from the University of New Hampshire, and a MS in finance from the Boston College Carroll School of Management. Jane is a Chartered Financial Analyst (CFA) charterholder.

Kevin D. Mahn joined Parsippany, NJ based Hennion & Walsh as a managing director in 2004. Serving as its chief investment officer, Kevin is responsible for the asset management activities of the firm.

He also serves as the portfolio manager for the SmartGrowth family of mutual funds and directs the creation and supervision of the various portfolios within the SmartTrust series of unit investment trusts. Additionally, Kevin is the author of the quarterly ETF Insights newsletter. Prior to Hennion & Walsh, Kevin was a senior vice president at Lehman Brothers where he held the positions of CAO of the high net worth product and services group as well as COO of Lehman Brothers Bank.

Kevin received his Bachelor's degree in business administration from Muhlenberg College and his MBA in finance from Fairleigh Dickinson University. He has also served as an adjunct professor at Fairleigh Dickinson University within the department of economics, finance and international business. Interviews with, as well as byline articles and insights from Kevin have appeared in/on CBS News, CNBC, Fox Business News, *Investor's Business Daily, Investment Advisor Magazine*, SmartMoney, *The Star-Ledger, The Daily Record, Reuters, Fund Action, The Street.com, Fox Business.com, Dow Jones MarketWatch, Ignites, Ticker Magazine, Money Management Executive, The Wall Street Transcript, Wall Street Reporter, Commerce Magazine* and *Investment News.*

Lisa Meyer is senior manager of business development at Dow Jones Indexes. She has authored numerous articles about the financial services, technology, media and healthcare industries. Lisa has made several television and radio appearances on news talk shows, as well as participated in conference presentations and panel discussions. She has a background in product development and journalism in the financial services industry. She has a Bachelor of Arts in English literature from Princeton University and a Master of business administration, international business and marketing research from Baruch College, Zicklin School of Business. Lisa also holds the Chartered Alternative Investment Analyst designation.

Thorsten Michalik graduated from the polytechnic in Constance with a degree in business and management administration. He started his career with a Swiss Bank in Zurich, as a trader for foreign exchange warrants, and later moved to the marketing of warrants and certificates in Germany. He joined Deutsche Bank in 2000, structuring and marketing equity derivatives, and in 2001 became responsible for marketing and press relations for warrants and certificates in Germany. He moved to Asia in 2004 and ran the warrants and certificate business for Deutsche Bank out of Hong Kong. Since mid-2006, Thorsten has been the head of db x-trackers, Deutsche Bank exchange traded funds business.

Manooj Mistry joined Deutsche Bank in May 2006 and is head of ETF structuring at db x-trackers, Deutsche Bank's exchange traded funds. Prior to Deutsche Bank, Manooj was with Merrill Lynch International in London where he was responsible for the development of the LDRS ETFs, the first ETFs to be launched in Europe and also worked on fund vehicles for the issuance of structured products. Manooj graduated in economics and business finance from Brunel University.

Imad A. Moosa is currently a professor of finance at Monash University, Melbourne. Before becoming an academic in 1991, he was an investment banker and a professional economist, and in that capacity he advised on currency strategies and indulged in exchange rate forecasting. Since becoming an academic, he has published some 150 articles and nine books. He has served in a number of advisory positions, including his role as an economic advisor to the US Treasury on issues related to the reconstruction of the monetary sector in Iraq.

Kathleen H. Moriarty concentrates her practice in financial services matters. She has extensive experience in the establishment and representation of exchange-traded investment companies (ETFs) and was instrumental in the early development of the structure, creation and registration of SPDRs. She has also advised clients on the establishment of various other US ETFs, including iShares, VIPERS, ProShares, and WisdomTree. Kathleen has been actively involved with ETF projects globally, including assisting the Stock Exchange of Hong Kong with the structure and creation of the Hong Kong Tracker Fund and representing the American Stock Exchange and NYSE Arca in connection with the cross-listing of DIAMONDS on the Singapore Exchange and Euronext N.V. She regularly advises foreign entities and delegations from both public and private sectors with respect to the regulation and operation of US ETFs.

Kathleen has also represented a variety of market participants in connection with the creation, structuring and development of other derivative securities and non-investment company exchange traded vehicles (ETVs), such as the SPDR Gold Trust. In addition, she represents and counsels broker-dealers and other institutional market participants in connection with trading issues and other securities laws matters relating to the purchase and sale of ETF and ETV shares. She also represents domestic and foreign ETF managers in connection with the licensing of financial indexes, such as Finans Portfoy Yonetimi A.S. in connection with the Dow Jones Istanbul 20, as well index providers licensing their financial products to ETFs.

Kathleen received her BA from Smith College in 1975 and her JD from the University of Notre Dame Law School in 1980. She is admitted to practice in New York. She is a member of the ABA Federal Regulation of Securities Subcommittee on Investment Companies and Investment Advisors and the Regulation of Futures and Derivative Instruments Committee.

Kathleen was named a New York Super Lawyer in 2007 and 2006 and received an honourable mention for her contribution to the Exchange Traded Funds sector at the Capital Link Third Annual Close-End Fund and ETF IR Awards. She sits on the editorial board of the *Journal of Indexes*. She is a frequent speaker, has published and appeared on national television on the topic of ETFs and ETVs.

Albert S. Neubert currently works for Information Management Network organising the indexing and exchange-traded funds conferences. He is also the executive director for the Index Business Association, the trade group for the index, indexing and index products marketplace. Albert is one of the world's leading consultants in the index business field where he develops new indexes, index-linked products, marketing and sales campaigns, business development programmes and event planning for clients. Prior to his consulting activities, he was senior director for global marketing and business development at Dow Jones Indexes and STOXX. Before his assignment with Dow Jones, he was responsible for the S&P Indexes global business development at Standard & Poor's Financial Information Services, a division of the McGraw-Hill Companies. At S&P Albert managed the S&P 500 and led the development of the S&P MidCap 400, S&P SmallCap 600 and SuperComposite 1500 Indexes. He was also involved in the creation of the S&P/BARRA Growth and Value Index series.

Albert has authored articles on index-related topics for publication in financial periodicals and books, including "Professional Perspectives on Indexing," "Indexing for Maximum Investment Results" and "Index Design and Implications for Index Tracking." He is also a frequent speaker at industry conferences and seminars. Albert holds a BA in finance from Pace University and an MBA from New York University.

John Prestbo is editor and executive director of the Dow Jones Global Indexes and is responsible for the development of new indexes for Dow Jones & Company. Since joining *The Wall Street Journal* in 1964 as a reporter in the Chicago bureau, John has held various positions including commodity news editor in New York and assistant managing editor and bureau chief in Cleveland. He was appointed vice president and editorial director of Dow Jones Radio 2 in 1981. John returned to the *Journal* as markets editor in 1983. He worked on the January 1993 launch of the Dow Jones World Stock Index and in April 1993 became its editor. In July 1996 the World Stock Index Group was renamed Dow Jones Indexes.

John has co-authored numerous books, including *News and the Market, Barron's Guide to Making Investment Decisions* and *The Wall Street Journal Book of International Investing*. In 1999 he edited *The Market's Measure*, an illustrated history of America told through the Dow Jones Industrial Average. John earned Bachelor's and Master's degrees from Northwestern University.

Ron Pruitt co-founded Placemark Investments and serves as chief investment officer. He is the architect of Placemark's overlay management philosophy, oversees the integration and ongoing interaction with sub-advisors and serves as chair of the Investment Committee overseeing the portfolio management team. Ron has been a guest speaker on numerous industry conferences speaking on topics of tax, wealth and overlay management and has published articles in *Investment Advisor* and *Senior Consultant* as well as contributions to *CFA magazine*, Financial Planning's *SMA Advisor* and *Financial Advisor magazine*.

After five years of distinguished military service, Ron led the implementation of Six Sigma initiatives within a business unit of General Electric, where he also taught the Six Sigma process.

A graduate of the United States Military Academy at West Point, Ron was a Kozmetsky scholar at the University of Texas at Austin's Graduate School of Business where he received his MBA. Ron is a CFA charterholder.

Kevin Rich is a managing director in the Global Markets Investment Products Group at Deutsche Bank and chief executive officer of DB Commodity Services LLC, which is the managing owner of several PowerShares DB commodity and currency based ETFs. He is responsible for providing currency and commodity-based investor solutions to the Deutsche Bank sales force in the Americas. Kevin holds a BS in business administration from Taylor University in Upland, Indiana and an MBA in finance from the New York University Leonard N. Stern School of Business.

Richard D. Romey is president and founder of ETF Portfolio Solutions, a fee-based investment advisory firm specialising in ETF portfolio management. Richard is the author of *Strategic Index Investing – Unlocking the Power of Exchange-Traded Index Funds*, one of the first books published on exchange-traded funds. He writes a quarterly newsletter that focuses on ETF investment strategies. Richard is a 1985 graduate of the University of Missouri-Columbia with a BSBA. He has over 22 years of experience in the investment management industry. Richard is a nationally recognised expert on exchange traded funds and ETF-based portfolio management. He is a frequent guest on financial radio and television programmes and is often quoted in financial publications. He has had numerous articles published regarding ETFs and ETF investment strategies and is a regular contributor to some of the most respected investment web sites on the internet.

Richard founded ETF Portfolio Solutions to offer investors an alternative to mutual fund-based portfolios and packaged financial products. His straight-forward and transparent approach to investing is designed to help investors achieve their goals and avoid the costly mistakes often associated with traditional mutual funds.

James Ross is a senior managing director of SSgA and president of SSgA Funds Management, Inc. He is responsible for product development, marketing and product management of all of SSgA's investment strategies offered through financial intermediaries. Prior to this role, James was responsible for the global product development of exchange traded funds. James also has extensive experience at both SSgA and State Street in all aspects of fund administration, fund accounting and custody services. Prior to joining State Street in 1992, he was employed by Ernst & Young as a senior accountant, responsible for auditing investment companies and insurance companies. James holds a Bachelor degree in accountancy from Bentley College and has passed the Certified Public Accountant exam in Massachusetts.

George U. "Gus" Sauter is the chief investment officer and a managing director of Vanguard. As chief investment officer, he is responsible for the oversight of more than US$900 billion managed by Vanguard fixed income and quantitative equity groups. The funds managed by these two investment groups include active quantitative equity funds, equity index funds, active bond funds, index bond funds, money market funds, and stable value funds. Gus is a member of the Council on the Graduate School of Business of the University of Chicago, the advisory board of the Journal of Investment Management Conference Series, and the *Journal of Indexes* Editorial Board. He is a past member of the equity markets committee of the Investment Company Institute, Institutional Traders Advisory Committee of the New York Stock Exchange, and the Nasdaq Quality of Markets Committee. Gus also has served on the trading committee of the Securities Industry Association and the AIMR Best Execution Task Force.

Gus joined Vanguard in 1987. Previously he was a trust investment officer with The First National Bank of Ohio. He received his BA in economics from Dartmouth College and an MBA in finance from The University of Chicago.

Kenneth R. Solow is a founding principal and the chief investment officer of Pinnacle Advisory Group, Inc, serving more than 500 families in the US and six countries, with more than US$600 million in assets under management. Offering creative financial solutions to individuals, business owners, and professionals since 1984, Kenneth currently directs the Research and Tactical Investment Policy for Pinnacle, and is a recognised speaker and author on active portfolio management.

John M. West is director and product specialist at Research Affiliates LLC, responsible for external communication of the firm's investment strategies and portfolio management processes. In this role, he actively participates in quantitative analysis, product development, and co-authors the monthly research piece in RALLC's *Fundamentals* newsletter. Previously, John was vice president and senior consultant at Wurts & Associates, an institutional consultant on the West Coast. At Wurts, he managed the firm's overall research effort including the development of capital market assumptions, new asset class opinions, alternative investments, effective portfolio processes, and spending policies. John graduated from the University of Arizona with a BS degree in finance. He holds the Chartered Financial Analyst designation and is a member of the CFA Society of Los Angeles. He is also a co-author of *The Fundamental Index® – A Better Way to Invest (2008)* and currently serves on the University of Arizona Investment Committee.

Preface

"Learning is like rowing upstream: not to advance is to drop back."
Chinese Saying

Exchange-traded funds (ETFs) have certainly covered a lot of distance since State Street Global Investor launched the SPDR 500, the first ETF to hit the US market, in 1993. After a relatively slow start that lasted until the mid-1990s, they began a long period of outstanding growth, even through the current financial crisis deemed by many experts as the most wrenching since the Great Depression.

According to a recent research report from Barclays Global Investors, at the end of the first quarter of 2009, 690 exchange-traded funds were listed in the US alone, with roughly US$430 billion in assets under management and an average daily trading volume of US$84.9 billion. Globally, the same report notes 1,635 ETFs with assets of US$635 billion from 87 different providers, and 66 new ETFs launched in 2009 alone.

This upbeat information on ETFs is confirmed by another revealing research report, from Financial Research Corp of Boston (FRC), showing that advisors have been increasingly using ETFs in their clients' portfolios, rising from a mere 25% of the advisors polled in 2003 to an impressive 71% in 2008. ETFs are no longer the sole domain of institutional investors, but have become a mainstream investment tool for advisers and individual investors alike.

Although ETFs largely started as a passive investing tool, there is no denying that they also owe their meteoric rise to their increasingly wide use by hedge funds and multi-asset managers within active asset allocation strategies. Indeed, throughout the current (and on-going) financial crisis, asset allocation has become an even more important driver of returns for active managers. As such, those who did not want to lose momentum in the markets are using ETFs to participate in sector or regional rallies.

Other active managers are of the opinion that this is the right environment for identifying the winners of the next business cycle. Considering the current massive dispersion in performance within sectors; the obvious difficulties in sorting the wheat from the chaff; and the significant expenses associated with stock picking in an environment that has never been more focused on fees than now, we should not be surprised if ETFs, which provide diversification with low fees, are being considered a suitable tool by such managers. In these pre-packaged sector portfolios, if one stock goes down, having other stocks within the sector may balance out the losses.

Since 1993, ETFs have evolved in both quantity and complexity. They have developed from their core long-only passive investment mandate to a satellite active tactical allocation tool. The newer ETFs are increasingly complex, not only focusing on sectors and narrow sub-sectors of the market as previously noted, but also on regional exposures, non-equity asset classes, or enhanced directional plays. Some allow investors to expand and fine-tune a traditional asset allocation based on core equity exposure; others, such as leveraged or inverse ETFs, are used to improve portfolio risk-adjusted performance. As such, we must be aware that while ETFs may offer the market valuable investment opportunities, there are also distinct risks associated with these investments that need to be fully understood. "What are they?," "How can they be used?," and "What do we need to know to protect ourselves before we invest?" are only a few of the questions addressed within these pages.

To effectively explore the increasing complexity of ETFs, this volume opts for a multi-author approach. It incorporates the perspectives of practitioners on the challenges facing ETF investors, as well as their insights on building ETF portfolios using the latest investment trends and strategies. Never before have this many professional perspectives on ETFs been collected in one place; the diversity of expertise gathered here offers the reader an unparallel exposure to all aspects of ETF features and use and an invaluable reference guide.

Acknowledgments

One of the most important duties of an academic is to accept the responsibility of communicating knowledge to his or her colleagues whenever the opportunity presents itself. In this spirit, when Risk Books approached me about authoring my second book on ETFs, I did not hesitate to accept the challenge, although experience told me this would be a demanding and time-taxing endeavor.

When I set out to develop an outline of this projected work, I struggled with the question of whether to proceed as a sole author, as with my first book, or to expand its reach by involving other professionals in the project. My interactions with many great practitioners and financial theorists at numerous ETF conferences made the decision easier: I am convinced that readers of this book will profit from such a broad array of perspectives and insights from well-known experts. A compilation of authors with proven expertise can more readily do justice to these versatile and ever-expanding financial products: ETFs have become too big and too complex for one person to tackle.

I began by contacting a long list of practitioners, each an expert in his or her field, for their opinion on what a new book on ETFs should cover and to gauge their interest in contributing chapters. I was overwhelmed by the enthusiasm and interest shown for the project by virtually all those I approached. If it were twice its current length, this book still could not address every topic that was identified as important by all these experts: I have had to pick and choose and condense in a manner that is pedagogically sound. As such, any omission of important topics is my sole responsibility: all the credit goes to these contributors.

The result is an array of chapters covering the most important issues that bear upon the ETF industry; effectively dealing with new methods of ETF performance evaluation, portfolio allocation, and the risk and returns that are imperative in understanding correct selection and monitoring of ETFs. Emphasis has been placed on understanding the applicability of the results as well as theoretical developments in this field. We believe this volume offers a truly comprehensive presentation of critical issues specific to ETFs, and will be a valuable resource for institutional investors, pension fund managers, endowment funds, and high-net-worth individuals, as well as academics and students working with ETFs.

My thanks must go to each of the contributing authors, for finding the room in their hectic schedules to invest the time and energy required to produce such a significant contribution to the literature on ETFs. They have proved once more that they are the driving force behind the dynamic market for these financial instruments. I also thank my wife Jacqueline and our children Harris and Hanna, for their ongoing patience and support throughout this project.

A. Seddik Meziani, PhD.

1

Indexes and Indexing

John A. Prestbo

Dow Jones

There has been a virtual contagion of index-based investment products since the mid-1990s. Many of them are exchange-traded funds (ETFs), a vehicle that made its US debut in 1993. ETFs look like open-end mutual funds – both are portfolios of securities – but trade on exchanges in real time like a stock. There were 698 ETFs in the US at the end of 2008, with aggregate assets of US$497.1 billion. Also gaining popularity are structured products, which commonly are bonds with index links. These investment vehicles do not pay interest but deliver a return based on predefined criteria regarding the underlying index's performance at maturity – such as the index rising above or falling below a specified level when the bond reaches maturity. These newer models joined older vehicles such as unit investment trusts and closed-end funds that in many, but not all, cases are based on indexes.

What unleashed this munificence of passive investment products? The narrow answer is "Black Monday", the one-day stock market crash on October 19, 1987, when the Dow Jones Industrial Average plummeted 508 points, or 22.6%. The market recovered over the next several weeks; the Dow actually ended 1987 with a 2.26% gain over the year before. In early 1988, the Securities and Exchange Commission (SEC) suggested future crashes might be muted by the existence of a market-basket instrument that could absorb some of the shock on individual securities created by waves of computerised trading that caused much of the downward spiral on October 19. No such instrument existed at the time, but the SEC said that "the concept of basket trading warrants consideration".

The next day, Wall Street started to create a basket instrument. After some trial-and-error attempts, the first ETF emerged five years later. It was based on Standard & Poor's 500-stock index, which is what the SEC had in mind in the first place. Because of their unprecedented structure, each ETF required "exemptive relief" from certain security regulations, meaning that the SEC allowed them to skirt some of the usual rules. For the following decade the SEC granted that relief only to applications for ETFs that tracked indexes. As the 21st Century settled in, the SEC occasionally deviated from that requirement, first with ETFs for oil and gold, and in 2008 with actively managed ETFs. Still, the vast majority of ETFs coming to market today are index-based. The SEC, in effect, created an industry.

The broader answer is that investing has evolved from the arcane ritual of the few into the everyday necessity of the many. Several factors contributed to this change, of course. Two current drivers are the projected shortfall in social security funds and the spread of 401(k) retirement plans. These plans require individuals to choose investments for their "defined contribution" from employers. The most common vehicle in these plans is ordinary mutual funds rather than ETFs. But more and more people are carrying the idea of index-based investing from the workplace into their own portfolios. Institutional investors, too, have come to appreciate the utility of highly liquid ETFs as part of implementing and managing their overall actively administered strategies.

As the ETF bandwagon grew bigger and faster, however, the concepts of indexes and indexed investing morphed into something quite different from what they were when they started. The competitive need of ETF sponsors to offer something new and different spawned the creation of indexes that mimicked investment strategies or tracked infinitesimal segments of the stock market. Ironically, the result is that "indexing" as an investment strategy is now a fuzzier concept than before, or, conversely, a riskier foray into securities markets than many investors may realise.

Before we examine that statement more closely, it is important to understand the history of indexes and indexed investing. Only then can the changes wrought in the past decade be fully appreciated.

INDEXES

In the beginning was the Dow, and the Dow was of the market, and the Dow was the market.

The US stock market, that is.

When Charles Henry Dow conceived of picking a few stocks, adding up their closing prices each day and dividing by the number of stocks he had selected, the stock market was a shadowy, dangerous place of ill repute. Bonds were the choice of the investor class in the closing two decades of the 19th Century. These were securities backed by real assets – railway equipment, maybe, or factory buildings; something tangible that would have value if the borrower (the bond issuer) went belly up. The investor might lose the income stream of interest payments, but would have something real that could be sold to recoup the lost capital.

Stocks, by contrast, were shares of ownership in incorporated businesses. Holders of these shares stood last in line for any recompense if the business failed, and in most such instances they got nothing. Moreover, the stock market was routinely marauded upon by manipulators who stopped at nothing to wrest control of companies from their startled owners and to one-up each other. The more notorious of them were called the "robber barons". It was Wild West capitalism in its rawest, most aggressive form.

This predatory capitalism caught the eye of Charles Dow. As a newspaperman in Providence, Rhode Island, he had gone west to cover a silver rush in Leadville, Colorado. He was part of an expedition that included, and was paid for by, a group of East Coast financiers. Not only did the young reporter (he was 27) learn the mining business, but also he was introduced to the financial world, warts and all, by his travelling companions.

Shortly after that exciting experience ended, he decamped to Manhattan. In time, he joined a financial news service, where he subsequently hired his Rhode Island friend Edward Jones. There, they learned about the markets as well as the financial dealings of large banks, railways and other businesses of the day. In 1882, they set up their own firm, Dow Jones & Co, in the basement underneath a soda shop at 15 Wall Street. Messrs Dow and Jones enlisted the financial help of their frugal Pennsylvania Dutch friend and colleague, Charles Bergstresser, whose unmelodious name was kept off the shingle.

The first Dow Jones stock index came two years later. It consisted of 11 stocks, nine of them railways (which at the time were the biggest companies in the US). Almost immediately he heard complaints that his list was too short, so in 1886 he raised the number to 20 and in 1887 to 30. Each time, he added a stock or two of industrial companies.

This was the period when manufacturing and service companies were emerging from their small-scale, family-owned status to be combined into large, powerful corporations. The apogee of this trend occurred in 1901 with the formation of United States Steel Corp, welding together eight steel and iron makers into what was then the biggest company ever formed. But Charles Dow had been attentive to this development for at least a decade.

By 1896 he felt the industrial sector had expanded to the point that it could sustain its own index. He introduced the Dow Jones Industrial Average in the *Wall Street Journal* on May 26 of that year, and subsequently revamped his previous index into the Dow Jones Railroad Average (which became the Dow Jones Transportation Average in 1970). His early recognition of industrials as the 20th Century growth engine of the US economy is a legacy largely unappreciated nowadays.

That is how regularly published stock-market indexes made it into the world. They really were averages until 1928, when a divisor other than the number of stocks was used in computation. At that point they were true indexes, but the "Average" name had stuck by then. The name was known on Main Street, too, as general newspapers picked up the industrial average as a shorthand way of communicating what was happening on Wall Street – and it was more palatable to quote from another newspaper (the *Wall Street Journal*) than from a stockbroker or other player in the investment game. This practice became habit when Wall Street earned at least a mention in the general news each day; and habit became tradition by the time the post-World War II bull market galvanised the nation's attention. The Dow Jones Industrial Average became the indicator to cite if a news story was citing only one.

Chapter two of market indexes began during the Roaring Twenties. Standard Statistics Co – one of the parents of the modern-day Standard & Poor's – began estimating stock-price indexes in 1923 on a weekly basis, and calculated them backwards to 1918.

The "all stocks" index was a forerunner of the S&P 500, which was created in 1957. Besides tracking many more stocks than the Dow Jones Averages, Standard Statistics picked up on the contention of Irving Fisher, professor of economics at Yale University, that measuring price without also measuring quantity was a meaningless exercise and perhaps misleading to boot. Standard Statistics weighted the stocks in its indexes by market value, or market capitalisation, as it is known in the investment trade, which is the number of outstanding shares multiplied by the market price.

The Standard Statistics index gained favour in academia. The driving force was Alfred Cowles III, the tubercular scion of a publishing family who became interested in the market when he started helping manage family finances from his convalescence in Colorado Springs. His efforts were directed initially towards finding consistently good market prognosticators; he could not, and eventually stopped trying.

In 1932, he founded the Cowles Commission for Research in Economics (which still exists today as the Cowles Foundation at Yale University, Cowles's alma mater), one of whose goals was to take the Standard Statistics methodology and create indexes back as far as possible – which turned out to be 1871. This immense body of data became a fertile field for research, which the Cowles Commission furthered by employing groups of bright academics to study, analyse and publish. One of those academics was Harry Markowitz, who went on to win a Nobel Prize for his work in exploring and defining stock-market risk and reward, as well as the benefits of portfolio diversification.

But the Dow Jones Industrial Average held onto its most-used status for its very simplicity – it could be computed in a minute or so with pencil and paper – while Standard Statistics had to push a much heavier maintenance load to get its indexes out once a week. Only when computing power reached an adequate level in the 1950s could Standard & Poor's generate a 500-stock index on a daily basis.

Meanwhile, stock indexes began mushrooming all over Wall Street, and beyond. Investment professionals found them to be useful tools for devising and monitoring their strategies, and investment firms discovered that putting their names on indexes was a classy promotion device. Several newspapers followed the *Wall Street Journal* in creating their own, as well. In the Cowles Commission's 1938 report on its extension of index history, the appendix listed and described 254 stock indexes in the US and 69 in the UK, plus at least one each for 20 other countries.

That is pretty much where things stood on the index-creation front until well after World War II. Following the creation of the S&P 500 in 1957 were two developments: first, Wilshire Associates, based in Santa Monica, California, a money-management firm and consultant to institutional investors, developed the Wilshire 5000 Index – the first index to include all exchange-listed stocks in the US, which at that time numbered around 5,000; second, Frank Russell & Co, also a consultant to institutional investors and a money-management firm, based in Tacoma, Washington, introduced its Russell 1000, 2000 and 3000 indexes in 1984. While its indexes were slimmer than the Wilshire 5000, Russell contended they were representative of the range of stocks that institutional money managers actually invested in.

Notice that all these indexes, from Dow Jones's selected blue chips to Wilshire's all-in treatment, were intended to reflect the overall stock market. To be sure, many of them focused on smaller segments, such as industrials and railways, but their various parts added up to a broad-market whole.

INDEXING

Market indexes existed for almost a century before indexing surfaced as an investment style. The idea of indexing was born from the marriage of modern portfolio theory (as espoused by William F. Sharpe and Harry Markowitz, among several others) and the burgeoning computer age. A key aspect of modern portfolio theory is asset allocation, which is simply deciding the mix of stocks, bonds, mutual funds and other asset classes in which to be invested. Each asset class has its distinct risk–reward characteristic, so each performs differently over time. As one kind of asset increases in value, another may be increasing to a lesser degree or even declining. Thus, an assortment of uncorrelated assets provides the best insurance against a major loss in any one asset.

This is diversification, and it is important within asset classes, too. Holding a broad array of stocks is less risky than holding just one, or several that are all in the same line of business. Buying a basket of stocks that replicates a broad-based index was proposed as a way of gaining "market exposure" without the cost of researching and selecting individual stocks. An academic paper in 1960 seems to be the first suggestion of such an approach, according to Peter L. Bernstein in *Capital Ideas*, but the first concrete proposal to create an indexed fund at an asset-management firm was made in 1969.

The man who proposed it, William Fouse, was working for Mellon Bank in Pittsburgh. Mellon said no, and Fouse moved on to Wells Fargo Bank in San Francisco. He proposed it again there, and this time he got the answer he was hoping for. But the fund, launched in 1971, was a flop. The index it tracked consisted of the approximately 1,500 common stocks on the New York Stock Exchange (NYSE), all equally weighted. Frequently rebalancing this portfolio as prices moved, new stocks appeared and others dropped out proved to be expensive and cumbersome. In 1973, Wells Fargo started another index fund that was based on the S&P 500, and in 1976 its original index fund was folded into this new one.

That index fund became the template for all that followed it, up to and including the original exchange-traded fund in 1993. But these initial index funds were aimed at institutional investors that had rubbed shoulders with the academics developing the concept. It was even the template for ETFs holding other assets, such as bonds, but they required some adjustments to accommodate the different characteristics of those securities.

John Bogle, who founded the Vanguard Group in 1974, used the template in 1975 to pioneer new ground – an indexed mutual fund marketed to average Mom and Pop investors. Initially named "First Index Investment Trust", it is now called the Vanguard Index 500, the largest mutual fund in the world, with US$82 billion in assets as of December 31, 2008.

Bogle is fond of recalling that the fund's success did not come quickly or easily. The initial offering raised just over US$11 million instead of the planned-for US$150 million. Cashflows into the new fund were minuscule for several years, and detractors ("Who wants to be operated on by an average surgeon?" asked one) took to calling it "Bogle's Folly". Eventually, it found traction, however, and, when the fund's assets surpassed US$500 million in 1987, other investment companies started to take notice. That first index mutual fund has now been joined by more than 360 others, including some from such previously all-active money managers as Dreyfus, Fidelity, Merrill Lynch, Morgan Stanley, Schwab, Scudder and T. Rowe Price.

Outside of academia, Bogle became the most prominent advocate of indexing as an investment strategy. In numerous books and speeches, he sang the praises of low-cost, passive investing as the strategy almost certain to leave the most money in investors' pockets over long stretches of time. In a 2005 speech, Bogle spelled out what he meant by an index fund: "An index mutual fund is a fund designed to return to investors 100% of the returns delivered by the stock market, less a nominal charge for expenses, simply by owning the preponderance of stocks in the market, weighted by the value of their capitalisations."

The "classic" index fund, he said, consisted of "(1) the broadest possible diversification, sustained over (2) the longest possible time horizon, operated at (3) the lowest possible cost, thereby assuring (4) the highest possible share of whatever investment returns our financial markets are generous enough to provide".

In the same speech, Bogle also articulated the case for favouring passive over active investing.

> [A]ll investors together [hold] the market portfolio. There's simply no way around that tautology. The problem, simply put, is that, individually, investors are constantly trading its component stocks back and forth with one another, and fall behind the market's return by the amount of their aggregate costs. The net result of all that shuffling of paper: the market portfolio remains unchanged, but the brokers and dealers who facilitate all those trades are enriched. And when investors don't do all that trading *directly* – and in today's financial system, in which financial intermediaries own 68% of all stocks, they *don't* – they do it *indirectly*, largely through agents such as … fund managers who engage in the same feverish activity, all the while arrogating yet another layer of costs – and an additional share of the market's returns – to themselves.

It was into this Bogle-defined investment world that ETFs ploughed like a huge meteorite, disrupting the previously clear line between active and passive portfolio management.

THE NEW LANDSCAPE

As the ETF bandwagon picked up steam at the end of the 20th Century, the brand-name, broad-market benchmark indexes were snapped up quickly by fund companies. Unsatisfied, they were desperate to issue even more ETFs to fatten their assets under management. The SEC was insisting that indexes underlie them. The result: indexes were created by the hundreds, many of them with reasonable investment purposes but too many with dubious *raisons d'être*.

One example is the trend to subdivide the market into industries and sectors, with ETFs on each. First came the logical segments – for instance, technology, oil and gas, and financials. Those were followed by somewhat finer breakdowns, such as semiconductors, oil equipment and services, and regional banks. But that granularity did not satiate the demand from expansion-intent ETF sponsors, so the slices became thinner and thinner.

There came to be ETFs not only for healthcare and biotechnology, but also for pharmaceutical companies specialising in drugs for treating cancer and autoimmune diseases. There was even an ETF of companies "on the verge" of having drugs to treat cancer holding 22 stocks with market capitalisations ranging from US$583 million all the way down to US$55 million. The investment rationale (as distinct from speculative appeal) for this ETF was not readily apparent and it was closed in 2008 during the market downturn.

Another example is the trend to "strategy indexes", which do not represent the market or subsets of it but rather emulate in rules-based fashion an active investment strategy intended to beat the market. There are "growth" and "value" strategies, dividend strategies, long-short strategies – the list goes on and on. Some people dispute whether these are really even indexes. Technically, they are. An index is simply a statistical device for tracking something quantitative – such as stock prices – over time. How the components are selected and how they are weighted within the index are about the only variables in index construction.

However, their technical qualification as indexes does not mean that investing in products based on them is "indexing". Even though these products are "passively" managed to track their underlying indexes, they are in fact vehicles of active management. If you buy a growth or value ETF, or an ETF composed of high-dividend-paying stocks or pharmaceutical stocks, you are betting that these market segments will do better than others. Putting money on your opinion is active management. If you buy an ETF of stocks selected by some "proprietary" methodology for having "the greatest potential for capital appreciation" – the phrase used in one prospectus – you are in a passively managed active strategy.

Indexing is not having a market opinion, or at least not backing it with real money. Indexing is the belief that in the long run the market as a whole outperforms any bets on particular slices of the market. Indexing is broad and consistent exposure to an asset class.

"If the original paradigm of indexing was long-term investing, surely using index funds as trading vehicles can fairly be described as short-term speculation," proclaimed Jack Bogle in that 2005 speech. He continued,

> If the original paradigm was the broadest possible diversification, surely holding discrete – even widely diversified – sectors of the market offers far less diversification ... If the original paradigm was minimal cost, it's clear that holding market sector index funds that are themselves low-cost still carries the substantial brokerage commissions, bid-ask spreads, and market impact costs entailed in moving money from one sector to another ... [S]ince the returns of investors in the aggregate fall short of financial market returns by the amount of intermediation and trading costs, the more we pay the intermediaries and the more we trade, the more we lose.

Why are these distinctions – active versus passive, classic versus *nouveau* – so important? One answer is that non-professional investors can become confused, believing that they are indexing when they are not. Moreover, the passively managed active strategies are every bit as volatile as straight active management. Sector funds are more volatile than broad-market funds, and require active decision making to roll from one to another. True indexing never delivers the best or worst performance; returns from indexing always are somewhere in the middle and therefore steadier over time. Indeed, that is one of the attractions for certain long-term investors – and one of the detriments for investors inclined to actively manage their portfolios in pursuit of superior performance.

What these distinctions add up to is that, like so many things, investing has become more complicated. Indexing does not necessarily mean passive portfolio management these days, and an index now could as easily be reflecting an active strategy as a broad, diversified market. These changes require increased awareness on the parts of investors, particularly those old enough to have absorbed into their vocabularies the earlier meanings of these terms.

Of course, paying more attention to investing details is the last thing most people want to do. For them, sticking with the classic indexing formula of building their nest eggs in passive broad-market funds is probably the safest and wisest course of action; fortunately, these are the kinds of index funds most likely to be found in corporate 401(k) plans. People for whom investing is an interesting avocation are the ones required by the transmogrified investment scene to push behind facile labels to discern the true characteristics of the ETF or other investment product.

Over time, markets change, institutions change, strategies change. The one thing that has not changed, though, is that hoary dictum, *caveat emptor* – "buyer beware". As long as there are investments to be made, this expression remains both eternal and universally applicable.

2

Conceptual Approaches to Indexes for Exchange-Traded Funds

David M. Blitzer

Standard & Poor's

Exchange-traded funds (ETFs) are relative newcomers to the investing world, dating back to 1993, when the first US ETF began trading. Stock indexes reach back much further, to 1884, when the Dow Jones published their first index covering 11 stocks. Modern stock indexes using market capitalisation weighting began in 1923, when the Standard Statistics Co, later Standard & Poor's, began publishing an index of 233 stocks. Despite this long history, indexes as investment tools did not reach individual investors until Vanguard began its S&P 500 index fund in 1976. While this fund may be one of the largest funds today, it began very small with a slow start.

While index mutual funds are seen as an adjunct to more exciting, though usually less successful, actively managed mutual funds, ETFs focus on indexes. The original idea behind ETFs was to create a way for investors to buy or sell an entire index portfolio in one trade. While these basket trades were available to large institutions, they were beyond the reach of individuals and many smaller institutional investors. The first US ETF was the SPDR, based on the S&P 500 and listed on the American Stock Exchange. As with Vanguard's pioneering mutual fund almost 20 years before, the SPDR was designed for investors who wanted to buy the US stock market. The S&P 500, covering some 80% of the total market value, is a highly liquid and very efficient way to gain exposure to the market. Index-based investing was becoming more popular and recognised, but was still focused on entire markets or large portions of markets rather than narrower sectors, styles or strategies.

In the 15 years since the introduction of the SPDR, the number of ETFs has expanded from that single beginning to several hundred funds covering a huge range of markets, styles, industry sectors and many other ways to classify and categorise stocks. Initially, the variation from one ETF to another was driven by what stocks were included. Beginning about five years ago, funds began to use different ways to weight the stocks, adding a second source of differentiation in the returns. More recently, the menu has also grown to include ETFs outside of equities, covering bonds and other fixed-income securities as well as commodities. This article looks at equity ETFs and does not discuss fixed income, commodities or other possibilities.

As the variety of ETFs exploded a second, more subtle, variation was introduced into their design and development. Originally ETFs, based on broad indexes, aimed to emulate or mimic the market's performance at minimal cost. If the market, as measured by a broad index such as the S&P 500, returned 10%, success for an ETF was to return the same 10%, possibly less a minuscule fraction for operating expenses. That fraction was driven down to single-digit-basis-point fees in some cases. However, no matter how many times analysts and economists argue, demonstrate or prove that index strategies outperform active investments, there are always investors who believe they can beat the market. They are not satisfied with ETFs that merely offer market performance. Following the terminology of the capital asset pricing model (CAPM), investment strategists distinguish between beta (β) returns generated by tracking the market and alpha (α) returns generated by superior investment skill. ETFs began as beta plays; most of the recent additions are either mixes of alpha and beta, or claim to be alpha plays. Market tracking ETFs are the beta-oriented ones; more targeted strategies that aim to outperform the broad market would be classified as alpha-oriented.

What is a beta question versus what is an alpha question depends on where you are looking. Suppose an investor is considering US stocks – the return the overall US market offers represents the return to their beta risk. If they decided to hold only large-cap stocks and excludes the mid-cap and small-cap sectors of the market, the difference between what they earned on large-caps and what the overall market would have given him is the alpha return. The investor's "active" decision to buy only large-caps restricted their portfolio and affected the results. If the investor were right – if they beat the overall market – the alpha would be positive and they would be happy. If it turned out to be the year for small-caps, the alpha is negative and the large-cap-only decision cost the investor something.

Suppose the same investor also decided to avoid any investments outside the US. That choice was also an active decision – in a year when US stocks returned 8% and the global stock markets (US and non-US) managed only 5%, our investor could claim an active (alpha) return of three percentage points.

Some indexes are designed to track and measure a specific market or market segment; returns earned by investing with these will be completely based on beta. Other indexes are designed to outperform a market – to provide alpha. The first step in classifying indexes is distinguishing the alpha generators from the beta producers. Figure 2.1 shows this split and how the classification differs between the two groups. The left side describes the two principal ways that alpha indexes attempt to achieve higher returns: varying the index weighting and selecting stocks based on investment strategies. The right-hand section lists the major categories of beta

Figure 2.1 The equity ETF family tree

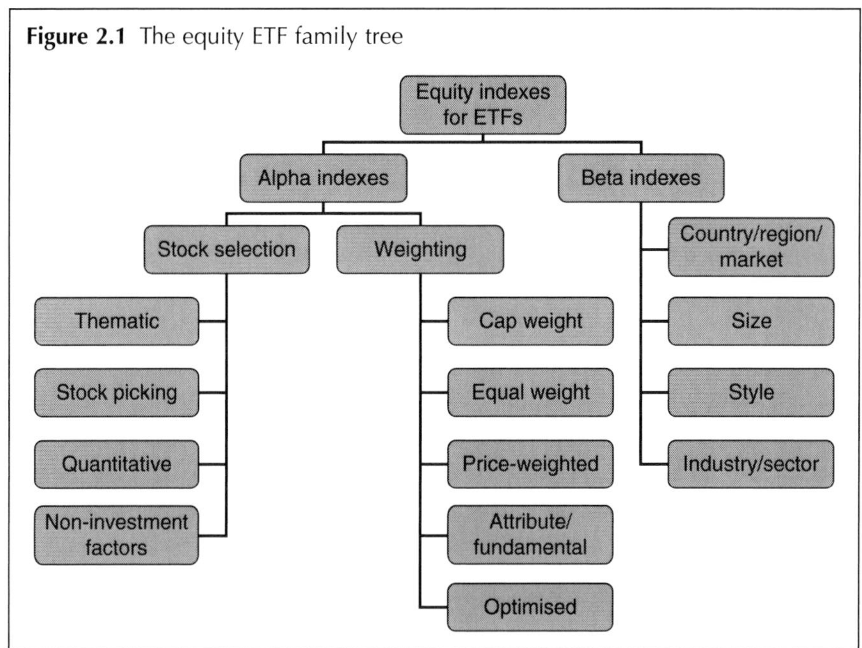

indexes. For these, the question is defining the market rather than making changes in hopes of outperforming the market.

ALPHA-SEEKING INDEXES

Purists may argue that an alpha index is an oxymoron, that indexes should simply track and mirror the market. One result of the growth of ETFs is the proliferation of indexes that use combinations of weighting and security selection in attempts to beat the market. Many of these are simply systematic descriptions of longstanding investment strategies, while a few may break new ground in investment tactics. The success of the alpha chasers is open to debate. It is widely recognised that key factors in the success of traditional beta-based index investing are low costs and low turnover. Some of the alpha-chasing ETFs tend to have both higher expense ratios and higher turnover, attributes that should be seen as warnings about performance.

Stock selection

Between stock selection and weighting, stock selection is the more obvious approach to improving performance. The stock-selection methods are broken into four broad categories, leaving issues such as only small-caps or industry concentration to the beta index group.

1. Thematic

Investment themes have been around as long as investors, or at least as long as stockbrokers selling to investors. The biggest theme of the last few decades was the dotcom boom, when anything Internet had to make you rich. More recent themes have been to focus on natural resources as a group or selected resources one by one, such as water resources and supply. The attractions are a catchy coherent story about how the market and the economy will develop combined with a way to gain investment exposure to a group of the "right" stocks. With an ETF, investors (or investment advisers) need not research each stock. Further, in their chosen themes their risks will be somewhat diversified. However, the level of diversification is not comparable to that of a broad-based index fund. Owning 25 dotcom stocks in March 2000 meant the only kind of diversification was diversified disaster.

2. Stock picking

Many investment organisations maintain and publish buy-hold-sell recommendations on large numbers of stocks. These recommendations can be used to define an index. The simplest approach is an index consisting of only the buys. If a brokerage house, investment advisory firm or other group has developed a consistent approach to stock selection and maintained a history of their recommendations, an index can be developed and backtested as well as tracked going forward. To some extent, these are essentially the focus or recommended lists that brokers often publish at the beginning of the year. The attraction to investors is to "invest with the pros" or to benefit from the stock analysts' research.

3. Quantitative

Among money managers and active investors, stock pickers often compete with the "quants", who use statistical models of stock returns to identify stocks they hope will outperform in the future. The same competition can be seen in the index world, where quant models challenge stock pickers and, to some extent, those extolling the latest investment theme. The appeal is similar to stock picking – benefit from the skill of the quant model builders at moderate cost and possibly have some diversification. The difference is that quants focus on statistics they can measure while stock pickers home in on hunches they believe are true.

4. Non-investment factors

This differs from the previous categories. At times investors impose religious, social or moral restrictions on their portfolios. One long-standing example is not holding any stocks of companies selling alcohol or tobacco products. More recently there is substantial interest in indexes screened to comply with Sharia law. Other examples include indexes where stock selection considers environmental, social or corporate governance criteria. While there are some analysts who argue that these kinds of restriction lead to higher returns, most often the restrictions are there for good and important reasons rather than in an attempt to pick better-performing stocks.

In most cases, a significant amount of research is required to consistently and accurately apply these restrictions. Using an index backed by professional research offers investments significant cost savings and economies of scale compared with individualised research. Indexes are an efficient way to comply with these non-investment factors indexes.

Weighting

How the stocks in an index are weighted can make a very big difference in the index's performance, far larger than most people realise. S&P publishes an equal-weighted version of the S&P 500 where each stock has a weight of one-fifth of 1% instead of being weighted in proportion to its market value. Equal weighting, compared with the usual market-cap-weighting approach, overweights smaller stocks and value stocks. From the end of 1999 – almost the peak of the dotcom boom – to August 2008, the S&P 500 is down 12.7% while the equal-weighted version of the S&P 500 is up 49%. The stocks in the two versions of the index are identical. Clearly, weighting matters quite a lot.

Cap-weighted

In a cap-weighted index, each stock's proportional weight is the ratio of its market value to the total market value of all the stocks in the index. In the same way, a stock's weight or importance in the stock market is the ratio of the stock's market cap to the total market cap of the market. Therefore, the returns, risks and other statistics of the index and the market are the same. Someone who wants to "buy the market" should buy an ETF based on a market-cap-weighted index. In most cases, cap-weighted indexes are float-adjusted so that the shares counted in calculating the index exclude stock that is closely held and not available in the market. An example of closely held stock are control blocks held by officers or directors of a company.

Cap weighting is attractive because the index and an ETF based on it will mimic the market very closely. With some weighting approaches, the weights need to be rebalanced from time to time because stock price movements will push the weights away from their targets. Cap-weighted indexes are self-adjusting, since the weight depends on the current price and shares of the stock rather than an external target. This means that ETFs should also be relatively inexpensive to operate compared with ETFs using other weighting rules.

Equal-weighted

Equal weighting is simple to explain and understand – the US dollar amount invested in each stock is the same when the index is rebalanced and the weights are set. Compared with cap weighting, this overweights any stocks with less then the average market value and underweights those with more than the average market value. Further, since value stocks tend to be small and growth stocks tend to be larger, it also overweights value stocks. Some investors believe this small-cap-value bias will lead to better than market returns.

Price-weighted

There are only a few price-weighted indexes in use today. Two that are well known are the Dow Jones Industrials in the US and the Nikkei 225 on the Tokyo stock exchange. Before computers, price-weighted indexes were preferred because the calculation is simple: add up the stock prices and divide by a scale factor. By comparison, calculating a cap-weighted index requires the index provider to track the number of shares of each company and calculate each market value before summing the values to get the index. For investment purposes, price-weighted indexes are not very attractive and can give surprising results. If there are two stocks, one priced at US$10 and one at US$100 in the index, the US$100 stock has 10 times the impact on the index whether it represents a larger or small company. If each stock rises 10%, the US$100 stock has 10 times the impact on the index as the US$10 stock, even though stock price without shares does not reflect the company's size or importance.

Attribute/fundamental weighting

This category includes a range of different ideas that have drawn a lot of attention in recent years. While the details differ, all these approaches depend on the idea that one can identify one or a few measurable attributes of a stock that can enhance its contribution to an index. For example, if one believes that stocks with high price-to-earnings or price-to-book ratios tend to be overpriced, then a weighting approach that mixes earnings or book values can offset the impact of the overpriced stocks. Likewise, if paying large dividends is an attractive attribute, then including dividends or dividend yields in the weighting will improve index results.

Similarly, some argue that revenues, book value or even employees are better measures of a company's size than market capitalisation and prefer to base index weights on these other size measures. Debates about attribute or fundamental weighting produced two kinds of claim and counterclaim: those based on performance and those tied to financial theory. Arguments on performance may never end since each month brings new data and new questions. The theoretical questions, but few answers, can be found in various scholarly journals.

For investors, the attractiveness of these approaches largely turns on past and hoped-for future performance. These indexes and associated ETFs should probably be considered quantitative strategies rather than true market indexes. As quant strategies, they work very well in some kinds of markets and less well in other markets. The question becomes which kind of market is best and when will we experience it.

Optimised weights

Stocks in indexes designed to support ETFs must be sufficiently liquid for the ETF manager to easily buy and sell shares when necessary to reflect index adjustments. Likewise, to assure smooth creation and redemption of ETF shares and efficient arbitrage between the ETF price and the underlying stocks, liquidity is essential. If an index has relatively few stocks and their sizes, or their liquidity levels, cover a wide range, the ETF may find it difficult to trade some of the less liquid components. Instead of excluding less liquid stocks, a better approach is to reduce their weight – and the amount an ETF would hold. This can be done by optimising the weights: reducing the weights of less liquid stocks while keeping other parameters such as the mix of industry sectors as close to the non-optimised weights as possible. Though actual calculations may be done with a computer-based optimiser, the idea is simply to stay as close as possible to the original weighting scheme while assuring that the ETF is workable.

A similar issue occurs in some markets where ETFs are subject to rules on diversification limiting the weight of the largest stock or the largest five or 10 stocks. Two common rules are "5/10/40" in the US and UCITS compliance in Europe. Both set limits on the weights of the largest stocks in the index.

BETA ISSUES

Market-wide or beta-oriented ETFs are simpler to discuss – there are fewer of them, they are all market-cap-weighted and none claim to choose only the "right" stocks. Moreover, the choices among indexes are more straightforward than choosing weighting schemes or stock-selection rules. A beta index is designed to track a market or a specific segment of the market. The design of the index must assure that all the stocks are sufficiently liquid to assure that trading, creation and redemption can proceed without excessive costs or delays. Further, there should be no question about what market or market segment is being covered. This section discusses the way these markets and segments are usually described.

Country/region/market

Indexes are usually defined in terms of the market or country they cover. In the US, where the NYSE and Nasdaq are the two major markets companies list on, most indexes draw from both markets. In most other parts of the world, market and country are synonymous. With increased interest in global investing, indexes that cover geographic regions, such as Europe, or groups of countries, such as emerging markets, are becoming more common.

For investors, the choice is largely one of deciding among different broad-based indexes, examining likely operating expenses and the reputation of the various ETF issuers. Often, investors and analysts tend to assume all indexes provide similar performance, that all ETF expenses are about the same and that there is little difference among large institutional money managers. All those statements are often wrong.

There are differences among ETFs and indexes when they track the same market. The number of stocks, their size, trading volume and any variation in trading will affect the costs of running the ETF and how closely it can track the index. Some indexes, such as the Russell series in the US, are largely rebuilt once a year. Others, such as the S&P 500 and S&P's other US indexes, make changes when market developments require. Different approaches result in different amounts of turnover and trading and different performance. For instance, the S&P SmallCap 600 and the Russell 2000 are both described as covering US small-cap stocks. However, one has 600 stocks and the other 2,000; one (the SmallCap) screens stocks for liquidity and profitability and the other does not. Finally, the S&P SmallCap 600 makes adjustments as necessary while the Russell 2000 completely rebuilds the index once a year. Over the last several years the S&P SmallCap 600 has provided higher returns.

Even where more than one ETF tracks the same index, there may still be differences based on operating characteristics of the ETF manager and the size of the ETF portfolio. All this means that investors must consider more than just which market they want when reviewing different ETFs.

Size

Company size – usually termed large-cap, mid-cap or small-cap – is used to segment markets and indexes. Two alternative approaches to defining size are absolute and relative sizes. Some indexes set specific size requirements based on market cap that are applied when a stock is added or when the index undergoes a periodic review. For example, in the S&P 500, stocks should be at least US$5.5 billion or more in market cap when they join the index. Most systems of global indexes covering numerous countries and maintaining consistent rules across countries use relative size. For example, in the S&P Global Equity Indexes, which cover more than 75 countries, size is defined on a relative basis. Companies are ranked by market cap from largest to smallest; the largest companies representing 70% of the total market are large-caps, the next 15% are mid-caps and the final 15% are small-caps. Because markets vary, a large-cap company in a modest size developing market might be smaller than some mid-cap companies in a developed market. In the S&P Global Equity Indexes, there is a second set of indexes that use absolute-size parameters to provide indexes with companies in specific market cap ranges.

Style

Style refers to classifying stocks as either growth or value. Growth stocks are perceived as enjoying rapid-earnings growth and having high valuations as measured by price–earnings or price-to-book ratios. Their rapid earnings growth makes them attractive, hence the high valuations. Value stocks might be thought of as having unrecognised values and often have low price–earnings or price-to-book ratios; value stocks also have higher-dividend yields and are more likely to pay dividends. The terms have been around for decades. Research by Eugene Fama and Kenneth French (1992; 1993) is usually cited as the start of quantitative work on indexes dividing stocks by style. They developed a model that explained stock returns with three factors covering the overall market return, returns related to company size and returns related to style. Their findings suggested that in the long run small-cap and value stocks outperform the market.

While the initial Fama–French work used one style factor, the ratio of book value per share to price, to determine style, most indexes now use multiple factors and a somewhat different approach. In the Fama–French approach, a stock can be either growth or value; it cannot have properties of both styles and it can not be without any style. Further, since stock prices shift much faster than book values, any move a stock makes between growth and value is almost always driven by its price. To address these issues, various index providers now use a number of financial measures including price–earnings, dividends, earnings growth and others, to identify growth or value stocks. Second, most indexes apportion stocks between growth and value – a stock might be 40% growth and 60% value rather than all of one style or all in the other. These changes reduce the amount of turnover from one style to the other and also lessen the overwhelming impact of stock price movements on the classification.

For investors choosing a style, ETF involves the particular index family and then the choice of growth or value. The same kinds of issue noted in the subsection "Country/region/market" above applies to choosing an index family for style – can an ETF efficiently track the index, and does the index's operating procedures create unnecessary turnover and trading or include too many illiquid stocks? The bigger choice may be between growth and value. Seldom do both do well – by construction both growth and value cannot outperform the market since they must add up to the market. Even if both growth and value offer positive returns, those who chose the style with the lower return will have chosen poorly.

Sectors and industries

The last classification tool for beta indexes and ETFs is the sector or industry. Stocks in different industries perform differently, and which sector does better changes from time to time. An investor who avoided financial stocks in the subprime credit crisis or who overweighted energy companies as oil rose to US$140 a barrel did better than others. You could play sectors or industries by looking at the covers of annual reports or looking companies up in the Yellow Pages. A more effective approach is to look for an ETF that tracks a particular sector index where the index is based on a comprehensive system of industry classification.

In 1999 and 2000, S&P and MSCI Barra developed the Global Industry Classification Standard (GICS) to provide consistent sector classification across the global equity markets. Today GICS classifies close to 50,000 companies into sectors, industry groups, industries and sub-industries. There are 10 sectors; at the other end of the scale there are about 150 sub-industries. Because these are applied across global index series such as S&P Global Equity Indexes, investors can choose ETFs focusing on sectors or more narrowly defined industry categories to gain targeted exposure in different markets. The result is that the efficiency of indexes and ETFs is available to those who believe they can recognise the next hot sector before its price peaks.

ETFs AND INDEXES

While indexes started some 110 years before ETFs, both began as tools to address entire markets in one package. In the last 10 or so years, both have developed more specialised variations to allow investors and analysts to target market segments with beta indexes or to utilise a wide range of strategies to outperform with alpha indexes.

REFERENCES

Fama, E. F. and K. R. French, 1992, "The Cross Section of Expected Stock Returns", *Journal of Finance* 47(2), June, pp. 427–65.

Fama, E. F. and K. R. French, 1993, "Common Risk Factors in the Returns of Stocks and Bonds", *Journal of Financial Economics* 33(1), February, pp. 3–56.

3

Alternatives to Cap-Weighted ETFs

John M. West, Robert D. Arnott

Research Affiliates, LLC

Capitalisation-weighted index funds have served investors well since their inception in the early 1970s. Likewise, exchange-traded funds (ETFs) mirroring these indexes are a more recent innovation allowing retail and institutional investors to efficiently gain exposure to broad or more focused areas of the equity markets. We are grateful to the pioneers who helped spawn index funds and their closely related ETF cousins. Both have cumulatively provided much-needed diversification and simplicity while providing investors with tremendous cost savings. As Jack Bogle constantly reminds us, "Costs matter!"

ISSUES WITH CAPITALISATION-WEIGHTED INDEXES

For all of their virtues, the capitalisation-weighted indexes that form the basis of the majority of ETFs suffer an important defect in their construction. In an inefficient market, in which prices and fair values differ, weighting individual stocks by market capitalisation will assuredly result in a portfolio that overweights overpriced stocks and underweights underpriced stocks. The result is a significant return "drag" incurred by cap-weighted indexes, relative to their opportunity set, because these pricing errors are linked to portfolio weights!

We aim to repair this flaw through weighting stocks by non-price measures of firm size such as sales or dividends. We find these Fundamental Index strategies add significant value by avoiding the return drag while simultaneously preserving the many favourable portfolio attributes associated with passive investing.[1] This radical yet simple idea is not just theory. As of mid-2008, there are now more than 40 Fundamental Index ETFs, trading all over the world, as against none just three years before. Combining ETFs, mutual funds and institutional portfolios, as of September 30, 2008, there is now over US$19 billion managed using Fundamental Index strategies, a remarkable sum for an idea that was first introduced barely three years before.

How has this simple idea gained such immense traction in so little time? To better understand the problem with cap weighting, let us drop our preconceptions about indexing and journey back to when the S&P 500 was created. Suppose you were on the investment committee at Standard and Poor's and were assigned the task of how to construct this expanded benchmark. Your goal was to establish a yardstick to measure the cumulative performance of stock market investors. Accordingly, you simply took the 500 companies on your list and determined how much they cumulatively advanced or declined each day, month or year. Naturally, this leads you to weight each stock by capitalisation. Add in the dividends paid over the appropriate time period to calculate the performance of the stock market. Feeling confident, you stride into the committee and make your proposal. It passes with flying colours – except for one dissenter. This committee member remarks, "True, this will measure the performance of the market but it will also put most of our money in the highest-priced stocks. Further, this 'cap weighting' will ensure increased exposure to the stocks that have recently rallied and decrease the weight to those that have recently faltered. Wouldn't it make more sense to try to measure the performance of the average company, not a basket that allocates to those with the highest prices? And what if investors decide to bypass managed funds and invest directly in the index? It surely seems that it would put too much in stocks that may be overpriced."

The likely rebuttal to these valid points would have focused on the fact that this new S&P 500 Index was not intended to be an investment portfolio. Managing portfolios is for the professionals. Surely they can beat this index!

Dean LeBaron, Jack Bogle, Charley Ellis, Bill Fouse and others realised in the mid-1970s that managed funds could not collectively beat this unmanaged group of 500 stocks after incorporating their fees. Today, 30-plus years of performance results validate these visionaries' then-revolutionary claims. However, we do ourselves and our clients a disservice by not questioning the cap-weighted index's construction, by not seeking improvement. The Fundamental Index concept does question the critical flaw in cap weighting. In so doing, we arrive at a solution for investors long dissatisfied with the hollow promise of active management and the propensity of traditional index funds to suffer after loading up on the hottest stocks, sectors and fads of the day.

MARKET EFFICIENCY

Our journey is built on a firm belief that the market is inefficient. In other words, today's collection of market prices fails to accurately reflect the fair values of the underlying companies. To believe the market perfectly prices thousands of equity securities every day is a bit far-fetched. Investors would need to clairvoyantly see years, indeed, decades of future cashflows to correctly determine the fair value of a firm. Sadly, none of us has such a crystal ball. History is littered with examples of immense mispricing in individual stocks, economic sectors and even broad markets. The Dutch tulip craze, the South Sea Co, the Nifty Fifty and the Internet bubble all are vivid examples of greed and euphoria carrying prices well above fair value. Only after prices crash do investors realise the magnitude of the pricing errors.

In a less-than-efficient market, we know that some stocks (and occasionally many) will be priced above or below their true fair value. Those that are priced above true value will have an erroneously higher capitalisation and, therefore, index weighting. These companies will comprise a larger portion of the cap-weighted index. Meanwhile, shares priced below fair value will comprise less of the cap-weighted index. As the overpriced subsequently underperform, their relative losses overwhelm the underpriced shares outperformance because the overpriced comprise more of the portfolio. In this way, we know that capitalisation-weighted indexes systematically overweight overpriced securities and underweight underpriced securities.

Consider the top 10 stocks in a cap-weighted portfolio. Some will get there because they are very large companies whose true value is accurately reflected in current prices. However, others will arrive on the list as a result of being overvalued. As this overpricing is realised and corrected by the market, the cap-weighted index suffers a major drag, as seen in Table 3.1, which summarises the top 10 stocks at any given point in time and their subsequent 10-year performance over the last 80 years.

The results are striking – on average three outperform while seven underperform. That is a darned lopsided coin to flip. We also discover that the average performance of the top 10 is 25% to 30% below that of the average stock in the S&P 500. This is a huge performance drag – we have got 20–25% of our money tied up in these underperformers.

THE RIDDLE OF EQUAL WEIGHTING

Conventional indexers acknowledge this shortcoming of cap-weighted indexes but assert that, unless we can determine which stocks are overvalued ahead of time, we have added little to the conversation. However, the cure is much simpler and requires virtually nothing in the way of a crystal ball. By simply breaking the link between price and portfolio weight, we randomise portfolio weights so that on average half of the portfolio is in overvalued stocks and half is in undervalued shares. As prices correct, we no longer structurally suffer from having a greater allocation to the overpriced. The relative gains and losses should cancel without a return drag.

Perhaps the simplest random weighting scheme is to simply take an index's constituents and equally weight them. Fortunately for our purposes, the Standard and Poor's group offers an equally

Table 3.1 Performance of top 10 stocks by capitalisation

	One-year (%)	Three-year (%)	Five-year (%)	10-year (%)
How often did the top 10 stocks in a cap-weighted portfolio outperform the average stock in the following period?				
1926–2006	44	40	37	31
1964–2006	38	35	30	27
By how much did the top 10 stocks underperform the average?				
1926–2006	–2.9	–11.1	–17.7	–29.4
1964–2006	–3.6	–15.9	–24.9	–36.9

Source: Research Affiliates

weighted variant of the S&P 500, the S&P Equal Weight Index (SP EWI) dating back to 1990. Each stock is given a 0.20% weight (ie, 1/500) regardless of its capitalisation or P/E ratio. On a quarterly basis, the portfolio rebalances the stocks with their drifting prices back to this equal weight. However, we find a very compelling return story despite its rudimentary construction.

By simply dividing by 500, the SP EWI achieves an excess return of 1.1% above the cap-weighted S&P 500 since its 1990 inception through December 2008. The results are particularly impressive relative to active mutual funds, likely garnering top decile rankings against relevant peer groups. The superior value added from such a simple strategy is largely attributable to "price indifference". Pricing errors are random – roughly half of the portfolio will be in overvalued stocks and half in undervalued. The resulting performance differentials should cancel. What is that worth? Equal weighting indicates 1.1%. Eliminating the return drag of price weighting is powerful indeed.

Equal weighing is illustrative of the problems embedded in cap weighting but it has issues of its own. Many of the original benefits of passive investing are lost with such an approach. Turnover increases, sector representation is skewed, economically inconsistencies abound – we give the same weight to Exxon Mobil as we do to stock number 500 – and capacity is drastically reduced.[2] This is the critical issue with equal weighing. Since we are required to invest the same amount in the very smallest companies as in the very largest, this strategy cannot be run on anything more than a trivial scale. Thus, equal weighting plugs the primary hole in the cap-weighted boat but simultaneously allows several new leaks to pop up. However, it indicates that the return drag from cap weighting is significant and can be cured.

THE FUNDAMENTAL INDEX AND RAFI

If capacity is the primary drawback of equal weighting, the next step in solving the flaw of cap weighing must concentrate on a manner in which to allocate more of the portfolio to larger companies. Fortunately, there are a host of ways to define company size. When news breaks of two companies merging, most publications will report the relative scale of the transaction by stating combined sales of x, combined profits of y, or combined number of employees by z. These are the measures of company size that Main Street thinks about.

Along these lines, we can create an index where the largest companies are identified and weighted by a Main Street measure of company size. For example, let us start with sales where we can construct a sales index first by identifying the top 1,000 sales companies over some period. The individual weights can then be determined by each company's relative scope. For example, Wal-Mart had annual sales of US$349 billion (trailing 12 months closest to June 30, 2007) while the top 1,000 companies by sales combined for US$8.8 trillion. Accordingly, Wal-Mart's weight would be 3.95% (US$349 billion/US$8.8 trillion). Repeat the exercise 999 more times and we arrive at a sales index.

In this same manner, a multitude of Fundamental Index variants can be constructed. Cashflow, dividends paid, book value and even number of employees can each be used to gauge company size and, therefore, form the basis of a Fundamental Index portfolio.[3] However, using only one fails to accurately capture the true "economic footprint" of a company. Is Wal-Mart the largest company in the US? If we use sales, yes. If we use dividends paid, it ranks only 18th. Furthermore, each individual metric has its own unique vulnerabilities.

- Sales: Relying only on sales to measure size may overemphasise companies with lower profit margins.
- Dividends: Many companies, particularly growth and emerging growth shares, do not pay dividends or use stock buybacks in lieu of dividend payments. Thus, broad representation is lost by solely using dividends. For example, 24% stocks in the S&P 500 and 62% of the stocks in the small-company Russell 2000 were non-dividend payers in September 2006 (Kittsley 2006).
- Cashflow: Companies with highly cyclical income will have their weights swing wildly in a profits-based index.
- Book value: A book-value metric may lead to over- or underexposure to companies with aggressive or conservative accounting practices.

For these reasons, our work focused on using multiple measures of firm size by using a composite approach of sales, cashflow, book value and dividends paid. For example, if Microsoft represents

4% of the total sales of the largest 1,000 US companies based on sales, 3% of total cashflow of the largest 1,000 equities based on cashflow, 2% of the total book-equity value of the 1,000 largest companies as measured by book-equity value and 1% of the total dividends of the largest 1,000 US equities based on dividends, then its composite weight would be $(4 + 3 + 2 + 1)/4$, or 2.5%. Taking a simple average of each company's relative scale in these four financial measures gives us a pretty good indication of its economic footprint. This straightforward composite is, of course, what we call the Research Affiliates Fundamental Index (RAFI) methodology. To reflect changing economic conditions, RAFI is rebalanced once per year.

The resulting portfolio can be expected to provide many of the favourable portfolio attributes expected by proponents of passive investing that equal weighting compromises. By using alternative measures of company size, most of our money will be allocated to the largest companies, ensuring capacity and liquidity similar to cap-weighted indexes. The portfolio and its sector allocations should broadly mirror the economy. Further, since stock prices loosely follow fundamentals, turnover should be low. Indeed, we witness historical turnover of 10% for the RAFI US Large Company Index versus 6% for a comparable cap-weighted portfolio.

Unless we believe that, systematically, big and small companies are always over- or undervalued, we have broken that structural and inherent link in cap weighting between over- and undervaluation and portfolio weight. By breaking it, what is that worth to us?

IS DATA CONSISTENT WITH OUR THEORY? FUNDAMENTAL INDEX PERFORMANCE

Simply put, the evidence that Fundamental Index portfolios beat cap weighting in the long run is overwhelming. Let us begin our historic retrospective first in US large companies that were the focus of our original work in the space.[4] Table 3.2 outlines the long-term returns of the four single metric indexes and the RAFI Composite against both the S&P 500 and the "Cap 1000" – an annually rebalanced portfolio of the top 1,000 US companies by capitalisation.

The S&P 500 posted an annualised return of 9.0% over the 47 years ended 2008, identical to the Cap 1000 figure of 9.0%. The RAFI Composite, equally weighting the four fundamental size metrics, posted an annualised premium over the S&P 500 of 190 basis points

Table 3.2 1962–2008 Fundamental Index performance

Index	Ending value of US$1 (US$)	Annual return (%)	Volatility (%)	Sharpe ratio	Tracking error (%)
S&P 500	57	9.0	15.0	0.29	1.6
Cap 1000	57	9.0	15.1	0.28	
Book	107	10.5	14.9	0.38	3.5
Cashflow	133	11.0	14.9	0.41	3.8
Sales	152	11.3	15.8	0.41	4.9
Gross dividend	114	10.6	13.6	0.41	5.2
RAFI Composite	130	10.9	14.7	0.41	4.0

Source: Research Affiliates

with a lower standard deviation. On average, the Fundamental Index approach delivers more in return with less risk. This positive relationship is quantified easily by the resulting superior Sharpe Ratio of 0.41 for RAFI versus 0.29 for the S&P 500.

One of the striking aspects of Table 3.2 is the tight clustering of annualised returns with the single metric fundamental indexes. Naturally, a list of the top dividend payers will be different from the largest sales firms, but the performance is very similar for all of these portfolios. Cap weighting is the only outlier – a full 190bp off the RAFI Composite and 150bp off the worst of the single metric Fundamental Index strategies. The 1.1% premium we previously outlined by equally weighting the S&P 500 is in line with these results, albeit under a different time horizon. This "clustering" of varying price-indifferent approaches in the 1.0–2.3% excess-return range indicates that the return drag from cap weighting is sizeable regardless of whether we eliminate it with dividend, sales, cashflow, book value or equal-weighting approaches. All randomise portfolio weights with prices, which should leave half our portfolio in overvalued stocks and half in undervalued.

Of course, 47 years is an incredibly long horizon, well beyond the holding period for most individual investors. Thus, slicing RAFI results into various market environments assists advisers and their clients in gaining a better understanding for Fundamental Index performance characteristics. Most obvious is examining historic results in bull and bear markets. We discover in Figure 3.1 that RAFI on average significantly outperforms cap weighting during periods of market turbulence, earning an annualised excess return of 5.0%

Figure 3.1 RAFI returns in different environments

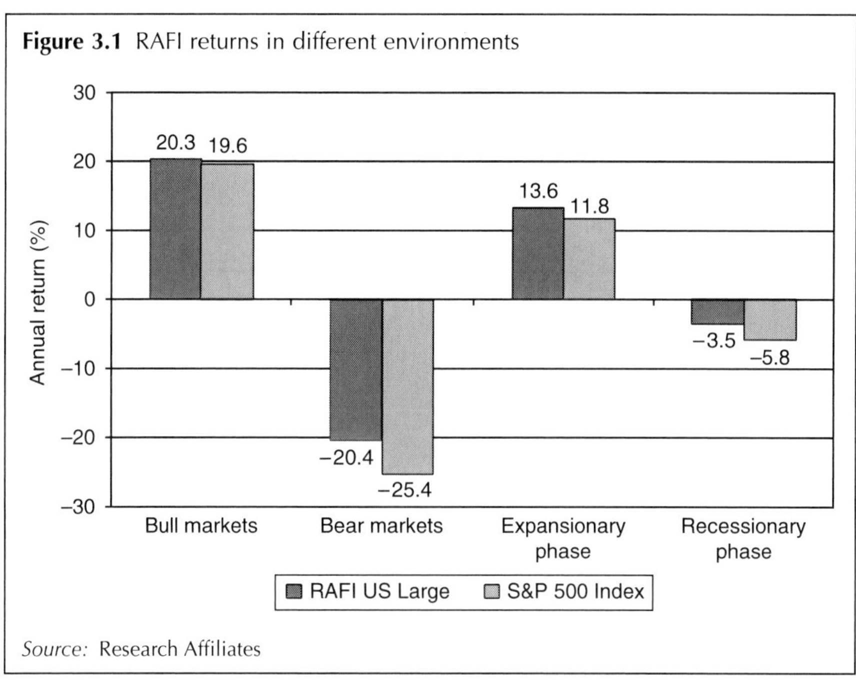

Source: Research Affiliates

per annum over the S&P 500. Likewise, recessions see excess returns of 2.3% for the RAFI methodology. Of course, most defensive strategies will give up these premiums when the market begins a new ascent. However, the Fundamental Index concept tends to hold its own, narrowly outpacing the S&P 500 by 0.7% and 1.8% in bull markets and expansions, respectively.

When has the Fundamental Index concept failed to outperform? It is a critical question for advisers, especially given investors' uncanny ability to sell even the most proven of strategies after periods of shorter-term underperformance. Figure 3.2 breaks down rolling five-year excess returns of RAFI versus the S&P 500. The performance is relatively consistently above the zero line, which indicates RAFI "wins" over most five-year windows since 1962. However, we can see three periods where the trend did not hold. Of these, two can be identified as bubble periods – the Nifty Fifty of the early 1970s and the dotcom/tech bubble of the late 1990s. In both cases, stocks that were later proven to be overpriced went on to become even more overpriced. As cap weighting structurally overweights the overpriced, such a period will be a brief boon for indexes such as the

Figure 3.2 RAFI US Large versus S&P 500: rolling five-year return (1967–2007)

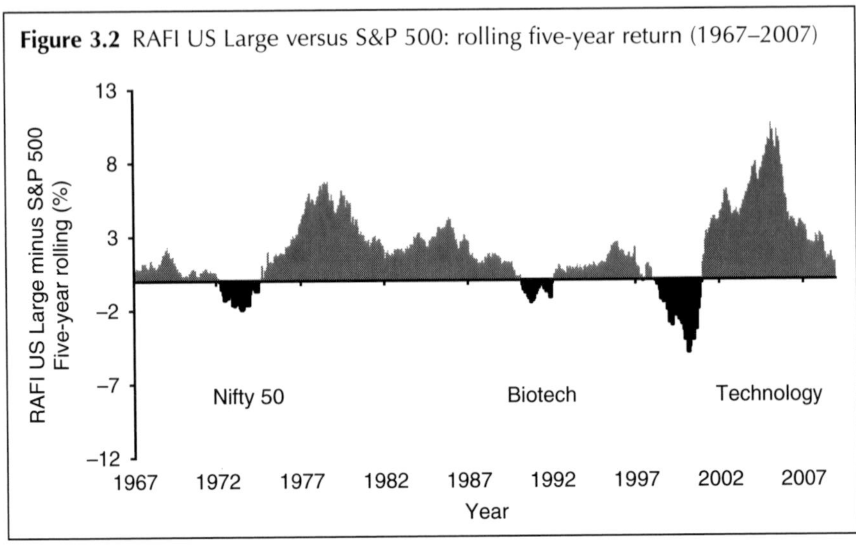

S&P 500 – until the market corrects itself. Then, mean reversion takes its toll and the Fundamental Index portfolio quickly recoups its relative losses. Another way to think about Figure 3.2 is to turn it upside down. Which index would you own? One that outperforms over most periods or one that outperforms only during brief periods mostly associated with speculative bubbles?

RAFI – A GLOBAL SOLUTION

One of the advantages of the Fundamental Index concept is its portability. It can be easily applied to other world equity markets in the exact same "four metric" fashion. The "Ex-US" applications also provide an excellent out-of-sample validation to the results seen in US large companies. Shortly after the publication of our work on US large companies in early 2005, Nomura Securities applied the methodology to the 23 developed country markets and found the RAFI approach added value over cap weighing in 23 of 23 markets dating back to the mid- to late 1980s. We update their analysis below in Table 3.3.

We find that, since Nomura's original work, one country, Switzerland, narrowly fell out of the value-added camp. However, 22 out of 23 countries with an average of 2.7% of value-added is a very impressive result – especially with no stock picking! Suffice it to say that the return drag from cap weighting is a global phenomenon.

Table 3.3 Global evidence for the Fundamental Index concept

23 country return statistics through December 31, 2008 (ranked by value added)

Country	**RAFI return (%)**	**MSCI return (%)**	**Value added (%)**	**Risk adjusted alpha (%)**	**Tracking error**	**Info ratio**	**Alpha *t*-statistic**	**Start date**
Ireland	11.2	3.1	8.1	7.9	9.1	0.89	4.20	1988
Austria	14.4	7.2	7.2	7.6	10.3	0.70	4.13	1984
Norway	13.6	9.4	4.1	4.3	6.5	0.64	3.29	1984
Hong Kong	18.3	14.5	3.9	3.9	6.4	0.61	3.04	1984
Portugal	8.9	5.1	3.8	3.8	8.1	0.46	2.24	1989
France	13.6	10.1	3.5	3.8	6.9	0.51	2.77	1984
Germany	11.2	8.0	3.2	3.7	6.0	0.53	4.02	1984
Japan	4.9	1.9	3.1	2.9	5.3	0.58	2.79	1984
UK	12.8	10.1	2.7	2.8	4.2	0.64	3.32	1984
US	11.7	9.8	1.9	2.3	4.7	0.40	2.51	1984
Belgium	10.6	8.9	1.7	2.0	5.5	0.30	1.98	1984
Netherlands	11.2	9.6	1.6	1.8	6.8	0.23	1.35	1984
Denmark	9.6	8.2	1.4	1.9	8.0	0.18	1.31	1984
Finland	11.4	10.0	1.4	3.4	19.6	0.07	1.10	1988
New Zealand	5.0	4.0	1.0	1.0	8.5	0.12	0.53	1988
Switzerland	9.3	9.6	−0.4	−0.3	4.2	−0.09	−0.34	1984
23-developed country average	13.3	10.5	2.7	3.1	2.8	0.96	5.78	

RAFI IN LESS EFFICIENT MARKETS

Developed-country large-company equities are typically thought of as the most efficient of the equity asset classes. They still suffer from mispricings – big and small – but the mountain of research coverage and ease of trading allow for these errors to be smaller than in less efficient categories such as small companies and emerging markets. Smaller amounts of research coverage and less liquidity foster mispricings that are much wider in magnitude. In such markets, the cap-weighted index allocates even more to the overvalued and even less to the undervalued! In this manner, the return drag from cap weighting rises.

Furthermore, the frequency of mispricings also increases in the cross section of inefficient markets such as small caps and emerging markets. A higher proportion of the universe can be expected to be priced well above/below fair value on any given day/month/year. Assuming these prices eventually revert towards fair value, the return drag from cap weighting is incredibly reliable in less efficient equity segments. Fundamental Index applications bypass this return drag and, in so doing, consistently exceed the cap-weighted alternatives.

Table 3.4 confirms our two claims – the Fundamental Index cumulative long-term advantage increases and becomes more consistent over intermediate stretches as we move down the "efficiency curve". The since-inception results for selected RAFI and representative cap-weighted indexes are shown along with a column for annualised excess return and rolling three-year "batting average". Starting with US large caps as a baseline, we see a per-annum premium of 1.9% while winning in 73.9% over rolling three-year periods. The Global ex-US RAFI witnesses 3.6% annualised value-added over the MSCI World ex-US Index while the three-year batting average increases to nearly 98%.[5] Small-company Fundamental Index investors in the US and Global ex-US would have earned an annual premium of 3.3% and 5.4% over their representative cap-weighted indexes with a remarkable three-year win rate of over 99% and 95% respectively. Emerging markets, intuitively the most inefficient market of all given rounds of fiscal turmoil and high transaction costs, extend the Fundamental Index premium to an astonishing 10.3% annually and have yet to experience a three-year performance shortfall since the inception of our data in 1994.

Table 3.4 RAFI in less efficient markets

	Start date	Return (%)	Volatility (%)	Value add (%)	% three-year wins (%)
RAFI US Large	1962	10.9	14.7	1.9	73.9
S&P 500	(47 years)	9.0	15.0		
RAFI Europe	1984	14.2	17.2	2.8	94.0
MSCI Europe	(25 years)	11.4	17.2		
RAFI Japan	1984	4.9	19.6	3.1	90.6
MSCI Japan	(25 years)	1.9	20.1		
RAFI US Small	1979	14.1	19.0	3.3	99.7
Russell 2000	(30 years)	10.8	19.6		
RAFI Global Ex US 1000	1984	12.6	16.5	3.6	98.5
MSCI World Ex US	(25 years)	9.0	17.3		
RAFI Int'l Small 1500	1999	10.1	15.7	5.4	95.3
MSCI EAFE Small Cap	(10 years)	4.7	18.3		
RAFI EM	1994	13.0	24.6	10.3	100.0
MSCI EM	(15 years)	2.7	24.2		

ETF STRATEGIES USING THE FUNDAMENTAL INDEX CONCEPT

Practical applications for ETFs tracking Fundamental Index strategies are nearly limitless. We encourage investors to use their imaginations! Any equity ETF application available in a cap-weighted format – countries, regions, size, style and so forth – can be swapped for a Fundamental Index tracking vehicle.[6] The many expected benefits of ETF index exposure are retained – broad representation, massive diversification, low turnover, tax efficiency and reasonable fees. However, the lone flaw in the cap-weighted index fund – its structural bias to overweight the overpriced and underweight the underpriced – and the associated negative alpha are cured. As we have shown, this lost performance is hardly trivial.

While the strategies using this concept are without bounds, we are aware of a few that seem to be more widely used since the launch of Fundamental Index ETFs in late 2005. First among them is using the Fundamental Index portfolio to hedge passive, broad market exposure. Infrequent bubbles are a recurring theme in the history of investments from the Dutch tulip craze of the 1600s to the tech run-up of the late 1990s. With certainty, it is not a question of if but when. Of course, its construction methodology assures the cap-weighted index will go along for the ride. A price-weighted index will keep on increasing its wager on the hot market segment. It seems sensible to provide some protection in our index fund exposure for this eventuality by diversifying a portion of funds into a price indifferent approach.

The two pronounced stock market bubbles of the last 50 years are excellent examples of why such "passive diversification" makes sense. In both the Nifty Fifty and the tech bubble, the Fundamental Index concept, as measured by the RAFI US Large Company, began to deviate its composition from the S&P 500 market portfolio. In Figure 3.3, we quantify this difference in the rolling three-year tracking error.[7] The Fundamental Index portfolio's tracking error dramatically rises as it annually rebalances the market's favourite stocks back to their fundamental size while the cap-weighted index allowed its winners to ride, magnifying its bet. In both periods, RAFI went on to produce sizeable relative gains as the new paradigm theme failed to materialise. Thus, a diversified passive approach with equal parts capitalisation and fundamentally weighted helps offset the wealth-eroding effect of speculative fad and bubble unwindings.

Figure 3.3 Tracking error of RAFI and S&P 500

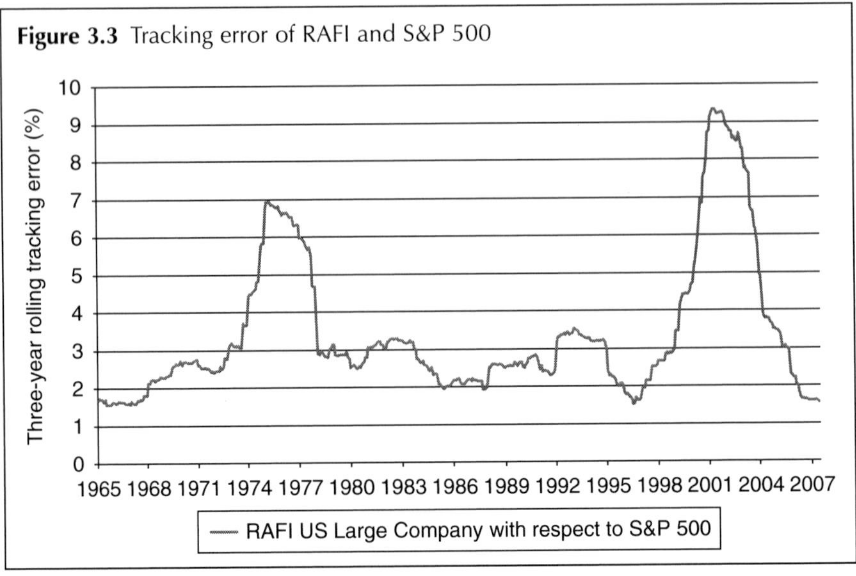

Meanwhile, a Fundamental Index portfolio behaves very much like a diversified core equity holding without these bubble episodes with a tracking error consistently in the 2–4% range, all the while adding incremental value over and above the S&P 500 in the majority – over 70% – of rolling three-year periods. Thus, this diversified passive approach is not a huge departure from a traditional core indexed portfolio.

Splitting passive exposure between these two orientations also makes sense intuitively from a style standpoint. We know the cap-weighted portfolio has a structural growth tilt – it gives twice the weight to each security with twice the market multiple and halves the weight to stocks selling at half the market P/E ratio. Growth stocks will always be overweighted in this kind of construct. Meanwhile, the Fundamental Index concept will assign the same weight to two companies with identical sales, cashflow, dividends and book value. If one is growing at a faster rate, it will be underrepresented, assuming the growth materialises in the future. Conversely, the slow grower will be overweight *vis-à-vis* its immediate prospects, thus ensuring a structural value orientation. We also know that the cap-weighted portfolio's growth bias will rapidly expand in bubbles as it allows these projected stars of tomorrow to become larger and larger positions. Blending a cap-weighted ETF's growth bias with the value tilt of a Fundamental Index ETF produces a more balanced growth/value orientation.

Another neat Fundamental Index ETF strategy revolves around increasingly popular sector funds. Advisers with a "top-down" macroeconomic view can quickly and efficiently take an exposure in a sector index ETF that has 20–100 individual names, thus eliminating the possibility of poor stock selection ruining an otherwise sound sector call. The Fundamental Index concept, as displayed in Table 3.5, has been applied to US and global economic sectors. The construction is simple by taking the sector holdings in the RAFI Large Company with its fundamental weights and comparing it with the cap-weighted sectors of the S&P 500. We find value-added in nine of 10 US sectors and 10 of 10 global sectors. Globally, Telecom saw the greatest value-add from selecting and weighting stocks on fundamental size metrics with per-annum excess returns of 4.9%. Consumer staples was at the other end but still a global consumer staples Fundamental Index portfolio posted an 80-basis-point annual premium over the MSCI Global Consumer Staples Index.

Thus, sector rotators now have an additional and potentially significant second source of excess returns. If an investor has a

Table 3.5 Fundamental Index sector performance

	US (1989–December 31, 2008)			**Global (1995–December 31, 2008)**		
	RAFI sector return (%)	**S&P sector return** (%)	**Value added** (%)	**RAFI sector return** (%)	**MSCI sector return** (%)	**Value added** (%)
Information technology	9.7	7.2	2.5	7.3	5.2	2.1
Utilities	9.5	7.1	2.4	10.9	8.2	2.7
Financials	8.7	6.5	2.2	5.5	2.8	2.7
Healthcare	12.2	10.2	2.1	11.1	9.4	1.6
Consumer staples	12.1	10.1	2.0	9.2	8.4	0.8
Energy	13.1	11.5	1.7	12.8	11.6	1.2
Industrials	9.2	7.5	1.7	5.8	3.7	2.0
Materials	6.7	5.5	1.3	8.8	4.8	4.0
Telecommunications	4.5	4.3	0.2	9.1	4.2	4.9
Consumer discretionary	4.1	5.8	−1.6	3.5	2.4	1.1

particular view on a sector and is proved correct with big returns, the Fundamental Index concept tends to keep pace in strong markets, implying full participation in this correct bet. Meanwhile, if the investor is wrong, the sector would falter badly and incur negative returns, but we know the Fundamental Index portfolios will generally cushion the downside quite markedly. That is true on the broad markets and within sectors. As a consequence, incorrect sector calls have a cushion while timely ones receive full participation – seemingly a very attractive way to invest in sectors. Incidentally, the same projected "cushion on the downside and participation on the upside" benefit would accrue to an investor that expresses top-down macro bets through country or regional allocations.

Fundamental Index sector ETFs also allow managers with sector-specific expertise to run a broader portfolio. For example, a stock picker with narrow expertise in financials and utilities can run a broader-value mandate. While a sizeable amount of the assigned benchmark may be in these predominately value sectors, the manager can fill in gaps in energy and consumer discretionary without giving up projected alpha at the overall portfolio level by using Fundamental Index sector ETFs.

One final implementation: Fundamental Index ETF strategy centres on the least efficient asset classes. Some advisers still cling to active management via mutual funds in small companies and emerging markets. Indeed, long-term peer-group data from performance-measurement firms indicates better odds for those willing to play the managed-fund game in these spaces.[8] Meanwhile, we previously found excess returns versus cap-weighted indexes – in line or higher than top quartile mutual funds – from simply shifting our passive approach to fundamental weights. For example, the Lipper Small Cap Core Mutual Fund Universe top quartile fund sported a 10-year excess return of 3.1% over the Russell 2000 Index as of December 31, 2008. The long-term value-add of RAFI Small Company is 3.3%. Yet, unlike active managers, the Fundamental Index concept in small companies (or emerging markets for that matter) maintains the positives of ETF index implementation – broad-coverage, high-capacity, intra-day trading and low fees. Accordingly, this ETF proposition deserves serious consideration as a one-stop alternative for filling an investor's small-company and emerging-markets allocations.

CONCLUSIONS

The Fundamental Index concept is not just theory: it is being used by institutional and individual equity investors today in a variety of geographical and company size mandates. Until December 2005, there were no Fundamental Index ETFs; three years later, there were more than 40, trading all over the world! Like other major indexes, a global index provider provides licences and data feeds to investment managers or plan sponsors to run Fundamental Index portfolios. Likewise, individual investors domiciled in North America, Europe, South Africa and elsewhere can access a host of exchange-traded funds linked to the Fundamental Index concept. In fact, by September 30, 2008, over US$19 billion in global assets are now managed in Fundamental Index portfolios, which we believe is substantial given the original publication of the idea was barely three years ago.

ETFs are a wonderful new tool. The vast majority are linked to cap-weighted indexes, where countless studies leave little doubt that most investors are better off versus actively managed and higher-priced mutual funds. However, should we rest on our laurels, especially when confronted with vast evidence that cap-weighted indexes underperform price indifferent alternatives? Perhaps it is because the theories of modern finance such as the capital asset pricing model and efficient markets hypothesis conclude the superiority of cap weighting.

This reminds us of something Yogi Berra said: "In theory there is no difference between theory and practice. In practice there is." We do our clients a disservice by looking the other way at the mounting evidence demonstrating that there is a better way. The Fundamental Index concept provides low-cost equity returns but in a matter more consistent with the frequent gaps between market prices and true fair values. Therefore, we consider it a new choice for ETF investors long dissatisfied with inefficient indexing in an inefficient market.

1 We should note that we have two patents pending on selecting and weighting indexes on fundamental measures of company size. We also hold trademark and registration rights on variations of "Fundamental Index" and "RAFI" on the Supplemental Register of the PTO in the US, as well as full trademarks in Europe and Japan. We respectfully ask investors to honour this intellectual property until the patents are decided.

2 Incidentally, one further shortfall of the SP EWI is its link to the Standard and Poor's committee-driven stock-selection process for the S&P 500, which typically adds stocks that have recently been successful and eliminates those that have struggled – in financial results

and presumably stock price. For this reason, we see the FTSE RAFI US 1000 exceed the return of equal weighting by 0.8% annually since the inception of the SP EWI.

3 Number of employees was tested in our original research but dropped, despite favourable performance, because of significant representation issues. For example, a fast-food burger flipper or a secretarial temp is given the same economic significance as a software engineer or a biochemist. As a result, McDonald's and Kelly Services routinely find their way into the top ten of an employment index.

4 US large company equities offered the longest testable time horizon (Arnott, Hsu and Moore 2005).

5 Both figures for Global ex-US are a bit misleading when trying to gain an intuition on the relative price efficiency of these markets. An interesting benefit accrues to a multi-country or global RAFI approach – country rebalancing. The average excess return among individual developed countries is 2.7%, but when combined into a Global ex-US portfolio it rises to 3.3%. In this application, the Fundamental Index avoids the cap-weighted drag of overloading on overvalued countries just as it does individual stocks or sectors in a single-country application such as US Large.

6 This assumes, of course, that the market in question has adequate depth (ie, number of names), avoids undue concentration (ie, 50% of the market is one stock) and has available, accurate financial data.

7 Tracking error is simply the standard deviation of excess returns above or below the benchmark and is an excellent measure of how close a portfolio's performance tracks its benchmark.

8 These figures need to be taken with a grain of salt. Survivorship bias artificially inflates the peer-group numbers as closed funds – and likely underperformers – are eliminated from the universe. Further, these excess returns accrue only to those willing to show the requisite patience in the active management game.

REFERENCES

Arnott, Robert D., Jason Hsu and Philip Moore, 2005, "Fundamental Indexing", *Financial Analysts Journal* 61(2), March/April, pp. 83–99.

Kittsley, D., 2006, "Dividend-Weighted Indexes: Tactical Plays, Not Broad Market Investments", *SSgA Viewpoints*, October.

Tamura, H., and Y. Shimisu, 2005, "Global fundamental indexes – Do they outperform market-cap-weighted indexes on a global basis?", Nomura Securities Co Ltd, Tokyo, Global Quantitative Research, October 28.

4

Mapping the ETF Universe

Richard A. Ferri

Portfolio Solutions, LLC

Index exchange-traded funds (ETFs) track securities indexes that are built on defined security selection and security weighting rules. Investors can gain extensive knowledge about an ETF by studying how the underlying index is constructed and maintained based on those rules. Knowledge about index construction rules puts an investor in a better position to make an informed investment decision.

ETF classifications methods are not new. There are several services that describe the type and style of funds available to the public. Equity ETFs are typically classified by company size and style factors, ie, large, small, value and growth. Fixed-income ETFs are typically classified by maturity and sector, ie, long-term, intermediate-term, short-term, government, investment-grade credit, non-investment-grade credit.

ETF classification by type and style serves the objective of a fund by defining the characteristics of securities held in an ETF, but it does not describe how securities are selected to be in the index or how securities are weighted in the index. The index classification mythology outlined in this chapter fills that gap. It defines how an index provider selects securities for an index and how those securities are weighted for that index.

Index categorisation by investment strategy is a two-part process. The first part defines the general index type that each ETF follows by either a market index or a strategy index, and the second part defines in more detail the methodology using an index strategy map.

A "market index" represents traditional market benchmarking techniques used for various asset classes. A "strategy index" represents customised investment strategies for investing in those asset classes. Market indexes are traditional measures that represent the universe that investors can choose from. It is the investable opportunity set of each asset class. In aggregate, the combined value of all securities held by investors makes a market index. ETFs that follow market index funds represent that market. In contract, strategy indexes represent alternative ways that investors can participate in the markets. By default, strategy indexes are not market benchmarks in that the providers intentionally design trading rules so those indexes do not track markets. The trading rules may include alternative security selection methods, alternative security weighting methods, or both.

After an index is categorised as either a market index or strategy index, further classification can be made using index strategy boxes (ISBs). ISBs and their accompanying tables give investors a quick and easy method for establishing how an index is constructed and maintained without having to comb through a fund prospectus or search an index provider's Website.

All indexes have rules for construction. There are two primary sets of rules establishing the security selection method and security weighting method. ISBs classify ETFs based on those two sets of rules. Each set of rules in an axis, and the rules for each axis are divided into three primary categories. The result is a set of nine boxes. Every ETF that follows an index falls into one of those boxes. The system can be applied to all asset classes, including stocks, bonds and commodities.

A free ISB database is available at www.ETGguide.com. Investors can quickly review ETFs for index strategy, and sort ETF products based on their underlying strategies. Users can also compare the fees of potential products using ISB methodologies to see if there are significant differences in cost. An example is shown later in this chapter.

There are many unfamiliar ETFs on the market today that are based on unfamiliar indexes. ETF classification by indexing rules is a natural next step in mapping out the marketplace. Product providers should encourage investors to understand the difference in structure, and be able to differentiate one product from another based on strategy. The adoption of ISB methodology is positive step for the ETF industry.

Your father's index fund

Measuring securities market performance dates back over 100 years to Charles Henry Dow's pioneering average. In 1884, Dow began to calculate the simply average of the prices of 12 mostly railway stocks that traded on the New York Stock Exchange. The average was published daily and providing investors with a feel for the direction of stock prices. Eleven of those stocks eventually became the basis for the Dow Jones Transportation Average.

Index methods advanced in the 20th Century as data-gathering methods improved and technology reduced calculation time. The most important innovation in index construction was that made by the Standard Securities Corp, now Standard & Poor's. In 1923, S&P constructed the first market-capitalisation-weighted index composite of 223 securities. The index later evolved into the S&P 500. Market capitalisation was accomplished by simply taking the price of each stock and multiplying it by the outstanding shares, and then adding all stock values together to form the total market value. This indicator measures the current value of all stock in an index. When dividend payments are calculated in, it forms a total-return index.

Capitalisation weighing is the standard index methodology around the globe. It also represents the theoretically mean–variance-efficient portfolio of securities in a given asset class. An outgrowth of this transformation is that capitalisation-weighted indexes have the lowest expected risk in a given asset class (among fully invested portfolios). In other words, they have a beta of 1.0 measured relative to the asset class. As such, market indexes have been pressed into duty as performance benchmarks against which to measure active management strategies. A manager has the choice to hold each security in the benchmark at the benchmark weight (which represents no active risk) or hold a greater or lesser weight (which represents some active risk). Active managers take bets against a benchmark and then their results are compared with the benchmark.

The principle that indexes are passively selected and capitalisation-weighted is so well founded in logic that it is hard for academics and learned professionals to separate the definition of the word "index" from the concept of market capitalisation. Yet that very idea is being challenged today by some people who claim that capitalisation-weighted indexes are not the best representation of investment value. They claim alternative securities selection methods such as fundamental weighting using dividends, earnings, revenue or a multifactor approach offer investors a better choice. One problem with this method is that the people marketing these claims cannot agree on consensus rules for constructing a standard, fundamentally weighted benchmark. The fundamental weighting methodologies are anything but uniform.

When a capitalisation-weighted index is well constructed, it represents the opportunity set for investors in an asset class. The returns on market indexes are the returns available from a fund or ETF benchmarked to that index, less a small fee. As a benchmark, market indexes have fostered many uses. The principal uses are:

- as the opportunity set that all investors can select from;
- as economic indicators used by central banks, academics and private enterprise;
- as proxies for asset class representation in asset allocation models;
- as benchmarks for comparing the skill of active investors; and
- as a standalone portfolio (although this was not an original purpose).

Market indexes are unquestionably important financial indicators. They are the standard applied throughout the world as valuation yardsticks. They are the benchmarks applied at the highest levels of economic analysis, including the US Federal Reserve. Broad market indexes are the preferred datasets used in fundamental research by all top academic institutions and private concerns. Virtually all asset allocation decisions are made using market index data, whether those decisions are being made by individual investors who use basic allocation models or by large institutional investors that use sophisticated modelling. In addition, market indexes are the yardstick by which all attempts to achieve superior performance through active management is measured. Last, but not least, over the last 30 years, market indexes have become the preferred indicators to use as benchmarks for index funds. No one market index is perfect for all uses and tradeoffs are inevitable; however, passively selected and capitalisation-weighted indexes are unquestionably the best representation for "the markets".

Market indexes are unbiased in selection and weighting. They are designed to measure markets, not outperform them. They are definitive reference points. They are stakes in the ground. Market indexes are the yardsticks that all investment decisions are measured against, and will be measured against for generations to come.

The first index funds and ETFs

Index funds and ETFs have their roots in long-established market indexes. They started with the very benchmarks that investment strategies have been measured against for years. In addition, the expense ratio of those funds remains very low compared with the active strategies that are measured against them. Low fees are a primary reason why market index funds outperform most active strategies.

The first public index fund was created by the Vanguard Group in 1975. It tracked a recognised market index, the S&P 500. Called the First Index Trust, the fund took in only US$11 million during its offering period, far below the US$50 million anticipated by Vanguard. Competitors ridiculed Vanguard founder, John C. Bogle, for launching a fund that gave investors only market returns. The idea, competitors said, was to beat the market. Sceptics anticipated that Vanguard would close the fund in a year. They were very wrong. Today, the Vanguard 500 Index Fund is the largest single public index fund available over US$100 billion in assets. Since 1975, The Vanguard Group has become the leader in public indexing and currently has more than US$500 billion in index products.

The first broadly traded ETF was launched in 1993 and it also tracks the S&P 500 index. SPDR S&P 500 is still the largest ETF on the market today with more than US$70 billion in assets and the most actively traded fund on the market. State Street is the second largest provider of ETFs by assets behind Barclays Global investors.

Not your father's index fund

Much has changed across the indexing landscape over the past decade. Even the very definition of the word "index" has drifted far away from its original intent as a proxy for broad market value. Gone are the days when index providers focused on creating the best benchmarks to use as market proxies. And gone are the days when investors intuitively understood that an index fund was a passively managed portfolio that tracks a recognised market benchmark. Today, a majority of new ETFs follow indexes that closer resemble active management strategies rather than passive, and thus they are referred to as strategy indexes.

Strategy indexes are not market indexes. Strategy indexes are designed by fund companies or index providers strictly to become an investment product. The creators of strategy indexes are not concerned with being a benchmark for market value, nor are they concerned with new indexes being used in economic analysis or in asset allocation decisions. The only purpose for a vast majority of strategy indexes is for launching commercial products.

Today, fund companies often dictate to the index providers how new indexes are to be created and how they will be maintained. The product providers go to index providers with active management ideas and ask the index providers to create a strategy with maintenance and trading rules. If strategy backtesting generates positive results relative to a market index over the period tested, the strategy becomes a new index and ultimately a new product that hypothetically "beats" the market.

The sad truth about indexing today is that the industry has lowered its standards. Indexing has degenerated to mean any mechanical trading strategy that has outperformed the market in backtesting and can be used to launch a new mutual fund or ETF. The fund company is paid a percentage based on the assets in a fund and the index company gets a piece of that. A snappy new product that follows a trendy new index may bring in billions in assets and millions in fees. The competition for index licensing fees has become intense. Index companies compete aggressively to create new indexes and administer new indexes brought to them by fund companies, and it does not really matter how viable these strategies might be in the future.

Little independent academic research is available that confirms the backtested results of most strategy indexes used to run a new fund. Investors have to take the product provider's word. Nonetheless, the Securities and Exchange Commission (SEC) allows fund providers to display the hypothetical index performance in marketing literature used by advisers, and any individual investor can easily access the backtested results through the fund provider's Website by saying they are an adviser. The investors who look at hypothetical index performance often are confused into thinking they are looking at actual live data. The SEC requires appropriate disclosures about hypothetical performance numbers in marketing literature, including a statement that fund performance is not index performance, but the disclosure is often in the fine print.

If strategy indexes are used only as investment products and not benchmarks, why are they now called indexes? There are two reasons this occurred. First, until 2008, the SEC required that all ETFs follow an index, although they did not define what an index was. That was left to the financial industry. Today, the SEC allows ETFs to trade that do not follow indexes. Thus, we have index ETFs and active ETFs. Second, active managers have been losing assets to index providers such as Vanguard for years. By redefining their active strategies as indexes, active managers could redirect some money destined for low-cost market index funds into their higher-cost, strategy index products.

Indexing is not what it used to be. Today, an index is any investment strategy that follows predefined rules for security selection and weighting, and then publishes the index constituents on a daily basis. Those rules create "market indexes" and "strategy indexes". Market indexes are asset-class benchmarks; strategy indexes involve active management decisions. It is helpful for investors to separate index funds and ETFs in that manner.

MAPPING THE INDEX UNIVERSE

Index providers follow predefined rules in the management of their indexes. The current constituents and weights of those indexes are provided to fund managers on a daily basis. The fund manager uses the index information to formulate their portfolio holdings, including any cash position. The fund holdings are then distributed to the authorised participants (APs) in a daily portfolio position file (PPF). The PPF is the basket of securities and cash the APs exchange for ETF shares during share creation, and the basket of securities they receive for a creation unit during a redemption.

Most index providers provide information about their index construction methods to the public. In addition, fund companies publish information about potential deviations from index holdings and when those deviations may be applicable. It is helpful when the index provider and fund manager publish detailed and clear index methodology and fund deviations information in plain English. An unsophisticated investor should be able to gain a working knowledge of the index methodology and fund management decisions from the published literature.

Most index providers and fund managers provide adequate information about their products for investors to understand their underlying strategies, although not always. Public information on some index products can be terribly confusing, misleading and, in a few cases intentionally vague. It would be expected that the providers of these funds would be forthcoming with information when asked given the competitive nature of the marketplace, but that is not the case. The response by those providers about their lack of disclosure is often that their methodology is "proprietary" or "part of a non-disclosure agreement" with another party, or no answer at all.

The index strategy map

Indexes follow rules for security selection and security weighting. These rules determine the constituents and weighting method for each index. The rules tend to fall into a few broadly discernible selection and weighting categories so that a rules-based categorisation system can be created. An index strategy map plots the security selection and weighting methods in a two-dimensional noughts-and-crosses diagram.[1]

Morningstar Incorporated popularised their noughts-and-crosses Morningstar style boxes in the 1990s to help investors identify the investment styles in fixed-income mutual funds. The two-dimensional style boxes provided investors with a quick overview of the types of securities each fund invested in. Equity funds use growth, blend and value on one axis and large-cap, mid-cap and small-cap on the other. Fixed-income style boxes categorise funds into the nine noughts-and-crosses boxes using the average maturity of a bond fund on one axis and the average credit quality of a bond fund on the other.

Unlike Morningstar style boxes, the index strategy map focuses on the rules used in index construction rather than what securities are owned. It is common for two mid-cap index ETFs to fall into the same Morningstar style box and different index strategy box.

It is also common for a small-cap-value ETF and a large-cap-growth ETF to be in different Morningstar style boxes and the same index strategy box. Morningstar style boxes are used to depict investment style while the index strategy map is used to depict index construction methods irrespective of style.

Index strategy boxes categorise each ETF based on its index construction rules for security selection and security weighting. The rows on the map represent security selection methodologies and the columns represent security weighting methods. The three rows, representing three broad security selection methods, are passive, screened and quantitative. The three columns, representing three broad security weighting methods, are capitalisation, fundamental and fixed. Each index strategy box represents a different mix of security selection and security weighting methods. Figure 4.1 illustrates the noughts-and-crosses design of the index strategy map.

Index strategy boxes and Morningstar style boxes work hand in hand when analysing index based products. Investors can use Morningstar to search for style-specific ETFs and then use the index strategy map to decide on an indexing methodology. For example,

Figure 4.1 Index strategy map

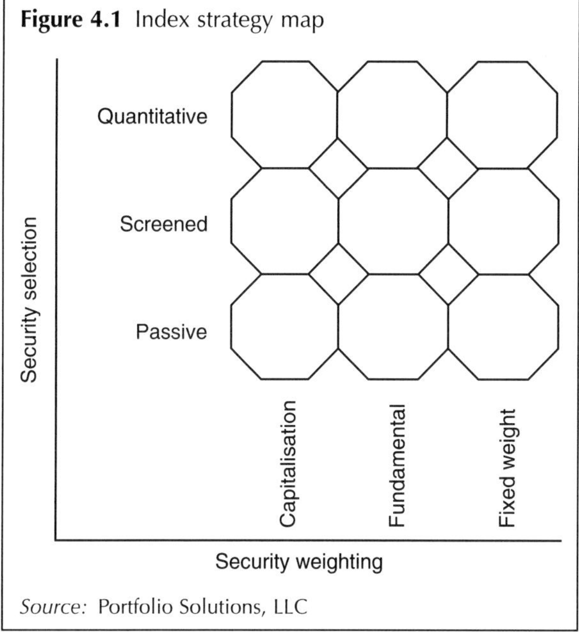

Source: Portfolio Solutions, LLC

assume an investor has decided to buy a large-cap US-value ETF. They can screen the ETF database at www.ETFguide.com to analyse the various indexing methodologies available in that style and select the type of large-cap US-value index product they are looking for. They may be seeking a very low-cost "market index" ETF that passively selects stocks and weights those securities according to their market capitalisations. Or they may be seeking to beat the market with a higher-cost "strategy index" ETF that uses a quantitative security selection process and alternative weighting method.

An appealing feature of the index strategy map is that it can be used for any asset class. The two-step process for index construction rules using security selection and security weighting is universal across equity indexes, fixed-income indexes, commodity indexes and multi-currency indexes. In addition, asset-class sectors and subsectors also fit cleanly into one of the nine index strategy boxes.

Index security selection

Index construction begins with a set of rules for security selection. Generally, index providers begin with a broad universe of securities. Depending on the type of selection process, the index provider may then whittle the list down to a portfolio of representative stocks that best suits their purpose. Some indexes have thousands of securities while others have only a couple of dozen.

Fund managers may represent an index in a fund using a variety of techniques. They can completely replicate all securities, sample the securities in the index, use derivatives that track the index, or a combination of sampling and derivatives. The important factor for index strategy map purposes is that the fund manager is attempting to replicate an index rather than how they do it. That makes the index selection rules the focal point of the security selection process in the index strategy map rather than fund-management techniques.

The three rows in the index strategy map represent three basic securities-selection methods used by index providers. At a base level, all index providers use one of these three basic methods as the primary means for selection in all indexes. It may appear at first observation that an index uses a combination of these methods or none of the methods, but, with deeper analysis, each ETF can be placed in one of the three security selection categories with confidence.

Securities are selected for indexes based on rules that are specified in advance and rigorously applied. These rules spell out the characteristics that a security must pose for inclusion in the index. Those characteristics must also be maintained for continued inclusion during reconstitution of an index.

Some rules tend to be universal across all indexes. One criterion for security selection in nearly all indexes is adequate liquidity or pricing. If a stock cannot be accurately priced because of infrequent trading, it is left out of most indexes. Another common exclusion rule is low price, such as stocks trading at less than US$2. Most indexes exclude investment companies such as ETFs and closed-end funds because those entities hold securities that trade on exchanges. Excluding investment companies and ETFs prevents double counting.

Differences in index security selection rules can be classified into three broad categories: passive, screened and quantitative. Indexes that select securities passively are attempting to represent a good cross-section of securities on a market. Screened indexes isolate specific segments of a market and eliminate all other segments. Quantitative selection is a "beat the market" approach to investing whereby a few securities are selected using advanced computer analysis. Table 4.1 lists the three broad selection categories and a sampling of strategies in each category.

The index strategy map is designed to place an ETF in one method of security-selection row that best represents the selection strategy. There are cases when an index could fit into two security-selection categories, or even all three. When selection is not clear cut, a holistic approach to security selection is needed to determent which one method best describes the single most important selection criterion that may effect performance.

Table 4.1 Security selection categories and a sampling of strategies

Passive	Screened	Quantitative
Full replication	Fundamental factors	Economic cycle
Sampling strategies	Thematic	Forward estimates
Buy-and-hold	Exchange-specific	Momentum/technical
Single securities	Qualitative factors	Proprietary

Source: Portfolio Solutions, LLC

Passive security selection

Passive security selection is the methodology most commonly used in global stock and bond index construction. The selection process provides a broad representation of securities on a market. There are no other biases in passive selection, meaning all industries and styles are represented by the index provider.

Passive selection does not require including all the securities on a market. There need be only enough constituents for the basket to reflect the natural price movement of a securities market. Securities are always selected across markets, so they are not exchange-specific or exchange-biased. For example, a passively selected US equities index has both New York Stock Exchange and Nasdaq securities.

Another trademark of passive selection is low turnover. In fact, passive selection typically has the lowest turnover of security selection types. Turnover is mostly the result of mergers and acquisitions and otherwise delisting of a security. New securities go into an index during regular reconstitution dates or when needed according to maintenance rules.

Passive selection: complete representation and sampling

The major broad-based US equity providers licensed by fund providers include Frank Russell & Co (Russell), Morgan Stanley Capital International (MSCI), Morningstar, Standard and Poor's (S&P), and Dow Jones Wilshire. Popular bond providers include Lehman Brothers (now owned by Barclays), Citigroup and Merrill Lynch.

Figure 4.2 Passive security selection

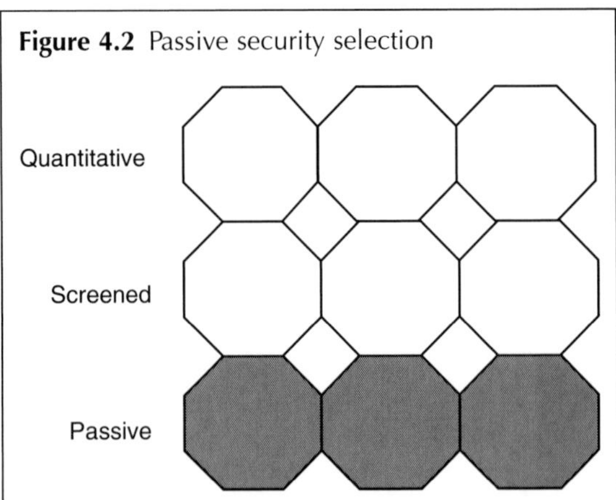

There are too many other providers with important indexes to mention them all here.

All of the above index providers have broad market indexes that attempt to capture the returns of the markets. The DJ Wilshire 5000 attempts to track the entire list of more than 5,000 US stocks. The Lehman Aggregate Bond Market attempts to capture the risk and return of the entire investment-grade bond market, excluding Treasury inflation-protected securities (TIPS).

Rather than use all the securities on an index, most index providers now use sampling methods. The idea is to construct indexes by selecting a basket of securities from a market in an attempt to replicate the characteristic and price movement of the entire market without having thousands of securities. Sampling makes fund managers happy because it is easier for them to manage actual portfolios and it reduces tracking error between their fund and the index. Most index providers place heavy emphasis on computer modelling to optimise their selections.

Some indexes sample the old-fashioned way. Rather than use a computer, they use a committee of human beings. The S&P 500 and the Dow Jones Industrial Average (DJIA) are placed under the passive selection category even though the securities are hand-selected by committee members. Neither indicator represents the entire market for large-cap stocks, yet the securities selected for both track closely an index that does include all stocks. As such, both the S&P 500 and the DJIA are considered to have passive security selection.

Passive selection: style, size, and industry sectors

Large index providers have index families. Families are created from a broad market index. For example, Frank Russell & Co of Tacoma, Washington, has the Russell family of passively selected stock indexes. Most Russell indexes are subsets of the Russell 3000 Index, which represents approximately 98% of the investable, free-float US equity market.

The Russell passive family of indexes is a hierarchy. It is divided into parts and the parts add up to the whole. The broad market index becomes value-and-growth indexes, and small-stock and large-stock indexes. Building back up, those indexes reconnect to form the Russell 3000. Figure 4.3 illustrates the family.

Figure 4.3 Russell 3000 index family

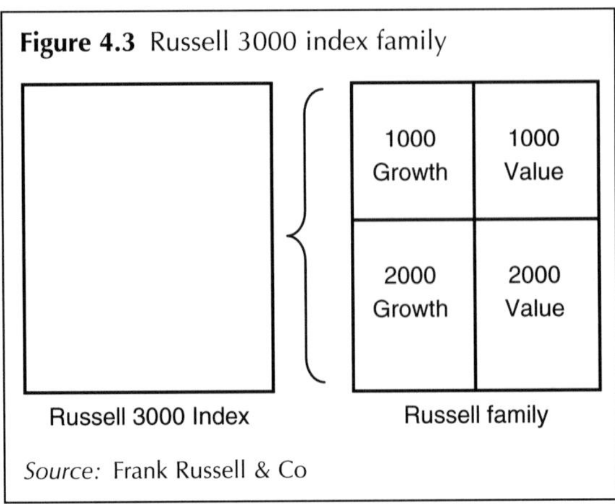

Source: Frank Russell & Co

Broad market index providers often slice the index into industry groups based on established industry classification methods. All the industry-sector indexes are also considered to be passive selection because it came from the broad market. Adding the industry sector indexes back together forms the broad market.

The providers of passively selected industry-sector indexes are not biased towards one industry sector or another. All sectors are equally available. It is up to the investor to decide which sector they choose to be in. Figure 4.4 is the decomposition of the S&P 500 index by industry. All stocks in the S&P 500 are in one of the industry sectors. The sector indexes are mutually exclusive so there is no overlap. Figure 4.4 is an illustration of the 10 passively selected S&P 500 industry sectors.

More passive selection methods

One ETF provider has created one-time securities baskets that hold a fixed portfolio. Holding company depositary receipts (HOLDRs) fill their trusts one time with the largest securities in an industry sector and hold that portfolio for many years. The advantage is extremely low-cost administration and no turnover. The disadvantage is that no new securities can go into a fund. Stocks are taken out of the basket due to mergers and acquisitions but no new companies can replace them. The cash is distributed.

There are many ETFs that follow the performance of a single security or item. Single securities are considered passive selection because it is just one security or item and it does not change. A gold

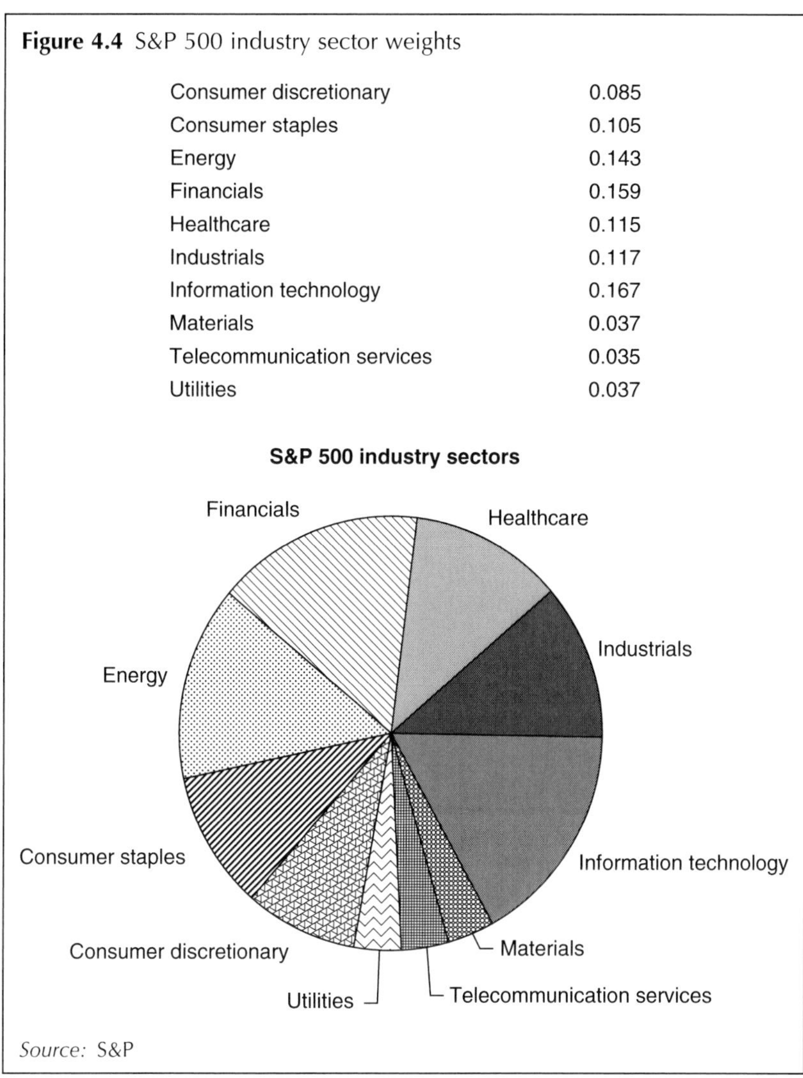

Figure 4.4 S&P 500 industry sector weights

Consumer discretionary	0.085
Consumer staples	0.105
Energy	0.143
Financials	0.159
Healthcare	0.115
Industrials	0.117
Information technology	0.167
Materials	0.037
Telecommunication services	0.035
Utilities	0.037

Source: S&P

fund represents passive selection because it holds only gold. Most currency ETFs hold only one currency and that currency never changes. Single commodities futures such as a near-term oil contract also fall under the category of passive security selection.

Screened security selection

Security screening is the second type of security selection method. With screened indexes, providers filter broad baskets of securities

Figure 4.5 Passive security selection

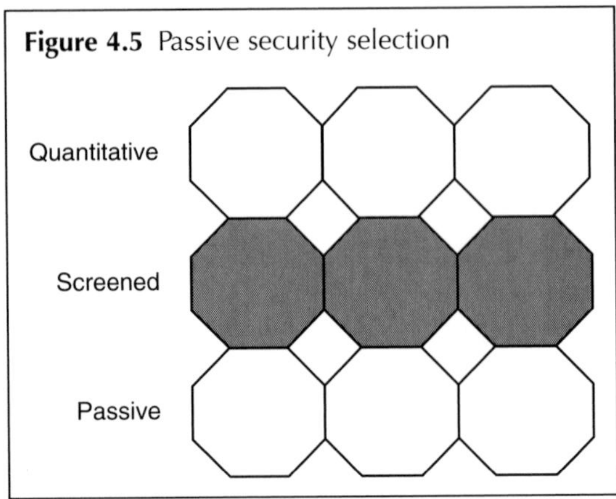

to weed out those that have undesirable characteristics. A simple example is social-awareness indexes. The social-awareness index provider eliminates all companies that their mandate considers to be socially unacceptable, such as tobacco companies and companies that pollute the environment.

Screening can be simple or complex, and the methodology is limited only by the imagination of the index provider. Screening can be based on religious, social, or environmental beliefs. It can be based on insider trading, price trend following, or certain fundamental qualities or a lack of those qualities, eg, eliminating stocks that have a high debt-to-equity ratio and no earnings. Screening can also eliminate securities that do not trade on certain stock exchange. For example, the Nasdaq-100 is a screened index because it includes only stocks that primarily trade on the Nasdaq with the exception of financial stocks, which are screened out.

Screened indexes require active management decisions in that the index providers make an active decision when they decide to eliminate certain types of securities and retain others. It is fair to say that ETF companies that follow these strategy indexes are following an active investment strategy.

Strategy indexes based on screens are not necessarily designed to "beat the market" although that is the goal of some. Rather, they are created as tailored portfolios to fit a specific investment theme or belief. That being said, many ETF companies do use screened indexes to promote their products as a "better way to index", although there is no evidence that ETFs benchmarked to screened indexes have or will outperform a comparable market index over the long term.

The providers of screened indexes start the process with a large universe of securities. Computers filter out securities that do not fit the parameters of what the provider is seeking. After screening is complete, the remaining list becomes the index constituents, or securities are sampled from the list to form the index constituents.

Securities that are eliminated from a screened index are completely gone. They no longer exist. Those securities do not go into an "undesirable index". For example, a socially responsible index provider does not maintain socially irresponsible indexes. Figure 4.6 illustrates the screening process. Notice that the unwanted securities are permanently eliminated by the process.

Examples of screened indexes

There are thousands of screens that can be applied to create custom indexes. The following paragraphs highlight a few of the more popular ones. By and large, the purpose of these custom indexes is to create and license investment products. Few custom indexes have any relevance in economic analysis, academic research, or asset allocation.

Dividend indexes. Stocks that pay regular dividends became quite popular after the tax law changes in 2003. The top tax rate on stock dividends was lowered to 15% if the shares were held more than 60 days. In addition, value stock investing became very popular in

Figure 4.6 Screened index security selection

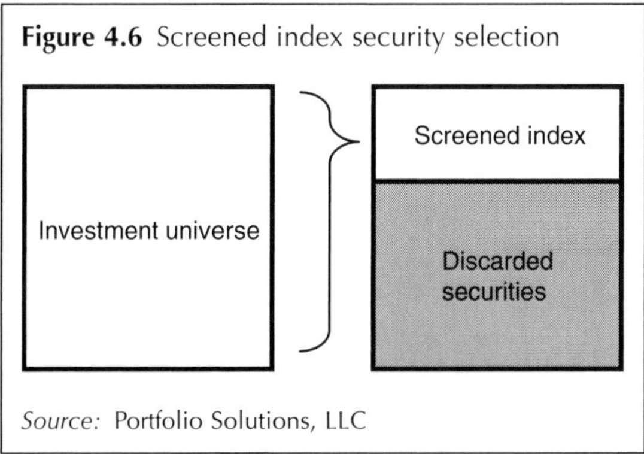

Source: Portfolio Solutions, LLC

the first half of the decade after the growth stock bubble collapse from March 2000 to March 2003. Those two events led to the creation of many dividend screened indexes followed by the launch of several ETFs that follow those custom indexes.

Dividend indexes have filters designed to sift through a basket of stocks looking for companies that pay regular cash dividends. Typically, an index provider starts with a universe of stocks composed of all exchanges. For example, the WisdomTree Dividend Index holds cash dividend-paying companies listed on the NYSE, AMEX and Nasdaq. According to WisdomTree, in 2008, there were approximately 1,500 dividend-paying stocks culled from a 3,500 stock universe that met minimum capitalisation and liquidity requirements.

Dividend indexes have strong value stock bias. Compared with non-dividend-paying stocks, companies that pay dividends typically are in mature industries, have lower price-to-earnings ratios (P/E), low price-to-book ratios (P/B), and low price-to-sales ratios (P/S). In addition, dividend indexes have a higher correlation with a passive value index than with a passive growth index. That means when the passive value index goes higher and the passive growth indexes goes lower, custom dividend indexes follow the value index.

Second- and third-dividend screens are typically applied to dividend indexes. Those screens may be designed to eliminate companies that have not increased their dividends in recent years, or pay out too much of the earnings as dividends, or have reduced their dividend. Index providers use as many screens as needed to tweak their custom indexes to just the right list of securities that they or their ETF firm client is actively seeking.

Exchange indexes. With the recent merger of the New York Stock Exchange (NYSE) and the American Stock Exchange (AMEX) in 2008, there are now two primary stock exchanges in the US: the NYSE and the National Association of Securities Dealers Automated Quotations system (Nasdaq). Each exchange has its own set of indexes based exclusively on the stocks that trade on those exchanges. The Nasdaq Composite Index includes only stocks that trade on the Nasdaq, while the NYSE Composite Index includes only stocks that trade on the NYSE. These are screened indexes because they include only stocks that trade primarily on one exchange.

The Nasdaq-100 Index includes 100 of the largest domestic and international securities based on the market capitalisation of the stocks that trade primarily on the Nasdaq. The index includes computer hardware and software, telecommunications, retail/wholesale trade and biotechnology. Banks and financial-services companies are screened out. The purpose of the industry screen is to give the Nasdaq-100 Index a growth stock bias. PowerShares QQQ tracks Nasdaq-100 Index and the trades on Nasdaq (symbol: QQQQ).

Socially responsible indexes. Socially responsible indexes are designed to reflect the way certain socially conscious investors select companies. As such, the indexes filter out companies involved in alcohol, tobacco and gambling, as well as controversial industries such as nuclear power, firearms and weapons-related defence contracting. Some socially responsible indexes also filter for subjective areas such as community relations, diversity, employee relations, environmental stewardship, human rights, product safety and quality, and corporate governance.

The KLD Select Social Index is a service mark of KLD Research & Analytics Inc. The index has been licensed for use by Barclay's Global Investors and is the benchmark for the iShares KLD Select Social Index ETF (symbol: KLD). The fund uses a representative sampling strategy in tracking the KLD Select Social Index.

The KLD Select Social Index consists of approximately 200 to 300 securities drawn from the universe of companies held in the Russell 1000 and the S&P 500 Indexes. Companies that do not meet KLD's financial screens of minimum market capitalisation, earnings, liquidity and stock price are also ineligible for inclusion.

In addition to screening out companies that make products that are offensive to some people, KLD screens for social and environmental performance based on seven qualitative areas. Those areas are environment, community, corporate governance, diversity, employee relations, human rights and product quality and safety.

Corporate action filters. Initial public offerings (IPOs) are companies that raise capital by selling common shares to investors for the first time. Once issued, those shares trade on a public stock exchange. Index providers can screen the markets to find IPO data and create custom indexes based on IPO information.

The US IPOX Composite Index is managed by Chicago index firm IPOX Schuster. The IPOX 100 Index measures the performance of the largest 100 companies in the US IPOX Composite as ranked quarterly by market capitalisation. The companies included in the index have had their IPO within 1,000 trading days (about four years). Since one or two large companies such as Google (symbol: GOOG) can dominate the index, individual securities are capped at 10% of the funds holdings. The First Trust IPOX-100 Index Fund (Symbol: FPX) follows the IPOX-100 index.

Quantitative security selection

Quantitative security selection strategies are designed to find securities that are believed to have superior performance potential. The strategies use sophisticated "black box" analysis to rank securities based on near-term attractiveness. The securities with the highest rankings are selected because, according to product providers, these securities have the highest probability of "beating the market".

A quantitative index holds a relatively small number of stocks, typically between 40 to 100 securities. That is in contrast to hundreds of securities in filtered indexes and sometimes thousands of securities in passively selected indexes. Figure 4.8 illustrates the narrow range of securities that are included in quantitative indexes.

Higher securities turnover is another quantitative selection characteristic, although trading does depend on the frequency at which the index provider reconstitutes its index. An index that is reconstituted

Figure 4.7 Quantitative security selection

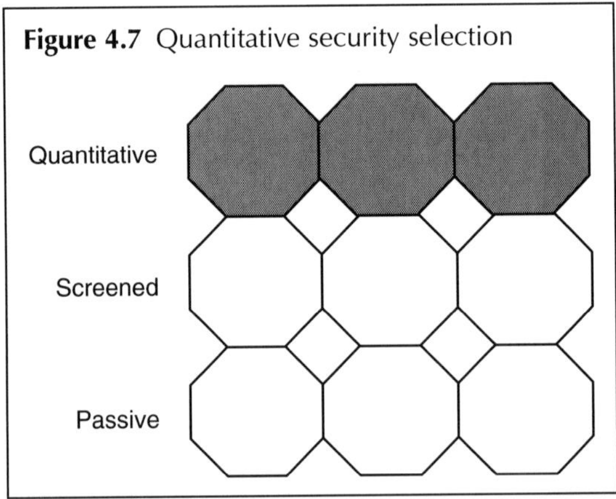

Figure 4.8 Quantitative index security selection

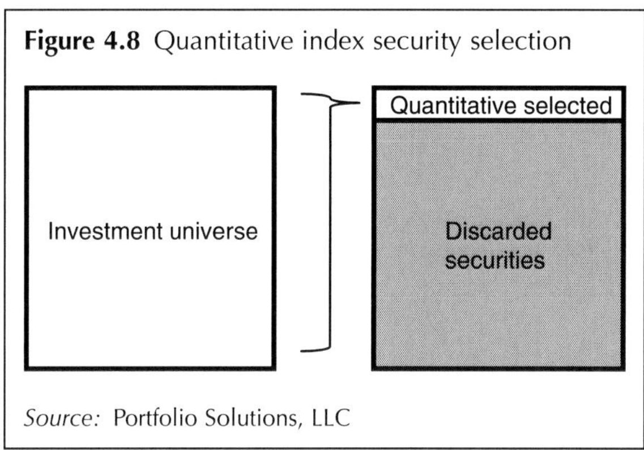

Source: Portfolio Solutions, LLC

annually might have a turnover of 50%, quarterly reconstitution might result in turnover of 100% per year, and monthly reconstitution might result in turnover of 250% per year.

How quantitative indexes select securities is often a dark secret. Most quantitative index providers are intentionally vague about their security selection methodology. According to the CFA Institute, index rules should be transparent enough so that any trained analyst can reconstruct an index and achieve the same investment results using historical data. However, the quant people say they do not want competitors reconstructing their indexes and stealing their secrets. Consequently, investors must place a lot of faith in ETF companies that use quantitative selection methods.

Universally, ETFs that employ quantitative methods charge higher fees than ETFs that follow indexing using filtered methods or passive security selection. Costs are an important consideration when selecting an indexing methodology.

Examples of quantitative security selection

The following are several examples of quantitative selection. The methods range from complex to eccentric.

Intellidex indexes. PowerShares was founded in 2002 by former Nuveen Investments sales and marketing executive H. Bruce Bonds. His idea was to use quantitative method to create indexes for use as benchmarks for ETFs. The methodology was initially developed by Bonds and then tweaked into a viable trading basked by analysts at AMEX. The Intellidex indexes are currently maintained by AMEX to satisfy the SEC requirement for a separation between the index provider and the fund company.

Details of Intellidex index methodology is not made public; what is known about Intellidex methodology is that it seeks to select stocks that meet certain quantitative criteria that are indicative of a potential stock growth. The system uses 25 selection criteria broken into four main groups: risk factors, momentum, fundamental growth, and stock valuations. Factors in the model include cashflow, historical trading range, analysts' consensus estimates, earnings growth, fundamental ratios, a consistent record of profitability and market liquidity. The exact sequence of the process and how much weight is given to each factor is not made available.

In May 2003, PowerShares launched its first two funds based on AMEX Intellidex indexes. PowerShares Dynamic Market Portfolio (symbol: PWC) begins with an initial universe of the 2,000 largest US-domiciled stocks by market and only 100 stocks end up in the index after quantitative methods are applied. The Dynamic OTC (Symbol: DYO) is similarly constructed and also has 100 stocks, although the initial universe of stocks is the 1,000 largest US-headquartered companies quoted on the Nasdaq.

Constituents in Intellidex indexes change quarterly during reconstitution. As a result, PowerShares ETFs that are benchmarked to those indexes tend to have high turnover ranging from 50% to 150% annually.

AlphaDEXes. First Trust's AlphaDEX ETFs were introduced in May 2007 to compete head to head with PowerShares Dynamic ETFs. The 16 AlphaDEX also attempt to "beat the market" using quantitative selection ETFs. The methodology takes existing S&P and Russell indexes and runs them through several quantitative models to find securities expected to outperform the existing benchmarks.

One difference between AlphaDEX and Intellidex is that the former is more transparent in its methodology. It gives investors all the nitty-gritty details about the security selection process.

Niche quantitative indexes. The PowerShares DWA Technical Leaders Portfolio (symbol: DWA) is based on the Dorsey Wright Technical Leaders Index. That index includes approximately 100 US listed companies that are believed to demonstrate powerful relative price-strength characteristics.

The index is constructed pursuant to Dorsey Wright "proprietary" methodology, which means there is not a lot of information available. The prospectus states that the index takes into account, among other factors, the price momentum and performance of each of the 3,000 largest US-listed companies compared to composite benchmark, and the relative performance of industry sectors and subsectors. The methodology evaluates companies quarterly and ranks them using a proprietary formula. Stocks that are selected receive a modified equal weighting in that large-cap stock have a certain fixed weight per company and small-cap stocks have a different fixed weight per company.

The PowerShares Value Line Timeliness Select Portfolio (symbol: PIV) is based on the Value Line Timeliness Select Index. The index seeks to identify a group of 50 companies that have the potential to outperform the US equity market. The index utilises the popular Value Line Ranking System, which comprises three categories: Timeliness, Safety and Technical. The equally weighted portfolio is rebalanced and reconstituted quarterly.

The Claymore/Clear Spin-Off ETF (symbol: CD) seeks investment results that correspond generally to the performance, before fees and expenses, of an equity index called the Clear Spin-Off Index. A spin-off occurs when a public company is separated from its larger parent firm and it subsequently trades on a stock exchange separate from its former parent. The Clear Spin-Off Index tracks those companies, although it is not simply a filtered index of spin-offs. Once the universe of spin-offs is established, each company goes through a rigorous quantitative analysis and only 40 stocks are selected for the Clear Spin-Off Index.

The Claymore/Ocean Tomo Patent ETF (symbol: OTP) seeks investment results that correspond generally to the performance, before fees and expenses, of an equity index called the Ocean Tomo 300 Patent Index. The index is an intellectual property index. It is a quantitatively selected index of 300 companies that own valuable patents. The evaluation of each company's patent portfolio is done by Ocean Tomo's, which calculates the relative attractiveness of the more than four million patents that have been issued by the US Patent and Trademark Office since 1983.

Index security weighting

Security selection is the first half of index construction and weighing those securities in the index is the second half. The weight allocated to each security in an index is important because different weighting schemes applied to the same basket of securities can have a profound impact on performance.

Index providers allocate securities in their indexes using three basic methods; capitalisation weight, fundamental weight and fixed weight. A capitalisation-weighted index bases the allocation on the relative market value of each security in that index. Fundamentally weighted indexes use financial ratios or qualitative factors to allocate among index constituencies. Fixed weighting assigns a fixed weight to constituents at the security level, industry level, style level or index level. Leverage, short (inverse) and long-short ETFs are also considered fixed-weighted indexes because the weighting of the entire index is a multiple of the index.

The three columns in index strategy boxes represent these three weighing methods. Most indexes fit easily into one of the three categories. There are a few indexes that could fit into two security weighing categories depending on how a person interprets the process. In those cases, the weighting methodology assigned is the one that best fits the index based on the how it compares to the weighting methods used by other indexes. For example, leveraged, inverse and long-short indexes may seem to be a good fit for the capitalisation-weighted category. However, it goes in fixed weight because the entire index is either 100% short (–1 times the index), 200% long (+2 times the index), or a fixed percentage long and short (+1.3 times long securities and –0.3 times short securities).

Table 4.2 lists the three broad weighting categories and a sampling of strategies in each category.

There are cases when an index could fit into two security weighting categories. When selection is not clear-cut, a holistic approach to security weighting is needed to determine which one method best describes the single most important weighting method that may effect index performance.

Capitalisation weighting

Capitalisation weighting is the intuitive method of security allocation because it reflects the investment opportunity set for all investors. For

Table 4.2 Sampled security weighting categories and sampled strategies

Capitalisation	Fundamental	Fixed weight
Full-cap	Financial factors	Equal weight
Free-float	Security price	Modified equal
Constrained	Momentum	Leveraged 2X, 3X
Liquidity	Qualitative factors	Short (inverse) –1X, –2X
Production	Time horizon	Long/short and 130/30

Source: Portfolio Solutions, LLC

Figure 4.9 Capitalisation weighting

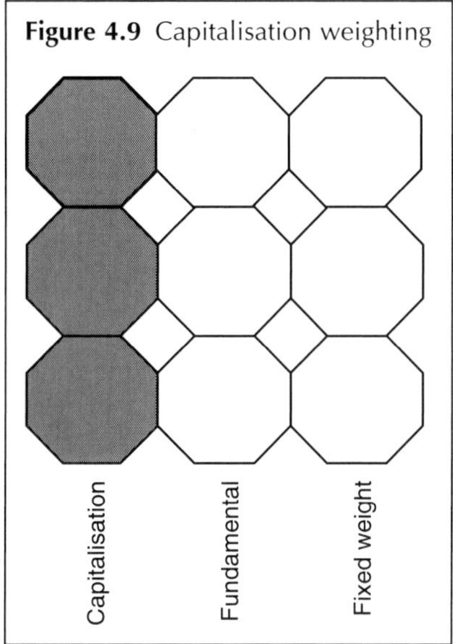

each stock in an index, capitalisation is simply the number of shares outstanding times its market price. Capitalisation-weighted indexes move with the total dollar value of securities in an index.

The market capitalisation of a company is calculated by multiplying the number of common shares outstanding by the current market price for those shares. For example, if a company has 200 million shares of common stock outstanding, and the current market price of that stock is US$50 per share, the market capitalisation of the company would be US$10 billion.

In a capitalisation-weighted equity index the market values of all constituents are added together. This naturally places a proportionally greater importance on large companies than on small companies, because large companies are worth more nominal dollars. The Russell 3000 has 3,000 stocks, but it is the largest 100 stocks that have the greatest influence on the index return.

The markets are an open auction. Willing buyers and willing sellers enter the securities markets each day to trade securities based upon agreed fair price. The value of a company stock or a bond on any given day can be thought of as the consensus price of all global investors. Some people argue that markets do a poor job deciding the fair market of companies. However, with millions of investors worldwide looking over the same data and interested investors coming to a fair and open agreement about price, that price is not likely to be too far off.

Types of capitalisation weighting

There are five basic types of capitalisation-weighted indexes: full-cap, free-float, capped (constrained), liquidity and single-security. The difference between full-cap and free-float is that the former includes the total value of all securities outstanding while the latter includes the value of only those shares that are available to all investors in the public markets. Capped equity indexes and constrained bond indexes preclude a few very large securities from dominating an index by limiting the amount in any single security or industry. Liquid indexes are useful in thinly traded markets to ensure that there is enough trading volume of securities to physically create investment products such as ETFs. Single-security indexes are made up entirely of one item, and that item is assumed to be capitalisation-weighted because it is traded as such.

Almost all capitalisation-weighted indexes were full-cap through the 20th Century. Every share of company stock outstanding was counted regardless of who owned it. A full-cap index counted shares that were restricted from sale, part of a private placement of stock, held by the government, and cross-held by other publicly traded corporations. Full-cap-weighted indexes have the advantage of reflecting the full market value of a company, which is good for economic study, but the disadvantage is that they hold shares that are not available in the public market, thus providing an inaccurate yardstick for creating index funds that represented the investable market.

Capitalisation-weighted methodology shifted by the millennium to free-float. A free-float (or float-adjusted) index includes only shares that are available in the public markets. Float-adjusted indexes more accurately measure the investable market universe available for purchase by the public. They also make easier benchmarks for index fund managers to replicate because the securities are available. In addition, free-float indexes also represent a better benchmark against which to judge the performance of active management.

Most full-cap index providers have switched to free-float. MSCI indexes completed the switch from a full cap to free-float in 2002 and indexing giant S&P completed its switch in 2005.

Liquidity is a major concern for product providers. A float-adjusted capitalisation-weighted index may be the best representative of the investable market. However, some securities in the index may be hard to buy or sell because those securities do not have an adequate volume of trading activity. A liquidity-adjusted index lowers the weight in securities that have limited trading activity, and that works well in some areas such as emerging markets. The next generation of capitalisation-weighted indexes may well be liquidity-adjusted to reflect better the ability to purchase securities.

Market can become dominated by a few securities. That creates a problem for some ETF structures that have to abide by the SEC's requirements for fund diversification. The concentrated security problem can be solved by benchmarking an ETF to a "constrained" or "capped" index. Those indexes place maximum-percentage caps on large positions in a capitalisation-weighted index to ensure that index products do not become overweighed in those securities. Typically the cap is between 5% and 10% on any single security. The excess amount is spread across all other securities in the index.

In the US alone, there are hundreds of capitalisation-weighted indexes covering all corners of the market. Broad, float-adjusted, capitalisation-weighted stock indexes providers include Dow Jones Wilshire, Russell, MSCI, Morningstar, Citigroup and Standard & Poor's – to name just a few. Most bond index providers use a full capitalisation weighting of sorts, although a more appropriate description would be "value-weighted". The driving factor for weighting bonds in an index is the market value of the bonds rather than the market value of the entity that issued them.

Capitalisation-weighted bond indexes include US Treasury bonds, corporate bonds, high-yield bonds, convertible bonds, mortgages, tax-exempt bonds and foreign bonds. Some leading providers of bond indexes are Lehman Brothers (now owned by Barclays), JP Morgan, Dow Jones and Merrill Lynch (now owned by Bank of America). Since many fixed-income indexes are dominated by one or two issues, several fixed-income index providers offer both unrestrained and constrained (capped) indexes.

There are no direct market-capitalisation-weighted indexes in the commodities markets, but there are attempts at economic weighting. Commodities are held in a variety of ways: long futures positions, over-the-counter investments, long-term fixed-price purchasing contracts, physical inventory at the producer, etc. That makes a complete accounting of the stock of commodities outstanding very difficult.

An easier way to achieve a market-capitalisation-like weighting in commodities is to count the amount of the commodity produced. The quantity of each commodity in the index is determined by the average quantity of production in the prior five years of available data. For instance, the impact that doubling the price of oil has on inflation and on economic growth depends directly on how much oil was produced. The appropriate weight assigned to each commodity is in proportion to the amount of that commodity flowing through the economy.

The only problem is that oil- and energy-related commodities dominate the markets, and overwhelm any production weighting methodology. Thus, many commodities indexes use restrictive caps on energy levels, or resort to modified equal weighting methodology.

The S&P GSCI (formally the Goldman Sachs Commodities Index) is world-production-weighted index. It holds as many commodities as possible, with the rules excluding commodities only to retain liquidity in the futures markets. Currently, the S&P GSCI contains 24 commodities from all sectors: six energy products, five industrial metals, eight agricultural products, three livestock products and two precious metals.

Fundamental weighting

Fundamentally weighted indexes use factors other than market cap to determine the weight of securities in an index. Those factors can

Figure 4.10 Fundamental weighting

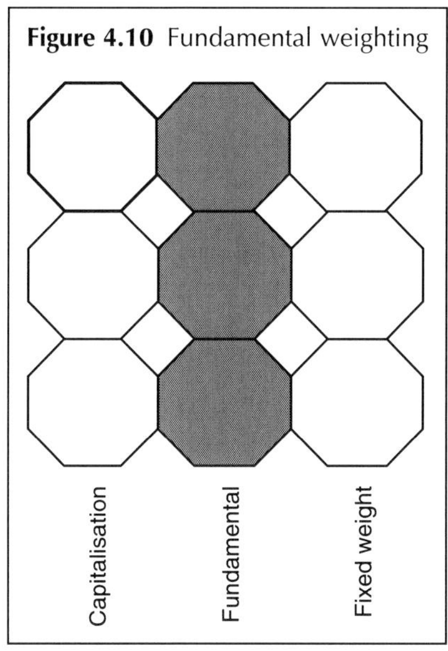

be derived from many different sources, the most common being corporate financial statements. Fundamental weighting based on financial statement data can be a single variable such as a company's dividend yield or earnings, or it can be a complex multifactor model that brings several pieces of financial data into an equation. Fundamental weighting can also be qualitative such as the level of environment stewardship and community involvement rankings. The weighting in a balanced index where asset classes take on variable weights can be based on economic factors, asset class valuations, or even the age of an investor.

Fundamentally weighted indexes are rebalanced periodically to realign the index with changing conditions. Consequently, the amount of trading taking place in a fundamentally weighted index is higher than in a capitalisation-weighted index. More trades implies higher costs in a fundamentally weighted portfolio over capitalisation weighing, and potentially less tax efficiency, although ETF managers have other methods to offset those taxable events.

A question of purity versus product

It is interesting to note that fundamentally weighted indexes are "in balance" only on the first day following a rebalancing, which is only a few times per year or less. After that, fundamentally weighted indexes shift in price based on changes in stock capitalisation. For example, assume that during semi-annual rebalancing a stock is given a 2% weighting in an index. Assume that over the next two months the stock doubles in value while the dividend remains the same. For the remaining four months the stock represents roughly twice as much as it should in the index because the dividend did not change and rebalancing is infrequent.

In addition, there is also an inherent flaw in calculating fundamentally weighted indexes that capitalisation-weighted indexes do not have. Different companies report fundamental data at different times throughout the quarter. Therefore, the weighting of each stock in a fundamental index should change as new information is known. But that is not the way fundamental indexes work. The provider waits until the next rebalancing period to make adjustments. Consequently, it can be easily argued that fundamentally weighted indexes are not "pure" in their message or methodology.

Why do fundamental index providers not rebalance daily as would be expected? Strategy indexes based on fundamental weighting are not designed to be benchmarks: they are designed to be investment products. For the sake of convenience to the index licensee, the index providers often choose to run indexes suboptimally because the licensee needs flexibility when trade the securities in the index. No fund company would license a pure fundamentally weighted index that rebalanced daily. That would be too cumbersome for the fund manager and too expensive for investors. As such, in this new era of indexing, product providers trading ease is a primary consideration when designing index construction rules.

The first fundamentally weighted indicator

The first US market indicator to use fundamental weighting is also the oldest market indicator known to US investors. The Dow Jones Industrial Average (DJIA), better known as the Dow, was unveiled by Charles Dow in 1896. It covered 12 large industrial stocks.

At the end of each trading day, Charles Dow simply added up the prices of the 12 stocks in the average and the sum total became the DJIA. Let us realise that stock price has nothing to do with a company's market capitalisation. A very large company can have a low stock price while a small company can have a high one. However, the computation of the DJIA was quite simple because the methodology was established during a time when stock price data was all recorded by hand.

Continuous adjustments have been made to the DJIA. Over the years, both the number of stocks and the "divisor" were used to best account for stock splits and buyouts. The DJIA gradually increased to 20 in 1916, and again to 30 in 1928 where it remains today. Nonetheless, the way the indicator was computed in the 19th Century is the same way it is computed today. The only difference is that today the averages are computed nearly instantaneously.

Today the DJIA is used for only two things: first, as a reference point for the media and stock market chatter ("How's the market?" "The Dow's up 30 today!"); second, Dow DIAMONDS (symbol: DIA) is a popular ETF with brokers and individual investors because it tracks the familiar DJIA.

Using financial statements to weight indexes

Fundamental weighting can be done using a simple single-factor model or a complex multifactor weighting methodology. The factors used to weight stocks typically come from balance sheets and income statements, but they can also stretch into more esoteric matters such as the amount of stock held by insiders.

Dividend-weighted indexes have become popular due to the outperformance of value stocks from early in the decade. Dozens of ETFs and open-end mutual funds were launched in the midst of the value stock boom. Many indexes were created that screened companies for cash dividend payments and then weighted those companies based on the dividend yield relative to all other dividend payers. Dividend-paying companies tend to have value characteristics over non-dividing paying stocks.

Multifactor weighting has been popularised by the heavily promoted Research Affiliates Fundamental Index series (RAFI). Research Affiliates is a quantitative management shop that developed a multifactor method for selecting and weighting stocks based on corporate sales, book value, cashflow and dividends. The process creates a value stock bias in a portfolio that accounts for most of the outperformance in those indexes, although RAFI claims that the widely known value premium in their indexes is alpha.

More fundamentally weighted strategies

The Claymore/Zacks Sector Rotation ETF (symbol: XRO) follows the Zacks Sector Rotation Index. The index overweights those sectors that are believed to outperform the S&P 500 on a risk-adjusted basis. The sector allocation methodology strives to overweight cyclical sectors prior to periods of economic expansion and overweight non-cyclical sectors prior to periods of economic contraction.

The Zacks Sector Rotation Index comprises 100 stocks selected from a universe of the 1,000 largest US listed stocks and ADRs based on market capitalisation. The index provider selects stocks using quantitative methods. Each quarter, the multifactor proprietary selection rules identify stocks that are believed to offer the greatest potential.

The industry sector allocation methodology weights each sector based on relative value, insider trading, price momentum, earnings growth, earnings estimate revision and earnings surprise, as well as quantitative macroeconomic factors focusing on the business cycle. Exposure to any one sector may range from 0% to a maximum of 45% of the index. Individual stock exposure within each sector is determined by relative market capitalisation within that sector. Individual issuers are capped at 5% of the total index.

Time horizon as a weighting factor

Life-strategy fund investing has become popular in recent years. These funds invest in indexes that consist of several different asset classes. The amount in each asset class changes based on the time left until a personal liability begins, such as retirement. As the time to the liability decreases, so does the index allocation to risky assets. In a life-strategy index, the index allocation to equities is reduced as retirement nears. The number of years to the liability is the fundamental weighting factor for asset classes in these new and increasingly popular indexes.

Fixed weighting

The third category of security weighting is fixed weight. The category covers a broad spectrum of weighting schemes including equal, modified equal, leveraged, inverse, and long/short methods such as market-neutral and 130/30 strategies.

Figure 4.11 Fixed weight

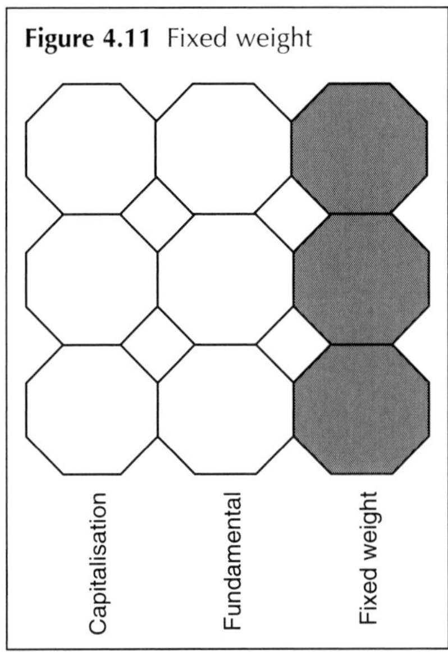

Equal weighting is the simplest form of weighing. All securities in an index are allocated the same percentage. If there are 100 securities, each gets a 1% weighting. If there are 50 securities in the index, they each get a 2% weighting.

The Rydex S&P Equal Weight (symbol: RSP) is an excellent example of an ETF that tracks a straight equally weighted index. The fund tracks the S&P Equal Weight Index (EWI), and product of Standard & Poor's. The fund will typically invest at least 90% of its assets in the securities of the S&P Equal Weight Index. It may also invest in options, futures contracts, options on futures contracts and swaps related to its underlying index, as well as cash and cash equivalents.

The S&P Equal Weight Index is the equal-weighted version of the widely regarded S&P 500. The index has the same constituents as the capitalisation-weighted S&P 500, but each company in the S&P EWI is allocated a fixed weight of 0.20%, rebalanced quarterly. When a company is added to the index in the middle of the quarter, it takes the weight of the company that it replaced.

In recent years there have been many ETFs launched that track equally weighted indexes. Many of those funds are thinly sliced sector funds that need to be equally weighted or else one or two stocks would dominate. Since some industry indexes are so narrow, the logical weighting method is equal weighting. That ensures that no single issuer dominates a sector index.

Modified equal weight is another method in the fixed-weight category. The term may sound like oxymoron, but it does describe the multilevel fixed-weighting methodology. Instead of using one equal weight, there are two or three levels of equal weights. Stocks are assigned to one of the levels based on a rank or size or some other factor. The difference between modified equal weighting and fundamental weighting is that the allocation of stocks using a modified equal-weight method is reset to a fixed percentage at rebalancing rather than to an arbitrary number based on the actual value of factors.

For example, an index might use an earnings rank score to assign weights. Stocks that have the highest rank in an index are given a fixed 3% weighting each; stocks in the second tier are allocated a fixed 2%; and stocks in the third and final tier are allocated a fixed 1%. Since turnover is high in a modified equal-weight index, typically those fixed allocations are adjusted quarterly or less frequently.

The PowerShares Dynamic Market Portfolio (symbol: PWC) is a good example of modified equal weighting. The ETF follows the Dynamic Market Intellidex Index. The index is a quantitatively engineered basket of 100 stocks thought to have superior investment characteristics. The largest 30 stocks by market capitalisation receive 70% of the index weighting (2.33% each) and the other 70 stocks receive 30% of the index weighting (0.43% each). The index is reconstructed each quarter. Stock weights are allowed to float between reconstruction periods.

Equally weighted and modified equally weighted indexes are "in balance" only on the first day following a rebalancing, which occurs only a few times per year or less. After that, equally weighted and modified equally weighted shift in price based on changes in stock capitalisation. For example, assume that during semi-annual rebalancing a stock is given a 0.5% weighting in an index. Assume that over the next two months the stock doubles in value. For the remaining four months the stock represents roughly twice as much as it should be. Why do equally weighted and modified equally weighted index providers not rebalance daily? Fund companies do not want to rebalance daily. It would be too cumbersome for the fund manager and too expensive for investors to rebalance daily.

Fixed-weight commodity indexes

There are many commodity indexes. Most are only a few years old. Almost all indexes benchmarked by fund companies are formed using commodity futures contracts. Several indexes track the same commodity futures contracts. However, there are significant differences in the weighting of commodity sectors.

The performance of a commodity index is greatly dependent on its weighting strategy. In 2006, the return of S&P GSCI was minus 15% and the return of the DJ-AIG was positive 2%. The S&P GSCI is a production-weighted index of commodity sector returns representing an unleveraged, long-only investment in commodity futures that is diversified across the spectrum of commodities. Since energy is the dominant commodity in the world today, the GSCI is highly dependent on oil prices. In contrast, the DJ-AIG index follows fixed diversification rules. No related group of commodities (eg, energy, precious metals, livestock and grains) may constitute more than 33% of the index as of the annual rebalancing of the components, and no single commodity may constitute less than 2% or more than 15% of the index. The difference in weighting methods caused a 17% difference in returns in 2006, and wide dispersions in annual returns on average.

Leveraged and short indexes

Several ETF providers have ventured into leveraged ETF and inverse ETF. These funds follow market indexes designed to generate two to three times the daily return of a market benchmark, or, in the case of an inverse index, return the opposite daily return of a market index. When an ETF attempts to return twice the performance of a markets index it is leveraged twice, or 2X. An ETF that shorts the return of a market receives the inverse return or –1X. Rydex and ProShares are innovators in these types of funds and have competing leveraged and inverse ETF products.

Fixed weights have a mid-cap bias

Fixed weighting can have a profound impact on equity index size characteristics over capitalisation weighting. The performance of an equity index takes on certain size and style biases as the percentage allocated to each security is spread more equally across all securities.

Equal weighting and modified equal weighting cause size shifts in a diversified index. Applying equal weighting to a broad basket of passively selected stocks creates a portfolio with mid-cap stock average capitalisation. At the beginning of 2009, the capitalisation-weighted S&P 500 had an average market capitalisation of approximately US$38 billion. In contrast, the equally weighted S&P 500 had an average market capitalisation of only US$8 billion.

The same basket of 500 stocks has a remarkable shift in market cap between the two weighting methods. The S&P 500 is a large cap index and the equal weight S&P 500 is a mid-cap index. In the early 2000s, mid-cap stocks significantly outperformed large-cap stocks. It should be no surprise that during the same period an equally weighted S&P 500 significantly outperformed the cap-weighted S&P 500.

It is no surprise why several index providers created fundamentally weighted indexes and equally weighted indexes during the first half of this decade given the rosy performance of value stocks and mid-cap stocks. And it is easy to understand why fund companies clambered to license those indexes soon thereafter. The mutual fund industry is widely known for following investment trends, and many new funds tend to launch in a hot style near the end of the trend.

The cost of strategy

How can index strategy maps be used? One way is to analyse the cost of the strategy. ETFs that follow market indexes are cheap. ETFs that follow strategy indexes are more expensive. Investors must weight the potential benefit of using a strategy index product against the guaranteed higher cost of that product.

The ETFguide.com database includes index strategy map information on all exchange-traded vehicles (ETFs, ETNs, HOLDRs, BLDRs). The database can be sorted using investment style and strategy. For example, the database can be used to find US long-only equity ETFs that follow broad US equity indexes and then place those funds in the appropriate index strategy boxes. The average fees of each box can then be analysed to determine the average cost of each strategy.

Figure 4.12 shows that, down of long-only US broad market index ETFs, expenses are based on index strategy. Passively selected

Figure 4.12 Strategy cost comparison by index strategy box

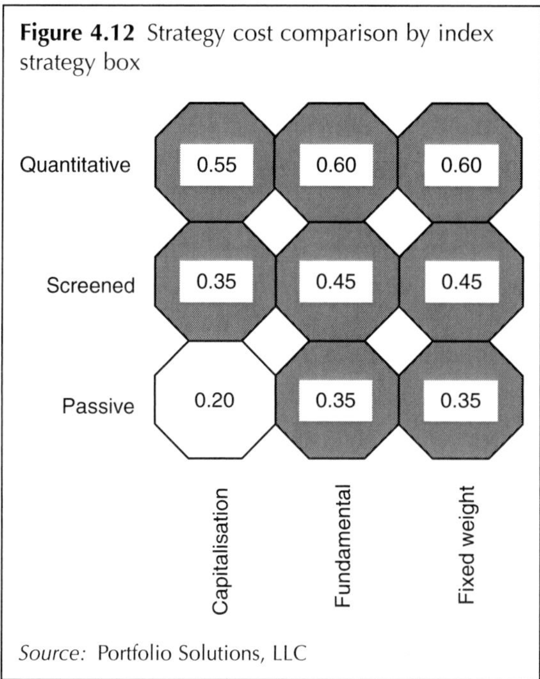

Source: Portfolio Solutions, LLC

and capitalisation-weighted market index funds charge on average 0.20% in annual fees. Thus, it can be said that basic beta exposure to various segments of the US equity markets cost 0.20% on average.

A fee of 0.20% for basic market beta exposure through passive security selection and cap-weighted ETFs is inexpensive relative to the alpha-seeking strategies in the other eight boxes. As security selection methods and security-weighting techniques become more complex, the fees charged by ETFs to manage portfolios to those indexes go up. There is a direct correlation between the complexity of the index and the cost of ETF management with quantitative security selection strategies that attempt to beat the market being the most expensive.

Index-strategy-map examples

Morningstar categorises the following three ETFs as large-cap blend:

- iShares S&P 500 Index (TICKER: IVV – 0.09% ER);
- WisdomTree US LC Dividend (TICKER: DLN – 0.28% ER); and
- PowerShares Dynamic Large Cap (TICKER: PJF – 0.60% ER).

Each of these funds invest primarily in large US companies; however, the strategy for security selection and security weighting is quite different in the index that each fund follows.

The iShares S&P 500 Index (IVV) seeks to replicate, before fees and expenses, the S&P 500 Index, a market-cap-weighted collection of US stocks. For all intents and purposes, the index is a large-cap vehicle, with mega-caps dominating the upper ranks. Below are the characteristic for security selection, security weighting and cost. Figure 4.13 illustrates the index strategy box for IVV.

- Security selection strategy – passive (reflects the large cap US market).
- Security weighting strategy – capitalisation (float-adjusted).
- Strategy cost – 0.09% expense ratio.

The WisdomTree US Large Cap Dividend (DLN) seeks to replicate, before fees and expenses, the WisdomTree LargeCap Dividend Index, which is composed of the 300 largest dividend-paying US

Figure 4.13 iShares S&P 500 Index (IVV) index strategy box

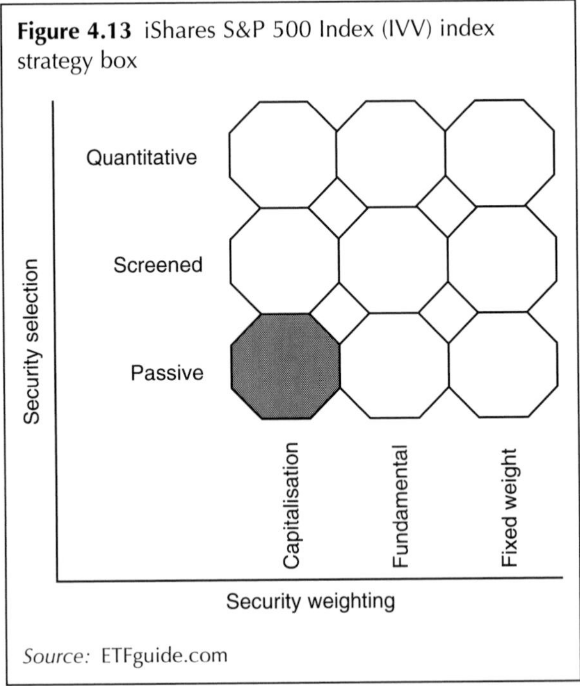

Source: ETFguide.com

companies as measured by market capitalisation. Stocks in the LargeCap Dividend Index are weighted by the US dollar value of cash dividends paid to shareholders. Below are the characteristic for security selection, security weighting and cost. Figure 4.14 illustrates the index strategy box for DLN.

- Security selection strategy – screened (dividend-paying companies only).
- Security weighting strategy – fundamental (by amount of cash dividend).
- Strategy cost – 0.28% expense ratio, which is 0.19% higher than IVV.

PowerShares Dynamic Large Cap Value Portfolio (PJF) seeks to replicate, before fees and expenses, the Dynamic Large Cap Value Index, which is part of the AMEX Intellidex index series. The index provider selects securities quarterly based on quantitative analysis and weights those securities using a modified equal-weighting methodology. Below are the characteristic for security selection,

Figure 4.14 WisdomTree US Large Cap Dividend (DLN) index strategy box

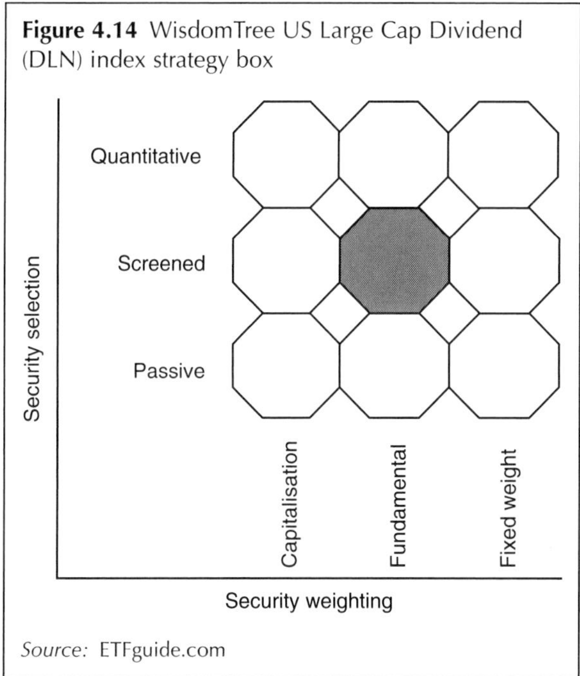

Source: ETFguide.com

security weighting and cost. Figure 4.15 illustrates the index strategy box for PJF.

- Security selection strategy – quantitative (25 factors are analysed).
- Security weighting strategy – fixed weight (modified fixed weight).
- Strategy cost – 0.60% expense ratio which is 0.51% higher than IVV.

All three ETFs are large-cap blend funds according to Morningstar, yet they each have very different investment strategies. Investors searching for a large-cap US blend ETF should refer to the database at ETFguide.com to isolate and compare strategies and costs quickly, and that will lead to better investment decisions.

SUMMARY

This chapter explained the differences between market indexes and strategy indexes. Market indexes are designed to capture the

Figure 4.15 PowerShares Dynamic Large Cap Value Portfolio (PJF) index strategy box

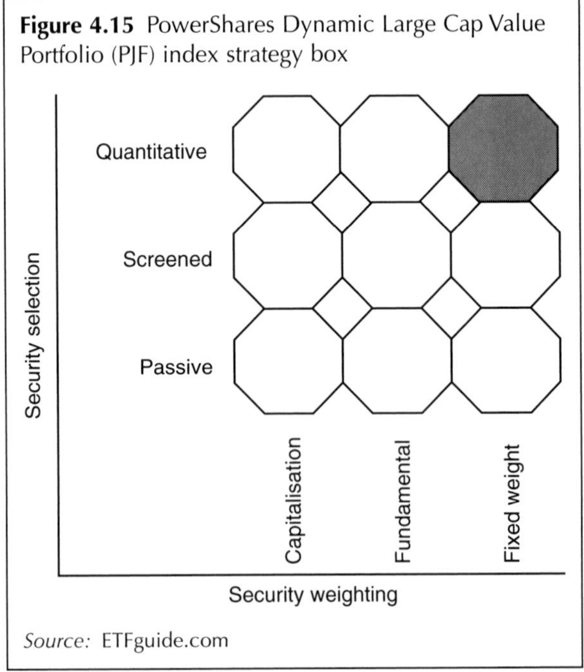

Source: ETFguide.com

performance of a financial market. Strategy indexes are set apart from market indexes by their alternative security selection and security weighting methods.

Those differences are expanded and illustrated using an index strategy map. Selection methods include passive, screened and quantitative. Security weighting can be in the form of capitalisation-weighting, fundamental-weighting and fixed-weight methods. Market index ETFs are categorised by passive security selection and capitalisation weighting. Strategy indexes fall in the other eight boxes.

Index strategy boxes are an easy method of analysis that categorises indexing selection and weighting rules. Strategy costs are also easy to isolate using index strategy map analysis. Use index strategy maps to isolate how an index is constructed and make more informed decisions about index product selection.

1 Noughts and crosses is the UK name for what is known as Tic-Tac-Toe in the US.

REFERENCES

Bernstein, Peter L., 1992, *Capital Ideas: The Improbable Origins of Modern Wall Street* (New York: Free Press).

Brinson, Gary P., L. Randolph Hood and Gilbert L. Beebower, 1986, "Determinants of Portfolio Performance", *Financial Analysts Journal* 42(4) (July/August), pp. 39–44; reprinted in *FAJ*'s 50th-anniversary issue: vol. 51(1), January/February 1995, pp. 133–8.

Cowles, Alfred, 1938, *Common Stock Indexes: 1871–1937* (2nd edn 1939) (Bloomington, IN: Principia).

Dimson, Elroy, Paul Marsh and Mike Staunton, 2002, *Triumph of the Optimists* (Princeton, NJ: Princeton University Press).

Ferri, Richard A., 2006, *All About Index Funds*, 2nd edn (New York: McGraw-Hill).

Ferri, Richard A., 2007, *The ETF Book* (Hoboken, NJ: John Wiley & Sons).

Graham, Benjamin, and Jason Zweig, 2003, *The Intelligent Investor* (New York: HarperCollins).

Grinold, Richard C., 1989, "The Fundamental Law of Active Management", *Journal of Portfolio Management* 15(3), Spring, pp. 30–7.

Ibbotson, Roger G., and Paul D. Kaplan, 2000, "Does Asset Allocation Policy Explain 40, 90, or 100% of Performance?", *Financial Analysts Journal* 56(1), January/February, pp. 26–33.

Markowitz, Harry M., 1952, "Portfolio Selection", *Journal of Finance*, March, pp. 77–91.

Phillips, Don, and Paul Kaplan, 2003, "What Comes Next? The Case for a New Generation of Indexes", *Journal of Indexes*, first quarter.

Pope, Brad, 2006, "Insights on Market Capitalization and Fundamental-weighted Indexes", Barclays Global Investors.

Sauter, Gus, 2002, "Index Rex: The Ideal Index Construction", *Journal of Indexes*, 2nd quarter 2002, URL: http://www.indexuniverse.com.

Schoenfeld, Steven A., 2004, *Active Index Investing* (Hoboken, NJ: John Wiley & Sons).

Siegel, Laurence B., 2003, *Benchmarks and Investment Management*, (Charlottesville, VA: The Research Foundation of the Association for Investment Management and Research).

Wiandt, Jim, 2001, "Passive Investing Trends", *Journal of Indexing*, 3rd quarter.

5

Legal and Regulatory Issues Related to ETFs and Certain Other Exchange-Traded Instruments

Kathleen H. Moriarty

Katten Muchin Rosenman LLP

The credit crisis of 2008 and resulting turmoil in the global financial markets have painfully reminded institutional and retail investors alike that a basic understanding of product structure, coupled with adequate diligence, is a key element of an informed investment decision. The bankruptcy of Lehman Brothers, for example, highlighted the differences among seemingly similar products, namely exchange-traded funds (ETFs) and certain other exchange-traded products such as exchange-traded commodities vehicles and exchange-traded notes.

The terms "exchange-traded fund" and "ETF" can be confusing because they are often used loosely to cover a wide variety of instruments traded on a stock exchange, including traditional closed-end funds, traditional foreign funds traded on their home country stock exchanges, exchange-traded grantor trusts such as HOLDRs and certain exchange-traded commodities vehicles, other investment programmes such as Folio,[1] publicly traded commodity pools, as well as exchange-traded notes. The term "exchange traded product" or "ETP" recently has been used as the inclusive term to cover all of these financial instruments and will be used in this chapter when referring to the universe of exchange traded products. As used in this chapter, the term ETF solely refers to a pooled investment vehicle that holds an underlying portfolio of securities, other assets and cash that is registered in the US with the Securities and Exchange Commission (Commission or SEC) under the Investment Company

Act of 1940 (1940 Act) as an investment company and is classified either as a unit investment company (UIT) or an open-end management company, commonly known as a "mutual fund" (open-end fund).

In contrast, an exchange-traded commodities vehicle or "ETC" is a special-purpose issuer not registered as an investment company under the 1940 Act that holds an underlying portfolio of physical commodities and/or other commodities, cash and other assets. Although ETFs and ETCs are subject to different regulatory regimes, they share certain characteristics. Most importantly, an ETF and an ETC each hold a portfolio of assets and issues equity securities which are listed and traded on a stock exchange like other shares of common stock. Like the common stock of corporations, each share issued by an ETF and ETC represents a ratable undivided interest in the enterprise of its issuer. As each ETF or ETC issuer is a pooled investment vehicle, not a manufacturer of goods or a service provider, its enterprise is directly tied to its portfolio assets.[2] Thus, were an ETF or ETC to liquidate, it would distribute its portfolio assets, net of all outstanding taxes and other obligations, on a *pro rata* basis to its outstanding shareholders, either in kind or in cash.

An exchange-traded note or "ETN", on the other hand, is not an issuer of equity securities such as ETFs and ETCs; in fact, it is not an issuer at all. Rather, an ETN is an unsecured general obligation (ie, a debt security), typically issued by a bank or other financial entity, such as Lehman. An ETN, therefore, is not backed by portfolio assets or other segregated property, hence the repayment of the note, when due, will be made by the issuer solely out of its general revenues or other assets. This means that the creditworthiness of the issuer is of paramount importance to a potential investor, because investors holding ETNs stand equal to all of the issuer's other general unsecured creditors. Therefore, the Lehman ETN investors are likely to receive little, if any, return of their investment proceeds after bankruptcy proceedings have been finalised.

This chapter will first discuss the major legal and regulatory issues involved in the structure and establishment of a US ETF and the secondary-market exchange trading of its shares. It will then explore some of the differences that exist between ETFs and ETCs.

REGULATORY REGIME APPLICABLE TO ETFs AND THEIR RELATED PARTIES

ETFs are subject to a variety of federal securities laws

Each ETF issues its securities for sale to the investing public, and so must register the offering with the SEC, which is an independent and quasi-judicial regulatory agency of the US government. The SEC has rule-making, exemptive, interpretive, investigative and enforcement powers. ETFs register the offering of their securities under the Securities Act of 1933 (1933 Act) and its rules.

"Often referred to as the 'sunshine law' or the 'truth in securities' law, the 1933 Act requires that investors receive material information, including prescribed financial data, concerning securities being offered for public sale; and prohibits deceit, misrepresentations, and other fraud in the sale of securities."[3]

In addition, each ETF lists its individual shares for trading in the secondary market on a US stock exchange and therefore is subject to various provisions of the Securities Exchange Act of 1934 (1934 Act) and its rules, as are the brokers who sell such shares to the public. The 1934 Act provides the SEC with broad authority over all aspects of the securities industry, including the power to register, regulate and oversee brokerage firms, transfer agents and securities exchanges, and prohibits certain types of conduct in the markets.[4] ETFs must also comply with the listing and trading rules adopted by the stock exchanges, which are self-regulatory organisations (SROs) that are required to adopt rules and implement measures to ensure market integrity and investor protection. Rules proposed by each SRO are adopted after review and approval by the SEC.[5] Each investment adviser to an ETF must be registered with the SEC under the Investment Advisers Act of 1940, which contains regulations designed to protect investors;[6] and securities professionals who execute transactions in ETF securities on behalf of investors, such as brokers, must be registered with FINRA, the Financial Industry Regulatory Authority (formerly the NASD) which is also an SRO.

Overview of the 1940 Act

Most importantly from a regulatory perspective, an ETF is an investment company and is therefore registered and regulated under the 1940 Act and its rules administered by the SEC.[7] Basic familiarity with the regulatory regime established by the 1940 Act and its rules is necessary to understand the structure and operation of an ETF, as well as why it differs from other ETPs that hold similar portfolio assets, or share other similarities.

The 1933 and 1934 Acts were designed around the "sunshine" concept of full and fair disclosure, each of which applies to certain practices and transactions conducted by the members of the securities industry in general. In contrast, the 1940 Act regulates the investment company industry in particular and establishes a substantive regulatory regime, implemented by prescriptive and proscriptive rules and regulations. The statute was adopted in response to the rapid growth of pooled investment vehicles and the serious problems experienced by their investors that arose during the 1920s and 1930s; it focuses on the problems and abuses that were peculiar to these unregulated investment vehicles, their advisers, distributors, custodians and other industry participants. The Congressional studies leading to the adoption of the 1940 Act examined the existing industry practices and identified a number of abuses that occurred[8] and the resulting statute was designed to address "major evils", which can be grouped loosely into three categories:

- failure to observe the usual principles of fiduciary duties and unscrupulous portfolio management practices (eg, embezzling, looting, dumping, insider trading, speculative investments and self-dealing);
- unfair or unsound capital arrangements (eg, pyramiding, excessive leveraging, paying dividends out of capital and preferential treatment of certain classes of shareholders to the detriment of others); and
- abusive or unfair fee arrangements and sales practices (eg, high-pressure sales techniques, switching, churning, discouragement of redemptions, high management fees and imbalanced profit-sharing arrangements for fund managers).[9]

Given the magnitude of these problems, Congress determined that the two-pronged approach of the 1933 and 1934 Acts – *caveat emptor* coupled with informed and adequate disclosure, adopted in connection with the sale of securities issued by industrial companies – was not sufficient to eliminate the structural and systemic abuses caused by unregulated investment companies managing pooled assets.[10] Indeed, the very nature of a large pool of money managed by unsupervised, sophisticated "insiders" on behalf of a numerous and disparate group of unsophisticated "outsider" investors seemed almost perfectly tailored to foster and facilitate the abuses catalogued in the Congressional studies. As enacted, the 1940 Act "regulates the organization of companies, including mutual funds, that engage primarily in investing, reinvesting, and trading in securities, and whose own securities are offered to the investing public. The regulation is designed to minimize conflicts of interest that arise in these complex operations".[11]

Therefore, the creation, establishment and operation of an investment company, as well as the sale and redemption of its shares, is extensively regulated, and what is not permitted under the 1940 Act cannot be undertaken without prior relief. As discussed below, because an ETF is a type of investment company not described in the 1940 Act or permitted by its rules, each ETF must first seek and receive from the SEC certain exemptions in order to be established, operate and offer its securities to investors for sale and redemption.

ETF as a "hybrid" investment company

An ETF is a "hybrid" investment company not currently permitted under the 1940 Act and therefore requires exemptive, no-action and other regulatory relief before it can operate.

It is a unique type of investment company in that its structure combines certain salient features of both open- and closed-end funds. Whether structured as a UIT or an open-end fund, each ETF issues, sells and redeems its securities once daily at their net asset value (NAV) only in a stated large number of individual units or shares (eg, 25,000 or 50,000), known as "creation units". Like securities issued by closed-end funds, however, the individual units or shares comprising a creation unit are not redeemable but instead are listed on a national securities exchange for trading in the secondary market throughout the day at current market prices.

Specifically, ETFs differ from traditional UITs and open-end funds in several important ways. For example, ETFs issue their units or shares only in creation units and almost exclusively "in kind", ie, in exchange for an actual deposit of the ETF's portfolio assets, plus a small amount of cash specified daily by the ETF to equal NAV.

In contrast, virtually all UIT units and open-end fund shares are issued in exchange for cash. Also, securities issued by an ETF are redeemed "in kind" and only in creation units, whereas UIT units and open-end fund shares are redeemed in individual unit/share size for cash. Furthermore, individual ETF securities are bought and sold only on the secondary market and without any interaction with, or input from, the ETF, whereas, all open-end fund shares are issued directly by the fund. In addition, individual ETF securities are bought and sold only for cash on the secondary market through market makers at current prices (which may or may not be at NAV) at all times during the trading day. In contrast, open-end fund shares are issued and redeemed directly with the fund, usually only once a day, and always at prices equal to NAV. Also, unlike open-end funds, ETFs do not utilise a traditional transfer agency function, because all ETF securities, whether individual or combined in creation units, are held solely in "street name" at the Depository Trust Co (DTC) in book-entry only form. Therefore, an ETF does not issue individual share certificates or know the identity of its individual shareholders. In addition, ETF securities, unlike UIT units and shares of open-end funds, can be sold pursuant to a variety of order instructions, such as market, limit and stop orders, and until recently, could be sold short on a "downtick".[12] Last, the actual composition of each ETF's portfolio assets is well known and widely disseminated on a daily basis, which is not the case with many open-end funds.

As this hybrid structure is not described, permitted or even contemplated by the 1940 Act,[13] each ETF must receive a set of exemptions from the application of this statue and the rules adopted under it (1940 Act Exemptions) prior to market introduction.[14] The most important of the 1940 Act Exemptions permits the ETF to issue shares redeemable only in creation units and allows individual ETF shares to trade intraday on a stock exchange at market prices that are not the current NAV for such shares.[15] It is important to understand that the 1940 Act Exemptions are granted by the Commission only to those persons who applied for the specified relief (applicants) and is applicable only upon the facts and conditions stated in the formal application submitted to the SEC. Hence, no other person may "use" or rely upon 1940 Act Exemptions granted by the Commission in its Exemptive Order to the applicants, and it is not an asset that can be bought or sold outright.

Exemptive authority of the SEC under the 1940 Act

Section 6(c) of the 1940 Act provides the SEC with the broad and general authority to grant exemptive relief from some or all of the 1940 Act's provisions if it "is in the public interest and consistent with the protection of investors and the purposes fairly intended by the policy and provisions of the Act".[16]

Section 6(c) is central to this regulatory structure and was deliberately designed to allow for the development and implementation of new investment company features and structures not contemplated when the 1940 Act was adopted. In describing the flexibility made possible by this grant of powers, President Roosevelt wrote:

> In the case of this legislation, it deserves notice that the investment trust industry insisted that the Congress grant to the Securities and Exchange Commission broader discretionary powers than those contemplated in the initial regulatory proposals. Not only is this a tribute to the personnel of the S.E.C. and an endorsement of its wisdom and essential fairness in handling financial problems, but it serves well to indicate that many businessmen now realize that efficient regulation in technical fields such as this requires an administering agency which has been given flexible powers to meet whatever problems may arise.[17]

Section 6(c) has provided the SEC with an important tool for regulating the ever-changing investment company industry. Many commonplace features and familiar structures offered by investment companies today exist as a direct result of the SEC's grant of relief under Section 6(c) to allow otherwise non-permissible arrangements under the 1940 Act; indeed, the money market fund has been cited as a prime instance of the type of investment company not originally foreseen at the time of the adoption of the 1940 Act.[18] So too, "ETFs owe their evolution to the willingness of the [SEC] and its staff to use the exemptive processes of the [1940] Act to enable their development."[19]

Under Section 6(c), the SEC is permitted to look outside the statute's express wording to its policy and purpose in granting exemptions. Section 1 of the 1940 Act declares that its "policy and purposes" are "to mitigate and, so far as feasible, to eliminate the conditions enumerated in this section which adversely affect the national public interest and the interest of investors".[20]

The conditions enumerated in Section 1 relate to the activities of investment companies, their nexus with interstate commerce, their importance to the national economy and the capital markets, and the means by which such companies are misused or otherwise adversely affect investors. The legislative history of the 1940 Act is largely in accord with the policy and purposes stated in Section 1. For example, the reports of the Senate Committee on Banking and Currency and the House Committee on Interstate and Foreign Commerce both state the importance of protecting investors and spurring investment in public companies.[21]

Despite the broad exemptive power provided under Section 6(c), the SEC sparingly exercises its authority to grant relief to applicants, and only after a finding that the three criteria stated in the section are met. The SEC carefully weighs the 1940 Act policies of investor protection and public-interest concerns against the needs of applicants and their desire to develop new products and services, and crafts narrow relief to achieve a balance between these sometimes competing goals. In practice, the SEC and its staff in the Division of Investment Management (Division) consider the goals of efficiency, competition and capital formation when reviewing applications for exemptive relief under the 1940 Act relating to innovative financial products. This is so for several reasons. First, the goal of capital formation is one of the policies mentioned by Section 1 and therefore warrants consideration.[22] Second, issues such as efficiency (including tax and arbitrage efficiency) and competition are relevant in analysing the stated purposes and proposed uses of a nonconforming investment company arrangement, structure or product.[23] Third, the goals of efficiency, competition and capital formation are often consonant with the public interest, investor protection and the policy and purposes of the 1940 Act; in other words, they further the 1940 Act's other stated goals. The SEC, aided significantly by its staff members in the Division, has historically analysed, weighed and balanced all these issues in deciding whether to grant unconditional or conditional exemptive relief, or to deny such relief in whole or in part.[24] As mentioned above, the ongoing innovation and development of financial products and structures in the investment company industry in general, and the ETF industry in particular, are proof that the multiple goals of the 1940 Act are carefully considered.

Obtaining exemptive relief from the 1940 Act

The 1940 Act provides that exemptions from some or all of its provisions may be made by order upon application to the SEC.

A written application is submitted to the SEC and contains arguments, precedents, factual representations and analysis as well as conditions and undertakings by the applicants. The application is subject to comment by the Division and, depending on the issues raised, by other divisions of the SEC, such as the Divisions of Markets and Trading (formerly, the Division of Market Regulation (1934 Act Division)), Corporation Finance, the Office of Economic Analysis, the Office of General Counsel and the Office of Compliance Inspections and Examinations. The applicants revise and amend the application in response to the written comments provided by the Division, as well as to add new facts or request additional relief. Once the application is approved by the SEC itself or by authority delegated to the Division, the public notice of the application and request for an order is published in the US Federal Register, generally for a period of 25–30 days. Usually an order is granted within several days following the expiration of the notice period if no public comments or requests for a hearing have been received. See Appendix A for a more detailed description of this process.

An ETF requires regulatory relief

The ETF structure does not fit neatly into certain provisions of other federal securities laws and rules. Given that the exemptive applications, no-action requests and other regulatory filings discussed below must be submitted to the appropriate regulator and relief must be received before launch, a new ETF is slower to reach the market as compared with certain other types of pooled investment vehicles such as open- and closed-end funds.

For example, in addition to the relief granted in the Exemption Order, each new ETF must receive the grant of regulatory relief from a variety of provisions and rules of the 1934 Act with respect to the listing[25] and trading of its shares. This relief is necessary primarily because such regulations contemplate that single-stock issuers and closed-end funds, not open-end funds or UITs, will list and trade their shares in the secondary market. As discussed below, relief is typically sought to permit, among other things, to allow broker-dealers and others to bid for, purchase, redeem or engage in other secondary-market transactions for an ETF's securities and its portfolio assets during a distribution or tender offer for portfolio assets and to permit margining of ETF securities without a thirty-day restriction under certain circumstances.[26]

In addition, because the ETF structure does not conform to the securities exchanges' equity-listing rules, special rules and standards relating to the listing and trading of ETF securities had to be adopted under Section 19(b) and Rule 19b-4 of the 1934 Act. Initially, an exchange's listing rule adopted for each new ETF related solely to a single product or family of products.[27] Eventually, after adopting a number of specific rules, the major exchanges worked with the SEC's 1934 Act Division to adopt "generic" ETF listing rules, which pertain to stated categories of ETFs.[28] The adoption of these generic rules has helped to speed up the regulatory process required in launching new ETFs. Note, however, that, if a new ETF cannot meet the requirements or fit into the parameters established by the "generic" listing rules, the listing exchange must apply to the SEC to adopt specific and appropriate listing rules under the 1934 Act designed for the ETF before its units/shares may be sold, bought or traded.

Also, no-action relief has also been sought and granted for beneficial owners of more than 5% of an ETF's shares/units, as well as for beneficial owners of more than 10% of the ETFs units/shares, so that such persons do not have to comply with reporting requirements imposed by Sections 13(d) and 16(a), respectively, of the 1934 Act.[29]

Each ETF listed and traded in the US secondary market requires exemptive, interpretive and/or no-action relief from various 1934 Act trading restrictions. Initially, each new standalone ETF or ETF family submitted a request for relief to the SEC, which was granted solely to those persons specifically named or described in the request.[30] After granting exemptive relief to a number of individual ETFs, the SEC's 1934 Act Division began to issue the relief described above to all new ETFs trading on any US registered national securities exchange that could meet certain defined criteria and fit within certain stated parameters (class relief). The class relief extends to ETFs that are "passively managed" index funds holding securities that meet certain stated parameters, including minimum public float values and average trading volumes. Only new ETFs unable to fully comply with the class-relief requirements need first obtain individual 1934 Act relief before their securities may be sold, bought or traded. See Appendix B for a more detailed description of the class relief.

In addition, many ETFs have received relief from the "prospectus delivery" requirements of the 1933 Act. The 1933 Act requires that, before sales of publicly offered securities may commence, a registration statement be filed with the SEC that includes a prospectus describing the salient characteristics and risks of such securities. It is unlawful, with certain exceptions, to sell or deliver after sale of a security unless a prospectus prepared for such security either accompanied or preceded such sale or delivery. Arguably, these provisions require prospectus delivery prior to, or at the time of, the confirmation of sale, for each ETF secondary-market trade involving a dealer. All the ETFs structured as UITs, as well as many structured as open-end funds, have received relief from the prospectus delivery obligation set forth in the 1933 Act. In addition, the exemptive relief granted to the Vanguard Index Funds permitting the issuance, sale and redemption of a new separate ETF share class (originally known as VIPERs) of certain of its existing Vanguard mutual funds included prospectus delivery relief.[31] This relief has been expressly conditioned upon the requirement that a "product description" summarising the salient features of the ETF be delivered to investors purchasing such ETFs as part of the primary listing exchange's rules.

Interpretive relief from NASD rules

As was the case with other statutes, regulations and rules adopted before the introduction of SPDRs, the Conduct Rules of the NASD (predecessor to FINRA) were designed to cover practices with respect to the issuance and sale of UIT and open-end fund securities but did not contemplate such practices with respect to ETF securities. Therefore, ETFs submitted request letters to the NASD seeking confirmation that these practices do not violate the Conduct Rules or NASD Interpretive Materials. The NASD has granted favourable interpretive relief, which is expressly conditioned on the continuing applicability of the ETF's 1940 Act order, as well as limited to the factual descriptions and legal representations contained in the ETF's request letter.

THE ETF STRUCTURE: COMPROMISE BETWEEN MARKETPLACE DEMANDS AND REGULATORY REQUIREMENTS

Background

ETFs were first developed in the US during the late 1980s and early 1990s in response to a demand for retail programme trading. At this time, only trading desks and large institutional investors were able to trade a large basket of securities (all of the constituent stocks of the S&P 500 Index,[32] for example) in a single buy order or sell order executed with a major brokerage firm. Treating such a stock basket as if it were a single stock was clearly a far more efficient and less costly method of buying or selling securities than entering 500 individual buy or sell orders. This facility was not available to smaller institutional and individual investors, who, by the late 1980s, were increasingly interested in easily tradable stock portfolios and comfortable with the concept of index investing. Index Participation Shares (IPSs) and Supershares were two predecessor products introduced to meet this demand, but they ultimately failed due to a variety of structural problems.[33] Therefore, the original ETFs were designed to provide many of the attractive features offered by programme trading, especially speed, efficiency and extremely low transaction costs, as well as the simplicity and flexibility inherent in a brokerage (as opposed to commodity) account and trading environment. Each of these ETFs was designed to fully replicate its underlying equity market benchmark[34] and therefore its portfolio assets comprised solely the constituent stocks of each such index, and cash.

The original ETFs fully replicated their underlying securities indexes

The first successful basket-traded product, the SPDR Trust, was launched in January 1993 using a relatively straightforward and transparent structure. Established as UIT, the SPDR Trust was designed to continuously issue and redeem its units of beneficial interest (SPDRS) by an "in-kind" exchange for the entire basket of the S&P 500 Index stocks at their daily NAV, as well as to list its individual SPDRS on the American Stock Exchange (Amex) for secondary-market trading at intraday prices. The Amex publicly disseminated SPDR prices and information about the SPDR Trust's portfolio assets during each trading day.

One of the Division's main concerns in reviewing the SPDR Trust's application for 1940 Act Exemptions was that the hybrid structure of the ETF was inherently unfair to small investors, who could not redeem their individual ETF shares at NAV but could only sell them on the secondary market, in contrast to large investors who could redeem their shares in creation units at NAV. The SPDR Trust applicants successfully argued that the price of an individual SPDR trading on the Amex would be very close to its actual NAV, both because the "in-kind" creation and redemption features of the SPDR Trust's structure provided ample and effective arbitrage opportunities and the various hedging capabilities made it easy and cheap. They reasoned that the continuous creation/redemption feature of the SPDR Trust structure allowed large market participants to take advantage of arbitrage opportunities arising from differences between the NAV of the SPDR Trust's portfolio assets and the price of individual SPDRs trading in the secondary market. Whenever this discrepancy grew large enough to produce a profit, arbitrageurs would execute the requisite purchase or sale transactions to realise the gain. The SPDR Trust applicants' argument proved correct; historically, this mechanism has facilitated price-correcting arbitrage activity and has acted to keep the trading prices of SPDRs closely aligned with the NAV of the SPDR Trust's portfolio assets. This feature has been replicated in each of the successor ETF products and has produced the same results; indeed, investors, traders, other market participants, analysts and securities regulators are keenly interested in the presence and efficacy of the arbitrage mechanism.

The SPDR Trust structure provided other features attractive to retail and institutional investors in addition to the arbitrage mechanism, such as the aforementioned ability to sell SPDRs short on a downtick and to place commonly used stock orders such as limit, market on close and stop-loss orders. Also, the SPDR Trust structure resulted in reduced costs and portfolio turnover, in large part due to the in-kind creation and redemption process discussed above. In addition, tax efficiencies were a positive, albeit unintended, consequence of this feature, which was designed and utilised primarily to achieve trading efficiencies, speed and lower transaction costs. In general, ETFs are subject to the same tax treatment as most open-end funds as well as many UITs, which elect for federal tax purposes to be treated as a "regulated investment company" (RIC) under Subchapter M of the US Internal Revenue Code. RIC status relieves such companies from a double layer of taxation on their income distributions. ETFs tend to be more tax-efficient in connection with recognition of capital gains and capital-gains distributions as compared to open-end funds and UITs holding comparable portfolio investments as a direct result of the relatively low portfolio turnover experienced by ETFs. Typically, ETF investors receive little in capital-gains distributions and realise capital gains only when they sell their units/shares.

Retail investors and institutional market participants have found a variety of uses for SPDRs since their introduction in 1993; their flexibility made them useful, both as tools and as investment products. Other products based on domestic stock indexes and modelled on the SPDR UIT structure, such as DIAMONDS[35] and QQQs[36] and were next introduced, along with similar exchange-traded products, such as WEBS[37] and CountryBaskets,[38] which were the first available ETFs based on international "equity market indexes" and offered US investors shares in index baskets of foreign equity securities.

The next generation of ETFs

More importantly from a development perspective, the WEBS funds and CountryBaskets funds expanded the basic ETF format itself by using an open-end fund structure. Although more complex and expensive than the UIT structure, the open-end fund structure affords far greater flexibility in portfolio management techniques. This design change was necessary for a variety of reasons, including that some of the designated international stock indexes underlying these ETFs were not sufficiently diversified to permit compliance with the RIC rules. A subtle shift in the investment objective of these ETFs therefore occurred: unlike the older ETFs structured as UITs, the WEBS and CountryBaskets funds could no longer simply seek to replicate their respective underlying indexes but instead were required to seek the investment performance of such benchmarks. As a result, the portfolios of the WEBS and CountryBaskets funds were not unmanaged baskets of stocks that simply acquired all of the component stocks in the same weight as that accorded by their underlying benchmarks, but rather were managed using traditional "passive" index investing techniques to achieve the investment performance of their underlying indexes. This trend was continued and expanded into the domestic ETF arena by the iShares Trust, which used the full array of these techniques, such as portfolio sampling and optimisation, for certain of its index series and therefore is permitted to invest up to 10% of each series' portfolio assets in securities not included in the relevant underling indexes as well as futures, option and swap contracts, cash and cash equivalents.[39]

As applications for 1940 Act Exemptions submitted by new ETFs increased in number, the SEC became more familiar with the structure and began to delegate its authority to grant relief under Section 6(c) to the Division upon the findings required by such section.[40] The ETF product range dramatically expanded both overseas and in the US during the years 2000 through 2007, when families of ETFs, such as iShares and Sector SPDRs, as well as VIPERS,[41] a novel exchange-traded share class of existing mutual funds, were introduced. These exchange-traded open-end funds provided investors with a wide array of investment opportunities based on unmanaged stock indexes which "sliced and diced" the domestic and global equity markets in different ways, including narrow-based sectors, style-based segments, country and regional segments.

The basic structure of the ETF continued to evolve as well. All of the ETFs mentioned above, whether UITs or open-end funds, were newly established investment companies, expressly designed to issue, offer, redeem and list their exchanged-traded securities as a single share class. As noted above, Vanguard, with the introduction of its VIPERS, took the next developmental step by adding an ETF share class to certain of the already-existing Vanguard Index Funds. This innovation required additional exemptions from provisions of the 1940 Act, primarily under Section 18 and Rule 18f-3, to accommodate VIPERS into the Vanguard Trust's multi-class structure.[42]

The ETF product category was further extended to encompass the use of new categories of portfolio assets, such as US Treasury obligations and highly rated corporate debt instruments. By the close of 2004, retail and institutional investors could chose from a wide array of ETFs to access multiple equity market segments and styles, as well as an expanding number of debt market investments.

The use of debt indexes expanded the concept of "passive" management by ETFs

The applications for 1940 Act Exemptions submitted by new ETFs intending to hold debt instruments as their portfolio assets raised certain structural and operational questions because, unlike stocks, government debt instruments are not listed and traded on securities exchanges but rather are bought and sold in a dealer market. The issues previously addressed in the equity-based ETF design and structure, particularly those relating to portfolio transparency, pricing mechanics/data, arbitrage opportunities, and liquidity of the underlying portfolio assets, were revisited, probed, and considered, and the Exemptive Orders for the original debt ETFs were granted by the Commission itself rather than by the Division under delegated authority.[43]

The discussion of the modifications to the basic ETF structure necessitated by the nature of the debt instruments themselves, as well as the particular construction methodologies of the underlying debt benchmark indexes, prompted the SEC to re-examine the concept of a "passively managed" index fund. For example, the ETF Advisors Trust intended to utilise as the benchmark for each of its funds a designated Ryan OTR Treasury Index, each of which uses the on-the-run (OTR) US Treasury yield curve.[44] Unlike most traditional financial indexes, which typically consist of a number of component securities, each Ryan OTR Treasury Index at any point is comprised of only one Treasury security because an OTR security is the most recently auctioned Treasury security of a stated maturity (eg, a two-year note or a 10-year bond).[45] When designing the structure of the ETF Advisors Trust and its funds, its adviser determined that it would be impractical and extremely costly for the funds to invest solely in the single component of its designated Ryan OTR Treasury Index. Therefore, in seeking investment results for each ETF that would generally correspond to the total return of its relevant index, ETF Advisors Trust stated in its application for 1940 Act Exemptions that it intended to invest in other US Treasury and high quality debt securities and related financial instruments meeting certain stated criteria.[46] The SEC viewed this portfolio strategy as an extension of portfolio management beyond the traditional "passive" index investing techniques utilised by the ETFs which had received prior relief.

The passive-versus-active portfolio management issue

In 2003, PowerShares introduced the next ETF innovation. Until then, ETFs had used pre-existing financial indexes that were designed as "benchmarks" to measure the return of a particular domestic or international market, sector or segment. By this time, many of the well-established indexes had been licensed by ETF issuers, and market demand spurred both new and existing third party index providers to develop additional benchmark indexes for use by ETFs. In addition, certain ETF issuers were becoming interested in the possible use of "dynamic" or "intelligent" rules-based indexes, rather than traditional benchmark indexes, as the basis for the selection and management of their ETF portfolio assets. Simply put, a "rules-based methodology" employs a stated objective method, such as quantitative analysis, to select and periodically rebalance an index designed to provide the potential for greater than average market return. A "rules-based methodology" usually subjects a designated universe of securities, say domestic large cap equity stocks, to the application of a series of objective factors or "screens" to arrive at, and periodically reconstitute, an index that has an inherent dynamic design. PowerShares ETFs were the first to use indexes employing "rules-based methodologies". Subsequently, other ETF applicants received Exemptive Orders to use different "rules based-methodologies" provided by third-parties.

As ETF issuers began expanding their product offerings by using "rules-based methodologies", the Division staff again raised "passive-versus-active" management issues. A chief concern was that an index resulting from a "rules-based methodology" could be altered more easily and frequently than a benchmark index and thereby, in effect, provide its ETFs with active portfolio management techniques disguised as a passive stock-picking methodology. The main factor that allayed the staff's concern was that the third-party index providers were unaffiliated with the ETFs as well as their advisors; this independence protected ETF investors from potential undue influence, index manipulation or other conflicts of interest.

Three years later, WisdomTree further extended innovation in this area when it expressly requested relief and received its Exemption Order permitting its ETFs to use the indexes provided by its affiliated index provider.[47] In the WisdomTree application for 1940 Act Exemptions, the applicants argued that there were no actual, as opposed to perceived, conflicts of interest between the ETFs and their affiliated index provider, because, among other things, each of the relevant parties would adopt policies and procedures to address any potential conflicts of interest. These would be specifically designed to limit or prohibit communication between index personnel and the employees of the portfolio manager with respect to issues related to the maintenance, calculation and reconstitution of the indexes. The applicants also argued that their proprietary rules-based methodologies, the indexes and the funds' portfolios would be transparent and made available to the public. In addition, the application for 1940 Act Exemptions also contained considerable detail with respect to how and when modifications to the "rules-based methodologies" would take place.

"Enhanced index" ETFs and "passive" versus "active" management

Also in 2006, seven years after first submitting its application for 1940 Act Exemptions, ProShares introduced its family of leveraged, inverse and inverse leveraged ETFs.[48] The application submitted by ProShares stated that the investment objective of each ETF was to seek daily investment results that correspond, (before fees and expenses) to a stated multiple of the performance, or inverse performance of a specific unaffiliated index. It also stated that the adviser intended to utilise its proprietary "rules-based methodologies" to determine the portfolio investments needed for each fund to achieve its stated investment objective. The ProShares application also explained that many of the ETFs would hold certain types of derivative instruments as portfolio assets in order to achieve their investment objective; in the case of the inverse and inverse leveraged funds, no equity securities would be held and only derivatives and other financial instruments would be used. In addition, the application described in detail the portfolio management strategies and investment techniques to be employed by the adviser to achieve the performance of a multiple or inverse multiple of a stated index.

The application submitted by ProShares in connection with their "enhanced" index funds discussed above also prompted the SEC and the Division to reflect on the nature of portfolio management ranging across the spectrum from "passively" to "actively" managed funds. Paul Roye, the director of the Division, noted in an October 17, 2002 address that the Division had received exemptive applications for ETFs that would seek to return a "multiple or an inverse multiple of an index", which approach, in the Division's view, "involve[s] elements of active management".[49]

In particular, the Division focused on the management techniques and methods discussed in the applications for 1940 Act Exemptions submitted by ProFunds and other applicants for new ETFs using "enhanced" indexes, as they related to the transparency of the underlying portfolios to be held by such ETFs. Staff members questioned whether the lack of full portfolio transparency, the potential increase in the frequency of portfolio turnover and the likelihood that portfolio changes might be less foreseeable than those experienced by traditional index funds would lead to a decrease in investor understanding and hamper efficient arbitrage activity. The Commission itself, and not the Division, granted the requested exemptive relief to ProShares.

SEC's ETF concept release

The continuing growth and innovation in ETF structure and design, exemplified by the debt-based, rules-based methodology and "enhanced" index funds, prompted the SEC to issue a concept release entitled "Actively Managed Exchange-Traded Funds" on November 8, 2001.[50] The concept release provides an excellent discussion of the structural, operational and regulatory background of ETFs existing at that time, and raises a variety of issues concerning the desirability and feasibility of permitting actively managed ETFs to be issued, sold and traded. The SEC issued the concept release to generate comments and ideas from a wide range of parties, including individual and institutional investors, shareholder organisations, financial planners, investment advisers, fund organisations, market makers, arbitrageurs, ETF sponsors and national securities exchanges.[51] Comments were sought with the explicit goal of allowing the SEC "to gain a better understanding of the various perspectives on the concept of actively managed ETFs" and thus to help it regulate these investment companies.[52]

The SEC sought guidance on a broad array of issues and sub-issues, including the uses, benefits and risks of actively managed ETFs; the distinction between index-based and actively managed ETFs; operational issues relating to actively managed ETFs, including transparency and liquidity of the portfolio assets; the potential discrimination among the different classes of shareholders and potential conflicts of interest for an ETF's investment adviser; and the concept of an actively managed ETF as a class of mutual fund. The concept release indicated that the SEC would likely regulate actively managed ETFs initially through the process of reviewing individual applications and granting exemptive relief from the 1940 Act, as it had done with prior ETFs.[53] In order to do so, the SEC noted, it would first have to make the required statutory findings under Section 6(c) and would use the comments generated by the concept release to help make these determinations.[54]

The concept release generated a range of responses from market participants and lawyers as well as the investing public,[55] which can be loosely divided into two categories: those approaching the concept release from a legal and policy standpoint, and those approaching it from a technical or economic standpoint. One theme running through the responses in both categories is that the market should be allowed to determine many of the questions posed by the SEC in the concept release. The commentators asserted that the SEC should focus its efforts in a descriptive, rather than prescriptive manner, so that informed market participants may knowledgeably make their investment decisions.

The SEC reviews and examines responses to a concept release in much the same manner as it does comments submitted in response to its formal notice and comment rulemaking. During this stage, the SEC applies its expertise and unique point of view to the subject and, consistent with its regulatory mission, determines how best to proceed. Although the SEC determined not to make a formal statement about the concept release, the Division has been examining and reviewing several applications for relief filed in respect of an actively managed ETF;[56] these are working their way through the review and comment process.

"Fully transparent" actively managed ETFs – the next product innovation

Recently, the SEC issued several exemptive orders to permit "fully transparent", actively managed open-end funds to operate as ETFs.[57] Unlike an index-based ETF, or one using "rules-based methodologies", a "fully transparent" actively managed ETF does not seek to track the return of a particular index. Instead, the adviser to an actively managed ETF, just like an investment adviser to a traditional mutual fund, selects securities consistent with the ETF's investment objectives and policies without regard to a stated benchmark, index or a set of mathematical rules. In contrast to its mutual-fund cousin, however, the "fully transparent", actively managed ETF, as its name suggests, is required to make public each day the identity of its securities and other portfolio assets. Although this development has expanded the possible array of ETF offerings, many market participants are sceptical that there will be more than a few portfolio managers willing to publicise their portfolio holdings and trading strategies on a daily basis. Nevertheless, this expansion into the realm of non-indexed based ETFs could, over time, spur innovative products not yet forseen.

THE PROPOSED ETF RULES

Growth in the number of US ETFs may accelerate once the ETF rules proposed by the SEC in early March 2008 are adopted and become effective.[58] Note that these proposed rules, as currently drafted, cover only new ETFs structured as open-end funds and not UITs[59] and, of course, do not relate to other non-investment-company exchange-traded vehicles, such as ETCs and ETNs. Most importantly, the proposed rules would permit certain registered investment companies to begin operation as ETFs without the delay and expense of first obtaining individual 1940 Act Exemptions from the SEC. The proposed rules would codify the existing Exemptive Orders granted to ETFs which permit the establishment and operation of both index-based and fully transparent active ETFs. The proposed rules also would codify the existing Exemptive Orders granted to certain ETFs, which permit unaffiliated funds to purchase and sell ETF shares in excess of the limits set forth in Section 12(d)(1)[60] of the 1940 Act, under certain conditions. In addition, the proposed rules would expand the scope of the existing Exemptive Orders in certain areas, such as permitting funds other than open-end funds and unit investment trusts (UITs) to acquire ETF shares in excess of the limitations imposed in section 12(d)(1) of the 1940 Act.

Proposed Rule 6c-11 would codify existing ETF exemptive relief

Proposed Rule 6c-11 would codify, and in some cases simplify, most of the previous 1940 Act Exemptions granted to existing ETFs. As currently drafted, Proposed Rule 6c-11 would apply to index-based ETFs as well as to fully transparent, active ETFs. Briefly, Proposed Rule 6c-11 would permit an ETF to (i) register under the 1940 Act as an open-end fund, (ii) redeem its shares in specified creation units in exchange for specified portfolio assets held by the ETF and (iii) list its shares on a national securities exchange where they would be traded intraday at negotiated market prices in the secondary market. Proposed Rule 6c-11 would require the intraday value of all ETF shares to be published at 15-second intervals throughout each trading day.

The proposing release makes clear that, apart from the existing requirements applicable to all open-end funds under the 1940 Act and its rules, Proposed Rule 6c-11 would not limit the types or quantities of portfolio securities that may be held by an ETF operating under the rule, nor would it limit the type of index that an index-based ETF may follow. Proposed Rule 6c-11 also would streamline and simplify certain requirements and conditions that were imposed by the prior Exemptive Orders granted to existing ETFs. For example, the proposed rule would not require a "firewall" to be established between an ETF and its affiliated index provider.

Proposed Rule 12d1-4 would codify much of existing Section 12(d)(1) relief

Proposed Rule 12d1-4 would broaden the scope of the existing ETF Exemptive Orders in providing an exemption to both registered and unregistered acquiring funds to permit such funds to invest in ETFs in excess of the percentage limits contained in section 12(d)(1) of the 1940 Act (Rule 12(d)(1) Limitations).

As drafted, Proposed Rule 12d1-4 would permit an acquiring fund to make an investment in an ETF up to 25% of the acquired ETF's outstanding shares without receiving an Exemptive Order from the SEC. In addition, Proposed Rule 12d1-4 would add two prohibitions with respect to redemption of an acquired ETF's shares.[61] First, an acquiring fund that relies on the proposed rule to invest in shares of an acquired ETF beyond the 3% limitation would not be permitted to redeem such shares, although it would continue to be able to sell them in the secondary market. Second, an ETF, its principal underwriter and any broker or dealer who relies on the proposed rule to sell acquired ETF shares in excess of the limitations imposed by Section 12(d)(1)(B) (12d1-4 entities) would be prohibited from redeeming those acquired ETF shares acquired by another acquiring fund that exceed the 3% limitation. Given that practical difficulties may be inherent in compliance with these requirements, the proposed rule includes a safe harbour for Rule 12d1-4 entities investing in of the 3% limitation.[62] Note that Proposed Rule 12d1-4 is not exclusive, therefore an acquiring fund may continue to rely upon existing Exemptive Orders that permit acquiring funds to invest in ETFs beyond the limits of Section 12(d)(1) but that do not restrict their ability to redeem ETF shares, subject to compliance with the conditions contained in such orders.

Proposed Rule 12d1-4 also would streamline certain conditions that were required in the prior Exemptive Orders granted to existing ETFs. For example, an acquiring fund will not be required to enter into a written "participation agreement" with, or to provide lists of certain affiliates to, an acquired ETF. In addition, Proposed Rule 12d1-4 would provide certain exemptions from various sections of the 1940 Act to permit an acquiring fund to enter into certain transactions with affiliated persons. Under the proposed rule, acquiring funds, including business-development companies (BDCs), would be permitted to deposit the underlying portfolio securities basket with the ETF and to purchase ETF shares in excess of the 5% limitations. Proposed Rule 12d1-4 would also provide limited relief from Section 17(e)(2) of the 1940 Act to permit an acquiring fund to pay commissions, fees or other remuneration to a second-tier affiliated broker-dealer without complying with quarterly board review and record-keeping requirements set forth in Rules 17e-1(b)(3) and 17e-1(d)(2).

Proposed Rule 12d1-4 would prohibit an acquired ETF from itself being or becoming a "fund of funds". In other words, the proposed rule will not permit a fund of funds of funds. Under the proposed rule, an acquiring fund could invest in an ETF that itself invests up to 10% of its assets in other ETFs.

Several commentators have observed that Proposed Rule 12d1-4, as written, expands the scope of relief beyond that previously granted in existing Exemptive Orders, which only permitted open-end funds and UITs to acquire ETF shares in excess of the limits in Section 12(d)(1).[63] Proposed Rule 12d1-4 would also allow closed-end funds, including BDCs, to do the same, provided that they comply with the stated conditions.

OTHER TYPES OF INVESTMENT VEHICLES ISSUE EXCHANGE-TRADED SECURITIES

US investment vehicles offering exposure to commodities and other non-traditional assets

In the US, there are a variety of well-established forms of investment vehicles other than open-end and closed end funds and UITs, that invest all or substantially all of their assets in various types of securities, derivatives and commodities, or otherwise provide exposure to non-traditional assets. A few examples are mortgage-backed securities issuers, asset-backed securities issuers and commodities pools, mentioned earlier. Some of these vehicles are not considered investment companies, due to specific sections of the 1940 Act. Examples include mortgage-backed issuers and asset-backed issuers who are exempted under Section 3(c)(5). In addition, there are other issuers that cannot qualify under the 1940 Act, usually because all or a large percentage of their portfolio assets are not traditional securities, such as equities and debt instruments.[64] In other cases, although the investment vehicles, such as hedge funds, hold traditional securities as portfolio assets, they are structured in such a manner that their securities are made available only to high-net-worth individuals and institutional purchasers, hence they are not registered with the SEC and their securities are not listed or traded on a securities exchange. Consequently, the regulatory regime applicable to these non-public vehicles is quite different from and often far less stringent than that applicable to ETFs.

Retail investors interested in participating in the opportunities offered by the commodities markets have long been able to acquire interests in a public commodity pool, which provide retail investors with an easy and relatively inexpensive way to invest in forwards, futures and options markets managed by one or more professional commodity trading advisers. Public commodity pools typically invest in a variety of futures contracts and futures-related interests, as well as Treasury bills and cash or cash equivalents. The range of these interests encompasses futures and options contracts on agricultural commodities, energy products, industrial raw materials, metals and a variety of financial instruments, as well as forwards, futures and options contracts on international currencies. Public commodity pools provide retail investors with many benefits, including access to professional management of the pool's assets at a relatively low minimum investment amount, daily pricing, liquidity, and liability limited to the actual amount invested, as well as a regulatory oversight regime involving the Commodities Futures Trading Commission (CFTC), the commodities exchanges, the SEC and the state securities regulators, which collectively impose suitability standards and disclosure requirements, as well as sales and promotional regulations. These benefits are similar to those provided to retail investors acquiring shares of open-end investment companies, apart from the regulatory oversight of the Commodities Exchange Act and the CFTC.

Despite these advantages, relatively few public commodity pools are currently offered, and, like all products, they have certain drawbacks. Many institutions cannot hold commodities outright or through a commodity pool, due to either statutory or internal restrictions. Also, the minimum investment amount is usually higher than that required to buy stock or mutual-fund shares and the suitability requirements are stricter. Further, because the pools offer professional management and engage in trading activity, there are related fees and trading costs to pay. In addition, public commodity pools are not structured with continuous creation/redemption features.

Exchange-traded vehicles holding and tracking investments that are not securities

The success of the ETF concept has spurred demand for easily tradable retail products holding a portfolio of one or more non-traditional assets, such as physical commodities. During the past five years, requests for exchange-traded vehicles holding or tracking investments such as gold, silver and crude oil have become more frequent. However, due to limitations imposed by the 1940 Act as well as the federal tax rules applicable to RICs, investment companies cannot hold portfolios that are entirely comprised of commodities, so there can be no true commodities ETFs. The demand in the US for ETF-like investment vehicles led to the development and launch of the StreetTRACKS Gold Trust[65] in November 2004, followed by iShares Comex Gold Trust in January 2005. Although ETF Securities Ltd had established and listed gold exchange-traded vehicles in Australia and the UK before this time,[66] the StreetTRACKS and iShares trusts were the first offered in the US to hold physical commodities (gold bullion) as portfolio assets while providing retail investors with an investment in exchange-traded vehicles that operate very similarly to ETFs.

The success of the US gold trusts indicated to the US marketplace that there is retail as well as institutional demand for unmanaged, low-turnover and low-expense commodity vehicles whose interests are traded on a securities exchange in a manner similar to ETF units/shares. Soon, these ETC products were followed by other exchange-traded vehicles holding various commodities and currencies, such as the Rydex Euro Currency Trust, DB Commodity Index Tracking Fund, iShares GSCI Commodity Indexed Trust, United States Oil Fund, LP and MacroShares $100 Oil Down Trust.[67] Demand for low-cost and transparent retail-exchange-traded products offering exposure to commodities and other non-securities asset classes continues to expand. There appears to be considerable interest in packaging a wide variety of assets such as base metals, real estate in various forms, single and multiple foreign currencies, coal, heating oil, natural gas, other energy-related products, baskets of assorted commodities tracked by an index, options volatility and other derivatives.

ETCs are regulated differently from ETFs

Although not ETFs, these investment vehicles share the important features of continuous creation and redemption of their securities, often partly or wholly in kind. If an ETC intends to offer and sell its securities (structured as participations, units, partnership interests and the like) to the general public, it must first register them under the 1933 Act and list them on a securities exchange; in this respect, these securities also resemble those issued by ETFs and are regulated in the same manner. However, some or all of the portfolio assets may be governed by a different set of regulations from those applicable to the portfolio assets of an ETF. For example, in the US, commodities and commodity futures are not securities; the regulation of securities markets and their related market participants is distinct from that of the futures markets and their related market participants, which are subject to the Commodity Exchange Act administered by the CFTC. Broadly speaking, the SEC regulates securities, options on securities and options on indexes of securities; and the CFTC regulates futures and options on futures.

Partly for historical reasons and partly reflecting the different nature and uses of the products traded as well as the nature and sophistication of the market participants, the regulatory concerns, issues, safeguards and requirements applicable to the commodities and futures markets are not the same as those applicable to the securities markets, although many are similar. For example, a sudden or rapid increase in the price of commodities, especially if caused by traders and speculators, has traditionally concerned commodities regulators and continues to be the case. Recently, this has become an important issue for securities regulators with the introduction of ETCs in the US market place. Among other things, the staff of the SEC's Division of Corporation Finance examines, questions and comments on a new ETC issuer's description of the relevant commodities market contained in its registration statement and prospectus with particular emphasis on liquidity, supply and demand issues. This is especially true for ETCs comprised of a single commodity, such as gold or oil.[68] For this reason, it is unlikely that a new ETC intending to invest in an unlimited amount of a single, highly illiquid, thinly traded commodity could satisfy the SEC registration process. Nevertheless, certain market participants have alleged that the demand for, and the resulting growth in the issuance of, ETCs during the past several years has strongly contributed to price increases in commodities backing these exchange traded vehicles.[69]

In addition, the structure of ETCs does not comfortably fit within the regulatory requirements of the 1933 Act nor the US Internal Revenue Code, and an intricate legal structure sometimes results when an ETC sponsor designs a product to meet all or most of investors' needs and demands. These and other related issues are prompting regulators to take a closer look at the structure of ETCs and the role they play in various markets. Recently, in response to the "enormous complexity" of certain commodity exchange-traded funds, Commission Chairman Mary Schapiro has stated that ETCs "are an issue on the agenda", indicating that she may add expertise in this area to the Commission's staff as well as work with the CFTC.[70] During the next few years, we can expect to see additional interest in this area, together with an increased demand for ETCs and the benefits they provide.

APPENDIX A

Typical timeline for the 1940 Act exemptive relief process

1. A draft application must be submitted to the SEC containing all relevant facts, explanations, descriptions and representations necessary for the grant to exemptive relief.

   a) Depending upon the complexity and or novelty of the relief being requested, the applicants may spend anywhere from four weeks to several months preparing their application for filing with the SEC.

b) Once filed, an application is a public document. Until January 2009, all 1940 Act exemptive applications were filed in paper format and could be retrieved only by obtaining a photocopy from the SEC's public reference room, which was often time-consuming and/or expensive. In Release Nos 33-8981, 34-58874 and IC-28476 (October 29, 2008), the SEC adopted rule revisions requiring that all 1940 Act exemptive applications be submitted electronically on its EDGAR system.

2. The SEC's administrative rule states that the first review should occur within 45–60 days after the submission of the application. After reviewing the application, the staff of the Division provides a set of written comments to the applicants.

   a) In practice, depending on the similarity to ETF Exemption Orders previously granted and the complexity of the applicants' request for relief, the Division staff typically provide first comments within three to six months after filing, and in some cases, considerably longer.
   b) Note also that events at the SEC may also further delay receipt of comments. For example, ProShares originally submitted a confidential draft application for 1940 Act Exemptions to the Division in December 1999 and filed a formal application with the SEC on December 5, 2000, but due to a delay caused by the issuance of the concept release, did not receive the first set of comments from the Division until April 16, 2002. In addition, major economic and market events may delay the Division's ability to comment quickly, because staff members will be redeployed to deal with ongoing crises involving investment companies. Two recent examples are the late trading "mutual fund scandal" of 2003 and Reserve Primary Fund's "breaking the buck" in September of 2008. See, "A Primer on the Mutual-Fund Scandal", Business Week, Amey Stone, September 22, 2003, URL: http://www.businessweek.com/bwdaily/dnflash/sep2003/nf20030922_7646.htm; and "SEC Sues Reserve's Bent and Son", Steve Stecklow and Diya Gullapalli, Wall Street Journal, May 6, 2009, URL: http://online.wsj.com/article/SB124154900090988321.html.

3. Applicants have 60 days to reply and file an amended application in response to the Division's written comments.

   a) The amended application is typically filed within two to four weeks following receipt of the comments, depending upon how extensive and/or controversial they are.
   b) Negotiation, clarification and amplification of contested issues raised by the comments are discussed by telephone conferences and, in rare cases, in person.

4. This process is then repeated, resulting in applicants' filing of additional amended applications in response to further comment letters and negotiations/meetings/phone conferences with the Division staff.

   a) This can become very time-consuming, especially if one or more of the SEC's other divisions or offices become involved in the issues raised by the application, such as the Division of Markets and Trading, Division of Corporation Finance, Office of General Counsel, Office of Compliance Inspections and Examinations and Office of Economic Analysis.

5. Once the application is in acceptable form, the SEC publishes notice of the request for orders in the Federal Register for 25–30 calendar days (20 days in exceptional cases) (order notice period).
6. Unless unusual SEC actions occur (see item 7 below), the exemptive order is signed by the Division pursuant to delegated authority. The order is issued and published several days after the order notice period expires.
7. There are several circumstances under which an exemptive order is not granted by the Division pursuant to delegated authority, but rather by the Commission itself, some of which are briefly described below. Each of these situations requires additional time before an order is entered.

   a) The most common example occurs when the staff of the Division decide that the application presents a novel request, (eg, the original ProShares application) or otherwise exceeds the scope of the delegated authority.

      i) In such cases, the Division staff will submit the application to the SEC Commissioners for their review. This will be accompanied by the Division's "action memo" recommending that the order be granted (or not).

ii) The Commission will then review the application and the action memo, and decide whether or not to grant the order.

b) An infrequent example occurs if, during the order notice period, a person with standing requests that the Commission hold a public hearing on the order (eg, the request by Standard & Poors to stop Vanguard from offering its new VIPER shares. See "S&P Asks SEC to Block New Vanguard Viper Fund", Mercer Bullard, special to the Street.com, November 1, 2000, URL: http://www.smartportfolio.com/funds/funds/1152940. html).

i) In such cases, the Division staff must consider the hearing request and draft a memo for the Commission's review.

ii) This memo sets forth the staff's analysis and recommendation to either accept or deny the hearing request.

iii) If the Commission accepts the request, a public hearing is conducted.

iv) The Commission will then conduct the hearing and decide whether or not to grant the order.

v) Although there is a right of appeal if the Commission declines to hold a public hearing, it is rarely used.

c) Another infrequent example occurs if the Commission, on its own initiative, decides to hold an open (ie, public) meeting in connection with the decision to grant the exemption order.

APPENDIX B
Selected ETF and Exchange Traded Vehicle (ETV) 1934 Act no-action letters

1. Regular Equity ETFs:

See letter to James F. Duffy, senior vice president and general counsel, Amex, dated January 22, 1993 (*1993 SEC No-Act. LEXIS 119*), re SPDRs, re Rules 10a-1, 10b-6, 10b-7, 10b-10, 14e-5 (formerly 10b-13), 10b-17, 11d1-2, 15c1-5, and 15c1-6; and
letter to Domenick Pugliese, Paul, Hastings, Janofsky & Walker LLP (March 8, 2007) File No. TP 07-49, URL: http://www.sec.gov/divisions/marketreg/mr-noaction/2007/hscompetf030807-msr.pdf: 10a-1, 10b-17, and 14e-5, Rules 101 and 102 of Regulation M, and Rule 200(g) of SHO.

2. Expanded equity ETF "Class Relief":

   See letter to Stuart M. Strauss, Clifford Chance US LLP (October 24, 2006), File No. TP-07-07, URL: http://www.sec.gov/divisions/marketreg/mr-noaction/etifclassrelief102406-msr.pdf at 2-3:

   "ETFs meeting the following criteria are granted exemptive and/or no-action or interpretive advice re Rules 10a-1, 10b-17, and 14e-5 under the Exchange Act, Rules 101 and 102 of Regulation M and Rule 200(g) of Regulation SHO, provided that the following conditions are satisfied:

   1. the ETF shares are issued by an open-end investment company or unit investment trust registered with the Commission under the Investment Company Act;
   2. the ETF consists of a basket of 20 or more component securities, with no one component security constituting more than 25% of the total value of the ETF;
   3. at least 70% of the ETF must be comprised of component securities that meet the minimum public float and minimum average daily trading volume thresholds under the "actively traded securities" definition found in Regulation M for excepted securities during each of the previous two months of trading prior to formation of the relevant ETF; provided, however, that, if the ETF has 200 or more component securities, then 50% of the component securities must meet the actively traded securities thresholds;
   4. ETF shares are to be issued and redeemed in creation-unit aggregations of 50,000 shares or such other amount where the value of a creation unit is at least US$1 million at the time of issuance; and
   5. the ETF must be managed to track a particular index all of whose components have publicly available last-sale trade information. The intra-day proxy value of the ETF per share and the value of the "benchmark" index must be publicly disseminated by a major market data vendor throughout the trading day."

3. "1934 Act Class Relief Letters", collectively:

   See letter to Securities Industry Association dated November 21, 2005, URL: http://www.sec.gov/divisions/marketreg/mr-noaction/sia112105.htm at 1, regarding an extension of relief granted in prior letters to ETFs and certain broker-dealers from

Section 11(d)(1) and Rules 10b-10, 11d1-2, 15c1-5 and 15c1-6 to include qualifying ETFs, subject to the following conditions:

"1. neither the broker-dealer AP nor any natural person associated with such broker-dealer AP, directly or indirectly (including through any affiliate of such broker-dealer AP), receives from the fund complex any payment, compensation or other economic incentive to promote or sell the shares of the ETF to persons outside the fund complex, other than non-cash compensation permitted under NASD Rule 2830(1)(5)(A), (B), or (C); and

2. the broker-dealer AP does not extend, maintain or arrange for the extension or maintenance of credit to or for a customer on shares of the ETF before 30 days have passed from the date that the ETF's shares initially commence trading (except to the extent that such extension, maintenance or arranging of credit is otherwise permitted pursuant to Rule 11d1-1).

For purposes of our response, qualifying ETFs are ETFs that satisfy all three of the following conditions:

1. the ETF shares are issued by an open-end investment company or unit investment trust registered with the Commission under the Investment Company Act;
2. the ETF shares are listed and trade on a market that has obtained approval from the Commission pursuant to Section 19(b) of the Exchange Act of a rule change regarding the listing and trading of the ETF shares on the market (or that is relying on Rule 19b-4(e) to list and trade the ETF shares); and
3. the ETF (a) consists of a basket of 20 or more component securities, with no one component security constituting more than 25% of the total value of the ETF, and is managed to track a particular index all of whose components are publicly available; or (b) solely for purposes of the exemptive relief for APs from Section 11(d)(1) of the Exchange Act, is an ETF with respect to which the staff of the Division of Market Regulation (Staff) has granted non-AP broker-dealers (as defined below) relief from the requirements of Section 11(d)(1) in a letter dated prior to the date of this letter, provided that the ETF has not changed in such a way as to materially affect any of the facts or representations in such prior letter."

See also, letter to Ira Hammerman dated July 18, 2005, File No. TP-05-47, URL: http://www.sec.gov/divisions/marketreg/mr-noaction/sia071805.htm, granting relief with respect to Rule 10a-1 in riskless principal transactions;
letter to Ira Hammerman dated January 3, 2005, File No. TP 05-11, URL: http://www.sec.gov/divisions/marketreg/mr-noaction/sia010305.htm re Rule 200(g) of SHO; and
letter to Clair P. McGrath, American Stock Exchange, dated August 17, 2001, File No. TP-00-133, URL: http://www.sec.gov/divisions/marketreg/mr-noaction/etifclassrelief081701-msr.pdf, for exemptive relief for equity-based exchange-traded index funds recites the conditions for the ETF "class exemption" for Rule 10b-10, Section 11(d)(1) and Rules 11d1-2, 15c1-5 and 15c1-6.

4. Foreign-equity ETFs:

   See letter to Kathleen H. Moriarty, Carter Ledyard & Milbum LLP, dated March 9, 2005, File No. TP 04-19, URL: http://www.sec.gov/divisions/marketreg/mr-noaction/vanguard030905.htm re International Index VIPERS;
   letter to Michael Simon, Milbank, Tweed, Hadley & McCloy, dated March 22, 1996, re CountryBaskets (*1996 SEC No-Act. LEXIS 387*) and letter to Tuuli-Ann Ristkok, and Stephen K. West dated March 22, 1996, File No. TP-95-21 (*1996 SEC No-Act. LEXIS 3860*) re Foreign Fund, Inc (later WEBs and now iShares MSCI); and
   letter to Donald R. Crawshaw, Sullivan & Cromwell, dated May 10, 2000, File No. TP 99-146 (*2000 SEC No-Act. LEXIS 626*).

5. Inverse-equity ETFs:

   See ProShares Trust letter dated January 24, 2007, File No. TP 07-32, URL: http://www.sec.gov/divisions/marketreg/mr-noaction/2007/proshares012407-msr.pdf re Section 11(d)(1), Rules 10a-1, 10b-10, 10b-17, 11d1-2, 14e-5, 15c1-5, and 15c1-6, Rules 101 and 102 of Regulation M and Rule 200(g) of Regulation SHO, class relief for inverse funds; and
   ProShares Trust letter dated June 20, 2006 (revised November 15, 2006), File No. TP 06-82 (http://www.sec.gov/divisions/marketreg/mr-noaction/proshares062006.pdf) re 10a-1, 14e-5, and 10b-17, and Rules 101 and 102 of Reg M and Rule 200(g) of SHO, and class relief applies (Rule 10b-10; Section 11(d)(1); Rule 11d1-2; Rules 15c1-5 and 15c1-6).

6. Debt ETF funds:

   See Ameristock Fixed-Income ETF Trust (June 29, 2007) URL: http://www.sec.gov/divisions/marketreg/mr-noaction/2007/ameristock062907-msr.pdf. The SEC will no longer respond to requests for relief from Section 11(d)(1) and Rules 10b-10, 11d1-2, 15c1-5, and 15c1- 6: class relief for fixed income ETFs;
   and letter to Benjamin Haskin of Willkie Farr & Gallagher LLP, April 9, 2007, File No. TP 07-57, URL: http://www.sec.gov/divisions/marketreg/mr-noaction/2007/fietfclassrelief040907-msr.pdf at 2-5: class relief for fixed-income exchange-traded funds re Rules 10a-1, 10b-17 and 14e-5, Rules 101 and 102 of Regulation M and Rule 200(g) of SHO:

   > "The relief granted herein extends to all fixed-income ETFs that continuously redeem, at net asset value, creation unit aggregations of shares, where the secondary-market price of shares do not vary substantially from the net asset value of such shares (which will be based on the value of the component securities).[3]
   >
   > Further, the fixed-income ETFs must meet the following conditions:
   >
   > - the fixed-income ETF shares are issued by an open-end investment company or unit investment trust registered with the Commission under the Investment Company Act;
   > - the fixed-income ETF shares are listed and traded on a national securities exchange or on a facility of a national securities association that has obtained approval from the Commission pursuant to Section 19(b) of the Exchange Act of a rule change regarding the listing and trading of shares on a national securities exchange or on a facility of a national securities association (or that is relying on Rule 19b-4(e) to list and trade shares);
   > - the fixed-income ETF seeks to: (i) provide investment results that correspond to the performance of a particular underlying index; (ii) exceed the performance of a particular underlying index by a specified multiple; or (iii) correspond to the inverse of the performance of a particular underlying index by a specified multiple;[4]
   > - the underlying index must consist of only fixed-income securities;
   > - the fixed-income ETF shares must be issued and redeemed in creation unit aggregations of 50,000 shares or such other amount where the value of a creation unit is at least US$1 million at the time of issuance; and

- the intraday proxy value of the fixed-income ETF per share and the value of the underlying index must be publicly disseminated by a major market data vendor during the trading day.

The relief is further subject to the "rule-specific" conditions set forth below…

The Staff hereby confirms the prior interpretations of Regulation M provided by the Commission and the Staff to issuers of fixed income ETFs (as discussed more fully below) where:

(i) no component security (excluding a Treasury security) represents more than 30% of the weight of the fixed-income ETF, and the five highest-weighted component securities in the fixed-income ETF do not in the aggregate account for more than 65% of the weight of the fixed-income ETF[5]; and
(ii) the fixed-income ETF (except where the fund consists entirely of exempted securities) must include a minimum of 13 non-affiliated issuers.

However, where the fixed-income ETF is wholly comprised of non-convertible fixed-income securities that are rated "investment grade" by at least one nationally recognised statistical rating organisation (as that term is used in Rule 15c3-1 in one of its generic rating categories that signifies investment grade), conditions (i) and (ii) above shall not apply.

The staff hereby confirm that fixed-income ETFs are excepted under paragraph (d)(4) of Rule 102 of Regulation M, thus permitting fixed-income ETFs to redeem shares during the continuous offering of the shares where the fixed-income ETF meets conditions (i) and (ii) set forth in the discussion concerning Rule 101 of Regulation M; provided however, that where the fixed-income ETF wholly comprises non-convertible fixed-income securities that are rated "investment grade" by at least one nationally recognised statistical rating organisation (as that term is used in Rule 15c3-1 in one of its generic rating categories that signifies investment grade), conditions (i) and (ii) above shall not apply."

7. Commodity ETVs:

See letter to Michael Schmidtberger, Sidley Austin Brown & Wood LLP dated January 19, 2006, File No. TP 06-31, URL: http://www.sec.gov/divisions/marketreg/mr-noaction/commodityidxtf011906.htm re DB Commodity Index Tracking Fund;

letters to Kathleen H. Moriarty, Carter, Ledyard & Milburn, dated December 12, 2005, URL: http://www.sec.gov/divisions/

marketreg/mr-noaction/streettracks121205.htm and November 17, 2004, File No. TP 04-21, URL: http://www.sec.gov/divisions/marketreg/mr-noaction/stgr111704.htm with respect to StreetTRACKS Gold Trust;

letters to David Yeres, Clifford Chance, dated January 27, 2005, File No. TP 04-77, URL: http://www.sec.gov/divisions/marketreg/mr-noaction/ishares012705.htm re iShares COMEX Gold Trust; and

letter to George T. Simon, Foley & Lardner, LLP, dated December 5, 2005, File No. TP 05-15, URL: http://www.sec.gov/divisions/marketreg/mr-noaction/eurocurrency120505.htm re Euro Currency Trust.

8. MACROS:

   See letter to MACRO Securities Depositor, LLC dated December 22, 2006, URL: http://www.sec.gov/divisions/marketreg/mr-noaction/macro122206-11d1.pdf re 11(d)(1) and Rules 10b-10, 11d1-2, and 10b-17.

9. ETNs:

   See letter to George White, Sullivan & Cromwell, dated July 27, 2006, File No. TP 06-90, URL: http://www.sec.gov/divisions/marketreg/mr-noaction/ipathetn072706.pdf re iPath Exchange-Traded Notes (linked to the Goldman Sachs Crude Oil Total Return Index) from Section 11(d)(1), Rule 10a-1, Rules 101 and 102 of Reg M, and Rule 200(g) of SHO.

1 A folio is a collection of stocks, funds and/or ETFs that can be bought, sold, rebalanced or customised in a single transaction that is offered through FOLIOfn Investments, Inc. See, URL: https://www.folioinvesting.com/whatfolios/index.jsp.

2 As will be discussed in this chapter, until recently, US ETFs were established to track a securities, commodities or other financial index, such as the S&P 500, or a multiple or inverse multiple of such an index, or to follow a rules-based method of selecting Portfolio Assets. In 2008, the SEC permitted the establishment of fully transparent actively managed ETFs (Fully Transparent Active ETFs).

3 See http://www.sec.gov/about/whatwedo.shtml, "Laws that Govern the Securities Industry".

4 Ibid.

5 Ibid.

6 Ibid.

7 See URL: http://www.sec.gov/answers/etf.htm. The text of the 1940 Act and its rules are available at URL: http://www.law.uc.edu/CCL/InvCoAct/index.html and URL: http://www.law.uc.edu/CCL/InvCoRls/index.html, respectively.

8 For reference to the major studies, reports and Congressional hearings conducted in connection with the adoption with the 1940 Act, see footnote 148 at page I-52 in volume 1 of the

four-volume treatise entitled "The Regulation of Money Managers", Frankel and Schwing, Second Edition (Frankel).

9 See, the Executive Summary contained in the US Securities and Exchange Commission, Division of Investment Management, "Protecting Investors: A Half Century of Investment Company Regulation" (1992), (1992 Study). URL: http://www.sec.gov/divisions/investment/guidance/icreg50-92.pdf.

10 See Frankel, Chapter 1.02 B for an excellent discussion of the problems and abuses that occasioned the adoption of the 1940 Act and its regulatory structure. See, also the brief but comprehensive explanation by Jerry W. Markham of foreign and US investment structures that predated the US mutual fund at 3 through 11 in "Mutual Funds and Other Collective Investment Mediums—A Comparative Analysis of Their Regulation and Governance" (May 21, 2006). bepress Legal Series. Working Paper 1386. URL: http://law.bepress.com/expresso/eps/1386.

11 See URL: http://www.sec.gov/about/whatwedo.shtml#laws.

12 Until recently, the relief from Rule 10a-1 under the 1934 Act (Uptick Rule), which prohibited short sales of a "reported security" on a "zero tick" or a downtick, proved to be extremely important to ETF secondary-market trading and liquidity. The Uptick Rule was eliminated on July 6, 2007, but on April 8, 2009 the SEC released several proposals, including a modified Uptick Rule, that would restrict short selling. As of this writing it is not yet known whether the SEC will provide relief from the application of these new rules, if adopted, to permit ETFs to be sold on a downtick.

13 The 1940 Act permits a registered investment company to be structured as a management company of either the open-end or closed-end variety, a UIT or a face amount certificate company, each with a prescribed set of features. See Section 4 of the 1940 Act.

14 The first US ETF, the SPDR Trust requested such 1940 Act Exemptions and received an order (Exemption Order) from the SEC granting such relief. See SEC Rel. No IC-18959 (September 17, 1992) (notice) and SEC Rel. No IC-19055 (October 26, 1992) (order) (collectively, SPDR Trust Order).

15 See, the exemptions from Sections 2(a)(32), 5(a)(1) and 22(d) of the 1940 Act as well as Rule 22c-1 thereunder in the SPDR Trust Order.

16 Section 6(c) of the 1940 Act states:

> "The Commission, by rules and regulations upon its own motion, or by order upon application, may conditionally or unconditionally exempt any person, security, or transaction, or any class or classes of persons, securities, or transactions, from any provision or provisions of this title or of any rule or regulation thereunder, if and to the extent that such exemption is necessary or appropriate in the public interest and consistent with the protection of investors and the purposes fairly intended by the policy and provisions of this title".

17 See, Statement of President Roosevelt, dated August 23, 1940 (reprinted in 4 Federal Securities Laws: Legislative History, 1933-1982 5230-31 (BNA 1983)).

18 See, David Silver, "The Investment Company Act of 1940: At the Frontiers," paper presented at the SEC's Major Issues Conference, November 2001, at footnote 2.

19 See, Tuuli-Ann Ristkok, "Exchange-Traded Funds," 34 Rev. Sec. Comm. Reg. 109 (May 30, 2001).

20 See, Section 1(b) of the 1940 Act.

21 See, footnote 148 of Frankel, supra.

22 See, Section 1(b) of the 1940 Act.

23 See, for example, the discussion at xxi through xxxvii of the Executive Summary in the 1992 Study.

24 See, Chapter 2 of Frankel which contains a detailed explanation of the exemptive process and an analysis of the various factors used by the SEC in determining whether to grant an order.

25 See, for example, the relief requested by WisdomTree Trust and its funds, which was granted in the Letter from James A. Brigagliano, Acting Associate Director, Division of Market Regulation (Division of Market Regulation), to Richard F. Morris, Esq. dated May 9, 2008,

File No. TP 08-39, with respect to certain WisdomTree Funds at URL: http://www.sec.gov/divisions/marketreg/mr-noaction/2008/wisdomtree050908-msr.pdf.

26 The relief from Rule 10b-17, as well as Rules 15c1-5 and 15c1-6, which contain notice and disclosure requirements, also was necessary because it enabled broker-dealers to execute secondary-market transactions in a rational and efficient manner.

27 See, for example, the original listing rules adopted by the American Stock Exchange and approved by the Commission for the listing of SPDRS in Release No. 34-31591 (December 11, 1992) and those for the listing of MidCap SPDRS in Release No. 34-35534 (March 24, 1995). Primary listing exchanges have adopted rules pursuant to orders granted under Rule 19b-4 of the 1934 Act to accommodate ETF trading. See, for example, Nasdaq Rules 4420(i) and 4420(j). and NYSE Arca Rule 5.2(j)(3) as well as Rules 8.201 et seq adopted to permit the listing of certain ETVs.

28 See, for example, NYSE Arca Equities Rule 5.2(j)(3).

29 See, for example, the no-action letter issued to the Select SPDR Trust on May 6, 1999 at URL: http://www.sec.gov/divisions/investment/noaction/1999/selectsectorspdr050699.pdf.

30 See, for example, the letter from James A. Brigagliano, assistant director of Market Reg., to Mary Joan Hoene, Carter, Ledyard & Milburn, dated November 1, 2002, File No. TP 02-126, URL: http://www.sec.gov/divisions/marketreg/mr-noaction/fitr110102.htm which, among other things, permitted broker-dealers and others to bid for, purchase, redeem or engage in other secondary-market transactions for ETF units/shares and portfolio securities during a distribution or tender offer for such portfolio securities.

31 See notes 41 and 42 below.

32 The S&P indexes, such as the S&P 500, are compiled by Standard & Poor's. "S&P 500", "Standard & Poor's 500", "Standard & Poor's Depositary Receipts" and "SPDRs" are trademarks of the McGraw-Hill Companies, Inc.

33 For example, IPs, novel stock basket products that were listed and traded on the Amex and the Philadelphia Stock Exchange in the late 1980s, were hybrid instruments that had elements of futures contracts as well as those of securities. The SEC and the Commodities Futures Trading Commission (CFTC) each contended that it had sole jurisdiction and regulatory responsibility for these products. Ultimately, the US Court of Appeals, in determining the proper characterisation of IPs, or in their words, deciding "whether tetrahedrons belong in square or round holes", decided that they were contracts of infinite duration based on the value of a specified securities basket and hence represented futures contract. As a result, trading in IPs on the Amex and Philadelphia Stock Exchange was suspended and all outstanding positions were liquidated.

34 See, for example, the SPDR Trust and the MidCap SPDR Trust, designed to generally correspond to the price and yield performance of the S&P 500 Index and S&P MidCap 400 Index respectively. See the propectus for the SPDR Trust: URL: http://www.sec.gov/Archives/edgar/data/884394/000095012309001718/y0087897e497.htm, and the prospectus for the MidCap SPDR Trust: URL: http://www.sec.gov/Archives/edgar/data/936958/ 000095012309003876/y0119197e497.htm.

35 "DIAMONDS" is a service mark of Dow Jones & Company, Inc.

36 The Nasdaq-100 Trust was rebranded as the "PowerShares QQQ Trust". "PowerShares QQQ Index Tracking Stock[SM]," "QQQQ®," "PowerShares QQQ Shares[SM]," or "PowerShares QQQ Trust[SM] are marks of the Nasdaq Stock Market, Inc. "Nasdaq-100 Trust" and "Nasdaq-100 Index Tracking Stock" are service marks of the Nasdaq Stock Market, Inc.

37 "WEBS" was the name of the family of ETFs which tracked certain of the MSCI international equity indexes that were compiled by Morgan Stanley Capital International. "WEBS" are now known as "iShares MSCI Series".

38 CountryBaskets Funds were another family of international equity ETFs. The CountryBaskets Index Fund, Inc ceased operations in March 1997 and deregistered as an investment company in 1998. See footnote 13 of the concept release cited in footnote 50, below.

39 See the discussion in the iShares "Statement of Additional Information" at 3 through 7, URL: http://us.ishares.com/content/stream.jsp?url=/content/repository/material/sai/sai_inc.pdf&mimeType=application/pdf.

40 See, for example In the Matter of The Select Sector SPDR Trust, *et al*, Rel. Nos. IC-23492 (October 20, 1998) (notice) and IC- 23534 (November 13, 1998) (order) which was granted by the Division pursuant to delegated authority.

41 Vanguard Index Participating Equity Receipts ("VIPERs"), recently renamed Vanguard ETF Shares. See the prospectus for the ETF Share Class of the Vanguard Growth Index Fund dated April 29, 2009 contained in post-effective amendment No. 114, File No. 2-565846: URL: http://www.sec.gov/Archives/edgar/data/36405/000093247109001014/indexfinal.txt.

42 See, In the Matter of Vanguard Index Funds, *et al*, Rel. Nos. IC-24789 (December 12, 2000) (order) and IC-24680 (October 13, 2000) (notice).

43 For example, the Commission itself granted the exemptive order to the iShares Trust by amending its prior orders to permit the issuance of ETFs holding US Treasury and certain other fixed income securities. See, In the Matter of Barclays Global Fund Advisors, Rel. Nos. IC-No. 25594 (May 29, 2002) (notice) and IC-25622 (June 25, 2002) (order).

44 See Ryan Indexes on the Ryan ALM, Inc website. URL: http://www.ryanalm.com/RyanIndexes/tabid/670/Default.aspx.

45 See, In the Matter of ETF Advisors Trust *et al*, Rel. Nos. IC-25725 (September 2, 2002) (notice) and IC-25759 (September 27, 2002). The Trusts were terminated and delisted in 1993. See URL: http://www.amex.com/amextrader/tdrInfo/data/wklyBulletins/2003/06202003wkly.pdf.

46 See note 44.

47 See the final application submitted by the WisdomTree applicants: URL: http://www.sec.gov/Archives/edgar/vprr/06/9999999997-06-023295, as well as the notice: In the Matter of WisdomTree Investments, Inc *et al*, Release No. IC-27324 (May 18, 2006) and the resulting order: Release No. IC-27391 (June 12, 2006).

48 See, In the Matter of ProShares Trust, Rel. Nos. IC-27323 (May 18, 2006) (notice) and 27394 (June 13, 2006) (order).

49 "Priorities in Investment Management Regulation", Paul F. Roye, director, Division of Investment Management, US Securities and Exchange Commission, keynote address at the Eighth Annual Advanced ALI-ABA Course of Study: Investment Management Regulation, Washington, D.C., October 17, 2002, URL: http://www.sec.gov/news/speech/spch592. htm.

50 See, Release No. IC-25258; File No. S7-20-01 (hereinafter the "concept release"). Page references to the concept release are to the Federal Register of November 15, 2001 (Volume 66, Number 221, at 57613-57624).

51 See concept release at 57615.

52 See note 51.

53 See note 52. ("We will then be able to evaluate better any proposals for these types of products as they are presented to us through the exemptive process on a case-by-case basis.")

54 In other words, the concept release was not issued in contemplation of a preliminary formal rule-making proposal.

55 It is interesting to note, however, that the concept release is not contemplated by the Administrative Procedures Act, which governs agency rule making. The concept release, it appears, is a step preliminary to the public notice of a proposed rule and the invitation of comments thereon. According to the SEC website, while the rule making process usually begins with a rule proposal, "sometimes an issue is so unique and/or complicated that the Commission seeks out public input on which, if any, regulatory approach is appropriate." URL: http://www.sec.gov/about/whatwedo.shtml (last modified May 30, 2001).

56 See, for example, Application by Claymore Securities Inc, *et al*, filed on April 22, 2008, File No. 812-13524-02: URL: http://www.sec.gov/Archives/edgar/vprr/08/9999999997-08-020882.

57 See WisdomTree Trust, *et al*, Rel. Nos. IC-28147 (February 6, 2008) (February 11, 2008) (notice) (WisdomTree Actively Managed ETF Notice) and 28174 (February 27, 2008) (order); Barclays

Global Fund Advisors, *et al*, Rel. Nos. IC-28146 (February 6, 2008) (February 11, 2008) (notice) and 28173 (February 27, 2008) (order); Bear Sterns Asset Management, Inc, *et al*, Rel. Nos. IC-28143 (February 5, 2008) (February 11, 2008) (notice) and 28172 (February 27, 2008) (order); PowerShares Capital Management LLC, *et al*, Rel. Nos. IC-28140 (February 1, 2008) (February 7, 2008) (notice) (PowerShares Actively Managed ETF Notice) and 28171 (February 27, 2008) (order).

58 Release Nos. 33-8901; IC-28193 (March 11, 2008) contain the Commission's proposal for public comment (proposing release) with respect to new rules 6c-11 and 12d1-4, as well as amendments to rule 12d1-2, under the Act and amendments to Form N-1A under the Act and the 1933 Act (collectively, "proposed rules"). URL: http://www.sec.gov/rules/proposed/2008/33-8901.pdf.

59 See, comment letter from Katten Muchin Rosenman LLP submitted to the Commission dated May 30, 2008 (Katten Letter), at 3 through 5. URL: http://www.sec.gov/comments/s7-07-08/s70708-18.pdf.

60 Section 12(d)(1) states, in pertinent part:

"A. It shall be unlawful for any registered investment company (the "acquiring company") and any company or companies controlled by such acquiring company to purchase or otherwise acquire any security issued by any other investment company (the "acquired company"), and for any investment company (the "acquiring company") and any company or companies controlled by such acquiring company to purchase or otherwise acquire any security issued by any registered investment company (the "acquired company"), if the acquiring company and any company or companies controlled by it immediately after such purchase or acquisition own in the aggregate –

i. more than 3% of the total outstanding voting stock of the acquired company;
ii. securities issued by the acquired company having an aggregate value in excess of 5% of the value of the total assets of the acquiring company; or
iii. securities issued by the acquired company and all other investment companies (other than treasury stock of the acquiring company) having an aggregate value in excess of 10% of the value of the total assets of the acquiring company.

B. It shall be unlawful for any registered open-end investment company (the "acquired company"), any principal underwriter therefor, or any broker or dealer registered under the Securities Exchange Act of 1934, knowingly to sell or otherwise dispose of any security issued by the acquired company to any other investment company (the "acquiring company") or any company or companies controlled by the acquiring company, if immediately after such sale or disposition –

i. more than 3% of the total outstanding voting stock of the acquired company is owned by the acquiring company and any company or companies controlled by it; or
ii. more than 10% of the total outstanding voting stock of the acquired company is owned by the acquiring company and other investment companies and companies controlled by them."

61 See, the discussion of the two provisions in the proposing release at 71-74, and the text of Proposed Rule 12d1-4 at 139-143.

62 The acquiring fund must provide a representation that none of the ETF shares that it is redeeming includes any acquired ETF shares acquired in excess of the 3% limitation in reliance on Proposed Rule 12d1-4, and the 12d1-4 entities have no reason to believe that the acquiring fund is redeeming acquired ETF shares acquired in excess of 3% limitation in reliance on Proposed Rule 12d1-4. See the text of Proposed Rule 12d1-4 at 139-143.

63 See, comment letter from Keith F. Higgins, Chair, Federal Regulation of Securities Committee, Section of Business Law, American Bar Association, submitted to the Commission dated May 29, 2008, at 7-8, as well as the Katten Letter at 16-17.

64 Section 3(a)(1) of the 1940 Act requires Investment Companies to mainly hold "securities" as Portfolio Assets. Section 2(a)(36) of the 1940 Act defines the term "securities" very broadly:

> ""Security" means any note, stock, treasury stock, security future, bond, debenture, evidence of indebtedness, certificate of interest or participation in any profit-sharing agreement, collateral-trust certificate, preorganization certificate or subscription, transferable share, investment contract, voting-trust certificate, certificate of deposit for a security, fractional undivided interest in oil, gas, or other mineral rights, any put, call, straddle, option, or privilege on any security (including a certificate of deposit) or on any group or index of securities (including any interest therein or based on the value thereof), or any put, call, straddle, option, or privilege entered into on a national securities exchange relating to foreign currency, or, in general, any interest or instrument commonly known as a "security", or any certificate of interest or participation in, temporary or interim certificate for, receipt for, guarantee of, or warrant or right to subscribe to or purchase, any of the foregoing."

65 Renamed SPDR Gold Trust in 2008.

66 The first ETV holding physical commodities was Gold Bullion Securities listed on the Australian Stock Exchange in 2003, see "Historic First As Gold Bullion ETF Is Launched", Journal of Indexes, April 1, 2003. URL: http://www.indexuniverse.com/component/content/article/7/1646.html?Itemid=23.

67 See the prospectus for:

(1) CurrencyShares British Pound Sterling Trust sponsored by Rydex Specialized Products LLC, dated February 8, 2008, URL: http://www.sec.gov/Archives/edgar/data/1353611/000089706908000251/cmw3234.htm;

(2) PowerShares DB Commodity Index Tracking Fund dated April 20, 2009, URL: http://www.sec.gov/Archives/edgar/data/1328237/000119312509085830/ds3asr.htm;

(3) iShares GSCI Commodity Index Trust dated January 26, 2009, URL: http://www.sec.gov/Archives/edgar/data/1332174/000119312509011198/d424b3.htm;

(4) United States Oil Fund, LP dated January 16, 2009, URL: http://www.sec.gov/Archives/edgar/data/1327068/000114420409002849/v136151_424b3.htm; and

(5) MacroShares $100 Oil Down Trust dated June 26, 2008, URL: http://www. macroshares.com/Public/common/DisplayLiterature.aspx?ID=01399ac4-5c53-4f68-a151-c6434a98187c) (Macros Prospectus).

68 See, for example, the discussion of the gold industry in the SPDR Gold Trust prospectus at 15-24, URL: http://www.sec.gov/Archives/edgar/data/1222333/000095012309004971/y01161sv3asr.htm#105) and the discussion of the world oil market in the Macros Prospectus at 50-57.

69 Michael W. Masters, "Are Index Investors Driving Up Commodity Prices?", excerpted from the testimony of Michael W. Masters of Masters Capital Management, LLC, as presented before the US Senate Committee on Homeland Security and Governmental Affairs on May 20, 2008, URL: http://www.indexuniverse.com/publications/journalofindexes/articles/140-november-december-2008/4679-are-index-investors-driving-up-commodity-prices.html.

70 Gail Marks Jarvis, "New SEC chair plans to investigate commodity exchange traded funds", Chicago Tribune, Your Money columnist, April 27, 2009, URL: http://www.chicagotribune.com/business/chi-biz-etf-sec-mary-schapiro-april27,0,7860093.story.

6

Understanding ETF Structures Important in Building Portfolios

Gus Sauter

Vanguard

In any industry, product structure rapidly adapts to limitations of current offerings or new market demands. The same is true of the US ETF industry, which has blossomed from a single-product marketed by a single sponsor in 1993 to more than 700 offerings from 24 providers by September 2008.

At a high level, there are several legal structures collectively referred to as exchange-traded funds, or ETFs. Perhaps the term "exchange-traded product" is more technically correct, although the ETF initialism still dominates the lexicon, and perhaps rightfully so, since these products have similar characteristics. ETFs are purchased and sold on the secondary market through brokers, and provide investors intra-day pricing and execution. ETFs may be sold short, bought on margin and purchased via stop and limit orders. Several ETF structures also feature an in-kind creation-and-redemption process that enhances tax efficiency relative to other investments, particularly active strategies. As with traditional mutual funds, investors in most ETFs are subject to reduced tax rates on dividends that are distributed quarterly and capital gains that are distributed annually.

The similarity among ETFs ends here, however. As ETFs have grown in popularity, key differences have emerged in their underlying structure. This structure, in particular, can affect tracking precision, tax efficiency, costs and ultimately performance. As a result, understanding the distinctions in structure can help advisers make more informed investment recommendations to their clients.

For the purposes of this chapter, we will examine the following exchanged-traded product structures that have been the most widely adopted by providers:

- unit-investment-trust (UIT) ETFs;
- standalone, open-end, management investment company ETFs;
- separate share-class ETFs, which is a variation of the open-end concept;
- grantor trusts, which are similar to ETFs; and
- exchange-traded notes (ETNs).

ALONG CAME A SPDR: FIRST ETFs STRUCTURED AS UNIT INVESTMENT TRUSTS

The first ETF in the US was a unit investment trust (UIT) that commenced operations in 1993. Known as the S&P Depositary Receipts Trust, Series 1, or SPDR 500 (ticker SPY), it was designed to track the S&P 500 Index of large-capitalisation US stocks. Like all investment companies, SPY registered with the SEC under the Securities Act of 1933 and the Investment Company Act of 1940. Before it could be brought to market, SPY had to obtain an SEC order that granted exemptions from several provisions of the Investment Company Act.

The UIT structure is simple and relatively inexpensive to operate, making it ideal at that time for an instrument such as a tradable index fund. Unlike an open- or closed-end fund, UITs do not have a board of directors or an investment adviser. Thus, costs are kept to a minimum.

While UIT-structured ETFs provide broad, low-cost exposure to the stock market or a segment thereof, they have some limitations. First, UIT ETFs are somewhat limited from the perspective of portfolio-management flexibility. They must be unmanaged, which means they must fully replicate the underlying target benchmark.

Because they cannot make discretionary investment decisions, UIT ETFs are not permitted to use optimisation strategies that other types of ETFs and index funds can employ to track broad market indexes. With an optimisation strategy, the portfolio manager will hold a representative sampling of the target benchmark that, in the aggregate, approximates the full index in terms of key characteristics, such as industry weightings and market capitalisation, as well as certain financial measures, such as price–earnings ratio and dividend yield.

On the other hand, the full replication strategy employed by UIT ETFs, whereby the same securities are held in the same weights as the underlying benchmark, reduces tracking error. The full replication strategy of the UIT structure makes these ETFs well suited to highly liquid large-cap indexes with relatively few (fewer than 1,000) securities.

The unmanaged nature of UIT ETFs means they are not permitted to invest in futures or other derivatives, because they are not part of the tracked index. Other ETFs and index funds utilise futures to facilitate cashflows or to equitise cash. For example, a manager may take a position in futures to simulate full investment in stocks or to reduce costs by buying futures instead of actual stocks when futures are cheaper.

As a result of their inability to make discretionary decisions, UIT ETFs are not permitted to lend securities. Securities lending has been a way for other ETFs to generate a modest level of income and partially offset transaction costs and operating expenses, thereby enhancing tracking precision and investor returns. While securities lending may entail some risk, ETF sponsors have tight controls in place and lend securities to approved broker dealers. For some ETFs based on broad domestic markets, the incremental return provided by securities lending may amount to just a few basis points (bp) annually; small-cap and international ETFs tend to earn more, with some enhancing their returns by about 10bp or more.

Perhaps the most important differences between these ETFs and their open-end successors (to be discussed shortly) is that the dividend proceeds that UIT ETFs receive from their portfolio holdings are accumulated and held in cash before they are paid out to shareholders, usually on a quarterly or other basis. This does not allow for them to be reinvested quickly in securities, which creates tracking error because the portfolio of the ETF is no longer in line with the underlying index due to the cash exposure. As a result, a drag on performance can occur in rising markets. In fact, this "cash drag" cost one exchange-traded vehicle an estimated 15bp per year during the bull market of the late 1990s. Conversely, in a bear market, this cash position can serve to modestly enhance returns.

In addition to SPY, other ETFs with a UIT structure include MidCap SPDRs (MDY), Diamonds, PowerShares QQQ (QQQQ), and BLDRS.

More recent SPDR products, including Select Sector SPDRs, have adopted the open-end management investment company format.

FROM SPDRs TO WEBS: NEXT GENERATION OF ETFs STRUCTURED AS OPEN-END FUNDS

In response to the portfolio management and dividend reinvestment limitations of UIT ETFs, the next wave of ETFs was organised as open-end management investment companies, which are commonly referred to as open-end ETFs. Also registered with the SEC under the Securities Act of 1933 and the Investment Company Act of 1940, open-end ETFs have the same tax treatment as all mutual funds and UIT ETFs but provide more flexibility to managers compared with the UIT structure.

Among the first ETFs of this kind were WEBS, an acronym that stood for World Equity Benchmark Shares. Introduced in 1996, WEBS were a series of 17 different single-country index portfolios that traded on the American Stock Exchange. WEBS were later renamed and marketed by Barclay's Global Investors under the iShares brand.

Along with iShares, other open-end ETFs currently include products from PowerShares and WisdomTree and the aforementioned Select Sector SPDRs.

Five years later, the ETF industry greeted yet another product innovation: an ETF as a share class of an existing conventional index mutual fund. Vanguard introduced in 2001 its first ETF, Vanguard Total Stock Market ETF (VTI). VTI is a share class of Vanguard Total Stock Market Index Fund (VTSMX), which was launched in 1992.

These two ETF types share many core characteristics and solved the drawbacks of the earlier UIT structure. Unlike their UIT brethren, open-end ETFs may utilise optimisation strategies if the liquidity or breadth of the securities in the benchmark makes it impractical to own every security. As a result, this structure is especially beneficial when tracking small-cap or other less liquid benchmarks or indexes with large numbers of securities. These ETFs may also lend securities to earn income and enhance returns. Finally, they may immediately reinvest dividends from holdings into securities for improved tracking.

Some may debate whether the open-end structure offers meaningful advantages over the UIT structure. The performance record of two prominent ETFs may shed some light on the issue. As shown in Table 6.1, there is very little difference in the performance of the

Table 6.1 Total-return performance of an open-end ETF versus a UIT ETF (for periods ended September 30, 2008)

	1 year (%)	3 years (%)	5 years (%)
iShares S&P 500 Index Fund	–21.98	0.16	5.09
SPDR S&P 500 ETF	–21.93	0.15	5.08
S&P 500 Index	–21.98	0.22	5.17

Source: Lipper Inc

iShares S&P 500 Index Fund, an open-end management investment company ETF that seeks to track the S&P 500 Index, and the SPDR S&P 500 ETF, a UIT ETF that tracks the same benchmark.

With the performance records being nearly identical over the various time periods, which structure is truly advantageous might be questioned. However, the annual swings in excess return are less for the open-end management investment company structure. And, over time periods when stocks provide a more typical 10% return, the cash drag inherent in the UIT structure has produced a greater shortfall. It is also interesting to note that most, if not all, ETFs that have come to market over the past five years have been of the open-end variety. An additional comparison now turns to how the standalone open-end structure compares with the newer share-class structure. The following section takes a closer look at ETFs issued as a share class of a conventional index mutual fund.

SEPARATE SHARE-CLASS ETFs: A BETTER MOUSETRAP?

It can be argued that the separate share-class structure brings several distinct advantages to the ETF. First, the ETF shares can be issued from an existing index fund with a large asset base. Starting with a critical mass of assets from an established fund is important for several reasons.

- Cost. Introducing an ETF share class of an established fund eliminates the start-up costs that weigh on the launch of a standalone ETF. The share-class ETF also leverages the economies of scale of an existing large pool of assets to minimise ongoing operating costs, or the expense ratio.
- Diversification. The critical mass of assets affords the share-class ETF a diversified portfolio from inception. Indeed, many share-class

ETFs are more broadly diversified than their standalone counterparts that cover the same market or market segment.

- Tracking precision. With an established base of assets, share-class ETFs can track the underlying benchmark with a greater degree of precision right from inception.
- Performance record. ETFs introduced as share classes of existing index funds can provide prospective investors with a relevant track record because the performance of other share classes, adjusted for differences in expense ratio versus the ETF share class, should reflect how the ETF class would have performed had it been in existence for longer periods.

Some ETF observers believe the share-class ETF structure has some drawbacks relative to the standalone variety. They believe that the fund's conventional share classes may saddle shareholders of the ETF class with potential taxable capital-gains distributions that accrued to the conventional share class. As a result, they suggest that share-class ETFs might be less "tax-efficient" than their standalone peers. In the next section, ETF tax efficiency is examined in greater detail.

THE TAX-EFFICIENCY DEBATE

Tax efficiency is more of an issue for stock ETFs than bond ETFs, because bonds typically do not generate significant capital gains. As ETFs gained momentum in the marketplace in the early 2000s, ETF sponsors aggressively touted a tax-efficiency advantage over mutual funds. ETFs are highly tax-efficient vehicles, primarily due to the advantages of indexing – a buy-and-hold, low-turnover approach. Beyond that, the tax efficiency of one ETF over the other has a lot to do with the portfolio's management strategy (broad index, narrow index, growth, value and so on) and accounting methodology used.

To a lesser extent, an ETF's tax efficiency is enhanced by the in-kind redemption process available to mutual funds. This enables the fund to redeem shares of the ETF for a portfolio of stocks representative of the underlying benchmark. Each individual stock comprises multiple tax lots and each lot has an associated tax cost basis. The US Internal Revenue Service code allows that in-kind redemptions from a fund do not trigger capital gains distributions to fund shareholders, so the ETF manager distributes the shares with the lowest-cost basis to departing investors, leaving only the higher-cost lots in the fund and making it less likely that capital gains will be realised and distributed. Both standalone and separate share-class ETFs (and all mutual funds, for that matter) have the ability to utilise the same in-kind redemption mechanism.

ETFs have been remarkably tax-efficient, but they are certainly not tax-free. In 2007, nearly 18% of ETFs tracked by Morningstar distributed taxable capital gains.

As mentioned earlier, some posit that share-class ETFs are less tax-efficient than standalone ETFs (including those with both the UIT and open-end structure). The argument focuses on the gains realised from sales of portfolio securities in the event of net redemption requests from holders of conventional shares. In theory, a large market decline might trigger large-scale redemptions of the conventional shares, forcing the managers to sell portfolio securities and realise gains. Because any capital gains generated would be allocated *pro rata* across all shares classes, the ETF holder would receive an unwanted taxable distribution.

This hypothesis has never materialised, however. In fact, the opposite has been true, as conventional index funds have generally enjoyed net cash inflows even during the declining market of 2000–2, and more recently in 2007–8. In addition, any sales that resulted from relatively modest redemptions led to realised losses, not gains, that can be carried forward to enhance the fund's tax efficiency in future years.

Interestingly, share-class ETFs have an additional tax management tool in their arsenal. The conventional share classes of such funds typically receive actual cash that can be used to rebalance the fund to changes in the underlying benchmark. Over time, the fund accumulates a large number of share lots, with a distribution of low-cost lots and high-cost lots. Should securities need to be sold from the fund in order to meet redemptions, the manager can sell the highest-cost lots potentially at a loss, thereby realising capital losses that may be used to offset any gains. Capital losses can be used to offset subsequent realised gains of a fund for up to eight years after the losses are realised, providing a cushion if it would ever be necessary.

The real issue is maximising after-tax returns

The goal of tax-efficient investing is not necessarily to minimise taxes, but to maximise after-tax total return. As such, after-tax returns (the performance of an investment after factoring in the impact of federal income taxes) should be a priority when establishing an asset allocation and selecting investments.

When it comes to evaluating after-tax returns, the following factors come into play: low costs, benchmark construction, tracking precision and qualified dividend income (QDI). Let us look at each in turn.

Low costs

Research has repeatedly shown a powerful relationship between low costs and returns. Every US dollar paid for management fees, trading costs and taxes is a US dollar less of potential after-tax returns.

Benchmark construction

Indexes based on investment styles or market capitalisation must be periodically reconstituted to ensure that they reflect the performance of the market segment they purport to measure. Both objectively and subjectively constructed indexes currently capture this concept, to varying degrees. In each case, the rebalancing usually results in market impact on the stocks affected and turnover and transaction costs.

ETFs tracking broad stock market benchmarks experience lower turnover and therefore tend to be more tax-efficient than those tracking more specialised markets. We consider the following as best practices for indexes:

- objective, not subjective, rules for index construction;
- market weightings that reflect only "floating" shares that are available and freely traded in the open market;
- market-capitalisation definitions that slightly overlap; and
- identification of a stock as "growth" or "value" using a variety of factors.

Tracking precision

Tracking precision shows the ability of the manager to accurately and efficiently match the return of the fund's target benchmark. Tracking precision is affected by several factors, including the number of holdings, the transactional skill of the portfolio managers and the structure of the product.

Equity index funds that fully replicate the holdings of their target index will typically have a lower tracking error than those using optimisation techniques. However, this also impacts on the use of "loss harvesting", which involves selling securities at a loss to offset capital-gains tax liabilities. The full replication of the index reduces the flexibility to harvest losses because of the 30-day wash-sale rule, in which a capital loss is deferred when the same or a substantially similar security is bought within 30 days before or after a sale. Conversely, funds that aggressively sample an index may have a greater opportunity to harvest losses, although they may experience greater tracking error.

The structure of the product can impact on tracking because of restrictions imposed on portfolio management. For instance, as noted previously, UIT ETFs may not track as precisely because of the cash drag from dividends and the inability to lend securities to generate income.

Qualified dividend income

The lower tax rate on QDI has been another factor in tax efficiency since its introduction in 2003, and can have a meaningful impact on some funds. This tax provision is set to expire at the end of 2010.

As shown in Table 6.2, the pretax returns of various ETFs with similar mandates and benchmarks can vary on a relative basis. Tax efficiency is shown in several ways: the capture ratio, which is the after-tax return divided by the target index return; and the tax cost, which is the amount of return surrendered to taxes.

STANDALONE OR SEPARATE SHARE CLASS: WHAT IT COMES DOWN TO

However modest the performance difference may be between the two types of open-end ETFs, the extra basis points do matter. The source of the outperformance may be directly related to the ETF's particular structure, as well as the manager's skill and experience, the fund's expense ratio and/or the spreads on the ETF shares.

GRANTOR TRUSTS: A NON-ETF STRUCTURE THAT ACTS LIKE AN ETF

The UIT ETF and open-end ETF structures are not conducive to investing in commodities. As a result, innovation led to the creation of new exchange-traded products. For example, a grantor trust structure

Table 6.2 Five-year annualised performance (NAV) of comparable ETFs through September 30, 2008 (sorted by capture ratio)

	Target index return (%)	ETF pre-tax return (%)	Tracking error (bp)	ETF after-tax returns (%)		Capture ratio		Tax cost (pre-liq.)
				Pre-liq.	Post-liq.	Pre-liq.	Post-liq.	
Vanguard Total Stock Market ETF	5.99	5.98	–01	5.70	5.18	0.95	0.86	–0.28
iShares Russell 3000 Index Fund	5.70	5.55	–15	5.24	4.74	0.92	0.83	–0.31
iShares Dow Jones US Index Fund	5.90	5.68	–22	5.35	4.84	0.91	0.82	–0.33
SPDR DJ Wilshire Total Market ETF	6.0	5.35	–65	5.02	4.56	0.84	0.76	–0.33

Sources: Vanguard, iShares.com, and statestreetspdrs.com

has been adopted by providers in order to offer a commodity- or currency-based product. Grantor trusts, which are not registered under the 1940 Act, have also been used for securities in a narrow sector or industry.

There are generally two types of grantor trust product: commodity and currency trusts, and Merrill Lynch's HOLDRs (Holding Company Depositary Receipts).

These products are technically not ETFs. But because they have similar characteristics – they hold a portfolio of assets and issue shares based on the value of those assets – they are traded on the stock market throughout the day, and may use an in-kind transaction process (there are some exceptions: for example, trusts that hold futures do not use an in-kind process) – they are generally included in discussions about ETF structures.

Grantor trusts are not subject to the same tax treatment as conventional index mutual funds and ETFs. Tax liabilities in a grantor trust flow through to investors, who must pay taxes on their share of the fund's realised gains each year even if they are not distributed. On the other hand, investors can take the realised losses for any securities that decline.

Grantor trusts are registered with the SEC under the Securities Act of 1933. Commodities trusts may also be subject to regulation by the Commodity Futures Trading Commission.

COMMODITY AND CURRENCY TRUSTS

Commodity and currency trusts can track an index. Currency trusts pay out dividends, as do certain types of commodity trust. Commodity and currency trusts may not be as tax-efficient as ETFs because of the tax treatment of the assets.

- Trusts that invest directly in precious metals are taxed as "collectibles" rather than securities, which means that gains are taxed at a maximum rate of 28% rather than the current 15% for long-term capital gains on securities.
- Realised gains on currency trusts are taxed at the shareholder's ordinary income tax rate.
- Commodity trusts holding futures receive dual tax treatment – 60% of gains are taxed at the long-term capital-gains rate (maximum of 15%), while the remaining 40% are treated as short-term capital

gains. The short-term gains are taxed at the shareholder's ordinary income tax rate, which can be more than twice as much. (The lack of tax efficiency noted here is also applicable to ETFs holding futures.)

Examples of commodity and currency trusts include SPDR Gold Trust, iShares Silver Trust and Rydex CurrencyShares.

HOLDING COMPANY DEPOSITARY RECEIPTS (HOLDRs)

Merrill Lynch created the first HOLDRs in 1998 to reassemble spun-off pieces of Telebras, a Brazilian telecom company. This structure was later expanded and applied to other areas of the market. HOLDRs are considered depositary receipts. They target a small group of niche stocks of sectors such as B2B services, Internet architecture, biotech and more.

HOLDRs do not track an index, but they do calculate and track a real-time basket value. The original composition of the underlying basket of securities stays fixed (unless a security is affected by a corporate action), with each security weighted equally or on a modified market cap basis. Because it is a fixed basket, the trust does not rebalance. The basket can become more concentrated as companies merge, are acquired or are spun off. This potential concentration can create a lack of diversification and volatility.

Here are some other characteristics of HOLDRs.

- Dividends are not reinvested and are distributed to investors.
- Investors in HOLDRs directly own the underlying securities (and get annual reports with voting proxies for all of them).
- When reconstitution events such as mergers and acquisitions or stock spin-offs occur, investors will receive that security in their brokerage account outside of their HOLDRs investment.
- Investors can unbundle stock from their basket and make a non-taxable exchange to defer realisation of capital gains. So, if the stock of a company in the basket has become unattractive, investors who no longer wish to own it can cancel their basket, take ownership of each of the underlying stocks and sell the undesirable one. This is especially beneficial if an investor wants to sell positions with the largest losses in an effort to manage taxes.
- Unlike ETFs, HOLDRs can be purchased only in 100-share increments.

Federal income tax laws treat owners of HOLDRs as directly owning the underlying securities.

LESS COMMONLY USED ETF "STRUCTURES"

Exchange-traded notes

ETNs are another type of investment that may be referred to as an exchange-traded product because they too have some characteristics similar to ETFs – namely, they are bought and sold on an exchange and they are linked to the performance of a market index or other benchmark (although ETNs do not own any of the securities in the index or benchmark).

The similarities end there, however. Non-currency and most ETNs are prepaid forward contracts, and, as such, are unsecured and subordinated debt notes issued by a financial institution. The issuer promises to pay the investor the total return of an index, less fees, upon the maturity of the note, often 30 years in the future. ETNs can be liquidated before their maturity by being traded on the exchange or by tendering a large block of securities directly to the issuing bank.

ETNs are backed only by the credit of the issuing bank. Thus, if the issuer experiences a reduction in its credit rating or goes bankrupt, the value of the ETN will be eroded. In fact, when Lehman Brothers declared bankruptcy, it had previously issued an ETN that has now become an unsecured creditor of the bankruptcy proceedings.

ETNs are treated for tax purposes as prepaid forward contracts that generally give rise to no current tax until they are sold or mature up to 30 years in the future. ETNs generally do not make interest payments and dividend distributions, so investors do not pay current tax on those. Investors instead generally realise capital gains or losses on the total return of the index, including any return pertaining to interest, dividends or short-term capital gain, when the note is sold or matures. The tax treatment of ETNs can thus currently be more favourable than that of ETFs: investors of non-currency ETNs can both defer paying tax on the total return of the index for up to 30 years, and then do so at favourable long-term capital-gain rates. Currency-based prepaid forward contracts, including ETNs, are taxed at ordinary income tax rates like currency trust products instead of at long-term capital-gain rates. However, as of the time of writing, the tax treatment for other types of ETN was still under regulatory

Table 6.3 Comparison of the most common ETF structures

	Unit investment trust ETF structure	Open-end management investment company ETF structure	Open-end, separate-share class ETF structure	Grantor trust structure	
				Commodity and currency trusts	Trust-issued depositary receipts
Examples	S&P 500 SPDR (SPY), S&P MidCap SPDR (MDY), Diamonds, PowerShares QQQ (QQQQ),BLDRS	iShares, Select Sector SPDRs, PowerShares, WisdomTree	Vanguard ETFs	SPDR Gold Trust, iShares Silver Trust, Rydex CurrencyShares	Merrill Lynch HOLDRs
Portfolio management flexibility	Limited – must be unmanaged and fully replicate index. Cannot use options, futures and securities lending	Flexible – can use optimisation techniques,options, futures and securities lending	Flexible – can use optimisation techniques, options, futures and securities lending	Limited to none	Limited to none
Dividends	Accumulates dividends and holds them in cash throughout quarter before paying shareholders	Immediately reinvests dividends and pays out to shareholders on specified schedule	Immediately reinvests dividends and pays out to shareholders on specified schedule	Currency trusts distribute dividends, as do certain types of commodity trusts	Dividends are not reinvested and are distributed to investors
Diversification	Yes	Yes	Yes	Maybe	Maybe
Can invest primarily in commodities	No	No	No	Depends on type	No
Cost-efficient	Yes	Yes	Yes	Yes	Yes

Tax-efficient	Yes	Yes	Yes	No	Maybe
Tracking precision	May not track as precisely because of cash from dividends and because they cannot lend securities to generate income. However, tracking issues may be overcome because they need to fully replicate index	Strives for low tracking error, but depends on portfolio management strategy	Similar to open-end, but may exhibit additional tracking precision because of greater number of securities held in underlying fund	Can track an index	Do not track an index, but they do calculate a real-time basket value and track that value
Investor ability to convert shares	No	No	Yes – investor can convert conventional shares to ETF shares	No	Investor can unbundle stock and make non-taxable exchange
Voting rights on underlying securities	Trustee only has voting rights	Manager only has voting rights	Manager only has voting rights	Trustee only has voting rights	Investors have voting rights
Registration	Securities Act of 1933 and Investment Company Act of 1940	Securities Act of 1933 and Investment Company Act of 1940	Securities Act of 1933 and Investment Company Act of 1940	Securities Act of 1933. Commodity trusts may also be regulated by Commodities Futures Trading Commission	Securities Act of 1933

discussion, as the taxation of prepaid forward contracts has never been confirmed by settled tax policy.

Continued innovation in structure is a testament to the appeal of exchange-traded products and it is important to understand them. These products have proliferated over the past 15 years. The first such products, ETFs, were carved out of the Investment Company Act of 1940. But, as new products were incompatible with the 1940 Act, innovations led to the use of other legal structures to create exchange-traded products with many characteristics similar to the original ETFs.

At the time of writing, more than 700 exchange-traded products had been created in the US alone, according to the Investment Company Institute. However, product proliferation may have gone too far, with more than 45 products being shuttered in 2008 alone.

As firms develop new investment ideas, they are likely to be offered in one of the current exchange-traded product structures discussed in this chapter or in yet another innovation. Regardless of how they are put together, an understanding of the structure's implications for tracking precision, tax efficiency and costs can help you determine whether they are a good fit for your clients' portfolios.

7

Finding the Right ETF for the Investor

Greg Friedman

Barclays Global Investors

Seemingly overnight, exchange-traded funds (ETFs) have taken the investing world by storm. The product first appeared in the early 1990s. Less than a decade ago, ETFs accounted for only US$36 billion in the US. Since then, assets under management by ETFs have grown to roughly US$600 billion.[1] Today, the three most actively traded equities – and six of the top 10 – in the US are ETFs. In fact, more than 25% of all equity trades in the US are with ETFs.[2]

Meanwhile, the ETF universe has expanded to include hundreds of products covering virtually every asset class, sector and style. From 2002 to 2006, 265 new ETFs were launched. In 2007 alone, however, a whopping 274 ETFs were launched.

The ETF explosion represents a true revolution in the investing world. With their simplicity, efficiency and ability to meet a wide range of investor needs, they represent an enormous opportunity for investors and advisers. However, their rapid growth also presents a significant challenge for investors, because with that opportunity comes even greater responsibility on the part of advisers to serve the best interests of the investor.

This chapter explores both sides of that question: the opportunities that ETFs present for investors and for financial advisers as a way to add value for clients; and a guide to navigating the ETF landscape to help advisers meet the responsibility of selecting the right ETF for clients' needs. In short, that should help them answer the question, "Is it right for the investor?"

HOW ETFs HELP ADVISERS DIFFERENTIATE THEMSELVES AND ADD VALUE

To begin, let us review the main features and benefits of ETFs. As described elsewhere in this book, ETFs are investment vehicles that combine key features of traditional mutual funds and individual stocks. ETFs are open-ended funds, which, like index mutual funds, generally represent portfolios of securities that track specific indexes. A distinct difference is that ETFs trade like stocks and can be bought and sold (long or short) on an exchange, and investors can employ the same trading strategies used with stocks.

ETF shares are created differently from traditional shares of stocks. Traditionally, a company issues a set number of shares through an initial public offering (IPO) and then the shares are traded in the secondary market. Volume is an indication of how many shares are available at a given price. ETF shares, however, can essentially provide unlimited liquidity through a process called creation and redemption.

With ETFs, authorised participants (APs) such as specialists on the exchange or institutional broker/dealers can create or redeem shares directly with the fund through an "in-kind" transfer mechanism. APs create ETF units by delivering a basket of securities to the fund equal to the current holdings of the ETF, plus a designated "cash component". In return, the APs receive a large block of ETF shares (typically 50,000 or 100,000 shares, depending on the fund), which investors can then buy and sell in the secondary market. Thus, ETF volume is an indication of how many shares have already traded, not how many shares could be traded.

This process also works in reverse, so, if an investor wants to sell a large block of shares of an ETF and there seems to be limited liquidity in the secondary market, the APs can readily take them in and redeem them.

The creation-and-redemption process is responsible for many of the benefits ETFs provide over traditional mutual funds. ETF investors interact with an exchange rather than with the fund company directly, which helps to minimise capital gains and maximise tax efficiency.

The unique structure of ETFs provides investors with a number of other benefits, however:

- lower cost;
- diversification;

- tax efficiency;
- transparency; and
- modularity.

ETFs are a lower-cost alternative to traditional mutual funds, with expense ratios that are typically well below those of both active and index mutual funds. For example, ETFs can carry expense ratios from nine to 75 basis points, which are typically substantially lower than the average active mutual fund, which typically can carry expense ratios over 100bp. While ETF transactions will most likely generate brokerage commissions, their lower expenses can offset those transaction costs for long-term investors.

Since most ETFs track indexes that comprise a basket of securities, they inherently provide instant diversification and are expected to minimise capital-gains distributions through lower portfolio turnover than actively managed funds. Unlike traditional mutual funds, where shareholder activity can contribute to capital-gains distributions, an ETF's creation and redemption structure eliminates the impact of shareholder activity on capital-gains distributions, thereby making them more tax-efficient.

ETFs are required to disclose on a daily basis the exact holdings of the fund, so you always understand precisely what you own and

Table 7.1 Average annual fees of traditional funds and ETFs

Morningstar fund category	Average active fund (%)	Average index fund (%)	Sample ETF and management fees (%)	
Large-cap	1.35	0.62	0.09	S&P 500
			0.15	Russell 1000
Mid-cap	1.49	0.56	0.20	Russell Midcap
Small-cap	1.56	0.70	0.20	Russell 2000
Diversified foreign equity	1.65	0.80	0.34	MSCI EAFE
			0.74	MSCI Emerging Markets
Fixed income	1.12	0.40	0.24	Barclays US Aggregate

Source: Strategic Insight, 2/08. The annual management fees of ETFs may be substantially less than those of most mutual funds. ETF transactions may result in record-keeping fees, but the savings from lower annual fees can help offset these costs

Notes: Expense ratios for ETFs tend to be significantly lower than those of traditional mutual funds. Higher expenses can adversely affect fund performance.

how much you are paying for it. This level of transparency is not disclosed by traditional mutual funds, although, to be sure, it is a concern only with actively managed funds, not indexed. With the myriad ETFs available tracking different indexes, investors can use the modularity of ETFs to create portfolios with different asset-class exposures and risk profiles. In short, they are like building blocks that can be combined in a range of ways to meet each investor's specific goals.

Financial professionals can use ETFs at virtually every stage of the investment process, from building an asset allocation to tactical strategies such as tax-loss harvesting. ETFs offer investors diversification, the ability to trade simply and easily, low expenses, tax efficiency and transparency. But perhaps the most important feature is their flexibility.

Table 7.2 describes portfolio strategies for ETFs.

As these examples illustrate, while ETFs are appealing with their simplicity and because they are easy to invest in, they also can be used in a wide range of sophisticated investing strategies. Advisers who utilise ETFs successfully in these sophisticated strategies are not only helping their clients meet their goals, but are also differentiating themselves and demonstrating a competitive advantage for their business.

GUIDELINES FOR SELECTING AN ETF

With so many ETFs to choose from, are you sure you are selecting the right one? Answering that question has grown much more difficult in recent years with the explosive growth of ETFs.

As the ETF landscape grows more crowded, it is more important than ever for anyone evaluating ETFs – whether to recommend for a client or as part of a due-diligence process for inclusion on a firm's platform – to understand how to differentiate among seemingly similar products. Many focus mainly on one explicit cost: the expense ratio. But there are other factors that investors should consider. For example, how accurately does the ETF capture the sector or asset class? Are there other implicit costs besides expense ratio? How liquid is the security? And choosing the wrong ETF can undermine the key advantages of ETFs: the ability to access an asset class cost-effectively with precision and transparency, and with sufficient liquidity.

Table 7.2 ETF portfolio strategies

Strategy	Objective	Example
Portfolio completion	Ensure a portfolio's complete diversification	Gain targeted exposure to sector and style segments and quickly and easily complete an asset allocation.
Cash equitisation	Maintain a fully invested market position	Use a broad-cap or total-market ETF to maintain full market investment, or use a style or sector ETF to maintain asset class weights during manager-transition or stock-selection process.
Tactical rotation among sectors, styles and market cap	Actively trade around research, earnings, economic data and sector calls	Use sector, style, or market-cap ETFs to establish, underweight or overweight positions according to tactical strategy or technical indicators.
Tax management	Manage for long-term tax efficiency	Use ETFs in place of high-turnover or tax-inefficient investment options to limit capital-gain distribution risk. Use ETFs during the 30-day wash sale holding period to remain fully invested while harvesting tax losses.
Risk management	Manage overall portfolio risk by incorporating index investments	Use ETFs for a standalone 100% index solution or combine with actively managed portfolios, funds or separate accounts to manage total portfolio volatility.
Concentration risk reduction	Diversify away from single security, asset class or sector concentration	Use a corresponding ETF sector fund to reduce single security risk or a broad market or complementary fund for single-sector or asset-class concentration.
Sophisticated and simplified fixed income investment	Precisely construct a customised, well-diversified portfolio	Select from the range of fixed-income funds to build a portfolio with specific duration, credit quality and sector exposure in the broad, corporate, TIPS and Treasury markets.

(*continued*)

Table 7.2 Continued

Strategy	Objective	Example
Yield enhancement	Add tax-efficient dividend yield to client portfolios	Enhance a client's well-diversified strategy with stock dividend yield, inflation-protected Treasury yield and corporate fixed-income yield.
Market-neutral investment	Ensure equal long and short exposure	Go long on a sector's stocks and short the corresponding ETF.
Select foreign investment	Tilt global-sector, regional and single-country markets	Implement a bullish single-country call while maintaining a broad developed- or emerging-market investment.

A framework for evaluating ETFs begins by viewing them through the lens of their unique structure, which combines the broad diversification benefits of a mutual fund with the tradability of an individual security. Against that backdrop, here are five guidelines to consider when evaluating an exchange traded product:

- take a look under the bonnet;
- consider total costs;
- look inside liquidity;
- assess the structure; and
- evaluate the provider.

Take a look under the bonnet

The importance of index construction

"What did the market do?" It is an age-old question, and it has long been answered by the performance of an index. While indicating the market's health and direction remains a primary function of indexes, today's investors also rely on indexes as tools for evaluating performance, modelling asset classes for asset allocation, and as the foundation for investment products such as index funds and ETFs.

Yet, while indexes are critically important to investors, the methodology index providers use to build an index and determine the weightings of securities within the index can vary considerably from provider to provider. Indeed, two indexes covering similar areas of the market – even those with similar names – can differ substantially from each other, resulting in divergent risk-and-return characteristics, stock and sector exposure, and fundamental attributes.

In addition, new indexes have entered the market alongside the traditional, well-established indexes. As more indexes appear, it is crucial for investors to understand the differences among indexes to ensure they use the right index for the right purpose.

Figure 7.1 shows what construction methodology can mean for the composition of an index, by illustrating the composition of three families of style indexes. Typically, companies classified as "value stocks" have low valuation ratios such as low price-to-earnings (P/Es), low price-to-book ratios (P/Bs), and so on, and companies classified as "growth stocks" have higher valuation ratios and higher-than-average earnings growth.

Each index family, however, has a different method for determining the "growth-ness" and "value-ness" of the index's member companies, and, as a result, the indexes can look different, as evidenced by the P/E ratio.

Figure 7.2 offers one example of what index construction can mean for the investor. Both indexes cover the same asset class (small-cap), but there are significant differences in the total returns between the two.

When index providers define the components of their indexes differently, it results in various securities in the index having dissimilar

Figure 7.1 Constructing methodology

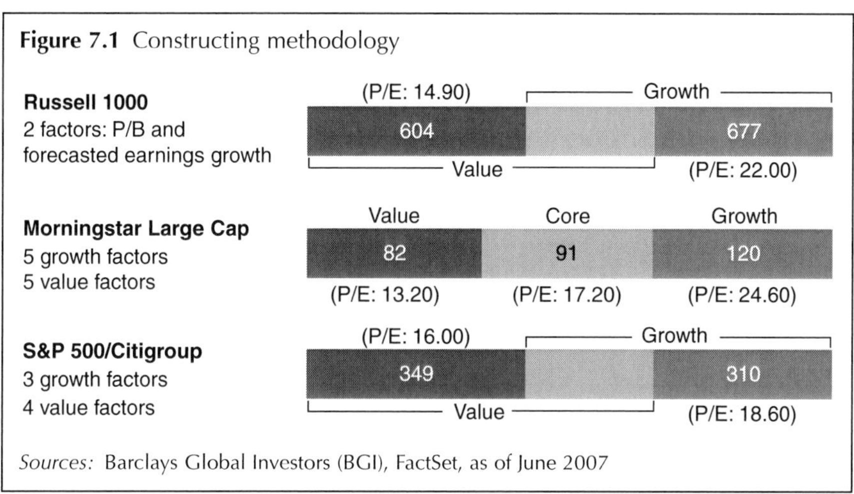

Sources: Barclays Global Investors (BGI), FactSet, as of June 2007

Figure 7.2 Small-cap index performance comparison

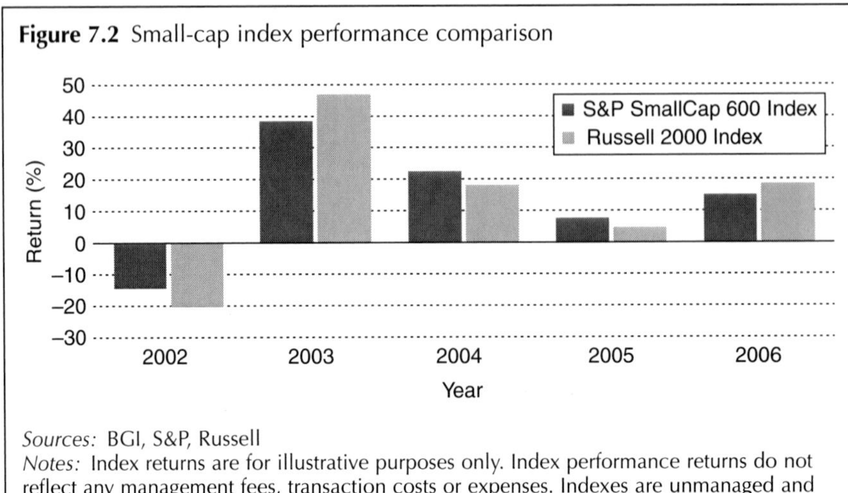

Sources: BGI, S&P, Russell
Notes: Index returns are for illustrative purposes only. Index performance returns do not reflect any management fees, transaction costs or expenses. Indexes are unmanaged and one cannot invest directly in an index. Past performance does not guarantee future results.

weights, which can lead to a portfolio having very different risks from what the investor first envisioned. For instance, as Figure 7.2 shows, the return difference is largely a result of meaningful differences in sector weightings. Investors should choose the index that best reflects the risk/return profile of their portfolio. But to do that they need to understand how the index is constructed – to know what they own.

As the innovator of index strategies, Barclays Global Investors (BGI) has done considerable research and analysed the various indexes.[3] We have developed a framework for evaluating indexes, specifically as it relates to differentiating among ETFs. In many cases, there is no right or wrong index to use, but we encourage investors to use what we term institutional-quality indexes. To determine how well an index rates, we look at five criteria.

1. Completeness. Does the index (or ETF) accurately reflect the overall investment opportunity set? The ideal index includes every security in its asset class, and it is possible for fund managers to construct a full-replication index fund containing all of the stocks in the index at their market-capitalisation weights. There is, however, a trade-off between breadth of market coverage and investability of the stocks in an index. For benchmarks that encompass small, illiquid stocks, for example, an

index that is not as broad and uses some replication may be desirable.

2. Objective, published rules. How transparent and publicly available are the rules governing the index's (or the ETF's) constituents? Objective rules allow the fund manager to predict, more or less accurately, which stocks will be added to and deleted from the index, enabling a fund to more closely track the index.
3. Accurate and complete data. Is return data for the index (or ETF) accurate, complete and readily available? Access to data allows investors to evaluate and compare indexes and ETFs within and across market categories.
4. Acceptance by investors. How well known and widely used is the index? An index that is both well known and widely used gives an investor comfort in the ongoing integrity of the index and the ability to make peer-group comparisons across indexes and ETFs. It may also allow investors and fund providers comfort that the index will most likely be maintained in the future, providing a benchmark for long-term investors. Historically, we have seen a number of instances where the success of an ETF (in terms of its growth in assets) has been tied to the index, especially when there are two or more ETFs covering a similar asset class.
5. Turnover and related costs. How low is the turnover of the index? Are the resulting rebalancing costs appropriate for the ETF? In general, the lower the turnover, the lower the rebalancing costs for the fund provider. Broad benchmarks favour lower turnover, yet timing and frequency of rebalancing vary among the index providers.

Well-constructed indexes tend to score well on all or most of these criteria, but investors choose different indexes for a variety of reasons. It is critical, therefore, that the investor knows exactly what is in that index.

Consider total costs

The importance of implicit costs

Expense ratio is usually the first thing that comes to mind when thinking of the costs associated with owning an ETF. There is no question that expense ratios are very important when it comes to selecting an ETF. But the expense ratio is just one component of the total costs associated with owning an ETF, or of managing a portfolio of ETFs.

Since ETFs are traded on exchanges, commissions are the most obvious example of other costs associated with ETFs. In addition, trading costs, rebalancing, and tracking error are examples of costs that many investors need to consider when owning an ETF. Expense ratios and commissions (known as explicit costs), together with these costs (known as implicit costs) add up to the total cost of owning an ETF.

For long-term, buy-and-hold investors, expense ratio may be the dominant cost. However, trading costs and rebalancing costs can also be important, especially for investors establishing and maintaining sizeable positions. Short-term holders of an ETF, those holding for less than one year, do not bear the full cost of an expense ratio. For those investors, commissions and other implicit costs can matter more.

Ultimately, implicit costs may be more important for some investors, especially those with larger holdings. For example, for investors making a sizeable trade, market impact is as important a consideration as commissions. Such investors need to understand what market impact is and where it shows up, and how to analyse implicit costs.

There are three main implicit costs to consider.

1. Trading cost. The market price for an ETF is typically reflected in the bid–offer spread. While most ETF investors trade on the secondary market within a few pennies of the bid or offer, larger transactions may require a creation/redemption by an authorised participant (AP) for best execution. There are several factors to consider when analysing ETF costs, including spread, market depth, and construction of the underlying basket of securities.
2. Rebalancing. An asset allocation is determined initially according to an investor's risk tolerance. Once the portfolio is implemented, each of the asset classes will have different realised rates of return; those varying returns will shift the optimum allocation originally selected and the appropriate risk levels for the client. To recapture the original risk/return characteristics, the portfolio will need to be rebalanced back to the target allocation. The investor should consider the trading costs involved in rebalancing.

3. Tracking error. Tracking error (the difference between the fund's gross performance and the index performance), can represent a potential drag on or boost to performance, and is reflected in the implicit costs for a portfolio. It is worth noting that tracking error does not incorporate a fund's expense ratio.

Implicit costs are not equal across ETFs and can overwhelm any expense advantage of one ETF over another. Consider the example in Figure 7.3, which compares the costs for two large-cap ETFs.

Look inside liquidity

Liquidity when you need it

What exactly is liquidity and why is it so important? Liquidity is the ability to trade when you want to without significantly affecting the price; it is an extremely important component when considering total cost. Poor liquidity can translate into greater trading costs (and total costs), as well as increased pressure on your fiduciary role as an adviser. After all, if you are transacting across many accounts, how does the price that the first client trading receives compare with that of the last client trading?

Unlike that of single stocks, ETF liquidity is unique, as it goes beyond spread and depth considerations. ETFs have an additional source of liquidity due to the creation/redemption mechanism, which allows large institutional trades to be executed without meaningful impact to the underlying markets. Additionally, the in-kind transfer of securities minimises the potential for taxable transactions and externalises the trading costs to the fund.

Although all ETFs use the creation/redemption process, there still are differences among specific ETFs. Two ETFs offering similar

Figure 7.3 Total-cost comparison for large-cap ETFs

	Explicit costs		Implicit costs			Total cost
	Expense ratio	Commission	Trading costs	Rebalance cost	Tracking error	
ETF 1	0.20%	+ 0.01%	+ 0.25%	+ 0.02%	+ 0.10%	= **0.58%**
ETF 2	0.40%	0.01%	0.10%	0.01%	0.05%	**0.57%**

Source: BGI

market exposure can trade quite differently. While most investors trade on the secondary market, both secondary and primary markets need to work well to ensure a transparent and efficient market with tight spreads, translating into lower costs. In short, when evaluating an ETF, it is imperative to examine both the liquidity of the underlying stocks – as well as the secondary market volume when measuring overall liquidity.

There are three questions to ask when measuring liquidity:

1. What is the spread, and how much volume can be traded there?
2. What is the depth of the market?
3. How far away from the bid–offer will I have to increase or decrease my price expectations to execute an order through creation/redemption?

Additionally, as ETFs have become more popular, their trading efficiency has increased due to natural supply and demand forces. In fact, tighter spreads than that of the underlying basket have emerged for several ETFs. Evidence of this improved liquidity is clear when looking at Figure 7.4 illustrating the tightening spreads of a small-cap and an emerging-market ETF, two products whose underlying securities would, at first glance, appear illiquid. The two funds present a paradox whereby, as they have grown, the ETFs now trade at a spread well inside the cost (cheaper) to transact the underlying basket of securities and are less expensive in which to transact.

Figure 7.4 Some ETFs deliver price efficiency through tighter spreads

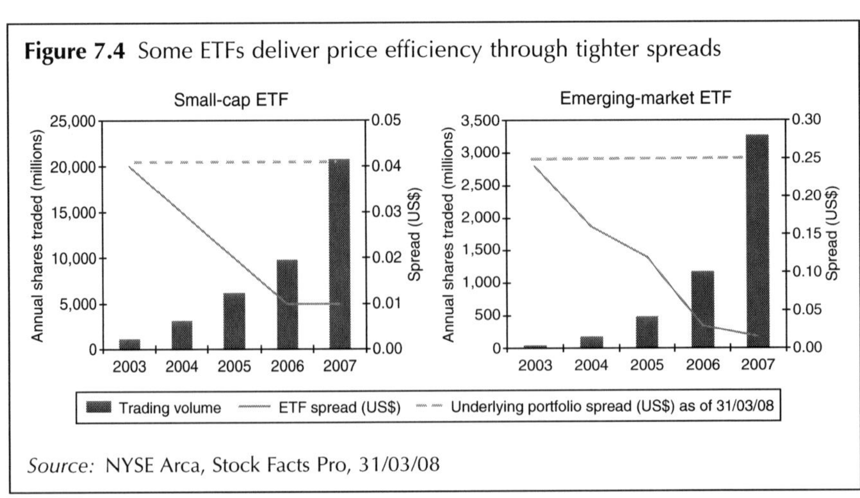

Source: NYSE Arca, Stock Facts Pro, 31/03/08

What distinguishes ETFs from one another is the depth of the secondary market. As is the case with individual stocks, a market is "deep" when there is significant volume of pending orders on the bid–offer preventing a large order from moving the price. The further one moves outside the bid–offer, the greater number of shares that can be executed – the number of shares is the market depth.

Figure 7.5 demonstrates the price efficiency of ETFs and the importance of market depth. Point A is a trade within the ETF quote, while Point B, representing a larger trade, is outside the quote but still cheaper than the underlying basket. ETFs are unique because an investor can theoretically create or redeem extremely large number of shares through the creation/redemption process and therefore have access to nearly unlimited market depth. Whenever an ETF is traded on an exchange inside the underlying portfolio quote, investors save money and receive "price improvement". In Figure 7.5, any price point between the arrows indicates price improvement resulting from trading the ETF versus the underlying basket.

Additionally, Point C underscores the importance of distinguishing among ETFs. ETF providers who work with market participants

Figure 7.5 Price efficiency of ETFs

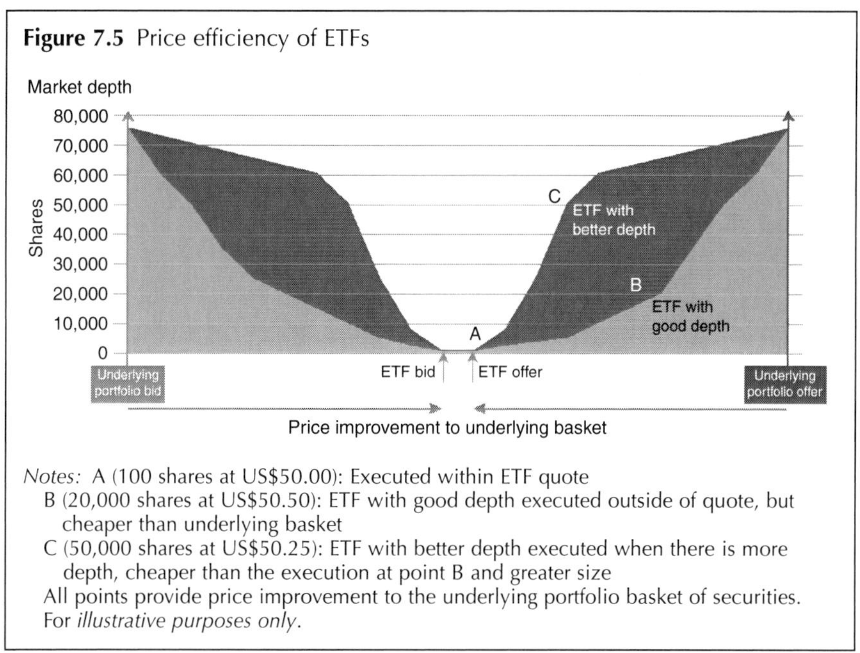

Notes: A (100 shares at US$50.00): Executed within ETF quote
B (20,000 shares at US$50.50): ETF with good depth executed outside of quote, but cheaper than underlying basket
C (50,000 shares at US$50.25): ETF with better depth executed when there is more depth, cheaper than the execution at point B and greater size
All points provide price improvement to the underlying portfolio basket of securities.
For *illustrative purposes only*.

to create efficient baskets that work for both the fund's benefit and to allow easier access for a multitude of market participants, typically see greater depth just outside the ETF bid–offer. This allows all investors to execute a greater number of ETF shares, while paying less than they would in the basket. It is important to recognise that market depth across ETFs can differ, and that difference will impact overall costs to the investor.

Assess the structure

The importance of product structure

As the exchange-traded product (ETP) universe has grown over the last several years, new products consisting of structures other than ETFs have emerged to meet new investor needs. Innovations in product structure have allowed ETPs to expand beyond the traditional, open-end fund structure associated with ETFs. Each structure has unique exposure, risk and tax implications. These nuances may make some structures – and products – more appropriate for some investors than others.

Among traditional ETFs, the various structures can ultimately lead to liquidity, tradability, and tracking-error differences. This, in turn, impacts on the cost to the investor of establishing and unwinding the position, as well as costs that the fund bears and which are then passed on to investors.

Table 7.3 describes the main features of various ETPs.

Evaluate the provider

The importance of experience

Experience matters. Size, scale, expertise and commitment vary across ETF providers, and those differences can impact on costs. How can an investor know if a provider's experience (or lack thereof) can affect costs? Specifically, investors should look at a provider's

- scalable operations to cross-trade and minimise costs and market impact;
- track record managing ETFs, including low tracking error and high tax efficiency;
- dedication to providing support and resources to investors, intermediaries and market participants; and
- deep knowledge of index construction and methodology.

Table 7.3 Comparison of structures

	ETFs	Unit investment trusts	Grantor trusts	Exchange traded notes	Limited partnerships
Registration	Investment Company Act of 1940	Investment Company Act of 1940	Securities Act of 1933	Securities Act of 1933	Securities Act of 1933
Recourse	Portfolio of securities	Portfolio of securities	*Pro rata* interest in the trust	Issuer credit	*Pro rata* interest in the partnership
Principal risk	Market risk	Market risk	Market risk	Market and issuer risk	Market risk
Tracking error	Low to moderate	Moderate	Moderate	Low	Moderate
Tax issues	Potential exposure to capital gains and losses of portfolio, although creation/ redemption mechanism works to minimise this. Dividends and interest income passed through to shareholders.	Potential exposure to capital gains and losses of portfolio, although creation/ redemption mechanism works to minimise this. Dividends and interest income passed through to shareholders.	Taxed as though investor effectively holds underlying security. Each investor takes a *pro rata* share of the income and expenses of the trust.	Capital gains only realised upon the sale, redemption, or maturity of the ETN. No dividend distributions.	Each investor takes a *pro rata* share of the income and expenses of the partnership.

Source: BGI

ETF providers should have extensive experience managing index investments, deep portfolio management skills and research teams to analyse and anticipate index changes. But, in addition, they should have the dedication to educate market makers, specialists and other potential primary market participants to ensure transparent and efficient primary and secondary markets with a commitment to producing unbiased education.

The ETF provider should be working with advisers and intermediaries, not in competition with them. A healthy partnership among providers, advisers and intermediaries (where the provider helps educate clients on how to use ETFs) is critical – for both advisers and providers.

With hundreds of ETFs in the market now, that kind of knowledge and experience as an index manager and ETF provider is more important than ever.

CONCLUSION

Evaluating ETFs often involves trade-offs. For example, an investor may prefer an ETF that is very liquid and has low trading spreads, even though it has a history of tracking error, because of the lower trading costs. In fact, the question investors should ask usually is not, "What is the best ETF?" Given their goals and the risk/return makeup of their asset allocation, the question advisers should ask is, "What is the right ETF for my client's portfolio?" And, by addressing that question, advisers will go a long way towards answering the most important question we in this industry face: "Is it right for the investor?"

1 Source: Factset. As of 31/05/08.
2 NYSE Arca, Bloomberg as of 30/06/07.
3 For more information, see *Investment Insights* on barclaysglobal.com.

8

ETFs: The More Efficient Way to Track an Index

Thorsten Michalik, Manooj Mistry

Deutsche Bank

ETFs have been around in Europe since 2000. By the end of the first half of 2008 497 ETFs with 1,627 exchange listings from 29 issuers were outstanding in Europe. Deutsche Boerse held the biggest market share by trading volume with 29.33%, followed by Euronext and the London Stock Exchange with 21.59% and 18.52% respectively.

In Europe the traditional ETF structure based on the fund owning all or a representation sample of the underlying benchmark has worked well in the early stages of the development of the market. However, institutional investors are increasingly demanding greater efficiency and lower overall costs in the products they hold and trade. This has led to the creation of a number of new ETFs, which are based on index synthetic replications as opposed to pure equity holdings. Currently, more than half of the outstanding ETFs in Europe are following this synthetic replication method. There are a number of benefits to be had from an ETF structured via a synthetic replication and, overall, these types of ETF have both significantly lower costs and tracking errors compared with traditional equity ETFs. Synthetic replication-based ETFs remove the risks of managing dividend flows compared with the index being tracked, meaning that the problems of cash drag and dividend receipt are no longer an issue. The same structure is also a more efficient means of replicating total-return indexes, especially with relationships to funds where dividends are sourced from a wide range of countries. Other costs that are faced with traditional ETFs include index turnover due to index changes, rebalances and corporate actions.

Figure 8.1 ETF market growth, Europe

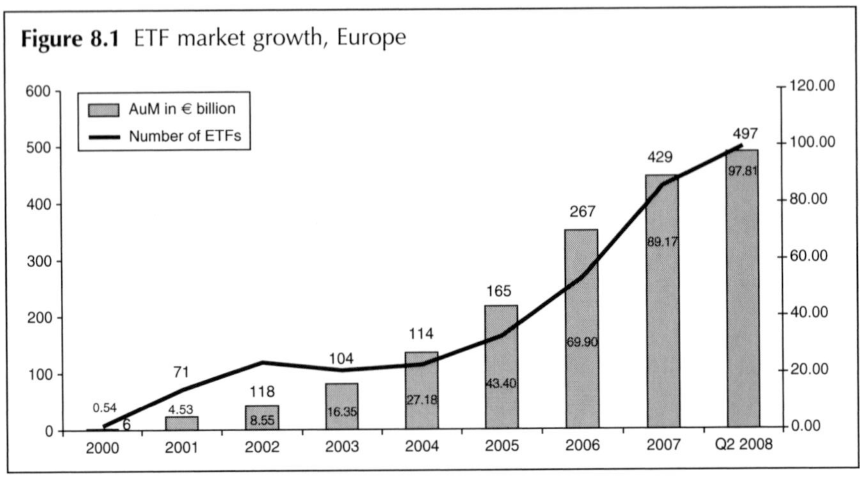

SYNTHETIC REPLICATION-BASED ETFs – CLOSE TO ZERO TRACKING ERROR

An index synthetic replication structure typically benefits a fund compared with owning the underlying equities due to the fact that the returns are based on the benchmark index. Effectively, the index synthetic replication ensures that the ETF will have performance, before any management fees, at least matching the designated index. In essence, all the risks and costs associated with running an ETF based on equities and measured against a total-return benchmark are passed on to the provider of the OTC swap. This means that a synthetic replication ETF, by the very nature of the returns that it now receives, is likely to be considerably more efficient than one based on the standard structure running the full basket of underlying equities.

The synthetic replication ETF framework has expanded from just the equity universe and now covers ETFs in the fixed-income, money-market and credit space. The main benefits from synthetic replication ETFs are low tracking error and certainty relating to costs, while investors also have the advantage of being able to take advantage of the liquidity in the underlying stocks. A good example would be for a broad index such as MSCI World. The underlying index has close to 1,800 stocks, which an investor could own as a fully replicated portfolio. However, this would tend to incur significant transaction costs and would likely have substantial ongoing maintenance costs with respect to corporate actions, takeover activity, dividend reinvestment and quarterly index rebalancing.

There are also multiple currencies to manage in the context of a world index. Investors have long used futures baskets to replicate broad-based benchmarks, but these also have constant ongoing costs with respect to futures roll, margins, execution risk and relatively high tracking errors.

An optimal basket of 10 local futures gives a tracking error of 153 basis points (bp). If investors wish to have greater operational efficiency by using fewer futures, the trade-off is in the form of higher tracking error with, for example, four futures giving a tracking error of 253bp. In contrast to this, a MSCI World synthetic replication-based ETFs can be expected to underperform its benchmark index by at most its total expense ratio of 45bp over the course of a year. In addition the tracking is likely to be extremely low, with the tracking error of the db x-trackers MSCI World ETF having ranged from 1 to 3bp. Investors face similar levels of efficiency with synthetic replication ETFs for broad benchmarks such as MSCI Europe and MSCI Emerging World. In the case of MSCI Europe a typical futures basket would have a tracking error of around 140bp, compared with 5bp for the ETF. With respect to the MSCI Emerging Market World benchmark, futures are generally inefficient with tracking errors as high as 541bp, while the ETF on the same index has a tracking error of 4bp. The charts below show how synthetic replication ETFs offer tightly controlled risk and performance relative

Figure 8.2 MSCI World ETF NAV vs. net TR index

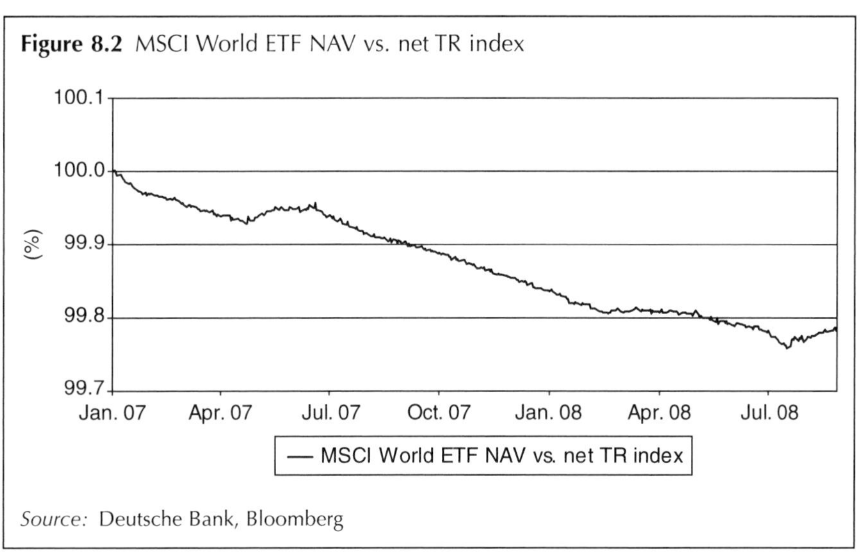

Source: Deutsche Bank, Bloomberg

Figure 8.3 Tracking error: MSCI World ETF NAV vs. net TR index (in basis points)

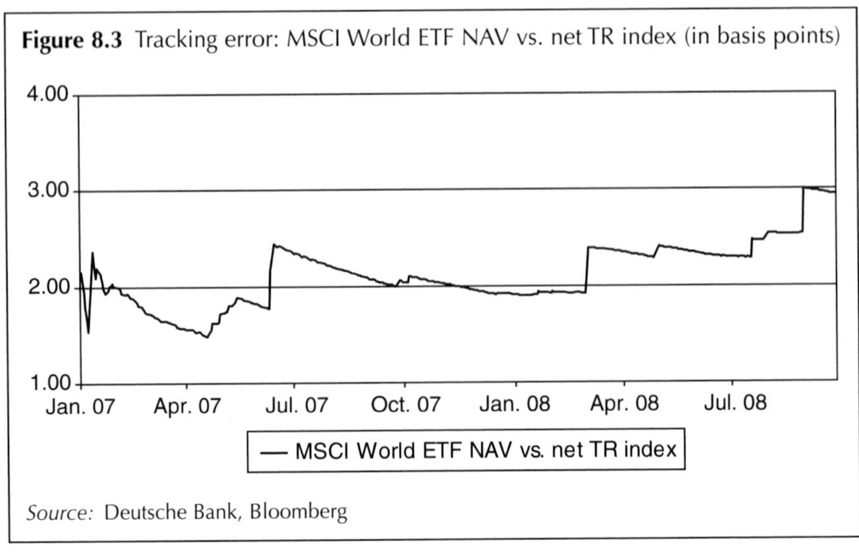

Source: Deutsche Bank, Bloomberg

Figure 8.4 Synthetic replication-based ETF vs. traditional ETF

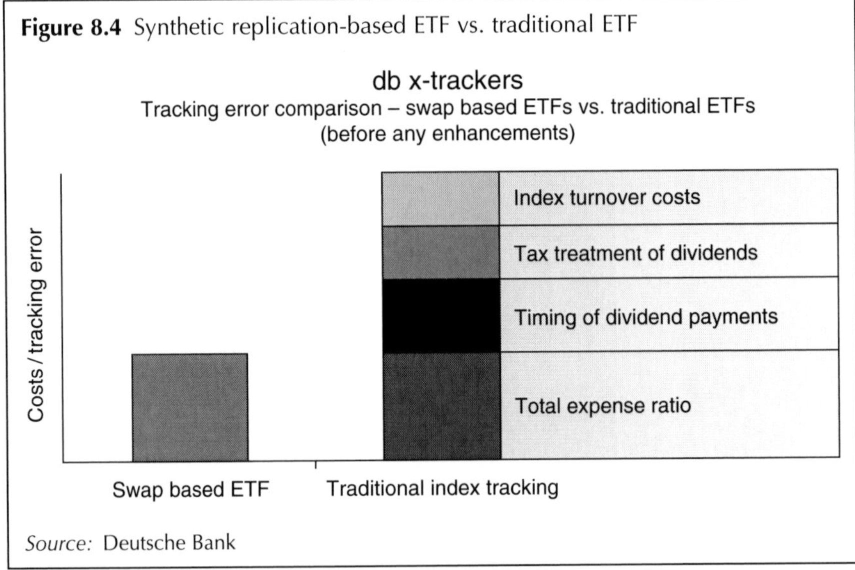

Source: Deutsche Bank

to their benchmarks, with the low tracking error being a significant feature. Another feature of the tracking error related to the futures baskets is that they tend to be very unstable and subject to significant increases or decreases depending on levels of market volatility. Synthetic replication ETF tracking errors are mainly a function of dividend factors relative to the benchmark.

Figure 8.5 Tracking error of 10 future baskets (MSCI World), in %

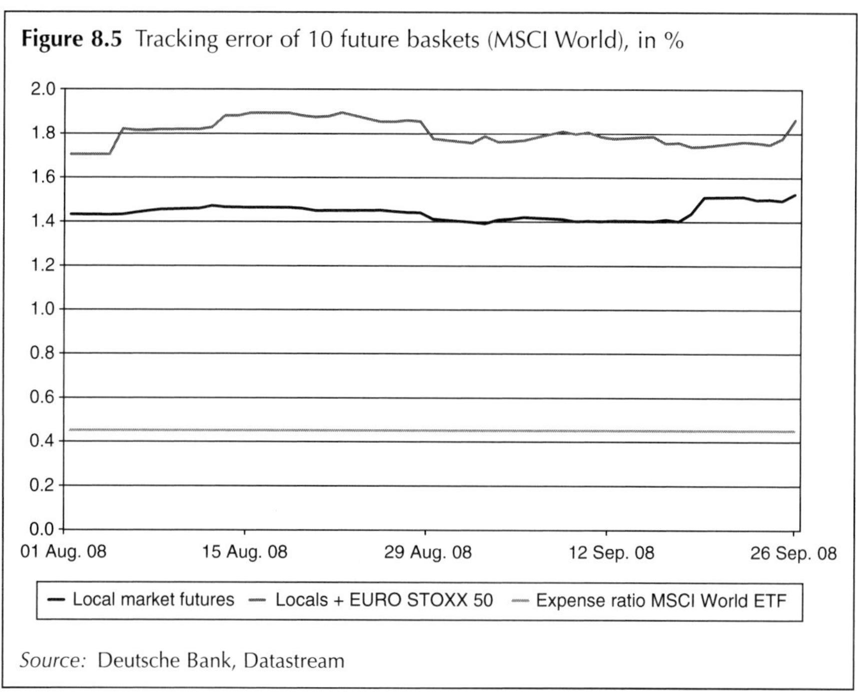

Source: Deutsche Bank, Datastream

Table 8.1 MSCI World future-tracking

Futures to track MSCI World				
Number of contracts	5	4	3	2
US	51.31	51.90	50.97	50.79
EURO STOXX 50	21.56	24.75	37.13	49.21
Japan	11.98	12.12	11.90	
UK	11.11	11.24		
Switzerland	4.05			
Tracking error (%)	2.44	2.53	3.15	5.60

Source: Deutsche Bank, Reuters

How synthetic replication ETFs can improve the performance of ETFs

Besides the stable tracking error, synthetic replication ETFs have a real advantage over the traditional way of full replication when it comes to generating enhancements while tracking a total-return index. Let us look at how a total return index works. STOXX, as with all index providers, have a matrix of the different tax rates that they

Table 8.2 Tracking errors summary

Futures to track MSCI World	
Developed benchmarks	
MSCI Europe	1.40%
MSCI EAFE	1.21%
MSCI Kokusai	1.25%
MSCI World	1.53%
Emerging benchmarks	
MSCI EM World	5.77%
MSCI EM Europe	11.04%
MSCI EM EMEA	10.47%
MSCI EM Eastern Europe	11.93%

Source: Deutsche Bank

apply when calculating net-return indexes. Given the constituents of the index and the relevant country rates that are used, we can estimate that the overall tax rate for the EURO STOXX 50 is currently close to 77.6%.

Timing of dividend payments

In order to be entitled to receive the dividend payment, investors have to buy the stock prior to the ex-dividend day. Many total-return indexes work on the assumption that dividends are paid and reinvested as soon as the stock goes ex-dividend. In reality, the average time between the ex-dividend and payment date is 22 days for US stocks, 38 for UK stocks and 74 days for Japanese stocks. This time lag in the dividend payment can cause a drag on the performance, especially in a rising market. In the case of the MSCI Europe this causes an estimated tracking error of 0.08% per annum (according to Deutsche Bank Index Research). The trend for companies to increase dividend payments and make special capital repayments heightens the importance of these timing issues for index-tracking funds such as ETFs. With synthetic replication ETFs dividends are reinvested on the ex-divided date and therefore this source of tracking error can be eliminated.

Index turnover

Apart from the need to manage dividend and cash reinvestments, ETFs that do full replication also have to deal with corporate actions

Table 8.3 Withholding taxes

Dow Jones STOXX withholding taxes		
Country	**Code**	**Withholding tax (%)**
Austria	AT	25.00
Belgium	BE	25.00
Finland	FI	28.00
France	FR	25.00
Germany	DE	21.10
Greece	GR	0.00
Ireland	IE	20.00
Italy	IT	27.00
Netherlands	NL	15.00
Portugal	PT	20.00
Spain	ES	18.00

Source: Deutsche Bank, STOXX

such as rights issues, takeovers, free-float changes and share issues and general rebalances. There is also the cost of additions and deletions from the index and the turnover that this can cause, together with the turnover that can be due to extraordinary rule changes. Typically, quarterly rebalance turnover for the EURO STOXX 50 is around 2.5%. Merger and takeover activity can significantly increase total turnover in any given year, even before we take into account the effect of the annual review. In 2007 turnover was above average due to the high level of merger activity even in large-capitalisation stocks, together with three additions and three deletions in the annual review. Running a full portfolio of index constituents will incur ongoing management costs that will typically detract from the overall returns, and these costs will impinge on the ability to match the index. Overall turnover has averaged 15% per annum if quarterly and annual changes and takeover-related activity are included. Investors can also gain revenue throughout the year by lending out stocks in their portfolios, although the returns for this in large-capitalisation stocks can be relatively meagre.

Generally, investors will find it difficult and operationally cumbersome to achieve returns that are significantly ahead of the total-return index and while managing risk effectively.

PERFORMANCE DIFFERENCE OF THE TRADITIONAL REPLICATION METHOD VS. THE SYNTHETIC REPLICATION-BASED APPROACH

Over the past two to three years the substantial growth in the use of exchange-traded funds in Europe has opened up a new market to institutional investors. Depending on the structure of the ETF, investors have been able to gain access to modestly enhanced returns at relatively low risk. Other characteristics of ETFs that have helped increase include the fact that they are simple to trade and settle just like ordinary shares while being open-ended collective investment schemes.

The traditional ETF structure is based on holding the full underlying equities but may also incorporate dividend enhancement, stock loan and derivative strategies in order to provide better-than-index returns. Alternatively, and this applies to the majority of cases, the traditional ETF structure that focuses on holding a full basket of underlying index equities is more likely to deliver performance broadly in line with the index, but overall underperformance due to the subtraction of management fees.

This divergence of performance with respect to the EURO STOXX 50 is shown in Figure 8.6 for two traditional ETFs, labelled ETF 1 and ETF 2.

An important aspect of the traditional ETF structure and total returns is the tracking error that is incurred, as this is a useful overall measure of the risks associated with capturing these returns. In the case of ETF 2, which has the higher enhanced returns, the tracking error versus the benchmark reaches a high of more than 60bp in June 2006, while even ETF 1, which performs broadly in line with the index, has a peak tracking error of around 50bp. Although the ability of some traditional ETF structures to enhance returns has helped boost interest in the use of ETFs to track various indexes, there remains a concern over the relatively high tracking errors that are often apparent. Investors ideally desire a combination of outperformance and low tracking error and hence low risk. Innovation in the ETF market has been mainly driven by the creation of synthetic replication-based ETFs.

These have allowed investors to capture benchmark returns and in some cases enhanced returns for a wide range of indexes ranging from relatively straightforward large-cap indexes to more difficult

Figure 8.6 Divergence of performance of traditional ETFs

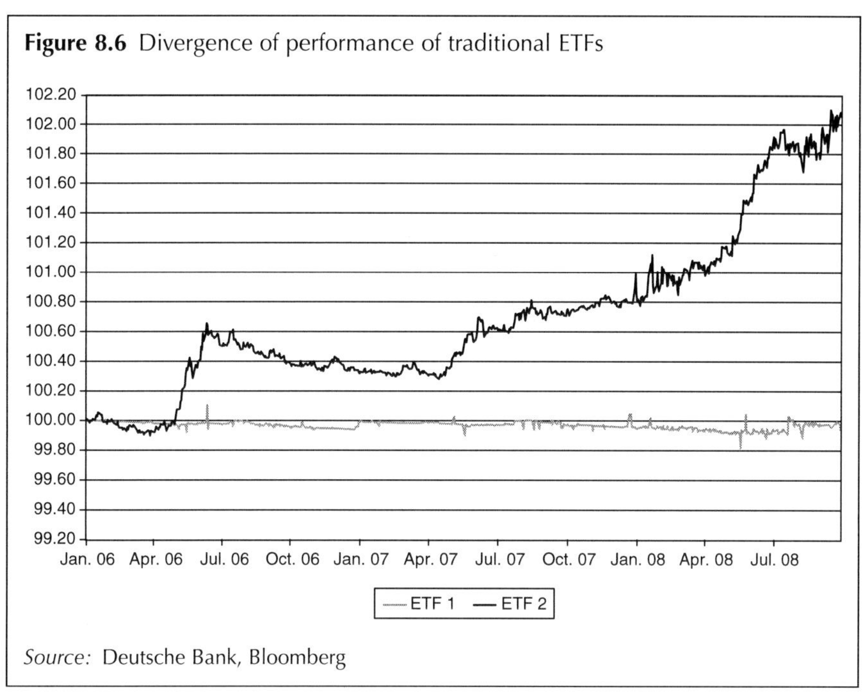

Source: Deutsche Bank, Bloomberg

Figure 8.7 Traditional ETF, tracking error (in basis points, 60-day)

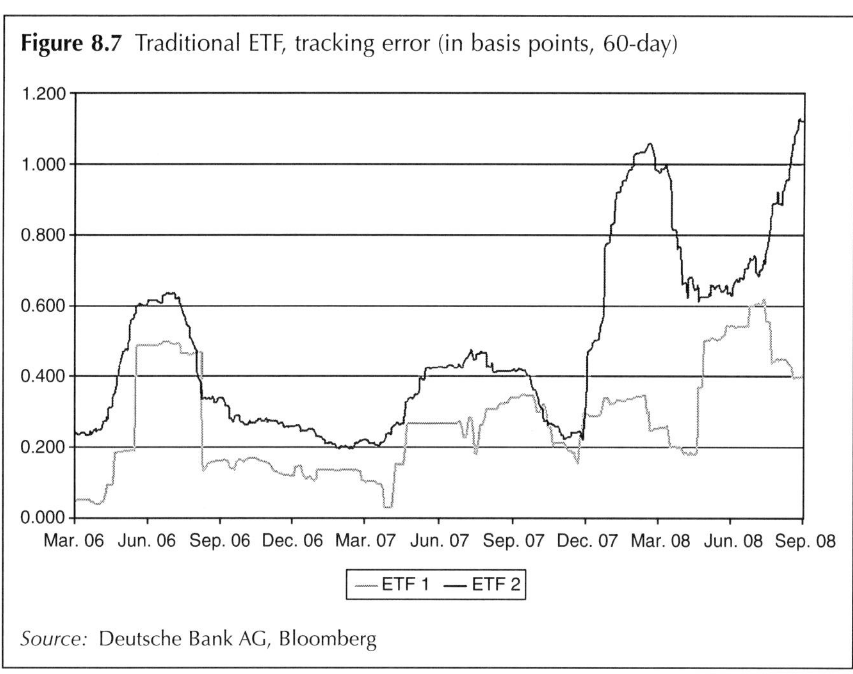

Source: Deutsche Bank AG, Bloomberg

Figure 8.8 Synthetic replication-based ETF vs. traditional ETFs (EURO STOXX 50, relative performance)

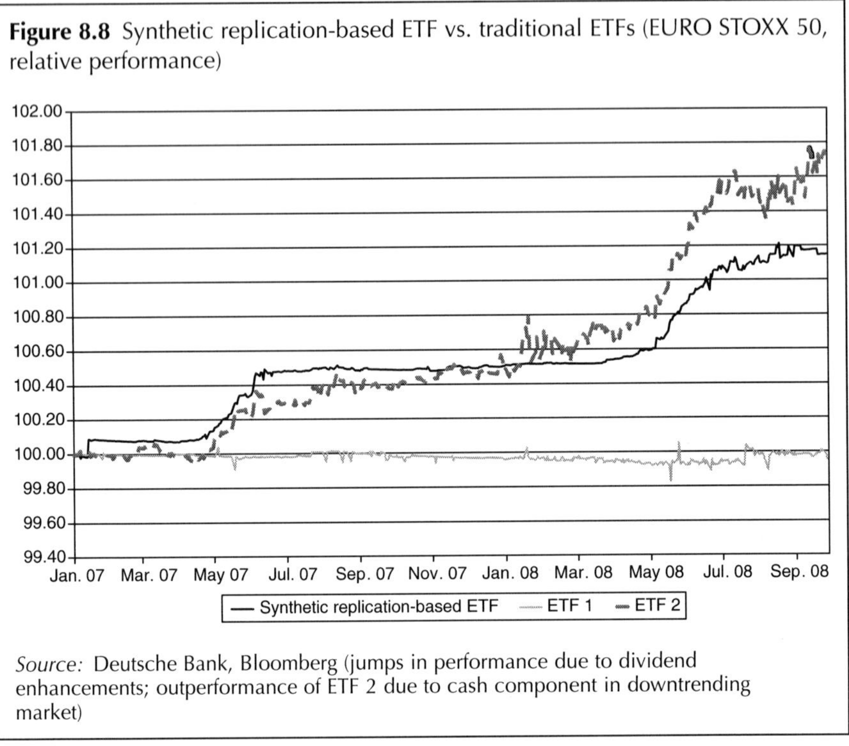

Source: Deutsche Bank, Bloomberg (jumps in performance due to dividend enhancements; outperformance of ETF 2 due to cash component in downtrending market)

emerging-market and even frontier-market indexes. An index synthetic replication structure typically benefits an ETF compared with owning the underlying equities, due to the fact that the returns are based on the benchmark index. Effectively, the index synthetic replication ensures that the ETF will have performance, before any management fees, at least matching the designated index. In essence all the risks and costs associated with running an ETF based on equities and measured against a total-return benchmark are passed on to the provider of the OTC swap. This means that a synthetic replication ETF, by the very nature of the returns that it now receives, is likely to be considerably more efficient than one based on the standard structure running the full basket of underlying equities.

The main advantage that synthetic replication ETFs offer is the more consistent profile of enhanced returns combined with overall lower tracking errors. In the case of synthetic replication-based ETFs the tracking error tends to rise mainly during peak dividend paying season as the ETF benefits from various dividend-enhancement strategies, while after that the tracking error falls sharply. A traditional fund structure with a single domicile will potentially be disadvantaged compared with funds that can use OTC swap that can more efficiently replicate index total returns, especially with relationship to funds where dividends are sourced from a wide range of countries. While it is not possible to bridge the gap fully between gross and net total-return indexes it is possible by the use of OTC swaps to manage exposure and the receipt of dividends more efficiently. This trend can be seen in Figure 8.9, where a synthetic replication ETF is compared with the same traditional ETF structures we have previously considered. The main differential, apart from the more stable performance relative to the benchmark, is that the tracking error has a peak of 28bp compared with close to 48bp for ETF 2, which also outperformed. Outside the main dividend season, the synthetic replication ETF has a tracking error of around 8bp compared with an average of close to 30bp for the traditional ETF structures.

DIFFERENCE IN THE CREATION/REDEMPTION PROCESS

Investors should focus on the creation and redemption process as being fundamental to the use of ETFs, especially in the case of

Figure 8.9 Creation/redemption process, traditional ETF

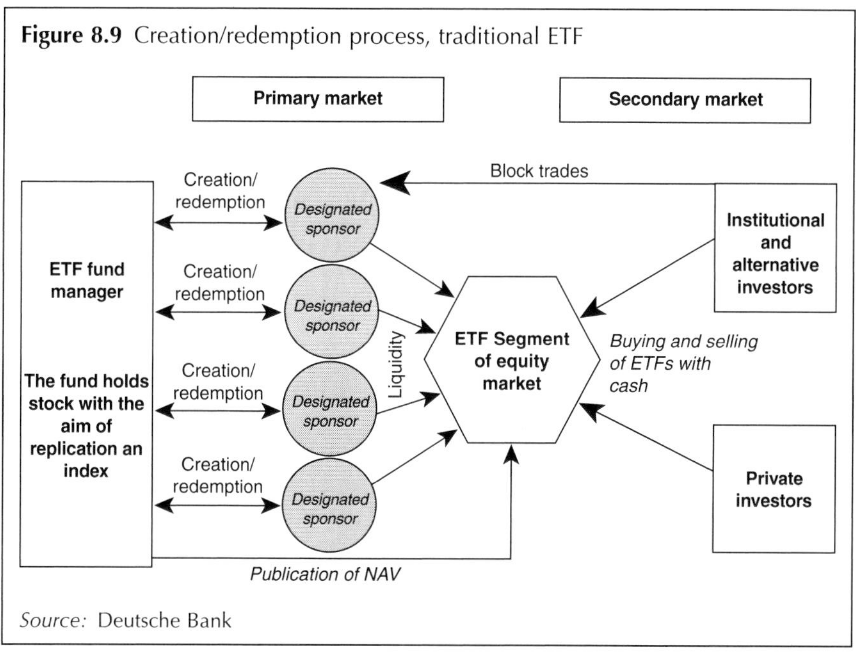

Source: Deutsche Bank

products where the ETF does not have significant on exchange liquidity. Typically, it is best for investors to deal through a broker that already has high cash equity flows. The ability to create ETFs by accessing natural flow can help lower costs by minimising market impact and trading costs. New units of an ETF can be created at the ETF's net asset value (NAV), either through the delivery of a basket of securities or cash. Investors need to go through an authorised participant in order to implement any creations or redemptions. Typically, there will be minimum size requirements and a fee may be charged. ETF providers and asset managers publish the net asset value for cash subscription, together with the composition of the perfect basket on a daily basis. This allows authorised participants to buy the securities that underlie the ETF and deliver these to the ETF asset manager, who then delivers the ETF shares to the purchaser. In this way, investors then hold and trade the ETFs just like shares.

Case study – how does a synthetic replication-based ETFs platform work?

The ETFs are sub-funds of an umbrella fund investment company domiciled in Luxembourg and comply with the relevant European

Figure 8.10 Creation/redemption process, synthetic replication ETF

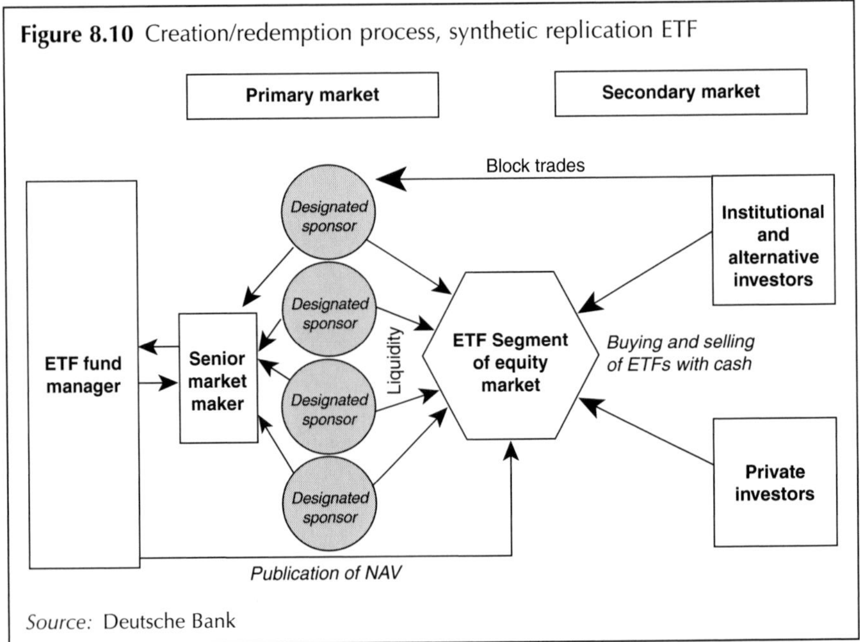

Source: Deutsche Bank

Figure 8.11 Swap details

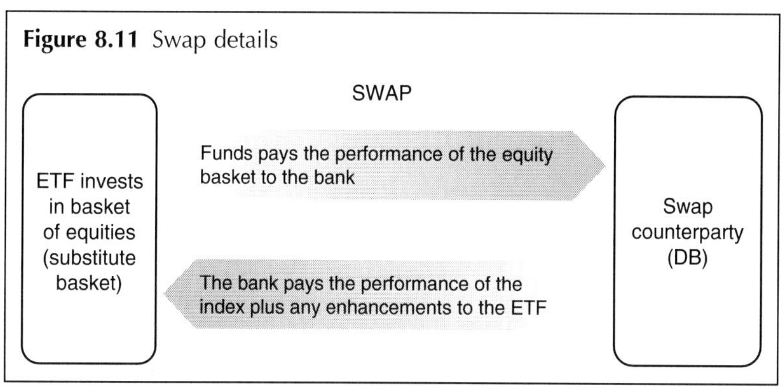

fund regulations relating to undertakings for collective investment in transferable securities (UCITS III). Under the terms of the prospectus the investment objective of each ETF is to replicate the performance of a specific index. The objective is achieved through an investment policy of purchasing a basket of securities (called the "substitute basket") and by entering into an index swap with a bank. The purpose of the index swap is to exchange the performance of the substitute basket for the performance of the index being tracked by the ETF.

Under the terms of the index swap agreement, the bank as the swap guarantees the performance of the index on a daily basis. In other words, the performance of the ETF will always be equal to the performance of the index before the accrual of the annual all-in fee.

The impact of the management fee can be further offset through the generation of enhancements by the swap counterparty. These enhancements can come from two sources: (i) lending of the underlying index constituents and earning income from this; and (ii) of dividends tax treatment. It should be possible in some cases for the bank to achieve a better tax treatment of dividends paid on the index constituents. For example, the db x-trackers Euro STOXX 50 ETF outperformed the underlying index by 1.02% per annum (since launch on January 4, 2007 to June 30, 2008), after taking into account the accrual of the annual all-in fee of 0.15%. That means the return advantage of the ETF to the index amounts to 1.25% since launch.

THE SUBSTITUTE BASKET

As mentioned above the assets of the fund are invested in what is called the substitute basket. For the db x-trackers ETFs tracking

Figure 8.12 EURO STOXX 50 ETF relative performance

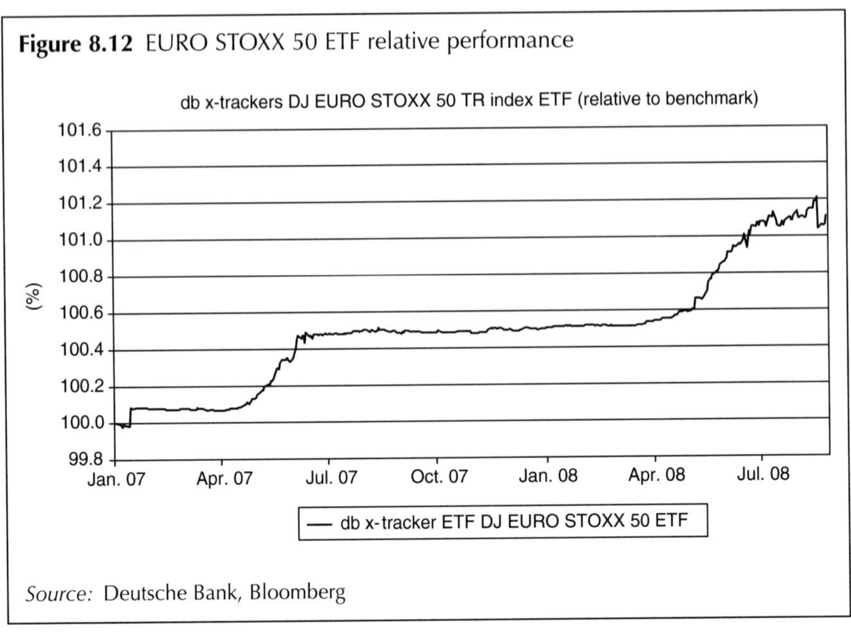

Source: Deutsche Bank, Bloomberg

equity indexes, the substitute basket typically comprises stocks, while for those on fixed-income indexes it typically comprises bonds and cash deposits. From the perspective of the performance of the ETF, the constituents of the substitute basket are not important, as ultimately this is delivered through the index swap in place with the bank. The substitute basket could even be constructed of stocks not related to the underlying index being tracked. For the db x-trackers ETFs, the substitute basket is constructed with the objective to keep the running costs of the ETF to a minimum and to satisfy the UCITS fund diversification requirements. So, for example, an ETF tracking a European index could have a substitute basket composed of US or Japanese stocks and vice versa. The constituents of the substitute basket do not have an impact on the performance of the ETF. This is going to be illustrated in the following example.

EXPOSURE TO SWAP COUNTERPARTY

A common question with synthetic replication ETFs is in relation to the risk exposure to the index swap counterparty.

Under the UCITS regulation a fund is subject to restrictions that are designed to ensure a sufficient risk diversification. Among others the fund is not allowed to invest more than 10% of the NAV in derivative instruments (which include the index swap). That is, the value of the index swap must not exceed 10% of the fund's NAV, which means that the level of exposure to the swap counterparty (or, in other words, the amount that the swap counterparty owes to the fund) is limited to a maximum of 10% of the fund's NAV.

EXAMPLES

In these examples the impact of the management fee is ignored in order to keep the explanations simple.

Day 1 – initial investment: Assume an initial investment at a NAV of €100 and a starting level of the index is €100. The €100 is invested in the substitute basket and the ETF enters into an index swap with a bank. The exposure to the bank under the index swap is zero at this stage.

Day 2 – index rises, substitute basket remains flat: Assume the index rises by 5% and the value of the substitute basket remains constant at €100. As the index has risen by 5% the new index level would be €105 and the NAV of the ETF will rise to €105. The exposure to the bank under the index swap is calculated as the difference between the index and substitute basket performance, which is €5 (€105 – €100) or 4.76% of NAV (€5/€105).

Day 3 – index rises, substitute basket rises: Assume the index rises by €2 to €107 and the value of the substitute basket rises by 2% to €102. As the new index level is €107 the NAV of the ETF will rise to €107. The exposure to the bank under the index swap is calculated as the difference between the index and substitute basket performance, which is €5 (€107 – €102) or 4.67% of NAV (€5/€107).

Day 4 – resetting the index swap: Due to UCITS restrictions, the exposure to the bank under the index swap cannot exceed 10% of the NAV of the ETF. In practice, if the exposure to the bank is due to reach 10% the index swap is "reset". This involves crystallising the gain in the index and reinvesting this in the substitute basket.

Assume the index level rises to €108 and the value of the substitute basket falls back to €100. The NAV of the ETF would be €108. The exposure to the bank under the index swap is calculated as the difference between the index and substitute basket performance, which is €8 (€108 – €100) or 7.41% of NAV (€8/€108).

The resetting of the index swap involves a payment of €8 from the bank to the ETF and these proceeds are invested in the substitute basket. This results in an increased value of the substitute basket to 108 and the value of the index is now 108, resulting in zero counterparty exposure to the bank.

Day 5 – index falls, substitute basket is flat: Assume the substitute basket remains at a value of €108 and the index falls by €4 to €104. The NAV of the fund will then also fall to €104. The index swap has a value of negative €4 (€104 – €108) or –3.7% of the fund's NAV.

If the index continues to fall or the substitute basket increases in value, the swap value approaches the critical threshold of –10% and a reset will be triggered. In this case stocks from the substitute basket will be sold to offset the negative value of the swap. The proceeds from selling the stocks are paid to the bank.

EXECUTION OF SYNTHETIC REPLICATION ETFs

It is important to offer an efficient and effective trading and execution service. Investors can benefit from tight bid–offer spreads and strong liquidity if they choose a dedicated ETF trading desk with a strong trading presence in the underlying markets and asset classes of the ETFs offered.

Investors can trade ETFs in one of three ways as follows.

1. On exchange during trading hours: ETFs can be traded on the exchange at the prevailing bid–ask price.
2. OTC during trading hours: When it comes to trading ETFs in volumes larger than those shown on the screen, a lot of the trades take place OTC in Europe. The benefit here is that large-size orders

Table 8.4 Swap example

	Index (€)	Substitute basket (€)	Synthetic replication value (€) to ETF	NAV (€)	Exposure to the bank	
					€	% of NAV
Day 1	100	100	0	100	0.00	0.00
Day 2	105	100	5	105	5.00	4.76
Day 3	107	102	5	107	5.00	4.67
Day 4 (before reset)	108	100	8	108	8.00	7.41
Day 4 (after reset)	108	108	0	108	0.00	0.00
Day 5	104	108	–4	104	–4.00	–3.7

can be traded at the same spread as shown on the screen without any market impact. This is a feature of trading on the European ETF market, where the large majority of trades take place OTC without any market impact.

3. OTC at the NAV: Some ETFs are UCITS funds where an independent NAV is produced by the fund administrator on a daily basis using the closing index levels. All of these ETFs can be traded at NAV. The advantage of this approach is that investors have further transparency of pricing, as they can buy based on the closing index level. This is particularly important when it comes to trading emerging-market underlyings or markets that are closed during European trading hours (eg, Asia).

SOME USES OF ETFs FOR INVESTORS

The wide range of ETF products currently available within Europe should allow investors to pursue a range of strategies. ETFs can be

Figure 8.13 Exchange trading

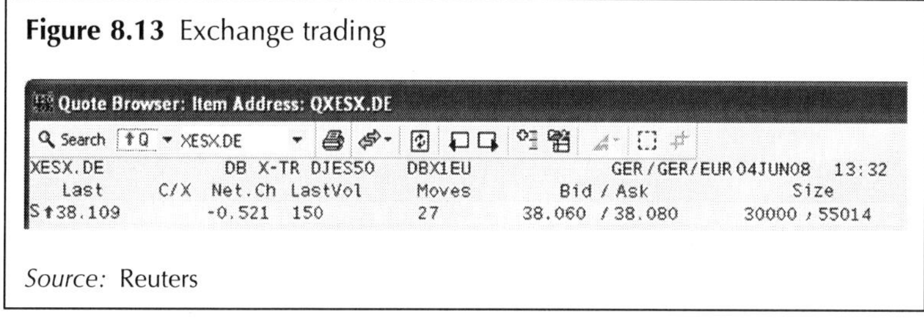

Source: Reuters

Figure 8.14 Market price and OTC offer

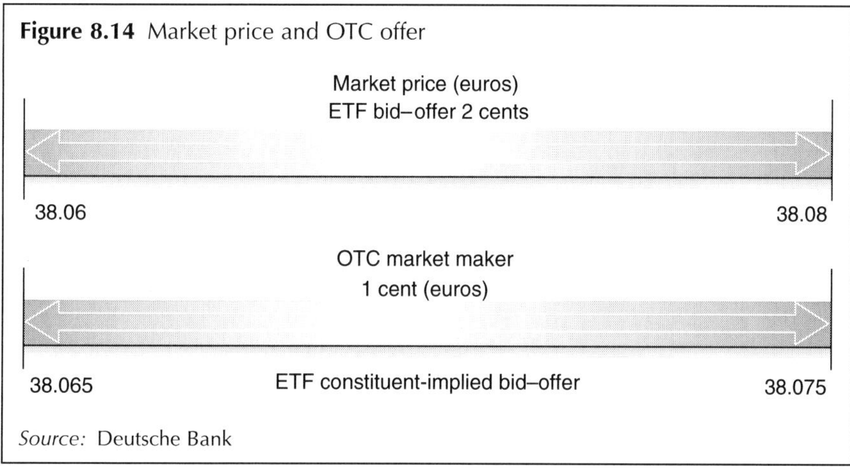

Source: Deutsche Bank

viewed as the building blocks of a portfolio and a highly flexible investment tool that can be used on both a long- and short-term basis. Below are some uses and strategies for the ETFs:

- asset allocation – both tactical and strategic;
- low-cost exposure to new markets and asset classes;
- cash management;
- core-satellite strategy;
- alternative to swap and futures;
- transition management tool; and
- performance enhancement through securities lending.

One of the fastest growth areas has been for ETFs that cover areas and asset classes that can be difficult and costly to trade and manage directly. This particularly applies to emerging markets, be it individual countries in Asia or Europe, or broad regions. The ability to trade markets as diverse as Brazil, Russia, India and Vietnam using ETFs that trade on a developed-market exchange is appealing compared with the complexities of handling trading, settlement, currency, corporate actions and custody in such markets.

Another trend observed by us has been that many investors concerned about counterparty or credit risk have switched out of products such as swaps and certificates (where there is 100% exposure) to synthetic replication ETFs (where the maximum possible exposure is 10%). The advantage of this is that investors can achieve the same level of efficient performance as a swap with much lower counterparty exposure.

Another fast-growing area in the ETF space relates to their use to gain exposure to different strategies. In the US market, short-related ETFs now account for more than 7% of all daily turnover, with the recent high levels of intraday volatility being particularly helpful in encouraging greater use of these products. In Europe, there is also a similar trend with both higher turnover and new ETF issuance in the area of short and leveraged ETFs. The main advantage to investors is that they can go long an ETF that creates positive returns in a falling market. This can be significantly easier for many investors to manage than either shorting futures or using a short OTC swap. A short-related ETF trades the same as a long ETF and so is just as simple to trade while offering returns normally only associated with a derivatives product.

THE RESULTS

Figure 8.15 compares the performance of the db x-tracker MSCI EUROPE TRN ETF with the performance of the underlying index. Regardless of market conditions the ETF always reflects the performance of the index less the all-in fee.

With index synthetic replication trackers, the advantages can be summarised as:

- more efficient index tracking;
- low tracking error versus benchmark index; and
- more product-creation possibilities, such as ETFs on emerging markets and short indexes.

FIXED-INCOME ETFs WILL BENEFIT THE MOST FROM THE SYNTHETIC REPLICATION-BASED APPROACH

The past two years have seen a surge in activity in the fixed-income ETF space with a significant number of new ETFs that cover a broad spectrum of indexes and maturities. This phenomenon has been apparent in both Europe and the US, although individual market trends have differed. In terms of assets under management, the

Figure 8.15 Efficient index tracking

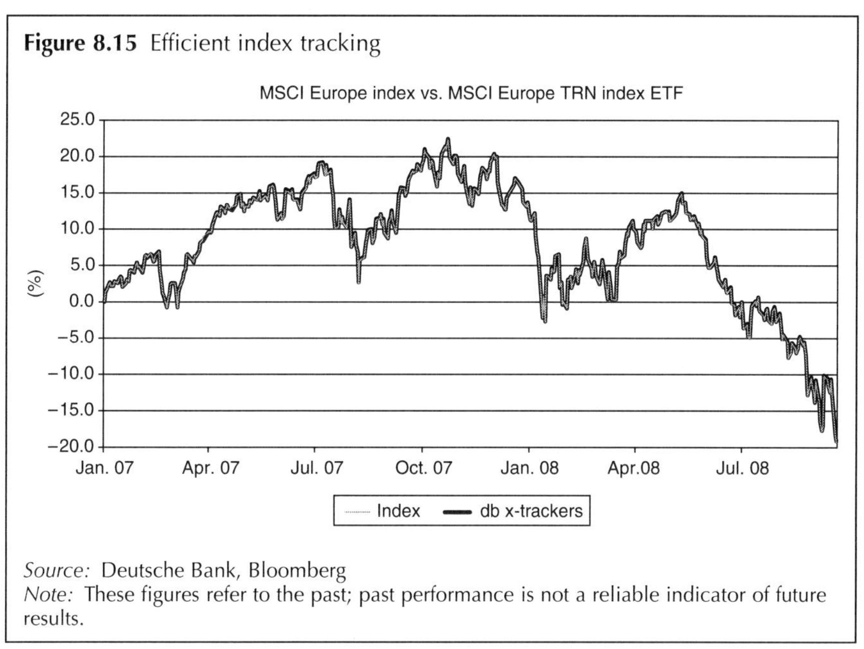

Source: Deutsche Bank, Bloomberg
Note: These figures refer to the past; past performance is not a reliable indicator of future results.

fixed-income space has experienced consistent growth over the past two to three years with both the US and Europe at or close to their peak levels.

Since the beginning of 2006, the assets under management of fixed-income ETFs have grown from €5.6 billion to €21.2 billion in Europe at the end of April 2008. This equals an annual growth of 80.3%. In contrast to this, the whole ETF market has grown by 12.72% per annum in the same period.

Assets under management in US fixed-income ETFs are at €27.6 billion, which is 7.3% of the total ETF assets in the US, whereas fixed-income ETFs in Europe count for 21% of the total assets in Europe.

Fixed-income ETFs have currently global assets under management of €50.4 billion; 54.74% are allotted to the US, 42.06% to Europe and 3.2% to the rest of the world. In terms of equity ETFs, the assets under management are 4.5 times bigger in the US than in Europe.

With 85 fixed-income ETFs available in May 2008, Europe had 27 more ETFs than the US, with 153 ETFs available worldwide. Fifteen percent of the average turnover in Europe falls upon fixed-income ETFs, while in the US it is only 1%.

The strong growth in Europe was driven by the huge inflows in money-market ETFs, which account for 28.5% of the assets under management of fixed income ETFs.

Regardless, if we consider Europe or the US, the growth of fixed-income ETFs will be much higher than the growth of ETFs based on equity indexes in the next few years. If pension funds, which manage more than 90% of their asset actively and have most of their money invested in fixed-income products, would rearrange their portfolio by putting 4% into ETFs, that would equal a doubling of the worldwide assets under management hold in ETFs.

CONCLUSION

ETF usage is expected to grow substantially in the medium term as more innovative and efficient ETF structures come to the market and offer more attractive performance characteristics to institutional investors. In terms of overall cost comparison with traditional ETF structures that own the underlying equity holdings, synthetic replication ETFs will bring enhanced returns to investors on a relative basis. There has also been a dramatic expansion in the number of indexes, styles and asset classes covered by ETFs with a particular emphasis on country-related products, international country exposure, regional indexes, sectors and, more recently, managed ETFs that offer leveraged returns. Fixed-income ETFs in Europe and the US have also been a major growth area, with a wide range of ETFs covering different maturities and strategies. By providing investors with the broadest set of opportunities, we believe that the ETF market can offer competitive solutions. This is especially likely in an environment where regulatory changes, such as the adoption of UCITS III, should benefit index-based products. The fact that ETFs remain easy to trade and settle in comparison with competing derivative and OTC instruments is likely to be a key factor in investor adoption of ETFs within their portfolio strategies. Investors are likely to derive the greatest benefit when using ETFs to gain exposure to broad diversified benchmarks and indexes.

9

ETF Strategies

Robert Holderith

Emerging Global Advisors, LLC

If you look back at most of the product innovations and investment strategies in the financial industry, you will find most were created as a response to the movement of the equity or fixed-income markets. Most of the necessary tools needed to build the products were available for many years before the strategies were delivered to the marketplace. This has not been the case for ETFs.

The limited number of ETFs, for many years, restricted a professional investor from creating even the simplest of asset-allocation models. Since the first fixed-income ETFs did not arrive on the scene until 2003, commodities until 2004 and inverse and leveraged until 2006, long-only equity strategies were the only portfolios that could be created without the use of a margin account. This is perhaps the most exciting thing about the evolution of ETF products. As additional unique ETFs become available, so do the opportunities to create new strategies. See Table 9.1.

THE INITIAL ETF CONCEPT

To better understand the types of portfolio that can be created using ETFs, we need to understand the initial ETF concept. Although numerous "alpha" ETFs exist today, the initial concept was to provide beta or market-based exposure. Whether it was domestic broad-based indexes, more narrow sector or industry exposures or broad-based country funds, the traditional ETF was always designed to be a single-trade alternative to purchasing a basket of names that were usually the members of an index. This single-trade methodology

Table 9.1 Exchange-traded funds product-development timeline, 1993–2008

	1993	**1994**	**1995**	**1996**	**1997**	**1998**	**1999**	**2000**
ETF product type	Domestic equity – Broad based			International equity – Single country		Domestic equity – Sector based		
	2001	**2002**	**2003**	**2004**	**2005**	**2006**	**2007**	**2008**
ETF product type	International equity – Broad based	Fixed income – Domestic taxable		Commodity – Single	Fundamental indexing	Inverse and leveraged		Actively managed

Sources: Yahoo, Bloomberg

greatly simplified the process of owning exposure either for limited-period monetisation or longer-term exposure plays. Only a handful of large institutions could practically implement the basket approach, since only large-scale purchases are practical for programme trading. Understanding this concept makes it easy to see why ETFs' major clients in the past and today are institutions.

Purchasing broad-based exposures has numerous efficiencies as well. Buying exposures instead of individual securities requires a less intensive top-down research effort. Since it has been suggested that most of the return of an individual security comes from market and sector exposure, you can likely accomplish your investment goals nearly as effectively, and likely with less risk, by purchasing an ETF instead of taking on risks specific to purchasing a single security.

BETA AND ALPHA INDEXES

There has been much debate as to the value of the aforementioned alpha indexes. Will they outperform their beta counterparts on a regular basis? Are they so similar in the makeup of their components they are likely to be too highly correlated to provide any meaning difference in return? We will not try to settle these issues here because we believe the point is not whether or not one will outperform the other over all phases of the market cycle – history has shown that no one strategy can provide eternal alpha throughout all economic ups and downs. The real issue for a portfolio manager is that, if some of these products do provide a lower correlation to their beta counterparts, are there strategies that we can create to benefit from this action? So, conceptually, alpha indexes do not have to outperform all the time. If we believe they will underperform, we can still use them. We can short them. The only question that needs to be answered here is: are there valid risk arbitrage strategies that can be created by shorting either the beta or the alpha index and going long the other? We will attempt to answer that question later in the advance strategies portion of this chapter.

HOW TO DEVELOP A STRATEGY

The author's training in this business has been consultative or client-based. He believes ETF strategy development should be viewed in the same light. A strategy is valuable to an investor only if it suits their particular need, whether it is capital appreciation, income, risk reduction or some combination of the three. A great equity strategy with solid risk-adjusted returns may not be valuable to some investors. A cash-equivalent portfolio may be suitable for an institution's operating capital account, but clearly not all investor types. Some portfolios need to be tax-sensitive while others do not.

One of the best things about ETF strategies is scalability. The ability to create numerous portfolio types for a single client is unique to ETFs. Investors with as little as a few thousand US dollars can easily have three of more strategies in their portfolios, limiting risk and creating multiple opportunities for creating non-correlating alphas.

Although there are unlimited types of strategy you can create, we are going to suggest they fall into two broad categories: fundamental and technical. We are all familiar with the difference between the two, so we will not cover them here, but a few important issues should be considered.

For technically based portfolios, consider the timeframe for investment, your trading expertise and quality of execution and your source of research. Many technicians believe technical analysis is best suited to providing relative-strength guidance more than anything else. Was your technically based portfolio created to benefit from this type of guidance, or is it an absolute-return strategy? Can you efficiently trade early or late in the day? What type of quote access do you have: Level 1 or Level 2? Do you have the time and resources to watch the market minute to minute? All these criteria and more must be considered before committing to a strategy whose success will be based on technical market signal.

Fundamentally based portfolios tend to be longer-term. At one point buy-and-hold was a favoured mantra on Wall Street. Towards the end of 2008, more investors were considering the benefits of a slightly more tactical and less strategic approach. As with technical analysis, your source of research and its intended timeframe are important considerations. You will also need to be very patient, as will your clients. Patience was hard to come by during the credit crisis of 2007 and 2008 and likely will be during any bear market stretches.

One comment on investor timeframes that we believe is valuable is that it is important to differentiate between strategic-allocation strategies and tactical strategies and the fact that you can combine the two. There are no absolutes in investing and portfolio building. A long-term strategic portfolio can have tactical attributes (and likely should) and, conversely, a tactical portfolio can hold positions for extended periods of time if the signals are in place to make such a commitment. The best strategists have the discipline to follow their plan and at the same time understand the value of flexibility when markets demand it.

Who you are as a portfolio manager, your training and expertise and the tools available to you should all be key determinants as to the type of strategies you can effectively manage. Many large wire-house broker dealers have programmes that allow a financial adviser to manage accounts on a fee basis and with discretion. The ability to manage portfolios the way you want to and trade effectively and efficiently without having to consult your clients is crucial to your success. Most of the aforementioned firms have platforms (Smith Barney has PM, UBS has PMP, Merrill Lynch has PIA, LPL has SAM, and so on) that provide an excellent portfolio-management environment and the tools needed to trade, act on research and otherwise fully implement a scalable ETF portfolio management business. Each has a trading system that allows you to create and save model portfolios, implement these models with a few keystrokes and even rebalance them quickly and easily. The author's previous firm had such a system. It revolutionised the way advisers managed their clients' portfolios, increased productivity and reduced trading errors by a huge margin.

Another important consideration is how many portfolio types, and variations on those portfolio types, you can effectively manage. The process of creating, researching, updating and overseeing more than 10 strategies can be overwhelming. You want to please as many clients as you can, but you do not want to compromise your ability to effectively manage. Keep in mind that you can combine existing strategies to create a different effect for each client, thereby personalising every portfolio. The above-mentioned trading tools provide the ability to manage many more portfolio types, but there are always practical limits to what can be achieved even with great technology.

ETFs AS COMPLEMENTARY PORTFOLIO COMPONENTS

As great an invention as they are, most advisers are likely not to invest 100% of their clients' assets in ETFs. Most advisers will be holding individual stocks or bonds, mutual funds or closed-end funds, or even have separate account portfolios as components of their clients' investment portfolio holdings. So we will first discuss ETFs as diversifiers or complements to existing strategies.

As shown in Table 9.2, there are about half a dozen broad ways to use ETFs as a complement to existing portfolios. We will look at each individually.

Increased exposure

For reasons fundamental or technical, you may want to increase your exposure to a market, sector, industry, country or even currency. If your overall strategy is still valid from a risk-and-return point of view and you have a broad range of exposures, but an opportunity comes along you would like to take advantage of such as having additional exposure to the US energy market or the anticipated strength of a currency, you may use an ETF to implement that opportunity. This works especially well for opportunities in the commodities and currency markets, where futures or swaps are usually the only way to obtain pure exposure.

Alternative exposure

Perhaps your portfolio has no exposure to emerging markets or domestic small-cap equities. Adding an ETF or two to a portfolio may be the best way to enter those markets with a single trade. Even a portfolio as small as US$10,000 can easily own 5% exposure through an ETF purchase. Most mutual funds do not provide pure commodity exposure for their investors (unless they are using ETFs). Copper, silver, gold and even coal can be easily purchased with ETFs.

Scalable exposure

Securities such as municipal and corporate bonds usually are US$1,000 each and very expensive to purchase in lots of fewer than 100.

Table 9.2 ETFs as complementary portfolio components

Increased exposure	Alternative exposure	Scalable exposure	Opportunistic hedging	Strategic hedging	Monetisation	Special situations

So even US$500,000 will likely get you only five issues. ETFs provide diversification at almost any scale for bond buyers. There are more than 30 fixed-income ETFs as of the end of 2008 and we can expect many more to surface over the years to come. Municipal bond buyers can sometimes find state-specific portfolios for additional tax benefits as well. US Treasury and corporate-bond ETFs have been available since 2002 and usually have volume that provides adequate liquidity for any investor. International, high-yield and emerging-market debt is also available in ETFs.

Opportunistic hedging

Opportunistic hedging describes purchasing short exposure that is nearly perfectly negatively correlated to a long position or positions already held. For example, if you are holding a US, domestic, large-cap-growth mutual fund and you are concerned about that area of the market but do not want to sell the fund, you can purchase an equal amount of short exposure through an inverse ETF or by shorting a long large-cap-growth ETF. As with all ETF strategies, opportunistic hedging can be easily implemented and undone with a single trade. The concept of obtaining inverse exposure for hedging purposes using ETFs is not new, but in the past required investors to borrow and short-sell long securities. There are now no fewer than five firms that offer inverse ETFs. Existing equity, bond and commodity positions can all be hedged through a long ETF purchase.

Strategic hedging

"Strategic hedging" is an academic term for creating what the hedge fund industry calls "long/short" or "variable long/short". Unlike opportunistic hedging, creating a long/short portfolio implies the purchase of both the long and the short positions at the same time. This process, if done correctly, can remove or greatly reduce market exposure or beta risk. Although beta is normally the key contributor to portfolio return, removing beta from a portfolio allows you to own fewer positions or expose your clients to markets that would normally be too volatile, such as emerging markets or small-cap. There are numerous ways to implement such a portfolio, but there is one constant. You will need to find a group of securities or an asset class or a country or a mutual fund manager that provides a return greater than the long version of your hedge. In other words, you can buy a small-cap equity manager and purchase inverse small-cap exposure. As long as the manager outperforms the index on a relative basis, whether the manager, on an absolute basis, makes money or loses money, you can benefit.

Monetisation

The use of ETFs to obtain temporary market exposure while a client is in between managers or reallocating between managers is one of the oldest ETF strategies. One trade can buy you almost any exposure needed as a short-term or long-term solution to maintaining a proper asset allocation. This strategy can also be used for tax-loss swapping or banking a portfolio loss without losing market exposure and violating tax-loss wash sale rules.

Special situations

There are numerous unique, one-off situations that clients can present you with. Some clients have restrictions on which types of securities they can own. Some have large positions that cannot be sold or hedged directly. Others may have trust accounts that require certain levels of diversification. It is not unusual for an endowment or other non-profit to forbid the use of futures or options or shorting. ETFs can provide a solution to all of these concerns.

ETFs AS PRIMARY OR EXCLUSIVE PORTFOLIO COMPONENTS

The exclusive use of ETFs as portfolio component pieces is not a new idea, although it has been possible to implement such a strategy only since 2002. The introduction of fixed-income ETFs and all the great tools that have followed have allowed almost any strategy to be created using only ETFs. We will cover a handful of portfolio ideas, from simple to complicated, to get you thinking about what you can actually implement.

Table 9.3 ETFs as primary or exclusive portfolio components

Traditional asset allocation	Neo asset allocation	Core and satellite	Trading strategies	Hedge fund strategies	Income strategies

Traditional asset allocation

"Traditional" is a very broad term in our business and it is more than a little ironic that the creation of a portfolio using the latest tools can be called traditional. Our use of the term here suggests a long-only, equity/fixed-income/cash portfolio as shown in Figure 9.1.

Neo asset allocation

The latest asset allocation models were built with the belief that asset classes such as commodities would act as a diversifier. This is not always the case but seems to occur often enough to include them. A neo or new asset-allocation concept is always subject to revision and will inevitably change over time. Figure 9.2 represents the thinking of many strategists and modellers from late 2007.

Core and satellite

This is an old strategy that was difficult to effectively implement until the introduction of ETFs. The idea here is simple: the majority

Figure 9.1 Traditional asset allocation

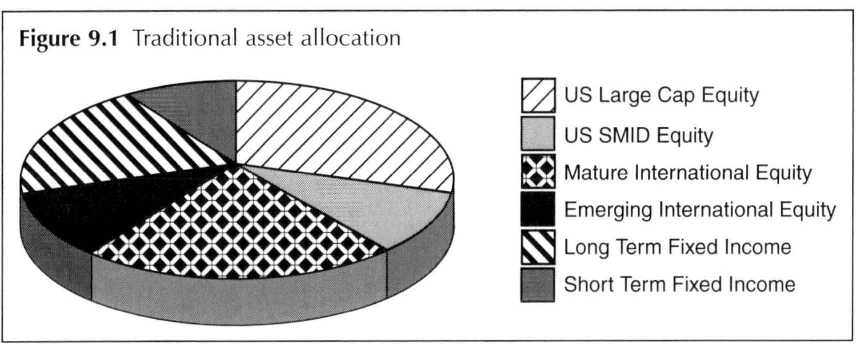

Figure 9.2 Neo asset allocation

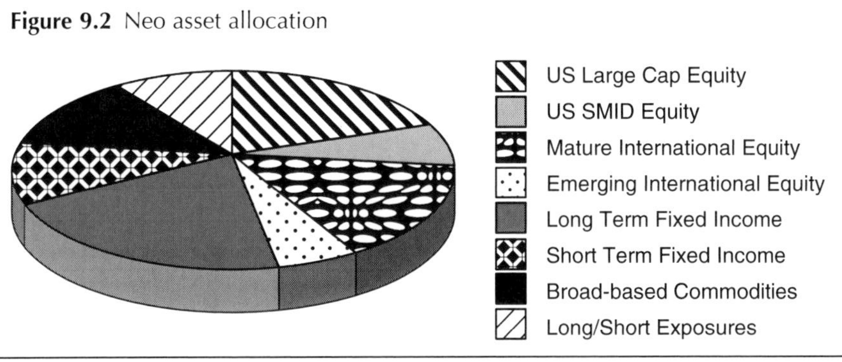

of your assets, usually 70% to 90%, are invested in your primary or core strategy; the satellite strategies are your "bets". These are usually tactical or opportunistic positions representing a short-term trade or opportunity. It is advisable that the satellite investments be a search for alternative exposures and not increased exposure of an asset class that already exists in your core investments. Narrow commodities, currencies and other specialised or narrow exposures are usually found here. One example is in Figure 9.3.

Trading strategies

This is a broad category, but an important one to include, since it is heavily used by ETF investors. The ability to instantly own intraday, liquid exposure is crucial to the success of any trader or tactical investor. Many ETFs turn over their entire portfolio (as calculated by total AUM divided by daily dollar volume) on a weekly basis. Figure 9.4 shows the chart of a highly traded ETF-tracked with Bollinger Bands.

Figure 9.3 Core and satellite

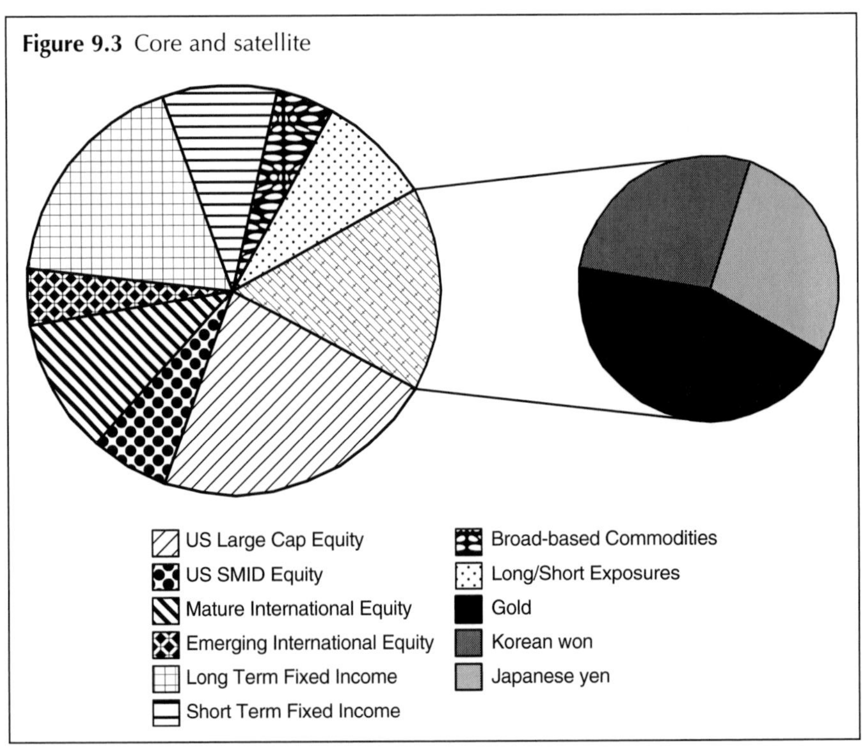

Figure 9.4 Bollinger Bands

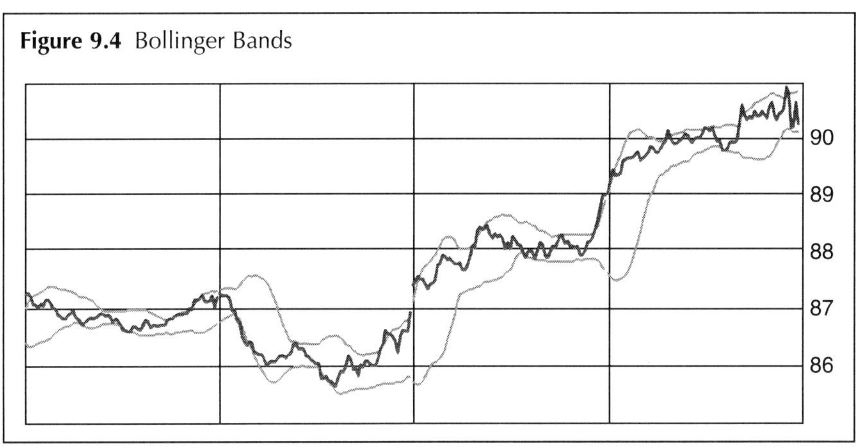

Figure 9.5 Variable long short – example is net long

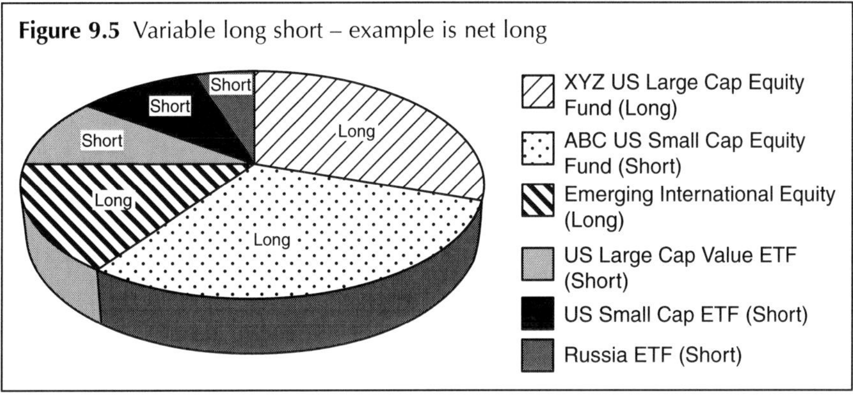

Hedge fund strategies

There are too many hedge fund strategies to list here, so let us cover just a few of the simplest. These strategies, as their name would suggest, allow you to create a portfolio that minimises your market or beta exposure. This exposure can be minimised on a variable basis (variable long/short), implemented as a net short portfolio or fully minimised (market-neutral) depending on your view of the market.

Income strategies

One of the big advantages ETFs may provide is a lower overall internal cost structure. The fees an ETF charges vary greatly, but historically they tend to be meaningfully less expensive on both the equity and fixed-income areas, providing greater cashflow simply due to

Figure 9.6 Market-neutral

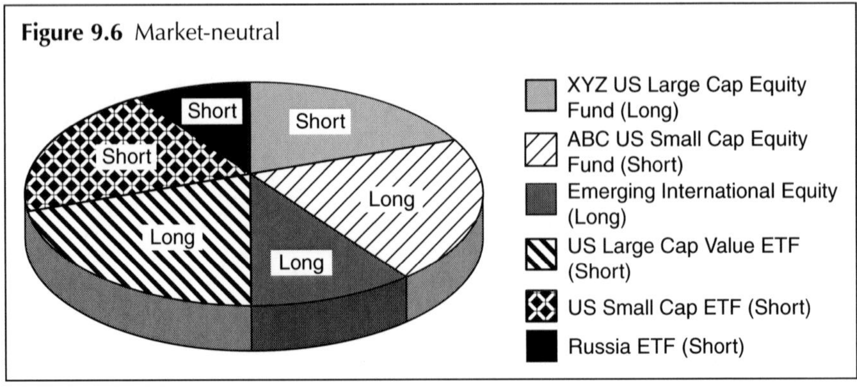

Figure 9.7 Income portfolio

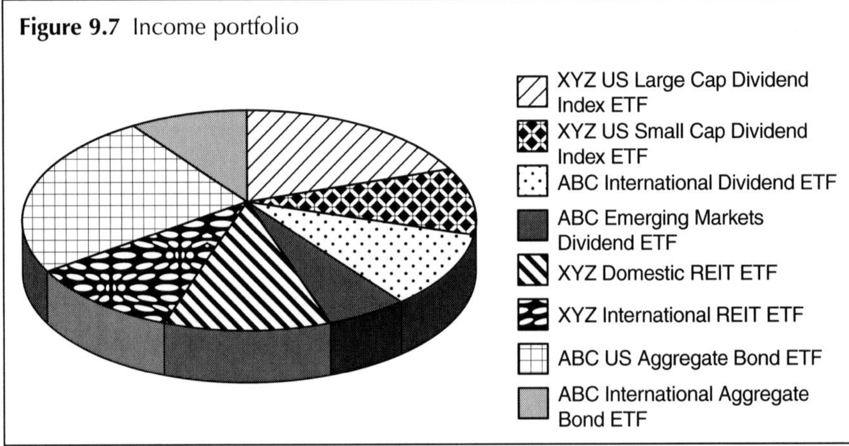

lower costs. As we have seen, it was not until 2002 that fixed-income ETFs became available. Before this time, investors needed to generate income from ETFs through less traditional sources. There are numerous dividend-weighted and REIT ETFs available today for both the domestic and foreign markets. Today, there are likely 100 or more ETFs that can be combined for creating a regular, meaningful flow of income.

10

Creating an All-ETF Portfolio

Richard D. Romey

ETF Portfolio Solutions

WHY CONSIDER EXCHANGE-TRADED FUNDS

In March of 1993, the American Stock Exchange launched the first domestically traded exchange-traded fund (ETF). It was an entirely new type of investment structure that combined the most attractive characteristics of traditional index mutual funds and common stocks. Like an index mutual fund, each ETF share represents ownership in a basket of securities designed to track a market index or benchmark. Like common stocks, ETFs trade throughout the day on organised exchanges, providing a level of liquidity and flexibility not offered by traditional mutual funds.

Based on the initial reaction from the financial services industry, which was less than enthusiastic, it is unlikely that the individuals involved with the development of this first ETF could have foreseen the dramatic impact their creation would ultimately have in the area of finance. There was no reason to believe that within a few years ETFs would have the mutual fund industry on the run; or that ETFs would replace mutual funds as the investment tool of choice for millions of investors. Yet, barely 15 years since the first ETF started trading, that is the reality.

In the area of investment management, ETFs are as revolutionary an invention as the telephone, the light bulb, the personal computer or the Internet. And, while some may feel that such an assertion is ridiculous, it is true. ETFs have revolutionised the way investors build and manage their portfolios by offering low-cost, easy, efficient access to hundreds of diverse asset classes, many of which were never before available to retail investors. Using ETFs, investors can build institutional-strength portfolios at a fraction of the cost of traditional mutual-fund-based portfolios.

Strategies once reserved for the wealthiest individual or institutional investor are now within reach of all investors. In this sense, ETFs have democratised investment management. No more are investors forced to settle for costly mutual-fund strategies or packaged financial products that make sense only for the companies selling them. They have a better choice. The slow, steady death of the mutual-fund industry has begun and ETFs are leading the charge.

ETF market share growth accelerates

In 15 years, ETFs have gone from nonexistent to over US$650 billion in assets under management, making them one of the fastest-growing investment products in the history of Wall Street. While traditional mutual funds still command a lion's share of the marketplace, with an estimated US$12 trillion in assets under management, ETFs are rapidly closing the gap. The threat ETFs pose to the mutual-fund industry was apparent at the Investment Company Institute's 50th Annual General Membership Meeting in May 2008. At the meeting, American Century Investments' president, Jonathan Thomas, said, "ETFs have cannibalised the actively managed space," referring to the rapid growth of ETFs and the impact it was having on traditional actively managed mutual funds.

When net new flows (NNFs) into ETFs and mutual funds are examined, we see why Thomas is concerned. Figure 10.1 shows that ETFs are garnering a larger and larger share of fund flows over the past several years. In 2008, ETFs had net new flows of US$177 billion compared with net outflows from mutual funds of US$224 billion.

As Figure 10.1 indicates, ETFs are taking a larger piece of the pie at the expense of mutual funds. According to William E. Koehler, chief investment officer of ETF Portfolio Solutions, through December 2008 a staggering US$224 billion flowed out of mutual funds while over US$177 billion flowed into ETFs. He believes investors are looking for a new investment paradigm and that a major shift in investor preferences is taking place.

The numbers of new ETFs created are also increasing at a rapid rate. From 1993 to 2000 a total of 92 new ETFs were launched. From 2000 to 2007 that number increased dramatically to over 450 new

Figure 10.1 ETF market share growth accelerates

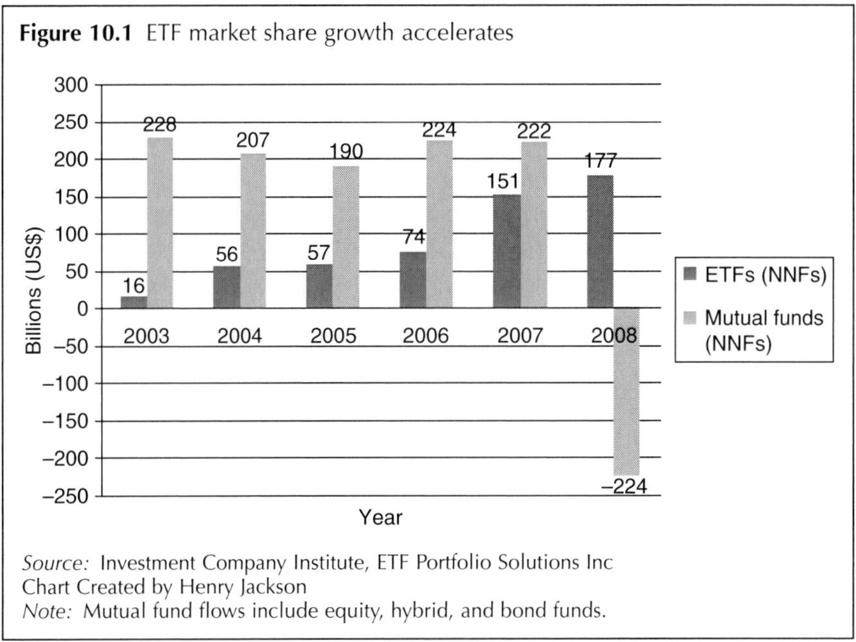

Source: Investment Company Institute, ETF Portfolio Solutions Inc
Chart Created by Henry Jackson
Note: Mutual fund flows include equity, hybrid, and bond funds.

ETFs. In 2008, there were 118 new ETFs introduced according to State Street Global Advisors. This included a number of new leveraged and inverse ETFs. At some point, the number of new ETFs will start to slow and should level out. That would be a very normal development. For now, investor demand shows no sign of slowing. Figure 10.2 illustrates the rapid growth in new ETFs offered over the last 15 years.

Why are ETFs growing at such a rapid pace and taking market share from mutual funds? Simply put, ETFs are a superior investment structure. They offer investors a number of significant advantages over mutual funds.

- ETFs are index-based: The vast majority of ETFs are designed to track the performance of an underlying index or benchmark. Over the years, indexing has proved very difficult for most actively managed fund managers to beat.
- ETFs offer inter-day liquidity: Unlike mutual funds, ETFs can be bought or sold throughout the day on organised exchanges. They offer investors a level of liquidity not available to mutual-fund investors.

Figure 10.2 ETFs experience rapid growth

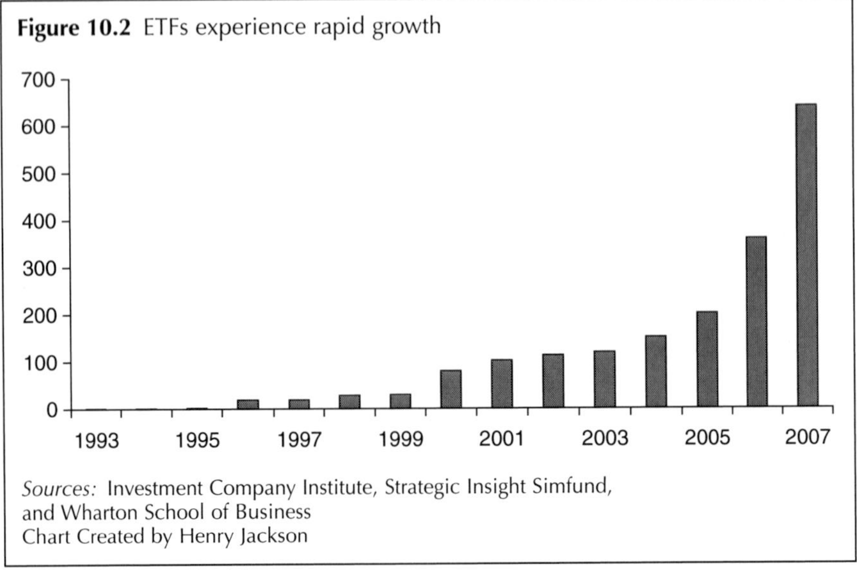

Sources: Investment Company Institute, Strategic Insight Simfund, and Wharton School of Business
Chart Created by Henry Jackson

- ETFs tend to have low internal operating expenses: All mutual funds, both load and no-load, have ongoing operating expenses. In fact, the ongoing cost of ownership represents the single largest expense for a long-term investor. Some funds charge fees in excess of 1.75%. In contrast, ETFs tracking broad-based indexes have average internal fees of less than 0.20%.
- ETFs are very tax-efficient: Unlike actively managed mutual funds, which typically pay large capital gains distributions to shareholders, ETFs limit taxable capital gains distributions to shareholders.

ETFs are the most important financial development in the last 30 years and the driving force behind a revolutionary change in the way investors build and manage their portfolios. There is no other investment vehicle today that combines the advantages associated with ETFs. Using ETFs investors can build and manage highly diversified, low-cost, tax-efficient investment portfolios customised to meet their specific risk and return objectives.

Three advantages of an all-ETF portfolio

In this chapter, we discuss how to use this powerful new type of investment tool to build a better portfolio. As we will see, an all-ETF portfolio offers a number of advantages over traditional mutual-fund and stock-based portfolios. Three key advantages, which we will overview, are lower fees, superior diversification and greater strategy flexibility.

The easiest way to improve performance, all else being equal, is to lower the investment-management fees you pay. The largest single cost associated with mutual-fund ownership is the ongoing management fees. All mutual funds, both load and no-load, have management fees, some in excess of 2% per year. There is an old adage in the investment-management industry about fees: "You get what you don't pay for." If you decrease the investment-related fees associated with a portfolio by 1% per year, it is possible to save tens of thousands of US dollars over the long run. Figure 10.3 shows how much you will pay over time, in fees and lost earnings, based on several different fee structures.

It has been said that diversification is the only free lunch in finance. Unfortunately, most investors fail to get the diversification they need. ETFs fare very efficient diversification tools because they are designed to track specific asset classes. They offer investors access to broad-based equity, fixed income and alternative asset classes. They also allow investors to easily segment these different asset classes by size, style and geographic region. ETFs allow investors easily and efficiently to implement the most basic to the most complex diversification strategy.

Figure 10.3 The cost of investment advice

Annual fees (%)	Actual fees paid and foregone earnings based on a US$100,000 investment and a 10% return, before fees and expenses				
	5 years (US$)	10 years (US$)	15 years (US$)	20 years (US$)	25 years (US$)
0.50	3,986.00	12,680.00	30,256.00	64,173.00	127,610.00
1.00	7,893.00	24,800.00	58,457.00	122,503.00	240,724.00
1.50	11,721.00	36,382.00	84,732.00	175,495.00	340,925.00
2.00	15,473.00	47,446.00	109,206.00	223,616.00	429,634.00
2.50	19,149.00	58,014.00	131,992.00	267,291.00	508,120.00

Source: US Securities and Exchange Commission Mutual fund Fees Calculator
Chart Created by Henry Jackson

ETFs offer investors the same trading flexibility, liquidity and portfolio strategies associated with stocks. For example, you can use a stop-loss or limit order when buying or selling shares of ETFs. You can purchase ETFs on margin, sell them short, and some even allow option strategies. ETFs are a more versatile tool than mutual funds, and that versatility transfers through to the portfolio. Using ETFs, investors can incorporate a wide range of portfolio strategies not available with a mutual-fund portfolio.

The advantages associated with an all-ETF portfolio are significant. In this section, we only addressed the cost savings, diversification and flexibility offered by ETFs. Throughout this chapter, these and other advantages will be discussed in detail.

BUILDING AN ALL-ETF PORTFOLIO

The starting point for every investor, regardless of portfolio size, is to develop a clear, concise, written portfolio plan. At the very least, the plan should outline the investor's goals, risk tolerance and time horizon. In the investment-management industry, we refer to this document as the investment policy statement (IPS). Institutional investors would never think of investing a penny without a plan. They typically have very detailed IPS covering all aspects of the portfolio process, and so should you.

The IPS serves as a roadmap or guide to help keep you on track. It provides guidance when you stray and offers a level of reassurance when the market goes through inevitable corrections or periods of extreme volatility. Unfortunately, most investors spend more time planning their summer holiday than they do planning their investment strategy. Unless you are willing to develop a detailed portfolio plan based on your goals and objectives and commit it to writing, you are not serious about succeeding.

When investors are told that they need a written IPS, questions such as these often arise: "Why does it need to be written?" "Can't I just make the investments and then watch them?" A written IPS serves two important functions: it helps you better understand your goals; and it is a reference manual that you can use over the years to insure that your portfolio is meeting your objectives. The value of having a written guide or instruction manual is clear. If you have ever tried to assemble a bicycle or toy, you know how difficult it can be doing it without written instructions. The author is sure there are some very talented individuals who could easily put together the most difficult project by simply looking at the parts and winging it. For most of us, that would lead to frustration, costly mistakes and a final project that is probably less than perfect.

If you try to assemble something without the directions you could well end up with extra parts. Or, when you are almost through, you realise you should have done something differently in step three and now you need to go back to correct it. Your portfolio is the same. If you try to wing it, you may succeed, but the odds are not in your favour. Messing up the assembly of a toy is one thing; messing up your financial future is another. The largest organisations in the world have detailed written investment plans – and you should, too.

While IPSs vary from one organisation or investor to another, they typically have three basic components.

1. Detailed strategic asset-allocation plan: Strategic asset allocation forms the foundation of a portfolio and is the key determinate of a portfolio's overall risk and expected return.
2. Implementation plan: The strategic asset-allocation plan simply shows which asset classes you want to own and in what percentages. The next step is determining the investment vehicle to implement the plan and specific guidelines for doing so.
3. Rebalancing strategy: How you rebalance, or choose not to rebalance, will have a major impact on the risk and return of the portfolio. Rebalancing is a critical part of the overall portfolio plan.

These three steps, covered in detail in the IPS, form the core of virtually every institutionally managed portfolio. The same three steps can help you build and manage a portfolio of ETFs that will put the odds of winning in your favour.

STRATEGIC ASSET ALLOCATION – DETERMINING YOUR PORTFOLIO'S RISK AND EXPECTED RETURN

Identifying the best long-term strategic asset-allocation mix for your portfolio, based on your risk tolerance and performance objectives, is one of the most important parts to building a portfolio. Asset allocation refers to how an investor chooses to allocate their portfolio among two primary types of assets: equities (stocks) and fixed-income (bonds). By altering the allocation mix among these two broad asset classes, it is possible to change the portfolio's overall risk and expected return. Most investors underestimate the importance of asset allocation. They are led to believe that finding the right mutual-fund manager or stock is the way to succeed.

One of the first studies that detailed the importance of asset allocation was published in 1986 by Brinson, Hood and Beebower. The study examined the returns of 91 large pension plans from 1973 to 1985. The researchers identified three factors that accounted for the majority of the variation in investment returns among the different investment portfolios. These were asset-allocation selection, individual stock selection and market timing. The study found that asset-allocation selection accounted for 93.6% of the variation in total returns over the time period used. In contrast, individual security selection accounted for only 4.2% of the variation in returns, while market timing accounted for only 1.7%. Other factors, such as luck, accounted for 0.5% of the variation in returns.

A number of follow-up studies have confirmed these results. For investors, the studies point out the importance of asset allocation. They make clear the need to focus most of your attention on the asset-allocation decision and spend less time and money on trying to pick winning mutual funds or individual stocks.

Asset allocation allows every investor to find the mix of stocks and bonds that will meet their specific risk-and-return parameters. By altering the percentage mix of a portfolio between stocks and bonds, using historic return data, it is easy to see how the overall risk and return of a portfolio changes. In Figure 10.4 we see the average return and risk associated with different asset allocation mixes.

The portfolios shown in Figure 10.4 are composed of the same two broad-based investments. The only difference is the way the portfolios are allocated between the two investments. The dramatic difference in risk and return shows the power of asset allocation.

From the chart, it is easy to see that altering the mix among stocks and bonds will change the portfolio's overall risk and return. However, these two asset classes (stocks and bonds) are very broad. Research has shown that it is possible to create subgroups within each of these categories. For example, stocks are often grouped based on the size of the company (large-cap, mid-cap, and small-cap) or by investment style (growth or value). For asset-allocation purposes, equity and fixed income is commonly divided into various subgroups or sub-asset classes, shown in Figure 10.5.

Figure 10.4 Risk and return associated with changing asset-allocation mix

Portfolio allocation		Three-year average annualised return* (%)	Worst 1 year loss** (%)
Stocks (%)	Bonds (%)		
100	0	13.08	–21.54
90	10	12.21	–17.94
80	20	11.32	–14.33
70	30	10.44	–10.73
60	40	9.55	–7.13
50	50	8.65	–3.52
40	60	7.74	0.80
30	70	6.83	3.69
20	80	6.12	3.21

Notes: Stocks are represented by the Russell 3000 Index, bonds are represented by the Lehman 7–10 Years US Treasury Index.
*Three-year performance data based on annual rebalancing from 31/05/2004 to 30/04/2007.
**Based on worst calendar year loss from 31/12/1986 to 31/12/2006.

Adding sub-asset classes to the allocation mix

By altering the allocation among various asset classes, like the ones shown in Figure 10.5, it is possible to improve on our basic asset-allocation model. As we saw earlier in this chapter, varying allocations of the Russell 3000 index and the Lehman Aggregate Bond Index produced a set of returns. By adding sub-asset classes, it is possible to create extremely sophisticated asset-allocation strategies and actually improve on the basic model. For example, the average annualised return and risk associated for a portfolio with an 80% allocation to equities and 20% fixed income can be improved. How do the risk and expected return of the portfolio change as we add sub asset classes? In Figure 10.6 we see how the overall portfolio changes by adding additional asset classes.

The advantage of adding additional asset classes to the portfolio allocation is clear. In each portfolio shown in Figure 10.6 it was possible to improve both the average annualised return and risk. Further, we did so without market timing, making complicated predictions about future returns, or by trying to guess which actively managed mutual-fund manager will beat the market. We accomplished this

Figure 10.5 Asset classes

Equity	
US equity	**Foreign equity**
Asset size Large-cap Mid-cap Small-cap Asset style Growth Value	Developed markets Growth Value Emerging markets

Fixed income	
Government	**Corporate**
Maturity Short Intermediate Long	Quality Investment-grade High-yield Maturity (Short, inter-, long)

task through improved diversification using the strategic asset allocation.

In Figure 10.7, a detailed list of asset classes and percentage allocation for nine different portfolios is shown. The portfolios range from aggressive to conservative and can be used to help you create an asset-allocation model for your portfolio.

Which allocation is right for you?

Accepting strategic asset allocation as the best way to build your portfolio is one thing; figuring out what allocation mix is best for you is another. Entire books have been written on this subject. Investment advisers, financial planners and brokers usually put a questionnaire in front of you that asks a lot of questions about how much you are willing to lose if the market drops.

Unfortunately, it is difficult to tell from the answers to some questions on a piece of paper how you will react when the market collapses. Most investors discover they have the wrong asset-allocation mix at the absolute worst time, when the market is down

Figure 10.6 Risk-and-return characteristics of two different asset allocations

Basic 80/20 asset allocation		Strategic asset allocation 80/20	
Equity:		**Equity:**	
Russell 3000 Index	80%	S&P 500 Index	20%
		MSCI EAFE Index	20%
		S&P Mid Cap 400 Index	20%
		S&P Small Cap 600 Index	20%
		Total equity	80%
Fixed income:		**Fixed income:**	
7–10-yr US Tsy Index	20%	7–10-yr US Tsy Index	10%
		1–3-yr US Tsy Index	10%
		Total fixed income	20%
Total portfolio	**100%**	**Total portfolio**	**100%**

Risk-and-return characteristics of portfolio allocation*			**Risk-and-return characteristics of portfolio allocation***		
Time period	**Avg. ann. return (%)**	**Standard deviation (%)**	**Time period**	**Avg. ann. return (%)**	**Standard deviation (%)**
3 yrs	1.79	8.86	3 yrs	2.62	9.57
5 yrs	5.78	8.23	5 yrs	7.89	9.12
10 yrs	4.67	11.18	10 yrs	7.23	11.39

Source: Barclays Global Investors
*Based on annual rebalancing as of 30/9/2008.

Figure 10.7 Strategic asset-allocation models

Asset class	Aggressive allocations			Moderate allocations			Conservative allocations		
	100/0	90/10	80/20	70/30	60/40	50/50	40/60	30/70	20/80
US equity broad-based asset classes									
Large-cap core	30.0	27.0	24.0	21.0	18.0	15.0	12.0	9.0	6.0
Mid-cap core	18.0	16.2	14.4	12.6	10.8	9.0	7.2	5.4	3.6
Small-cap core	10.0	9.0	8.0	7.0	6.0	5.0	4.0	3.0	2.0
Total US equity	58.0	52.2	46.4	40.6	34.8	29.0	23.2	17.4	11.6
Foreign equity									
Developed markets large cap	30.0	27.0	24.0	21.0	18.0	15.0	12.0	9.0	6.0
Emerging markets	12.0	10.8	9.6	8.4	7.2	6.0	4.8	3.6	2.4
Total Foreign Equity	42.0	37.8	33.6	29.4	25.2	21.0	16.8	12.6	8.4
Total US equity broad-based allocation	**100.0**	**90.0**	**80.0**	**70.0**	**60.0**	**50.0**	**40.0**	**30.0**	**20.0**
Fixed income									
US Treasuries (7–10 years)	0.0	5.0	10.0	15.0	20.0	25.0	30.0	35.0	40.0
Interm. Investment-Grade Corp	0.0	5.0	10.0	15.0	20.0	25.0	30.0	35.0	40.0
Total fixed-income allocation	**0.0**	**10.0**	**20.0**	**30.0**	**40.0**	**50.0**	**60.0**	**70.0**	**80.0**
Total portfolio	**100.0**	**100.0**	**100.0**	**100.0**	**100.0**	**100.0**	**100.0**	**100.0**	**100.0**

dramatically and a large part of their net worth has disappeared. That is when the financial experts are telling you to hold the course and wait it out.

Another way to try and find the right allocation mix is to look at the potential losses in terms of actual US dollars instead of percentages. For example, it is pretty easy to say that you can take a 20% loss in your portfolio. It is another to say you can take a loss of US$40,000 based on a US$200,000 portfolio. What the author likes to do is show investors the following table and ask them where the pain starts to come in. In Figure 10.8 a spreadsheet is used to help you determine the corresponding US dollar loss associated with various percentage losses.

Be honest with yourself. Determine the maximum acceptable level of pain you can handle and then pick a strategic asset allocation model that has historically lost less in bad years. Remember, strategic asset allocation provides only a guide for what type of risk and return you may see. Your actual returns could be very different and your losses far worse. It is not a perfect science.

Your tolerance for risk will probably change over time. For example, as you near retirement it might make you feel more comfortable to have less of your portfolio exposed to equities. When you are younger it tends to be easier to take a longer-term view and look past current market fluctuations.

IMPLEMENTATION – ETFs OFFER THE BEST SOLUTION

Once the strategic asset-allocation plan is completed, the next step is to determine the best investment tool to implement the allocation

Figure 10.8 US dollar losses based on percentage losses

Portfolio value (US$)	Portfolio loss in percentage and dollars				
	–5.0% (US$)	–10.0% (US$)	–15.0% (US$)	–20.0% (US$)	–25.0% (US$)
50,000.00	(2,500.00)	(5,000.00)	(7,500.00)	(10,000.00)	(12,500.00)
100,000.00	(5,000.00)	(10,000.00)	(15,000.00)	(20,000.00)	(25,000.00)
200,000.00	(10,000.00)	(20,000.00)	(30,000.00)	(40,000.00)	(50,000.00)
300,000.00	(15,000.00)	(30,000.00)	(45,000.00)	(60,000.00)	(75,000.00)
400,000.00	(20,000.00)	(40,000.00)	(60,000.00)	(80,000.00)	(100,000.00)
500,000.00	(25,000.00)	(50,000.00)	(75,000.00)	(100,000.00)	(125,000.00)
750,000.00	(37,500.00)	(75,000.00)	(112,500.00)	(150,000.00)	(187,500.00)
1,000,000.00	(50,000.00)	(100,000.00)	(150,000.00)	(200,000.00)	(250,000.00)

mix. It is at this point that many investors and investment advisers take an interesting leap of logic. They implement the asset-allocation plan using actively managed mutual funds.

As we saw in an earlier section, strategic asset allocation is a diversification strategy based on the idea that how you allocate your portfolio among different asset classes is more important than individual stock selection or market timing. At the heart of every actively managed mutual fund is the belief that the fund's manager can add value through superior stock selection or market timing, the very idea that asset-allocation theory disproves. The additional costs associated with individual stock-selection strategies add additional hurdles for the fund manager to overcome. Traditional actively managed mutual funds attempt to do the very thing that asset-allocation theory tells us provides little or no value. Therefore, when an investor or investment adviser creates an asset-allocation plan and then implements it using actively managed mutual funds, they are being intellectually dishonest since one contradicts the other.

For asset allocation to work, you need an investment tool that closely mirrors both the expected return and risk of the underlying asset class in the model. Actively managed mutual funds do not offer pure asset-class tracking. In contrast, exchange-traded funds do making them the best way to implement an asset-allocation strategy.

For asset-allocation purposes, ETFs offer investors a combination of advantages not offered by actively managed mutual funds, index-based mutual funds or common stocks. When implementing an asset-allocation plan, there are several key features ETFs offer.

- Index-based tracking: ETFs are index-based and indexing is the best way to track specific asset classes.
- Inter-day liquidity: ETFs allow investors actively to manage and rebalance their portfolio throughout the day. Mutual funds, in contrast, limit when investors can make changes to their portfolio.
- Limit style drift and cash drag: Actively managed mutual funds tend to hold cash and shift from one investment style to another. This can hurt the effectiveness of your asset-allocation plan.

Strategic asset allocation is the best way to build a portfolio. It works only if the right investment tools are used to implement it. Actively managed mutual funds can actually mitigate many of the advantages asset allocation provides.

Choosing the right ETFs to implement your portfolio when multiples exist

Based on the advantages they offer, there is no questioning that ETFs are the best tool for investors to use when implementing an asset-allocation strategy. They are institutional-strength tools that allow investors to implement, easily and efficiently, virtually any asset-allocation strategy, from the most conservative to the most aggressive. However, with close to 700 ETFs available, how do you choose which ETFs you should use?

The first step is to segment the ETF market based on the type of index or benchmark the ETF is tracking. The list in Figure 10.9 provides a good breakdown.

To implement the asset-allocation plan we simply need to find an ETF that tracks the same or similar index that we want access to. For example, if our strategic asset-allocation model is based on the S&P 500 index, we would want to find an ETF that tracks the S&P 500 index. Likewise, if large-cap stocks are represented using the Russell 1000 in our strategic asset-allocation model we would want to find an ETF that tracks the Russell 1000 index.

When there are several ETFs tracking the same index, it is important to consider the following factors:

- the internal expense ratio of the ETFs;
- index tracking error of the ETF; and
- tracking strategy (full replication or sampling) trading volume and price spread

Figure 10.10 provides an example of how some ETFs may track the same underlying index or asset class. As you can see, the instances of the same index being tracked by more than just a couple of ETFs are rare.

When implementing the strategic asset-allocation plan, the goal is to find ETFs that track the same underlying asset class as used in developing the plan. This is usually easy to do and allows you to match the allocation plan very closely.

REBALANCING YOUR PORTFOLIO

In the previous sections, we examined the benefits of strategic asset allocation and discussed how to implement the plan using ETFs. In this section, our focus shifts to the final component of the IPS. It is

Figure 10.9 Example of some of the available equity ETFs by asset class

Broad-market ETFs

ETF name	Symbol	Expense ratio (%)
iShares Russell 3000	IWV	0.20
iShares S&P 1500	ISI	0.20
SPDR Wilshire Total Market	TMW	0.20
Vanguard Total Stock Market	VTI	0.07

Large-cap ETFs

ETF name	Symbol	Expense ratio (%)
iShares Russell 1000	IWB	0.15
iShares Russell 1000 Growth	IWF	0.20
iShares Russell 1000 Value	IWD	0.20
iShares S&P 500	IVV	0.09
iShares S&P 500 Growth	IVW	0.18
iShares S&P 500 Value	IVE	0.18
SPDR S&P 500	SPY	0.10
Vanguard Mega Cap 300	MGC	0.13

Mid-cap ETFs

ETF name	Symbol	Expense ratio (%)
iShares Russell Mid Cap	IWR	0.20
iShares Russell Mid Cap Growth	IWP	0.25
iShares Russell Mid Cap Value	IWS	0.25
Vanguard Mid Cap	VO	0.13
Vanguard Mid Cap Growth	VOT	0.13
Vanguard Mid Cap Value	VOE	0.13
SPDR Wilshire Mid Cap	EMM	0.25
SPDR Wilshire Mid Cap Growth	EMG	0.25
SPDR Wilshire Mid Cap Value	EMV	0.25

Small-cap ETFs

ETF name	Symbol	Expense ratio (%)
iShares Russell 2000	IWM	0.20
iShares Russell 2000 Growth	IWO	0.25
iShares Russell 2000 Value	IWN	0.25
Vanguard Small Cap	VB	0.10
Vanguard Small Cap Growth	VBK	0.12
Vanguard Small Cap Value	VBR	0.12
SPDR Wilshire Small Cap	DSC	0.25
SPDR Wilshire Small Cap Growth	DSG	0.25
SPDR Wilshire Small Cap Value	DSV	0.25

Figure 10.10 Example of multiple ETFs tracking the same underlying index

Underlying Index	ETFs Tracking the Index
S&P 500 Index	iShares S&P 500 Index ETF SPDR S&P 500 Index ETF
MSCI EAFE	iShares EAFE Index ETF Vanguard Europe/Pacific ETF
Lehman Aggregate Bond	SPDR Lehman Aggregate Bond ETF iShares Lehman Aggregate Bond ETF Vanguard Total Bond Market ETF

important to have a rebalancing strategy in place to help ensure your portfolio stays on track. Remember, everyone has a rebalancing strategy whether they know it or not. If you choose not to rebalance, the market does it for you. Unfortunately, the market does not know your risk tolerance and goals and may not always provide you with the optimal mix.

Why is it important to rebalance your portfolio? As soon as you implement your portfolio market changes will alter the mix. Over time, these changes can dramatically change the risk of your portfolio. For example, a portfolio has an initial 15% allocation to large-cap growth stocks. Over the next few years growth stocks far outperform other asset classes, leaving the portfolio with a 25% allocation in large-cap growth stocks. By not rebalancing, the investor let the portfolio get riskier than intended.

This is what happened during most of the 1990s. Growth stocks in general, and large-cap growth stocks in particular, did very well. If an investor did not rebalance their portfolio by the end of the decade they had a far greater allocation to growth stocks than intended. The portfolio would have greater risk.

When the market corrected, from 1999 through 2001, the hardest hit were large-cap growth stocks. By not rebalancing on a regular basis your portfolio became riskier and riskier. The market corrects and you get hammered. If you had started with a diversified portfolio and continually rebalanced throughout the 1990s, when the correction came your portfolio would have held up better than many.

A systematic rebalancing plan would have helped moderate the decline, since it would have kept you from getting too far away from the intended asset-allocation model. Two of the most used strategies for rebalancing a portfolio are based on a given point in time and tolerance bands. Each has positives and negatives, which we will discuss.

Following an acceptable range or "tolerance bands" when rebalancing is becoming more popular. One reason is that computer technology and easily available pricing data make it far easier to manage than just a few years ago. Using this method, we determine tolerance bands for each asset we own. For example, for broad-based asset classes the band may be 20%. As long as the asset class stays within 20% of the initial allocation, no changes are made. If large-cap stocks were initially 10% of the portfolio, they would not be rebalanced until they reached 12% or fell to 8% of the portfolio. These bands are calculated as follows:

- upper limit: initial allocation 10% + (initial allocation 10% × tolerance band 20%) = 12%; and
- lower limit: initial allocation 10% – (initial allocation 10% × tolerance band 20%) = 8%

Once the bands are set the portfolio is monitored on a regular basis. You might like to review weekly to determine if any asset class has moved outside of its tolerance range. When an asset moves beyond its range, you simply rebalance it back to it is original allocation.

The most commonly used rebalancing strategy is to rebalance based on a predetermined time such as annually, semiannually, quarterly or monthly. Even though this is the most used and touted by many financial professionals, it has a number of shortcomings.

The problem with this approach is that it does not take into consideration that the markets are fluid, continually changing. A recent example is from 2007. The market started strong and by September many asset classes had posted returns in excess of 15% to 20%. The market started correcting in October and by December was essentially at the level it was at the start of the year.

For investors rebalancing annually, in December, they missed out on the huge market run-up from January to September. They did not move out of top-performing asset classes and reap the rewards associated with a strong market. Instead, they watched their profits disappear and did nothing. Markets are continually moving and changing, so you need a rebalance strategy that reflects that. Using tolerance bands, you rebalance when the market tells you, not on some predetermined point in time.

THE NEXT STEP – GETTING STARTED

Once you have determined your optimal strategic asset allocation, decided which ETFs to use and decided on the best rebalancing strategy, the next step is to implement the portfolio. In the implementation phase you take your plan, from the IPS, and put it into action. It is at this point that many investors freeze up and doubt takes over. What if the market goes down after I invest? Am I doing the right thing? Should I go with a different plan?

While it is important to evaluate and analyse your investment strategy thoroughly, there comes a point when you must take action. Otherwise, you spend your entire life waiting. By not making a decision to invest you are deciding to do nothing, which is often the wrong decision. More money is lost because investors fail to take action than by market declines. Some investors hold poor-performing, expensive investment products because they are afraid of change. Another reason is that they do not want to sell at a loss. They would rather hold on and hope their investment comes back instead of moving to a better situation.

Unless you are suddenly handed a large sum of money, you will probably need to sell some or all of your current investments to implement a new strategy. It is hard to do. After all, you liked the investment enough to buy it. Selling is an admission that you made a mistake. However, if you stay with inferior investments you will lose valuable time and opportunity. Over the long run, failing to act is the main reason most investors fail to achieve their goals.

When you have decided to change your portfolio and are ready to start, the most important question that must be resolved is whether to go it alone or seek out help. There are advantages and disadvantages to both, which need to be considered.

Going it alone

The decision to manage your own portfolio often turns on a question of time and enjoyment – more specifically, how much time you have to devote to the management of your portfolio and whether or not you enjoy doing it. Before you decide to manage your own portfolio you must be sure you are willing to commit the time and energy necessary. If you have a habit of getting enthusiastic about a project and then losing interest after the newness wears off, do not try to manage your own portfolio. You will only end up regretting it.

There are many things that we have the time and ability to do, but simply do not enjoy. Likewise, there are many things we have the time to do, but do not do well. If you enjoy managing your own money and you have the ability to stick with it and the time to do it, then you should. Before taking on your portfolio management you need to ask yourself some tough questions and be honest with your answers. The author would recommend the self-test shown in Figure 10.11.

If your total score is over 10, you should do fine managing your own money. If your score is under 10, you might want to find outside help.

Treat yourself as you would any other money manager. You need to decide on a benchmark to judge your performance and set up a routine to review your portfolio. It is important that you ask yourself tough questions. Evaluate your performance as harshly as you would evaluate a hired money manager. If you find it is more than you want to do, you should consider hiring a professional money manager to help you with your ETF portfolio.

Figure 10.11 Questions to consider before managing your own portfolio

For every "Yes" answer give yourself 3 points. For every "No" answer give yourself 1 point.

Questions to consider	Score
1 Do I have the time?	________
2 Do I enjoy it?	________
3 Can I remain calm during times of market volatility?	________
4 Do I have the knowledge, or can I acquire the knowledge necessary to build and manage my own portfolio?	________
5 Do I have the ability to stick to my portfolio plan regardless of market or economic activity?	________
6 Can I think and act independently instead of following the "crowd"?	________
Total score	________

Seeking out help

If you do not have the time or desire to manage your own portfolio you will need to find help. Find an adviser with similar investment beliefs as you have. If you go to a broker who believes they can pick winning stocks and ask them to manage an ETF-based portfolio following the strategies suggested in this chapter, you will probably get a very cool reception.

When searching for help, use the following guidelines and questions. These are only a few of the questions you might want to ask. Remember, no question is off limits. It is your money and they work for you. Too often, investors are made to feel as if they work for the broker or adviser. The broker acts as if they are doing you a favour to manage your portfolio. That is unacceptable.

Consider the questions, shown in Figure 10.12.

FINAL THOUGHTS

In this chapter we tried to provide a roadmap to help you create and manage a portfolio entirely comprising ETFs. It may seem like a very simple, almost basic, approach, but it works. Wall Street has a habit of making money management seem more difficult than it is.

Figure 10.12 Questions to ask a potential financial adviser

1. How do you get paid? (This is a tough one for some investors to ask, but it is important to know.)
2. If the adviser is paid based on an asset-based fee, find out what the expenses are associated with the underlying investments they will be using to manage your portfolio.
3. How long have you been advising clients?
4. What is the average account size you manage and how much do you have under management?
5. What types of investment tools do you use and why?
6. How often will I hear from you regarding my account?
7. Can I have a list of references who have used your services?
8. What are your overriding investment beliefs?

The strategies put forth in this chapter can help every investor build a portfolio that meets their goals. However, it is up to you to follow through. You need to take the next step and decide that you are ready to move in a new direction. The hardest part is to step up and commit to doing it. Investing is too important to leave to chance. Your financial future depends on it. Become informed, learn about the investment strategies put forward in this book and get started today.

REFERENCE

Brinson, G. P., L. Randolph Hood and G. L. Beebower, 1986, "Determinants of Portfolio Performance", *Financial Analysts Journal*, July–August.

11

Exchange-Traded Funds and Tactical Asset Allocation

Michael E. Kitces, Kenneth R. Solow

Pinnacle Advisory Group

Tactical asset allocation may best be defined by contrasting it with the more traditional industry method of portfolio construction, popularly known as strategic asset allocation. Strategic asset allocation is a method of building portfolios where the percentage weightings of the asset classes in the portfolio are presumed to deliver the most "efficient" mix of return and portfolio volatility. The intellectual and academic foundation for constructing portfolios in this manner is built from modern portfolio theory (MPT) (Markowitz), the efficient-markets hypothesis (Fama), and the capital asset pricing model (CAPM) (Sharpe).

Harry Markowitz's famous paper (1952) is credited as being the granddaddy of modern financial thought, and Markowitz's ideas about portfolio construction continue to resonate in every corner of the institutional money-management industry today. Essentially, Markowitz concluded that investors must be interested in the risk and reward of their entire portfolio, as opposed to being interested only in the investment characteristics of the individual securities that comprise the portfolio. Markowitz's essential breakthrough was to realise that investors were interested in total portfolio risk as well as return, and that the characteristics of an overall portfolio may be different than the mere sum of its parts. He gave us statistical tools to select from a given mix of securities (or asset classes) the appropriate allocation for an optimal portfolio that would maximise expected return for a given level of risk. Today, the idea of constructing portfolios that lie on an efficient frontier of possible portfolio constructions is ubiquitous to modern investing. At the time, though, applying the tools of normal distributions, average returns, variance and correlations, to develop a model for portfolio construction, was a novel way to view the aggregate portfolio construction.

Sharpe significantly advanced Markowitz's work by giving us the CAPM, and with it a methodology to short-cut the many calculations needed to identify the cross correlations, standard deviations and average returns, for every security (or asset class) in a portfolio. His contributions established the industry standard measures of beta and alpha, to quantify (respectively) the risk of an asset relative to the market and the amount that an investment has outperformed its expected risk and return based on the CAPM model. Alpha in turn became the Holy Grail for all investment managers.

The last part of the intellectual and academic basis for strategic asset allocation is the efficient market hypothesis originally proposed by Eugene Fama in the early 1960s. Fama's idea assumed that financial markets price assets perfectly efficiently based on available information – in other words, to assume that markets (at least in the aggregate) must know all available information and that therefore all information would always be fully reflected in the market price. And, even if no one market participant knew everything, it could be assumed, based on the law of large numbers, that when you put together millions of investors, all of whom have access in the aggregate to all available public information about a security, and all of whom are pursuing their own individual best interests, their estimate of the true value of a security would be so efficient that it would be virtually impossible for any one investor to "beat" the market.

At the intersection of the work of Markowitz, Sharpe and Fama was the quintessential idea that if asset prices fully reflect all available information at all times, and a market portfolio can be constructed that maximises the efficiency of returns for a given level of risk, and risk itself can be measured by the volatility of the market itself, then a passive, strategic portfolio could be constructed that could not be improved upon.

This conclusion is somewhat ironic, though, since, when Markowitz first crafted his paper on portfolio selection, the first paragraph suggests that the portfolio construction process involves two stages where "the first stage begins with observations and experience and ends with beliefs about the future performances of available securities". Over the years the institutional investment industry used Fama's Efficient Markets Hypothesis as a reason to eliminate the need for the first stage of the portfolio construction process as originally proposed by Markowitz, because with efficient markets there was no longer any need to establish relevant beliefs about the future performance of asset classes. Instead, investors using MPT and CAPM could use past data about security performance in order in run these models under the assumption that markets were efficient and investors would reward asset classes with similar risk premiums, correlations and standard deviations in the future as they had in the past.

As stated earlier, the result of these three famous bodies of work is that strategic investors can build a multiple-asset-class portfolio that is assumed to lie on an efficient frontier of all possible portfolios which can be constructed from the universe of asset classes available to the model. This strategic portfolio construction does not change due to changing economic conditions because the underlying theory supposes that markets are efficient. Each asset class in the portfolio is normally "rebalanced" back to the target percentage weightings determined at the beginning of the investment process, typically either on a calendar basis or on a rules basis. Finally, for most strategic, buy-and-hold investors, they will decide whether to use indexes to invest in each portfolio asset class, or they will decide to use active managers, in the form of either mutual funds or separate account managers, to invest each asset class. For strategic investors, the most important decision to be made about active management pertains to whether they should use active managers to invest within each asset class, as opposed to actively managing the amongst asset classes themselves. To the extent an active manager is used, it is generally only in the belief that the particular sub-segment of the market may be less than perfectly efficient (such that an active manager may provide value), but is still in the context of an overall asset allocation that is presumed to be optimally efficient with the proper level of risk, based on MPT and CAPM.

One last practical point about strategic asset allocation is worth mentioning. In the strategic thought process, the expected performance of asset classes is assumed to appear over long periods of time. To the extent that the portfolio might not deliver expected returns over any shorter-term time horizon, it is still presumed that "time diversification" will eventually allow multiple periods of disparate performance to average out to the anticipated long-term return. As a result, investors are routinely asked to be patient until expected returns appear at some point in the future. Functionally, this means that investors are asked to endure whatever short-term volatility the market delivers in exchange for achieving expected returns over longer-term periods of 20 years or more. The volatility of strategic portfolios is usually managed by the percentage allocation to the most volatile asset class in the portfolio, generally classed as stocks or equities (which will typically include both US and international stocks as a subset). Higher stock allocations are associated with higher and less predictable portfolio volatility in the short term, but are assumed to deliver higher long-term returns for investors in the long run.

TACTICAL ASSET ALLOCATION

Tactical asset allocators reject many of the basic assumptions underlying the strategic, buy-and-hold approach. As a result, they focus on actively changing the asset allocation of the portfolio based on their changing perceptions of value opportunities that are presented by the marketplace at any point in time. Instead of believing that markets are efficient, tactical asset allocators believe that markets are inefficient, and that examples of the "herd behaviour" of investors are so overwhelming that they cannot be ignored. Examples of market bubbles and investor panics surround us, and it is hard to deny the "madness of crowds" when considering the recent history of the Nasdaq bubble, the real estate bubble and now the credit bubble, all of which speak of the incredible ability of investors to suspend common sense in pursuit of profits in a bubble environment.

In fact, there are several important assumptions necessary for MPT and CAPM that tactical investors would take issue with. Some of these include the following.

- There are no transaction costs in buying and selling securities; no brokerage fees, no spreads, and no taxes of any kind.
- An investor can take a position in any security they wishes of any size without moving the market. Liquidity is infinite.

- Investors are indifferent to the tax consequences of investing and do not care about dividends and capital-gains distributions.
- Investors are rational and risk-averse. They will always demand the highest possible returns for a tolerable level of risk.
- Investors, as a group, have the same investment time horizon. A short-term speculator and a long-term investor have the exact same motivation to invest.
- Investors all measure risk the same way. All investors have the same information and will buy or sell based on an identical assessment of the investment regardless of their situation, and all expect the same thing from the investment.
- Investors seek to control risk only by the diversification of their holdings.
- Investors can lend or borrow at the risk-free rate, and can also sell short without restriction.
- Investor psychology and other sources of potential endogenous uncertainty have no effect on the market.

Many of these assumptions are obviously simplistic and do not need to be commented on here. Nonetheless, investors who follow the passive, strategic asset allocation approach at least inherently assume that the discrepancies of some of these assumptions can be reasonably ignored. On the other hand, investors who choose tactical asset allocation reject the idea that these assumptions can be safely ignored when implementing a portfolio strategy. For tactical investors, there is both a need to find a more robust theoretical basis for investment decisions than the reliance on efficient markets, and a belief that such a framework can be utilised successfully.

In addition to being troubled by the many tortured assumptions necessary to bring strategic asset allocation models to equilibrium, tactical investors are also aware of the large and growing body of research that shows that stocks do not, in fact, always deliver expected historical returns over all long-term time periods. Instead, it has become evident that the price/earnings (P/E) multiple of the market at the time of purchase, as well as whether or not the P/E multiple rises or falls over the subsequent holding period for the stock market, is a major determinant of market returns.

Ed Easterling, director of Crestmont Research, constructed the chart represented by Table 11.1 to illustrate the point. Easterling

Table 11.1 20-year returns ending 1999–2005 (87 periods)

Decile	Compound annual total returns by decile range			Average beginning P/E	Average ending P/E
	From (%)	To (%)	Average (%)		
1	1.20	4.50	3.20	19	9
2	4.50	5.20	4.90	18	9
3	5.20	5.40	5.30	12	12
4	5.40	5.80	5.60	14	12
5	5.90	7.20	6.70	14	14
6	7.20	8.80	8.30	17	18
7	9.00	9.30	9.20	15	17
8	9.40	10.80	10.40	11	20
9	11.00	11.90	11.70	12	22
10	11.90	15.00	13.40	10	29

Source: Crestmont Research – Total returns shown net of gains, dividends, and transaction costs of 2%

groups the returns of the S&P 500 index (adjusted for dividends, and reduced by an expense factor for trading costs) into 10 deciles from lowest to highest returns. He evaluates 87 different 20-year periods in his study, with end-years from 1919 to 2005. For each of the nine 20-year periods within each performance decile, he gives us the range of compounded annual returns for the stock market as well as the average return per decile. Finally, he gives us the average beginning and ending P/E ratio for the stock market for each decile. Easterling uses the P/E data from Robert Shiller at Yale University, who in turn utilises 10 years of trailing inflation-adjusted earnings to normalise his P/E calculations.

The results of the study are startling for those who expect that buying and holding stocks for 20 years is long enough to assure that expected average past returns will be realised. Instead, the data shows that buying stocks in situations where the P/E multiple is high and declines during the subsequent 20-year period can clearly and consistently lead to the lowest 20-year annualised returns. In this case, the range of 20-year annual returns when buying the market at high valuation levels (when the P/E multiple averaged 19) was an extremely low 1.2% to 4.5%, with an average of only 3.2%. Of course, the data also shows that buying stocks when the P/E multiple is low and expanding results in much better-than-average returns over the subsequent 20-year period. In this case, buying and holding the market when the P/E multiple is a low 10 results in average annual subsequent returns of 13.4%.

The data overwhelmingly supports the idea that market valuations have a dramatic impact on subsequent expected returns from buying and holding stocks, even over long periods of time – emphasising the importance of market valuation and challenging the underlying passive strategic assumption of efficient markets. As a result, tactical investors conclude that it is unreasonable to believe that buying and holding at high valuations will earn average returns (they will be lower), and likewise that buying and holding at low valuations will not earn average returns either (they will be higher). Therefore, the most fundamental approach to tactical investing is to try to identify markets or asset classes that have good value, and overweight them in the portfolio, or, alternatively, to find markets or asset classes that have especially poor value, and underweight them.

The primary problem with strategic asset allocation is that buying and holding the market when it has poor value will almost certainly result in disappointing returns (and likewise that failing to own more of the market when it has favourable value may leave additional return opportunities on the table). The problem with tactical asset allocation is trying to define what constitutes good and bad value. Different practitioners will define good value in a variety of different ways, yet ultimately the goal is the same. Tactical investors want to actively manage the asset allocation of the portfolio in order to take advantage of market or investor inefficiencies in order to earn excess returns over time.

ENDOGENOUS RISK AND FORECASTING THE NEWS

The basis for actively managing portfolios can be broken down into two separate and distinct philosophies, both of which can be defended by recent academic literature and real-world observation of portfolio results.[1]

One approach for actively managing portfolios relies on the idea that investors are responsible for a significant percentage of price volatility in investment markets. Although this notion is rejected in traditional economic theory, where price movements are only the result of exogenous risk (news) that causes prices to change and any other volatility is simply due to the unpredictable random walk of stock prices, tactical investors believe that endogenous risk (the aggregate behaviour of market participants themselves) can be a major cause of price movement. One tactical asset-allocation strategy is to forecast the behaviour of investors and anticipate their subsequent impact on prices. Typical investment strategies that rely on this type of portfolio construction are momentum investing strategies, many risk arbitrage strategies and any other strategy that attempts to profit from price overshoots and undershoots that are the result of the mass psychology of investors. As investors in the aggregate move the markets to pricing extremes, thereby causing the price of an asset to deviate from its intrinsic fair value, opportunities are created for investors to profit either during the movements towards the extremes, or as prices move back from the extremes towards fair value.

The second type of tactical philosophy attempts to better forecast the news than the consensus of investors. This strategy is very much akin to traditional value investment strategies that require investors to understand the fundamentals of the broad markets, sectors, industries or individual securities that comprise their portfolio. Proponents of this strategy strive to understand global macroeconomic trends and their subsequent impact on the market cycle to position the portfolio to take advantage of value opportunities before they are recognised by the consensus. For tactical asset allocators, though, this top-down valuation approach to the markets tends to focus on evaluating the value of asset classes themselves (and sometimes also sectors and industries), and not necessarily the underlying stocks that comprise those market segments, thus literally reflecting the name tactical asset allocation as opposed to tactical "stock selection".

Perhaps the most important and least obvious point to be made about tactical asset allocation is that it assumes that investors will try to earn excess returns over and above market returns. A basic premise of the efficient-markets hypothesis is that investors cannot reliably be expected to outperform the market, and therefore the best that investors should hope for is to earn the most efficient market return, as defined by the cross section of returns and risk. Because of this belief, strategic investors place the highest possible weight on minimising taxes and expenses, since they are a drag on investors being able to earn what are otherwise assumed to be the best possible returns – market returns. For strategic investors, theoretically there is no other way to deliver market-beating returns at the level of the portfolio's asset allocation without, by definition, changing the risk of the portfolio. Ironically, if strategic asset allocators do wish to achieve market-beating returns, they believe (the obvious exception being the subset of investors who index all of their holdings) that excess returns can be earned only by employing active money managers to manage the securities underlying each asset class in their portfolio, but not the asset classes themselves. There seems to be a clear conflict in their belief in buying and holding asset classes because markets are efficient, and their willingness to utilise active managers to beat the market of securities that comprise each asset class.

Tactical investors, on the other hand, believe that there are many market inefficiencies to be found in their evaluation of the value characteristics of asset classes, and therefore they will actively manage their asset allocation in order to maximise return and minimise risk for their investments. Of course, tactical investors will also evaluate the relative benefits of using active managers to invest each asset class. The clear difference is that tactical investors could use a variety of passively managed investment choices such as index mutual funds and especially exchanged-traded funds to invest each asset class in their portfolio, yet still be actively managing the asset allocation of the portfolio itself based on the investment opportunities that present themselves at the time. The belief and intent to earn excess returns is a primary motivation for tactical asset allocators, but, moreover, tactical asset allocators believe that other investors are seeking the same excess returns – and that some may fail in the attempt to do so and cause securities to become mispriced – and opportunities for excess return will themselves be created in the process.

Figures 11.1 and 11.2 present a simple comparison of strategic asset allocation versus tactical asset allocation. Figure 11.1 shows a simple, strategically managed portfolio in two different valuation regimes. In the high-P/E valuation regime and the low-P/E valuation regime, the asset allocation remains the same. The investor will rebalance the portfolio back to these exact target weights, on either a calendar basis or a rules basis, regardless of the current or forecast valuation of the stock market, as the prices of the securities fluctuate

Figure 11.1 Strategic portfolio

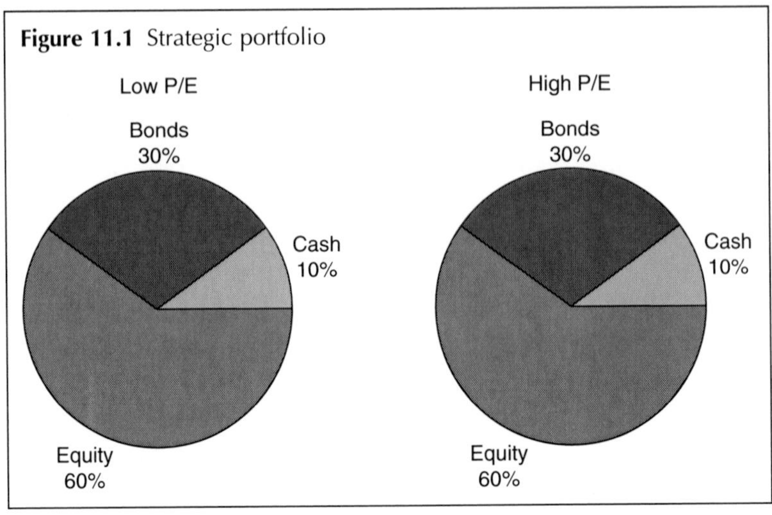

Figure 11.2 Tactical portfolio

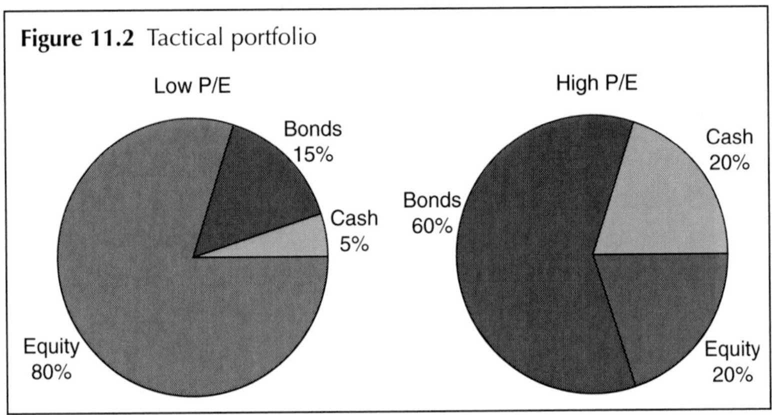

over time. In Figure 11.2, the tactical investor has significantly changed the asset allocation of the portfolio based on the change in the valuation of the financial markets. In the low-P/E environment the investor has overweighted the equity allocation of the portfolio, because stocks are likely to outperform their historical average returns when purchased at low valuations. On the other hand, the investor has underweighted stocks in the portfolio in the high-P/E environment. This tactical change in portfolio construction reflects the investor's belief that it is unlikely that average historical equity returns can be achieved when the asset classes are acquired at high starting valuations.

HOW DO YOU IMPLEMENT TACTICAL ASSET ALLOCATION STRATEGIES?

Active portfolio management is art as much as it is science. There is no "right" way to actively and tactically manage portfolios – except to acknowledge that all approaches fundamentally assume that asset classes may become mispriced and that these mispricings, or their subsequent corrections, can be forecast and anticipated and invested. The various methods for implementing tactical asset allocation, in practice, generally reflect the personal style and investment beliefs of the investor who is implementing the strategy. It is certainly a frustration for students of portfolio construction to find out that there is no one correct method to learn, and that the techniques that are successful for some will not necessarily be implemented effectively by others.

Nonetheless, we have already identified two basic methods for approaching active management. One method tries to take advantage of endogenous price risk in the financial markets, and is the basis for many trend-following and momentum-based investment strategies, as well as many strategies that try to take advantage of risk arbitrage opportunities to earn excess returns. The second method, which attempts to better forecast the news, tries to utilise a fundamental grasp of macroeconomic and market-cycle trends to adjust portfolio construction in a manner that will earn excess returns through the market cycle.

Next we present two simple examples of how these tactical strategies might be implemented by active tactical asset allocation managers using exchange-traded funds currently available in the financial markets. In the first example the investor relies on quantitative decision making to drive active management decisions. In the second example, the investor relies on qualitative judgement to make active management decisions. Ultimately, most investors will use both types of analysis to some degree when making tactical asset allocation decisions that impact their portfolio construction.

Market-neutral – a tactical approach to arbitrage

An investor who wants to take advantage of their own ability to choose asset classes or sectors in a manner that will seek to outperform the market can do so with a simple market-neutral investment strategy. In this case, the investor will be "long" a variety of exchange-traded funds that exhibit certain momentum characteristics that the investor believes will allow them to outperform the general market. In our example, the investor notices that the consumer staples sector ETF, the biotech industry ETF and several energy sectors, including the energy services ETF and the energy industry ETF, are all dramatically outperforming the broad market in terms of their relative strength to the S&P 500 index, and in terms of their absolute price momentum over the past six months. The investor uses computer software to evaluate the relative strength trends for these sectors, as well as to draw trend lines on price charts showing where prices are relative to long-term price movements. The investor buys these ETFs in equal weights in order to create the "long" allocation in the portfolio.

In order to manage the risk of their long positions, the investor will use 33% of the available portfolio capital in order to acquire two leveraged inverse ETFs that will short the S&P 500 and the small-cap Russell 2000 indexes. By using 2X leverage in the inverse funds, the investor effectively creates the opportunity for more return because there is more capital at risk in the market due to the underlying leverage. The portfolio construction, assuming a US$1,000,000 total portfolio, looks as follows:

Description	Portfolio %
Consumer staples	US$165,000 (16.5%)
Biotech	US$165,000 (16.5%)
Energy	US$165,000 (16.5%)
Energy services	US$165,000 (16.5%)
Total long positions	**US$660,000 (66%)**
Inverse 2X S&P 500 index	US$260,000 (26%)
Inverse 2X Russell 2000 index	US$70,000 (7.0%)
Effective short positions	**US$330,000 (33%)**
Cash	US$1,000 (1%)
Total	**US$1,000,000**

The net result of this strategy is that the investor's total portfolio has effectively hedged out the systematic market risk with short positions (assuming the ratio of S&P 500 large cap stocks to Russell 2000 small cap stocks is a fair representation of overall systematic market risk), and the available return (and potential risk) lies entirely in the difference in returns between the long and short positions. This is because the portfolio's aggregate long weighting (US$660,000) balances against the portfolio's aggregate short weighting (US$330,000) invested, as with 2X leverage it will perform as a US$660,000 offsetting position on a daily basis. If the long ETFs are market performers, and if the portfolio is perfectly hedged, meaning that the short positions perfectly offset the long positions, there is no resulting gain or loss. In such a situation, any gains or losses on the long positions will offset an opposite-magnitude portfolio loss or gain (respectively) on the short positions. For example, if the long positions rise in value by 10%, and the shorted indexes also rise by 10%, the investor will make US$66,000 on the long positions (US$660,000 × 10%), and will lose US$66,000 on the short positions (US$330,000 × 10% × 2 leverage), producing a net return of 0%.

However, if the investor's momentum strategy pays off, the investor gets to benefit from the excess returns that the long positions will earn over and above the short returns. For example, if the aforementioned sectors rise by 15% in the aggregate, but the market indexes as a whole rise by only 10%, the portfolio will earn +15% (US$99,000) on the long positions, and will lose US$66,000 (which is 10% loss at 2X leverage on US$330,000) on the short positions. The net result of earning +15% on the long positions and –10% on the short positions is a positive return of US$33,000 (3.3% of the original portfolio), in this case by successfully forecasting the outperformance of the long sector positions relative to the aggregate market indexes. Notably, this return opportunity is available regardless of market direction. Had the long positions declined by 10% while the market declined 15% (also producing a 5% relative outperformance of the targeted sectors, similar to the prior situation where both positions went up instead of down), this would have produced a US$66,000 loss from the long positions, a US$99,000 gain from the short positions, and again a net return of +US$33,000.

By utilising this approach, the investor is effectively profiting from a risk arbitrage position between the targeted long positions expected to outperform and the shorts that were used to hedge them. Remarkably, the portfolio itself may also exhibit very little aggregate volatility – since the systematic risk of the portfolio is hedged out, the only valuation fluctuations will be the net return difference between the long and short positions from day to day, and the tactical asset allocator can manage these relative exposures on an ongoing basis.

For a tactical investor, though, any trend that produces the anticipated outperformance of the targeted long positions would not be expected to persist for ever. Eventually, a new tactical opportunity would be expected to arise (and the value of the old tactical position would decrease), as the securities either reach a pricing extreme, or alternatively return to fair valuation (depending on what the investor was investing towards in the first place). Thus, from this point forward, the investor might tactically adjust the portfolio in several ways, including:

- rotating the long positions, based on subsequent momentum studies, to different asset classes or sectors that exhibit a more favourable outlook at a future point in time; and
- changing the mix of inverse S&P and Russell 2000 ETFs that are being used as hedges to create a market-neutral base for the long/short relative performance; and
- changing the leverage of the inverse S&P and Russell 2000 ETFs to produce more magnified absolute returns (or theoretically changing the leverage of the long positions as well to accomplish the same goal).

It is also notable that, although the above example was based on a long position in the target asset classes and a short (hedging) position in the underlying market indexes, the reverse portfolio construction could be applied as well. If an investor anticipated a significant underperformance of certain asset classes or sectors, the investor may very well hold long positions in the underlying market indexes, and short positions in the asset classes, expected to produce outsized unfavourable returns. Again, in such a situation, the net return to the investor will be represented by the difference in returns between the long and short positions.

Economic cycle rotation – a long only tactical strategy

Rotation throughout the economic cycle – classically done via sector rotation – is an active tactical investment strategy that recognises that the market is made up of different asset classes and sectors that have different risk-and-return characteristics in different parts of the economic cycle. Over the years, investors have recognised that, if they can forecast the current and next stage of the market cycle, they can take advantage of their beliefs to earn excess returns by rotating their stock ownership to those sectors that tend to outperform in each part of the cycle.

Table 11.2 shows the 10 S&P 500 sectors and how they tend to perform relative to the economic market cycle. Note that the terminology of cyclical versus non-cyclical refers to each sector's performance during economic expansions and contractions. Non-cyclical sectors tend not to be impacted by economic slowdowns and are considered to be defensive in nature by investors in such times. Cyclical sectors are the opposite of non-cyclicals, and their profits and performance tend to be highly correlated to economic expansions and contractions.

Investors can rotate among sectors based on their belief about the current and next stage of the market cycle. (This may mean investors remain fully long in the markets throughout – the rotation adjustments can be derived solely from allocations amongst sectors, not by altering the net equity exposure.) Unlike our previous example, where our investor used momentum strategies to determine which sectors to own, in this case the investor relies on research to reach a qualitative conclusion about the prospects for the economy. For example, assume an investor believes that the current economic environment represents a "short and shallow" recession and that the economy should begin to recover by the end of the year. In this case, the US portfolio allocation could be weighted towards the consumer staples ETF, the healthcare ETF, and the utilities ETF. Depending on

Table 11.2 Ten S&P 500 sectors and how they fit in the market cycle

Sector	Description
Consumer staples	Non-cyclical
Healthcare	Non-cyclical
Utilities	Non-cyclical
Financials	Early-cyclical
Consumer discretionary	Early-cyclical
Technology	Cyclical
Materials	Cyclical
Industrials	Cyclical
Energy	Late-cyclical
Telecom services	Late-cyclical

the investor's views and investment time horizon, the investor might use recent price weakness in financials and consumer discretionary to start building positions in the early cyclical part of the market, anticipating the coming economic recovery and early stage of a new economic growth cycle. The investor "rotates" among the sectors as the economy works its way through the overall economic cycle and the investor can earn excess returns versus just holding the broad market by either not owning the worst performing market sectors, or being overweight the best performing sectors.

Rotating through the economic cycle does not need to rely solely upon tactical shifts among domestic US sectors, though. Other tactical asset class adjustments based on economic analyses might include:

- rotating from stocks to bonds at the end of the growth phase of the economic cycle where profits are expected to slow (a headwind for stocks) and interest rates are likely to be cut (a boost for bond total returns);
- rotating from conservative bonds to aggressive bonds at the end of the contraction phase of the economic cycle, where such "high-yield" bonds will likely provide extremely high spreads relative to conservative bonds (providing a total-return boost via yield) and are also likely to experience price increases as the default rate declines in the emerging growth phase of the economic cycle;
- rotation from domestic equities to foreign equities where the foreign economy is at a more bullish stage of the economic cycle than the domestic economy; and
- rotation towards commodities based on the supply and demand economic outlook for the commodity based on the domestic and/or global growth environment.

In both cases that we have illustrated (the market-neutral approach and the economic cycle rotation), the portfolio strategy is tactical in that the investor is trying to earn excess return over and above the market return by making dynamic shifts in portfolio allocation over time. In each case the investor is forecasting price changes and investing accordingly, as opposed to assuming that past performance will eventually appear over long periods of time. In each case the investor does not delegate the active management decisions to other managers, but is making the portfolio decisions themselves in order to earn excess returns.

MAKING AND IMPLEMENTING TACTICAL ASSET ALLOCATION FORECASTS

In the end, virtually all implementation of tactical asset allocation is predicated on forecasting. Thus at its core, tactical asset allocation inherently assumes that (a) aspects of the economic cycle can be forecast and (b) that the cycle's impact on the prices of securities is not necessarily already reflected in the price. This provides the tactical asset allocator the opportunity to invest on the basis of a forecast, and to generate more desirable risk/return results pursuant to the strategy.

Consequently, the approach itself requires the investor to make forecasts, and, moreover, that the forecasts be made more effectively than the market in the aggregate. As discussed earlier, the impact of both endogenous market risk and the fact that much of the market does appear to fail to fully anticipate news can create opportunities for investors to forecast more effectively than the market. Nonetheless, such forecasting certainly is not easy.

Thus, from a practical perspective, the implementation of tactical asset allocation requires a heavier research burden than the passive strategic approach. The investor will be required to do significant macroeconomic top-down research analysis to formulate views on the status of the economy and its anticipated changes in the future. The investor will also need to evaluate the valuation of many asset classes, so that the relative and absolute risk-and-return opportunities can be properly considered. It is necessary to have access to extensive (albeit publicly available) economic data, and utilising additional independent research is recommended (both to help provide a breadth of views to the economic forecast, and also to identify potential opportunities the investor may not have yet been studying/observing).

Because of the depth and breadth of economic information analysed, developing quantitative models is often a desirable approach to be certain that all available information is fully incorporated. Using a modelling approach can provide a more rigorous framework to analyse a high volume of disparate data, and can to some extent help "protect" the investor from viewing data in a manner to confirm preconceived biases and notions. Ideally, data instead should be used to identify opportunities in the first place.

To some readers, the depth of research involved in tactical asset allocation may seem very similar to the research conducted for individual securities analysis. To a large extent, it is. The primary difference is the focus on evaluating asset classes as a whole, as well as market sectors and industries, rather than individual securities. By focusing at the asset-class level, the investor eliminates much of the individual company risk associated with stock selection, while maintaining the overall value and opportunity for applying research-based forecasting to the investment markets. In addition, to the extent that the majority of the investment marketplace currently focuses on either strategic passive investing or individual security analysis (and, in the case of the latter, most investment managers are constrained to security selection within a finite segment of the market), there may be additional opportunity for investors to focus on a neglected segment of the overall markets – making tactical shifts among the relative investment merits between asset classes.

THE BENEFITS OF USING ETFs TO IMPLEMENT TACTICAL ASSET ALLOCATION STRATEGY

Notably, in all of the examples discussed in this chapter, the investor has been using ETFs, because this investment vehicle can be a particularly effective fit for implementing tactical asset allocation strategies. ETFs offer tactical investors numerous benefits for the construction and implementation of tactical portfolios, including breadth of investment choices, intra-day pricing, trading expense, diversification, low cost, tax efficiency and static construction.

Breadth of investment choices

Investors can find ETF products to invest in virtually all of the investment styles as defined by the Morningstar style boxes. Investors have several choices for large-cap, mid-cap and small-cap indexes, as well as growth and value. In addition to style choices, all of the US market sectors are available in ETFs, as well as many of the sub-industries within the sectors. For example, an investor can choose to invest in the Healthcare SPDR or iShares, or they can choose to invest in healthcare sub-industries of the healthcare sector, such as biotech and medical equipment. While all of the S&P industry groups are not yet available to investors, the products are being developed quickly and are likely to be available soon.

In addition to the US market, most countries can be invested in through the ETF marketplace. If they care to, investors can structure a country-specific approach to their international equity allocations with little difficulty, using a similar economic-cycle-based tactical outlook approach. There is a great deal of interest in the universe of emerging-market ETFs as the emerging theme continues to grow in popularity.

Aside from the universe of US and international equity ETFs, there is also a growing pallet of fixed income ETFs to choose from. Investors can roll up and down the credit scale with choices of corporate bond, junk bond or Treasury and agency bond ETFs. In addition, investors can move along the yield curve by choosing among different fixed-income ETFs with different maturities. The low cost of ETFs in general makes them an attractive alternative for fixed-income allocations to portfolios.

In addition to traditional long positions, inverse ETFs allow investors to short various market indexes. Notably, this also gives investors the opportunity to create effective short positions in qualified accounts, when they would not otherwise be able to do so. As shown in the earlier examples, inverse ETFs also allow investors to creatively leverage their portfolio construction to better manage risk.

Finally, there are a growing number of alternative investment choices available in the ETF marketplace. ETF choices in the alternative space include investments in gold, commodities, domestic and foreign real estate, various types of hedge fund exposure, and other non-traditional investments. For many affluent investor portfolios, the opportunity to invest via an ETF may provide a way for the investor to obtain exposure to an asset class that otherwise would not be practical or feasible to own (or, at least, not in a brokerage-account-based environment).

Intra-day pricing

The fact that ETFs are priced throughout the business day makes them an ideal investment vehicle for active managers with short- or intermediate-term investment horizons. In volatile markets, significant extra returns can be earned by effective execution of the entry or exit timing from a position.

Trading expense

ETFs trade like a stock and investors typically pay the same brokerage fees for ETF transactions as they would to purchase and sell individual securities. With trading costs at most custodians and brokerage firms plummeting due to competition, the cost of implementing tactical asset allocation has never been lower. At an average cost of US$9.95 per trade, doing 100 transactions per year in implementing an active tactical strategy costs less than US$1,000, an insignificant amount relative to the size of institutional or affluent investor portfolios.

Diversification

ETFs allow investors to invest in multiple sectors and industries and still be diversified within each investment theme. Instead of choosing the two or three highest-quality stocks in each sector, country or other asset class, the ETF allows for a much greater level of diversification, and safety, for investors. Many ETFs own 50 to 100 stocks within their defined asset-class space, which allows for company risk to be minimised in a dramatic way to focus on only the systematic risk (and opportunity) of the particular asset class.

In the end, ETFs are often an effective tool to obtain a "pure play" investment in a particular narrow asset class, while maintaining the diversification of multiple stocks within the asset class to minimise individual company risk.

Low cost

ETFs typically have very low expense ratios relative to other active management choices such as mutual funds and separate accounts, providing a unique opportunity to own well-diversified exposure within narrowly defined asset classes so that the tactical asset allocator can focus purely on tactical investment decisions.

The low expenses help to defray trading costs for more active tactical asset allocators, and at the margin help investors to minimise any diminishment of long-term returns due to expense costs while obtaining the other advantages discussed in this section.

Tax efficiency

Because of the structure of ETFs, where like-kind exchanges are used to create the ETF units for buys and sells, investing in ETFs is relatively tax-efficient compared with many other pooled investment vehicles that might otherwise be used for tactical asset allocation implementation. Investors can concentrate on the cost basis of their shares, without worrying as much about unexpected and unplanned for tax distributions from the shares at year-end.

Static construction

Although some exceptions apply, most ETFs are constructed on a static basis, where the underlying composition of securities changes little (if at all), and if any changes occur they are clear and well communicated. This allows an investor to obtain exposure to a particular asset class, confident that the nature and character of the exposure will remain consistent throughout the holding period. This is markedly different from implementing tactical asset allocation using other active investment vehicles (such as actively managed mutual funds or separate accounts), where the investment manager of the vehicle may also be making changes to the underlying positions that may alter the asset class exposure in unanticipated ways. By maintaining a static construction of the ETF's underlying securities, the tactical asset allocator can focus on initial security selection and then hold the investment passively while monitoring the overall portfolio. If the ETF's security holdings were not static, the investor would need to constantly monitor whether the underlying securities were being altered in a way that might cause asset class or style drift, which in turn could lead the portfolio to end out holding an investment that was not consistent with the original tactical goal.

ISSUES AND CONCERNS ABOUT ETFs AND TACTICAL INVESTING

ETFs are excellent investment tools for tactical investors, and some of their drawbacks as a "generic" investment product are mitigated by the fact that tactical or active managers may not hold the securities in their portfolios for long periods due to the trading strategies that they may pursue. Nonetheless, there are several issues that investors should be aware of when adding ETFs to their portfolios.

Perhaps the most important concern about ETFs is the construction of the underlying index that is used to map the holdings of the ETF. In 1999, Standard and Poor's, in conjunction with MSCI, created the Global Industry Classification Standard (GICS), which sorts more than 26,000 companies and 29,000 industries worldwide into sectors, industry groups and industries. According to MSCI, their system covers more than 95% of the world's equity market capitalisation. It is the GICS system that divides the S&P 500 index into 10 different major sectors and further divides the market into 24 industry groups and 64 industries. Unfortunately, sometimes the capitalisation-weighted construction of these groups is so highly concentrated in just a few stock issues that the ETF that is available to invest in a specific industry or country theme is not well diversified.

For example, let's consider the US telecom industry. There are several ETFs to choose from in the space, including the two domestic choices – iShares Dow Jones US Telecom Fund (IYZ) and the Vanguard Telecom Services VIPERS (VOX) – as well as one global choice, the iShares Global Telecom Sector Index Fund (IXP). Investors considering the IYZ iShares Dow Jones Telecom Fund will find that this ETF currently (as of 2008) has 71.2% of its assets in its top 10 holdings. The weightings for the top two holdings are AT&T (22.47%) and Verizon Communications (15.4%). The resulting investment of 38% in just two stocks may give some investors pause. IYZ may not offer the kind of diversification that was wanted for an investment in the US telecom space. Investors will find that the other choices are less concentrated in terms of their holdings, and, if this is a concern, might consider other options. On the other hand, some investors may wish to utilise IYZ nonetheless, noting that the capitalisation-weighted exposure arguably is a reasonable representation of the economic realities of that industry.

Another issue is that this ETF has an expense ratio of 0.48%. While it is still inexpensive compared with most actively managed funds, in today's competitive marketplace it is hardly a bargain. Finally, the market capitalisation of this particular ETF (as of 2008) is US$564 million, so most institutional and individual investors should have no liquidity issues in entering and exiting this position. However, there are several ETFs that trade very few shares on an average trading day and institutional investors must be careful that the bid–ask spread on these acquisitions will remain reasonable given a relatively large purchase compared with the usual daily trading volume, and furthermore that acquiring or exiting a large position will not itself significantly impact the price of the trade.

Finally, there are several ETF products marketed today that offer some element of active management in terms of the ETF holdings. These ETFs utilise quantitative models to adjust the holdings of the security, usually on a quarterly basis. Depending on the investor's objectives, the investor must be careful that the character of the ETF does not change as the holdings are given new weights within the ETF structure, or the investor may end up holding exposure to a different asset class or stock composition than originally intended. In addition, care should be taken to be sure that tracking error (relative to the target asset class) or outright relative performance of the ETF remains within the investor's comfort zone.

A HOME RUN FOR TACTICAL INVESTORS

Overall, ETFs remain a remarkably effective investment choice for investors who want to use active tactical asset allocation strategies. As the industry continues to offer new ETF products, investors will be able to be even more creative in constructing portfolios that meet the needs of today's challenging market conditions. The startling number of ETF choices both in the US and globally, as well as new ETF products for alternative investments, makes it certain that tactical investors will continue to view ETF investments as a viable implementation vehicle for their portfolios. As mentioned above, the number of inverse ETFs will also continue to find popularity with investors, especially in today's volatile market climate. Combined with the traditional benefits of ETF investing, including diversification of holdings, low costs and high tax efficiency, the ETF marketplace will remain a home run for tactical investors for the foreseeable future.

1 Some of this discussion is drawn from the work of Mordecai Kurz of Stanford University, and also from H. "Woody" Brock PhD, director of the research firm Strategic Economic Decisions (SED), who originally proposed the academic basis for active management in their paper, "The Logical Justification of Active Management".

REFERENCE

Markowitz, Harry, 1952, "Portfolio Selection", *Journal of Finance*, 7(1), pp. 77–91.

12

Option Strategies Using ETFs

A. Seddik Meziani

Montclair State University

"Whatever is good to know is difficult to learn"
Greek Proverb

Purchasing ETF options has become a viable and effective way to provide fast and cost-effective portfolio risk control for investors who chose to invest in ETFs, based on our review of the numerous ETF options currently available (see list in Table 12.1). In order to make strategic or tactical changes to investment portfolios as market conditions change, it is important to understand certain features of option contracts.

In this chapter, we will introduce defensive investment strategies using options on ETFs. We will first begin with the most basic ones to give the reader who has yet to be properly introduced to these strategies an understanding of how options work. We will then go on to show how these tools can be combined to produce a number of exciting option strategies capable of effectively insulating an investment portfolio.

We will make every attempt to avoid baffling the reader; we ask in return that the reader keeps an open mind to this fascinating subject and plan to invest some time here to become acquainted with several ideas that could be important to preserving investment portfolios.

BASIC OPTIONS CONTRACTS

An option is a contract that gives its holder the right (but not the obligation) to buy (or sell) shares of a given asset at a predetermined

Table 12.1 List of options on ETFs

Name	Symbol	Option symbol	Name	Symbol	Option symbol
Biotech HOLDRS	BBH	BBH, KEE, OEE, PJH, WQK, XEI, YEE, ZWA	Select Sector SPDR-Energy	XLE	DPY, GKJ, GQQ, HGH, JSK, ORJ, WHA, XBT, XGF, XLE, XTG, XXM
Broadband HOLDRS	BDH	BDH, FGH, FML, LAV	Select Sector SPDR-Financial	XLF	VKP, WFS, XJZ, XLF, YUW
Claymore S&P Global Water Index ETF	CGW	CGW	Select Sector SPDR-Health Care	XLV	VMJ, WLH, XLV
Claymore/BNY BRIC ETF	EEB	EEB, JIK, JUE	Select Sector SPDR-Industrial	XLI	VS, WHM, XDL, XLI
DIAMONDS	DIA	BQD, BQQ, BQS, DAU, DAV, DAW, DAZ, DIA, DIH, DIJ, DWZ, HLK, OHP, OMO, OVG, YCK, YKL, ZAV	Select Sector SPDR-Materials	XLB	BMK, OJL, WFP, WXX, XJB, XLB
Euro Currency Trust	FXE	FLN, FNK, FXE, XXF, YXO	Select Sector SPDR-Technology	XLK	NHV, VQP, WQD, XLK
First Trust Amex Biotechnology Index Fund	FBT	FBT	Select Sector SPDR-Utilities	XLU	ORU, WGT, XKJ, XLU
Internet HOLDRS	HHH	HHH, WHB	Semiconductor HOLDRS	SMH	OTO, SMH, SZS, YRH
Market Vectors – Coal ETF	KOL	CFO, KOL, QLE	Utilities HOLDRS	UTH	LBT, UTH
Market Vectors Russia ETF	RSX	RKM, RSX, RZU, VWH, WWJ	Vanguard Consumer Staples ETF	VDC	VDC
MidCap SPDRs	MDY	DYJ, LDE, LEY, LSP, MDY, OVW, XTY, YLU	Vanguard Emerging Markets ETF	VWO	EOY, JWM, VWO
Oil Service HOLDRS	OIH	KXF, KXN, LHF, LLB, OHQ, OID, OIH, OOL, OSD, YYW, ZJO, ZJP, ZJY	Vanguard Europe Pacific ETF	VEA	QNE, VEA
Pharmaceutical HOLDRS	PPH	OYJ, PPH, WIG	Vanguard European ETF	VGK	GJQ, GKV, VGK

PowerShares Dividend Achievers Portfolio	PFM	PFM	Vanguard Extended Market ETF	VXF	ERR, VXF
PowerShares Dynamic Banking Sector Portfolio	PJB	PJB	Vanguard FTSE All-World ex-US ETF	VEU	UEN, VEU
PowerShares Dynamic Consumer Discretionary Sector Portfolio	PEZ	PEZ	Vanguard Financials ETF	VFH	FGY, VFH
PowerShares Dynamic Energy Exploration & Production Portfolio	PXE	PXE	Vanguard Growth ETF	VUG	GHW, QFP, VUG
PowerShares Dynamic Industrials Sector Portfolio	PRN	PRN	Vanguard Health Care ETF	VHT	VHT
PowerShares Dynamic Large Cap Value Portfolio	PWV	PWV	Vanguard Industrials ETF	VIS	JVU, VIS
PowerShares Dynamic Oil Services Portfolio	PXJ	PXJ	Vanguard Information Technology ETF	VGT	TKY, VGT
PowerShares Dynamic Small Cap Growth Portfolio	PWT	PWT	Vanguard Intermediate-Term Bond ETF	BIV	BIV
PowerShares Dynamic Small Cap Value Portfolio	PWY	PWY	Vanguard Pacific ETF	VPL	JCL, VPL
PowerShares Dynamic Technology Sector Portfolio	PTF	PTF	Vanguard Short-Term Bond ETF	BSV	BSV
PowerShares Golden Dragon Halter USX China Portfolio	PGJ	PGJ, POJ	Vanguard Small-Cap Value ETF	VBR	VBR
PowerShares High Growth Rate Dividend Achievers Portfolio	PHJ	PHJ	Vanguard Total Bond Market ETF	BND	BND

(continued)

Table 12.1 Continued

Name	Symbol	Option symbol	Name	Symbol	Option symbol
PowerShares Lux Nanotech Portfolio	PXN	PXN	Vanguard Total Stock Market ETF	VTI	JTI, VGW, VTI
PowerShares Water Resource Portfolio	PHO	PHO	Vanguard Utilities ETF	VPU	VPU
PowerShares WilderHill Clean Energy Portfolio	PBW	PBW	Vanguard Value ETF	VTV	UDV, VTV
ProShares Short Dow30	DOG	DJH, DOG, SIW, SRW, UHM	iShares COMEX Gold Trust	IAU	IAU
ProShares Short MidCap400	MYY	MYY	iShares Cohen & Steers Realty Major	ICF	ICF, ICV, IJE
ProShares Ultra Dow30	DDM	DAO, DDM, DMB, HXD	iShares Dow Jones US Real Estate Index Fund	IYR	BHW, BJN, IYD, IYR, LGW, ZPE
ProShares Ultra Financials	UYG	UUF, UYG, UZP, YJD, ZYW	iShares FTSE/Xinhua China 25 Index Fund	FXI	FJJ, FXI, IKI, VHF,YOF
ProShares Ultra MidCap400	MVV	ANM, GLY, MVV	iShares Lehman 1–3 Year Treasury Bond Fund	SHY	SHY
ProShares Ultra Oil & Gas	DIG	DHB, DIC, DIG, DPB, DXY	iShares Lehman 20+ Year Treasury Bond Fund	TLT	ILT, KCU, TLT, TTJ, VJL, YLI, YXD
ProShares Ultra Real Estate	URE	UQF, URE	iShares Lehman 7–10 Year Treasury Bond Fund	IEF	IEF, IKS
ProShares Ultra S&P 500	SSO	SOJ, SSO, SUA, SUC	iShares Lehman Aggregate Bond Fund	AGG	AGG
ProShares UltraShort Dow30	DXD	DOF, DSD, DXD, DXW, DZD, DZQ, DZS, UDA, UDK, UEH	iShares Lehman TIPS Bond Fund	TIP	TIP, TZB
ProShares UltraShort FTSE/Xinhua China 25	FXP	FAT, FHP, FIM, FXJ, FXP	iShares MSCI EAFE Index Fund	EFA	EFA, EFE, EJU, LXL, ZST
ProShares UltraShort Financials	SKF	RIY, SKD, SKF, SUX	iShares MSCI Emerging Markets	EEM	EEM, EFF, EGH, MBY, YSV, YVK, YZO, ZYX

ProShares UltraShort MidCap400	MZZ	MZZ, UJF	iShares MSCI Hong Kong Index Fund	EWH	EWH
ProShares UltraShort Oil & Gas	DUG	DOE, DUG, DZG	iShares MSCI Mexico Index Fund	EWW	EDM, EJZ, EQM, EWW, KUU, LKM
ProShares UltraShort QQQ	QID	DMR, DYM, QID, QOI, QOJ	iShares MSCI Taiwan Index Fund	EWT	EWT
ProShares UltraShort S&P 500	SDS	JZA, JZB, JZG, JZI, JZN, SBJ, SCF, SDS, SQF, SRJ, SRY, SSH, SXW	iShares MSCI-Brazil Index Fund	EWZ	ESZ, EWZ, WKB, WWB, YEK, ZYL
SPDR Barclays Capital TIPS ETF	IPE	IPE	iShares MSCI-South Korea Index Fund	EWY	EHT, EJY, EWY, XYW, YQX, ZJT
SPDR DJ Wilshire International Real Estate ETF	RWX	RFT, RGU, RWX	iShares Nasdaq Biotechnology	IBB	IBB, KDG, XEF
SPDR DJ Wilshire REIT ETF	RWR	RDJ, RWH	iShares Russell 1000 Growth Index Fund	IWF	IOB, IWF
SPDR Homebuilders ETF	XHB	KHG, XHB, XJL, XXJ	iShares Russell 1000 Index Fund	IWB	IBW, IES, IWB, YIK
SPDR KBW Bank ETF	KBE	KBE, KEJ	iShares Russell 1000 Value Index Fund	IWD	IDH, IFT, IWD
SPDR KBW Regional Banking ETF	KRE	KRE	iShares Russell 2000 Growth Index Fund	IWO	IKB, IWO, IZP, IZT
SPDR Lehman 1–3 Month T-Bill ETF	BIL	BIL	iShares Russell 2000 Index Fund	IWM	DIW, IOW, IQQ, IQS, IQX, IQZ, IWM, JZW, OJM, WIM, WOI, WYV, YNE, YNL
SPDR Lehman High Yield Bond ETF	JNK	JNK	iShares Russell 2000 Value Index Fund	IWN	IRG, ITV, IWN, IZZ, WCQ, WNX, ZSH
SPDR Lehman Long Term Treasury ETF	TLO	TLO	iShares Russell 3000 Index Fund	IWV	ILV, IWV

(continued)

Table 12.1 Continued

Name	Symbol	Option symbol	Name	Symbol	Option symbol
SPDR Russell/Nomura Small Cap Japan ETF	JSC	JSC	iShares S&P Latin America 40 Index Fund	ILF	FBB, ILF
SPDR S&P 500	SPY	CYU, CYY, FYN, FYS, JBG, JCA, OBM, OBV, RDQ, ROQ, RQQ, RQY, SFB, SIY, SPY, SUE, SWG, SWV, SXO, SYH, SZC, YAZ, YQA, YQN	iShares S&P MidCap 400 Growth Index Fund	IJK	IJF, IJK, IJV
SPDR S&P BRIC 40 ETF	BIK	BIK	iShares S&P MidCap 400 Index Fund	IJH	IAJ, IGH, LYE
SPDR S&P China ETF	GXC	GXC, UZQ	iShares S&P MidCap 400 Value Index Fund	IJJ	IJJ, IJM, IJY
SPDR S&P Dividend ETF	SDY	SDY	iShares S&P SmallCap 600 Growth Index Fund	IJT	IEU, IJT
SPDR S&P Metals & Mining ETF	XME	EXF, HEO, MVQ, XME, XXE	iShares S&P SmallCap 600 Index Fund	IJR	IJN, IJO, JIN
SPDR S&P Oil & Gas Equipment & Services ETF	XES	GNP, XES	iShares S&P SmallCap 600 Value Index Fund	IJS	IJW, ISD
SPDR S&P Oil & Gas Exploration & Production ETF	XOP	XOA, XOP	iShares Silver Trust	SLV	SLV, YMK
SPDR S&P Retail ETF	XRT	KDB, VGB, WGV, XRT, XRY	iShares iBoxx $ High Yield Corporate Bond Fund	HYG	HYG, JYH
Select Sector SPDR-Consumer Discretionary	XLY	LMP, XLY, XPW, ZMP	iShares iBoxx $ InvesTop Investment Grade Corporate Bond Fund	LQD	LQD
Select Sector SPDR-Consumer Staples	XLP	ORF, XLP, YLV	streetTRACKS Gold Shares	GLD	GCZ, GLD, GVD, GVH, GVJ, KFF, KRK, OQA

Source: ETF and ETP Industry Review-End of Q4 2008/Barclays Global Investors

price within a specified period of time. This set price is called the strike, or exercise price. An option is said to be in the money when its exercise would produce profits for its holder. The option would be out of the money when exercise would be unprofitable. There are two basic option types: call options and put options. You also should become familiar with the terms "American option" and "European option".

An option that can be exercised at any time before it expires is called an American option; a European option allows for exercising the option only on the expiration date. Whether the option is American in form or European has everything to do with when it can be exercised and nothing to do with where it is traded. In fact both forms are traded on both sides of the Atlantic as well as in the rest of the world. Because they allow more leeway than their European counterparts by giving their holders the flexibility to exercise them at any point during the life of the contract, American options generally will be more valuable. In the rest of the chapter, we will refer to American options unless specified otherwise.

Investment strategies from the perspective of the buyer of call options

A call option gives its holder the right to purchase an asset for a specified price, or strike price, on or before a specified expiration date. A put option conveys to the owner the right to sell an asset at the agreed-upon price. Investors who expect the price of the underlying asset to rise in the near future generally buy call options. Put options, on the other hand, are bought by investors who believe that the price of the asset will fall over the same investment horizon.

As an example, consider the February expiration call option on a share of Standard & Poor's depositary receipt (SPDR 500) with an exercise price US$100.00, selling on February 2, 2009 for US$4.00. This option expires on February 20, 2009. Until the expiration date the purchaser of the calls may buy shares of the SPDR 500 for US$100.00 a share.

If the SPDR 500's price remains at or below US$100.00 a share at expiration, the out-of-the-money call will expire as worthless. It clearly would make no sense to exercise the option to buy shares of the SPDR 500. At above US$100.00, on the other hand, the purchase is justified as the call is in-the-money. If the SPDR 500 sells, say, for US$110.00 on February 20, the option would be likely to be exercised as it would give its holder the right to buy this ETF for US$100.00 a share when it is worth US$110.00. Under such a favorable scenario, the value of the option on the expiration date would then be:

Value at expiration: SPY price – Strike price
= US$110.00 – US$100.00 = US$10.00

The value at expiration of the call option is stated as follows:

$$\text{Payoff to call holder} = \begin{cases} V - X & \text{if } V > X \\ 0 & \text{if } V \leq X \end{cases}$$

The following shorthand notation can be used to express these possibilities:

$$\text{Max}[0, V - X] - \text{Call Premium}$$

where V is the market value of SPDR 500, and X is the exercise (strike) price of the option. "0" represents the possibility that the call could expire out-of-the-money if V is less than X. This formula emphasises that the payoff cannot be negative. That is, if the market value of the option is less than its strike price, exercise does not occur and the call expires with zero value.

Figure 12.1 shows the value of the option increasing as the market price of the ETF moves above US$100.00. The dashed line in Figure 12.1 illustrates the net profit to the holder of the call.

The net profit is calculated as the gross profit minus the cost of the option in the third row of the schedule shown in Table 12.2.

This schedule indicates that at option expiration, the investor suffers a loss equal to the price of the call (US$4) if the price of the SPDR 500 is less than or equal to US$100. This loss, however, is limited to the total premium paid for the call, no matter how low the underlying ETF declines. Since each contract normally covers 100 ETF shares, the total loss per contract will be US$400, which corresponds to the 100 calls purchased. This loss, however, could appear trivial compared to the leverage potential of this transaction if the price of SPDR 500 rises well above the break-even point before February 20 when the option expires.

Figure 12.1 Payoff and profit to call holder

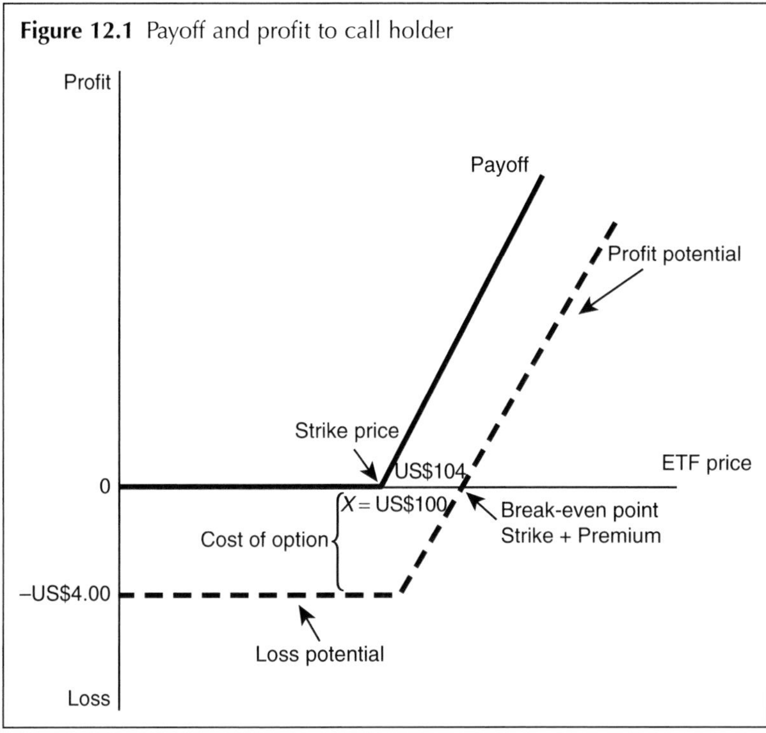

Table 12.2 Value at expiration of the call with exercise price at US$100.00

SPY price (US$)	60.00	70.00	80.00	90.00	100.00	110.00	120.00	130.00
Option value (US$)	0.00	0.00	0.00	0.00	0.00	10.00	20.00	30.00
Profit (US$)	**(4.00)**	**(4.00)**	**(4.00)**	**(4.00)**	**(4.00)**	6.00	16.00	26.00

The break-even point is US$104 since the payoff to the call, $V - X$ = US$104 – US$100 = US$4 corresponds to the premium paid for the call. The break-even point can also be seen as the call's strike price plus the premium paid for the option. Figure 12.1 shows the profit potential for the call holder as unlimited as the price of the ETF continues to rise.

Note that ETF options have a smaller contract size than index options because they are listed on financial products generally representing about 1/10th the price of the underlying index. In addition to their increasing availability when compared with the situation to the early 2000s, this undoubtedly has helped them become popular with investors who often back out at the much larger numerical strike price of index options.

As an illustration, the SPDR 500 closed at US$90.24 on December 31, 2008, while the S&P 500 index ended its run the same year at US$903.25. In the case of the SPDR 500, the notional value covered by the option amounted to US$9,024 (US$90.24 times 100 shares of the underlying ETF), a fraction of the US$90,325 cash value of the S&P 500 index, calculated as the year-end value of the index times US$100.

From the perspective of a portfolio manager who buys call options on the SPDR 500 in the expectation that the overall market will rise prior to the expiration of the option, the purchase of the call will yield a large return if this expectation comes true. The size of the return will depend on how high the price of the SPDR 500 is in relation to US$104, identified as the break-even point in our working example. If, for example the price of the SPDR 500 skyrockets to US$125 on or before February 20, then the same call option would be worth the difference between the new market price and the strike price, herein US$25 (US$125 – US$100) or US$2,500 per 100-share contract. Hence, our investor would have turned a 25% increase in the ETF price into a 525% increase in the option premium [(US$25 – US$4/US$4)].

Because of the leverage potential of the transaction, which is virtually unlimited compared to a limited loss of US$400 per 100-share contract, call buyers often appear to buy calls for speculative purposes. Call options, however, could also be purchased for other purposes. For example, they might also be used to implement a prudent tax strategy. Suppose the SPDR 500 has lost quite a bit of its value as has happened in 2008, but that our investor still likes its long-term prospects. In this case our portfolio manager could have sold it at the end of November 2008 then bought a call option that is exercised outside of the wash sale period, a period defined by the Internal Revenue Service as equal to 61 calendar days, so that the transaction is not disallowed by the US tax code. This strategy effectively allows our portfolio manager to harvest capital losses by using them to offset capital gains without violating the wash-sale rule. If our manager's opinion of the SPDR 500's prospects turns out to be true, this tax strategy not only will have helped reduce the portfolio's tax liability but also allowed the manager to reestablish a position in the ETF at the lower exercise price.

Investment strategies from the perspective of the seller (writer) of call options

Let us now look at the position of an investor who sells these options. If the investor sells, or "writes" a call, they promise to deliver shares if asked to do so by the call buyer. In other words, the buyer's asset is the seller's liability. If the share price of the ETF is below the strike price when the call matures, the buyer will not exercise the call and the writer's liability will be zero. If, on the other hand, the price of the ETF share rises above the strike price, the buyer of the call will exercise and the seller must give up the shares. If this is the case, the seller loses the difference between the share price and the exercise price received from the buyer. Unfortunately for the seller, it is the buyer who always has the option to exercise; option sellers simply do as they are told. One consolation is: if the call is in-the-money for the buyer, the losses for the seller are reduced by the proceeds from selling the option. The profit of the buyer is also reduced but by the cost of purchasing the call.

Going back to our working example, an increase in the price of the SPDR 500 above the strike price does not make the payoff for the seller of this call nearly as beneficial as for the buyer of the call. On the contrary, as the price of the SPDR 500 climbs and the call option becomes in-the-money for its buyer, the seller of the call stands to face large losses when it is exercised. If they do not own the underlying ETF, the writer of the call is forced to purchase the asset at the market price (*V* as denoted above) and sell it to the call buyer at the lower exercise price (*X*), suffering in the process losses which could be huge depending on the spread between *V* and *X*.

Continuing with our illustration, suppose that the price of the SPDR 500 rises to US$125 with an exercise price of US$100. By buying it in the open market the call writer is in effect losing US$21 (US$125 – US$100 – US$4) per ETF that must be purchased, for a loss of US$2,100 per 100-share contract. Note that US$4 must be subtracted from the loss since it corresponds to the premium pocketed by the seller.

When the seller of a call does not own the underlying ETF, the situation is referred to as an uncovered or naked call option. This does not mean, however, that the situation of the seller of the call would be any better if he or she had owned the ETF. This situation is referred to as a covered call option. If the SPDR 500 was previously purchased at US$100 a share, an opportunity cost of US$21 (US$25 reduced by the call premium of US$4) per ETF is still incurred because of the missed opportunity to pocket the difference by selling it at the spot price in the open market. The reader could also think of this scenario as a missed opportunity to pocket a windfall profit of US$21 per ETF or US$2,100 per 100-share contract.

A naked call option could be, however, worse than a covered call option for the writer of the call if the ETF is illiquid because its underlying basket is hard to purchase in the open market.

This does not mean, however, that the writer of the call cannot profit. In this case the situation is simply reversed, as the seller's profit is equal to –1 times the buyer of the call's profit. In this scenario, the profit from writing the call can be stated as follows:

$$\text{Payoff to call writer} = \begin{cases} (V - X) & \text{if } V > X \\ 0 & \text{if } V \leq X \end{cases}$$

Figure 12.2 depicts the payoff and profit diagrams for the call writer as the mirror images of the corresponding diagrams for call holders shown in Figure 12.1.

The break-even point for the option writer also is US$104. The negative payoff at that point offsets the premium received when the call was written. If the market value of the SPDR 500 remains lower than its exercise price at or before February 20, then the option expires out of the money for the buyer of the call, whereas the writer of the call retains the US$400 (the US$4 corresponding to the call premium times 100 shares) referred to earlier. The US$400 becomes their profit.

Utilising ETF puts as portfolio insurance

A put option represents the right to sell the underlying instrument at the exercise price within some future period. Unlike for a call, the holder of a put will not exercise the option unless the asset is worth less than the exercise price. As such, the value of the put at expiration equals:

$$\text{Payoff to put holder} = \begin{cases} 0 & \text{if } V \geq X \\ (X - V) & \text{if } V < X \end{cases}$$

Figure 12.2 Payoff and profit to call writer

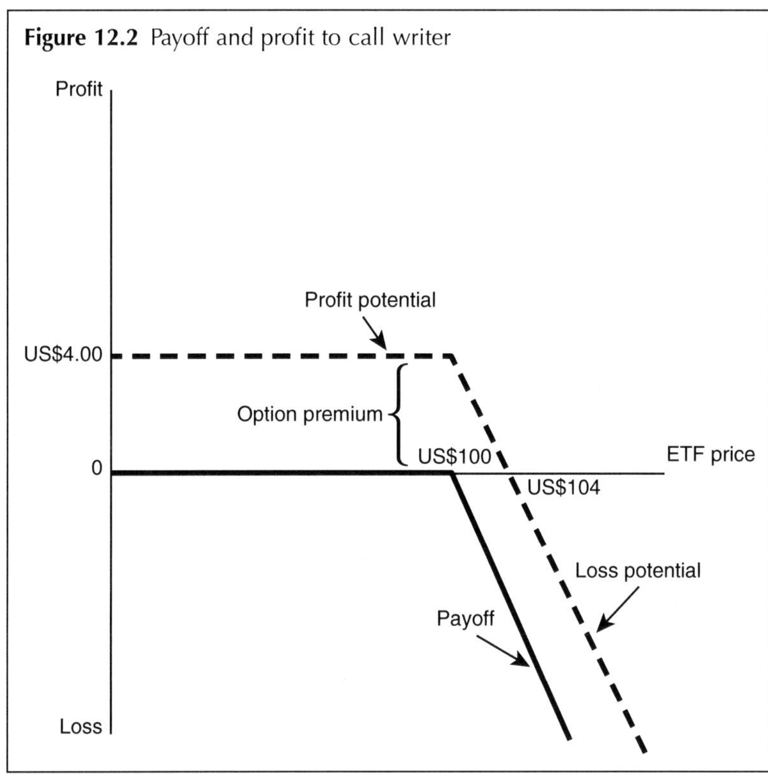

or in other words

$$\text{Max}[X - V, 0] + \text{Put Premium}$$

This is called the option's boundary conditions. Its payoff can be graphed easily. Figure 12.3 represents the put option. The solid line illustrates the payoff at expiration to the holder of the put option. The payoff to the holder of a put option at maturity starts at its highest value then decreases in value as the price of the underlying instrument increases until it has zero value. This occurs when the asset's price (V) equals the exercise price X. At this market price and higher ($V \geq X$), the put is certainly worthless and is said to be out-of-the-money. The dashed line represents the put option owner's profit, net the initial cost of the put.

Consider the option's payoff at maturity. If the underlying asset's price at maturity is greater than the exercise price, what is the option

Figure 12.3 Payoff and profit to put holder

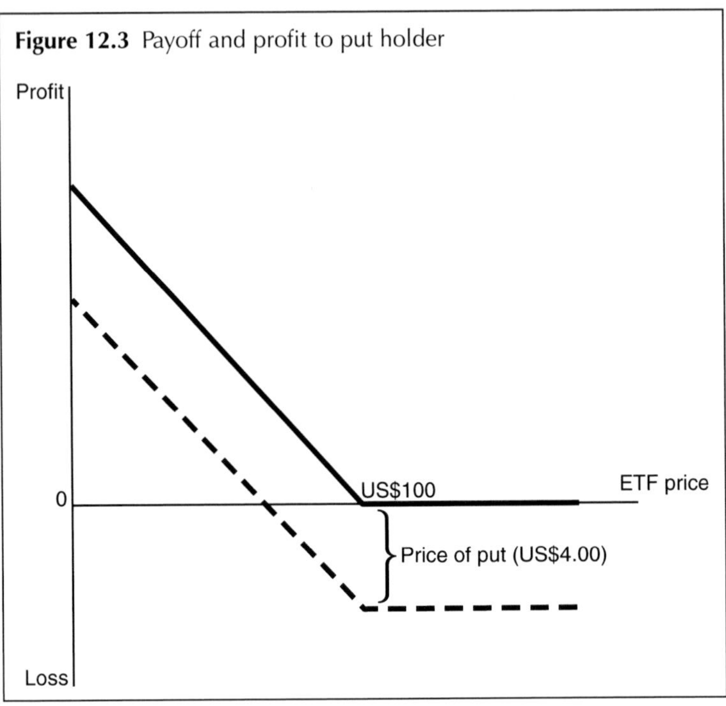

worth? Continuing with our working example, say the SPDR 500 climbs above its exercise price of US$100. A put option gives its holder the right to sell the asset at US$100, but this right is worthless as the SPDR 500 is selling for more than US$100. The holder would not exercise the right to sell the ETF shares at the exercise price. If, on the other the price falls below US$100, say US$90, the put option is in-the-money. By purchasing the SPDR 500 in the open market at US$90 and exercising the put at US$100, the holder of the put will clear US$10 per share minus the price of the put. If the put costs US$4, the net profit per ETF share would then be US$6 or US$600 per 100-share contract. Hence, selling the ETF at the exercise price generates a profit of $X - V$.

How about the payoff to the writer (seller) of a put option at maturity? The writer is pleased only when the asset price (V) is greater than the exercise price; herein when the price of the SPDR 500 is above US$100. In this case, the option expires worthless for the buyer of the put and the writer pockets the put premium worth US$40 per 100-share contract [US$4 × 100]. If, on the other the price drops below US$100, then $V - X$ represents the loss to the writer of the option. At a market price of US$90, the net loss to writer of the put per ETF share is also US$6 (US$90 – US$100 + US$4) or US$600 per 100-share contract.

Figure 12.4 is a graphical representation of the payoff and profit generated by a put option from the perspective of the writer of the option (short put). When the market price of the underlying ETF is above the strike price (ie, US$100), the option expires worthless and the writer profits by keeping the premium collected when selling the put. Note, on the other hand, that the writer of the put could face potentially huge downside loss potential if the price of the underlying ETF collapses. This could be especially damaging for the put writers who do not have a position in the underlying ETF. This situation is known in the market as a naked or uncovered put. The put writer will face the obligation to buy the underlying ETF at the put strike price from those who purchased the option from him at a time when the market price of that same ETF is significantly lower. The only limit to the loss potential for a naked put writer is that the ETF price cannot drop below zero.

Figure 12.4 Payoff and profit to put seller

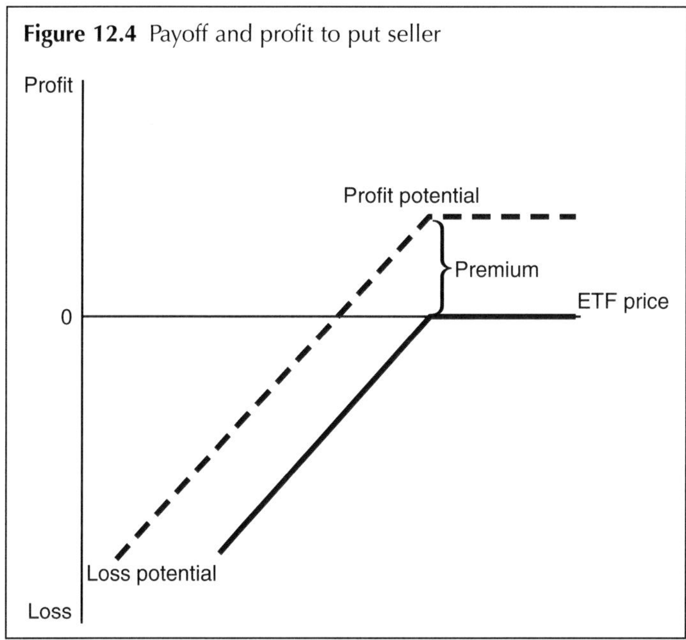

MORE INVOLVED OPTION STRATEGIES

As mentioned earlier, options can also be combined to produce more involved trading strategies. As such, a number of payoff patterns can be devised by combining puts and calls. The following structures constitute some of the better-known option strategies.

Protective put

Going back to our buyer of a put, the value of the position could also be bearish on the asset price when the holder uses it as a hedge against the price of the underlying ETFs going down. In this case, the buyer is not buying the put as an instrument of speculation; the SPDR 500 was purchased at the exercise price from the writer of the put when the option was in-the-money not to net a profit but rather as a hedging tool for a pre-existing portfolio of ETFs. This position is known as a protective put strategy.

Protective put strategies limit losses and therefore provide portfolio insurance for an investor who has concerns about ETF price declines in the near term. Purchasing puts while holding shares of underlying ETFs guarantees a payoff at least equal to the put option's exercise price regardless of what happens to ETF prices.

Indeed, in bear market conditions, protective puts can be very useful (and very expensive) hedging instruments as losses become bounded. The asymmetry of the losses with and without a protective put option as shown in Table 12.3, clearly demonstrates the

Table 12.3 Protective put

Price SPDR 500 (US$)	Potential loss per 100-share contract	
	without put option (US$)	with put option (US$)
50.00	**(5,000)**	0.00
60.00	**(4,000)**	0.00
70.00	**(3,000)**	0.00
80.00	**(2,000)**	0.00
90.00	**(1,000)**	0.00
100.00	0.00	400.00
110.00	0.00	400.00
120.00	0.00	400.00
130.00	0.00	400.00

value of this position. A rational investor would certainly prefer to pay a US$400 premium per 100-share contract (and even more if the option becomes significantly more expensive) to avoid a loss of, say, US$4,000; corresponding to a per-share price of US$70.00. This price is in fact very close to what the SPDR 500 was selling at around the end of February 2009.

In this case, the put option is analogous to an insurance policy written on the ETF. The price paid for the put (the premium) insures the value of the underlying asset. If the price of the SPDR 500 at maturity is above the exercise price, then the protective put as an insurance tool is discarded as worthless. On the other hand, the put (insurance) is cashed in (exercised) to protect the value of the portfolio if the price of the SPDR 500 drops below US$100.

At a strike price (X) of US$100 and the SPDR 500 selling, say, at US$60 ($V$), the holder of the option will not allow the protective put to expire unexercised since the right to sell at US$100 protects the ETF share holder against potential losses equal to US$40 per share ($X - V$) or US$4,000 for each 100-share contract owned. Note that the holder of the protective put could incur a loss if the option were to expire unexercised ($V \geq X$), but the loss in this case would be limited to the cost of the put, which is US$400 (US$4 × 100) per 100-share contract assuming the protective put was purchased earlier at US$4 in a more favourable market environment. A smart portfolio manager, however, should balance this bounded loss against the important fact that no matter how much the underlying ETF decreases in value, while the protective put is outstanding it guarantees the holder of the option the right to sell the SPDR 500 at the put's strike price of US$100.

Figure 12.5 compares the profit on the protective put strategy with that of the ETF investment. The solid line which represents the profit on a protective put strategy is displaced downward by the cost of the put. Notice that potential losses are limited to the cost of establishing the position (price of the put). The dashed line which represents the profit on the SPDR 500 without protective put shows that the profit on the ETF is zero as long the market price (V) remains equal to the strike price (X). The profit increases for every US dollar change above the strike price. Figure 12.3 also shows that without a protective put, the losses are unbounded as the market price of the ETF moves below X. Hence derivatives do not mean only risk. They can also be used as an effective risk management tool.

Figure 12.5 Protective put

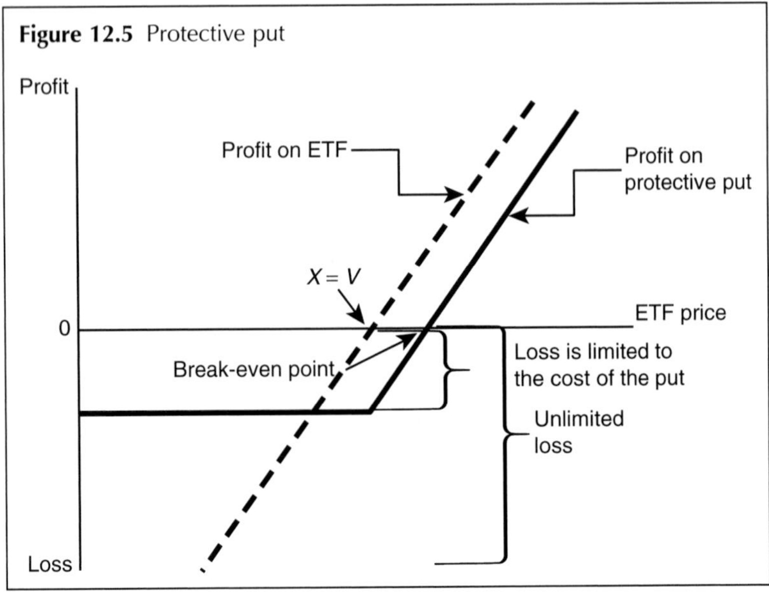

Covered call

A covered call strategy consists of purchasing ETF shares while simultaneously writing an equivalent amount of call option contracts on those ETFs. This strategy is also known as a "buy-write" since it involves both. The call is "covered" because it is fully collateralised by the shares held in a brokerage account in contrast to naked option writing when a call is written without an offsetting ETF position.

Although covered calls can be written in any market condition, this strategy is most often used by investors who expect little change in the price of the ETFs held and as such would boost income (in addition to dividends) by the premium collected if the market were to behave according to expectations.

As shown in Figure 12.6, this strategy offers limited protection from a decline in price of the underlying ETF. Capital gains, on the other hand, are forfeited should the ETF price rise above the strike price of the call. In essence, the sale of the call options means the call writer has sold the claim to any value above the exercise price in return for the initial additional income from selling the calls.

Say an institutional investor bought the SPDR 500 at US$80 a share while simultaneously writing an equivalent number of call contracts with an exercise price (X) of US$100 per share. Expecting little action

Figure 12.6 Covered call

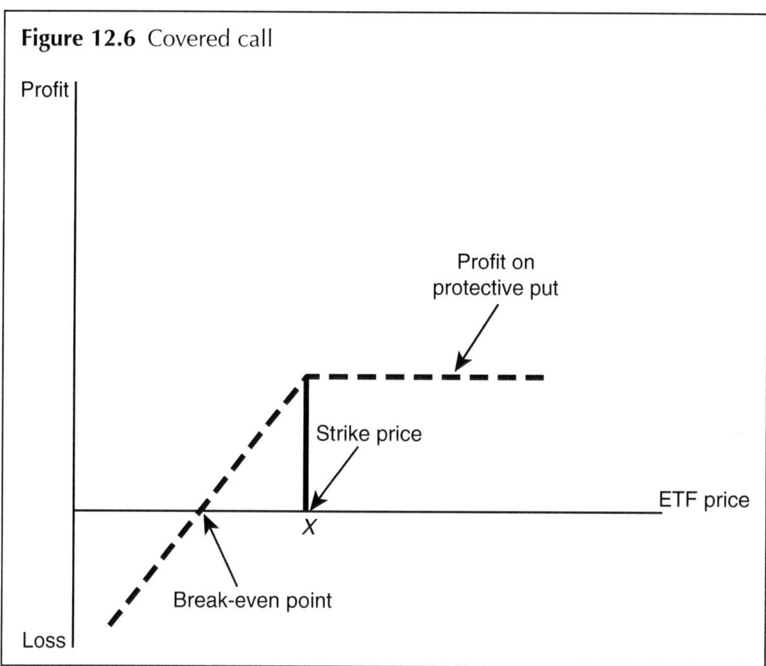

in the market in the near future, our risk-neutral investor settled on a call expiring in 60 days with a price of US$400 (US$4 × 100 shares) per 100-share contract. This means that US$400 in additional income can be picked up for each 100 contracts written.

As long as the market behaves as expected, this investor will get to appreciate the dividends accruing from the underlying ETF shares along with voting rights and the extra income from writing the calls. Maximum profit indicated in Figure 12.4 occurs if the price of the underlying ETF is at or above the call's strike price. In this instance, the writer of the call does not need to buy the SPDR 500 in the market, but needs to simply deliver the shares held, effectively selling at the exercise price. In this instance, the investor gets to keep the option premium (US$400 per 100-share contract) but clearly misses out on the opportunity to pocket the capital gains, which could be substantial.

Note that the break-even point is truncated (below *X*) since any loss accrued from a decline in the price of the shares held is offset by the premium the investor received from the initial sale of the call option. This loss will remain unrealised as long as the underlying shares are not to be sold.

OTHER OPTION STRATEGIES: FINANCIAL ALCHEMY WITH OPTIONS

Puts and calls can also be combined to establish popular position known as straddles, spreads or collars.

Straddle

A long straddle is considered a useful strategy by ETF investors who are anticipating large price swings but are uncertain about the direction of the move. In this case a position is established by buying both a call and a put on the underlying ETF, with both options having the same expiration and same strike price. Suppose that you and the market believe that the alterations to the financial regulations being discussed by the Senate's Banking Committee will be capable of significantly transforming the way the banking sector currently operates. If the ruling is meaningful and far-reaching, this would spur renewed optimism about prospects for the banking sector. On the other hand, a ruling perceived as only bringing cosmetic changes to the current situation will, in your opinion and that of the market, undermine any hopes for further improvement in the banking sector's fortunes and as a result banking ETF share prices will continue downward.

Being unsure of the debate's outcome, herein the banking ETF will make a big move but you do not know which way; you may chose to buy the same number of puts and calls (long straddle) on the underlying ETF in order to capitalise on large price movements in either direction. Your market position is generally considered to be a neutral strategy since the equal ratio of calls and puts effectively neutralises directional risk because the purchased contracts have approximately a 50% chance of finishing in-the-money or out-of-the-money by expiration. The greatest risk in this case is no movement in the ETF price and both options expiring worthless.

The payoff to a straddle can be presented as follows:

$$\begin{array}{lcc} & V<X & V\geq X \\ \hline \text{Payoff of call} & \left\{\begin{array}{l} 0 \\ \\ (X-V) \end{array}\right. & \begin{array}{c} \text{if } V-X \\ \\ 0 \end{array} \\ +\text{Payoff of put} & & \\ =\text{Total} & X-V & V-X \end{array}$$

X and V represent the option's strike price and the price of the underlying ETF, respectively. Note that the payoff of the ETF portfolio is always positive except for when $X = V$. In this case it has zero value. You might wonder why all investors do not adopt such a neutral strategy?

To answer this question, we may want to show how this position might look. Say the underlying banking ETF currently trades around US$30 a share. Because a straddle position is opened with a strike price closest to the current share price, we set the straddle strike price at US$30. You purchase 50 calls at US$5.50 and 50 puts at US$5.00 on the ETF to prepare for a big move in either direction. At these prices, since you are buying both a put and a call, every straddle will cost you US$10.50 for a total of US$52,500 per 100-share contract. Here is what the straddle will look like:

Long straddle				
		Unit price		Price per 100-share contract
Buy	1	50 call at US$5.50		US$27,500
Buy	1	50 put at US$5.00		US$25,000
Total			US$10.50	US$52,500

Note that the price of a call would be higher than that of a put if the ETF trades above the strike price of the straddle. Similarly, the price of a call would be lower than the price of a put if the ETF trades below the straddle strike price. We are assuming that the ETF is trading slightly above the strike price at the time the straddle position is established. Many would call this position balanced when the difference between the put's price and the call's price is less than US$1.00 as it is in this case. People who are versed in option theory also refer to this situation as delta-neutral.

Going back to our illustration, the US$52,500 paid for the straddle will be the most you can lose if the banking ETF continues to trade at around US$30 by expiration. However, before we get too concerned by the likelihood of losing this amount, let us review the situation in light of what could happen in case of a drastic swing in the price of the ETF in either direction.

Since the position could profit from big moves in either direction, it has both a downside and upside breakeven point. The upside breakeven point corresponds to the straddle's strike price plus the cost of the straddle (US$30 + US$10.50 = US$40.50) whereas the down-side break-even point is obtained by subtracting the cost of the straddle from the strike price (US$30 – US$10.50 = US$19.50). The area between these two break-even points is often referred to as the "dead zone". Table 12.4 below shows that when the price of the ETF leaves this so-called dead zone, the holder of the straddle begins to make a profit. Note that as the price of the underlying ETF goes up, the call part of the straddle gains in value, while the put's value drops and vice versa.

The payoff to a straddle is presented in Figure 12.7. The solid line, which illustrates the payoff, shows that the payoff is always positive except at the one point where the position has zero value, $V = X$. The dashed line, which represents the profit, is truncated due to the cost of the straddle (price of the put plus price of the call). It also dips below zero within the aforementioned dead zone.

Figure 12.7 also implies that buyers of a straddle position expect that one side of their position, either the call or the put, to go deep in the money otherwise their outlay for the purchase of both options is lost. In other words, making the purchase is their way to make a bet on the future increase in the volatility of the underlying ETF. The value of the straddle is in fact highest when the ETF makes extreme upward or downward moves from the strike price X. Conversely, investors who write these straddles by selling puts and calls are *de facto* betting on little future volatility in the price of the ETF. They pocket the option premiums hoping that the ETF price will stay within the dead zone, the contract is in-the-money, before option expiration.

Table 12.4 Long straddle

X = US$30 ending ETF price (US$)	Cost of straddle (US$)	Payoff (US$)	Profit or loss/share (US$)
10.00	10.50	20.00	9.50
20.00	10.50	10.00	**(0.50)**
30.00	10.50	0.00	**(10.50)**
40.00	10.50	10.00	**(0.50)**
50.00	10.50	20.00	9.50
60.00	10.50	30.00	19.50
70.00	10.50	40.00	29.50

Figure 12.7 Value of a straddle at expiration

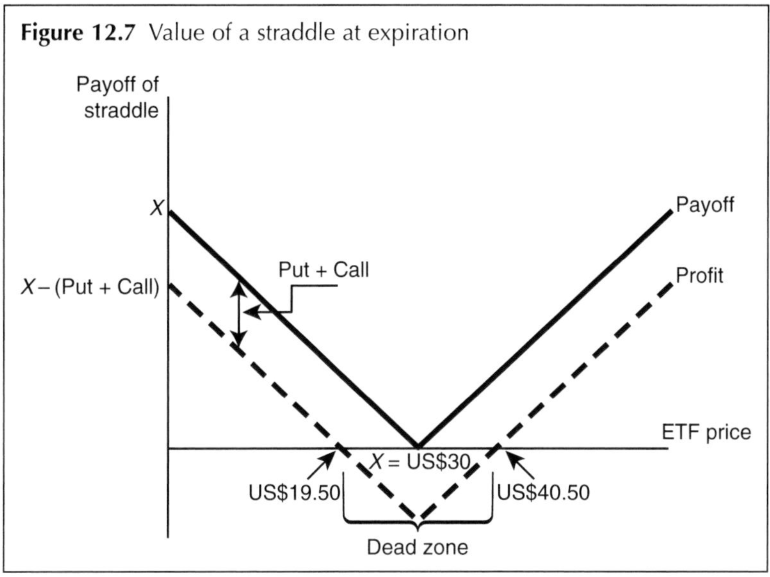

There are certainly many variations to a straddle position. If for example, an investor buys two puts and one call on the ETF with the same exercise price and maturity date, the position is called a strip. Conversely, if two calls and one put are purchased, then the position is referred to a strap.

Option spreads

Depending on how technical investors want to get, they can also combine several option strategies to establish more complex positions known as option spreads. Option spread strategies go by different names such as bear spread, bull spread, butterfly spread, calendar spread, call spread, cartwheel to name a few. Just like the other option strategies described so far, option spreads can be used to lever risk up for speculation or down for hedging purposes. A sample of these option strategies is described below.

Bull spread using calls

The "bull" in a bull spread option refers to the fact that those who employ this strategy are of the opinion that we are in a moderately bullish market environment. Hence, the price of the underlying ETF is going to moderately rise before the option expiration date. Under this strategy, two investment positions are concurrently established.

The same investor simultaneously buys (long call option) and writes (short call option) a call option with identical expiration dates but different strike prices. The long call option has a lower strike price (X_1) than the short call option (X_2). The payoff of a bullish spread at expiration will look as follows:

	ETF price range		
	$V \leq X_1$	$X_1 < V \leq X_2$	$V \geq X_2$
Payoff from long call option, exercise price = X_1	0	$V - X_1$	$V - X_1$
+ Payoff from short call option, exercise price = X_2	0	0	$-(V - X_2) = X_2 - V$
= Total	0	$V - X_1$	$X_2 - X_1$

Bullish spreads have three outcomes to distinguish: the lowest price region where the market price of the underlying ETF at expiration (V) is below X_1 and thereby X_2 since the exercise price of the long call option is lower than the exercise of the short call option, a middle zone where V is between the two exercise prices, and a high-price zone where V exceeds X_2 and X_1 since the former was established as being higher than the latter.

As an illustration, suppose an investor buys US$5 a call (US$500 per 100-share contract) with a strike price of US$60 ($X_1$) and sells for US$3 a call (US$300 per 100-share contract) with a strike price of US$65 ($X_2$). The payoff from this bull spread position will look as follows:

	ETF price range		
	$V \leq$ US$60	US$60 $< V \leq$ US$65	$V \geq$ US$65
Payoff from long call option, exercise price = X_1	0 – US$5	V – US$60 – US$5	V – US$60 – US$5
+ Payoff from short call option, exercise price = X_2	0 + US$3	0 + US$3	$-(V - X_2)$ = US$65 – V + US$3
= Total	–US$2	V – US$62	US$3

Figure 12.8 expresses the payoff and profit of a bullish spread. It shows that investors who established a bull call spread investment strategy are presented with two palpable benefits. The premium received from the short option partially offsets the price paid for the long call option. Hence the risk of losing the premium paid for the long call option is partially hedged. Also, if the strike price on the written call is exercised at the higher price X_2, then those shares can be bought at the lower price X_1 by exercising the purchased call.

Although this strategy represents a great benefit for those who want to hedge their portfolios of ETFs against undue risk (the maximum loss is limited to the net debit between the price received for the written call and the price paid for the call ($C_2 - C_1$ in Figure 12.8), the written call does however limit the upside maximum profit otherwise. In this instance, the maximum profit ($X_2 - X_1$) occurs when both purchased and written option are in-the-money: the underlying ETF increases in price and the investor exercises the long call at the strike price of US$60 ($X_1$), but sees their upside maximum profit cut short when the holder of the short call option also exercises his or right to purchase the underlying ETF at US$65 ($X_2$) as soon as the market price reaches that price. The break-even point in Figure 12.8

Figure 12.8 Value of a bullish spread at expiration

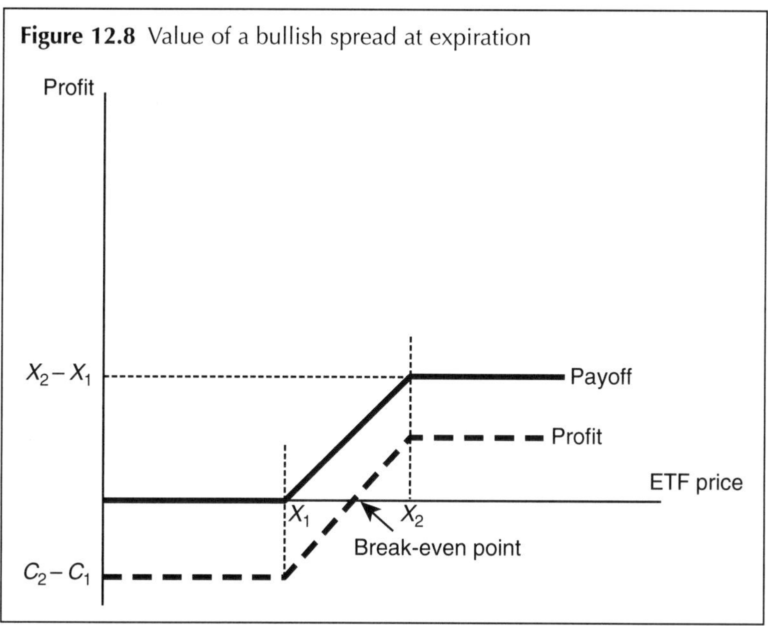

is equal to the strike price of the long call option (ie, US$60) plus the net debit paid (US$5 – US$3) for a total of US$62.

Bear spread using calls

The "bear" in a bear spread call option reflects a negative feeling on the market in general or on a particular ETF. Using our banking ETF example, if a particular investor believes that the banking sector has yet to reach bottom, they may create a bear call spread by purchasing call options at an exercise price X_1 and simultaneously selling the same number of call options with a lower exercise price X_2 on the same underlying ETF, say the SPDR Financial (XLF). Recall that in the case of a bull call spread, calls are sold at a higher exercise price X_2. Both options expire the same month. Just as the holders of bullish spreads benefit from ETF price increases, those who bet on bearish spreads benefit, on the contrary, on price decreases.

Suppose XLF is trading near US$9 in March 2009 and our investor decides to establish a bear call spread position by simultaneously selling 10 APR 9 calls for US$1,500 [US$1.5 × 10 × 100 contracts] and buying 10 APR 11 calls for US$1,000 [US$1 × 10 × 100 contracts], giving him a net credit of US$500 for entering this trade. If XLF moves lower as expected, both calls will expire worthless and the US$500 premium will be collected as profit by our investor. Because the difference between the price of the long and the price of the short calls results in a net credit, the bear call spread is often referred to as a credit spread.

If the price of XLF had rallied instead to, say, US$12 then both calls will expire in-the-money. The maximum loss in this case will be the difference in the two strike prices minus the net premium received plus any commission paid as given by the formula below:

$$\begin{aligned}\text{Maximum Loss} = {} & \text{Strike Price of the Long Call} \\ & - \text{Strike Price of Short Call} \\ & - \text{Net Premium Received} \\ & + \text{Commission Paid}\end{aligned}$$

Continuing to ignore commission paid for simplicity's sake, the maximum loss for our investor is calculated as follows:

$$\begin{aligned}\text{Max Loss} = {} & [(\text{US\$10} - \text{US\$9})(10 \text{ contracts} \times 100 \text{ shares})] \\ & - \text{US\$500} = \text{US\$500}\end{aligned}$$

Hence the upside risk of a bear call spread is limited. The break-even point of this position is determined by adding the net premium received to the strike price of the short call. The bear call spread graph is shown in Figure 12.9.

Note that strategies based on spreads also involve investment strategies based on put bull spread (Figure 12.10) and put bear spread (Figure 12.11). The first option strategy is established with a long put option and a short put option with a higher strike price. The maximum profit in this case is limited to the net credit collected for the spread whereas the maximum loss is the difference between the two strike prices minus the net credit collected. The net credit is the difference between the premium received for the short option net of the premium paid for the long option. A put bull spread is used by investors who are bullish on the direction of the market. Since a put bull spread uses put options instead of call options, its payoff is a flipped image of a call bull spread.

Figure 12.9 Bear call spread

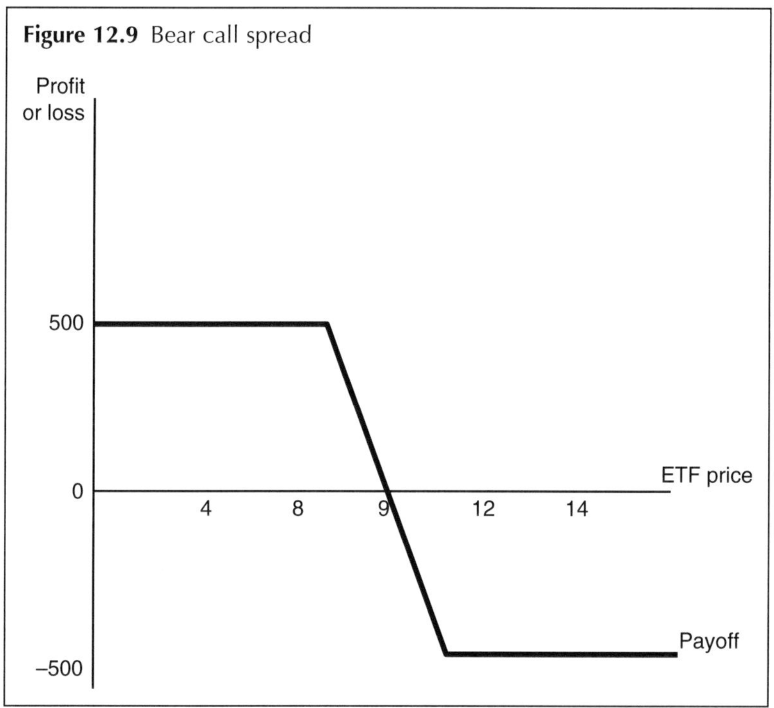

Figure 12.10 Put bull spread

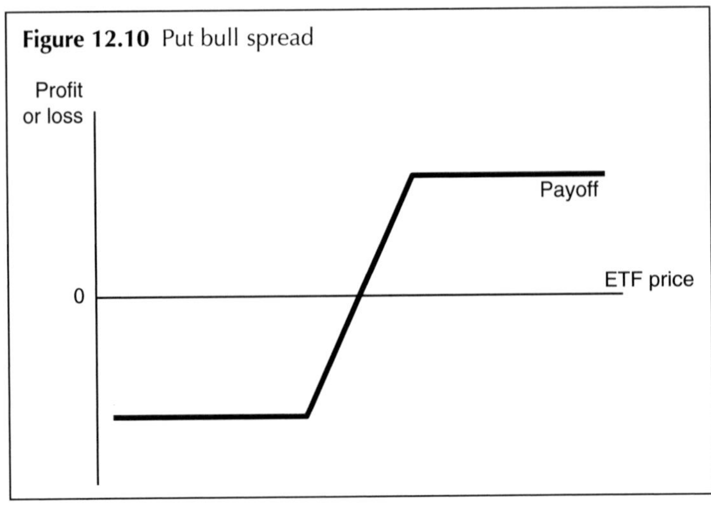

Figure 12.11 Put bear spread

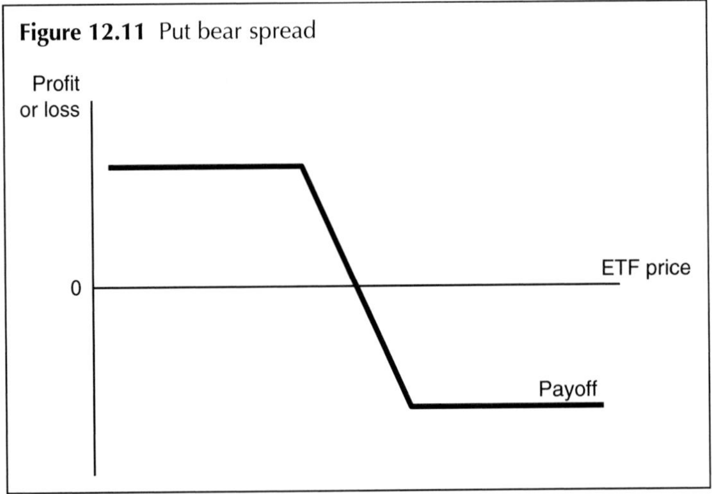

Collars

In a declining market, protective collars could represent cheaper portfolio insurance than buying puts which tend to become increasingly expensive in such an environment. This is especially true for investors who have a target wealth goal but are unwilling to assume losses beyond a certain threshold. It is a strategy that derives its name from the constraints imposed on both losses and profits.

Obviously this strategy starts with a long position in shares of an ETF. Suppose our investor has purchased 2,000 shares selling at

US$100 a share. Next our investor decides to bracket the value of the portfolio between two bounds. The lower bound (a floor) is set by buying a protective put with a strike price below the current price of the ETF. The investor buys a put with a strike, say US$90. Simultaneously, our investor writes a call with a strike price US$110 (a cap or ceiling), to help defray the cost of the put. The call represents the upper bound of the collar and as such its strike price must be set above US$100, the price at which the ETF was purchased.

Note that it is common practice for investor to have the floor at a level of approximately 80% to 90% of the current market price, and the ceiling set at a price of equal value. Note also that if the general market sentiment is bearish, the income from the call will only partially cover the cost of the put, meaning in this case that the net outlay for the two options positions is negative.

If the strike price on the call is set at US$110 then writing the call also means that this investor must forego the portfolio's upside potential. If the price of the ETF moves above US$110, the buyer of the call will ensure that our investor will not do better than US$110 by calling away the ETF. As such, while a collar strategy could be a satisfactory strategy for investors whose main purpose is to protect an ETF portfolio in a period of pronounced market volatility, it could be on the other hand a directional play filled with regret for those who did not expect the market to rally.

Figure 12.12 shows the payoff from a collar position. It shows that purchased protective puts can provide the downside protection an ETF portfolio might need. In return for downside insurance, investors who establish a collar position are also willing to make the trade-off of limited profit potential on the upside by writing calls to finance at least in part the cost of the purchased puts. The dashed line shows what could happen to an unprotected portfolio. The downside risk of such a portfolio looks quite daunting.

CONCLUSION

Numerous news stories relate options to financial disasters but much less is said about their benefits. In fact, a number of these options strategies were introduced to respond to the demands of an increasing number of sophisticated investors who have been requesting their use on a regular basis to hedge risks in today's increasingly complicated markets.

Figure 12.12 Collar

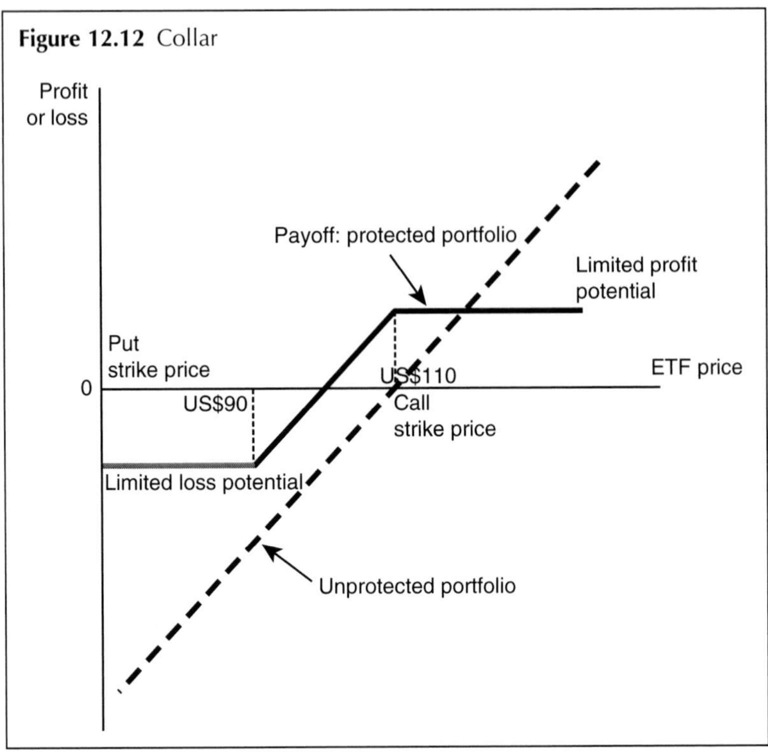

In response, numerous option strategies were devised to manage risks and those described and analysed in this chapter are only the tip of the iceberg of what is being used in the market. As we have seen, for a relatively modest premium, investors can safely hedge their risks and as such avoid significant losses to their portfolios due to adverse market movements. In fact market research shows that most investors use option strategies for hedging purposes.

The downside of establishing options strategies is their use for speculative purposes. In the recent past, it was assumed that a certain class of investors whether individuals or institutions could bear the risk involved in speculating with options. More recent news however has taught us that this is no longer the case: no one is too big to fail. Those who failed are either not sufficiently knowledgeable about the risks involved or levered up the risk way too high in the pursuit of outlandish returns.

In sum, this chapter emphasises that option strategies can and should be used to protect wealth but the leverage inherent in option contracts makes them potentially risky, especially to those who do not have reasonable knowledge of them. Rather than shying away from them in light of recent events, investors seeking to hedge their risks will be well served by these complex option strategies as long as clear policies regarding their use are established and audit procedures are adopted to ensure that the safeguards are put in place. These procedures must be established and supported by the right team of investment professionals.

13

The Present and Future ETF Bond Market

James Ross

State Street Global Advisors

Fixed-income asset. Debt investment. Bond. By whatever name, a rose is a rose is a rose – or is it? Twenty years ago, fixed income was a relatively simple asset class. It was generally accepted that the fixed-income portion of a traditional 60/40 portfolio likely comprised treasuries and municipal bonds. Today, fixed income is increasingly diverse, with assets ranging from corporate and credit bonds to inflation-linked bonds, convertibles, and even emerging-market debt.

Not only has the asset class diversified, but so too have the vehicles by which investors can access this market. Today, investors can buy not only individual bonds, but also bond mutual funds and exchange-traded funds (ETFs) that track bond indexes. In fact, the introduction of bond ETFs in 2002 helped to break down many of the barriers to bond investing for the average investor, decreasing the high investment minimums that individual bonds demand and the relatively high expenses that active bond funds typically require. Bond ETFs also offer greater relative liquidity and pricing transparency by virtue of their daily trading on the secondary market. In addition, bond ETFs can deliver diversity equivalent to (and sometimes better than) bond mutual funds.

However, this increased variety in the number and type of bond investments carries a price. That price is complexity, and complexity can breed confusion. For evidence, look no further than the recent credit crisis. Sparked first by the subprime lending meltdown, the ensuing credit crunch revealed investors' misconceptions about the perceived safety of fixed-income investments. In some cases, investors mistakenly believed their fixed-income exposure to be equivalent to cash and were caught off-guard by illiquidity and panic selling that broadly drove down prices.

NOT YOUR FATHER'S BOND MARKET

Recent events have presented the investment management community with a remarkable opportunity to shed light on the tremendous variety of fixed-income investments available today. This is, after all, not your father's bond market. In fact, a 20% allocation to fixed income in the last year would have yielded a significant divergence in returns depending on the fixed-income asset type (Table 13.1). For example, investors with exposure to Treasury inflation-protected securities (TIPS) and international treasuries would have fared far better than those allocated to convertibles, T-bills or high yield bonds.

Knowledge of the drivers and risks for various fixed-income assets, as well as the unique attributes of vehicles used to acquire this exposure, is a prerequisite to constructing diversified portfolios that precisely match your clients' wealth and income goals.

In this chapter, we will take a closer look at the multiplicity of fixed income today. More specifically, we will look at the ways

Table 13.1 Performance of 80/20 hypothetical portfolios

As of 30/09/2008			
	1 year (%)	**3 years (%)**	**5 years (%)**
LB Global Ex Treasury Blend	–20.54	2.86	8.19
LB Municipal Blend	–21.70	2.08	7.63
LB US Corp Blend	–22.68	1.64	7.29
LB US High-Yield Blend	–24.19	1.66	7.73
LB Treasury Blend	–19.76	2.99	8.08
LB T-Bill Blend	–23.33	2.13	7.67
LB MBS Blend	–20.05	2.91	8.13
LB US Convertibles Blend	–25.38	1.31	7.50
LB US Credit Blend	–22.30	1.83	7.41
LB US TIPS Blend	–20.28	2.66	8.15
Lehman US Aggregate Bond Index*	3.66	4.15	3.79
80% MSCI AC World Index 20% Fixed			

Source: StyleAdvisor and Lehman Brothers, SSgA Strategy & Research as of 30/09/2008
*As of November 2008, all Lehman indexes were renamed to Barclays Capital.

fixed-income ETFs may be revolutionising investing for you and your clients, offering benefits previously reserved only for institutional investors.

Fixed-income market growth

Fixed-income assets have been growing at a fast clip over the past decade. Currently, the global fixed-income market measures US$27.6 trillion. That's nearly one-third larger in size than the global equity market, which totals US$19.8 trillion, after a significant decline in the three month period from the end of July to October 2008. In the US, the fixed-income market is only slightly smaller than domestic equity, measuring US$12.1 trillion and US$12.8 trillion, respectively.[1]

Growth in fixed-income assets has likely been propelled by the volatile equity market along with the impending wave of baby-boomer retirees, many of whom are shifting their retirement assets into income-generating investments. Not only have assets been increasing, but so too have the number of fixed-income investment vehicles. What accounts for the rapid growth of this asset class, and what might the future hold for bond investors?

Inflation and interest rates: their impact on bonds

When we look back to 2001, in the wake of the technology bubble, investors faced tight credit spreads and abysmal equity market performance. In an effort to stimulate the economy and pump liquidity back into the market, during 2001 to June 2003 the Federal Reserve lowered the Fed funds rate 13 times, ultimately bottoming out at 1.00%.[2]

The aggressive policy worked. The US economy not only recovered – it flourished. The housing market and other real estate sectors expanded rapidly. As the global economy grew stronger overall, oil and commodity prices skyrocketed in response to increased demand. The Federal Reserve increased the Fed funds rate 17 times, climbing to 5.25% over a three-year period in an attempt to stave off inflation.[3] Interest rates rose sharply while the US dollar declined. US equity performance, which had been weak relative to years past, turned downright ugly. This prompted investors to shift assets into fixed income or cash. Shortly thereafter, the bottom fell out of the housing market, subprime losses hit, and credit dried up.

It was then that the Federal Reserve began to reverse its policy. Investors fled to short-term treasuries, away from longer-term issues and US equity. But, despite having cut interest rates eight times by 3.75% since September of 2007,[4] inflation is still up 4.6% over last year and concerns persist. On a seasonally adjusted basis, inflation eased a bit in August and September, down from 7.9% in June of 2008.[5]

Though inflation has eased a bit from its 17-year high in July 2008, largely due to a drop in oil and energy prices, the Federal Reserve still faces the threat of stagflation, where a weak US economy persists amid high inflation. This environment also presents unique challenges for investors seeking fixed-income exposure, especially since high inflation erodes the real value of bonds. If it was not apparent before, it is painfully evident now that all bonds are not alike, nor are they altogether "safe". For investors seeking to build diversified portfolios in this environment or any other, it is critical to understand how market events and pressures influence the performance of different types of fixed-income assets – from a risk, return and yield perspective.

FIXED-INCOME RISKS AND OPPORTUNITIES

Duration matters

Duration is a measure of a bond's sensitivity to interest rates, a primary determinant of bond performance. When interest rates fall, bond prices usually rise. When this happens and new issues come on to the market with lower yields than older securities of the same duration, the higher coupon on the older securities becomes more valuable. Conversely, as long-term interest rates rise, the price of long-term bonds decreases. The older issues with lower coupons are worth less in the new higher-rate environment, since investors could buy new issues with higher coupons.

In general, bonds of longer duration carry greater risk due to the potential volatility in interest rates over time and the erosive power of inflation. Duration, however, is only one piece of the bond investor's puzzle.

Credit quality counts – a lot

In addition to duration, credit quality is an important determinant of bond performance. Credit quality took centre stage in the wake of the 2007 subprime market fallout, as some investors lost their entire investment principal due to issuer default. There are various tools investors use to assess credit quality. The official statements bond issuers produce regarding their financial health is one example. Most investors, however, rely heavily on the credit ratings developed by ratings agencies. Credit ratings are determined by the rating agency's assessment of the issuer's ability to fulfil its debt obligations.

Credit ratings, whether downgrades or upgrades, have a tremendous impact on bond trading and credit spreads. The credit spread is the difference in yield between a corporate bond and a Treasury bond. It represents the potential compensation investors receive for taking on the higher risk associated with corporate bonds relative to Treasuries. Investment-grade companies with higher credit ratings are deemed more creditworthy and are thus able to borrow money at lower rates than companies with lower credit ratings.

The credit spread between corporate and Treasury securities generally widens as the economy slows, or as inflation rises. The spread between corporate and Treasury securities typically narrows as the economy grows or interest rates decline.

Investors should not rely blindly on credit ratings to assess risk, however. In the past, even bonds with high credit ratings have defaulted.

Liquidity risk

Certain segments of the bond market can be very thinly traded. Municipals, high-yield bonds, convertibles and some emerging-market debt are not particularly liquid markets.

If liquidity is limited, investors should expect wider bid–ask spreads in pricing.

Call risk

Certain types of bond are subject to call risk, whereby the issuer reserves the right to call back, or redeem, its bonds from investors prior to the maturity date. With callable bonds, investors face the risk that corporations will redeem these bonds when the coupon rates they are paying are higher than current interest rates. This enables the issuer to save money by calling back old bonds, potentially at below-market prices, and issuing new bonds with lower coupons.

Market risk

Just like any investment, bonds are subject to prevailing market risk. As we saw recently, in an environment of economic uncertainty or negative sentiment, bonds may be marked down below their par value – forcing the investor to hold them until maturity in order to receive full principal payment.

Watch the yield curve

The yield curve, which tracks the interest rates of treasuries against their maturities, can provide a good visual indicator of the market environment for bond investors (Figure 13.1). Economists and investors watch for three primary types of yield curve – normal, flat and inverted – to assess which way the market is moving and to identify potential bond opportunities.

Normal curve

A normal yield curve indicates that the yields of bonds of equivalent quality are increasing as their maturity extends, to account for the added risk of longer durations.

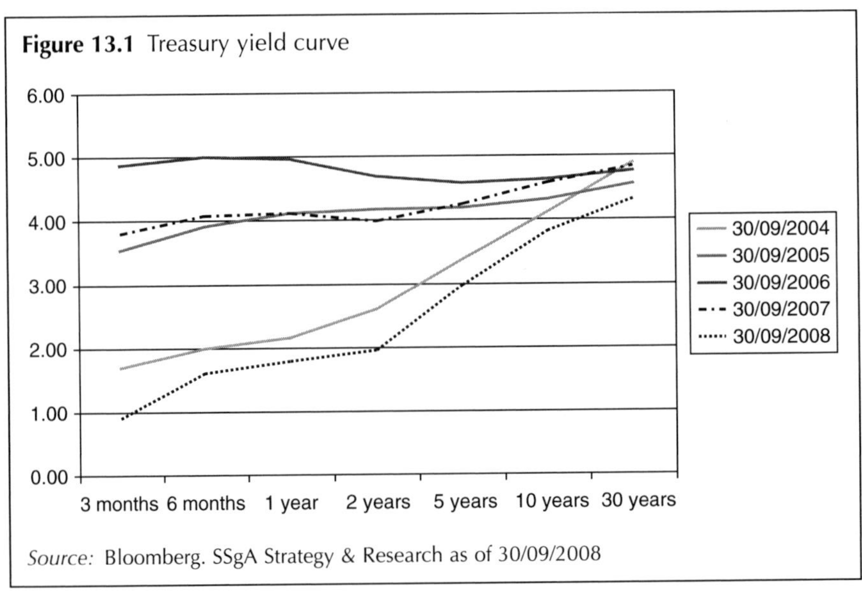

Figure 13.1 Treasury yield curve

Source: Bloomberg. SSgA Strategy & Research as of 30/09/2008

Steep normal curve

A steep yield curve typically indicates a strengthening economy. This results in concern that inflation could rise. The curve reflects the expectation that longer maturities should increase to cover that potential increase in inflation. The greater the slope of the curve is, the wider the spread between short-term and long-term interest rates.

Flat curve

A flat yield curve can signal a slowdown in the economy and, at the least, characterises a transitional period for the economy. When the Federal Reserve raises interest rates to pre-empt inflation, the curve typically flattens. Short-term yields generally rise to reflect rate hikes, while long-term rates fall as inflation expectations moderate.

Inverted curve

An inverted yield curve occurs when short rates are higher than long-term rates, reflecting aggressive Federal Reserve rate hikes that the market fears will slow the economy too much. An inverted yield curve is a rare event and frequently precedes a bear market or recession.

BONDS BEHAVING DIFFERENTLY

Fixed-income asset types respond differently under varying market conditions, resulting in very different risk-return profiles and yields. Variability in performance from one fixed-income asset type to the next, and from one year to the next, can be significant (Table 13.2).

When assessing bond performance, the coupon, or fixed-interest rate, is only part of the equation. The current bond interest rate provides investors with the actual yield of the bond, determined by calculating the bond interest rate as a percentage of the bond's current price. A bond trading below its par value may offer an attractive yield. However, as that bond nears maturity, its price should move back toward par value, thus reducing its current yield but providing price appreciation.

Conversely, a bond trading above its par value may have a less attractive yield that will increase as it approaches maturity but

Table 13.2 Periodic table of bond returns

1998	1999	2000	2001	2002	2003	2004	2005	2006	2007	YTD 2008
Lehman Global Ex-US Treasury Bond 18.21%	Lehman T-Bill 1–12 Month 4.69%	Lehman US Treasury Index 13.52%	Lehman US Credit Index 10.40%	Lehman Global Ex-US Treasury Bond 21.91%	Lehman US Corporate High-Yield 28.96%	Lehman Global Ex-US Treasury Bond 12.06%	Lehman US Municipal Bond 3.53%	Lehman US Convertibles Index 13.33%	Lehman Global Ex-US Treasury Bond 10.93%	Lehman US Treasury Index 4.58%
Lehman US Treasury Index 10.03%	Lehman US Corporate High-Yield 2.39%	Lehman US Municipal Bond 11.69%	Lehman US Corporate Investment Grade 10.30%	Lehman US Treasury Index 11.79%	Lehman US Convertibles Index* 27.69%	Lehman US Corporate High-Yield 11.14%	Lehman T-Bill 1–12 Month 3.05%	Lehman US Corporate High-Yield 11.87%	Lehman US Treasury Index 9.02%	Lehman US MBS Index 3.84%
Lehman US Aggregate Bond Index 8.67%	Lehman US MBS Index 1.86%	Lehman US Aggregate Bond Index 11.63%	Lehman US Aggregate Bond Index 8.42%	Lehman US Credit Index 10.53%	Lehman Global Ex-US Treasury Bond 18.20%	Lehman US Convertibles Index 9.61%	Lehman US Treasury Index 2.79%	Lehman Global Ex-US Treasury Bond 7.29%	Lehman US Aggregate Bond Index 6.96%	Lehman T-Bill 1–12 Month 1.93%
Lehman US Corporate Investment Grade 8.59%	Lehman US Aggregate Bond Index –0.83%	Lehman US MBS Index 11.16%	Lehman US MBS Index 8.22%	Lehman US Aggregate Bond Index 10.27%	Lehman US Corporate Investment Grade 8.24%	Lehman US Corporate Investment Grade 5.40%	Lehman US Corporate High-Yield 2.74%	Lehman US MBS Index 5.22%	Lehman US MBS Index 6.90%	Lehman Global Ex-US Treasury Bond 0.80%
Lehman US Credit Index 8.57%	Lehman US Corporate Investment Grade –1.94%	Lehman US Credit Index 9.39%	Lehman US Treasury Index 6.75%	Lehman US Corporate Investment Grade 10.12%	Lehman US Credit Index 7.70%	Lehman US Credit Index 5.24%	Lehman US MBS Index 2.61%	Lehman US Municipal Bond 4.85%	Lehman US Convertibles Index 5.62%	Lehman US Aggregate Bond Index 0.64%

Lehman US MBS Index 6.96%	Lehman US Credit Index –1.95%	Lehman US Corporate Investment Grade 9.07%	Lehman US Corporate High-Yield 5.28%	Lehman US Municipal Bond 9.60%	Lehman US Municipal Bond 5.32%	Lehman US MBS Index 4.70%	Lehman US Aggregate Bond Index 2.43%	Lehman T-Bill 1–12 Month 4.82%	Lehman US Credit Index 5.11%	Lehman US Municipal Bond –3.19%
Lehman US Municipal Bond 6.48%	Lehman US Municipal Bond –2.07%	Lehman T-Bill 1–12 Month 6.21%	Lehman US Municipal Bond 5.13%	Lehman US MBS Index 8.75%	Lehman US Aggregate Bond Index 4.11%	Lehman US Municipal Bond 4.47%	Lehman US Convertibles Index 2.02%	Lehman US Aggregate Bond Index 4.33%	Lehman T-Bill 1–12 Month 5.01%	Lehman US Credit Index –6.83%
Lehman T-Bill 1–12 Month 5.40%	Lehman US Treasury Index –2.56%	Lehman Global Ex-US Treasury Bond –2.82%	Lehman T-Bill 1–12 Month 4.43%	Lehman T-Bill 1–12 Month 1.80%	Lehman US MBS Index 3.07%	Lehman US Aggregate Bond Index 4.34%	Lehman US Credit Index 1.96%	Lehman US Corporate Investment Grade 4.31%	Lehman US Corporate Investment Grade 4.56%	Lehman US Corporate Investment Grade –8.58%
Lehman US Corporate High-Yield 1.87%	Lehman Global Ex-US Treasury Bond –6.39%	Lehman US Corporate High-Yield –5.86%	Lehman Global Ex-US Treasury Bond –3.97%	Lehman US Corporate High-Yield –1.40%	Lehman US Treasury Index 2.24%	Lehman US Treasury Index 3.54%	Lehman US Corporate Investment Grade 1.67%	Lehman US Credit Index 4.26%	Lehman US Municipal Bond 3.37%	Lehman US Corporate High-Yield –10.07%
					Lehman T-Bill 1–12 Month 1.11%	Lehman T-Bill 1–12 Month 1.24%	Lehman Global Ex-US Treasury Bond –8.81%	Lehman US Treasury Index 3.08%	Lehman US Corporate High-Yield 1.88%	Lehman US Convertibles Index –18.95%

Source: StyleAdvisor and Lehman Brothers, SSgA Strategy & Research as of 30/09/2008
Note: As of November 2008, all Lehman indexes were renamed to Barclays Capital.
*Lehman US Convertible Index Inception Date January 2003.

will experience a decline in price over time and may result in a loss of principal. Factoring both yield and price is essential to understanding a bond's total return potential (Table 13.3). Investors who select bonds primarily based on higher coupon rates without taking into consideration potential changes in the price of those bonds due to market factors may find themselves with total returns that are lower than the total returns of bonds with lower fixed-interest rates.

Table 13.3 Price plus coupon equals bond total return

As of 30/09/2008						
	1 quarter (%)	1 year (%)	3 years (%)	5 years (%)	10 years (%)	20 years (%)
Global Treasury Ex-US Price	1.93	0.36	−1.54	−0.60	−0.61	0.57
Global Treasury Ex-US Coupon	0.88	3.52	3.49	3.51	4.02	5.90
US Credit – Price	−7.78	−10.21	−4.77	−3.70	−1.81	−0.19
US Credit – Coupon	1.48	5.98	5.88	5.84	6.42	7.38
US Mortgage Backed Securities – Price	0.49	1.51	−0.09	−0.35	0.18	0.65
US Mortgage Backed Securities – Coupon	1.37	5.54	5.52	5.47	6.06	7.27
US Treasury – Price	1.21	4.01	1.03	−0.14	0.07	0.85
US Treasury – Coupon	1.08	4.55	4.71	4.61	5.29	6.41
US Treasury: US TIPS – Price	−4.08	3.85	1.85	2.52	3.92	N/A
US Treasury: US TIPS – Coupon	0.56	2.27	2.43	2.57	3.09	N/A
Municipal Bond – Price	−4.38	−6.44	−2.84	−1.90	−0.75	0.48
Municipal Bond – Coupon	1.20	4.86	4.83	4.83	5.04	5.78
US Corporate High-Yield – Price	−11.03	−18.71	−6.88	−3.70	−4.18	−2.18
US Corporate High-Yield – Coupon	2.31	9.01	8.44	8.33	8.93	9.82
US Corporate Investment Grade – Price	−9.22	−12.22	−5.64	−4.27	−2.15	−0.37
US Corporate Investment Grade – Coupon	1.52	6.13	6.00	5.95	6.50	7.42
Lehman US Aggregate Bond Index*	−0.48	3.66	4.15	3.79	5.20	7.23

Source: StyleAdvisor and Lehman Brothers, SSgA Strategy & Research as of 30/09/2008
*As of November 2008, all Lehman indexes were renamed to Barclays Capital.

The real measure of a bond's performance, then, is total return, which is affected by changes in interest rates and other market events.

Government bonds

Treasuries

Government-backed credit such as T-bills, notes and bonds, are available in different maturities and are suitable investments for nearly every type of investor. US treasuries are generally considered to be the least risky of all fixed-income assets. However, while they carry lower risk, government bonds are not risk-free.

Short-term treasuries are often attractive investments in rising-rate environments. Since these bonds mature relatively quickly, investors get their principal back and can continue to reinvest in new bonds with higher coupons as older ones mature. In this way, they put their money to work more effectively as rates rise.

Long-term treasuries, on the other hand, lock investors into a fixed interest rate for longer periods of time. Because they are locked in, investors lose the opportunity to invest in bonds with higher coupons in a rising-rate environment, even while new bonds are being issued. Long-term treasury bonds are particularly vulnerable to inflation, too, since inflation erodes purchasing power and thus the real value of these bonds.

US agency

US agency bonds are bonds issued by various government agencies or instrumentalities that have either the direct backing of or a line to the US Treasury. These bonds generally carry an implied AAA rating and enable investors to take on a small degree of credit risk relative to treasuries. As recent history made painfully clear, however, these bonds are not without risk.

Treasury inflation-protected securities (TIPS)

When inflationary concerns arise, demand for inflation-linked assets naturally increases. Like nominal treasuries, Treasury inflation-protected securities (TIPS) are backed by the US government and are generally low-risk and highly liquid. Recent years have seen other developed and developing nations create and issue similar inflation-linked securities. Unlike nominal treasuries that have a fixed principal, TIPS rise with inflation, preserving an investor's purchasing power. While the inflation-adjusted principal on TIPS is not paid until maturity, inflation-adjusted interest payments on TIPS are paid semiannually. When TIPS mature, they are redeemed at their inflation-adjusted principal or par value – whichever is greater.

Securitised bonds

Mortgage-backed securities

Mortgage-backed bonds grew in popularity since 2002, likely due to the Federal Reserve's long-term relaxed policy stance. The prevailing low interest rates spurred a boom in the mortgage markets from 2002 to 2006. Attractive conditions made mortgage debt easy to acquire and also affordable, prompting an explosion in the housing markets.

Mortgage-backed bonds are essentially pools of individual mortgage loans that have been packaged and offered for sale by government agencies such as the Government National Mortgage Association (Ginnie Mae), the Federal Home Loan Mortgage Corp (Freddie Mac) and the Federal National Mortgage Association (Fannie Mae).

Commercial mortgage-backed securities

Commercial mortgage-backed bonds are pools of commercial mortgages (such as those for shopping malls, office buildings and apartment buildings) that have been packaged for sale.

Investors seeking income may be drawn to both types of securitised bonds described above, since they pay interest monthly, along with a portion of principal. Generally speaking, principal payments may accelerate when interest rates are declining due to the impact of refinancing. Alternatively, payments may decrease when rates are rising. Minimums for these bonds can be quite high; and, there is risk associated with these investments, as many investors abruptly discovered when the subprime market imploded.

Credit bonds

With credit bonds, investors are essentially lending money to the issuer. In exchange, the issuer agrees to pay the holder regular payments at a fixed interest rate. These bonds are not backed by the government (see "Credit quality counts – a lot" above). Instead, the bondholder assumes the credit risk, or default risk, of the issuer.

This is the primary risk investors face with these securities. Credit bonds fall into two major categories.

- Investment-grade corporate bonds: High-quality, or "investment-grade", corporate bonds tend to offer higher yields than treasuries, because they are not backed by the full faith and credit of the US government but by the issuing corporation. These companies are considered investment-worthy due to their solid financial condition typically validated through their debt ratings. However, they are considered more vulnerable to default risk compared with the US Treasury and seek to compensate investors for taking on the additional risk via higher coupons.
- High-yield bonds: High-yield bonds are not investment-grade bonds, and so carry a higher level of issuer credit and liquidity risk than other corporate bonds. Issuers of high-yield bonds are often companies with riskier business models or less predictable cashflows. These securities are more attractive investments when spreads are wide and inflation lower. Investors, after all, want to be compensated well for the high risk associated with these investments.

Tax-exempt municipal bonds

Tax-exempt municipal bonds offer investors tax-free income, at least at the federal level. Some state and local municipals also deliver income exempt from state and local taxes as well. While the yields on tax-exempt bonds tend to be lower, investors in higher tax brackets can potentially capture after-tax returns that outperform taxable bonds. Table 13. 4 illustrates what a taxable bond would have to yield in order to deliver benefits equivalent to tax-exempt municipals.

In other words, an investor in the 28% tax bracket would have to invest in a taxable bond with a yield of 6.25% in order to receive the same after-tax return as a tax-exempt bond yielding 4.50%.

- General obligation versus revenue: General obligation bonds are backed by the government itself and are considered to be relatively secure. Revenue bonds, backed by a specific source of municipal revenue (eg, highway tolls), may be less secure but typically offer higher yields.
- Insured versus uninsured: Some municipal bonds are covered by insurance that guarantees the bond's scheduled payment of

Table 13.4 Taxable bonds versus tax-exempt municipals

Tax-free yield (%)	Income tax brackets* (%)						
	15%	**25%**	**28%**	**33%**	**35%**	**40%**	**45%**
3.00	3.53	4.00	4.17	4.48	4.61	5.00	5.45
3.50	4.12	4.67	4.86	5.23	5.38	5.83	6.36
4.00	4.71	5.33	5.56	5.97	6.15	5.57	7.27
4.50	5.29	5.99	6.25	6.72	6.92	7.50	8.18
5.00	5.88	6.67	6.94	7.47	7.69	8.33	9.09
5.50	6.47	7.33	7.64	8.21	8.46	9.17	10.00
6.00	7.06	7.99	8.33	8.96	9.23	10.00	10.91
6.50	7.65	8.67	9.03	9.71	10.00	10.83	11.82
7.00	8.24	9.33	9.72	10.45	10.77	11.67	12.73
7.50	8.82	10.00	10.42	11.20	11.54	12.50	13.64
8.00	9.41	10.67	11.11	11.94	12.31	13.33	14.55
8.50	10.00	11.33	11.81	12.69	13.08	14.17	15.45
9.00	10.59	12.00	12.50	13.44	13.85	15.00	16.36
9.50	11.18	12.67	13.20	14.18	14.62	15.83	17.27
10.00	11.76	13.33	13.89	14.93	15.38	16.67	18.18

*Taxable equivalent yield (TEY): $\frac{\text{tax exempt yield}}{(1 - \text{tax rate})}$.

interest and repayment of principal upon maturity. Insured municipals generally offer lower yields than their uninsured peers. The insurance, however, does not protect an investor against interest rate risk or market risk; and, recent market events have highlighted risks of insurance for municipal bonds.

International bonds

US Treasury bonds represent less than a quarter of the developed world's treasury bonds outstanding. There is a world of opportunity open to investors in the international bond markets. Offering low correlations to US fixed-income and other major US and global asset classes, international bonds offer exposure to a diverse array of economic, inflation and interest rate cycles. And, since non-US treasuries are denominated in currencies other than the US dollar, they provide exposure to different exchange rates, potentially reducing volatility in returns and offering a hedge against US dollar weakness.

It is important to note, however, that by virtue of being international investments, these bonds carry additional risks compared with their US equivalents. Historically, international bond markets have done a fairly good job of rewarding investors for taking on these risks, especially when these bonds are used to further diversify an existing fixed-income portfolio.

Convertible bonds

Convertible bonds are corporate bonds that can be redeemed for a predetermined amount of company stock prior to maturity and at the discretion of the bondholder. They tend to offer lower yields, or interest rates, to compensate for the holder's privilege of being able to turn the bonds into equity, typically done when a company's stock is performing well.

ETFs: A BETTER BOND MOUSETRAP

Growth in the absolute number and assets of fixed-income ETFs is robust. In fact, of the 10 largest ETFs launched in 2008, three were bond funds, with currency and commodity ETFs rounding out the majority of those remaining. As of September 30, 2008, there are 51 fixed-income ETFs in the US with assets totalling more than US$49 billion. That figure represents more than 8% of total US ETF assets. There were 552 new ETFs in registration, 23 of which were fixed-income.[6]

Looking at cashflows for the past year, we can see that growth in fixed-income ETFs is even more impressive, having garnered more

Table 13.5 US ETFs as of September 2008

Subsector	AUM (million)	Number of funds
Credit	4,636.99	4
Emerging markets	110.57	1
High-yield	1,335.04	3
International	1,131.70	2
Investment-grade agg	13,083.27	9
MBS	530.97	1
Municipal	1,690.04	14
Short	1,786.86	1
Short-term	1,792.67	6
TIPS	8,220.38	2
Treasury	15,373.99	8
Total	49,692.48	51

Source: SSgA Strategy & Research as of 30/09/2008

than US$12 billion in new assets. That is a larger share of new ETF assets than commodities, currencies and international equity ETFs combined (Hougan 2008).

A closer look at the unique attributes of fixed-income ETFs may reveal what accounts for this increasing popularity with investors.

Diversification

ETFs offer investors instant diversification across issuers in a single trade. These ETFs also make it easier for investors to diversify their total fixed-income exposure based on sector, duration and credit quality. As illustrated below, over the long term, fixed-income assets are generally lowly or negatively correlated with one another and with other major asset classes (Table 13.6).

Liquidity and pricing transparency

Most individual bonds trade in an over-the-counter (OTC) negotiated market, which makes price transparency and liquidity difficult for all but large institutional investors. Due to their listing on the exchange and resulting continuous pricing, ETFs bring a degree of pricing transparency to fixed income, particularly the more illiquid segments of the market, such as corporate and municipals.

And, since ETFs disclose their portfolio composition at the end of each day, they make it easy for an investor to know exactly how they are invested. Comparatively, mutual funds are required to reveal their constituents only semiannually.

No investment minimums

Unlike individual bonds and many active bond mutual funds, ETFs have no investment minimums. Investors can purchase as few as one ETF share or as many shares as they like. In a market long dominated by institutional investors with huge amounts of capital, ETFs are an equaliser for the average investor. Difficult-to-reach segments of the bond market are now accessible to investors from Wall Street to Main Street.

Lower expenses

Fixed-income ETFs typically have expense ratios slightly lower than their index mutual fund counterparts and significantly below the expenses paid for active bond funds (Table 13.7).

Table 13.6 Long-term bond correlations

	October 1998–September 2008																		
	1	2	3	4	5	6	7	8	9	10	11	12	13	14	15	16	17	18	19
1) Lehman Global Ex-US Treasury Bond	1																		
2) Lehman US Municipal Bond	0.38	1																	
3) Lehman US Corporate Investment Grade	0.41	0.76	1																
4) Lehman US Corporate High-Yield	0.04	0.26	0.48	1															
5) Lehman US Treasury Index	0.51	0.65	0.69	–0.1	1														
6) Lehman T-Bill 1–12 Month	–0.08	0.04	0.04	–0.15	0.16	1													
7) US Mortgage Backed Securities Index	0.43	0.63	0.66	0.02	0.84	0.25	1												
8) Lehman US Credit Index	0.43	0.77	1	0.44	0.74	0.06	0.7	1											
9) MSCI AC World Index	0.08	–0.02	0.12	0.56	–0.34	–0.08	–0.2	0.08	1										

(continued)

Table 13.6 Continued

	October 1998–September 2008																		
	1	**2**	**3**	**4**	**5**	**6**	**7**	**8**	**9**	**10**	**11**	**12**	**13**	**14**	**15**	**16**	**17**	**18**	**19**
10) S&P 500	–0.04	–0.03	0.07	0.52	–0.35	–0.04	–0.19	0.04	0.95	1									
11) Dow Wilshire 5000	–0.05	–0.03	0.09	0.56	–0.35	–0.06	–0.19	0.05	0.95	0.98	1								
12) Russell 2000	–0.07	–0.01	0.08	0.57	–0.31	–0.09	–0.2	0.05	0.75	0.72	0.83	1							
13) Dow Wilshire REIT	0.1	0.17	0.14	0.34	–0.07	–0.07	0.01	0.13	0.3	0.31	0.32	0.42	1						
14) Dow Wilshire Global Ex-US RESI	0.31	0.26	0.32	0.53	–0.05	–0.1	0.06	0.3	0.68	0.58	0.57	0.49	0.53	1					
15) Dow AIG Commodity Index	0.25	–0.01	0.18	0.13	0.02	–0.07	–0.04	0.16	0.2	0.05	0.08	0.08	–0.07	0.23	1				
16) MSCI EAFE Index	0.21	0.02	0.15	0.53	–0.28	–0.1	–0.17	0.12	0.96	0.83	0.85	0.72	0.28	0.72	0.27	1			
17) S&P/Citigroup EM World BMI	0.04	–0.03	0.15	0.58	–0.28	–0.12	–0.2	0.12	0.83	0.71	0.75	0.67	0.26	0.67	0.32	0.8	1		
18) S&P/Citigroup Global BMI	0.08	–0.01	0.14	0.57	–0.33	–0.09	–0.2	0.1	0.99	0.94	0.96	0.79	0.31	0.69	0.22	0.96	0.84	1	
19) Lehman US Aggregate Bond Index	0.51	0.77	0.86	0.14	0.94	0.16	0.91	0.89	–0.16	–0.18	–0.17	–0.16	0.03	0.12	0.06	–0.11	–0.13	–0.15	1

Source: StyleAdvisor, SSgA Strategy & Research as of 30/09/2008
Note: As of November 2008, all Lehman indexes were renamed to Barclays Capital.

Table 13.7 Average expense ratios of fixed-income investment vehicles

	Average expense ratio (%)
Fixed-Income ETF	0.23
Fixed-Income Index Mutual Fund	0.52
Fixed-Income Active Mutual Fund	0.94

Source: Bloomberg as of 30/09/2008

Trading flexibility

Like all ETFs, fixed-income ETFs can be purchased on margin and sold short. In addition, investors can place stop-loss and limit orders.

Long-term performance

The long-term returns of bond indexes are competitive with those of other major asset classes (Table 13.8).

Regular income

Individual bonds generally pay a fixed rate of interest in regular six-month intervals until the bond reaches maturity. ETFs, in contrast, typically pay income interest on a monthly basis, making them appealing for investors seeking steady income.

No maturity date

With individual bonds, investors often hold them to maturity to receive par back rather than selling the bonds in the market. In doing so, they give up gains they might have acquired from rolling down the yield curve. In other words, they could have potentially seen a higher return on their investment if they had sold while the bond price was still above par. On the other hand, in a rising-rate environment, if the investor can hold a bond to maturity and does not have to sell a bond when the price is below par, the investor benefits by getting back their principal. While holding the bond, the investor sacrificed the potential to invest in other bonds with higher coupons.

ETFs, with their perpetual duration, automate the roll. They automatically trade holdings as needed to maintain index tracking and duration. Investors reap the benefits via regular dividend payments.

Table 13.8 Long-term returns of bonds versus other major asset classes

As of 30/09/2008						
	1 year (%)	**3 years (%)**	**5 years (%)**	**10 years (%)**	**15 years (%)**	**20 years (%)**
Lehman Global Ex-US Treasury Bond	4.51	5.40	5.48	4.84	5.98	7.18
Lehman US Municipal Bond	−1.86	1.86	2.84	4.24	4.96	6.28
Lehman US Corporate Investment Grade	−6.78	0.05	1.45	4.22	5.33	7.03
Lehman US Corporate High-Yield	−11.24	1.05	4.39	4.43	5.90	7.45
Lehman US Treasury Index	8.73	5.79	4.47	5.36	5.96	7.31
Lehman T-Bill 1–12 Month	3.00	4.23	3.25	3.53	N/A	N/A
US Mortgage Backed Securities Index	7.02	5.52	4.84	5.68	6.20	7.35
Lehman US Convertibles Index	−21.10	−0.84	3.26	N/A	N/A	N/A
Lehman US Credit Index	−4.80	0.86	1.94	4.50	5.52	7.17
MSCI AC WORLD INDEX	−26.47	1.79	8.53	4.78	6.84	7.32
S&P 500	−21.98	0.22	5.17	3.06	8.40	9.95
Dow Wilshire 5000	−21.26	0.56	6.00	3.98	8.31	9.87
Russell 2000	−14.48	1.83	8.15	7.81	8.23	9.47
Dow Wilshire REIT	−12.46	5.18	13.43	13.04	11.36	10.26
Dow Wilshire Global Ex-US RESI	−38.25	0.36	12.86	11.45	7.05	N/A
Dow AIG Commodity Index	−3.66	1.90	10.15	9.98	8.59	N/A
US Dollar Index	2.22	−3.90	−3.07	−1.89	−1.03	−1.03
MSCI EAFE Index	−30.12	1.58	10.16	5.42	5.49	5.41
S&P/Citigroup EM World BMI	−31.95	10.34	19.30	14.59	N/A	N/A
S&P/Citigroupl Global BM	−26.62	1.81	8.97	5.84	N/A	N/A
Lehman US Aggregate Bond Index	3.66	4.15	3.79	5.20	5.86	7.23

Source: StyleAdvisor, SSgA Strategy & Research as of 30/09/2008
Note: As of November 2008, all Lehman indexes were renamed to Barclays Capital.

In addition, the payoff from maturing bonds held by the ETF is automatically reinvested, freeing long-term investors from the hassle of reinvestment.

Tax considerations

Since fixed-income ETFs must maintain their target maturity, they may trade more frequently than many equity ETFs. Changes in the composition of a fixed-income index prompt trading in the ETF tracking the index. Typically, bond ETFs rebalance on a monthly basis to maintain index tracking. Many fixed-income benchmarks are reconstituted on a monthly basis to account for the continual evolution of the fixed-income market, as new issues emerge and older securities mature. Rebalancing prompts trading, which can trigger capital gains and result in a tax liability for investors.

USING FIXED-INCOME ETFs

With fixed-income ETFs, investors have the tools they need to build fixed-income portfolios that not only support long-term goals, but possess the flexibility and liquidity needed to respond quickly to shifts in the bond markets.

Strategic asset allocation

Fixed-income ETFs can be used to cost-effectively diversify total portfolio risk while maintaining the liquidity needed to adjust fixed-income exposure in response to market and interest rate shifts. Diversifying fixed-income risk is made easier and less costly with ETFs.

Combining fixed-income assets of varying risk-return profiles in a single fixed-income portfolio should result in better risk-adjusted returns. As noted previously, the long-term correlations among fixed-income asset types are attractive. It makes sense, then, that combining these asset types with varying correlations into a single portfolio would potentially result in better diversification and improved long-term risk-adjusted returns.

Prior to ETFs, implementing this level of fixed-income diversification was a costly and time-intensive endeavour at best, and altogether impossible at worst, due to high investment minimums for most types of bonds or bond mutual funds.

By virtue of their flexible trading attributes, lack of investment minimums and higher relative liquidity, fixed-income ETFs enable the average investor to diversify within and across specific fixed-income asset types, resulting in portfolios primed to capture high-performing segments of the fixed-income markets while mitigating the risk of underperformers.

Portfolio completion

Fixed-income ETFs can be used to fill gaps in your clients' existing fixed-income portfolios. For example, whereas purchasing individual international treasury bonds may be cost-prohibitive or too risky for many investors, ETFs make it possible for the average investor to add exposure to this attractive segment of the fixed-income market.

Tactical positioning

By virtue of trading on exchanges and their subsequent relative pricing transparency and liquidity, fixed-income ETFs can be used to adjust portfolios quickly in response to inflation, interest rates and shifts in the economy overall.

For example, we can see from Table 13.9 that the short-term correlations of various fixed-income types are more attractive than their longer-term coefficients. Furthermore, the returns of different fixed-income assets can vary considerably even over a relatively short three-year period.

US dollar hedge

Since 2003, until very recently, the value of the US dollar has fallen dramatically. For investors seeking to hedge the US dollar's decline, international bonds may prove attractive, especially inflation-linked securities. The appreciation in the value of the underlying currencies of international bonds could potentially increase their yield and return. Inflation-linked international bonds offer the added protection against inflation in exchange for a slightly lower coupon (Table 13.10).

Alternatively, should investors believe the US dollar will strengthen, they may choose to sell short exposure to international treasuries or international government inflation-linked bonds via ETFs that track these segments of the international fixed-income marketplace.

Table 13.9 Three-year returns and correlations for fixed-income assets

	October 2005–September 2008																			
	1	**2**	**3**	**4**	**5**	**6**	**7**	**8**	**9**	**10**	**11**	**12**	**13**	**14**	**15**	**16**	**17**	**18**	**19**	**20**
1) Lehman Global Ex-US Treasury Bond	1																			
2) Lehman US Municipal Bond	0.23	1																		
3) Lehman US Corporate Investment Grade	0.32	0.64	1																	
4) Lehman US Corporate High-Yield	–0.04	0.58	0.71	1																
5) Lehman US Treasury Index	0.61	0.14	0.32	–0.29	1															
6) Lehman T-Bill 1–12 Month	0.34	0.14	0.23	0.1	0.38	1														
7) US Mortgage Backed Securities Index	0.49	0.35	0.4	0.01	0.85	0.37	1													
8) Lehman US Convertibles Index	–0.02	0.48	0.7	0.91	–0.33	0.08	–0.1	1												
9) Lehman US Credit Index	0.36	0.64	1	0.67	0.4	0.26	0.47	0.65	1											

(continued)

Table 13.9 Continued

	October 2005–September 2008																			
	1	**2**	**3**	**4**	**5**	**6**	**7**	**8**	**9**	**10**	**11**	**12**	**13**	**14**	**15**	**16**	**17**	**18**	**19**	**20**
10) MSCI AC World Index	−0.03	0.36	0.53	0.83	−0.4	0.07	−0.15	0.92	0.48	1										
11) S&P 500	−0.21	0.45	0.47	0.85	−0.41	0.1	−0.1	0.86	0.42	0.92	1									
12) Dow Wilshire 5000	−0.21	0.43	0.46	0.85	−0.43	0.06	−0.13	0.88	0.42	0.93	0.99	1								
13) Russell 2000	−0.27	0.31	0.26	0.69	−0.47	−0.12	−0.21	0.73	0.22	0.77	0.85	0.89	1							
14) Dow Wilshire REIT	−0.15	0.27	0.12	0.52	−0.22	0.04	0.09	0.44	0.11	0.45	0.61	0.62	0.69	1						
15) Dow Wilshire Global Ex-US RESI	0.06	0.37	0.54	0.84	−0.28	0.23	0	0.82	0.51	0.87	0.81	0.81	0.67	0.58	1					
16) Dow AIG Commodity Index	0.4	−0.03	0.4	0.29	0	−0.05	−0.01	0.42	0.38	0.33	0.06	0.1	−0.02	−0.17	0.25	1				
17) MSCI EAFE Index	0.06	0.35	0.53	0.79	−0.36	0.08	−0.15	0.89	0.49	0.98	0.84	0.85	0.7	0.37	0.88	0.39	1			
18) S&P/Citigroup EM World BMI	0.11	0.2	0.48	0.63	−0.3	0.04	−0.13	0.81	0.44	0.92	0.73	0.75	0.61	0.23	0.76	0.48	0.92	1		
19) S&P/Citigroup Global BMI	−0.02	0.35	0.52	0.82	−0.4	0.06	−0.16	0.92	0.47	1	0.91	0.92	0.78	0.44	0.87	0.34	0.98	0.92	1	
20) Lehman US Aggregate Bond Index	0.57	0.53	0.75	0.26	0.83	0.41	0.88	0.19	0.8	0.07	0.06	0.04	−0.1	0.04	0.17	0.16	0.08	0.08	0.06	1

Source: StyleAdvisor, SSgA Strategy & Research as of 30/09/2008
Note: As of November 2008, all Lehman indexes were renamed to Barclays Capital.

Table 13.10 International inflation-linked bonds as US dollar hedge

As of 30/09/2008				
	1 year (%)	**3 years (%)**	**5 years (%)**	**10 years (%)**
Lehman Global Inflation Linked Ex-US Index	0.67	6.21	8.62	7.71
Lehman US Treasury: US TIPS	6.19	4.32	5.15	7.11
US Dollar Index	2.22	–3.90	–3.07	–1.89
Lehman US Aggregate Bond Index	3.66	4.15	3.79	5.20

Source: StyleAdvisor and Lehman Brothers, SSgA Strategy & Research as of 30/09/2008
Note: As of November 2008, all Lehman indexes were renamed to Barclays Capital.

Interest rate hedge

ETFs enable investors to underweight or overweight exposure to a specific fixed-income asset type in response to interest rate movements. Amid the current uncertainty in the bond markets, with stagflation still a threat, investors may be wary of investing in longer-duration bonds. When unsure of which way the Fed will move on interest rates, or when they believe interest rates will rise, many investors opt for short-term bond exposure. Shorter-duration fixed-income ETFs offer perpetual short-term exposure to minimise interest rate risk.

Investors with a strong conviction in future rate hikes may opt for an even more aggressive strategy by shorting longer-duration-bond ETFs. While such a strategy could reap higher returns, it also carries more risk.

Core/satellite strategies

ETFs have created new core/satellite possibilities for fixed-income portfolios. Investors may choose to acquire efficient, low-cost core exposure through an aggregate fixed-income ETF and then take smaller bets on duration or credit risk with ETFs of specific maturities or credit ratings. Or, after satisfying their core exposure, investors may opt to spend the majority of their risk budget on individual bonds or active bond funds they believe will outperform the market. International bonds and high-yield ETFs or mutual funds could also be preferred satellite investments.

Instead of an aggregate core, investors may decide to create a core comprising relatively risk-free treasuries and money market funds, and then invest more of their risk budgets in satellite investments that exhibit greater volatility in price and performance, such as international bonds, municipals or convertibles.

Sector rotation strategies

As illustrated previously (Table 13.2), markets are variable and cyclical. Segments of the fixed-income market perform differently from one year to the next in response to various inflationary pressures, interest rate movements and economic events. Some investors believe they can capitalise on these cycles in performance by rotating among different sectors. With fixed-income ETFs, implementing a sector rotation strategy is relatively simple. As with all sector rotation strategies, there is a degree of timing involved on the investor's part, where they must have conviction in the future performance of a particular segment of the fixed-income market.

Transition strategies

Fixed-income ETFs are optimal vehicles for transitioning portfolio assets from one fund manager to the next. Rather than holding cash, investors can maintain their fixed-income allocation and stay invested in their chosen fixed-income market while assessing where or with whom to invest next. Whereas once money markets or individual short-term treasuries may have been the transition vehicle of choice, investors now have an increasingly diverse number of fixed-income ETFs to choose from. Fixed-income ETFs not only offer investors the opportunity to remain fully invested in a specific segment of the fixed-income market, but they also provide the flexibility and liquidity needed to move cash quickly into a new investment or fund when the opportunity is ripe.

Retirement strategies

Bonds have always had a reputation for capital preservation and income, making them choice investments for the risk-averse, as well as for retirees and those approaching retirement. The introduction of fixed-income ETFs only enhances the bond's appeal and usefulness as a wealth preservation and income-generating tool.

Let us start with the obvious: bonds may be a lower-risk alternative, making them attractive to retirees who need to preserve their money. T-bills, treasury notes and bonds offer investors capital preservation along with modest-interest income payments.

The second most obvious benefit: steady income. Because fixed-income ETFs typically pay out interest income monthly, they may offer retirees a better tool for managing their retirement income and spending than many individual bonds or bond mutual funds.

Taking the longer view on retirement, inflation-linked ETFs may help investors not only to generate steady income, but to match future or predicted liabilities. Predicted healthcare costs for retirees, for example, are staggering. A couple retiring in 2010 can expect to pay more than US$200,000 in out-of-pocket healthcare costs – and that is not including long-term care (Table 13.11). Inflation-linked ETFs may be one means for investors to ensure that the assets they set aside to meet future liabilities keep pace with inflation.

Laddered portfolio strategies

If you invest in bonds with the same maturity and they all mature when yields on new bonds are lower, you will be forced to reinvest your money at the lower rate. Laddering a portfolio, or buying bonds of different and ascending maturities, can be a smart way to diversify fixed-income exposure and mitigate interest rate risk. But laddering individual bonds can be an expensive and cumbersome strategy to maintain. As individual bonds mature, an investor will need continually to rebalance the portfolio and reinvest as needed to ensure the portfolio is at all times diversified among bonds of

Table 13.11 Predicted out-of-pocket healthcare costs

Retirement year	Single (US$)	Couple (US$)
2010	102,966	205,932
2020	141,752	283,503
2030	188,899	377,798
2040	245,767	491,534

Source: Center for Retirement Research, Boston College, February 2008

varying maturities. And, with the minimums that bonds require, implementing and managing a laddered strategy can be both time- and capital-intensive.

Alternatively, bond ETFs offer perpetual duration, eliminating the need to continually rebalance a laddered portfolio. For example, once you invest in a short-term treasury ETF, the ETF does the work for you to ensure continual exposure to bonds of short duration. In addition to their perpetual duration, ETFs carry relatively low expenses and require no investment minimums.

CRITERIA FOR SELECTING FIXED-INCOME ETFs

There are several criteria investors should consider when selecting fixed-income ETFs.

Quality and construction of underlying benchmarks

Just as any chain is only as strong as its weakest link, an ETF is only as strong as its underlying benchmark. The quality and objective of an underlying benchmark, determined by its construction methodology, must be a consideration when selecting the right ETF for your needs.

Size and skill of fixed-income ETF manager

Size matters when it comes to fixed-income investing. A larger-sized fixed-income asset manager may be able to negotiate lower transaction costs and leverage other operational efficiencies, resulting in potentially lower costs for investors. While critically important when selecting active ETFs, manager skill is still a vital consideration when selecting traditional fixed-income ETFs. A large and experienced manager with intimate knowledge of OTC markets may be able to price securities more easily, a challenge in a market that has historically lacked transparency.

Credit quality and volatility ratings for bond ETFs

Such as the bonds themselves, some fixed-income ETFs are rated by large agencies like Standard & Poor's and Moody's, at the request of the ETF sponsor. S&P, for example, assigns credit and volatility ratings to more than 26 different fixed-income ETFs. Ratings range from "AAAf" to "CCCf", where the "f" denotes that it is a fund rating.

THE EVOLUTION OF FIXED-INCOME ETFs: WHAT IS ON THE HORIZON?

If the equity ETF market is any indicator of what is to come, the future of the fixed-income ETF marketplace is likely to be characterised by continued innovation and growth.

More focused international ETFs

We should see the international bond ETF market grow increasingly segmented. In 2009, we are likely to see emerging-market debt ETFs tracking local currencies come to market. In addition, there seems to be an appetite for country-specific government bonds.

Active ETFs

Following the trend in the ETF marketplace, growth in active fixed-income ETFs will likely increase. But their successful development and long-term viability rely on a number of factors. Among them are: the ability to disclose portfolio holdings; the development of platforms to support these products; and the capability to meet regulatory requirements, which are only likely to increase in the wake of the passage of the Emergency Economic Stabilisation Act of 2008.

Blended portfolios

Bond ETFs will likely play a larger role in the creation of blended portfolios such as target-date mutual funds, sometimes referred to as asset-allocation or life-cycle funds. Target-date funds themselves are growing in number and assets. That trend will likely continue per the Pension Protection Act, passed in August of 2006. This legislation paved the way for employers to use target funds as the default auto-enroll option for 401(k) plans or other employer-sponsored retirement plans.

According to a Hewitt Associates report, automation is becoming standard in 401(k) plans and investment defaults have grown more diversified, with 50% of plans defaulting to target-date funds. Assets invested in target-date now comprise more than 9% of US 401(k) assets. As of September 2008, fixed-income and stable-value assets comprised more than 33% of US 401(k) assets.[7]

Since bond ETFs are traded on the exchange, pricing is more transparent – an advantage relative to some types of individual bonds. Transparent pricing is critical for mutual funds that have to be priced daily.

Income portfolios combining high yield with long maturity

Where will income be found? It just may be the question of the decade, in large part prompted by the number of baby boomers looking to transition their retirement assets into income-generating investments. Also, dividends on stocks have gradually waned over the last decade, making them less reliable sources of income than they once were. While dividend ETFs have certainly grown in favour, the fixed-income ETF market presents opportunities for even more innovation in this area. We may well see more income-oriented ETFs emerge, whereby higher-yielding bonds are combined in a single portfolio with long-duration bonds of higher quality.

Cash ETFs

While we saw earlier that many investors might consider short-term treasuries as an alternative to money markets, it is unlikely that we will witness the emergence of ETFs that invest in ultra-short-term investment-grade securities with maturities of less than three months. These investments will share many characteristics with money markets. However, while money market funds are not required to disclose holdings daily, ETFs are. They may be preferable to investors desiring greater transparency and, again, no investment minimum.

ETFs BREATHE NEW LIFE INTO STODGY OLD BONDS

The variety of fixed-income vehicles available today is quite remarkable, considering where we were only a decade ago. What we have covered in this chapter is likely just the tip of the iceberg in terms of the asset class's continued evolution. In a world riddled with uncertainty, one thing is for sure: the ETF is a game changer for fixed-income investors. Never before have investors had such transparent and cost-effective access to the fixed-income markets, especially segments that have typically been the most opaque and difficult to price.

Within the past few years, we have experienced both positive and negative market cycles – including some especially difficult ones for fixed income. ETFs have historically performed as expected – even throughout the most turbulent of times. For investors seeking products that deliver the precise fixed-income exposure they say they are going to deliver, the ETF is a creditable choice.

1 As of September 30, 2008. Global equity market capitalisation is measured by the MSCI AC World Index. Global Fixed Income is measured by the Lehman Multiverse Index. US equity market capitalisation is measured by the Dow Jones Wilshire 5000 Index. US Fixed-Income market cap is measured by the Lehman US Universal Index. SSgA Strategy & Research.
2 Federal Reserve.
3 Federal Reserve.
4 Federal Reserve.
5 Bureau of Labor Statistics of the US Department of Labor.
6 SSgA Strategy and Research as of 30/09/2008.
7 Hewitt Associates. The Hewitt 401(k) Index, September 2008.

REFERENCE

Hougan, Matt, 2008, "ETF Investors Spread it Around", URL: http://www.indexuniverse.com, August 12.

14

Sector Investment through ETFs

Jane Li

FundQuest Incorporated

The performance of different sectors within a market index can vary significantly. For instance, the S&P 500 Index was down 13% over the 12 months from July 1, 2007 to June 30, 2008, while the energy sector gained 23%, the healthcare sector dropped 12%, and the financials sector lost over 44% during the same period. The second half of 2008 was extremely difficult for equity investors as all sectors suffered heavy losses and the S&P 500 index lost 28% of its value. However, some sectors held up better than other sectors. For instance, the healthcare sector declined "only" 12%, compared to the financials sector's 36% loss and the energy sector's 40% drop.

Sector allocation is often one of the major factors contributing to a portfolio's performance. Many portfolio managers make active sector bets and sector rotations based on their top-down macro forecasts.

However, before making any decision on sector investment it is important to understand the features and risks associated with various sectors. In this chapter we will address the following issues:

- the classification and definition of different sectors;
- comparing two different sector investment vehicles: ETFs and open-end mutual funds;
- using exotic beta and real alpha to evaluate the benefits of sector investment;
- how to integrate sector exposure into portfolio construction; and
- how to select sector ETFs.

SECTOR DEFINITION AND CLASSIFICATION

An economy can be divided into various sectors to define the proportion of the population engaged in the activity sector. The activities include producing raw material and basic foods, manufacturing finished goods, providing services to the general population and to businesses, etc.

Broad-based market indexes are designed to represent the performance of a whole stock market – and, by proxy, reflect investor sentiment on the state of the general economy. More specialised indexes track the performance of specific sectors of the market. Stocks are classified into different sectors and industries based on what companies actually do.

There are many different ways to classify sectors. Below, we will compare three common classification systems: Global Industry Classification Standard (GICS), Industry Classification Benchmark (ICB) and Morningstar Sectors Classification.

MSCI and S&P developed the Global Industry Classification system jointly. GICS has the longest history among the three systems and may be the best known. GICS classifies companies into 10 sectors: energy, materials, industrials, healthcare, financials, telecommunications, utilities, consumer discretionary, consumer staples and information technology. Each sector is further divided into industry groups, industries and subindustries. The GICS structure consists of 10 sectors, 24 industry groups, 67 industries and 147 subindustries.

ICB was developed by Dow Jones and FTSE. ICB classifies companies and securities based on their source of revenue or where it constitutes the majority of its revenue. The structure is based on 10 industries, 18 super-sectors, 39 sectors and 104 subsectors.

Morningstar divides the stock universe into three major economic spheres or super-sectors: the information economy, the service economy and the manufacturing economy. Within each of these super sectors, four specific groups are defined for a total of 12 sectors.

Table 14.1 provides a side-by-side comparison of three classification systems.

In general all three systems are very similar, but not the same. The consumer and technology categories are the most different among the systems, as Table 14.1 shows. GICS divides the consumer category into consumer discretionary and consumer staples sectors,

Table 14.1 Sector classification systems

GICS	ICB	Morningstar
10 sectors	**10 industries**	**12 sectors**
Energy	Oil and gas	Energy
Materials	Basic materials	
Industrials	Industrials	Industrial materials
Healthcare	Healthcare	Healthcare
Financials	Financials	Financial services
Telecommunications	Telecommunications	Telecommunications
Utilities	Utilities	Utilities
Consumer discretionary		
Consumer staples		
Information technology	**Technology**	
	Consumer goods	**Consumer goods**
	Consumer services	**Consumer services**
		Business services
		Software
		Hardware
		Media

while ICB and Morningstar divide the consumer category into consumer goods and consumer services.

The GICS consumer discretionary sector encompasses those industries that tend to be most sensitive to economic cycles. It includes both manufacturing and services segments. The GICS consumer staples sector is comprised of companies engaged in businesses that are less sensitive to economic cycles. It includes manufacturers and distributors of food, beverages and tobacco and producers of non-durable household goods and personal products. It also includes food and drug retailing companies as well as supermarkets and consumer super centres.

We cannot directly map the consumer discretionary sector in GICS to either the consumer goods or the consumer services industry/sector in ICB or Morningstar. You would need to combine the two consumer categories of each for them to be equal.

Both GICS and ICB classify "Technology" as one sector, while Morningstar divides "Technology" into software and hardware sectors. Morningstar also has two additional sectors: media and business services.

According to Morningstar, the media sector includes companies that own and operate broadcast networks and those that create content or provide it for other media companies. These companies are usually included in the consumer discretionary sector in GICS.

The business services sector includes advertising, printing, publishing, business support, consultants, employment, engineering and construction, security services, waste management, distributors and transportation. These companies are generally included in the industrials sector in GICS.

The weights of sectors or industries are not the same for each system. Therefore, we need to know which system, GICS, ICB or Morningstar, is referenced when we read about or plan sector weights or industry weights.

Even within the same classification system, sector weights are not constant, they can change significantly over time due to the development of the economy. We will use the S&P 500 Index as an example. The S&P 500 Index is one of the most widely watched stock market indexes. The index contains the stocks of 500 Large-Cap corporations, most of which are American, and is considered to be a bellwether for the US economy. Many index funds and exchange-traded funds (ETFs) track the performance of the S&P 500 Index by holding the same stocks as the index, in the same proportions, thus attempting to match its performance (before fees and expenses).

The S&P 500 Index uses GICS to classify sectors. Figures 14.1 and 14.2 and Table 14.2 demonstrate how the sector weightings within the S&P 500 Index have changed in the past.

During the 12-month period from December 31, 2007 to December 31, 2008 the financials sector lost ground as many banks, mortgage companies and primary brokerage firms saw their stock plummet during the credit crisis. The weighting of the financials sector in the S&P 500 Index shrank from 17.6% to 13.3% in just 12 months. The healthcare and consumer staples sectors gained the most weight at the expense of the financials sector. As of the end of 2008, the healthcare sector almost tied information technology, becoming one of the largest sectors in the S&P 500 Index.

The changes in sector weightings were more broadly spread and amplified over an extended period. As indicated in Table 14.1, the telecommunication services sector counted for almost 10% of the S&P 500 Index in 1993, while today it weighs only 3.8%. The consumer discretionary sector was the largest loser over the past 15 years in terms of sector weight. During the same period, the technology

Figure 14.1 Sector weightings changes over one year

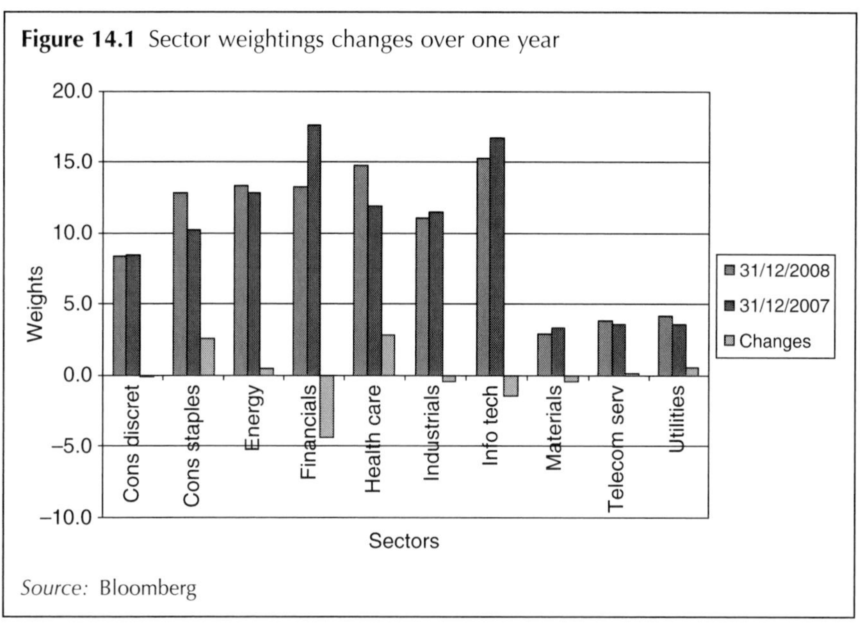

Source: Bloomberg

Figure 14.2 Sector weightings changes over 15 years

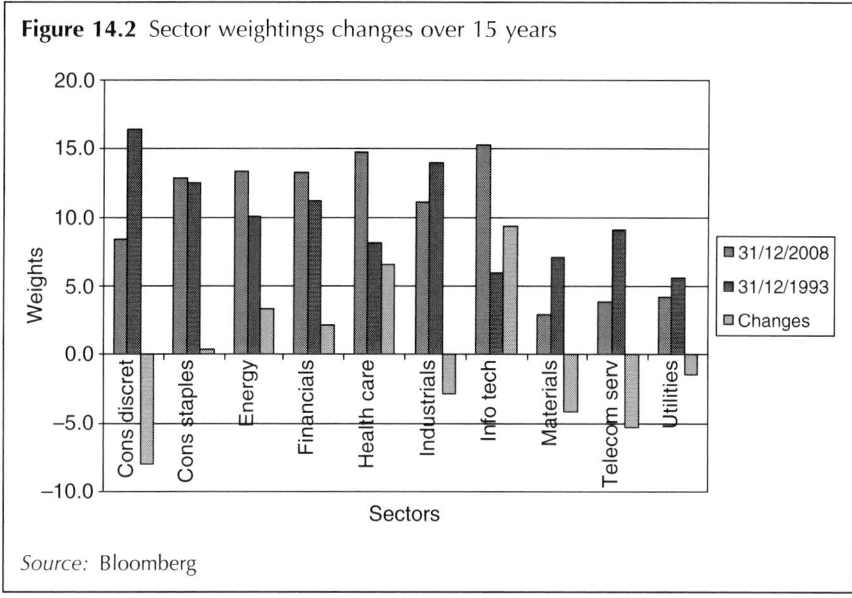

Source: Bloomberg

sector almost tripled its weighting in the index, and the healthcare sector gained 6.6% in sector weight during the period.

Many sector ETFs are based on different systems. For example, State Street and Vanguard sponsored sector ETFs are based on the

Table 14.2 Changes in sector weightings

S&P index sector weighting	% weight	% weight	1-year	% weight	15-year
Name	31/12/2008	31/12/2007	Changes	31/12/1993	Changes
Cons discret	8.4	8.5	−0.1	16.4	−8.0
Cons staples	12.9	10.2	2.6	12.5	0.4
Energy	13.3	12.9	0.5	10.0	3.3
Financials	13.3	17.6	−4.3	11.2	2.1
Healthcare	14.8	12.0	2.8	8.2	6.6
Industrials	11.1	11.5	−0.4	13.9	−2.9
Info tech	15.3	16.7	−1.5	5.9	9.3
Materials	2.9	3.3	−0.4	7.1	−4.2
Telecom serv	3.8	3.6	0.2	9.1	−5.3
Utilities	4.2	3.6	0.6	5.6	−1.4

Source: Bloomberg

GICS system, while Barclays sponsored sector ETFs are based on the ICB system.

In the following analysis, we will follow Morningstar's category classification and focus on US ETFs and open-end mutual funds classified in the "speciality" categories. There are eight "speciality" categories in the Morningstar system: communications, financial, health, natural resources, precious metals, real estate, technology and utilities. See the Appendix for the definition of these categories.

COMPARING SECTOR ETFs AND OPEN-END MUTUAL FUNDS

Investors can obtain exposure to sectors via either sector ETFs or open-end mutual funds. An ETF is similar to a mutual fund but trades like a stock throughout the day. ETFs combine the features of mutual funds with individual securities. ETFs usually aim to track certain market indexes, while most open-end mutual funds aim to outperform certain market segments through active portfolio management.

There are a few open-end mutual funds that are designed to track indexes, and some ETFs claim to be "actively managed". We will not focus on these funds since they remain a tiny fraction of sector investment.

According to the Morningstar database more than 800 ETFs existed in the US as of June 30, 2008, out of which 279 ETFs fell into eight speciality categories. In other words, more than 30% of ETFs focused on investing in certain specific sectors. We are not surprised by these findings. Over the past few years, since ETFs following traditional broad indexes have become ubiquitous, ETF sponsors have been competing on offering "niche" ETFs that focus on specific sectors, industries or even subindustries.

There are approximately 7,000 distinct open-end mutual funds in the US, of which only around 400 funds are speciality funds. That is fewer than 6% of existing open-end mutual funds.

In the following analysis we studied the historical performance of 2,770 ETFs and open-end sector mutual funds, including obsolete funds, in eight speciality categories. Obsolete funds are usually liquidated or merged with other funds. If a fund offers different share classes, we treated each share class as a different fund to capture the impact of different expense ratios on portfolio returns.

We included obsolete funds in this study to reduce survivorship bias: the tendency for companies or mutual funds to be excluded from a database because they no longer exist. Mutual funds with poor performance tend to be dropped by mutual-fund companies, generally because of poor results or low asset accumulation. This phenomenon, which is widespread in the fund industry, results in an overestimation of the past returns of mutual funds. For example, a mutual fund company's selection of funds today will include only those that have been successful in the past. Many losing funds are closed and merged into other funds to hide poor performance.

In our study, we took this important issue into account when analysing past performance. We analysed approximately 1,000 obsolete funds in our database and included their historical asset base and returns during their existence when calculating category composite performance. By including obsolete funds in the population when calculating category averages, the data better reflects the reality of the category's historical returns.

Open-end funds are a traditional sector investing vehicle. While ETFs have a much shorter history, they have recently gained popularity. Total assets in open-end sector funds still significantly outweigh that of ETFs. In fact, 70% of sector investing assets are gathered by open-end mutual funds, while only 30% are invested in ETFs. However, the average size of each ETF is much bigger than the average size of each open-end fund.

The expense ratio is an important differentiator between sector ETFs and open-end mutual funds. Table 14.3 lists the simple average expense ratios and asset-weighted average expense ratios of different types of sector funds. ETFs offer lower expense ratios by both measurements.

We also found that the asset-weighted average expense ratios were much lower than the simple average expense ratios. That is to say, in general, funds with lower expense ratios were much bigger in terms of assets under management than funds with higher expense ratios. Two factors could have contributed to this outcome. First, large funds can spread their costs over a bigger asset base, which helps achieve economies of scale, lowering the average expense ratios. Second, funds with below average expense ratios are more attractive to investors than funds with higher expense ratios.

ETFs and open-end funds have different average lifespans. Open-end funds that are still live today have an average lifespan of almost nine years, while existing ETFs have been around for less than three years. Obsolete open-end funds on average survived more than five years before being liquidated or merged, while obsolete ETFs on average survived less than two years.

In Tables 14.4, 14.5 and 14.6, we provide the breakdown of the number of funds in each of the eight speciality categories as of June 30, 2008.

Table 14.3 Sector investment (as of June 30, 2008)

	ETFs	Open-end funds	Total
Number of sector funds	285	2,485	2,770
Total assets (US$ million)	117,872	278,864	396,736
Percentage of sector assets (%)	30	70	100
Average size of the funds (US$ million)	422	226	262
Simple average expense (%)	0.56	1.66	1.62
Asset-weighted average expense (%)	0.28	1.02	0.73
Number of obsolete funds	6	917	923
Average lifespan of obsolete funds (year)	1.70	5.16	4.64
Average lifespan of live funds (year)	2.73	8.93	7.04

Source: FundQuest/Morningstar

Table 14.4 Number of sector ETFs in study (as of June 30, 2008)

Category	Live ETFs	Obsolete ETFs	Total ETFs
Speciality communications	10		10
Speciality financial	25		25
Speciality health	42	1	43
Speciality natural resources	111	2	113
Speciality precious metals	14		14
Speciality real estate	30		30
Speciality technology	32	3	35
Speciality utilities	15		15
Total	279	6	285

Source: FundQuest/Morningstar

Table 14.5 Number of sector open-end funds in study (as of June 30, 2008)

Category	Live open-end funds	Obsolete open-end funds	Total open-end funds
Speciality communications	50	48	98
Speciality financial	146	71	217
Speciality health	205	141	346
Speciality natural resources	252	31	283
Speciality precious metals	73	43	116
Speciality real estate	455	126	581
Speciality technology	272	383	655
Speciality utilities	115	74	189
Total	1,568	917	2,485

Source: FundQuest/Morningstar

Table 14.6 Number of sector funds in study (as of June 30, 2008)

Category	Total live funds	Total obsolete funds	Total funds
Speciality communications	60	48	108
Speciality financial	171	71	242
Speciality health	247	142	389
Speciality natural resources	363	33	396
Speciality precious metals	87	43	130
Speciality real estate	485	126	611
Speciality technology	304	386	690
Speciality utilities	130	74	204
Total	1,847	923	2,770

Source: FundQuest/Morningstar

The natural resources category has the largest number of ETFs in the market. Hundreds of ETFs have been brought to the market within the past few years, when commodities and energy experienced a fully charged rally. It is well known in the industry that investors tend to chase performance. Therefore, it is not surprising that many new offerings were focused on the sizzling natural resource arena.

The real estate category has the largest number of live open-end mutual funds (455). Open-end mutual funds have a much longer history than ETFs and many open-end real-estate funds were launched during the housing bubble era. The technology category has the second largest number of live funds but by far the largest number of obsolete funds. Hundreds of technology funds were brought to the market in the late 1990s that later became casualties when the technology bubble burst in 2000.

In combination of ETFs and open-end mutual funds, the real estate (485) and natural resources (363) categories have the largest number of offerings and the communication (60) category is the smallest.

Table 14.7 gives an overview of assets allocated in each of the eight speciality categories.

The natural resources sector is by far the most popular sector, representing 36% of total sector fund assets. Real estate is the second-largest sector in terms of total assets. The housing bubble was a main contributor to the asset growth in the real estate sector. However

Table 14.7 Assets of sector funds (million as of 30/06/2008)

Category	ETFs	Open-end funds	Total	Weight (%)
Speciality communications	1,459	3,253	4,712	1
Speciality financial	13,560	6,630	20,190	5
Speciality health	9,722	41,647	51,369	13
Speciality natural resources	44,524	98,274	142,798	36
Speciality precious metals	26,681	22,834	49,516	12
Speciality real estate	9,096	60,534	69,630	18
Speciality technology	8,462	26,091	34,553	9
Speciality utilities	4,366	19,601	23,967	6
Total	117,872	278,864	396,735	100

Source: FundQuest/Morningstar

after the bubble burst and shattered the financial markets, investors switched gears and poured tons of money into the booming commodity and energy areas. Although the real estate category still has the largest number of funds, total assets in real estate funds are less than half that of the natural resources category.

EVALUATING THE BENEFIT OF SECTOR INVESTMENT (MEASURED BY EXOTIC BETA AND REAL ALPHA)

Both ETFs and open-end funds can provide investors with exposure to sector investing and there are hundreds of ETFs and thousands of mutual funds to choose from.

Investors should ask the following questions before making decisions in sector investing:

- Has sector investing historically outperformed broad market investing?
- Should investors choose passively managed ETFs or actively managed open-end mutual funds? Have active managers added value in sector investing?
- Have active managers done relatively better in certain categories than in other categories?

In this section we will address these questions by using two measurements, exotic beta and real alpha, to evaluate the relative performance of sector ETFs and active mutual funds.

Exotic beta is a concept that was first introduced in the hedge fund world. It refers to a premium associated with exposure to a particular asset class. In other words, exotic beta measures the return derived from exposure to some systematic risk factors (such as credit risk, liquidity risk and volatility risk) that is common to a particular asset class, but not directly correlated to traditional stock or bond markets. These risk premiums vary by investment category.

Real alpha is the additional return truly stemming from the unique ability and skill set of fund managers. It is the active alpha that can be ported on to completely unrelated betas. Real alpha measures manager skill. Studies suggest that only a small fraction of hedge fund returns are actually accounted for by real alpha.

See the Appendix for the methodology of calculating exotic beta and real alpha.

The study sought to identify:

- speciality categories in which active managers provided value through their unique investment management capabilities in excess of the category's index movement; and
- speciality categories that have generated excess returns through risk premiums not correlated to the broad markets.

In this analysis, we studied the historical performance of 2,770 ETFs and open-end sector mutual funds, including obsolete funds, in eight speciality categories. If a fund offered different share classes, we treated each share class as a different fund. We included obsolete funds in this study to minimise survivorship bias.

Returns were analysed net of management fees and other expenses.

The data of this study covers a 15-year span from July 1, 1992 to June 30, 2008. We further segmented the time span into five mutually exclusive three-year trailing periods:

- July 1, 1993 to June 30, 1996;
- July 1, 1996 to June 30, 1999;
- July 1, 1999 to June 30, 2002;
- July 1, 2002 to June 30, 2005; and
- July 1, 2005 to June 30, 2008.

Traditionally, many investors and researchers use the three-, five-, 10- and 15-year trailing periods when evaluating investment performance. Recent performance can have a heavy impact on returns over all time periods since the three-year returns are also captured in the five-, 10- and 15-year trailing periods. Our methodology avoids this redundancy by removing the overlap in the trailing periods.

We also analysed managers' performance patterns in different market environments. We divided the 15-year period from July 1, 1992 to June 30, 2008 into four periods based on the market cycle:

- (Bull1) July 1, 1993 to March 31 2000;
- (Bear1) April 1, 2000 to September 30, 2002;
- (Bull2) October 1, 2002 to June 30, 2007; and
- (Bear2) July 1, 2007 to June 30, 2008.

We calculated the asset-weighted average exotic beta and real alpha of each speciality category for each time period. The asset base of each fund at the beginning of each time period was used in calculating the asset-weighted category average.

Tables 14.8 and 14.9 list the results of the study.

Real alpha

In general, we recommend using active managers for investment categories deemed to have consistently generated positive real alpha through manager skill. Specifically, we suggest using an active approach if the investment category generated positive real alpha over at least four of the five time periods in the study, or if the average real alpha for all time periods was above 1.5%. Conversely, we recommend adopting a passive approach for investment categories that have underperformed for at least four of the five time periods of the study, or if the average real alpha for all time periods was below –1.5%.

Investment categories that fall outside these two definitions are considered to have performed in line with their sector benchmarks, and either active or passive management could be appropriate.

An investment category was considered to have generated positive real alpha if its asset-weighted real alpha exceeded +0.5% for the time period. If the asset-weighted average real alpha was below –0.5%, we consider the category to have underperformed for

Table 14.8 Historical three-year real alpha (July 1, 1993–June 30, 2008)

Category	July 1, 1993–June 30, 1996	July 1, 1996–June 30, 1999	July 1, 1999–June 30, 2002	July 1, 2002–June 30, 2005	July 1, 2005–June 30, 2008
Speciality communications	0.77	1.96	–11.74	7.25	2.65
Speciality financial	2.68	–2.47	0.81	–0.15	–1.66
Speciality health	0.81	–2.65	6.05	2.70	2.26
Speciality natural resources	0.64	–0.26	9.08	4.58	5.61
Speciality precious metals	8.04	–4.31	0.29	15.48	26.33
Speciality real estate	–0.23	0.39	–1.02	1.69	–0.16
Speciality technology	–0.27	–6.01	–10.96	–4.31	1.74
Speciality utilities	2.36	1.78	–4.29	5.70	4.04
Total	2.35	–2.04	–3.59	0.88	2.64

Source: FundQuest

Table 14.9 Historical real alpha in bull and bear markets (July 1, 1993–June 30, 2008)

Category	Bull1: July 1, 1993–March 31, 2000	Bear1: April 1, 2000–September 30, 2002	Bull2: October 10, 2002–June 30, 2007	Bear2: July 1, 2007–June 30, 2008
Speciality communications	4.75	–12.99	4.53	–3.45
Speciality financial	–0.99	3.17	–0.34	–4.48
Speciality health	1.35	1.59	3.36	1.05
Speciality natural resources	–0.06	10.34	2.12	11.62
Speciality precious metals	–0.96	6.00	20.11	36.16
Speciality real estate	–0.55	–1.01	1.25	–0.45
Speciality technology	–1.35	–8.98	–2.09	5.72
Speciality utilities	3.18	–9.95	8.97	1.66
Total	1.44	–6.17	1.90	4.21

Source: FundQuest

the time period. If the asset-weighted average real alpha fell between +0.5% and –0.5%, we consider the category neutral.

We further make specific recommendations for different market cycles. If the investment category generated positive real alpha in both bull market periods in the study, we suggest utilising an active approach in the category during bull markets. If the investment category generated negative real alpha in both bull market periods, we suggest utilising a passive approach in the category during bull markets. If the investment category fell outside these two definitions, we considered the category to be neutral in bull markets, and either active or passive management could be appropriate. A similar rule applies in bear market periods.

Actionable conclusions

Based on the results of our real alpha analysis, we found no meaningful difference between active and passive investing approaches within the general sector investment universe. However, once the universe was broken down into distinct speciality categories, there were significant performance differences.

We found that both active and passive investments have strengths and weaknesses. Utilising active managers might be more

Table 14.10 Active/passive recommendation based on real alpha

Category	Bull markets	Bear markets	General
Speciality communications	Active	Passive	Active
Speciality financial	Neutral	Neutral	Neutral
Speciality health	Active	Active	Active
Speciality natural resources	Neutral	Active	Active
Speciality precious metals	Neutral	Active	Active
Speciality real estate	Neutral	Passive	Neutral
Speciality technology	Passive	Neutral	Passive
Speciality utilities	Active	Neutral	Active
Total	Active	Neutral	Neutral

Source: FundQuest

favourable than passive in certain categories, but less favourable in others.

In general market conditions we recommend active investing in the communication, health, natural resources, precious metals and utilities categories and passive investing in the technology category. In the financials and real estate categories, the study found no meaningful difference between active and passive investing approaches.

We also found that active managers in the communications and utilities categories tended to add more value in bull markets than in bear markets, while active managers in the natural resources and precious metals categories tended to add more value in bear markets. Managers in the healthcare sector have added value in both bull and bear markets.

Exotic beta

In terms of exotic beta, a category was considered to have consistently provided a specific risk premium on top of broad market returns if its asset-weighted average exotic beta was above +0.5% for at least four of the five time periods in the study, or if the average exotic beta for all time periods was above 1.5%. In general, we recommend an overweighting of these categories, which are more likely to obtain above-market returns.

Similarly, if the asset-weighted average exotic beta was below –0.5% for at least four of the five time periods of the study, or if the average exotic beta for all time periods was below –1.5%, we

Table 14.11 Historical three-year exotic beta (July 1, 1993–June 30, 2008)

Category	July 1, 1993–June 30, 1996	July 1, 1996–June 30, 1999	July 1, 1999–June 30, 2002	July 1, 2002–June 30, 2005	July 1, 2005–June 30, 2008
Speciality communications	–1.60	–1.05	2.53	0.18	1.21
Speciality financial	–1.65	–1.08	7.11	1.37	–9.57
Speciality health	2.47	–0.26	1.49	1.84	–1.89
Speciality natural resources	–0.88	–0.95	6.09	10.59	16.51
Speciality precious metals	–13.56	–29.83	15.15	–0.29	3.83
Speciality real estate	–1.79	–1.34	10.10	13.49	–0.15
Speciality technology	3.39	1.52	23.44	2.37	0.69
Speciality utilities	–7.83	0.21	–0.33	3.03	5.49
Total	–4.95	–2.22	10.59	3.78	2.63

Source: FundQuest

Table 14.12 Historical exotic beta in bull and bear markets (July 1, 1993–June 30, 2008)

Category	Bull1: July 1, 1993–March 31, 2000	Bear1: April 1, 2000–September 30, 2002	Bull2: October 1, 2002–June 30, 2007	Bear2: July 1, 2007–June 30, 2008
Speciality communications	0.34	1.09	–1.27	7.70
Speciality financial	–4.16	11.37	0.50	–19.62
Speciality health	3.71	5.16	–1.05	–3.07
Speciality natural resources	–0.98	6.18	15.96	28.39
Speciality precious metals	–15.46	30.52	1.94	–0.64
Speciality real estate	–3.05	15.13	10.05	–0.36
Speciality technology	6.80	9.09	–2.06	9.88
Speciality utilities	–4.13	0.98	2.71	12.38
Total	–2.91	7.73	1.38	6.52

Source: FundQuest

consider the category to have generated fewer premiums than broad market returns. We recommend an underweighting of these categories, which are less likely to obtain above-market returns.

Investment categories that fall outside these two definitions are considered neutral.

We further make specific recommendations for different market cycles. If the investment category generated positive exotic beta in both bull market periods in the study, or if the average exotic beta for both bull market periods was above 1.5%, we suggest overweighting the category during bull markets. If the investment category generated negative exotic beta in both bull market periods in the study, or if the average exotic beta for both bull market periods was below –1.5%, we suggest underweighting the category during bull markets. We follow a similar rule in the bear market analysis.

Actionable conclusions

Risk premiums vary by investment category. We found that, in general, the healthcare, natural resources, real estate and technology categories generated positive exotic beta, while the financials and precious metals generated negative exotic beta. We also found that exotic beta was not stable over different time periods. No category was able to generate positive exotic beta over all five of the three-year periods and the bull and bear markets.

Sector investing appears to add more value during bear markets, as all but the financials category generated positive exotic beta in bear markets. In bull markets, we recommend overweighting the healthcare, natural resources, real estate and technology categories, and underweighting the financials, precious metals and utilities categories.

Table 14.13 Allocation recommendation based on exotic beta

Category	Bull markets	Bear markets	General
Speciality communications	Neutral	Overweight	Neutral
Speciality financial	Underweight	Underweight	Underweight
Speciality health	Overweight	Overweight	Overweight
Speciality natural resources	Overweight	Overweight	Overweight
Speciality precious metals	Underweight	Overweight	Underweight
Speciality real estate	Overweight	Overweight	Overweight
Speciality technology	Overweight	Overweight	Overweight
Speciality utilities	Underweight	Overweight	Neutral
Total	Underweight	Overweight	Overweight

Source: FundQuest

We believe overweighting categories that have historically generated positive exotic beta returns in a tactical asset allocation may enhance portfolio performance against the broad markets. However, we must keep in mind that the exotic beta was not constant over time. Periodically a portfolio's tactical asset allocation needs adjustment based on market conditions and changes in capital market assumptions.

HOW TO INTEGRATE SECTOR INVESTMENT INTO PORTFOLIO CONSTRUCTION

Sector investing is very common in practice. However, the ways that investors use sector funds can be very different. Some own a broad index fund as a core position and then selectively overweight their portfolios in a particular sector by buying ETFs or open-end mutual funds of that sector. Others do not own a core broad index fund. Instead, they own only funds that provide exposure to sectors in which they are confident. Still others may not own a core broad index fund, but own funds in all sectors. They determine weights in each sector that can deviate from the overall market weights, then reallocate or rebalance from time to time.

We recommend investors maintain well-diversified portfolios, only using sector investing as a supplement to their core portfolios to enhance, not reduce, diversification.

As indicated in Table 14.14, many sector categories have low correlation with the broad markets and other sector categories. Correlation coefficient is a measure that determines the degree to which two variable's movements are associated. The correlation coefficient will vary from –1 to +1. A –1 indicates perfect negative correlation and +1 indicates perfect positive correlation. In general, the lower the correlation coefficient, the higher potential benefit for diversification.

A sector investment that provides potential positive exotic beta and low correlation with other asset categories is desirable because these features might reduce portfolio volatility and boost portfolio returns.

Figure 14.3 demonstrates the benefits of including these categories in portfolio construction. See the Appendix for the assumptions used for this illustration.

In Figure 14.3 we compare two efficient frontiers: the dashed line represents the efficient frontier constructed with two major market

Table 14.14 Correlation coefficients between asset categories (data period: 01/07/1993–30/06/2008)

	1	2	3	4	5	6	7	8	9	10
1. S&P 500	1.00									
2. Lehman US Aggregate Bond Index	**0.02**	1.00								
3. Communications	0.85	**−0.07**	1.00							
4. Financials	0.80	**0.09**	0.55	1.00						
5. Health	0.59	**0.03**	0.65	**0.39**	1.00					
6. Natural resources	0.50	**0.00**	**0.40**	**0.45**	**0.34**	1.00				
7. Precious metals	**0.18**	**0.06**	**0.19**	**0.18**	**0.20**	0.57	1.00			
8. Real estate	**0.38**	**0.08**	**0.29**	0.55	**0.30**	**0.34**	**0.28**	1.00		
9. Technology	0.78	**−0.09**	0.90	**0.44**	0.70	**0.40**	**0.19**	**0.23**	1.00	
10. Utilities	0.73	**0.12**	0.68	0.65	0.53	0.59	**0.23**	**0.43**	0.55	1.00

Source: Zephyr

Figure 14.3 Efficient frontiers comparison

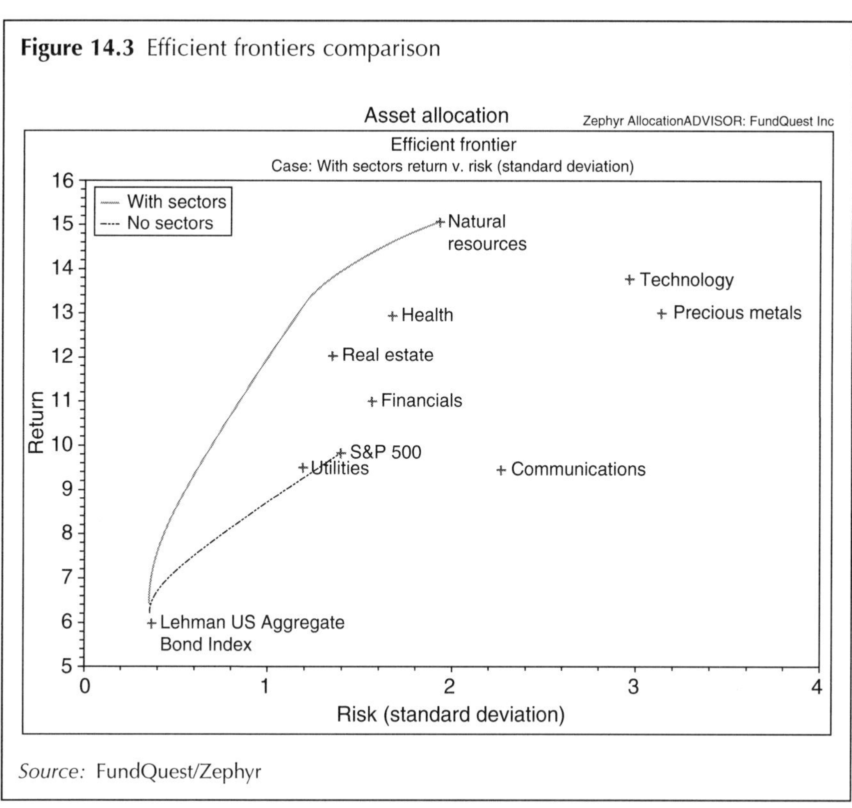

Source: FundQuest/Zephyr

indexes: the S&P 500 Index and Barclays Capital (formerly Lehman Brothers) US Aggregate Bond Index; the solid line represents the efficient frontier constructed with the abovementioned two indexes plus eight sector speciality categories. Including these categories significantly lifted the efficient frontier upward and shifted it to the left. The new efficient frontier is also much longer than before. That is to say, the inclusion of these sector categories helped to construct more efficient portfolios with higher returns, lower risk, or both.

The actual weighting of each sector in a portfolio depends on the investor's risk profile. All portfolios on the efficient frontier are "optimal" portfolios given the available asset classes, providing the best expected return at a certain risk level. Each efficient portfolio might call for a different combination of sector allocations. Again, investors need to review their capital market assumptions and re-optimise their portfolios periodically.

HOW TO SELECT SECTOR ETFs

Once investors have made the decision on sector allocations, they can hunt for the "best-of-breed" investment vehicle within a specific sector. ETFs are not necessarily the top option for all sectors.

As indicated in the earlier section "Evaluating the benefit of sector investment (measured by exotic beta and real alpha)", active funds have generally outperformed their benchmarks and generated positive real alpha in several sectors: communications, healthcare, natural resources, precious metals and utilities. Therefore, in general, active funds appear to be better choices than ETFs in these sectors.

However, in the Technology sector, on average, active managers have trailed their benchmarks and failed to add value to investors. Hence, ETFs might be a superior option in the technology sector. In the financials and real estate sectors, active managers have performed generally in line with their benchmarks. Both active funds and ETFs can be solid options in these two sectors.

In this section, we will discuss only how to select ETFs. How to select active mutual funds is another big topic that is beyond the scope of this study.

Selecting ETFs was almost a no-brainer during the early 1990s, when only a handful of ETFs were available in the market. But today,

Table 14.15 Performance comparison of four financials ETFs (performance as of June 30, 2008)

Name	Ticker	Total returns three months	Total returns (%) rank category three months	Total returns one year	Total returns (%) rank category one year	Standard deviation one year
Financial Select Sector SPDR	XLF	−18.24	78	−42.32	83	23.10
iShares Dow Jones US Financial Services	IYG	−19.79	81	−45.23	91	25.14
PowerShares Dynamic Financials	PFI	−5.22	19	−20.98	17	15.09
Vanguard Financials ETF	VFH	−16.40	70	−38.73	62	21.56

Source: Morningstar

with more than 800 ETFs competing for investor money, it is not that easy to identify the best choice.

Here we will compare four financial ETFs: Financial Select Sector SPDR (XLF); iShares Dow Jones US Financial Services (IYG); PowerShares Dynamic Financials (PFI); and Vanguard Financials ETF (VFH).

Basing your assessment just on the name of the ETFs, you might think they are similar creatures. However, if we take a closer look, we will soon realise that each fund provides a different risk profile and exposure to a variety of industries in the financials sector.

First let us take a look at recent performance. We see a wide range of dispersion of returns. Fund selection definitely matters to a portfolio's performance.

Over the past three-month and one-year periods as of June 30, 2008, iShares Dow Jones US Financial Services was the worst-performing fund within the group, while PowerShares Dynamic Financials held up best during the same time periods. The difference between their one-year return was as wide as 24%. For the past 12 months, the Vanguard Financials ETF, the second-best performing ETF, trailed PowerShares Dynamic Financials by 17%, but topped iShares Dow Jones US Financial Services by over 6%.

Table 14.16 Industry weightings

Name	Ticker	Commercial banks %	Thrifts and mortgage finance (%)	Diversified financial services (%)	Consumer finance (%)
Financial Select Sector SPDR	XLF	15.57	3.27	23.61	4.60
iShares Dow Jones US Financial Services	IYG	24.11	5.47	31.16	5.67
PowerShares Dynamic Financials	PFI	7.21	0.00	1.12	2.66
Vanguard Financials ETF	VFH	17.54	4.16	20.60	3.63

Name	Ticker	Capital markets (%)	Insurance (%)	REITs (%)	Real-estate management and development (%)
Financial Select Sector SPDR	XLF	19.74	24.72	8.26	0.21
iShares Dow Jones US Financial Services	IYG	28.38	0.29	0.00	0.00
PowerShares Dynamic Financials	PFI	24.85	64.16	0.00	0.00
Vanguard Financials ETF	VFH	15.61	25.60	12.16	0.62

Source: Morningstar

Much of the performance difference can be explained by their different exposure to various industries within the financial sector. PowerShares Dynamic Financials concentrated almost two-thirds of its total assets in the insurance industry and had little exposure to the hard-hit commercial banking and diversified financial services industries. On the other hand, more than half of iShares Dow Jones US Financial Services' total assets were invested in the commercial banking and diversified financial services industries, and it had almost no exposure to the insurance industry, which has been a relatively bright spot during the recent credit crisis.

Table 14.17 Portfolio characteristics

Name	Ticker	Expense ratio	Total holdings	Turnover	Primary prospectus benchmark
Financial Select Sector SPDR	XLF	0.23	91	15.00	S&P 500 Sec/ Financials TR
iShares Dow Jones US Financial Services	IYG	0.48	137	9.00	DJ US Financial Services TR USD
PowerShares Dynamic Financials	PFI	0.72	61	50.00	Dynamic Fincl Sector Intellidex PR USD
Vanguard Financials ETF	VFH	0.22	514	12.00	MSCI US IMI/ Financials GR USD

Source: Morningstar

Financial Select Sector SPDR and Vanguard Financials ETF are more diversified than the other two ETFs, therefore their returns stand in the middle of the group. Although PowerShares Dynamic Financials' short term performance is much better than Financial Select Sector SPDR and Vanguard Financials ETF, we believe Financial Select Sector SPDR and Vanguard Financials ETF are better options for investors who want to have a broad exposure to the financial sector.

The industry allocation of these four ETFs is very different because they are not designed to follow the same index. Financial Select Sector SPDR (XLF) tracks the S&P 500 Sec/Financials TR index; iShares Dow Jones US Financial Services (IYG) tracks the DJ US Financial Services TR USD index; PowerShares Dynamic Financials (PFI) tracks the Dynamic Fincial Sector Intellidex PR US dollar index; and Vanguard Financials ETF (VFH) tracks the MSCI US IMI/Financials GR US dollar index.

We also found that PowerShares Dynamic Financials was the most concentrated fund within the group with only 61 holdings, compared with Vanguard's 500 plus holdings. PowerShares Dynamic Financials also had the highest expense ratio and turnover ratio within the group. A high expense ratio can erode a fund's long-term performance, and a high turnover ratio might incur higher trading costs and/or trigger more taxable capital gains distributions.

Therefore, when investors select sector ETFs, it is very important for them to look beyond returns and truly understand each ETF's tracking index, holdings, industry exposure, expense ratio, turnover, etc.

SUMMARY

In this chapter we have compared three sector classification systems: GICS, ICB and Morningstar and reviewed the historical changes of sector weightings in the S&P 500 Index. We gave an overview of the sector investment universe and explored the landscape of each sector speciality category.

We analysed the historical performance of 2,770 ETFs and open-end sector mutual funds, including approximately 1,000 obsolete funds, in eight speciality categories over the past 15-year period from July 1, 1993 to June 30, 2008. We calculated real alpha and exotic beta for each sector speciality category over various trailing time periods.

Based on the results of real alpha analysis, we found that both active and passive investments have strengths and weaknesses. Utilising active managers may be more favourable than passive in certain sector speciality categories, but less favourable in others. Active managers' capability of adding value may vary in bull and bear markets.

We also found that some speciality categories have provided positive exotic beta, a specific risk premium on top of broad market returns, over various time periods. We believe overweighting categories that have historically generated positive exotic beta returns in a tactical asset allocation may enhance portfolio performance against the broad markets.

We further illustrated the benefit and strategy of integrating sector investment into portfolio construction. Finally, we used four financial ETFs as examples to explain how to select sector ETFs.

Sector investing provides investors with great flexibility and opportunities in portfolio management. However, if investors fail to maintain well-diversified portfolios, they might expose themselves to significant sector-specific risks and potentially suffer heavy losses if the performance of different sectors diverges greatly and works against the investors' expectations. The investment environment is very dynamic and constantly changing. It is crucial for investors to maintain a long-term focus, but also periodically review their portfolio construction, re-optimise the asset allocation and re-evaluate security selections.

APPENDIX

Definition of Morningstar speciality categories

Speciality communications portfolios concentrate on telecommunications and media companies of various kinds. Most buy some combination of cable television, wireless communications and communications-equipment firms as well as traditional phone companies. A few favour entertainment firms, mainly broadcasters, film studios, publishers and online service providers.

Speciality financial portfolios seek capital appreciation by investing primarily in equity securities of US or non-US financial services companies, including banks, brokerage firms, insurance companies and consumer credit providers.

Speciality health portfolios focus on the medical and healthcare industries. Most invest in a range of companies, buying everything from pharmaceutical and medical-device makers to HMOs, hospitals and nursing homes. A few portfolios concentrate on just one industry segment, such as service providers or biotechnology firms.

Speciality natural resources portfolios focus on commodity-based industries such as energy, chemicals, minerals and forest products in the US or outside of the US. Some portfolios invest across this spectrum to offer broad natural resources exposure. Others concentrate heavily or even exclusively in specific industries including energy or forest products.

Speciality real-estate portfolios invest primarily in real-estate investment trusts (REITs) of various types. REITs are companies that develop and manage real-estate properties. There are several different types of REIT, including apartment, factory-outlet, healthcare, hotel, industrial, mortgage, office and shopping-centre REITs. Some portfolios in this category also invest in real-estate operating companies.

Speciality-technology portfolios buy high-tech businesses inside or outside the US. Most concentrate on computer, semiconductor, software, networking and Internet stocks. A few also buy medical device and biotechnology stocks and some concentrate on a single technology industry.

Speciality utilities portfolios seek capital appreciation by investing primarily in equity securities of US or non-US public utilities including electric, gas and telephone-service providers.

Assumptions and inputs for sector allocation analysis

Methodology

Alpha is a portfolio measure of the difference between actual returns and expected performance, given a level of risk as measured by beta.

$$\text{Portfolio return} = \text{alpha} + \text{beta} \times (\text{market risk component})$$

In other words, alpha is the excess return, on a risk-adjusted basis, that active fund managers generate over and above their benchmark. The volatility of the residual returns is its active risk. A positive alpha figure indicates better performance than beta would predict. In contrast, a negative alpha indicates underperformance, given the expectations established by the beta. It is generally believed that positive alpha is easier to find in less efficient markets, while capturing alpha is very difficult in larger and more liquid asset classes.

Alpha can be used to directly measure the value added or subtracted by a manager. Alpha depends on two factors: (i) the assumption that market risk, as measured by beta, is the only risk measure

Table 14.18 Analysis inputs

	Forecast		Date		Constraint	
	Return (%)	Risk (%)	Start	End	Min (%)	Max (%)
Assets						
S&P 500	9.80	14.00	01/07/1993	30/06/2008	0	100
Lehman US Aggregate	6.00	3.70	01/07/1993	30/06/2008	0	100
Communications	9.50	22.70	01/07/1993	30/06/2008	0	100
Financials	11.00	15.60	01/07/1993	30/06/2008	0	100
Health	12.90	16.70	01/07/1993	30/06/2008	0	100
Natural resources	15.10	19.30	01/07/1993	30/06/2008	0	100
Precious metals	13.00	31.40	01/07/1993	30/06/2008	0	100
Real estate	12.00	13.50	01/07/1993	30/06/2008	0	100
Technology	13.80	29.60	01/07/1993	30/06/2008	0	100
Utilities	9.50	11.90	01/07/1993	30/06/2008	0	100

Source: Zephyr

necessary; and (ii) the strength of the linear relationship between the portfolio and the benchmark, as it has been measured by R-squared.

In addition, a negative alpha can sometimes result from the expenses that are present in the returns of a manager, but not in the returns of the comparison index.

Beta measures the sensitivity of a portfolio relative to the market; a portfolio with a beta of one will exactly track the market.

Exotic beta

The concept of exotic beta was first introduced into the hedge fund world. Exotic beta refers to a premium associated with a particular asset class exposure. Some studies suggest that hedge fund returns are composed of three portions: traditional beta, exotic beta and real alpha.

$$\text{Portfolio return} = \text{real alpha} + \text{exotic beta} \times (\text{particular asset class risk component}) + \text{traditional beta} \times (\text{market risk component})$$

Traditional beta refers to the return derived from exposure to traditional stock or bond markets, while exotic beta refers to the return derived from exposure to other systematic risk factors (such as credit risk, liquidity risk, volatility risk) common to each family of hedge fund strategies.

Real alpha

Real alpha is the additional return truly stemming from the unique ability and skill set of the hedge fund manager. It is the active alpha that can be ported on to completely unrelated betas. Real alpha measures the manager's skill. Recent academic analysis suggests that only a small fraction of hedge fund returns are actually accounted for by real alpha.

The main sources of returns are the risk premium derived from exotic betas. Ibbotson and Chen (2006) suggest that, during the time period from January 1995 to April 2006, on average, hedge funds have generated an alpha of 3.04% and returns from the betas of 5.94%. The 3.04% alpha measured here is traditional alpha, which includes the returns from exotic betas. Real alpha is hard to find and expensive to access, while exotic beta is relatively easy to find and cheap to get.

In this study, we applied the concepts of real alpha and exotic beta to the mutual-fund world. We calculated the best-fit alpha and traditional alpha of funds in each asset category.

We believe the best-fit alpha represents the real alpha, and the difference between the best-fit alpha and traditional alpha reflects the return derived from the exotic beta embedded within each asset category. Exotic beta is an important source of return, and also provides the benefit of diversification. Measuring each asset category's exotic beta can help optimise a portfolio's tactical asset allocation.

Regression analysis

Mathematically, alpha is a regression coefficient. In calculating it, we deducted the return of the three-month T-bill from the total return of both the portfolio and benchmark. Thus, the alpha figures shown here may be lower than those published elsewhere.

We believe that this calculation represents the fact that every investor has choices about where to place their money.

Traditional alpha was calculated for each portfolio by using a standard set of benchmarks for each asset group. In the US, we use the following benchmarks for alpha statistics: S&P 500 Index for US stock portfolios, MSCI EAFE for international stock portfolios, Barclays Capital (formerly Lehman Brothers) US Aggregate Bond Index for taxable bond portfolios, and Barclays Capital (formerly Lehman Brothers) Muni Index for municipal bond portfolios. In this study, we focus on sector funds, thus only the S&P 500 Index is used as the benchmark for traditional alpha calculation.

Best-fit alphas are calculated using the market index that shows the highest correlation (R-squared) between a portfolio and an index over the most recent certain time periods based on the best-fit R-squared. The indexes that were regressed against portfolios in calculations are shown in the following list:

- NYSE Arca Tech 100
- Dow Jones Financial
- Dow Jones Healthcare
- Dow Jones Telecommunications
- Dow Jones Utility
- Goldman Sachs Natural Resources

- JSE Gold (US$)
- MSCI AC World ID
- Standard & Poor's 500
- Wilshire REIT

Next, we calculated the exotic beta.

Since,

portfolio return = traditional alpha + traditional beta
× (broad market index risk component)

portfolio return = best-fit alpha + best-fit beta
× (best-fit index risk component)

and,

portfolio return
= best-fit alpha + exotic beta
× (particular asset class risk component) + traditional beta
× (broad market risk component)

return from exotic beta
= exotic beta × (particular asset class risk component)
= best-fit beta × (best-fit index risk component)
– traditional beta × (broad market index risk component)
= traditional alpha – best-fit alpha

Therefore, return from exotic beta is the difference between traditional alpha and best-fit alpha.

REFERENCE

Ibbotson, R., and P. Chen, 2006, "The A, B, Cs of Hedge Funds".

15

Real Estate Investment Trust ETFs

Brad Case

NAREIT

The dawn of exchange-traded funds (ETFs) has come at an important time for investors. Participants in traditional defined-benefit pension plans often had a big advantage over individual investors: they were able to invest in the full universe of asset classes, and achieve superior portfolio performance using superior asset allocations. With ETFs, though, individual investors can now gain exposure to every asset class necessary for a well-diversified, optimally performing portfolio. A critical piece of the new asset-class universe is ETFs focusing on real-estate investment through Real Estate Investment Trusts, or REITs.

REAL ESTATE AS A SEPARATE ASSET CLASS

Many investors underestimate the importance of real estate in their portfolios. Most investment advisers say that the key is to construct a portfolio that achieves efficient portfolio diversification. It is more than just "not putting all your eggs in one basket" – that is a different kind of diversification (what economists call granularity) that protects investors from bad events that may hit one investment (say, Enron stock) but not other investments in the same asset class (say, stocks). Efficient diversification means having investment in different asset classes.

An asset class is a set of investments that all share a similar expected return pattern – that is, they all (1) have roughly the same expected return, (2) have roughly the same expected volatility, and (3) are highly correlated. That third point is the most important one: high correlations among different investments in the same asset class mean that when one investment is doing poorly, the other investments in the same asset class are likely to be doing poorly as well. The reason why an efficiently diversified portfolio includes investments in different asset classes – with low correlations between asset classes – is that, when investments in one asset class do poorly, investments in another asset class are not likely to be doing poorly, so the value of the portfolio as a whole will be more stable.

The four fundamental asset classes are (1) cash, (2) bonds, (3) real estate and (4) stocks. They may go by different names: for example, cash may be called "T-bills", and bonds are often called "debt securities" while stocks are "equity securities". Sometimes an asset class is divided into sub-classes: for example, stocks may be divided into sectors (information technology, industrials, etc) or styles, such as "small-cap growth" and "large-cap value".

Table 15.1 is a correlation matrix that shows the difference between asset classes and sub-classes. Correlations among the four core domestic asset classes are all quite low, no more than 40%. In contrast, the four domestic stock market styles are all highly correlated both with the broad domestic stock market (76–94%) and with each other (mostly 63–79%). Likewise, the selected domestic stock market sectors are all highly correlated both with the broad domestic stock market (75–85%) and with each other (mostly 63–73%). Low correlations among asset classes give investors the opportunity for efficient portfolio diversification, whereas high correlations among sectors or styles of the same asset class do not.

Asset allocation is the process of deciding which share of your portfolio should be invested in each asset class; once you have decided the allocation, then you can choose an ETF to gain exposure to that asset class. Each ETF gives the investor granularity – that is, exposure to a large number of investments in that asset class. It is the well-selected portfolio of ETFs from different asset classes that gives the investor diversification.

Some investors may use ETFs to gain exposure to alternative asset classes as well, such as commodities. But alternative investments are not critical to a well-constructed portfolio, while the basic four – cash, bonds, real estate and stocks – are. Mark J. P. Anson, the former chief investment officer of the California Public Employees'

Table 15.1 Correlations among asset classes, styles, and sectors

	Asset classes*				**Stock market styles**				**Stock market sectors**			
	Cash (%)	**Bonds (%)**	**Real estate (%)**	**Stocks (%)**	**Large-cap growth (%)**	**Large-cap value (%)**	**Small-cap growth (%)**	**Small-cap value (%)**	**Consumer discretionary (%)**	**Financials (%)**	**Industrials (%)**	**Information technology (%)**
Asset classes*												
Cash	*100*	14	–5	6	7	9	–1	–2	3	10	8	6
Bonds	14	*100*	11	0	4	1	–10	–3	–7	9	–5	–4
Real estate	–5	11	*100*	40	24	47	38	68	35	45	37	17
Stocks	6	0	40	*100*	94	91	83	76	85	75	84	84
Stock market styles												
Large-cap growth	7	4	24	94	*100*	80	71	56	78	65	78	88
Large-cap value	9	1	47	91	80	*100*	63	76	85	88	88	65
Small-cap growth	–1	–10	38	83	71	63	*100*	79	63	39	58	76
Small-cap value	–2	–3	68	76	56	76	79	*100*	66	59	66	51
Stock market sectors												
Consumer discretionary	3	–7	35	85	78	85	63	66	*100*	71	79	67
Financials	10	9	45	75	65	88	39	59	71	*100*	73	44
Industrials	8	–5	37	84	78	88	58	66	79	73	*100*	63
Information technology	6	–4	17	84	88	65	76	51	67	44	63	*100*

*Asset classes, styles and sectors are represented by the following indexes: 1-month US Treasury bills (cash), Barclays Capital US Aggregate Bond Index (bonds), FTSE NAREIT Equity REIT Index (real estate), Dow Jones Wilshire 5000 (stocks), S&P 500/Citigroup Growth (large-cap growth), S&P 500/Citigroup Value (large-cap value), Russell 2000 Growth (small-cap growth), Russell 2000 Value (small-cap value), S&P 500 Consumer Discretionary Sector, S&P 500 Financial Sector, S&P 500 Industrial Sector, and S&P 500 Information Technology Sector.

Retirement System (CalPERS), made this point in his book, *Handbook of Alternative Assets*:

> "Real estate is not an alternative to stocks and bonds – it is a fundamental asset class that should be included within every diversified portfolio. Equity, fixed income, cash, and real estate . . . are the basic asset classes that must be held within a diversified portfolio."

Burton G. Malkiel, the Chemical Bank chairman's professor of economics at Princeton University, makes the same point in his book, *The Random Walk Guide to Investing*: "Basically, there are only four types of investment categories that you need to consider: cash, bonds, common stocks, and real estate." David F. Swensen, the chief investment officer for Yale University's endowment, says it in his book, *Unconventional Success: A Fundamental Approach to Personal Investment*: "Core asset classes encompass stocks, bonds and real estate". (Separately, Swensen describes a "basic formula for creating an investment portfolio likely to give you good returns while still managing risk" that comprises allocations of 30% to US domestic stock investments, 20% to foreign stock investments, 30% to bonds and 20% to real estate.)

REIT ETFs: SUPERIOR REAL ESTATE INVESTING IS OPEN TO INDIVIDUALS

REIT ETFs are not the only way to invest in the real-estate asset class, but they are among the very best ways for any investor to do so. REIT ETFs select and invest in REITs, which are individual companies that own and (generally) manage real-estate assets such as office or apartment buildings, hotels, and even specialty real estate such as timberlands or high-tech data centres. Investors have access to the real estate asset class through a variety of ETFs, including the following 19.

1. Domestic REIT industry

- First Trust S&P REIT Index Fund (FRI: http:www.ftportfolios.com/Retail/etf/etfsummary.aspx?Ticker=FRI);
- iShares Cohen & Steers Realty Majors Index Fund (ICF: http: www. cohenandsteers.com/opmc_overview.asp?cusip=7);
- State Street Global Advisers DJ Wilshire REIT ETF (RWR: http: www.ssgafunds.com/etf/fund/etf_detail_RWR.jsp);
- Vanguard REIT ETF (VNQ: https://personal.vanguard.com/us/FundsSnapshot?FundId=0986&FundIntExt=INT).

2. Domestic REIT sectors

- iShares FTSE NAREIT Real Estate 50 Index Fund (FTY: http:// www. ishares.com/product_info/fund/overview/FTY.htm);
- iShares FTSE NAREIT Industrial/Office Index Fund (FIO: http://www.ishares.com/product_info/fund/overview/FIO.htm);
- iShares FTSE NAREIT Residential Index Fund (REZ: http://www.ishares.com/product_info/fund/overview/REZ.htm);
- iShares FTSE NAREIT Retail Index Fund (RTL: http://www.ishares.com/product_info/fund/overview/RTL.htm);
- iShares FTSE NAREIT Mortgage REITs Index Fund (REM: http://www.ishares.com/product_info/fund/overview/REM.htm).

3. Domestic real-estate industry

- iShares Dow Jones US Real Estate Index Fund (IYR: http:www.ishares.com/product_info/fund/overview/IYR.htm);
- ProShares Ultra Real Estate (URE: http:www.proshares.com/funds/ure.html).

4. Global/international real-estate industry

- Cohen & Steers Global Realty Majors ETF (GRI: http://www.cohenandsteers.com/opmc_overview.asp?cusip=25);
- First Trust FTSE EPRA/NAREIT Global Real Estate Index Fund (FFR: http://www.ftportfolios.com/Retail/etf/etfsummary.aspx?Ticker=FFR);
- iShares S&P World ex-US Property Index Fund (WPS: http://www.ishares.com/product_info/fund/overview/WPS.htm);
- PowerShares FTSE RAFI International Real Estate Portfolio (PRY: http://www.invescopowershares.com/products/overview.aspx?ticker=PRY);
- State Street Global Advisers SPDR DJ Wilshire Global Real Estate ETF (RWO: http://www.ssgafunds.com/etf/fund/etf_detail_RWO.jsp);
- State Street Global Advisers SPDR DJ Wilshire International Real Estate ETF (RWX: http://ssgafunds.com/etf/fund/etf_detail_RWX.jsp);
- WisdomTree International Real Estate Fund (DRW: http://www.wisdomtree.com/etfs/fund-details.asp?etfid=49).

5. International real-estate, country-specific

- Claymore/AlphaShares China Real Estate ETF (TAO: http://claymore.com/fund/Overview.aspx?ID=4bf8ddf5-a4c6-434c-a873-9a0400b2a89e).

And while REIT ETFs do not yet have a long track record – the oldest one started in 2000, and only four existed before late 2006 – the underlying REITs have a history of more than 35 years of producing (1) strong returns, (2) moderate volatility, (3) superior risk-adjusted performance, (4) effective diversification against other asset classes, (5) granularity within individual REITs as well as across the real estate asset class, (6) consistently strong dividend income and – and these are important attributes that are undervalued by too many investors – (7) transparency and strong corporate governance.

RETURNS, VOLATILITY, AND RISK-ADJUSTED PERFORMANCE

It can be dangerous to look at the historical performance of an investment that has a short track record. As an example, the First Trust S&P REIT Index Fund (FRI) started on May 8, 2007, just four months after the beginning of a downturn in the REIT market. As a result, the ETF's performance since inception has been scary: –19.95% annualised as of June 30, 2008. But the ETF closely tracks the S&P REIT Composite Index, which since the end of 1989 has produced total returns averaging +12.0% per year. The same is true of the iShares FTSE EPRA/NAREIT North America Index Fund (IFNA), whose total return was –16.4% annualised since its inception on November 12, 2007 – but it tracks the FTSE EPRA/NAREIT North America Real Estate Index, whose total return has averaged 14.3% per year since the end of 1989.

The three iShares ETFs that track property sectors of the US REIT industry all started trading on May 1, 2007, and all have produced similar annualised returns since inception: –19.8% for the iShares FTSE NAREIT Industrial/Office, –14.7% for the iShares FTSE NAREIT Residential, and –23.7% for the iShares FTSE NAREIT Retail. But the underlying indexes have a much longer period of strong returns: +14.6% per year for the FTSE NAREIT Industrial/Office, +11.6% for the FTSE NAREIT Residential, and +13.6% for the FTSE NAREIT Retail, all since the end of 1993. When an ETF is designed to track closely an underlying index, it is important for investors to look to the index for more useful historical performance data.

As a general conclusion, the performance of the REIT indexes that support REIT ETFs have, on a long-term basis, shown (1) returns slightly stronger than the broad US stock market, (2) volatility about the same as or slightly less than the broad stock market, and (3) significantly better risk-adjusted performance than the broad stock market. Table 15.2 shows average annual returns, the standard deviation of monthly returns (a measure of volatility), and the Sharpe Ratio (the most commonly used measure of risk-adjusted performance) for the FTSE NAREIT Equity REIT Index and three common stock market indexes: the Dow Jones Wilshire 5000 (a total-market

Table 15.2 Risk-adjusted returns of REITs and stock market indexes

Period	Equity REITs	DJW 5000	S&P 500	Nasdaq
Average annual returns				
5 years (%)	14.30	9.78	7.58	7.16
10 years (%)	10.65	4.54	2.88	1.93
15 years (%)	11.65	9.94	9.21	8.19
20 years (%)	11.43	10.89	10.44	9.20
25 years (%)	12.03	11.28	11.26	8.21
30 years (%)	13.88	12.68	12.36	10.32
35 years (%)	13.28	11.46	10.92	9.33
Volatility				
5 years (%)	5.00	2.76	2.71	4.17
10 years (%)	4.47	4.40	4.31	8.20
15 years (%)	4.04	4.04	4.02	7.16
20 years (%)	3.90	3.98	3.96	6.69
25 years (%)	3.78	4.25	4.22	6.55
30 years (%)	3.95	4.36	4.27	6.46
35 years (%)	4.05	4.51	4.40	6.37
Sharpe ratio (risk-adjusted performance)				
5 years	2.39	2.71	1.96	1.19
10 years	1.62	0.41	0.06	—*
15 years	1.95	1.54	1.37	0.63
20 years	1.84	1.70	1.60	0.78
25 years	1.88	1.53	1.54	0.53
30 years	1.98	1.53	1.49	0.69
35 years	1.80	1.22	1.13	0.54

*Sharpe Ratio is not meaningful when average annual returns are less than the total return on 1-month Treasury bills.

index), the S&P 500 (a large-cap index), and the Nasdaq (a small-cap growth stock index). Over every period ending June 30, 2008 – periods that included a sharp REIT market downturn in 2007/08 – equity REIT returns outpaced stock returns with comparable volatility and much stronger risk-adjusted performance.

Figure 15.1 shows another way to compare the returns and volatility of equity REITs and the broad US stock market. Over any two-year investment period from June 1973 through June 2008, there was only an 8% likelihood that US equity REITs would suffer negative returns. A loss was much more likely in non-REIT equities: 9% in the broad stock market (the DJW 5000), 11% in large-cap stocks (the S&P 500), and 16% in the Nasdaq. And there has never been a five-year period during the last 35 years when equity REITs produced negative total returns, while five-year losses were 3% likely in the broad stock market, 9% likely among large-cap stocks, and 11% likely among Nasdaq stocks.

DIVERSIFICATION WITH RISK-ADJUSTED PERFORMANCE

We have seen that the real-estate asset class – which investors can access efficiently through REIT ETFs – has a very low correlation with other asset classes, along with high returns, moderate volatility and strong risk-adjusted performance. Figure 15.2 shows just how rare is this combination of diversification potential and strong risk-adjusted returns.

Figure 15.1 REITs are less likely to produce investment losses

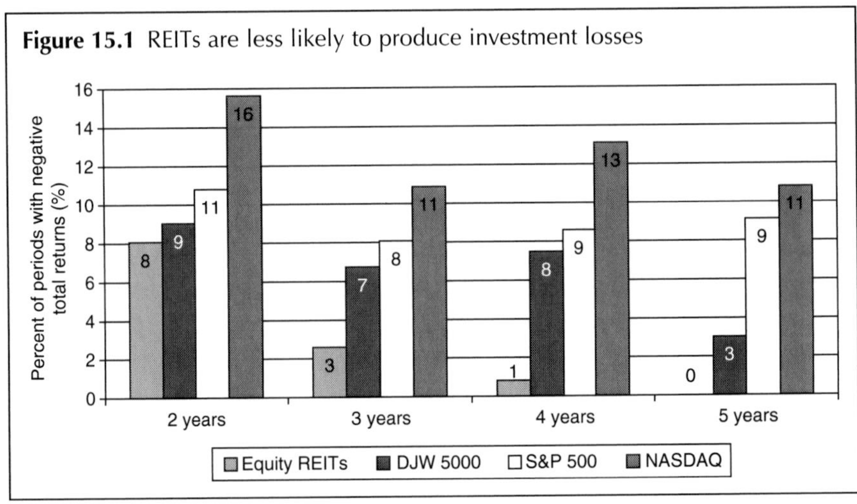

Figure 15.2 Risk-adjusted performance and diversification power

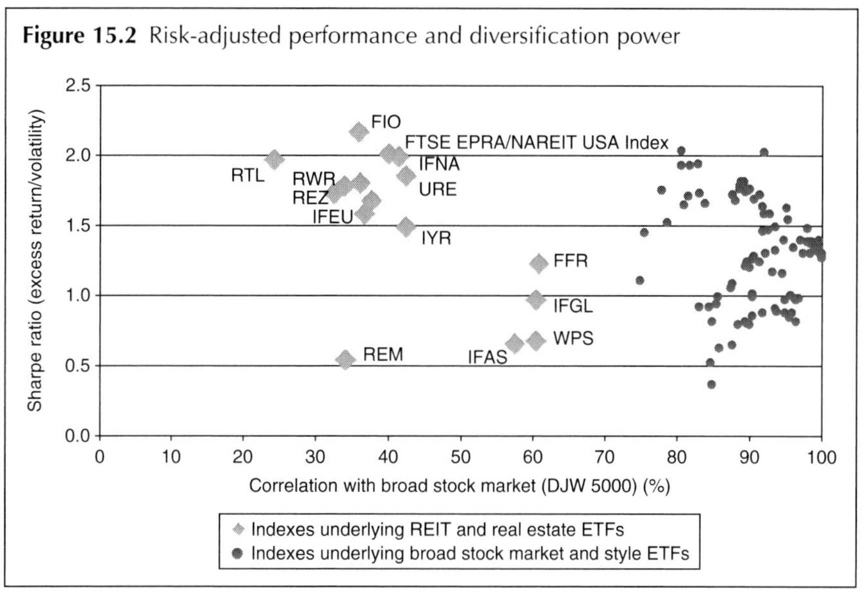

The horizontal axis on Figure 15.2 shows correlation with the broad stock market since the end of 1993: investors achieve portfolio diversification by choosing assets with low correlations, so they want assets on the left side of the chart. The vertical axis shows risk-adjusted performance over the same period: investors achieve strong risk-adjusted performance by choosing assets with high excess returns and low volatility, so they want assets near the top of the chart. The dots show every index of either the broad US stock market or specific investment styles (eg, small-cap growth, large-cap value, etc) for which data is available back to the beginning of 1994, while the diamonds show every index underlying a REIT or real-estate ETF for which data is available for the same time period.

As the chart shows, investors cannot hope to diversify their investment portfolios by choosing ETFs focusing on different stock market styles: even the lowest correlations between investment styles and the broad stock market are 75%. In contrast, most REIT ETFs had correlations between 36% and 42%, and only a few – FFR (global REIT), IFGL (global ex-US REIT), WPS (global ex-US property), and IFAS (Asia) – had correlations above 50%. At the same time, most REIT ETFs provided very strong risk-adjusted returns: only those four plus REM (mortgage REITs) had Sharpe ratios below 1.5, while most stock-market-style indexes had Sharpe ratios below 1.27. Literally no stock market investment style ETF has combined both strong risk-adjusted performance and diversification power, while nearly all REIT ETFs accomplished that double goal.

GRANULARITY

Besides diversifying their portfolios by using REIT ETFs to gain efficient access to the real-estate asset class, investors also achieve granularity – that is, exposure across many different assets within an asset class – by investing through REIT ETFs. The publicly traded equity REIT industry encompasses some 117 companies (and there are 31 other REITs that invest in real-estate financial assets or both financial and real assets). Most REITs specialise in one property type, but investing in even one broad REIT ETF gains the investor a share in the ownership of all commercial property types: industrial and warehouse facilities, office buildings, apartment buildings, retail properties (including regional malls, neighbourhood shopping centres and freestanding stores or restaurants), hotels and resorts, self-storage facilities, nursing homes and other healthcare facilities, cinemas, manufactured home communities, data centres, timberlands and even a railway. And, while a few REITs concentrate on properties in a certain part of the country, investing in a REIT ETF gains the investor nationwide real estate exposure – as shown in Figure 15.3, which shows the locations of nearly 30,000 REIT-owned properties throughout the US.

TRANSPARENCY AND CORPORATE GOVERNANCE

Investors have a potential secret weapon in choosing the best-performing investments. Academic research suggests that both transparency and strong corporate governance are associated with superior risk-adjusted investment performance. Transparency means that the assets you are investing in are well-defined and can easily be valued. REITs are among the most transparent investments because their property holdings are publicly reported, the properties themselves can easily be appraised, and (like other stock market investments) the REITs are followed by a community of equity analysts. (As an example of a non-transparent investment, the value of a pharmaceutical company may fluctuate wildly depending on whether or not its newest drugs are likely to gain regulatory

Figure 15.3 Locations of 30,000 REIT-owned properties in the US

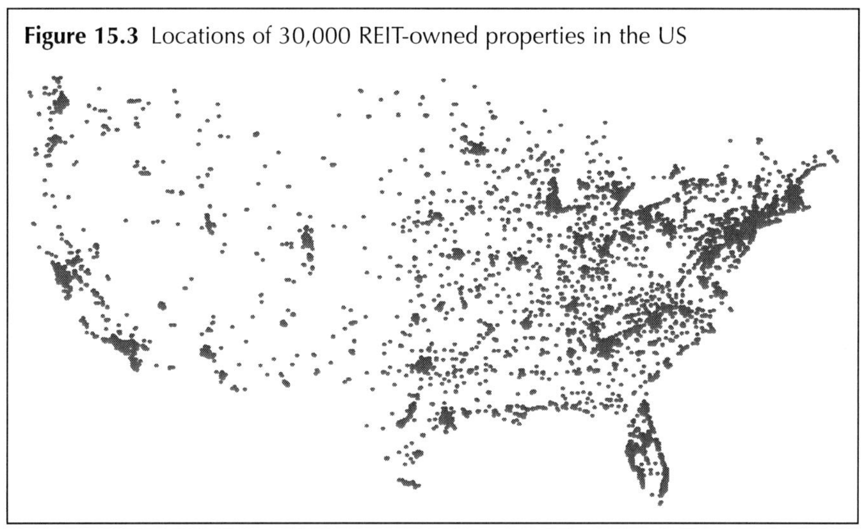

approval. During the tech-stock boom, many companies were valued highly based on unproven new technologies, only to find their company values evaporate when their products were finally brought to the market.)

Corporate governance covers a variety of practices, such as whether the board of directors and key committees can exercise independent supervision over company management. According to the Corporate Governance Quotient (CGQ) computed by RiskMetrics, the real-estate industry (primarily REITs) is among the top industries in overall quality of corporate governance. The managers of a REIT ETF may well choose to invest in those REITs that are the most transparent and have the strongest corporate governance. For the individual ETF investor, though, it is more important that the entire REIT industry be transparent and have strong corporate governance.

DIVIDEND INCOME FROM REIT ETFs

For many investors – especially those in or near retirement – it is especially important that their portfolio include investments that generate significant current income. Many income-oriented investors believe that only bonds, and some bondlike stocks (such as utilities), provide strong current income – and those investments typically offer low total returns, meaning that the investor has to pay for current income by accepting less growth in future overall portfolio wealth.

Because REITs own and manage commercial real estate, they generate significant current income in the form of net operating income, or rents, as well as the gains on selling properties. More importantly, REITs are actually required to distribute at least 90% of their taxable income in the form of dividends to shareholders – and most REITs pay dividends much higher than the requirement. That means that a large share of the total return on REITs comes to REIT ETF investors in the form of dividend income. For example, since January 1990 – the start date for the indexes that underlie several REIT ETFs – the average equity REIT has provided income returns averaging almost 7.5%, amounting to almost two-thirds of the total return of 11.9% per year.

Best of all for investors who hold REIT ETFs in taxable accounts, much of the dividend income from REITs is taxable at the long-term capital-gains tax rate, rather than at the higher tax rate for ordinary income. In 1998, 83% of REIT dividends were taxable at the ordinary income rate, but by 2006 that share had declined to 55%, meaning that almost half of the dividend that investors receive through REIT ETFs is taxable at the lower long-term capital-gains rate.

REIT ETFs AND INFLATION HEDGING

Many investors have never worried about inflation: during the 15 years from 1993 through 2006 the annualised inflation rate averaged only 2.55%, less than the return on even the safest investments. But inflation started to surge in 2007, and during the first half of 2008 it averaged more than 8% on an annualised basis. That means that ETF investors now have to think about inflation hedging – choosing ETFs whose returns are likely to keep pace with rapid price increases.

There are three classic inflation hedges, all of which can be accessed through ETFs: Treasury inflation-protected securities (TIPS), commodities, and real estate. TIPS guarantee that the income will adjust to the inflation rate – but this adjustment happens up to six months after the inflation is measured. More important, this income adjustment does not guarantee that the total return will keep up with prices, and the total return on TIPS has been only in the 7–8% range. Commodities tend to offer strong returns during inflationary months, but are extremely volatile, meaning that commodities have very poor risk-adjusted returns; moreover, commodity returns tend to be especially terrible during months when inflation turns out to be more moderate.

Real estate is (like commodities) a natural inflation hedge. Properties with long-term leases, such as office buildings and shopping malls, have inflation protection built right into the leases, while properties with short-term leases, such as apartment buildings and hotels, are able to adjust the lease rates between rentals. The result is that real estate tends to provide a strong income stream even during inflationary times. Not only that, but because investors know that operating income will adjust with inflation, they tend to drive up the stock values of REITs and REIT ETFs when they expect inflation to increase.

More important, the indexes that REIT ETFs follow have combined strong inflation protection with strong returns and moderate volatility as well as portfolio diversification – a combination that neither of the other two inflation hedges has provided. In the period 1993–2007, during months when inflation was relatively high the income alone from REITs averaged 6.4% per year, comfortably ahead of the inflation rate and far higher than the paltry 1.8% income return for non-REIT stocks.

More importantly, as the left side of Figure 15.4 shows, during those same high-inflation months REIT total returns have averaged 13.0% per year, second to commodities but far greater than either TIPS (10.0%) or non-REIT stocks (7.7%). And, unlike commodities, REIT returns do not fall apart when inflation eases: as the right side of Figure 15.4 shows, during low-inflation months over those 15 years, REIT returns held steady at 13.0% per year, better than non-REIT stocks (12.4%), TIPS (6.2%), and of course commodities (minus 2.6%).

Figure 15.5 shows the percentage of six-month periods of relatively high inflation during 1993–2007 when total returns on each asset exceeded the inflation rate. REIT total returns beat inflation in 79% of inflationary periods – better than commodities (which lost money, on average, during non-inflationary periods) and far better than non-REIT stocks (66% inflation coverage) and TIPS (60%). Fifteen years of historical performance as the most dependable inflation hedge suggest that, in the future, REIT ETFs may continue to be the strongest component of an inflation-protected portfolio.

Figure 15.4 Asset-class returns in high-inflation and low-inflation environments

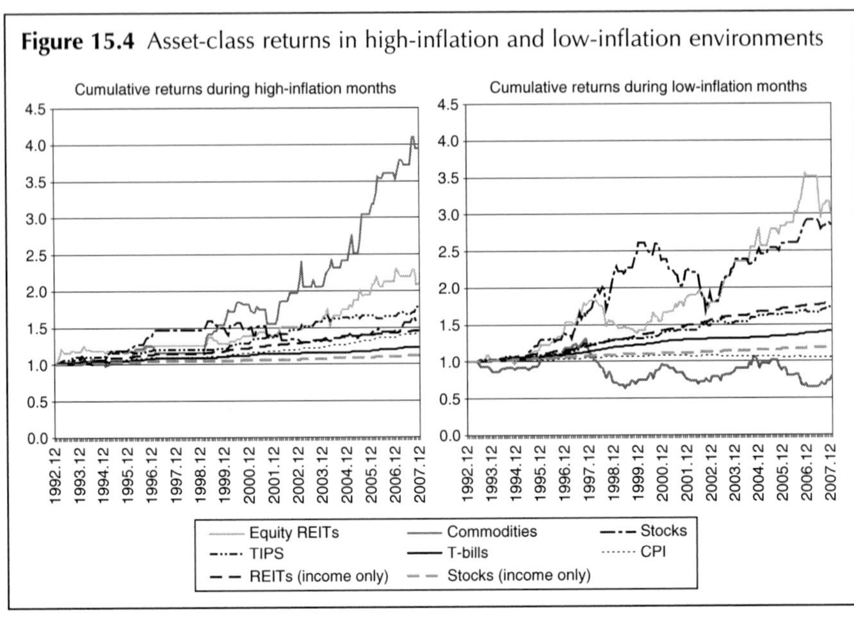

Figure 15.5 REIT returns cover high inflation rates more effectively than other assets

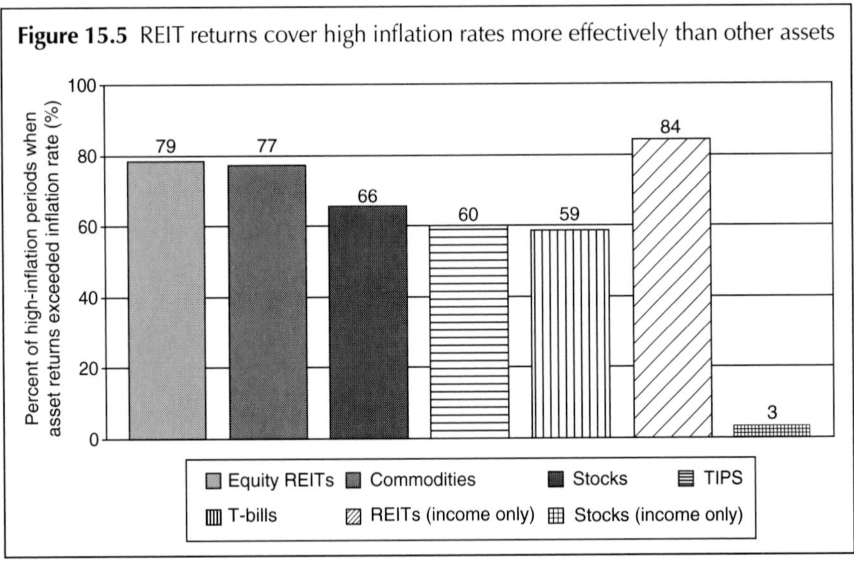

REIT ETFs IN A GLOBAL PORTFOLIO

The ease of global investing through ETFs has hugely expanded the accessible asset universe for even the smallest individual investors, and sophisticated investors scour the world for strong risk-adjusted returns that are uncorrelated with the US stock market. Yet it turns out that there is essentially no equity investment worldwide that can be expected to beat ETFs based on the US REIT industry.

Figure 15.6 is similar to Figure 15.2 but shows risk-adjusted performance (the vertical axis) and correlation against the US stock market (the horizontal axis) for hundreds of global and non-US stock market benchmarks in addition to domestic stock benchmarks. Global investing does bring diversification benefits: the benchmarks underlying global and non-US stock ETFs are typically less highly correlated with the broad US stock market than are the benchmarks underlying domestic stock market investment style ETFs such as growth, value, small-cap, or large-cap ETFs.

Surprisingly, though, very few of the global stock investments have provided risk-adjusted performance as strong as that of most REIT ETFs – including domestic-only REIT industry ETFs such as RWR and FRI – and virtually none has provided as much portfolio diversification. While the availability of global stock ETFs has expanded the universe of investment opportunities, it does not seem to have improved on the combination of risk-adjusted performance and diversification power available through REIT ETFs.

In 2008 the stock market research firm Ibbotson Associates (a subsidiary of Morningstar) conducted a study to estimate the role that

Figure 15.6 Risk-adjusted performance and diversification power

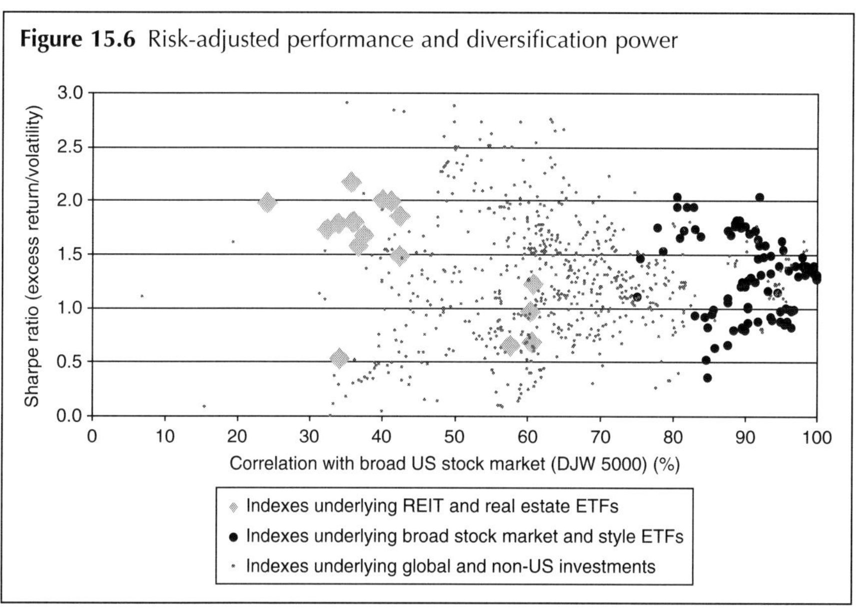

real estate should play in an optimal global investment portfolio. Rather than basing their analysis solely on historically observed returns, Ibbotson Associates projected future return series for US and global stocks, bonds and real estate along with cash. On the basis of this forward-looking analysis, Ibbotson concluded that real estate should comprise between 11% and 34% of the total portfolio, depending on the investor's risk tolerance, with moderate-risk investors keeping about 21% of their assets in real estate. As Figure 15.7 shows, Ibbotson also concluded that between one-third and one-half of the real estate allocation should be invested in North America (US and Canada), with Europe accounting for between one-quarter and one-third, and Asia for the remainder.

ANALYSING REIT MARKET DYNAMICS

Although investors should not depend on being able to "time the market" with any consistent success, it may be helpful to consider how to identify particularly good times to invest in REIT ETFs. Two useful pieces of information in analysing REIT market dynamics are (1) the duration of historical bull and bear markets in the REIT industry, and (2) the relationship between REIT stock prices and the underlying value of the properties that they own.

Figure 15.7 Asset allocations in Ibbotson's optimal forward-looking portfolios

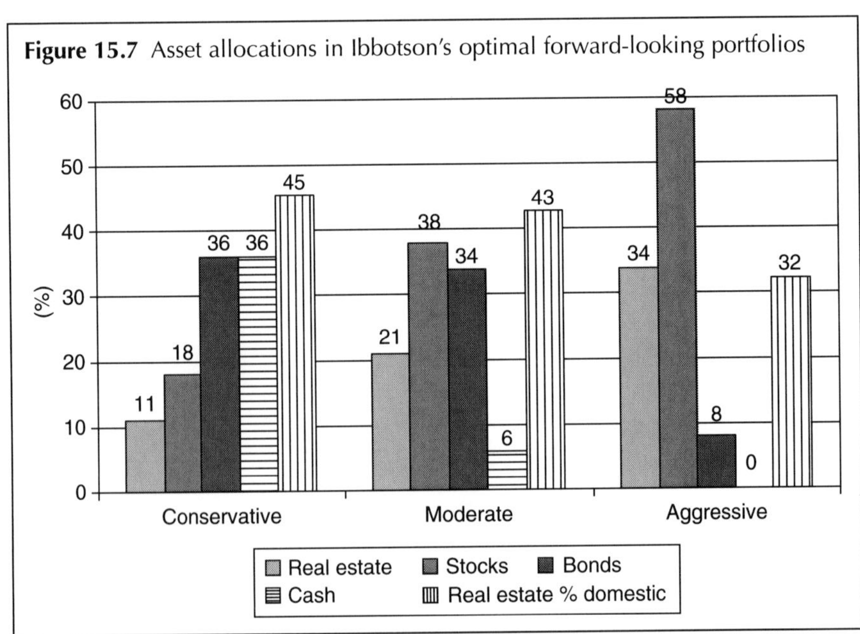

Figure 15.8 compares REIT total returns during three historical bear markets: the first started in August 1989 and reached its lowest point in October 1990; the second started in December 1997 and reached its trough in November 1999; and the third started January 2007. In both of the first two cases, REITs lost about 24% in total return during a bear market lasting between 13 and 23 months – and then began extended bull markets lasting more than eight years during which total returns averaged more than 20% per year.

The second useful piece of information is the relationship between REIT stock prices and underlying property values. REIT equity analysts estimate the net asset value, or NAV, of the underlying real estate that each REIT owns, as part of the process of forming their investment recommendations. The company Green Street Advisors, for example, publishes a monthly newsletter in which its analysts estimate the NAV for a large number of REITs. Green Street also computes the ratio of current stock price to NAV for each company, and publishes the average premium (if positive) or discount (if negative) for the equity REIT industry as a whole. REITs generally trade at a premium of perhaps 3%, representing the value of the company's management of its real-estate assets; a discount implies that investors can purchase a share in the ownership of the company's assets for less than their estimated value.

Figure 15.8 REIT total returns during three market downturns

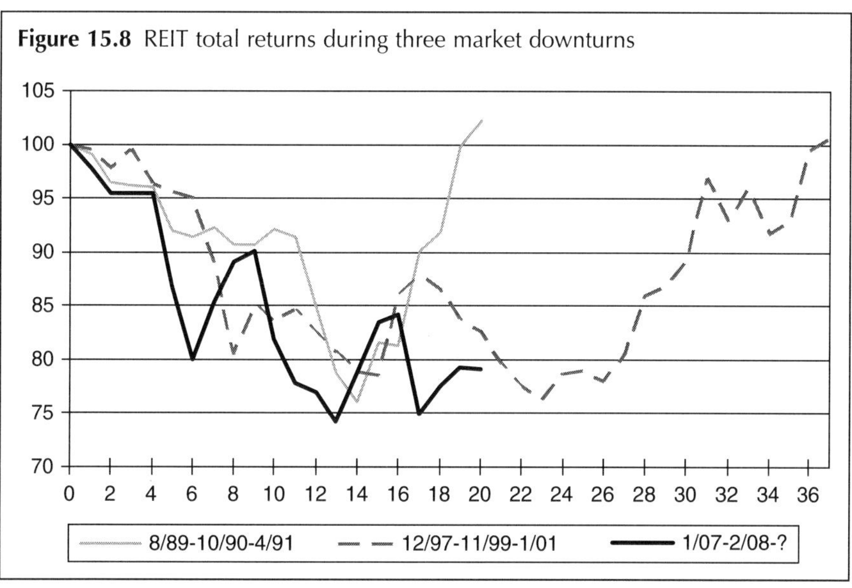

Investors who purchase REIT stock at times when it is trading at a discount have historically realised extraordinarily high returns, as the left side of Figure 15.9 shows. For example, investors who purchased REITs or REIT ETFs during months when they were trading at an industry average discount of at least 10% enjoyed returns over the next two years that were higher than stock market returns by about 13% in each year. Even those investors who purchased REITs or REIT ETFs when they were trading at a premium of up to 5% enjoyed returns that exceeded the stock market by about 5% each year. There is no measure yet of the premium or discount to NAV of specific REIT ETFs, but it may well be that the industry-wide premium/discount estimates published by companies such as Green Street indicate whether REIT ETFs are trading at a similar premium or discount.

In contrast, a piece of information that history suggests is not helpful in predicting REIT market dynamics is the current state of the underlying commercial property market. This is because REIT

Figure 15.9 Total-return difference between equity REITs and S&P 500

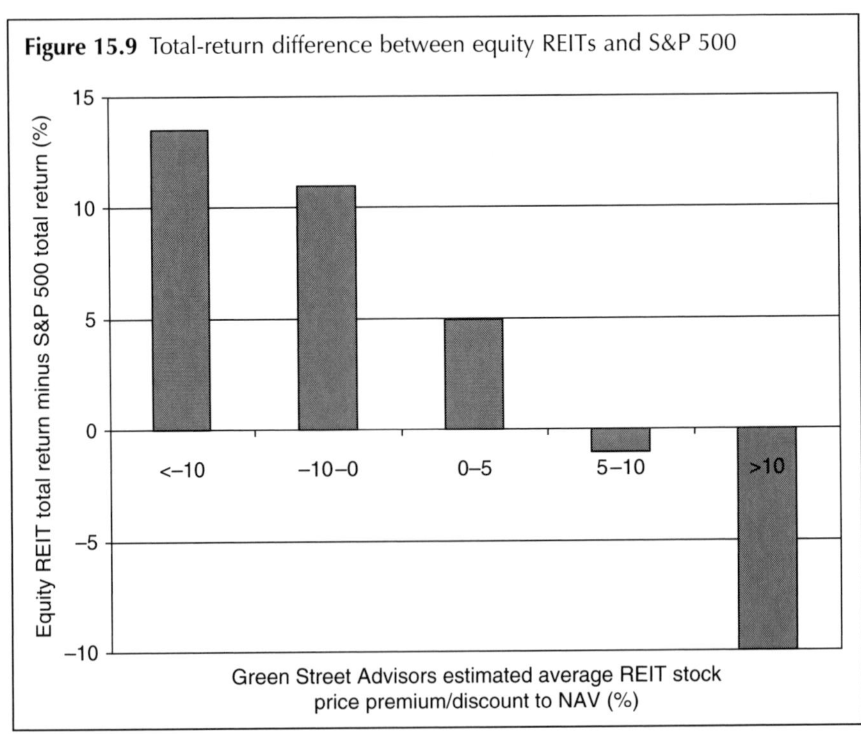

returns have generally led underlying property values by between one and two years, so investors cannot use today's news about property values to predict tomorrow's movements in REIT stock values.

As an example, Figure 15.10 compares the (smoothed) history of REIT total returns and underlying property values for four years, from the end of 1989 – when a severe REIT bear market began – through the end of 1993. The REIT bear market lasted just 13 months and was followed by a long bull market; by the end of 1993, REIT returns had increased more than 107% from their lowest point. Underlying property values continued to increase during the entire REIT bear market, but then started a downturn lasting more than two years; by the end of 1993, property values were still down almost 10% from their peak.

SUMMARY

Exchange-traded funds have made it easy and inexpensive for investors to form well-diversified portfolios comprising multiple investments in each asset class, both domestically and globally, but investors still have to face the most important decision: how much of their portfolio to invest in each asset class. REIT ETFs provide

Figure 15.10 REIT returns and underlying property values, 1989–1993

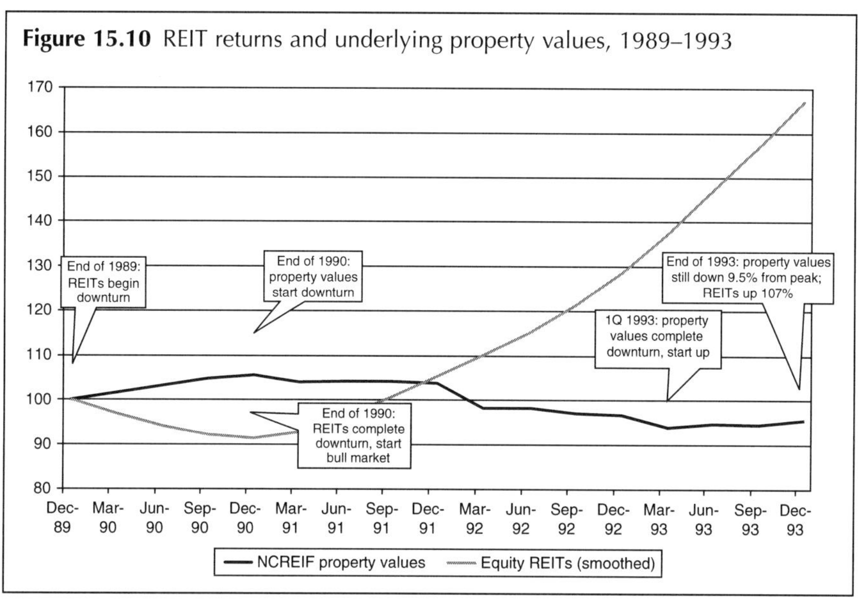

investors with a wide range of important benefits: strong returns, moderate volatility, superior risk-adjusted performance, effective diversification, granularity, transparency, strong corporate governance, strong and tax-favourable dividend income, and effective global exposure.

Highly regarded investment experts such as Mark Anson, Burton Malkiel, David Swensen and Ibbotson Associates have emphasised that real estate is a critical piece of a well-performing diversified investment portfolio, and several, including Ibbotson Associates, have recommended that investors allocate between 11% and 34% of their total portfolio to real estate. REIT ETFs give investors a leg-up in putting those recommendations to work.

16

Commodity ETFs

John T. Hyland

United States Commodity Funds LLC

This chapter is an attempt to explain to the professional and layman the structure and uses of exchange-traded funds (ETFs) that are based on energy-related commodities such as crude oil. It is not the goal of this chapter to discuss how to analyse the movements of commodity prices and make investment decisions about future commodity price trends. That would be an entire book unto itself. Rather the goal is to leave the reader with a firm understanding of how commodity-based ETFs came to be, the differences among them, how they are used and some of their benefits and risks.

This chapter is divided into three sections. The first section describes the commodity ETF universe in general, and energy-commodity ETFs in particular. This section takes a step-by-step approach and shows how energy-commodity ETFs are created and operate.

The second section discusses the four main ways in which investors can look to make use of energy-commodity ETFs in their portfolios and trading strategies. Some of these approaches are ones that can be considered by most investors and that could be implemented using virtually any commodity-based ETF. Other approaches are more narrowly focused and would actually work only with a portion of the commodity ETF universe.

Finally, the third section contains more detailed information about certain important topics mentioned in the first two sections. One key "special topic" is the portion that discusses the impact of the shape of the futures curve on price movements of commodity-based ETFs and their total returns. If an investor or investment professional is not familiar with "backwardation" and "contango", they may wish to jump to the back of the chapter and refresh their knowledge of this unusual feature of futures.

The chapter concludes with some discussion of the future of the energy commodity universe. Some of the trends that the ETF world has seen with equity ETFs will sooner or later be seen in the commodity ETF world.

ENERGY-COMMODITY ETF: HISTORY, CONSTRUCTION, AND OPERATIONS

A brief history of an ETF sector

ETFs have existed in the US since 1993. That was the year that the first ETF, based on the Standard & Poor's 500 Index, was launched in the US. Over the next decade a large number of ETFs were created and launched by different firms. Initially, most were based on established US stock indexes. However, as time went on and the well-known domestic stock indexes were all taken, ETF sponsors had to look further to come up with new, but potentially interesting, areas.

The ETF sponsors started to branch out in several new directions. One was to launch ETFs based on bonds and not stocks. A second was to work with index firms such to create completely new, and often very custom, stock indexes upon which an ETF could be based. A third direction was to "go global" and base ETFs on foreign stock indexes. All of these new approaches required the ETF sponsors to adapt their existing processes and procedures to new investment areas. Each new area had its own particular quirks and problems. However, most of these new approaches could be done within the existing legal structure of ETFs as used in the US.

Eventually, one of the few areas left untouched was that of actual commodities. ETF sponsors left this until fairly late in the game for several reasons. The first is because, while it is legally very straightforward to create an ETF that would own a basket of stocks of companies involved in a particular area of the commodity world, gold miners or oil companies for example, the rules were not very friendly for the commodities themselves. ETFs in the US were at that time all registered under the Investment Company Act of 1940. The 1940 Act is the part of Federal securities law that regulates mutual funds (legally, a mutual fund is actually an "investment company"). For a variety of both tax and regulatory reasons, it is difficult if not impossible for a mutual fund to actually own either physical commodities or futures contracts based on commodities. In addition, while an ETF using stocks or bonds is regulated by the Securities and Exchange Commission (SEC), one using commodities would be regulated by both the SEC (since it is a public security), and by the Commodity Futures Trading Commission (since it could be deemed to be a commodity pool). A commodity-based ETF was going to be a bit more complicated than an ordinary ETF and so the ETF sponsors held off tackling these issues.

A second major issue was that transferring ownership of listed futures based on commodities works very differently from the way it does for stocks or bonds. As a result, the standard approach used by stock and bond ETFs when creating or redeeming baskets of the ETF's shares in exchange for baskets of the underlying stocks or bonds would not work with commodities. ETF sponsors would have to come up with a new way to handle the creation or redemption process in order to devise a workable new structure.

Finally, for much of the first 10 years of ETFs in the US, the commodity markets were fairly slow and uninteresting to most mainstream investors. As a result, ETF sponsors did not expect to see strong demand for these new, and more complicated, ETFs and held off working on the sector.

Starting in the early part of the current decade, ETF sponsors turned their attention to commodities. The first ETF based on a commodity launched in the US was one based on gold, which came public in 2003. A second gold ETF from a different sponsor was brought to market a few months later. To avoid the limitations of the 1940 Act, both of these registered instead under the Securities Registration Act of 1933. The 1933 Act is that portion of US securities laws that regulates the registration of ordinary companies that plan to trade publicly. For example, Apple Computer, GE and Chevron would all be registered as 1933 Act companies. A 1933 Act company can own physical commodities or listed futures. In the case of the two gold ETFs, their investments actually consisted of physically owning gold bullion.

With the first commodity ETFs in the market, work commenced on bringing to market other ETFs that would provide additional exposure to commodities. In early 2006, the first ETF that owned futures contracts, as opposed to the actual commodity, was launched. That ETF, the Deutsche Bank Commodity Index Tracking Fund (ticker: DBC), actually held a basket of six different commodity futures. Included in that basket were futures based on crude oil. It was launched in March of 2006. In April of 2006, the first ETF was launched that used futures contracts based on a single commodity. That ETF, the United States Oil Fund, LP (ticker: USO), invested solely in crude oil futures.

Within a year of the launch of the DBC and USO, a large number of new commodity-based ETFs were launched. Some were based on baskets with a large number of different commodities contained within them. Others were based on a smaller number of related commodities such as all agricultural commodities, or all energy-related commodities. Finally, a number were based on a single commodity. Aside from gold and crude oil, other single-commodity ETFs that have come out includes ones based on silver, natural gas, copper, nickel, petrol (or gasoline in the US) and heating oil.

Table 16.1 ETF timeline

1993
1st Equity ETF – S&P 500 "Spider" (ticker: SPY)
2004
1st Commodity ETF – Gold (ticker: GLD)
2006
1st Commodity Basket ETF – Powershares DB Liquid Commodity Index (ticker: DBC)
1st Crude Oil ETF – United States Oil Fund (ticker: USO)
1st Energy Sub-basket ETF – Powershares DB Energy (ticker: DBE)
2007
1st Natural Gas ETF – United States Natural Gas Fund (ticker: UNG)
1st Multi-month energy-commodity ETF – United States 12 Month Oil (ticker: USL)
2008
1st Gasoline ETF – United States Gasoline Fund (ticker: UGA)
1st Heating Oil ETF – United States Heating Oil Fund (ticker: UHN)
1st Inverse Energy-commodity ETF – Powershares DB Crude Oil Short (ticker: SZO)
1st Levered Energy-commodity ETF – Powershares DB Crude Oil Dbl Long (ticker: DXO)

CURRENT STATE OF THE US MARKET

By mid-year 2008, there were more than 50 different commodity-based ETFs with more than US$30 billion in combined assets in the US. Roughly speaking, a third of these commodity ETFs are based on large, diversified baskets of commodities, a third are based on smaller sub-baskets of related commodities and a third are based on a single commodity such as gold, silver or crude oil.

There are currently five established broad-based commodity indexes. They include the S&P GSCI Commodity Index, the Dow Jones-AIG Commodity Index, the Reuters CCI (formerly the old CRB Index), the Deutsche Bank Liquid Commodity Index and the Rogers International Commodity Index. Each of them contains some component of energy commodities within its basket of holdings, but the weightings can vary a great deal. For example, the CCI Index has approximately a 17% weighting to energy commodities, while the S&P GSCI Commodity Index has over 70%.

Among the commodity sub-basket ETFs, several exist that have a 100% weighting to energy. They typically include in their holdings four or more different energy commodities, including crude oil, natural gas, gasoline and heating oil.

Among the most active of all of these commodity-based ETFs were the ones based on a single energy commodity. In particular, at the present time those ETFs focused on either crude oil or natural gas have seen a great deal of acceptance by the investing community and have large amounts of trading volume. Other energy-based commodity ETFs have been more recently introduced and it remains

Table 16.2 Major commodity indexes

	Reuters CCI (old CRB)	DJ-AIG	Rogers International	DB Liquid	S&P GSCI
Number of commodities	17	19	36	6	24
Agriculture (%)	47.04	29.47	30.65	22.50	14.94
Energy (%)	**17.64**	**33.00**	**44.00**	**55.00**	**71.54**
Industrial metals (%)	5.88	19.97	14.00	12.50	8.09
Livestock (%)	11.76	7.44	3.25	0.00	3.17
Other (%)	0.00	0.00	1.00	0.00	0.00
Precious metals (%)	17.64	10.12	7.10	10.00	2.27

Note: As of May, 2008.

to be seen how readily they will be widely accepted by investors. All told, there are more than a dozen energy commodity-related ETFs in the market as of mid-2008 targeting crude oil, natural gas, gasoline, and heating oil.

WHAT'S IN A NAME?

ETF, ETS and ETN

Before proceeding further a brief look at the nomenclature used in the ETF marketplace is in order. The SEC has a legal definition of what constitutes an ETF. The SEC's view is that an ETF is an investment pool that shares the following five characteristics:

- it is registered under the mutual fund regulations (ie, it is a 1940 Act company);
- it is listed and traded on a public exchange;
- it tracks some sort of index or price series;
- it holds a basket of investments related to its index or price series; and
- it allows broker-dealers to create or redeem shares at net asset value (NAV) in large blocks.

However, we have already discovered that the commodity-based "ETFs" do not exactly meet the SEC definition. The five significant points of these newer vehicles are as follows:

- it is registered under the ordinary company listing rules (ie, it is a 1933 Act company);
- it is listed and traded on a public exchange;
- it tracks some sort of index or price series;
- it holds a basket of investments related to its index or price series; and
- it allows broker-dealers to create or redeem shares at NAV in large block.

These newer vehicles are sometimes called exchange-traded securities (ETSs) or exchange-traded commodities (ETCs). Except for being registered under the 1933 Act, and not the 1940 Act, they appear to be just like ETFs. How much of a difference does, or should, this make to investment professionals and investors? The answer is that it is not clear that the SEC's stricter definition should really matter to investors. The legal structures are different (and have different tax consequences, as we will discuss later), but are otherwise legal equivalents. As a practical matter, people within the ETF industry as well as those on Wall Street do not really draw much of a distinction between the two legal approaches.

However, to make matters a bit more complex, some of the newest legal structures used to bring to market commodities in the ETF world are neither 1940 Act nor 1933 Act investment pools. Instead, a major Wall Street firm or commercial bank will bring to market a special sort of zero coupon bond. This bond's price movement is designed to mimic the movement of a commodity-based index or price series. In this case, these exchange-traded notes (ETNs) have the following characteristics:

- they are not registered under either the 1933 Act or the 1940 Act, but are instead registered as a bond;
- they are listed and traded on a public exchange;
- they track some sort of index or price series;
- they do NOT hold a basket of investments related to its index or price series; and
- they allow broker-dealers to create or redeem shares at NAV in large block.

From a practical standpoint, there are two notable differences between the ETN structure and either the ETFs or ETSs described above. First, the tax treatment of ETNs varies from that of either an ETF or an ETS. This we will discuss later. Second, unlike with an ETF or ETS, with ETNs there is no pool of assets that actually belong to the investors. Instead the investor has a promise to pay by the issuing bank. How much of a source of concern is that for investors? If the issuing bank were to run into difficulties the investors could find themselves in line with other creditors of the bank and at risk of losing money. Offsetting that risk is that investors could always sell their shares in the ETN in the marketplace, assuming they acted before the bank ran into serious difficulties or actually filed for bankruptcy.

There is only limited history to guide investors on this topic. There existed in the US marketplace ETNs offered by both Bear Sterns and Lehman Brothers at the time of their collapse in 2008. It appears that the Bear Sterns ETFs, issued by a company that was bought by JP Morgan before it went bankrupt, are going to be largely unaffected. However, shareholders in the Lehman ETNs are not so lucky. They found themselves as general creditors of Lehman and may end up recovering only a small portion of their pre-bankruptcy NAV.

Generally speaking, the ETF industry and Wall Street tend to view ETNs in the same way as they view exchange-traded securities and, for that matter, ETFs themselves. However, the demise of Lehman Brothers and the problems facing the owners of shares of the ETNs issued by them may cause the marketplace to re-evaluate the credit risk inherent in ETNs. There is a real risk that the marketplace for any ETN shares could reflect not only the price movement of the particular commodity, but also a discount based on concerns about the issuing bank.

For the purposes of the balance of this chapter, we will use the term "ETF" to describe all three structures unless otherwise indicated.

THE MECHANICS OF A TYPICAL ENERGY-BASED COMMODITY ETF

To give the reader a better understanding of how energy-based commodity ETFs work, let us walk through the structure and daily processes in some detail. Let us assume that an established sponsor of ETFs wanted to launch an ETF on a commonly traded energy commodity. We will assume that the commodity is some form of crude oil, although almost any energy-related commodity would fit the example.

Step One

The ETF firm files a prospectus under the 1933 Act to register a new fund that will invest in crude oil futures contracts and be listed on an exchange. It has a defined investment objective as well as a defined list of what would be acceptable investments within the portfolio. The investment objective could be its NAV rise, or fall, each day in the same amount in percentage terms as that of the crude oil benchmark it is seeking to track.

Step Two

At least one Wall Street firm will agree to fill the role of the initial market maker at the designated exchange. A larger number of broker-dealers may also decide to make a market in these new shares, either on the exchange or via some form of electronic market, but there will always be at least one firm.

Step Three

Once the registration has been effectively declared by the SEC (and the CFTC), the new ETF would seek a listing on an exchange such as the New York Stock Exchange, or on the Nasdaq.

In this example, we will assume that the fund's NAV at the start will be US$50 per share. The actual choice of initial NAV price is largely arbitrary. Also in this example we will assume that the price of the particular type of crude oil that it seeks to track is currently US$100 per barrel. At the time of the launch one or more of the market makers might purchase from the fund some amount of shares, delivering to the fund cash representing the number of shares purchased times US$50. When buying, or "creating", shares a broker-dealer must do so in certain large sized blocks. These blocks, known as creation and redemption baskets, are usually in 50,000 or 100,000 share increments.

Assuming that the broker-dealers elected to create one million shares at the onset, the fund would receive US$50 million prior to the start of trading. If the targeted crude oil future was trading at US$100 a barrel, and assuming that the futures contract stipulated 1,000 barrels per contract (which is typical), a single contract would have a nominal value of US$100,000. The fund would need to buy approximately 500 contracts to fully invest all of its assets. The fund would deposit an amount equal to around 10%–20% with the futures broker as a margin deposit. On that deposit it would receive an interest rate equal to prevailing short-term rates. The fund would deposit the rest of the cash into other short-term or cashlike investments and also receive a short-term return. The fund quite often will attempt to target receiving an average yield on its cash equal to that of the 90-day Treasury bill.

Step Four

Once the fund is listed and public trading commences, investors interested in owning exposure to crude oil will buy and sell shares by placing trades with their brokers. The movements in the market price of the fund during the day should mirror the movement of the futures oil contracts as measured in percentage terms. So if the oil contracts price was to rise 1% on the first day of the ETF's trading, from US$100.00 to US$101.00, then you would expect the price of the ETF to also rise 1% from US$50.00 to US$50.50. If the price of the oil contracts were to fall 1%, you would expect the price of the ETF to fall accordingly.

The exchange that lists the ETF will usually release throughout the day an "indicative NAV". This is not an official NAV, which is calculated only once at the end of the day, but it will give investors a rough guide as to what the ETF should be worth based on its holdings throughout the day. During the trading day the actual market price will tend to fall somewhere right above, or right below, the value that the futures contract would suggest as investors buy and sell shares. These premiums or discounts usually reflect the relative number of buyers and sellers at any particular time and can change rapidly.

Step Five

The market makers for the ETF on the exchange will generally make quotes to buy, or sell, shares with a "spread" between the bid and the offer, which represents their potential profit for making an active market for investors. For example, if at 11:15 am the "fair value" of the ETF based on the movements in the futures contracts it holds was US$52.50, the market makers might post quotes offering to buy shares at US$52.45 or sell them at US$52.55. The 10 cent "spread" represents their opportunity to make a profit by making a market in the security.

As the market makers conduct their business they may find that they are either ending up selling more shares than they are buying, or the reverse. If they are selling more shares into the market than they are buying, the market maker may find at the end of the day they are now "short" thousands of shares. The market makers may need to create more shares to accommodate their trading volume and to allow them to rebalance their inventory. They do so by placing an order with the ETF to buy more shares in 50,000 or 100,000 share increments. The order is placed by the broker-dealer while the trading is still occurring, but the actual price at which the broker-dealers will buy new shares will be at the end-of-the-day official NAV. Once the broker-dealer's order has been accepted, and the NAV established at the close of the day, the broker-dealer will typically receive the new shares and pay for them on T-3, as would be the case with most listed securities. The broker-dealer can then turn around and deliver these shares to the firms that had bought shares from the market maker.

Unlike a traditional stock ETF, where the broker-dealer delivers to the ETF a basket of the underlying stocks as payment for the new shares, with commodity futures the broker-dealer will deliver cash to the fund who will buy the futures contracts themselves. This is because, unlike as with stocks or bonds, you cannot transfer ownership of a futures contract from one investor to another.

Alternatively, the situation may arise where the broker-dealer finds that the marketplace is selling them more shares than they are buying and at the end of the day the market maker is now "long" thousands of shares. In that case the broker-dealer may redeem shares in the same fashion as they create shares to once again rebalance the market maker's inventory. The difference with a redemption is that, on T-3, the broker-dealer delivers shares to the fund and receives cash back.

Once the fund is up and running and trading volume has increased to the point where creations and redemptions routinely occur, then there are a number of other points investors should be aware of about the operations of the ETF. Some of the more important ones are listed below.

Calculating the NAV

The fund calculates its NAV at the end of each trading day. The NAV calculation is not in anyway impacted by the trading of the ETF shares in the equity market. Rather it is impacted by the change in the value of the oil futures contracts it owns. If the 500 oil futures contracts purchased at the onset at a price of US$100.00 a barrel were to finish the day or week at US$104.50, then the total value of all the portfolio holdings would be US$52,250,000 (US$104.50 × 1,000 barrels per contract × 500 contracts). Since in this example there are still only 1,000,000 shares outstanding, the NAV would equal US$52.25.

Interest yields and the NAV

In addition, the NAV calculation will be effected positively by the amount of interest the fund earns on its large cash holdings, as well as negatively by the amount of its management fee and other operating expenses (including paying brokerage commissions on its buying and selling of futures). If the fund was earning an average of 2.6% annualised on its cash holdings, and had combined management and brokerage expenses of around 0.80%, then the net effect would be that every day the NAV would be positively impacted on to the tune of 1.80% annualised, or about 0.005% per day. In a day when the price of the oil contracts went up 1%, the fund's NAV would go up 1.005%. If the price of the oil contracts went down 1%, then the NAV would drop 0.995%. Although the daily impact of the interest earned and the expenses is very small, it will add up over time. This is particularly true when short-term interest rates are high.

Buying and selling futures by the fund

Since it is up to the fund to buy or sell futures contracts, it is important that the fund execute those trades at the "right" price. Most commodity-based funds use as their defined benchmark the end-of-the-day prices for their particular commodity. It is important that the ETF match its targeted benchmark. As such, the fund will typically want to always buy or sell at the end-of-the-day settlement price. If the fund ends up not being able to buy or sell all of the contracts they are trading at the settlement price the fund will incur a small amount of tracking error compared with its benchmark.

If the fund received a creation order for a single basket of 100,000 shares on the second day of trading assuming that the oil futures contracts were worth US$104.50, then the NAV would be US$52.25. A market maker ordering the creation basket would have had to place their order before the end of the trading day. Once the NAV is established, the value of the 100,000 share creation basket can be established. In this case the basket is worth US$5,225,000, which the market maker will owe to the fund in cash on T-3. However, the fund needs to buy some amount of futures contracts to accommodate the increase in shares. To keep the fund's current and future NAV on track, the fund would need to buy 50 more contracts. What is more, the fund would aim to buy them at the closing, or "settlement", price on the same day as the order is placed.

A typical order flow for a creation or redemption could involve the market maker's ordering a creation basket at 12 noon, New York time. This in turn causes the fund to place an order for 50 more contracts on the futures exchange where the futures contracts trade. The futures order would indicate that the buyer, the fund, wants to get the end-of-the-day settlement price. For some exchanges that day's trading ends at 2:30 pm and the settlement price is released soon after. For the fund, it must usually wait until after it stops trading, typically at 4 pm, before it calculates its NAV based on the 2:30 pm oil futures prices. Between the time the market maker orders the creation basket and the time the fund's NAV is determined, the price of the futures contracts might rise, or fall, a great deal. However, that will not change the fact that a single 10,000-share basket will still equal 50 futures contracts. Movements in the futures contracts will be mirrored in the NAV and the ratio will remain the same.

The impact of arbitrage

The creation and redemption process is essential to all ETFs. One of the things it helps accomplish is to keep the ETF from trading at a large premium, or large discount, to the underlying value as measured by the NAV. If an ETF were to trade too high above its indicative NAV, the market maker could profitably sell shares to buyers and then do a creation at NAV (and so at a zero premium), and deliver those shares to investors. The impact of increasing the supply of shares would act to reduce the premium in the price down to a modest level. If on the other hand the ETF was trading at a large discount to NAV, the broker-dealer would act to buy the shares cheaply in the open market and turn around and redeem them at NAV, locking in a profit. In this case reducing the number of shares outstanding would force the discount to narrow.

Hedging by broker-dealers

Broker-dealers making a market in a commodity-based ETF do not themselves typically want to be exposed to the price movements in crude oil. As such, whenever they buy large amounts of the ETF shares, and are thus now "long" crude oil exposure, they will sell an offsetting amount of the crude oil futures contracts to hedge their oil position back to zero. By the same token, if they are selling shares to investors they may find themselves "short" crude oil and will buy an offsetting amount of crude oil futures contracts. As a result, any gains or losses the market maker experiences will be related to the job they do in making a market in the shares and not from movements in the direction of the commodity itself.

Paying dividends

Although the commodity ETF is earning interest on its cash, it will typically not pay out that interest to its investors in the form of monthly or annual dividends. Rather, the cash will remain part of the fund and always be part of the NAV calculation.

"Rolling" the contracts forward

Unlike owning stock, an ETF that owns futures contracts has to deal with the fact that all futures contracts eventually expire. In most cases if you own the futures contract at the point of expiration you will have to accept delivery of the physical amount represented by the contracts. Not surprisingly, a commodity-based ETF does not really want to turn US$100 million worth of oil futures contracts into US$100 million worth of actual barrels of oil. As a result, their self-described benchmark will indicate at what point they will sell futures contracts that are close to expiring and buy replacements.

For example, a crude oil ETF that on January 1 owns US$100 million worth of February contracts might plan to sell them all two weeks before they expire and replace them with US$100 million worth of March contracts. The act of selling the near month and buying one further out is referred to as "rolling" the position. As when the fund buys or sells to accommodate creations and redemptions, the fund would want to roll the contracts at the settlement prices on the day they roll. In this example, that would involve selling the February contracts at the roll day settlement price and buying the March contracts at the same time, also at their settlement price.

Leverage and commodity ETFs

It is very common in the commodity investing world to make use of leverage. An investor with US$100,000 to invest might use it as margin to purchase US$1 million worth of crude oil futures. Should the price of oil rise, the investor's returns will be magnified. Should the price fall, the losses would be magnified as well.

By comparison, most commodity ETFs do not seek to use leverage. If investors invest US$100 million into a crude oil ETF, the fund would seek to only purchase US$100 million worth of contracts. This could mean that the fund might deposit US$10 million as a margin deposit and will hold onto the rest in cash or cash equivalents. As a result, the fund's NAV movement will more closely match the actual movements of the benchmark contract without the extreme gains or losses caused by leverage. However, there are some commodity-based ETFs that do make use of leverage. Most typically, they use 50% leverage to produce a daily result that is exactly twice the result of the commodity benchmark.

"Shorting" energy commodity exposure

Although at first glance most investors view investing in commodity ETFs as a way to gain "long" exposure to the area, in fact virtually any commodity ETF can be sold short. In this way an investor can take a position that will benefit if the commodity declines in value.

As with any short sale, the investor will arrange to borrow shares from their broker and then sell them at the current price. At some point in the future the investor will need to buy the shares back, ideally for less than they sold them for, and return them to the broker. A brokerage firm will charge the investor for loaning them the shares. Although in theory any ETF can be shorted, in reality the ease of doing so is somewhat dependent on both how active a market there is in the particular ETF and which broker firm an investor is looking to to execute the trade. Any brokerage firm that is very active in making a market in a particular ETF can usually easily arrange a loan of shares. By comparison, many firms that are not active in market making, including many discount brokerage firms, are not good candidates to help arrange a short loan.

One new development to help make it easier for investors to take a short position in a particular commodity is the creation by ETF sponsors of "inverse" or "short" commodity ETFs. These funds are mirrors of the traditional long ETF and as a result, their NAV will go up if the commodity futures price goes down. Of course, the reverse is also true and their NAV will go down if the commodity price rises.

Options on energy-commodity ETFs

A fairly recent development is that stock exchanges are now listing options on many of the energy-commodity ETFs. Like any other stock, the options have a strike price and an expiration date and can be either a put or a call. A crude oil ETF trading around US$75 a share might have a dozen or more puts and calls with strike prices both above and below its current price as well as with expiration dates ranging throughout a number of months. However, only those energy-commodity ETFs that have a great deal of volume in the ETF are typically seeing much volume in the options. As a result, investors must take care to make sure that the options that they may have an interest in actually have enough volume to allow taking and liquidating positions without having to incur too high trading costs. Typically, information about the options on an energy-commodity ETF can be found on the website of the stock exchange that is the primary listing of the ETF.

USING ENERGY-COMMODITY ETFs IN A PORTFOLIO OR TRADING STRATEGY

The four ways to use an energy-commodity-based ETF

At first glance investing in energy-commodity-based ETFs may seem a daunting task. However, a fairly simple analysis framework may help reduce the task to more manageable portions. There are essentially four very different ways that an investor can approach using energy-commodity ETFs. These different approaches vary based not only on the time horizon of the investor, but also on what the underlying rational is for making any such investment as well as the particular attributes of the commodity being reviewed. It is very important for any investor to consider which of these approaches they are looking to employ as well as how suitable a particular energy commodity, or energy-commodity-based ETF, is for their intended use.

In brief an investor can use an energy-commodity ETF because:

- they want to take a directional position on the price of that commodity;
- they want to hedge another position, which consists of another commodity, an equity, or some other investment;
- they want to hedge an actual physical exposure that they have to the underlying commodity or to a related commodity; or
- they are looking to hold the position as part of a long-term portfolio strategy that seeks to maximise returns and minimise risks.

Each of these approaches would be approached in a very different fashion by a potential investor. Furthermore, some of these approaches, depending on the commodities, are either very difficult to implement or essentially impossible.

Directional investments

The most obvious way to look at investing in any commodity-based ETF is one in which the investor has a particular viewpoint on the price direction of the commodity or commodities. This directional approach can be used whether an investor is looking at a broad basket of commodities, a sub-basket of commodities or a single-commodity ETF. This approach can also be used regardless of whether the commodity is energy-related, agriculture-related, precious metals or any other commodity exposure. With the directional approach, the investor has reasons to believe that the price trend will be up (or down) over some reasonably defined time period and as a result, they wish to be long (or short) exposure to that particular commodity using a suitable ETF.

In one sense, this is the simplest approach because, once the investor's view on the commodity or commodity basket's direction has been determined, it a straightforward task to implement the strategy.

Their view could be based on prevailing supply-and-demand factors for the commodity, on related currencies that impact on the commodity, on technical analysis of the recent trading of the commodity, on the weather or on political events that might impact on the price of the commodity. As a general rule, many investors would likely make such investment with a short-term or intermediate-term time horizon. Either the scenario they envision comes to pass or it does not. In either case they might envision closing the position within weeks, months or perhaps a year or so.

Limitations. Unlike the other three broad approaches to using commodity ETFs, the directional approach is not limited by the nature of the commodities.

Multiple-investment strategies and hedging

While the directional approach is the most straightforward, the multiple-asset approach can be the most complicated. In many respects this approach is the type of investment or trading strategy most likely to be employed by a hedge fund. In this instance, the investor is typically going long, or short, an energy-commodity ETF while at the same time going long, or short, another investment such as a stock, an option, or another commodity ETF. Unlike with the directional investor first mentioned, the object here is not to benefit by correctly anticipating whether the commodity price is going higher or lower. Rather it is typically a relative-value strategy that seeks to benefit when the price relationship of the two investments moves in a particular way.

As an example, an investor might elect to be long crude oil and short natural gas. Such an investor is not concerned that prices of crude oil or natural gas might rise or fall, but is instead interested in the change in the spread between the two. In this case, long crude and short natural gas, the investor will benefit if prices go up or down as long as oil goes up more, or goes down less, than natural gas. Even within a single commodity, the investor may elect to go long one commodity ETF that owns the front-month contracts and go short another ETF that is based on the same commodity but owns different contract months, and attempt to profit on the relative changes in the price of the contracts. For example, most crude oil ETFs own the front-month contract of crude oil. However, a few own a different month or even a range of months. Buying one ETF and shorting the other is a strategy that assumes that the shape of the futures price curve will get either steeper or flatter, and profit accordingly.

Alternatively, an investor might elect to be long the commodity ETF and sell, or be short, an out-of-the-money call option on the same commodity ETF. In this situation, usually known as a "buy/write" strategy, the investor is implicitly assuming that, at least in the near term, the price of the commodity is not going to rise quickly. If they are correct they will collect the premium for selling the call and retain the ETF after the option expires. If they are wrong, the ETF shares will be called away from them at a higher price and they will lose the potential gain above that level, but they will still have the premium (and have sold at a higher price than when they executed the buy/write).

A third possible combination strategy is to use the commodity ETF to hedge the commodity exposure of an equity. This would allow the investor to break the price of the stock into two parts. For example, assume an investor thought that Exxon was overpriced based on a comparison of its value versus that of other oil majors. At first glance it would seem that shorting Exxon's stock would be a viable strategy. However, if the investor did so and the next day an oil tanker owned by Shell blew up in Nigeria or got hijacked by pirates off the coast of Somalia, possibly causing the price of crude oil to spike, they could see the price of Exxon run up and their short position badly underwater. Their problem is that part of Exxon's stock price movement reflects it as a company, but part of it reflects the movement of oil prices. However, if the investor calculated that a third of Exxon's price movement was all about oil and the rest was the company's prospects, they might arrange to go long the oil ETF while simultaneously shorting Exxon. In this case they might go long US$1 of the commodity ETF for every US$3 of Exxon they short. If they are correct as to their estimate of what percentage of Exxon's is the oil and what percentage is not, they have now hedged out the oil factor. Of course, they now have to be correct, with the oil factor taken out, that Exxon is overvalued. Alternatively, they could think that Chevron was undervalued but were afraid that oil prices might fall. In that case they would go short a crude oil ETF in some proportion of going long Chevron.

Limitations. Obviously, the number of ways that an investor can combine being long or short energy-commodity ETFs, energy-related stocks or energy-related options is limited only by the creativity of the investor. It can also be constructed in such a way as to add or lower a great deal of risk in the strategy. However, the choices the investor has are still limited to finding appropriate matching investment choices. With some commodities – crude oil and gold, for example – there exists a large universe of equities whose price movement to at least some degree reflects the movement of the commodity price. As of late 2007, for example, the total global market cap of equities of companies that were in the oil or energy business was in excess of US$2 trillion. The equity market cap of gold-related stocks, mostly mining companies, was over US$100 billion. But at the time there was only one stock in the world that was primarily a play on silver. In attempting to measure the ability to combine commodity ETFs with other investments, not all commodities are created equal! However, the very nature of these strategies that involve "pairs" of investment choices requires that the commodity ETF and the other investment have a strong correlation in their price movements. That also means that an ETF that represents a basket of commodities, or even a basket of energy commodities, may not be enough of a pure play to achieve the desired price relationship. As a result, only a certain subset of the commodity ETF world will actually be usable to apply any of these strategies. Finally, in order to do any of the option-related strategies, such as the buy/write, it is obvious that the ETF would need to have options that are listed on it and trade in the marketplace. Not all energy-commodity ETFs have active option markets, so that will also tend to limit the universe a bit.

Commodity ETFs in a multi-asset-allocation portfolio

While the multiple-investment strategy is typically more the approach a hedge fund or other sophisticated investor would take, the asset-allocation approach is more for the buy-and-hold investor. Over the years investors and academics have concluded that there is an enormous benefit to creating a portfolio that consist of different asset classes and investments that are each expected to produce, over time, acceptable total returns while at the same time are not expected to move up and down in value together in lockstep. The asset-allocation plan of 30 years ago – which consisted of allocating money among large-cap US stocks, high-quality bonds and cash – has now evolved by adding exposure to small-cap US stocks, foreign stock, high-yield or foreign bonds, and real estate stocks (REITs). The addition of these other asset classes typically broke into mainstream thought after some early adopters, often sophisticated endowments and pension plans, started adding such investment classes to their mixes with successful results. This was often accompanied by academic studies that looked back at the returns and correlations of returns and concluded that there was a sound factual basis for adding the new investment class to the mix.

Over the last half-dozen years, a number of major endowments and pension plans have started adding commodities to their list of acceptable asset classes. At the same time, some landmark studies have been published reviewing the merits of adding commodities to asset-allocation models. Perhaps the best known of these is a 2005 study done by Rouwenhorst and Gorton, which is sometimes referred to as the "Yale" study (although Gorton is from Wharton). Their study lent a great deal of support to the notion that commodities offered total returns that were competitive with the returns of equities and bonds, but without being strongly correlated. A similar study by Buyuksahin, Haig and Robe (2007) also concluded that they found no evidence that the correlation of commodities to stocks and bonds has risen in recent years.

Most studies that focus on commodity correlations and returns in the context of a multi-asset-allocation study focused on baskets of commodities such as the Dow Jones AIG Commodity Index or the S&P GSCI. From those results many investment professionals have concluded that a 5–15% weighting to commodities may be appropriate for a well-designed asset-allocation portfolio.

Most studies have not specifically focused on the impact of just using energy commodities in a model. However, evidence suggests that energy commodities when used by themselves should provide similar benefits to those found within the baskets. Buyuksahin, Haig and Robe found that the energy-heavy S&P GSCI was essentially uncorrelated to the S&P 500 over various time periods measured between 1991 and 2007. They also reached the same result when measuring a basket of energy commodities against the S&P 500 (not surprising, the correlation of energy commodities and the S&P GSCI was over 0.96). Finally, they found that energy commodities did not strongly correlate with other, non-energy commodities.

Table 16.3 compares the correlation over the last 10 years of three of the four major energy commodities traded as futures in the US: crude oil, natural gas and heating oil (gasoline is not included, because a change in the US government gasoline standards meant that two different gasoline contracts existed during this time period). Clearly none of the three energy commodities strongly correlate with stocks, US or global, or US bonds. Interestingly, natural gas only moderately correlates with crude oil or heating oil. It does not come as a surprise, however, that heating oil does correlate strongly with crude oil.

If energy commodities do not strongly correlate with traditional asset classes such as stocks and bonds, what might have been the

Table 16.3 Ten-year correlation matrix 1997–2007

	Large-cap US equities	**US govt bonds**	**Global equities**	**Crude oil**	**Natural gas**	**Heating oil**
Large-cap US equities	1.000	–0.237	0.949	–0.037	–0.008	–0.065
US govt bonds		1.000	–0.259	0.033	0.197	0.065
Global equities			1.000	0.040	0.029	–0.003
Crude oil				1.000	0.344	0.802
Natural gas					1.000	0.480
Heating oil						1.000

Source: Bloomberg

result of including an energy commodity in a diversified portfolio? Since academics have tended to focus on commodity indexes and not individual commodities in their studies, we will need to create a small study ourselves. Table 16.4 compares the results of a diversified investment split equally in one case into five traditional asset classes, and in another case split equally into the same five assets plus an investment into crude oil futures that target always owning the front-month contract (and rolling it forward each month).

The results are interesting. The crude oil investment lost money in two years, 1998 and 2001, but only one of those years was a down year for the S&P 500. In two other years, the S&P 500 lost money but crude oil made money. Overall, the presence of crude oil helped to increase the portfolio's annual total return over this time period by 3.55% a year, while only increasing the standard deviation of the portfolio by 1.04%.

Readers are cautioned that future results for crude oil may not be as favourable as during this time period. Furthermore, the results might have been very different if we had selected a different energy commodity over the 10-year time period, or a basket of energy commodities. For example, although heating oil and gasoline have tended over the last 40+ years to have similar annual total returns to crude oil, natural gas has tended to lag its liquid cousins.

Limitations. The primary limitation of using commodity ETFs as part of a strategy is the lack of much in the way of third-party studies, particularly academic papers, that examine the historical results of using such commodities. As noted, the majority of studies have focused on baskets of commodities. With the exception of gold – for whose inclusion in and impact on portfolios' risks and return there is a long history of studies – individual commodities have not yet received a great deal of attention. However, with the case already being made for commodity baskets, the next logical step is for economists to focus their attention on individual commodities. In that case it would seem likely that crude oil will soon join gold as a frequently studied candidate for asset diversification.

Commodity ETFs and hedging a physical cost or liability

Of the four approaches to using commodity ETFs, the one with the most limited universe of potential investors, is the approach that

Table 16.4 Hypothetical diversified portfolio total returns including crude oil exposure (1998–2007)

Year	90-day T-bill (%)	Lehman Agg Bond (%)	S&P 500 (%)	Russell 2000 (%)	MSCI EAFE (%)	Crude oil front month (%)	Traditional portfolio (%)	With oil portfolio (%)
1998	5.02	8.69	28.58	–2.55	19.93	–26.67	11.93	5.50
1999	4.87	–0.82	21.04	21.26	27.03	117.32	14.68	31.78
2000	6.32	11.63	–9.10	–3.02	–14.17	11.01	–1.67	0.44
2001	3.67	8.44	–11.89	2.49	–21.44	–22.30	–3.75	–6.84
2002	1.68	10.26	–22.10	–20.48	–15.94	58.94	–9.32	2.06
2003	1.05	4.10	28.68	47.25	38.59	5.28	23.93	20.82
2004	1.43	4.34	10.88	18.33	20.25	35.04	11.05	15.04
2005	3.34	2.43	4.91	4.55	13.54	43.82	5.75	12.10
2006	5.07	4.33	15.79	18.37	26.34	5.09	13.98	12.50
2007	4.77	6.97	5.49	–1.57	11.17	61.99	5.37	14.80
Annualised return (%)							**6.77**	**10.32**
Standard deviation (%)							**9.46**	**10.50**

Source: Bloomberg

has investors using a commodity ETF to hedge their own expenses or liabilities. In addition, the small universe of investors for whom this technique would apply will find that most commodity-based ETFs are not suitable for their needs.

A simple example of whom this approach might work for would be the client of an investment adviser who operates some sort of business or farm. That particular business could have a large exposure to one or more particular commodities. For example, it could be a small trucking firm for whom diesel fuel or gasoline is a major part of their operating budget. To reduce the risk to the business posed by the volatility in the energy commodity markets, the client might elect either to purchase a suitable energy-commodity ETF to essentially "lock in" their price, or buy an option on the energy-commodity ETF. In a simple example, they could hedge US$200,000 worth of future gasoline expenses by either buying some amount of a gasoline ETF, or by buying a "call option" on a gasoline ETF.

(Note: Although at present there is not a diesel fuel ETF, there is a heating oil ETF. For decades energy traders have used heating oil futures as a proxy for diesel fuel.)

If the operation was large enough – think of an airline such as Southwest – they might operate on a large enough scale that they would skip the energy-commodity ETF and just buy the futures contracts, or options on futures contracts, directly. In that way they avoid having to pay the ETF's expenses, although presumably they have to pay their own energy traders, and they can more precisely target the exact exposure they want. For smaller business, which lack the scale or internal expertise, this may not be practical and they may find it easier to use commodity ETFs or options on commodity ETFs.

A business using this approach has several factors to consider. First, there must be a suitable ETF that closely matches its needs. This is one reason why there is only a fairly small number of commodity ETFs that this approach would be suitable for in the market. Although a large number of small or medium-sized businesses might want to hedge their gasoline or heating oil costs, no firm that size really needs to hedge a large basket of commodities such as the ones found in the S&P GSCI or Dow Jones AIG. In fact, it is not likely that a small-to-medium-sized business would need to hedge the sort of exposure represented by one of the sub-baskets, such as an all-agriculture or all energy-basket.

Furthermore some of the individual commodities that are traded, and that might be the basis of a single-commodity ETF, may not be ones where many small or medium-sized businesses would really attempt to hedge their costs. Coal, for example, tends to be bought and sold among a small number of very large firms that are more likely to use futures or swaps than a commodity ETF.

Second, the commodity ETF they are looking at must correlate reasonably well to the need they have in their business. It is unlikely that there is a 1:1 relationship between the business's needs and the commodity ETF. For example, the gasoline used to form the basis of the listed futures contracts, and a gasoline ETF, is typically wholesale. The gasoline that is actually used by a business is typically retail and includes non-commodity expenses in the form of federal or state taxes. As a result, the business would have to assume that they it have to buy more, or less, of the commodity ETF to effectively hedge its exposure.

A third factor is that the business would have to calculate what the impact would be on its hedge of the transaction costs to buy and sell the ETF, as well as the annualised expenses of the ETF itself.

Finally, if the commodity ETF is based on futures contracts, in particular using a single month as its benchmark, then the total return of the commodity ETF will be impacted on by the shape of the futures curve. Depending on the commodity and the particular market, the business's hedge may benefit or be hurt by a futures market that was in backwardation or in contango.

Limitations. The reality is that any particular commodity-based ETF may be only an approximate fit to use as a hedging tool for a small or medium-sized business. However, it does have the advantage of ease of use and relatively low cost. For a firm lacking scale and internal expertise, it may be an approach worth considering.

PAYING THE TAXMAN!

Differences in ETFs

An investor in a commodity ETF in a taxable account needs to be aware of how capital gains and ordinary income generated by ETFs are reported to investors and how they will be treated by the Internal Revenue Service (IRS) – the taxable implications for non-US investors are beyond the scope of this chapter.

As described earlier in the chapter, ETFs, ETSs and ETNs do differ is in their tax treatment and reporting. Since all of the commodity-based "ETFs" are actually either an ETF or an ETN, it is important to understand how the taxes differ and how they are similar.

Mutual fund and ordinary ETF tax rules

Let us first view how taxes and tax reporting are handled by an ordinary mutual fund or stock-owning ETF. Under IRS regulations, a mutual fund does not itself pay fund-level taxes. Rather, all realised gains and earned income are given to shareholders in the form of capital gain and ordinary income dividends by the end of the year. A mutual fund or ETF does not report to shareholders any unrealised gains on stocks or bonds that the fund owns but have not yet sold. Most stock and bond ETFs obtain and dispose of most of their portfolio holdings by transfer with the market makers who are creating and redeeming shares. This allows the ETF to minimise any actual realised long-term or short-term capital gains as the ETF itself rarely actually sells the stocks and books the gain. In February of the following year the investor will typically receive a Form 1099 breaking out their share of short-term capital gains, long-term capital gains, and ordinary income, which represents the dividends that were declared by the ETF or mutual fund. It is important to remember that it does not matter if the investor actually takes the dividends or leaves them at the fund to be reinvested. The tax-reporting obligation is the same.

Commodity-based ETSs

Most commodity-based ETSs have a different tax treatment compared with a mutual fund or ETF. Remember that commodity-based exchange traded securities are not set up as 1940 Act mutual funds and so cannot use the same section of the tax code to avoid fund level taxes. Also remember that, like an ordinary ETF, an ETS does own a portfolio of futures contracts or other assets. To avoid fund-level taxes, a commodity-based ETS may elect to be taxed as a limited partnership. Under this regime, the ETF itself does not pay fund-level taxes on any of its gains or ordinary income. Instead, the long-term capital gains, short-term capital gains and ordinary income are passed on to the shareholders. So far this sounds like the tax treatment of an ordinary ETF. However, there are four key differences between taxes in an ETF and taxes in a commodity-based ETS.

First, a commodity-based ETS does not have to actually declare capital gain or income dividends in order for shareholders to be obligated to report them in their tax filing. Most ETSs will elect to retain the gains and interest in the fund, where they will remain part of the NAV. In that sense, it is a bit like a mandatory reinvestment.

Second, under partnership tax-reporting rules, it does not matter whether or not the fund sold the investment by the end of the year in order to be included in the gain. All gains, whether realised or not, are reported. This may seem to be a big difference compared with mutual funds/ETFs who report gains only on securities that have actually been sold. From a practical standpoint, this particular rule actually has only a small impact. This is because most commodity-based ETSs sell some or all of their futures contracts each month (when they "roll"), and so, by the end of the year, only a small portion of their gains or losses are unrealised.

A third difference is that, unlike a mutual fund or ETF, a commodity-based ETS reports capital losses as well as gains to its investors. If a mutual fund at the end of the year has a certain amount of realised capital losses it must wait until it has capital gains to make use of the loss. It may not pass the realised loss to shareholders, who could use it to offset their gains elsewhere. However, under partnership rules, if the ETS has losses, those losses will be reported to the investor, who may use them in their own tax filings to offset gains in other portions of their portfolio.

Finally, the owner of a commodity-based ETS will not receive a 1099 tax-reporting form. Instead they will receive a K-1 tax-reporting form. Although the K-1 form looks more complicated, in many respects it is not much more challenging than a 1099. The form will break down all capital gains, or losses, into long-term and short-term gains or losses. If the fund gained its exposure to the commodity by using futures contracts, as most do, all gains and losses will be assumed under IRS regulations to be 60% long-term and 40% short-term, regardless of how long the fund actually owned the futures contracts. In addition, the K-1 will report to the investor their share of the interest that the fund earned on cash or other investments. This is reported as ordinary income. Finally, the K-1 will report how much of the operating expenses of the fund belongs to each shareholder. This is treated as a deduction, as it represents the investor's share of business expenses.

If an investor sells their shares in the commodity-based ETF, the K-1 will contain additional information. A key concept for investors to bear in mind here is that all the reported figures that the K-1 provides every year regarding gains, losses, interest and business expenses not only affect the investor's current reported results, but also impact on the cost basis of the shares when the investor sells them. If a shareholder bought shares in 2007 of a fund for US$50 and received a K-1 in early 2008 informing the investor that their share of the fund's capital gains was US$3, they would have to report the US$3 as a gain on their 2007 tax filing. However, it would also mean that their cost basis starting in 2008 would go up from US$50 to US$53. So, if they turned around and sold their shares for US$53 in early January of 2008, they might have no gain in 2008 to show for their disposition of the shares that they bought at US$50. Most K-1s will contain some form of running total that accrues the adjustments over time to aid investors with their cost basis calculations.

Exchange-traded notes

Readers need to remember that ETNs differ from ETFs and ETSs in two ways. First, an ETN is technically a type of bond and is thus a debt security. An ETF and an ETS are equity securities. Second, an ETN does not own any assets and so has no portfolio holdings. Instead the issuing bank promises to pay a return that would be similar to the results you would get if you owned such a portfolio. Lacking a portfolio, there are no capital gains or losses to be realised.

The firms that sponsor ETNs have indicated in their prospectuses that they are of the opinion that a buyer of an ETN does not have to report any gains, losses, or ordinary income from owning the security until they sell the investment. As an example, an investor might buy the ETN in 2006 for US$50 a share. The shares could rise in value over the next two years as the value of the benchmark commodity rose. But, unlike with an ETS, each year the investor would not report any gains or interest unless they sold their shares. At first blush this sounds like a better tax treatment than that of an ETS, and maybe even better than that of an ETF! But, as with many things, there is no free lunch.

The issue is that, although the issuers of such ETNs have stated that they believe their opinion is the correct tax interpretation, the IRS has not agreed to that view. In fact, the IRS has indicated that it is reviewing the ETN sponsor's claim. It may be that the IRS will conclude that the ETN sponsor's view is correct. However, there is a real chance that they may conclude that ETNs must send out 1099s, K-1s or some similar tax-reporting form every year just as an ETF or ETS does. Worse yet, they could make the reporting requirements retroactive. In that case investors might have to file amended filings to adjust their past tax filings to the new requirement. At the present time it is not possible to determine what the eventual outcome will be of this IRS review.

ENERGY COMMODITIES IN THE US AND GLOBALLY

In a modern economy such as the US, there are a number of energy-related commodities that are routinely traded both among energy-related businesses and within the investing community. At the same time, there are other energy commodities that do not actively trade and thereby are not suitable in very active markets.

There are four major energy commodities that trade in the US. The most important of the major commodities is crude oil. Crude oil is traded both by energy-related companies that produce, ship or refine crude oil and by investors and speculators who seek to gain returns by trading exposure to crude oil. Crude oil is itself is not used as a final product in a modern economy, but is instead turned into a variety of other energy commodities as well as industrial products such as plastics. Since crude oil is refined into a wide range of products, it is perhaps the single most important commodity traded in the world.

The second most important energy commodity in the US is natural gas. Although natural gas itself is not used in as many ways as crude oil, in certain key areas, such as the production of electricity and the heating of homes and business, it is essential.

Finally, there are two products distilled from crude oil that are actively traded in the US. The first is heating oil. Heating oil is an important source of residential and commercial heating for certain parts of the US, in particular the northeast. However, heating oil is also chemically very similar to diesel fuel. As a result, the price of heating oil has long served as a proxy for the price of diesel fuel.

The second of the major distilled energy products is gasoline. Unlike some of the other energy commodities, the use in a modern economy of gasoline is very concentrated in one particular area of economic activity: automotive transportation. However, since it is safe to say that the US economy runs on gasoline, it remains a very important commodity. When a refinery processes crude oil it would typically be able to turn about 50% of it into gasoline and 25% of it into heating oil (or diesel). The remaining amount would be a wide range of both energy products and industrial products.

Aside from the four major energy commodities traded in the US, there are some others that are used by consumers or business and can also be traded by investors or other interested parties. These include commodities such as low-sulphur diesel fuel, uranium, propane and ethanol. However, these other energy commodities at the present time are seeing only limited amounts of trading by non-industry participants. In some cases this may be because it has been only recently that investors could find a means to trade these commodities. In other cases it could be because the small size and narrow appeal of a particular commodity make it less desirable for investors to dabble in its trading, or because investors have other ways to gain exposure to a particular commodity.

For example, although there has been a great deal of interest in recent years in alternative energy sources to those derived from crude oil, it was only in 2007 that a futures contract was listed on either uranium or ethanol. It may be that over the next few years interest in these two commodities will grow, but at the present time trading in these by non-industry participants remains limited. Propane has been traded far longer than either of these two new entries, but it appears to have only a very limited appeal to non-industry players. Diesel fuel by comparison certainly has a large potential base of interested participants. However it suffers both from the fact that a future was listed on it only in 2007 and the fact that many interested participants have long been accustomed to trading heating oil as a proxy for diesel fuel. Since futures trading in heating oil commenced in 1978, it may be some time before a large number of investors and other trading participants gravitate to the new diesel fuel contract.

Certain important energy commodities, such as coal, jet fuel and electricity, are not routinely traded outside industry participants. Typically, these energy commodities lack listed futures contracts that would make it easier for non-industry investors to access these markets. However, over time it may be reasonable to expect that these other commodities will also become of greater interest and new futures contracts will be listed covering these commodities.

Of course, there are other energy commodities that trade outside of the US. Major centres of such energy commodity trading include London, Dubai, Singapore and Japan. Since all modern economies have similar energy needs, the energy commodities traded in these other locations tend to be similar to the ones traded in the US, but with certain local or regional differences. London is a major trading centre for crude oil, in particular the type of light, sweet crude oil that comes from the North Sea oilfields and is known as "Brent North Sea". In addition, other energy commodities are also traded in London that include natural gas, heating oil (known as "gas oil" in Europe), gasoline and diesel. Dubai is a trading centre for a variety of crude oils produced and exported from the Middle East. In 2007, the Dubai government established a new commodity futures exchange and commenced listed futures trading in a particular variety of crude oil from the region. Finally, Japan and Singapore remain important centres of energy trading for the Asian region.

Physical commodity variations

Although some of the commodities tend to be very standardised from a physical standpoint, others are not. Gasoline's actual chemical makeup, as it is produced by a refinery, is strictly defined by the oil companies that manufacture it, the car makers who build cars for it and the governments who regulate its use and environmental impact. As a result, although every few years the standards are updated, as a general rule "gasoline is gasoline". The same is largely true of many other energy commodities such as heating oil and natural gas.

By comparison, there is a huge variation in crude oil as it comes out of the ground. Depending on the actual oilfield where it comes from, certain types of crude oil may be physically heavier or lighter. They may also contain varying levels of impurities such as sulphur. Crude oil that contains low levels of sulphur is referred to as "sweet", while crude oil with large amounts of sulphur is referred to as "sour". From the standpoint of a refinery, the lighter a crude oil is, and the less sulphur it contains, the easier it is to turn into gasoline and other valuable products. So crude oil that is light and sweet is more valuable than crude oil that is heavy and sour.

Worldwide, there are more than 60 major variations of crude oil based on the geography where the crude comes from as well as its physical characteristics. However, since it would be difficult for the oil industry and investors to individually price every variation, the marketplace has largely settled on a few particular varieties as the standard product, or "benchmark". For North America, the standard benchmark is West Texas Intermediate (WTI), a light, sweet crude oil. The prices of all other types of crude oil in North America are based on the price of WTI with an appropriate premium or discount added to their market value depending on whether they are lighter or heavier, sweeter or sourer, than WTI. In Europe and other parts of the world, the standard benchmark is typically Brent North Sea, although there is growing use of a third benchmark based on heavier and more sour Middle Eastern crude oil variation.

Global versus regional consumption and trading

Certain commodities are fully global in terms of their production and consumption. Others are not as global and regional or national factors may be much more important. Crude oil is certainly a good example of a totally global commodity, as it is produced in a large number of countries and can easily be physically moved from one country to another by either pipeline or tanker. As a result, from a price and financial standpoint, the trading of crude oil is a fully globalised marketplace. Demand anywhere in the world can impact on the price of crude oil in another country such that an increase or decrease in demand in China will immediately affect the price of crude oil in Spain. A supertanker loaded in Saudi Arabia and bound for Rotterdam can have its cargo resold, and the ship rerouted to Houston, if prices in the US move higher.

At the other end of the extreme is natural gas. For physical reasons, it is difficult and very expensive to move natural gas except by pipeline. As a result, natural gas markets tend to be regional and based on the existence of a network of pipelines. Canada and the US form one major regional market, while Russia and Europe form another. With the emergence of liquefied natural gas (LNG) tankers, it is possible to move natural gas from one region to another. However, LNG capacity remains small and the process expensive.

As a result, a spike in natural gas demand and prices in China will have less impact on natural gas prices in the US than a similar spike in crude oil demand and prices.

Many of the refined products, such as diesel, gasoline and heating oil, can be transported by tankers. As a result, they can move between markets such as North America and Europe. At the same time they may not meet the exact specifications for the new market. For example, diesel in the US and diesel in Europe may not be identical. As a result, the markets would tend to be more globalised than natural gas, but somewhat less so than crude oil.

Seasonal versus non-seasonal usage patterns

Certain energy commodities, such as crude oil, do not display a great deal of seasonality in their demand or in their market pricing. On the other hand, some of the other commodities are very seasonal. As an example, gasoline use in the US peaks in the summer and declines in the winter, while heating oil use peaks in the winter and declines in the summer. As a result, an investor looking at prices of heating oil or gasoline for delivery in future months will detect a very pronounced seasonal cycle with prices for futures rising and falling based on seasonal demand.

Exchange-traded versus cash or OTC

Economic exposure to energy commodities can be obtained in four primary fashions. These methods range from those that involve physical movements of the commodity to those that involve purely financial arrangements in which no commodity ever changes hands.

The first method is to contract directly with another firm to actually buy physical barrels of oil with a stated delivery that will occur in the very near future. As an example, consider a contract to buy 10,000 barrels of crude oil for delivery in three days at a location to be specified. In addition, the particular physical characteristics of the crude oil would have to be stated in the terms of the agreement. This form of trading is referred to as the "cash market". The price paid in the cash market is also sometimes referred to as the "spot price". It tends to be the province of commodity-producing and commodity-consuming participants, since it presumes that the buyer or seller actually either has the physical commodity in hand or can accept delivery of it. In the case of crude oil, for example, the buyer might be a refinery while the seller might be a major oil company. Such trading is between two parties and, unlike with the stock market, there is no central trading facility for buyers and sellers to meet. This means that in certain respects the cash market for commodities represents an "over-the-counter" (OTC) market. In addition, lacking a central trading platform means there is no single place where the value and terms of these trades are maintained. However, certain financial information firms, such as Platts (the energy market division of McGraw-Hill), do collect reported trades and disseminate representative pricing to market participants. Because the cash market essentially presumes that the participants have the ability to physically make or accept delivery of the commodity within a few days, this market is not generally used by purely financial players in the commodity markets. Since the performance of the contract is dependent on both parties being able to fulfil their obligations, the cash market does present participants with a high degree of counterparty risk in that the other side of the trade may not be able to perform its part under the contract.

The second method of trading commodity exposure is in the "forward" market. This market is similar to the cash market except that the delivery called for occurs later than in the immediate future. As a result, it would be possible for a participant who does not intend to make or accept delivery to trade in the forward market, since they would presumably have some amount of time to arrange to sell their obligation to another participant prior to the time that delivery is called for by the contract. However, the majority of financially orientated commodity investors or traders would tend not to use the forward market as a means to invest in commodities. Like the cash market, the forward market does not trade on an exchange and is essentially an over-the-counter market. In addition, reported market pricing is typically obtained from firms such as Platts. Finally, the forward market also presents participants with a degree of counterparty risk.

The third method of investing in commodities is to buy or sell listed futures contracts on an established futures exchange. The principal exchange in the US for trading energy-commodity-related futures contracts is the New York Mercantile Exchange (Nymex), while the principal exchange outside of the US is the London-based ICE (formerly the International Petroleum Exchange). A futures contract is a standardised contract to buy/sell a set amount of the commodity with an intended delivery as of a certain date or range of dates. In addition, the physical characteristics of the commodity that is to be delivered are strictly defined, as is the location where delivery must be made to satisfy the terms of the contract.

As an example, an investor may elect to buy or sell futures contracts on Nymex calling for delivery of 1,000 barrels (42 gallons per barrel) of certain types of light, sweet crude oil with delivery to be made in Cushing, Oklahoma. Nymex will list contracts for delivery at the start of each month, beginning with the next month and extending out six years. An investor on January 1, 2009, looking to buy crude oil exposure could invest in any one of a number of standardised crude oil futures contracts with the shortest-term one calling for delivery in February 2009, and a different contract calling for delivery for each month extending out to December of 2014.

Unlike with the cash market or the forward market, prices for the commodity as traded on an exchange are disseminated to investors and the public as the trading occurs. In addition, when an investor agrees to sell a contract calling for delivery of a commodity, and another investor buys that contract, the two investors do not depend on a third party to perform under the terms of the contract. Rather each investor's counterparty is a central clearing house owned by or affiliated with the futures exchange. As a result, neither investor has a significant amount of counterparty risk using listed futures. Finally, futures contracts do not require the buyer of the contract to pay for the contracted amount unless they take delivery. However, to ensure that both parties are able to fulfil their obligations under the terms of the futures contract, both parties must maintain some amount of cash or other assets on deposit with their futures brokerage firm (known as a "futures commodity merchant"), which is the investor's margin requirement. The exact amount of margin that must be maintained varies by commodity and exchange, but typically represents an amount equal to 5% to 20% of the current market value of the contract. If the contract declines in value, the buyer of the contract will be required to add to their margin account. The same would be true for the seller of the contract if the price was to rise.

The final form of trading of commodity exposure is in purely financial arrangements, where no actual oil is expected to change hands. These are typically done as a form of an OTC arrangement between two parties. The most common arrangement is for these trades to be structured as "swaps". In a swap, the buyer and seller of the swap agree to exchange an amount of money at some point in the future based on changes in the price of the commodity (either a cash price or a price derived from the listed futures market). If the price of the commodity that the swap is based on goes up, the buyer of the swap is owed more money from the swap. If the price goes down, the seller of the swap is due money from the buyer. Swaps are normally only invested in by major, sophisticated financial institutions.

TERM STRUCTURE OF COMMODITY FUTURES

Commodity futures differ from ordinary equities in that they, like a bond, have an eventual "maturity date". In reality, what commodity futures have is a last date of trading known as the "expiration date". This is an investor's last chance to sell their long position for cash, or close out their short position by buying an offsetting long position. After expiration, the owner of the commodity future (the "long" investor) must be prepared to receive delivery of the physical commodity, while the seller of the commodity future (the "short" investor) must be prepared to actually deliver the commodity. Depending on the actual commodity, typically 98–99% of all contracts are closed out before expiring. So only a handful of commodity future investors plan to take or make delivery. They are mostly firms that are actually in the production or use of the commodity on an industrial basis.

However, aside from creating a deadline by which time an investor will normally want to close out their futures position, the fact that a commodity future contract has an expiration date means that commodity futures, like bonds and options, have a time component to them that is different from a stock. Unlike shares in IBM, each futures contract has a finite life and another contract must come after it. At any given time, there will be a wide range of futures contracts for a given energy commodity, each calling for expiration and delivery in some future month. An exchange such as Nymex will list contracts for every month up to three years (in the case of gasoline and heating oil), six years (in the case of crude oil) and even 12 years (natural gas).

Because getting 1,000 barrels of crude oil next month is not the same as getting 1,000 barrels in six months, each contract will have its own price reflecting the market's judgement of not only where prices might be going over the next few months, but also how supply and demand might change in the intervening months. Thus commodity futures can produce a term structure of prices in much the same way the yield on bonds produces a yield curve.

The prices of a given commodity might drop off the further you get from the current front month. In the futures market such a pattern is known as a "backwardated" market. An example of a backwardated market is shown in Figure 16.1, in which the price of the individual futures contracts drops as you move from first month to the seventh month.

The opposite of a backwardated market is one in which the price of the further out contracts are higher than the front-month contract. Such a market is known as a "contango" market (see Figure 16.2).

Figure 16.1 Backwardation

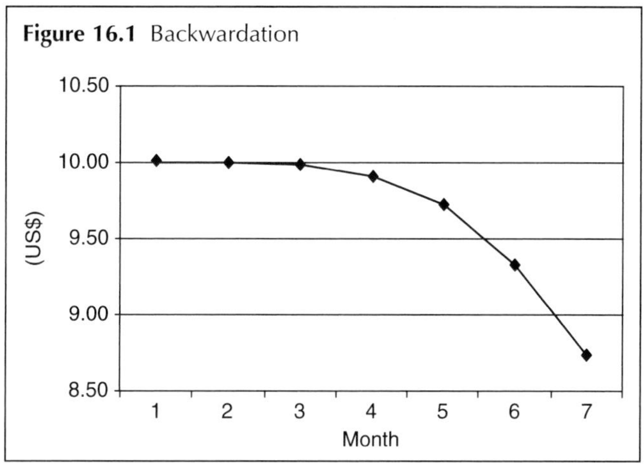

Figure 16.2 Contango

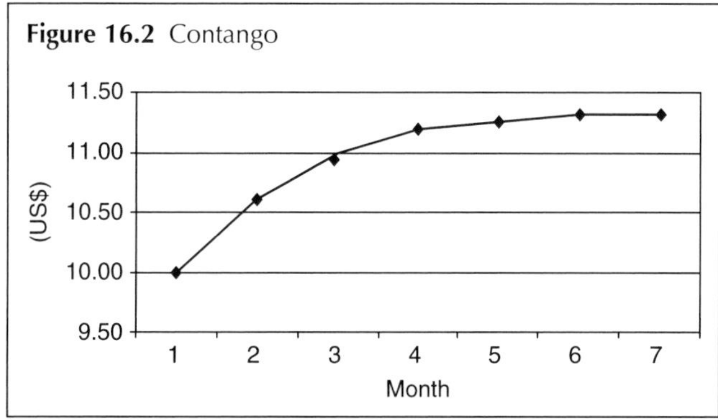

Finally, the futures market for a particular commodity might include aspects of both backwardation and contango. This would typically be true of a commodity that has a strong seasonal bias to its pricing. In the energy world, this could include, for example, either heating oil, whose price tends to peak in early winter and bottom out in early summer, or gasoline, whose price tends to peak in early summer and bottom out in early winter. An example of a seasonal futures chart is in Figure 16.3.

There are a number of factors that impact on the shape of the futures curve. The front month price is most closely tied to the "spot" price being paid by the actual users or consumers of a commodity. As such it reflects the current balance between supply and demand. By comparison, seasonal demand patterns, investors' expectations about future price movements, current and long-term supply-and-demand expectations, inventory levels, political uncertainty, currency levels and the cost of financing, are all factors that can cause the price of further-out contract months to be either higher or lower than the front-month contract. Various economists, including John Maynard Keynes, have come up with explanations as to why a commodity market is, or should be, in one state or another. However, no theory or model seems to do a very good job of forecasting when and why changes in the shape of the futures curve will occur. For example, crude oil futures have been traded in the US since 1983. It has spent approximately 62% of that time in a backwardated market. However, it can switch and has switched into a contango market without any advance warning.

Figure 16.3 Seasonal commodities

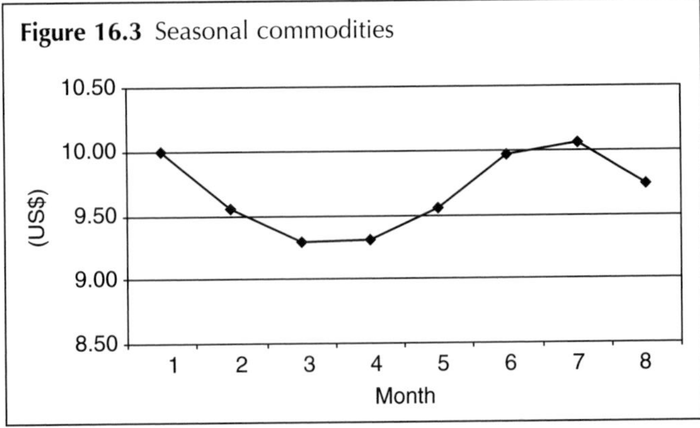

For an investor in a commodity ETF that uses futures contracts, the shape of the futures curve can be very important because it impacts on the total return that an investor will receive over time from the investment. Figures 16.4 and 16.5 will help explain how this works.

Assume that an investor buys a commodity ETF that once a month sells the front-month contract, when it is close to expiring, and buys the second-month contract. One month later the ETF will repeat the trade. Assume that, on the day the ETF "rolled" its position forward, the investor bought the ETF (or you can assume that the investor directly purchased the futures contract themselves, since the result will be the same). At the time they made their trade the front-month contract was trading for 1% more than the second-month contract. Finally, assume that over the next month the prices

Figure 16.4 Backwardation example A

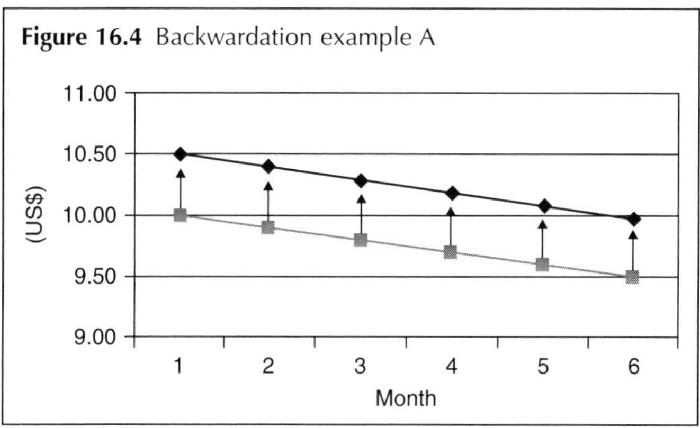

Figure 16.5 Backwardation example B

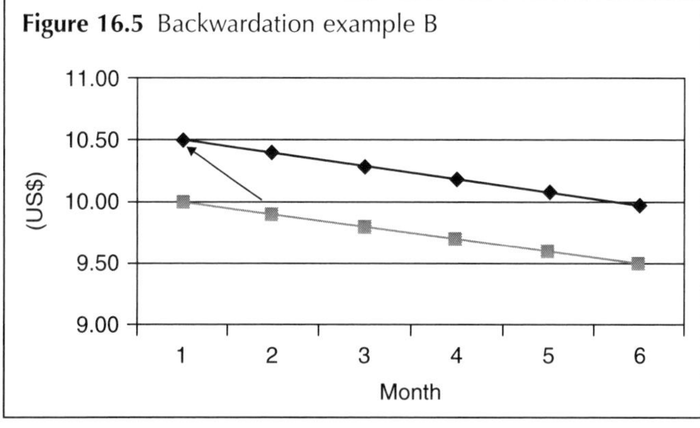

of all the futures contracts rose by 5%, but the shape of the curve remained unchanged. In that case what would have occurred is shown in Figure 16.4, backwardation example A.

However, the total return for the ETF or the investor is not up 5%. That is because their second-month contract not only went up in value, but it also became the new front-month contract over the course of the month. As such it was impacted on by both the overall change in the futures curve and the difference between the value of the second month and the front month. Figure 16.5, backwardation example B shows how the second-month contract gained both because prices overall went up and because it became the front month. So, if the difference between month 1 and month 2 was 1%, then the commodity ETF gained 5% plus 1% over the course of the month. In this example, backwardation added 1% to their monthly return.

Using the same example, if the market remained in backwardation but prices across the curve fell 5%, what would have happen to the ETF or the investor? In that case they would have lost only 4% as is shown in Figure 16.6, backwardation example C.

The example from a contango market is just the mirror image of the backwardated market. In the case of a generally rising market across all months, the owner of the second-month contract will tend to underperform the average change in prices because of the negative effect of contango. On the other hand, if the market is generally falling, the impact of contango will be to increase the overall loss.

Generally speaking, the impact of backwardation tends to be most strongly felt at the front end of the futures price curve, often between

Figure 16.6 Backwardation example C

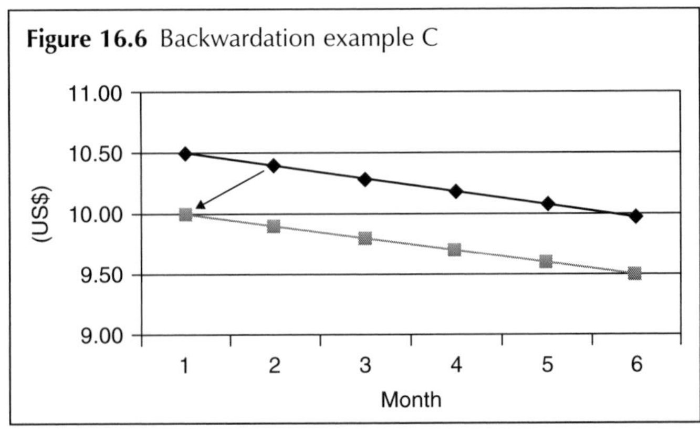

Figure 16.7 Contango example

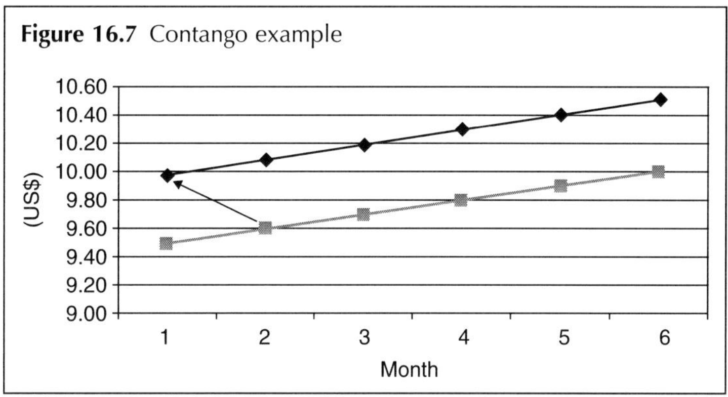

the front month and the second month. At the same time, these tend to be the most liquid futures months and the ones that many commodity ETFs will use to benchmark themselves off and purchase for their portfolios. As a result, many investors will be impacted on by backwardation and contango as they make use of commodity ETFs.

If a commodity ETF wishes to minimise the impact of backwardation and contango on its total return, there are two alternative approaches to benchmark and portfolio construction. The first is to select as a benchmark the movement of a wide range of futures contracts spread over several months, or even a year, instead of just targeting the front end of the futures price curve. Such an approach will typically mean that over time the total return of the ETF will be less negatively impacted on by the effect of contango than a front-month-only approach, but it will also be less positively impacted on by the effect of backwardation. An alternative approach is for the manager of the ETF to select as their benchmark an index that adjusts the target contract months based on the shape of the futures curve in a semiactive attempt to earn more when the futures market is in backwardation, and lose less in contango, than if the benchmark remained fixed on a single month or range of months. However, there can be no guarantee that such a tactic will actually produce superior results to either the front-month-only approach or to the approach of spreading the contracts out over time.

Comparing energy-commodity ETFs

In one sense picking the correct commodity fund is as easy (or hard) as counting to three.

Step 1: Choose your commodity

Depending on which of the four investment strategies we have already discussed is the one you are looking to implement, you will be deciding to invest in either a sub-basket of energy ETFs, generally as part of a strategy, or an individual energy commodity, in which case you could be doing any one of the four strategies. At the present time a single-commodity ETF will typically be crude oil, natural gas, heating oil or gasoline, although in the next few years that could expand to include other choices such as ethanol, uranium, non-US commodities and even solar energy. In any case the choice of which of the four investment strategies you are contemplating determines the choice of individual commodities.

Step 2: Determine the term structure you are interested in for your strategy

Depending on exactly what you are planning to do, the expected time horizon of your investment holding period and the current shape of the futures price curve, you may elect to go with a commodity ETF that owns the front-month contract only or one that owns futures contracts spread across time. Generally speaking, the front-month-only choice is a better one if either you have a short-term time horizon – in which case backwardation and contango will have only limited impact – or you have a longer time horizon and the commodity market is in backwardation (if you are going long) or in contango (if you are going short). If you are looking at a long-term investment, particularly if the commodity you select is in contango, you would likely opt for a commodity ETF that owns contracts spread out over several months, since that would tend to diminish the negative impact of contango.

Step 3: Select the particular ETF among the remaining choices based on cost, structure, and features

Although you may have started with a universe of 20 or more commodity ETFs, by the time you have selected the particular single commodity or sub-basket you will reduce your choices to a handful. After you make a decision as to whether you want a front-month-only or a multiple-month ETF, your choices drop even further. At this point you may have only two or three fairly similar choices in the ETF marketplace. To select among these remaining choices you will likely look at two factors: cost and ETF structure. For cost, it is easy to compare the annual operating cost of the remaining choices and select the ETF with the lower overall cost. This is particularly true if the intended holding period is medium or long-term. If the intended holding period is short-term, or if the annual operating costs between two choices are nearly identical, then you should look at the difference between your choices in the bid–ask spread, since they are quoted on an exchange. Typically, the ETF with the most average daily volume will also have the narrowest spread.

The issue of structure is essentially deciding whether or not you want to accept the extra credit risk that comes with using an ETN as opposed to a portfolio-owning ETF. Of course, if your intended strategy calls for you to buy or sell commodity ETF options, you have to pick a commodity ETF that has options listed on it at an exchange. Not all do. Finally, your broker can advise you as to whether or not they can arrange to borrow shares to allow you to short a particular commodity ETF. Typically, it is much easier to arrange a short sale for a more actively traded ETF than for a less actively traded ETF.

As an example, if you think the Chinese economy will report a big positive jolt next month, and that will fuel a spike in oil consumption and prices (strategy number 1, "directional"), and you expect to exit your position within two months, it is likely you would (1) choose a crude oil ETF, since it is the most global of the energy commodities; (2) choose one that owns the front-month contract, since they react the most to positive, and negative, news and your time horizon makes you more or less indifferent to backwardation and contango; and (3) choose the most active ETF with the lowest bid–ask spread since the difference in annual operating expenses between two otherwise similar ETFs will not matter over such a short time period while the bid–ask will matter. 1-2-3!

UPCOMING EVOLUTION IN THE ENERGY-BASED COMMODITY ETF SECTOR

Although the energy-based commodity ETF sector is only a few years old, it is not too soon to start contemplating future evolutions in the sector. By looking at the evolution of the stock and bond ETF sectors it may be possible to anticipate some of the future changes in the energy market segment. Here are some changes that are likely to occur over the next few years.

More choices of energy commodities

There are more than 30 commodities that are currently traded in the US. Of those, more than half a dozen are energy-related commodities. In addition, certain energy-related commodities do not even trade as listed futures. However, at the present time only West Texas Intermediate (WTI) crude oil, natural gas, unleaded gasoline and heating oil currently have single-commodity ETFs that offer exposure to the particular commodity. There are a number of other energy commodities that could be used as the underlying commodity for an ETF. These include low-sulphur diesel, ethanol, uranium, various grades of coal and additional grades of US crude oil other than WTI. Electricity production itself is a traded commodity that could be placed within an ETF vehicle. Finally, the emergence of newer forms of energy commodities such as solar, geothermal and biodiesel could offer additional choices. Having created the basic structure for crude oil and other commodities, all that is really needed for ETF sponsors to bring to market new ETFs based on any of these other energy-based commodities is the belief of the sponsors that sufficient investor demand exists to support these new entries.

Foreign commodities

The world has become ever more global over the years and the commodity markets are no different. Just as 20 years ago an investor would not have automatically thought about investing in foreign stocks or bonds, today most US investors would not automatically think about commodities traded outside the US. However, the commodity markets do not stop at any border and there are other markets, and other commodities, to consider investing in, either directly or through an ETF.

For example, although WTI crude oil is the primary benchmark in the US for oil prices, outside the US there are other important crude oil benchmarks. Crude oil from the North Sea oilfields actively trades in London as "Brent North Sea" crude oil and acts as the benchmark for much of the rest of the globe outside of North America. Like WTI, the benchmark represents an especially valuable type of crude oil known as "light, sweet" crude oil. A new crude oil benchmark, representing a heavier form of crude oil, has recently developed in Dubai. If global production of crude oil tilts towards heavier grades of crude oil, then it is possible that over time this new benchmark may become more important than either Brent or WTI. Commodities that already trade in the US, such as diesel, natural gas and heating oil, all trade in Europe or in Asian markets. Often those markets have different supply-and-demand dynamics from those of their US counterparts and offer investors additional investment options.

Leveraged and inverse ETFs

The original group of commodity ETFs did not use leverage as part of their investment process. However, taking a leaf from the equity ETF sector, we are already seeing ETFs in the commodity area that offer investors various levels of leverage within the structure of the ETF. A typical approach in the equity ETF area that is being adopted by the commodity ETF sector is one in which the ETF essentially uses 50% leverage. As a result, its daily percentage return would usually be double that of the movement of its underlying commodity or commodity future. For example, a "double-up" crude oil fund would go up 2% in a day if the crude oil futures contract went up 1%. Of course, if the price of crude oil fell 1%, the double-up fund would fall 2%.

Another adopted approach from the equity ETF universe is that of an "inverse" fund. An inverse fund is one that moves in the opposite direction to the commodity or commodity future. If crude oil went up 1%, the inverse oil fund would go down 1%. Essentially, an inverse fund offers an investor similar returns to what an investor would see if they were short the commodity (or a long commodity ETF). In the equity ETF world there are not only double-up funds, and inverse funds, but there are also "double-down" funds, which are essentially leveraged short funds.

Playing the curve and embedded strategies

The first generation of commodity-based ETFs typically targeted the returns that came from owning the futures contract that is the closest to expiration. This is because the front-month contract in most commodities is the one that is most actively traded as well as the one that is the focus of most of the investor attention. When the first commodity ETFs were created it was easier to base them on the front-month contracts due to both the pre-existing investor interest and the greater amount of liquidity in the underlying futures contracts. However, their investment returns of owning futures contracts other than the front month can differ from the front month. There are situations and markets where an investor might prefer to own an ETF based on a different month from the front month, as the returns might be expected to be better. In some cases an investor might want to own a range of months. Newer generations of commodity ETFs are being brought to the market that offer investors the opportunity to own a 12-month "strip" of contracts that represent equal holdings in each month from the front month to the current twelfth month. As investors become more knowledgeable about commodity futures they will demand, and ETF sponsors will provide, a wider range of commodity exposures divided by both commodity and contract month.

Another area of development likely to be adopted from existing ETFs in other sectors is one in which the commodity ETF's benchmark or investment objective contains some form of an embedded strategy. Such an approach already exists in other ETF sectors. For example, a stock ETF could be one in which the ETF always buys the highest-yielding stocks in a particular index and at the same time always shorts the lowest-yielding stocks in the same index. In a currency ETF, the ETF could always own the highest-yielding currencies out of a major group of different currencies and always sell the lowest-yielding currencies in the group. Such ETFs take complicated investment strategies and prepackage them into easy to access ETFs. It remains for the investor to decide whether the particular strategy is one they want to use, but once they have made that decision the ETF allows them to make a single trade to implement the strategy. In the case of energy-based commodities, it could be possible to develop an ETF that allows investors to make a single trade to implement a strategy based on the differences between crude oil prices and gasoline prices (the difference between the two is known as the "crack spread"), or a different ETF that would allow investors to take positions relating to the difference between natural gas prices and electricity prices (known as the "spark spread").

CONCLUSION

As with other investment innovations of the last few decades, the emergence of energy-based commodity ETFs should not be thought of in terms of creating something that is automatically something an investor should rush out and buy. Rather, they should be thought of as a new set of tools for investors to make use of in constructing portfolios or implementing trading strategies. Like all good tools, they should be made as robust as possible, and should be as simple as possible, yet still capable of doing their job. Investors need to be mindful that, just as a sharp knife will allow them to do many useful things, it can cut the user.

Commodity-based ETFs are not a magic bullet that suddenly makes investment gains automatic. The addition of a range of new "tools", in particular ones that have traditionally provided returns that differ from other pre-existing "tools", does represent a net benefit for investors. As with any new tool, it is up to the user to learn how to use them appropriately to help them construct their desired outcome.

17

Trading Strategies Using Currencies and Currency-Based Exchange Products

Kevin Rich

Deutsche Bank

Exchange-traded products, whether exchanged-traded notes (ETNs) or exchange-traded funds (ETFs), offer many attractive features for investors to utilise in adding currencies to their investment portfolios. The ETF/ETN wrapper provides transparency to underlying currency holdings, intra-day liquidity, and low-cost, efficient access to the underlying markets. But, before we discuss taking currency exposure or implementing currency strategies with exchange-traded products, we first have to understand the currency markets, and the returns those markets have to offer.

WHY CURRENCIES?

The currency market is the largest financial market in the world. From an investment perspective, traditionally, currencies were viewed as a zero-sum game, with no inherent return, and simply a source of uncompensated risk. Because of these misconceptions, historically currencies were not utilised as an asset class in the way that equities and bonds had.

This traditional view, however, is changing, as institutional investors, plan sponsors and consultants have come to recognise what many absolute-return investors have always believed: that currency investing can provide a significant source of returns that have a negative to low correlation to equities and bonds.

OVERVIEW OF THE CURRENCY MARKETS

While there is a large amount of historic data on equities and fixed-income instruments going back several decades, the currency markets developed into what we see today at a much later stage. Prior to 1971, exchange rates between currencies were set under the Bretton Woods system, where countries committed to maintain the exchange rate of their currencies within a range around a fixed value. The Bretton Woods system collapsed in 1971 as the US left the gold standard. Following the collapse of Bretton Woods, currency managers had very few alternatives to access the underlying markets and were restricted to a handful of global macro funds and managed commodity trading adviser (CTA) programmes. The majority of market participants typically viewed currencies as an unavoidable source of secondary risk. These managers initially traded individual currency pairs, later moving on to trade currency options, as well as indexes composed of static currency baskets. The development of options and indexes provided more effective and practical tools for expressing tactical views on individual or groups of currencies.

In the ensuing period, the explosive growth in currency turnover has been accompanied by rapid progress in both the perception and management of currency risk. By the late 1990s, it was largely accepted that currencies provide a source of return as well as risk. This new perspective led to the development of rules-based indexes, whose currency composition changed dynamically over time. These indexes aimed to capture returns from widely known investment strategies such as the carry trade, which is based on investing in high-yielding currencies through funding in the low-yielding currencies.

Today, it is also possible to wrap the performance of currency managers into investment-friendly indexes. At the same time, the discussion on currency returns and risk has moved on to the possibility that some indexes represent the "beta" of currency markets, while others the "alpha". In this way, currency markets may finally get a returns "benchmark" similar to bond and equity markets. Clearly, the currency product offering has expanded significantly.

As the currency markets have evolved, so has the makeup of players in these markets. Analysing the participants in the currency markets today, we see a relatively low percentage of players as "profit seekers" relative to "liquidity seekers". Profit seekers systematically make their profits at the expense of liquidity seekers, or phrased differently, liquidity seekers pay a premium in the form of profits to profit seekers in return for the provision of liquidity. We will discuss these participants in more detail later.

DIVERSIFICATION

Investors are increasingly looking to add "low-correlated" assets as alternative investments to their portfolio, which offer returns in line with their expectations, while offering further diversification to their portfolios. Just as commodities, real estate and private equity are used as alternatives, based on their low to negative correlation with equity and fixed-income markets, currency investments also offer these same features.

The addition of currencies to a portfolio of bonds and equities can significantly enhance the quality of returns by reducing the volatility of returns and duration and magnitude of significant phases of underperformance. While many view currencies as a slice of a diversified portfolio's allocation to alternative investments, others argue that a more proper allocation to currencies is comparable to those of bonds and equities. In like fashion, some investment professionals consider a funded currency investment to supplant a portfolio's allocation to cash or fixed-income instruments by providing returns analogous to a fixed-income product with an imbedded currency overlay.

CURRENCY INDEX CONSTRUCTION

In addition to using simple currency pairs or baskets of currency pairs, investors also use indexes to invest in currencies. Why are currency indexes gaining popularity among investors? For the reasons that investors use equity, bond or commodity indexes to invest in those markets: they provide diverse and cost-effective market access, they are a means of outsourcing expertise in a particular market and they are simple to trade.

There are some obvious factors that dictate how an investment friendly index is designed, including:

- liquidity considerations;
- availability of reliable market data;
- fixing sources (particularly relevant for FX which often trades on an over-the-counter (OTC) basis rather than on an exchange where exchange closing levels can reliably be used); and
- frequency of roll.

But there are also some more esoteric factors that are a valuable part of the intellectual property that non-specialist investors seek. Such factors that we pay a great deal of attention to are:

- roll mechanism – preventing market front-running of positions that an index is required to implement and minimising the "footprint" a large notional index leaves in the market; and
- robustness – making sure that there is a sound economic rationale behind index rules and that the parameters in the index are not overly optimised to give the best historic performance over a specific backtesting period – this last point is often overlooked; however, investors should be particularly aware that an over-complicated set of index rules can have parameters optimised in such a way that it is unrealistic to assume historic performance can be matched after the index based product launches.

CURRENCY MARKETS: MONEY LEFT ON THE TABLE

Research has shown that currency markets have historically delivered consistent excess returns over time, often equivalent to or stronger than equity markets. The systemic returns from the currency markets were evident by the profitability of three widely followed strategies: carry, momentum and valuation. The actual track record of currency managers further supports the profitability of currency investments.

Yet the presence of these returns raises more questions than it answers. As the most liquid in the world, shouldn't currency markets be efficient, and so not allow consistent profit opportunities? How can a zero-sum game, where for every long position there is a short position such as in currency markets, offer systematic returns? Who are the systematic losers who supposedly leave "money on the table"? If they exist, what share of the market do they consist of? And is that share declining? In the following pages we attempt to answer these questions.

WHAT DO WE MEAN BY EFFICIENT MARKETS, AND DOES IT WORK?

The currency markets are the most liquid in the world with a daily turnover of close to US$3.98 trillion according to the Bank for International Settlements, which makes them multiple times larger then bond and equity markets. So, of all the financial markets, currency markets should perhaps conform closest to what economists call an "efficient market", that is, a market, where prices reflect all available information, and so traders and investors should not be able to earn excess returns over time. Yet reality has a habit of providing obstacles to many economic theories, and currency markets are one such obstacle.

In order to show why the classical efficient-market hypothesis does not hold for currency markets, we simply need to see what the hypothesis would predict for currency markets, and compare that with the real world. The efficient-market hypothesis assumes that market participants are risk-neutral and behave rationally. The former means that they care only about the expected return of holding foreign currency and not the risk, and the latter generally means that investors know the true model of the underlying economy and markets, use all publicly available information and stick to the principles of logic. Given these assumptions, one of the predictions of the hypothesis would be that uncovered interest parity should hold; or, put another way, carry trades should not consistently make money over time. Another would be that momentum or trend-following strategies should not be profitable.

After more than 30 years of academic work in this area, the overwhelming consensus is that, in the real world, uncovered interest parity does not hold, and so currency markets are not efficient according to the classical definition. Academic work has also shown that trend-following strategies have been profitable at various points in time. It would appear that, for the efficient-market hypothesis to work market participants would need to be either extremely risk averse or irrational, neither of which sits well with most economists. In fact, the fundamental tenet of how market participants are represented in the efficient-markets hypothesis appears to be completely ill suited to apply to currency markets.

NEW THEORIES FIGHT BACK

Of course, some avenues of academic research have proved to be more satisfying. Behavioural economics delves into the irrationality of investors, and provides some explanations for observed market dynamics. Other approaches that broadly retain the assumption of rationality and have interesting-sounding names such as rational beliefs and endogenous uncertainty, adaptive market hypothesis and order flow-based models, have all proved to conform to market reality.

In essence, they are based on a world where market participants have different beliefs of what drives currency markets, have different objectives that they may be maximising, and often have different information at various times. In such a world, investors can earn systematic returns over time, but not without taking risks, and there is room for "smart" investors to outperform the "average" investor.

Therefore, these theories of currency markets suggest that market participants need not be irrational for currency markets to deliver consistent excess returns over time, but instead they need to be shown to have differing objectives and beliefs regarding what drives markets. If that can be shown, then in theory at least, currency markets may offer systematic returns to those willing to take risk.

THE PARTICIPANTS IN THE CURRENCY MARKETS

As briefly mentioned earlier, there are three categories of participants in the currency markets: profit seekers, liquidity seekers (those who pay a premium in the form of profits to profit seekers in return for the provision of liquidity) and currency dealers.

Before we discuss currency dealers we will focus on the other two groups of market participants: profit seekers and liquidity seekers. The former has the sole objective of entering into currency transactions in order to make a profit from movements in currencies, while the latter has the objective of ensuring they can access the currency markets whenever they need to engage in a cross-border transaction. Examples of profit seekers would be a hedge fund or currency overlay manager. Examples of liquidity seekers would be: a corporate that needs to enter into a currency transaction to set up a factory abroad; an international equity investor who needs to buy a foreign currency in order to invest in a foreign equity market; a bond manager who always currency-hedges their foreign bond exposures; a central bank that needs to buy or sell currencies in order to maintain an exchange-rate policy.

In such a world the liquidity seekers are willing to pay a premium to induce profit seekers into currency markets. As a result, this segmentation would lead to profit seekers generally making profit over time, while liquidity seekers would generally lose money over time in return for achieving other objectives.

Research has shown profit seekers appear to make up at most 50% of the market, which leaves the rest as non-profit-seekers. Additionally, this share appears to be falling over time. Therefore, there appears to be strong grounds for profit seekers to have consistent profit opportunities over time at the expense of liquidity seekers.

Currency dealers are the intermediaries between profit seekers and liquidity seekers, and so in many ways they are the reactive segment of the market. That is, were the profit seekers or liquidity seekers not to place any orders, the dealer or interbank volumes would dry up. Currency dealers step in to provide the necessary liquidity in the very short run in situations where profit seekers, in addition to the usual liquidity seekers, also become liquidity seekers. Dealers are induced to provide this liquidity by receiving the bid–offer spread.

In theory, as long as currency market participants have different motives, sources of information and beliefs regarding what drives currencies markets, currency markets can provide systematic excess returns to those willing to take the risk.

HOW TO INVEST IN THE CURRENCY MARKETS

So far in this chapter we have discussed the history of the currency markets, the various participants in the markets and their objectives, the theory of available returns versus reality, and the rationale for allocating a portion of your portfolio to currencies.

Once an investor decides to allocate to currencies, they must also determine the strategy they will utilise and the tools or products they will invest in. The following sections of this chapter discuss the investment strategies and the tools available to implement these strategies:

- Directional views of spot, forwards and options;
- Carry investing;
- Purchase-price parity (PPP), or valuation; and
- Momentum investing.

Note that, as the market continues to evolve and new products are launched, the examples and lists of available tools should be viewed as representative of the tools available at the time this chapter was written. There are many sources available to keep abreast of the products as they come to market.

DIRECTIONAL VIEWS OF SPOT, FORWARDS AND OPTIONS

Traditionally investors who allocated money to the currency markets did not have their own specific views of the values of one currency over another, and typically employed CTAs, who would invest in the markets on their behalf. In contrast, today there is a deluge of easily available information on specific currency pairs or on the value a one currency versus a currency basket.

To implement a directional view on a currency, investors could:

- enter the futures market themselves by trading currency futures and options on the futures markets;
- trade on retail focused currency account that uses the spot/forward markets (examples are http://www.dbfx.com, www.fxcm.com, www.forex.com);
- purchase a structured note with an embedded directional currency view; or
- invest in exchange-traded products.

Table 17.1 carries a list of some US exchange-traded products that will give an investor directional currency exposure to a single currency versus the move in the US dollar.

Another way of implementing a directional view in a broader sense would be to use a basket approach. The two ETFs in Table 17.2 offer a directional view on the US dollar versus a basket of six major currencies:

These two ETFs use the USDX futures contract traded on ICE Futures (formerly the New York Board of Trade). This contract represents a basket of the following currencies at the specified fixed weights versus the US dollar:

- Euro 57.6%
- Japanese yen 13.6%
- Sterling 11.9%
- Canadian dollar 9.1%
- Swedish krona 4.2%
- Swiss franc 3.6%

CARRY INVESTING

One of the most widely known and profitable strategies in currency markets are carry trades, where an investor systematically sells low-interest-rate currencies and buys high-interest-rate currencies.

Table 17.1 US exchange traded products – directional currency pair exposure

Product	Issuer	Symbol
US listed currency		
CurrencyShares Australian Dollar Trust	Rydex Invest.	FXA
CurrencyShares British Pound	Rydex Invest.	FXB
CurrencyShares Canadian Dollar Trust	Rydex Invest.	FXC
CurrencyShares Euro Currency Trust	Rydex Invest.	FXE
CurrencyShares Japanese Yen Trust	Rydex Invest.	FXY
CurrencyShares Mexican Peso	Rydex Invest.	FXM
CurrencyShares Swedish Krona Trust	Rydex Invest.	FXS
CurrencyShares Swiss Franc	Rydex Invest.	FXF
CurrencyShares Russian Ruble Trust	Rydex Invest.	XRU
WisdomTree Dreyfus Chinese Yuan Fund	WisdomTree AM	CYB
WisdomTree Dreyfus Brazilian Real Fund	WisdomTree AM	BZF
WisdomTree Dreyfus Euro Fund	WisdomTree AM	EU
WisdomTree Dreyfus Indian Rupee Fund	WisdomTree AM	ICN
WisdomTree Dreyfus New Zealand Dollar Fund	WisdomTree AM	BNZ
WisdomTree Dreyfus Japanese Yen Fund	WisdomTree AM	JYF
WisdomTree South African Rand Fund	WisdomTree AM	SZR
ProShares Ultra Short Euro	ProShares	EUO
ProShares Ultra Yen	ProShares	YCL
ProShares Ultra Short Yen	ProShares	YCS
ProShares Ultra Euro	ProShares	ULE
US listed currency ETN		
iPath EUR/USD Exchange Rate	Barclays Capital	ERO
iPath JPY/USD Exchange Rate	Barclays Capital	JYN
iPath GBP/USD Exchange Rate	Barclays Capital	GBB
Market Vectors Double Long Euro ETN	Van Eck Funds	URR
Market Vectors Double Short Euro ETN	Van Eck Funds	DRR
Market Vectors-Renminbi/USD ETN	Van Eck Funds	CNY
Market Vectors-Rupee/USD ETN	Van Eck Funds	INR
Barclays Asian and Gulf Currency Revaluation ETN	Barclays Capital	PGD
Barclays gems Asia 8 ETN	Barclays Capital	AYT

Carry trades exploit the widely observed "forward-premium puzzle" or "forward-rate bias", which suggests that systematically buying high-interest-rate currencies and selling low-interest currencies may be profitable. This is because the existence of a risk premium, the use of different models to forecast currencies by

Table 17.2 US exchange traded products – directional broad US dollar exposure

Product	Issuer	Symbol
PowerShares DB US Dollar Index Bullish Fund	DB Commodity Ser	UUP
PowerShares DB US Dollar Index Bearish Fund	DB Commodity Ser	UDN

rational market participants, or the differing constraints and objectives faced by market participants.

Contrary to classical notions of efficient markets, carry trades have made money over time. Academics believe the reason this is possible is that investors who employ the carry trade expose themselves to currency risk. Investors taking this risk are rewarded by positive returns over time.

A parallel to the carry strategy in the fixed-income markets is where investors look to earn a higher "term premiums" by increasing duration.

We see a similar "puzzle" in the equity markets. Equities have tended to significantly outperform relatively risk-free assets over the long run. This would be expected, as equities are riskier. However, theory would suggest that US equities should outperform T-bills by 1%, yet in reality they have outperformed by closer to 7%. This divergence between theory and reality has come to be known as the "equity premium puzzle". The currency markets possibly provide an even bigger puzzle: the "forward-premium puzzle" or "forward-rate bias", as discussed above. In this case, not only does theory underestimate the magnitude of a currency's performance, it also gets the direction wrong. Consequently, investors have had a consistently profitable, though at times volatile, investment strategy in the form of buying carry trades.

Investors can implement a carry strategy in several ways. Using actual bank accounts denominated in different currencies, an investor could borrow in one currency, transact in the currency spot market, and then deposit those proceeds in a bank account denominated in that currency. Investors could also use the spot forward OTC currency markets, the currency futures market, or structured notes. All of these methods will require challenges in structuring and maintaining the strategy, and could result in different tax outcomes. The simple and straightforward method we will discuss in this chapter is using ETFs to capture carry.

Implementing carry using ETFs

While an investor could create their own carry strategy using a combination of the individual single ETFs noted above in the section, "Directional views of spot, forwards and options", that would be fairly complicated, requiring short sales of the long ETFs, and potentially an inefficient approach from a capital-allocation perspective versus using a carry ETF.

There are two carry-based exchange-traded products in the US. The first to launch in the market was the PowerShares DB G10 Currency Harvest ETF (symbol DBV).

DBV uses the three-month interest rate to rank G10 currencies each quarter. The ETF buys the top three yielding currencies and sells the bottom three currencies. In this way, it is regularly invested in the three largest carry trades in the G10 world.

DBV invests in US three-month Treasury bills, and then uses those bills as collateral to enter G10 currency futures contracts. The ETF rebalances and reselects currencies on a quarterly basis, and gives investors long exposure to the three highest-yielding currencies within the G10, and short exposure to the three lowest yielding currencies within the G10.

The second carry exchange-traded product available is the iPath Optimized Currency Carry ETN, symbol ICI. ICI uses an optimised carry strategy versus the equally weighted strategy deployed by DBV. Optimised carry attempts to underweight or overweight the long and short currency exposure relative to implied volatility in the currency markets.

Equally weighted carry versus optimised carry

There are two schools of thought on the most effective way to capture carry returns in the market. Those who feel that an optimised carry strategy is preferable to an equally weighted carry strategy suggest that you should increase or decrease leverage based upon implied currency volatility versus target volatility. This concept is termed "mean variance optimisation", and proponents of this feel it provides a more robust way to capture carry than simply allocating in an equally weighted fashion.

On the other hand, those in the equally weighted camp suggest that it is inconsistent to incorporate carry, which is based on the notion that markets are inefficient, with mean-variance optimisation, which assumes that markets are efficient. The argument continues that assuming carry trade returns are normally distributed is not correct, as a handful of daily observations can have a significant impact on returns, and that assumptions of stable volatilities and correlations are also not reflected in the real world, and tend to trigger a deleveraging of portfolios at the wrong time.

The positive for investors is that the wide array of exchange-traded products includes both optimised and equally weighted carry strategies, so investors have alternatives for each depending upon which view they take on the benefits of optimisation.

EM carry

The same concepts that apply to opportunities for carry returns using G10 currencies also apply when extended to emerging-market currencies. The attractiveness of adding emerging currencies is that a global basket may be able to enjoy higher returns than one purely focused on G10 currencies.

By expanding the universe of currencies beyond those used in G10 carry to include the more liquid EM currencies, you should be able to improve on the prospective returns, assuming the following. First, the positive carry that is captured should be higher, so even in range-bound markets returns should look respectable. Second, some high-yielding currencies are less likely to be overvalued, thus providing more scope to capture spot returns.

The more pressing question, though, would be whether the risk premiums associated with emerging-market currencies are sufficiently low for the yield on those currencies to be worth earning. That is, investors need to evaluate whether the odds of a large depreciation are sufficiently low to make consistently owning EM currencies worthwhile.

What does theory say? How does reality compare?

According to the risk-neutral efficient-markets hypothesis, the expected gain from holding one currency rather than another should be offset by the loss of interest in holding this currency rather than the other. This is generally referred to as the "uncovered interest parity" (UIP) condition. From an investor's perspective, this would imply that investing in currencies with high interest rates by borrowing in currencies with low interest rates (ie, carry trades) should not deliver consistent profits over time. That is, the high-interest currency should depreciate. The reality could not be more different.

A broad consensus has emerged that the theory does not conform to reality, at least over short- to medium-term horizons. Studies that look at the sensitivity of currencies to interest rate differentials (the beta) have found values closer to –1, than the +1 that theory would predict. The only time horizons over which UIP appears to hold is over the very short period that spans the time interest is paid on currency positions each day, and the long-run (five years onwards). Therefore, explanations are needed on the failure of UIP and the efficient-markets hypothesis.

Adjusting the assumptions seems to help

Underlying the efficient-markets hypothesis is that market participants are risk-neutral and are endowed with rational expectations. The former implies investors care only about expected returns and not risk, while the latter generally implies investors know the true model of the underlying economy and markets, use all publicly available information and stick to the principles of logic.

Much work has been done to test both assumptions. Relaxing the assumption that investors are risk-neutral, and instead assuming they are risk averse, allows for the possibility of earning excess returns (ie, the forward-rate bias) to compensate for a risk premium. However, most studies show that investors must be extremely risk-averse or that consumption should be highly correlated with currencies for the forward-rate bias to be as large as it is. Neither of these is realistic.

Several explanations have been posited on whether investors do not form expectations in the way that the efficient-markets hypothesis would suggest. Investors may be irrational, or, if they are rational, they are unsure of the true model of the market. In the latter case, investors may come up with different models of what drives currencies even using the same data – that is, they have "rational beliefs". Investors in carry trades are therefore being rewarded for the "uncertainty" of currency markets. Finally, if market participants are different in other ways, for example by being non-profit-maximisers or by having different risk limits, then it may not always be possible for sufficient capital to be allocated to carry trades for the forward-rate bias to disappear. Only when expectations of positive returns are very high would that likely be the case.

VALUE INVESTING

Valuation investing in currencies is based upon the assumption that, in the long-run, currencies tend to move back to their fair value based on purchasing-power parity (PPP). While in the short to medium run currencies can deviate from their PPP values due to trade, information and other costs, the theory supporting valuation investing suggests that investors can profit from currencies as they revert to their fair values over the long run.

Valuation strategies attempt to exploit this long-run trend for currencies to move towards their "fair value" by systematically buying "undervalued" currencies and selling "overvalued" currencies.

A parallel to PPP in the equity markets is incorporating a "fundamental" metric such as earnings or revenues to portfolio selection.

Do fundamentals matter?

In a seminal paper, written almost 25 years ago, it was shown that using fundamentals-based models to forecast currencies could not outperform tossing a coin. Matters were made worse by the fact that, even if the fundamental data was known in advance, the result still held. Under this theory, even if an investor were able to predict correctly the coming year's values for inflation, growth, money supply and interest rates, then we could still not forecast currencies better than tossing a coin!

Every few years or so, the work has been updated to include additional models and currencies. The most recent comprehensive update found that, depending on what criteria were used to assess the success of a model, some fundamentals-based models do show some promise – though it appears that what works for one currency may not work for another. The models cover factors including PPP, money supply (sticky prices), debt and net foreign-asset positions (composite). The upshot is that, on the criterion of accuracy of "direction of change", PPP tends to outperform the random walk over long time horizons. Interestingly, it also appears to outperform more recently popularised models such as ones that include productivity and net foreign-asset positions. It would therefore appear that the best fundamental model to use would be the simplest, PPP.

The resurrection of PPP

The earliest versions of PPP theory have been traced to the Salamanca School of 16th-Centrury Spain. Its continued use to this day attests to its allure (to economists, at least). The idea behind PPP is that a unit of currency should buy the same basket of goods in one country as the equivalent amount of foreign currency, at the going exchange rate, can buy in a foreign country. If that were not the case, then there would be the possibility of arbitrage. The *Economist*'s "Big Mac Index" is an example of the theory in popular form, where the price of Big Macs from around the world are compared in a common currency to see which currencies are over- or undervalued.

When testing PPP, economists have tended to stick to goods that are able to be traded, since that should be where PPP is most likely to hold. Of course, transportation and information costs may make arbitrage difficult, and so it may not be expected that PPP holds at all times. Moreover, productivity differences between countries may also lead to departures from PPP. Notwithstanding these issues, empirical studies show some evidence that PPP holds in the long run. These studies show that it takes between three and five years for half of the deviation from PPP to be corrected. The length of the deviations has proved to be a puzzle to economists.

Part of it may be explained by a more technical point of how individual goods' prices are aggregated up to price indexes – that is, when PPP is tested the price indexes between countries may contain different goods or different weights between goods. A big-picture explanation is that currencies may adjust in a nonlinear fashion. When currencies are not too far from PPP levels, the scope for arbitrage may be limited as the transport and other costs may offset any potential arbitrage gains. However, if currencies were to deviate significantly from PPP, then arbitrage forces come into play and may induce a more rapid reversion to PPP. Studies appear to support this dynamic and suggest that, when currencies are close to their PPP level, their behaviour is close to a random walk, while, when they deviate significantly from PPP, they tend to mean-revert.

Turning PPP into an investment strategy

One of the dilemmas of using PPP in any investment strategy is deciding which PPP measure to use. A direct approach would use the actual price levels of some combination of goods and services and compare these across countries to arrive at an actual level of PPP (such as the Big Mac Index). Alternatively, price indexes, such as the consumer price index, could be used, but then PPP levels would have to be derived by assuming that some earlier base period represents equilibrium. While this approach allows a price index to be picked that contains more tradable goods, there is scope for data mining by choosing the base period that results in PPP working best.

For this reason, professional investors prefer to use the direct approach, and opt to use the Organisation for Economic Co-operation and Development's (OECD) PPP values. The OECD calculates direct PPP values in order to make international GDP comparisons, rather than as a tool to forecast currencies. Therefore, it is more robust and comprehensive than other direct PPP measures.

As discussed earlier, PPP tends to work best when currencies are at valuation extremes. However, looking back for each currency to see which extremes tend to see the quickest mean-reversion may not fare so well out of sample. Therefore, it is preferable to take a ranking approach of G10 currencies to avoid having to pick discrete thresholds. This is accomplished by calculating each currency's deviation from PPP, and then ranking the currencies by how under- or overvalued they are. We then buy the three most undervalued currencies and sell the three most over-valued currencies. This is assessed every three months.

MOMENTUM INVESTING

Momentum investing in currencies attempts to exploit the trend over time, which suggests that using past prices may be informative to investing in currencies. This is due to the existence of irrational traders, the possibility that prices provide information about non-fundamental currency determinants or that prices may adjust slowly to new information.

A widely observed feature of currency markets is that many exchange rates trend on a multi-year basis. Therefore, a strategy that follows the trend typically makes positive returns over time. The segmentation of currency market participants with some acting quickly on news while others respond more slowly is one reason why trends emerge and can be protracted.

A parallel to currency momentum strategies in the equity markets is investing in a market-capitalisation-weighted equity index, which is effectively employing a long momentum strategy.

Academics jump on to the trend

Currency investors have been using some form of trend-following strategies for decades. The most recent surveys indicate that technical analysis is used as much as fundamental analysis by currency market professionals. Yet academics have been reluctant to analyse the phenomena. Indeed, from 1960 to 1994, only 11 academic papers had been written on the subject for currency markets. Since then, 33 papers have been written. Part of this was likely due to the scepticism many academics felt towards technical analysis, as it was in clear violation of the standard efficient-market hypothesis, which states that the current price contains all available information, so using past prices should prove to be futile for investors. Of course, most studies have now shown that trend-following strategies have been profitable in violation of the standard efficient-markets hypothesis. They show that the most statistically significant profits occurred before the 1990s, and then returns appear to have experienced a sharp drop in the early 1990s.

Several explanations have been put forward to explain why trend-following strategies have been profitable (and why profits have fallen since 1990). These include the existence of irrational traders (noise traders), the possibility that prices adjust slowly to new information, the possibility that prices provide information about non-fundamental currency determinants and, finally, the existence of temporary market inefficiency. There is some evidence for each one of these, though the last one is perhaps the most concerning for currency investors.

The extinction of trend-following returns?

Several factors may alleviate concerns of the possibility that trend-following returns will no longer occur. First, the duration of very high returns in the 1970s and 1980s may perhaps be too long for an inefficiency to have existed. Also, it would be unclear why other widely known strategies that violate the standard efficient-markets hypothesis, such as carry trades, have not shown a decline in returns. Moreover, the decline in trend-following returns did not occur gradually, but instead very rapidly in the early 1990s. Second, and perhaps more important, the strength of currency trends in the majors showed sharp declines from the early 1990s onwards (particularly US dollar/Japanese yen). That is, the major exchange rates exhibited large and durable trends in the 1970s and 1980s, but the 1990s saw more range-bound markets. It would be unlikely that a greater number of trend followers in currency markets in the early 1990s resulted in the disappearance of multi-year trends in currency markets. Instead, larger macroeconomic developments were the likely cause. These would include the efforts of policymakers to stabilise currencies through the Louvre Accord finally bearing fruit in the early 1990s, and, importantly, the marked decline in the volatility of growth and inflation across the G10 world seen since the early 1990s. Looking ahead, the macro environment could well change, and so generate larger trends.

Therefore, it would appear that there are grounds to believe that trend-following strategies may well work in the future, particularly if prices continue to show evidence of adjusting slowly to information and of containing non-fundamental currency determinants. The question then is what strategy best captures this.

Keeping the momentum going

In the literature on trend-following or momentum strategies, approaches have varied from using simple currency returns to moving average crossover rules to more complex Markov switching models. The essence of all these approaches is that they profit when currencies trend, and that they cover the time horizon over which fundamental models have little forecasting power (that is, over the short to medium run). These need to be retained in any strategy. Additionally, switches in signals should be kept to a minimum to reduce transaction costs. Bearing all of these factors in mind, two questions need to be answered.

- What type of momentum rule should we use (eg, a moving average)?
- Which currency pairs should we use?

For the rule, we opt for using 12-month changes in spot exchange rates – an even simpler approach than using a moving average crossover. It has the advantage of minimising the frequency of signal changes, while remaining within the time horizon where trend-following rules are effective. Picking which currency pairs to apply this rule to is more problematic, as there would be scope to data-mine, and pick crosses that have worked well in the past. However, a ranking of the changes in spot across all G10 currencies would sidestep this issue. Our approach therefore ranks all G10 currencies by their change over the past 12 months, and then we buy the top three performing currencies and we sell the bottom three performing currencies. We assess the ranking each month. In this way, the choice of currency pairs is left to the strategy itself.

WHAT DRIVES RETURNS IN CURRENCIES?

Broadly speaking the major factors that drive returns in the currency markets are volatility, global liquidity, trending markets and deviations from purchasing-power parity.

Let us look at these more closely

Carry: The three main drivers of carry trade performance are as follows.

- Currency market volatility: When volatility is low, capital tends to flow from low-yielding to high-yielding currencies. Investors become more willing to assume currency risk to take advantage of differing interest rates across currencies. These capital flows tend to create a virtual cycle of positive carry returns, as they contribute to depreciation in low-yielders and corresponding appreciation in high-yielders, and encourage further carry-trade activity. In contrast, high volatility combined with risk-aversion not only discourages these types of flows, but is usually associated with an abrupt unwind of existing carry-trade positions. The large FX carry losses during the Russia/LTCM crisis of 1998, and the credit crisis of 2007 to 2008 (still going in early 2009), events were both associated with such unwinds.
- Liquidity: Broadly speaking, when real yields are below trend, carry tends to perform well; but, when they are above trend, carry performs less well.
- Valuation: This is a key medium-term driver of carry performance. When carry crosses are close to purchasing-power parity,

FX carry tends do well, as valuation is less of a constraint on carry cross appreciation. In contrast, large carry unwinds have usually been associated with an average overvaluation level in the dbCR FX carry basket of more than 20%.

Momentum investing: The driver behind momentum returns is intuitively straightforward: the strategy performs well when FX markets exhibit strong trending behaviour.

Valuation: Valuation investing returns are also intuitively simple to understand. This strategy delivers better returns when currencies deviate excessively from purchasing power parity.

STRUCTURE OF EXCHANGE-TRADED PRODUCTS

As you have read throughout this book, exchange-traded products provide many benefits to holders in allowing them to access markets, portfolios or strategies in a simple, transparent, liquid and cost-effective way. These benefits are very true of currency-based exchange products, allowing investors to take currency positions in their securities accounts without the complexity of transacting in the OTC or futures markets.

The products that list on the stock exchanges and provide these currency returns are structured in various forms, so it is prudent for an investor to understand what benefits or risks may be associated with each type of underlying product structure. Following is a list of the more prevalent structures that underlie most exchanged traded products.

40 Act Funds

The majority of ETFs traditionally in the US have been structured as Registered Investment Companies, or "40 Act Funds". These are mutual funds that primarily hold a basket of securities as their investment. In order for the 40 Act Funds to list on an exchange, they are given regulatory exemptions to list on US national stock exchanges with creation and redemption features. These funds are called "40 Act Funds" because they are regulated under the Investment Company Act of 1940, which regulates investment companies. While a 40 Act Fund can hold securities that have some form of embedded currency exposure, it is not the ideal structure to provide a pure currency exposure. For example, a 40 Act Fund holding the ADR of a UK-based company would have some US dollar/ sterling risk along with the performance of the company itself, but is a much different investment from holding the actual US dollar/ sterling currency pair.

Trusts

ETFs that hold deposits in bank accounts of a currency to provide returns are often structured as grantor trusts. When an investor buys a share of the ETF, they are usually viewed as holding their *pro rata* share of the currency in the underlying trust, and, as a result, receives the interest earned on that deposit (sometimes less a spread). For example, the CurrencySharesSM Euro Trust (symbol FXE), managed by Rydex, holds euros in a bank account in the name of the trust, and pays the euro interest earned on a monthly basis, less a basis-points spread.

Exchange-traded notes

Exchange-traded notes (ETNs) are a more recent development as an underlying structure for exchange-traded products across all asset classes. When comparing ETNs with ETFs, it is important to note that ETNs and ETFs share most of the benefits around intra-day liquidity, cost-effectiveness and price transparency that have made ETFs so popular with investors, with the following differences:

- ETNs guarantee an index return, while ETFs may have tracking error; and
- ETNs carry the credit risk of the issuer of the notes, while ETFs are valued based on the actual holdings of each funds.

ETNs that provide currency returns allow the issuer and investor great flexibility in the strategies and returns offered through the note.

What does your exchange-traded product hold?

As we have just discussed, there are a few different underlying legal structures for exchange-traded products. In order to provide the currency return or exposure within each product you will see that those structures could hold various instruments to provide the return. Following is a list of the instruments the exchange product may hold. Investors should look at the prospectus for the instruments they are considering to see exactly what the product may or may not be invested in at any time.

Deposits

A very straightforward way for an exchange product to provide its investors the specific exposure is simply to hold that currency in a bank account owned by the fund. Interest earned on that deposit (normally less a spread) would be for the benefit of the investors, and typically distributed as income to the investors on a periodic basis.

Futures

Another very straightforward way for an exchange product to provide its investors the specific exposure is to hold exchange-traded futures contracts in a futures account owned by the fund. The equivalent of the interest of what would have been earned on an actual deposit would be priced into the value of the futures contract, so would accrue for the benefit of the investors, but would not be distributed as income on a deposit, but rather would show in the capital appreciation of the fund.

Spot/forward

The traditional and most liquid way to take currency exposure is through the OTC spot/forward market. While an exchange product would typically not transact or hold OTC spot/forward contracts in the name of the fund, it is important to understand the depth of the underlying liquidity offered and available in the spot/forward market, as this allows futures and other associated instruments to be fairly valued. Additionally, the issuer of a currency-based ETN would most likely use the spot/forward markets to hedge its obligation to investors on the notes. As in the futures, the equivalent of the interest of what would have been earned on an actual deposit would be priced into the value of the forward contracts, so benefit would accrue to the holder of the OTC instrument for the benefit of the investors, but would not typically be distributed as income on a deposit, but rather would show in the capital appreciation of the fund.

Non-deliverable forward

Non-deliverable forwards (NDFs) are OTC forward contracts that cash-settle, as opposed to physically settle with the underlying currencies. Typically, NDFs are issued around currencies that have liquidity or delivery restrictions. The same beneficial ownership points made for deliverable forwards relative to instruments held by exchange products hold true for NDFs.

OTHER CONSIDERATIONS

There are several other considerations investors should be aware of when utilising a currency-based exchange-traded product. They should look to the prospectus and marketing materials provided by the issuers of the products to gain an understanding relative to these points.

Categorisation of returns: We spoke earlier about where the currency returns are derived from, but investors should also understand how those returns will be reflected in the value of the exchange product. A product that provides a total return may capture the interest related to a currency in the value of the shares, or possibly distribute that periodically.

Taxes: The structure of the exchange product and the instruments the products holds will drive the way the returns are taxed. Investors should read the prospectus carefully to determine whether returns and distributions are taxed as income or as short-term or long term gains. Additionally, the timing of recognition of gains and how those gains are communicated to investors are important as well. Again, investors should look to the prospectus for the appropriate tax treatment.

Tracking error: For those exchange-traded currency products that hold instruments with the objective to track and underlying index, investors should look at how closely the traded price and net asset value (NAV) of the product track the underlying index. Any material deviation from the index either intra-day or over a

Table 17.3 US exchange traded products – carry strategies

Product	**Issuer**	**Symbol**
PowerShares DB G10 Currency Harvest	DB Commodity Ser	DBV
iPath Optimized Currency Carry ETN	Barclays Capital	ICI

Table 17.4 US exchange traded products – currencies

Exchange-traded product name	Issuer	Exchange	Bloomberg ticker
US listed currency			
CurrencyShares Australian Dollar Trust	Rydex Invest.	NYSE Arca	FXA
CurrencyShares British Pound	Rydex Invest.	NYSE Arca	FXB
CurrencyShares Canadian Dollar Trust	Rydex Invest.	NYSE Arca	FXC
CurrencyShares Euro Currency Trust	Rydex Invest.	NYSE Arca	FXE
CurrencyShares Japanese Yen Trust	Rydex Invest.	NYSE Arca	FXY
CurrencyShares Mexican Peso	Rydex Invest.	NYSE Arca	FXM
CurrencyShares Swedish Krona Trust	Rydex Invest.	NYSE Arca	FXS
CurrencyShares Swiss Franc	Rydex Invest.	NYSE Arca	FXF
CurrencyShares Russian Ruble Trust	Rydex Invest.	NYSE Arca	XRU
WisdomTree Dreyfus Chinese Yuan Fund	WisdomTree AM	NYSE Arca	CYB
WisdomTree Dreyfus Brazilian Real Fund	WisdomTree AM	NYSE Arca	BZF
WisdomTree Dreyfus Euro Fund	WisdomTree AM	NYSE Arca	EU
WisdomTree Dreyfus Indian Rupee Fund	WisdomTree AM	NYSE Arca	ICN
WisdomTree Dreyfus New Zealand Dollar Fund	WisdomTree AM	NYSE Arca	BNZ
WisdomTree Dreyfus Japanese Yen Fund	WisdomTree AM	NYSE Arca	JYF
WisdomTree South African Rand Fund	WisdomTree AM	NYSE Arca	SZR
ProShares Ultra Short Euro	ProShares Advisors	NYSE Arca	EUO
ProShares Ultra Yen	ProShares Advisors	NYSE Arca	YCL
ProShares Ultra Short Yen	ProShares Advisors	NYSE Arca	YCS
ProShares Ultra Euro	ProShares Advisors	NYSE Arca	ULE
US listed currency – style			
PowerShares DB G10 Currency Harvest	DB Commodity Ser	AMEX	DBV
PowerShares DB US Dollar Index Bullish Fund	DB Commodity Ser	AMEX	UUP
PowerShares DB US Dollar Index Bearish Fund	DB Commodity Ser	AMEX	UDN
US listed currency ETN			
iPath EUR/USD Exchange Rate	Barclays Capital	NYSE Arca	ERO
iPath JPY/USD Exchange Rate	Barclays Capital	NYSE Arca	JYN

(continued)

Table 17.4 Continued

Exchange-traded product name	Issuer	Exchange	Bloomberg ticker
iPath GBP/USD Exchange Rate	Barclays Capital	NYSE Arca	GBB
iPath Optimized Currency	Barclays Capital	NYSE Arca	ICI
Barclays GEMS Asia 8 ETN	Barclays Capital	NYSE Arca	AYT
Market Vectors Double Long Euro ETN	Van Eck Funds	NYSE Arca	URR
Market Vectors Double Short Euro ETN	Van Eck Funds	NYSE Arca	DRR
Market Vectors-Renminbi/ USD ETN	Van Eck Funds	NYSE Arca	CNY
Market Vectors-Rupee/USD ETN	Van Eck Funds	NYSE Arca	INR
Barclays Asian and Gulf Currency Revaluation ETN	BGI	NYSE Arca	PGD

Table 17.5 South African exchange traded products – currencies

Exchange-traded product name	Issuer	Exchange	Bloomberg ticker
Other listed currency			
Newrand	Trackhedge Managers Proprietary Ltd	Johannesburg	ZAR

Table 17.6 German exchange traded products – currencies

Exchange-traded product name	Issuer	Exchange	Bloomberg ticker
European listed currency			
db x-trackers DB Currency Carry ETF	db x-trackers	Deutsche Borse	XCCR GR
db x-trackers DB Currency Returns ETF	db x-trackers	Deutsche Borse	XCCR GR
db x-trackers DB Currency Momentum ETF	db x-trackers	Deutsche Borse	XMOM GR
db x-trackers DB Currency Valuation ETF	db x-trackers	Deutsche Borse	XVAL GR

period should be noted and understood. There are instances where an index may reference a close, or settle, price which is different from the trading time of the stock exchange. In cases such as this, the difference between trading price and an earlier underlying settle price is explainable and justified.

Bid–offer spreads and liquidity: Investors should take note of how wide the spread is between the bid and the offer on the stock exchange, and use limit orders where appropriate if the bid–offer is unreasonably wide. Typically, newer exchange products may have wider spreads until the product attracts increased trading activity. Liquidity should be reviewed at two levels: first, how liquid the underlying markets are in which the exchange product invests; second, how liquid the exchange product is.

Credit risk: Investors should understand whether the instruments with the exchange product or the product itself carries any credit risk.

Leverage: If the exchange product is utilising leverage, investors should understand how that leverage either amplifies their opportunity for returns or increases their risk. Leverage can also be used to take on a level of risk utilising less capital.

ETFs (FROM DEUTSCHE BANK RESEARCH)

Tables 17.3, 17.4, 17.5 and 17.6 provide the list of currency-based exchange products as compiled by Deutsche Bank's Research Department (as of July 2008).

The author would like to thank the members of the Deutsche Bank Currency Research and Strategy groups for their extensive contributions and assistance on this chapter. Various research and strategy pieces produced over the past year by Bilal Hafeez and George Saravelos have been used to inspire or directly included within this chapter in outlining the case for currencies and how currency strategies are deployed in the markets.

18

International Equity ETFs

Kirk Kinder

Picket Fence Financial

As in the rest of the marketplace for exchange-traded funds (ETFs), the growth in international equity ETFs has been explosive. With the recent rise in emerging economies and the two-year decline in the US dollar, investors have recognised that adding international equities to an otherwise all-domestic portfolio can lower portfolio risk while increasing returns. In turn, this led to the impressive growth in the international ETF landscape. Currently, international ETFs hold US$166 billion in investors' assets and comprise 27% of overall ETF assets.

While the proliferation of international equity ETFs helps investors by providing scores of choices and strategies, it also requires more due diligence. Investors must parse through the numerous holdings to find the most appropriate vehicle for their portfolio. This chapter plans to provide investors with an overview of the international equity ETF world. With more than 160 ETFs dedicated to the international environment, it is beyond the scope of this chapter to cover each offering thoroughly. Instead, the focus will be on a few key areas. First, the reasons international assets belong in a portfolio are discussed along with arguments to use international ETFs. Next, the methodologies of the index providers will be examined. Finally, a review of the traditional broad-based ETFs will be conducted followed by a summary of the focused, speciality products.

THE CASE FOR INTERNATIONAL

Before describing the actual international ETF products, it is important to understand why investors should include international

Table 18.1 S&P 500/EAFE correlations, 1970–2007

Time period	Correlation (%)
2002–2007	0.91
1970–1988	0.623
1989–2007	0.614
1972–1976	0.874

Source: Dimensional Fund Advisors

equities in a portfolio. An argument exists in the financial world that investors do not benefit from adding international equities to their portfolios. Proponents of this claim point to rising correlations between the US and international markets. They also argue that most large US international firms derive a considerable portion of their sales from international markets, so adding international companies creates redundancy, not diversification.

Correlations between the US and international markets have increased recently. Over the past five years, the correlation between the Standard & Poor's (S&P) 500 and the Europe, Australia and Far East (EAFE) benchmark has reached 0.91. A correlation of 1.0 represents identical market movements.

However, correlations tend to fluctuate over time. This strong relationship may not hold in the future. Since 1970, the correlation between the S&P 500 and the EAFE benchmark averaged 0.618. This long-term average comprises shorter periods with correlations above and below the average. As it does today, the period 1972/76 exhibited a strong correlation of 0.874. Investors who abandoned international equities after this period missed the chance to own an asset class with a low correlation to the US equity market. In 1996, the EAFE registered a 0.25 correlation to the S&P 500. The key is to focus on long-term trends, not short periods. Ibbotson Associates conducted a study and found that the correlation benefits emerged more prominently as the data moved from monthly returns to annual and from five-year rolling returns to ten-year (Korn 2005).

Investors can still improve the risk/return parameters of their portfolio by including global equities even with increased correlation levels. Table 18.2 shows the improvement in the Sharpe Ratio for a portfolio consisting of 80% US and 20% international allocation at

Figure 18.1 Equity portfolio Sharpe Ratio improvement for different levels of correlation (assumed 80/20 US/international allocation)

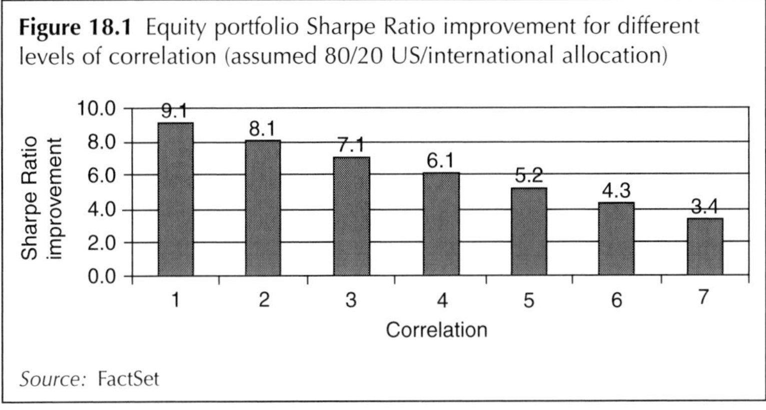

Source: FactSet

Table 18.2 S&P 500/international small-cap correlations 1970–2007

Time period	Correlation (%)
1970–1988	0.459
1989–2007	0.374

Source: Dimensional Fund Advisors

different correlations. Certainly, a lower correlation between the two asset classes provides a better risk-adjusted return, but investors can experience a stronger Sharpe Ratio even with higher correlations (Brandhorst 2002).

Even if investors decided to forgo using international investments tied to the EAFE (large company, developed markets) due to the recent correlation, they would be remiss if they ignored the diversification benefits of international small-company stocks. This asset class has an even lower correlation to US stocks than the EAFE. The primary reason is most small company stocks generate a large percentage of their revenues from their local economy.

In fact, the variation in the performance of country economies justifies an allocation to international equities, large or small. Figure 18.2 shows the randomness of stock market returns by country for the developed markets. Since each country's stock market is affected by local economic and market forces, investors can diversify the returns of the US stock market with an allocation to international equities.

Figure 18.2 Equity returns of developed markets

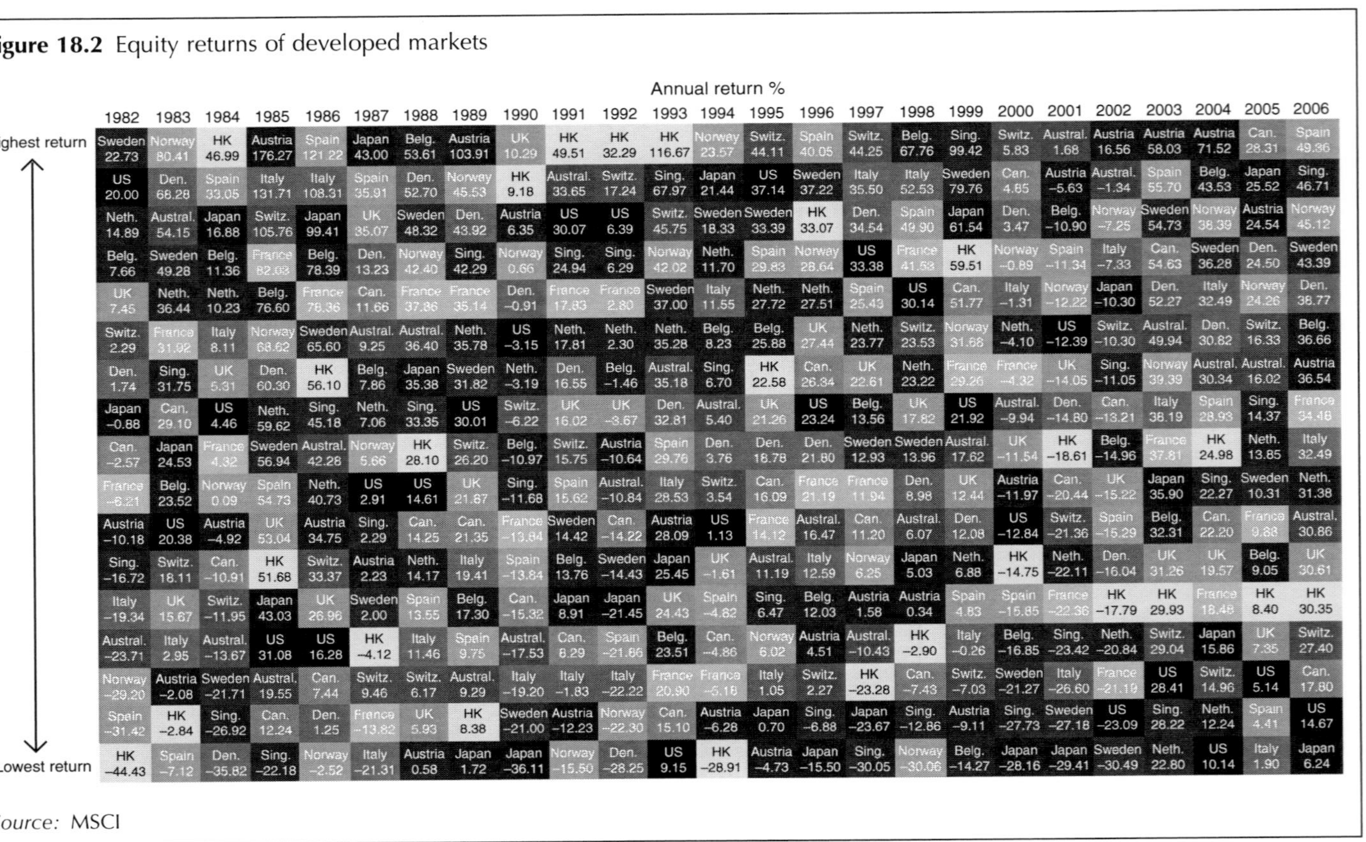

Annual return %

	1982	1983	1984	1985	1986	1987	1988	1989	1990	1991	1992	1993	1994
Highest return	Sweden 22.73	Norway 80.41	HK 46.99	Austria 176.27	Spain 121.22	Japan 43.00	Belg. 53.61	Austria 103.91	UK 10.29	HK 49.51	HK 32.29	HK 116.67	Norway 23.57
	US 20.00	Den. 68.28	Spain 33.05	Italy 131.71	Italy 108.31	Spain 35.91	Den. 52.70	Norway 45.53	HK 9.18	Austral. 33.65	Switz. 17.24	Sing. 67.97	Japan 21.44
	Neth. 14.89	Austral. 54.15	Japan 16.88	Switz. 105.76	Japan 99.41	UK 35.07	Sweden 48.32	Den. 43.92	Austria 6.35	US 30.07	US 6.39	Switz. 45.75	Sweden 18.33
	Belg. 7.66	Sweden 49.28	Belg. 11.36	France 82.03	Belg. 78.39	Den. 13.23	Norway 42.40	Sing. 42.29	Norway 0.66	Sing. 24.94	Sing. 6.29	Norway 42.02	Neth. 11.70
	UK 7.45	Neth. 36.44	Neth. 10.23	Belg. 76.60	France 78.36	Can. 11.66	France 37.86	France 35.14	Den. −0.91	France 17.83	France 2.80	Sweden 37.00	Italy 11.55
	Switz. 2.29	France 31.92	Italy 8.11	Norway 68.62	Sweden 65.60	Austral. 9.25	Austral. 36.40	Neth. 35.78	US −3.15	Neth. 17.81	Neth. 2.30	Neth. 35.28	Belg. 8.23
	Den. 1.74	Sing. 31.75	UK 5.31	Den. 60.30	HK 56.10	Belg. 7.86	Japan 35.38	Sweden 31.82	Neth. −3.19	Den. 16.55	Belg. −1.46	Austral. 35.18	Sing. 6.70
	Japan −0.88	Can. 29.10	US 4.46	Neth. 59.62	Sing. 45.18	Neth. 7.06	Sing. 33.35	US 30.01	Switz. −6.22	UK 16.02	UK −3.67	Den. 32.81	Austral. 5.40
	Can. −2.57	Japan 24.53	France 4.32	Sweden 56.94	Austral. 42.28	Norway 5.66	HK 28.10	Switz. 26.20	Belg. −10.97	Switz. 15.75	Austria −10.64	Spain 29.76	Den. 3.76
	France −6.21	Belg. 23.52	Norway 0.09	Spain 54.73	Neth. 40.73	US 2.91	US 14.61	UK 21.67	Sing. −11.68	Spain 15.62	Austral. −10.84	Italy 28.53	Switz. 3.54
	Austria −10.18	US 20.38	Austria −4.92	UK 53.04	Austria 34.75	Sing. 2.29	Can. 14.25	Can. 21.35	France −13.84	Sweden 14.42	Can. −14.22	Austria 28.09	US 1.13
	Sing. −16.72	Switz. 18.11	Can. −10.91	HK 51.68	Switz. 33.37	Austria 2.23	Neth. 14.17	Italy 19.41	Spain −13.84	Belg. 13.76	Sweden −14.43	Japan 25.45	UK −1.61
	Italy −19.34	UK 15.67	Switz. −11.95	Japan 43.03	UK 26.96	Sweden 2.00	Spain 13.55	Belg. 17.30	Can. −15.32	Japan 8.91	Japan −21.45	UK 24.43	Spain −4.82
	Austral. −23.71	Italy 2.95	Austral. −13.67	US 31.08	US 16.28	HK −4.12	Italy 11.46	Spain 9.75	Austral. −17.53	Can. 8.29	Spain −21.66	Belg. 23.51	Can. −4.86
	Norway −29.20	Austria −2.08	Sweden −21.71	Austral. 19.55	Can. 7.44	Switz. 9.46	Switz. 6.17	Austral. 9.29	Italy −19.20	Italy −1.83	Italy −22.22	France 20.90	France −5.18
	Spain −31.42	HK −2.84	Sing. −26.92	Can. 12.24	Den. 1.25	France −13.82	UK 5.93	HK 8.38	Sweden −21.00	Austria −12.23	Norway −22.30	Can. 15.10	Austria −6.28
Lowest return	HK −44.43	Spain −7.12	Den. −35.82	Sing. −22.18	Norway −2.52	Italy −21.31	Austria 0.58	Japan 1.72	Japan −36.11	Norway −15.50	Den. −28.25	US 9.15	HK −28.91

	1995	1996	1997	1998	1999	2000	2001	2002	2003	2004	2005	2006
Highest return	Switz. 44.11	Spain 40.05	Switz. 44.25	Belg. 67.76	Sing. 99.42	Switz. 5.83	Austral. 1.68	Austria 16.56	Austria 58.03	Austria 71.52	Can. 28.31	Spain 49.36
	US 37.14	Sweden 37.22	Italy 35.50	Italy 52.53	Sweden 79.76	Can. 4.85	Austria −5.63	Austral. −1.34	Spain 55.70	Belg. 43.53	Japan 25.52	Sing. 46.71
	Sweden 33.39	HK 33.07	Den. 34.54	Spain 49.90	Japan 61.54	Den. 3.47	Belg. −10.90	Norway −7.25	Sweden 54.73	Norway 38.39	Austria 24.54	Norway 45.12
	Spain 29.83	Norway 28.64	US 33.38	France 41.53	HK 59.51	Norway −0.89	Spain −11.34	Italy −7.33	Can. 54.63	Sweden 36.28	Den. 24.50	Sweden 43.39
	Neth. 27.72	Neth. 27.51	Spain 25.43	US 30.14	Can. 51.77	Italy −1.31	Norway −12.22	Japan −10.30	Den. 52.27	Italy 32.49	Norway 24.26	Den. 38.77
	Belg. 25.88	UK 27.44	Neth. 23.77	Switz. 23.53	Norway 31.68	Neth. −4.10	US −12.39	Switz. −10.30	Austral. 49.94	Den. 30.82	Switz. 16.33	Belg. 36.66
	HK 22.58	Can. 26.34	UK 22.61	Neth. 23.22	France 29.26	France −4.32	UK −14.05	Sing. −11.05	Norway 39.39	Austral. 30.34	Austral. 16.02	Austria 36.54
	UK 21.26	US 23.24	Belg. 13.56	UK 17.82	US 21.92	Austral. −9.94	Den. −14.80	Can. −13.21	Italy 38.19	Spain 28.93	Sing. 14.37	France 34.46
	Den. 18.78	Den. 21.80	Sweden 12.93	Sweden 13.96	Austral. 17.62	UK −11.54	HK −18.61	Belg. −14.96	France 37.81	HK 24.98	Neth. 13.85	Italy 32.49
	Can. 16.09	France 21.19	France 11.94	Den. 8.98	UK 12.44	Austria −11.97	Can. −20.44	UK −15.22	Japan 35.90	Sing. 22.27	Sweden 10.31	Neth. 31.38
	France 14.12	Austral. 16.47	Can. 11.20	Austral. 6.07	Den. 12.08	US −12.84	Switz. −21.36	Spain −15.29	Belg. 32.31	Can. 22.20	France 9.88	Austral. 30.86
	Austral. 11.19	Italy 12.59	Norway 6.25	Japan 5.03	Neth. 6.88	HK −14.75	Neth. −22.11	Den. −16.04	UK 31.26	UK 19.57	Belg. 9.05	UK 30.61
	Sing. 6.47	Belg. 12.03	Austria 1.58	Austria 0.34	Spain 4.83	Spain −15.85	France −22.36	HK −17.79	HK 29.93	France 18.48	HK 8.40	HK 30.35
	Norway 6.02	Austria 4.51	Austral. −10.43	HK −2.90	Italy −0.26	Belg. −16.85	Sing. −23.42	Neth. −20.84	Switz. 29.04	Japan 15.86	UK 7.35	Switz. 27.40
	Italy 1.05	Switz. 2.27	HK −23.28	Can. −7.43	Switz. −7.03	Sweden −21.27	Italy −26.60	France −21.19	US 28.41	Switz. 14.96	US 5.14	Can. 17.80
	Japan 0.70	Sing. −6.88	Japan −23.67	Sing. −12.86	Austria −9.11	Sing. −27.73	Sweden −27.18	US −23.09	Sing. 28.22	Neth. 12.24	Spain 4.41	US 14.67
Lowest return	Austria −4.73	Japan −15.50	Sing. −30.05	Norway −30.06	Belg. −14.27	Japan −28.16	Japan −29.41	Sweden −30.49	Neth. 22.80	US 10.14	Italy 1.90	Japan 6.24

Source: MSCI

Figure 18.3 World market cap and US market cap as percentage of world market cap 2004 – present

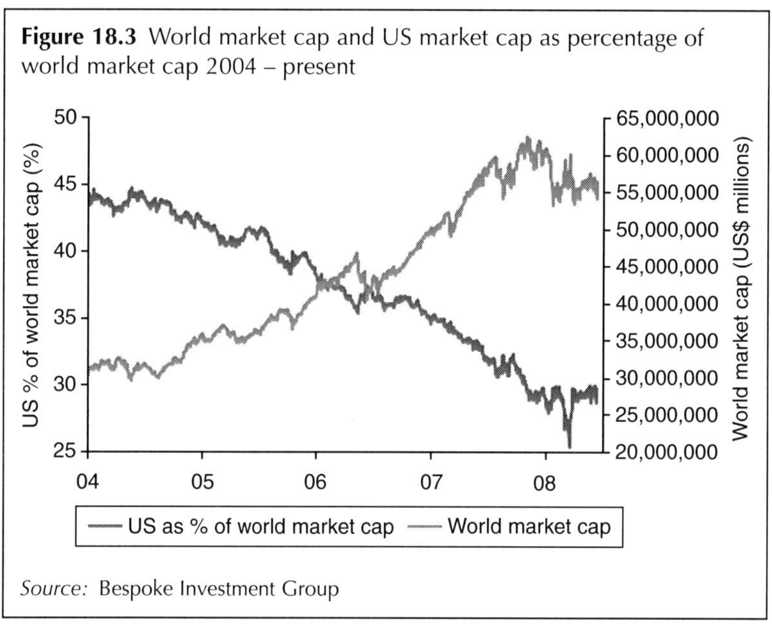

Source: Bespoke Investment Group

Another reason to consider international equities is increased investment opportunities. In 1960, the US made up 68% of the world's market capitalisation. Today, this number is closer to 30%. While this percentage fluctuates over time, investors are bypassing a large percentage of the world's investing opportunities when they ignore international markets.

Once investors decide to include international equities in their portfolios, the next step is choosing the appropriate allocation. If markets are truly efficient and stock prices reflect all available information, then the proper allocation should be based on market capitalisation, which means directing 70% to international investments. However, this allocation probably is not feasible for a couple of reasons. As previously mentioned, the world's market capitalisation is constantly adjusting. Maintaining the appropriate mix of US and international equities in such a volatile environment would make portfolio management cumbersome, costly and tax-inefficient. Investors would constantly be modifying positions to maintain the underlying allocation. Also, most US investors are mentally anchored to the domestic market. The performance of the US market is discussed daily by the various news organisations, as well as

Figure 18.4 Annualised change in portfolio volatility when combining US and international equities

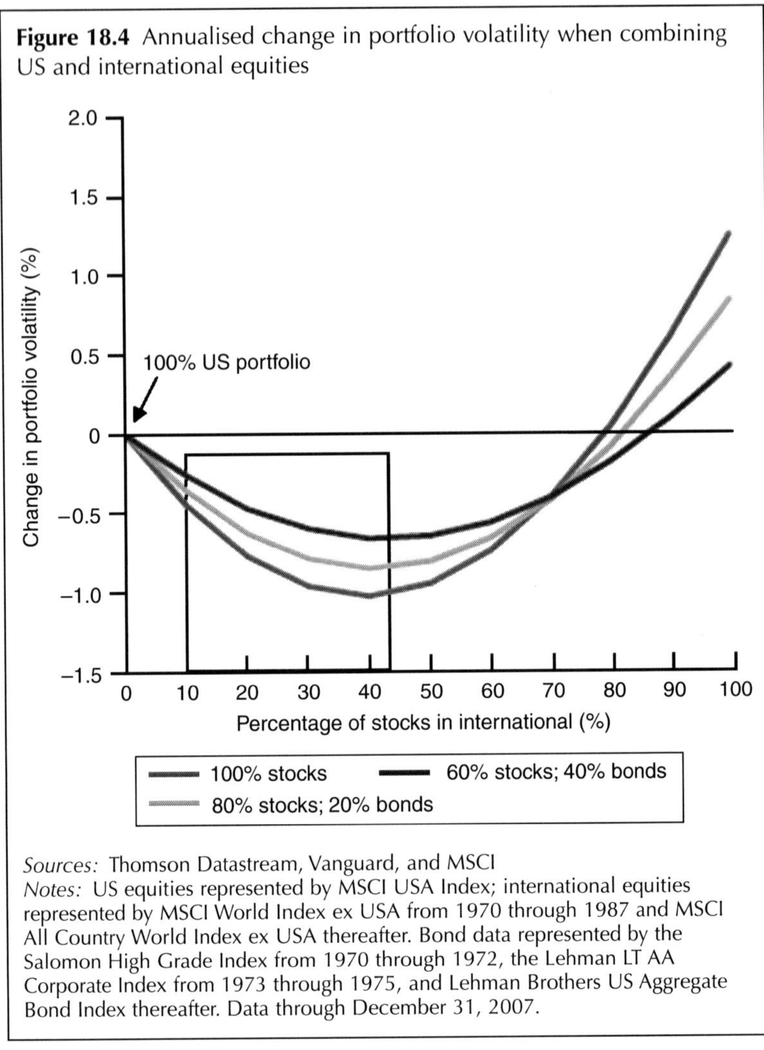

Sources: Thomson Datastream, Vanguard, and MSCI
Notes: US equities represented by MSCI USA Index; international equities represented by MSCI World Index ex USA from 1970 through 1987 and MSCI All Country World Index ex USA thereafter. Bond data represented by the Salomon High Grade Index from 1970 through 1972, the Lehman LT AA Corporate Index from 1973 through 1975, and Lehman Brothers US Aggregate Bond Index thereafter. Data through December 31, 2007.

US residents. Most investors would find it difficult to deviate so far from their home market.

Fortunately for investors, a market-cap-weighted approach may not be the most effective practice. According to a study conducted by the Vanguard Group, investors benefit by directing as little as 10% of their portfolio to international equities. Vanguard's research also found that the benefit of adding international equities diminishes after reaching a 40% allocation. The results of this study are presented in Figure 18.4. The Vanguard study examined the effect of incrementally adding international equities to three different portfolios: 100% equity, 80% equity/20% fixed income, and 60% equity/40% fixed income.

At a 10% allocation to international equities, investors were able to reduce overall portfolio volatility by 25 to 50 basis points (bp) depending on the chosen portfolio. A 20% allocation reduced portfolio volatility between 50 and 85bp. With a 40% international allocation, portfolio volatility decreased between 75 and 114bp. After a 40% allocation to international equities, the volatility of the portfolios increased.

While the 40% allocation was optimal from a risk standpoint, it may not be the optimal allotment for some investors. Other factors need to be considered when making this decision. First, investing internationally carries higher fees. For instance, the Vanguard Total US Stock Market ETF has an expense ratio of 7bp annually while the Vanguard FTSE All-World ex-US ETF, which covers the world's stock market outside the US, charges 25bp on an annual basis. The lower portfolio volatility may not outweigh the additional costs for many investors. Currency risk is another reason investors may avoid a 40% allocation to international securities. While currency risk bears little impact over the long term (and actually assists in lowering long-term correlations), it does affect returns and volatility over the short term (Philips 2008). Of course, the anchor to the US markets, which was mentioned previously, may be another reason investors opt for lower international equity exposure. However, investors should recognise that adding a modest allocation to international equities provides significant benefits to a portfolio.

CASE FOR USING ETFs

After deciding to add international equities to a portfolio, the next question for investors is how to access the asset class. The avenues available to purchase international equities are plentiful: actively managed mutual funds, individual equity positions, American Depository Receipts (ADRs), hedge funds, separately managed accounts, options, index mutual funds and ETFs, to name a few. Of course, choosing the instrument is only one part of the decision. ETFs offer investors several advantages over the other methods mentioned.

ETFs provide investors with style consistency, broad diversification and lower costs. When index providers create an index, they attempt to accurately represent an entire market (or segment of the market). To truly represent the underlying market, the index usually includes the vast majority of the market's securities. These indexes change only as the market changes. Since ETFs attempt to replicate an index, they provide investors with a consistent allocation with a broad array of holdings. Actively managed instruments tend to vary as the active manager(s) makes bets on particular segments or strategies. This often leads to style drift or a heavy concentration on a particular segment of a market. The largest advantage for ETFs relative to the actively managed instruments is the costs. Morningstar estimates that the average diversified foreign-equity mutual fund charges 1.81% per year whereas the comparable ETF charges just 35bp annually. Studies conducted by the Vanguard Group show that this extra expense usually results in lower investor returns over the long term. Vanguard examined the percentage of active fund managers who beat their benchmark over various rolling 10-year periods starting in January 2003 through October 2006. As Figure 18.5 shows, roughly 70% or more of active fund managers failed to beat their benchmark over these time frames. This includes funds focused on global, European and US markets. This study discovered that the

Figure 18.5 Active management versus benchmark

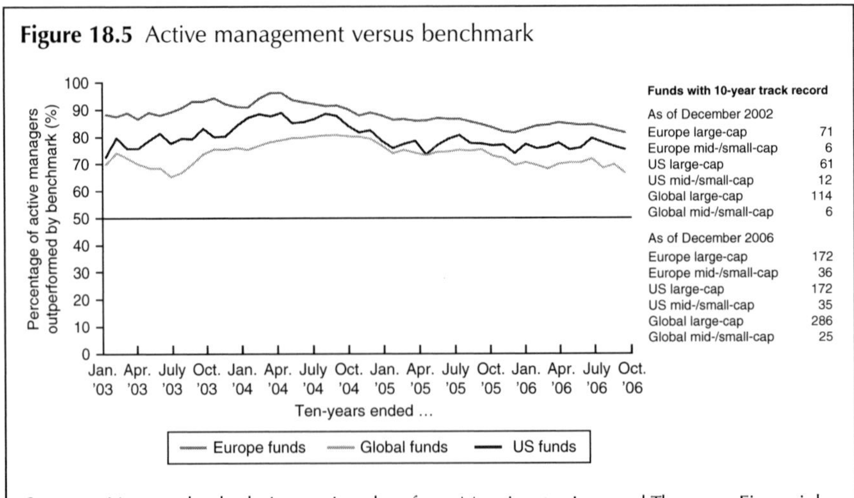

Sources: Vanguard calculations using data from Morningstar Inc, and Thomson Financial
Notes: European market represented by MSCI Europe Index; global market represented by MSCI All Country World Free Index; and US market represented by MSCI USA Index. Returns were compared to FTSE and Dow Jones benchmarks with similar results. All returns are in euros.

average underperformance for actively managed funds was 1.53% for global funds, 2.31% for European funds, and 2.85% for US large-blend funds. These variances strongly correlate to the difference in cost structure between active and indexed funds.

Index mutual funds also offer investors these benefits, but the international ETFs are superior to index mutual funds regarding costs. For instance, the Vanguard Group offers both index mutual funds and ETFs for international equities. However, the internal expense ratio for the two instruments differs considerably. Table 18.3 shows comparison of a few Vanguard holdings.

The comparison in Table 18.3 is based on Vanguard's investor share index fund and not its Admiral share, which offers lower expense ratios but requires a substantially higher initial deposit or account balance.

Even beyond the Vanguard holdings, ETFs maintain this low-cost advantage compared with index mutual funds. According to Morningstar, the average annual expense ratio for a diversified foreign equity index fund is 1.07%. The average ETF in this category charges 0.35% annually on average. There are probably several reasons for the lower costs in the ETF marketplace, such as the creation/redemption process, administrative fees, marketing and competition, but this discussion is beyond the scope of this chapter.

Proponents of active management claim that these benefits of ETFs are outweighed by the inefficiency of the international equity marketplace. As with the small-cap universe, active managers argue that the international markets do not garner the analyst and institutional coverage that the large, blue-chip US stocks do, especially in the emerging-markets arena. This lack of transparency allows active management to outperform passive instruments such as ETFs. However, in most cases, these active managers are comparing their performance to the Morgan Stanley Capital International/Barra

Table 18.3 Average ETF and index fund expense ratios

Asset class	ETF expense ratio (%)	Index fund expense ratio (%)
All World (ex-US)	0.25	0.40
Developed Europe and Asia	0.15	0.22
Emerging markets	0.25	0.37

(MSCI) EAFE index, an extensive index representing the stock markets of 21 nations.

While the EAFE is a well-constructed index, it may be too broad. The regional economies that make up the EAFE are not integrated or strongly correlated. Since the EAFE is strictly based on market capitalisation without regard to the region, this has resulted in an inconsistent allocation to the various regions of the EAFE. For instance, during the 1980s, the EAFE heavily favoured Japan in its composition. After Japan's economic malaise began, the index altered its allocation in favour of the European countries. Essentially, the index construction rules are guaranteeing performance chasing. As one region outperforms the other, the index will increase its allocation to that region. Once that region declines, the index reduces its percentage to the region.

Despite this drawback of the EAFE, the argument that active management tops this index is unsupported. Data provided by Morningstar shows that active management has been unable to consistently provide higher returns to investors compared with the EAFE.

Figure 18.6 EAFE regional allocation 1970–2005

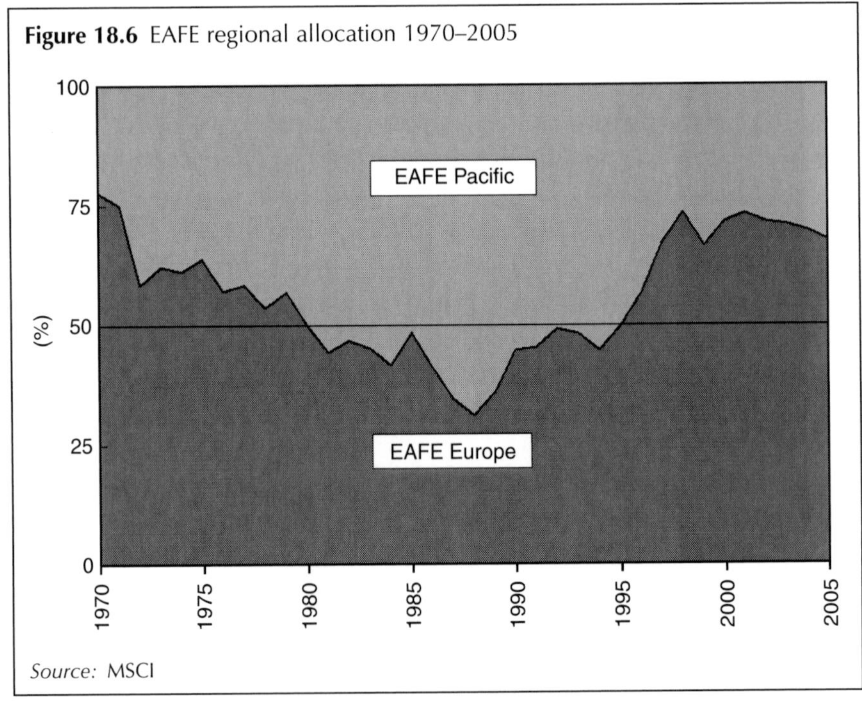

Source: MSCI

Table 18.4 shows the returns of actively managed international equity mutual funds and the EAFE for the three previous decades. The actively managed funds include funds that invested in emerging markets as well as the regions represented by the EAFE. Also, the data does not incorporate survivorship bias. If the data excluded funds that invested in emerging markets and included defunct or closed funds, the results would probably favour the EAFE even more.

Rather than turning to active management, investors looking to optimise their international equity allocation may want to create static regional allocations with a systematic rebalance. According to a study performed by Rick Ferri, a money manager with Portfolio Solutions and an author of several books on asset allocation and index investing, investors could have substantially increased their returns and lowered their overall risk by slicing and dicing their international allocation regionally. The table below shows the results

Table 18.4 Actively managed international fund performance versus EAFE performance

Category	1980s (%)	1990s (%)	2000s (%)
Foreign Large Growth	16.80	11.93	1.38
Foreign Large Blend	18.29	9.65	2.13
Foreign Large Value	19.36	10	5.52
Foreign Stock	18.28	10.40	3.11
EAFE	22	7	5.30

Source: MSCI and Morningstar Inc through July 2008

Table 18.5 EAFE versus slice and dice allocations

Portfolio allocation	1990s (%)	2000s (%)	1989–2007 (%)	Annual standard deviation (%)
EAFE	7	5.30	5.90	18.20
40% Europe/40% Pacific/ 20% Emerging	11.60	6.80	8.90	14.80
20% Europe ex-UK, 20% UK, 20% Japan, 20% Pacific ex-Japan, 20% Emerging	14.30	10.10	11.70	14.40

Source: MSCI (MSCI emerging data goes back only to 1989; data does not account for transaction or tax costs)

for three portfolios. The first portfolio is the EAFE, net dividends. The second portfolio is 40% allocated to the developed regions of the Pacific and Europe with 20% invested in emerging markets. The final portfolio breaks the developed markets into four regions (Europe ex-UK, UK, Japan and Pacific ex-Japan) and includes emerging markets as well. All portfolios assume an annual rebalance.

Investors employing this strategy would clearly have outperformed the EAFE and the average actively managed fund. The static allocation with the annual rebalance ensured that investors were selling high and buying low as each regional economy experienced superior and lagging performances.

INTERNATIONAL INDEX METHODOLOGIES

As previously mentioned, it is essential for investors to conduct proper due diligence before investing in an ETF. The first step in that process is understanding how the index providers create their indexes. While each index provider has its own proprietary methodologies for creating indexes, each provider begins building its global and international indexes by focusing on the countries. Countries are grouped together to form regions, and regions are combined to form the international and global indexes. This section provides a broad overview of the major index providers methodology.

FTSE

Launched in 1987, the FTSE All-World Index Series is a free-float-adjusted, market-cap-weighted set of indexes that use a clearly defined set of ground rules to create their indexes. FTSE breaks the indexes into three segments based on market capitalisation: the FTSE Global Equity Series (Large, Mid, and Small Cap), the FTSE All-World Index Series (Large and Mid Cap), and the FTSE Global Small Cap Indexes.

FTSE follows a strict process to determine if a country or security is eligible for inclusion in an index. FTSE does this by:

- parsing the global market into regions;
- grouping countries into the appropriate region;
- applying criteria to determine if the country is eligible for inclusion in the indexes;
- classifying the eligible countries into developed, advanced emerging or secondary emerging market;

- analysing the country's securities for inclusion; and
- categorising eligible securities by market capitalisation.

FTSE created seven regions (Asia Pacific ex-Japan, Developed Europe, Emerging Europe, Japan, Latin America, Middle East and Africa, and North America) to organise each country. While quarterly reviews are performed, FTSE reviews the countries and securities in each region only once a year to minimise turnover.

For a country to be eligible for inclusion in an FTSE index, it must meet the following criteria:

- permission for direct equity investment by non-nationals;
- availability of accurate and timely data;
- nonexistence of any significant exchange controls that would prevent the timely repatriation of capital or dividend;
- demonstration of significant investor interest in the local equity market; and
- adequate market liquidity.

If a country meets FTSE's requirements, it is then classified as developed, advanced emerging or secondary emerging. FTSE has primary and secondary factors that determine a country's classification.

After creating the regional and country classifications, FTSE then applies size, liquidity and free-float constraints before including a security in an index. FTSE begins by discarding any companies in the bottom 2% of market capitalisation and includes only companies with a market capitalisation of at least US$100 million.

FTSE tests liquidity for a security by examining turnover. FTSE reviews the daily trading of a security for a month and focuses on its median trading day (the middle of its monthly ranges). A security meets the liquidity test if during its median trading day at least

Table 18.6 FTSE regional review dates

Date of meeting	Region(s) to be reviewed
March	Asia Pacific ex-Japan
June	Latin America Emerging Europe Middle East and Africa
September	Developed Europe Japan
December	North America

Table 18.7 FTSE index qualifications

Primary factors	Secondary factors
Data quality Free flow of foreign exchange GDP (per capita) Market breadth: number of eligible companies Market depth: number of industrial sectors Reliable price information Stock market capitalisation versus GDP Unrestricted/low restrictions on foreign investment	Efficient settlement systems Liquidity – minimum stock market turnover Market maturity Membership of economic group or common currency block Total-stock market capitalisation

0.05% of its shares are traded. For new security inclusions, this 0.05% measurement must be met in 10 of the previous 12 months. If a security has been trading for less than 12 months, it must meet this 0.05% threshold in every month since its listing. An existing constituent to an FTSE index needs to turn over only 0.04% of its shares for four of the previous 12 months to pass the liquidity test. FTSE bases liquidity from data provided by the exchange where the security is listed. If there is more than one exchange, FTSE aggregates the data.

To pass the free-float screen, a security must have more than 5% of its shares available for purchase by outside investors. For any security with less than a 15% free float, it must have a market capitalisation of at least US$5 billion for a developed country and US$2.5 billion for an emerging country.

Once a security passes the rules test, it is placed into the appropriate index by its market capitalisation. FTSE attempts to minimise turnover by creating buffer zones to determine cut-off points between large-, mid-, and small-cap. Table 18.8 shows how FTSE determines to which market cap weighting a company belongs.

Standard and Poor's

S&P takes a different approach to creating its global and international indexes. Rather than building one broad-based index, S&P creates seven distinct and separate indexes and groups these together to create its international and global indexes.

Table 18.8 FTSE market capitalisation inclusion percentages

	Eligible for inclusion (%)	Eligible for exclusion (%)
Large-cap	68	72
Mid-cap	86	92
Small-cap	97	99

The global benchmark for S&P is the S&P Global 1200. The S&P Global 1200 is similar to the FTSE All-World Index Series in that it is a market-cap-weighted and float-adjusted index. However, it differs from the other global indexes in that S&P does not attempt to capture the world's available market capitalisation. S&P's goal is to create a highly liquid and tradable index with a consistent number of stocks. S&P does not try to capture the entire market cap universe, just enough to adequately serve as a barometer for the underlying markets. The S&P Global 1200 covers approximately 70% of the world's market capitalisation compared with more than 90% for the other global indexes.

As previously mentioned, S&P uses a composite of seven regional indexes to create its global benchmark. The regional indexes are the S&P 500, regarded by many as the pre-eminent benchmark representing the US stock market, the S&P Europe 350, the S&P/Topix 150 (Japan), S&P/TSX 60 (Canada), S&P/ASX All Australian 50, S&P Asia 50 (Asia ex-Japan), and S&P Latin America 40. Each regional index is maintained by a separate S&P index committee. While each committee is independent, the guidelines for stock selection are consistent. The criterion for selection is based on size, liquidity, profitability and sector/market representation.

The S&P Global 1200 consists of mostly blue-chip stocks with large market capitalisations. Each stock's weighting in the index is based on its float-adjusted market capitalisation. Like the other global indexes, S&P bases float on the shares available for trading on public exchanges. Shares held by insiders, the government or other private sources are excluded from the float calculation.

To measure liquidity, S&P examines the annual US dollar value traded as well as the annual volume traded, days per year traded and float turnover. The index committees include only companies with the highest US dollar or volume trades, and they generally set a minimum float turnover of 30% per year for inclusion.

One area where all S&P indexes vary from other market-cap-weighted indexes is the profitability criterion. The index committees critique the financial stability of all the companies before and after inclusion in an index. S&P does this to reduce index turnover; however, this criterion introduces an active element to the index process not seen with its market-cap-weighted competitors.

Another unique factor of the S&P indexes is the use of sectors. Every index is developed around the 10 sector classifications of the Global Industry Classification System (GICS). Every holding is categorised into one of the 10 GICS sectors, and the index committees strive to keep the sector weightings consistent with the underlying market economies. This devotion to sector weightings has allowed S&P to create numerous sector indexes to complement its regional benchmarks.

Since the S&P maintains a consistent number of companies in each index, the indexes change only if a company is deleted from the underlying index. Deletions usually occur because of mergers, acquisitions, spin-offs, bankruptcies or delistings. When a company is added, the index committee focuses on maintaining the sector representation of the underlying index. If the addition is an initial public offering (IPO), the index committee requires six months of adequate liquidity.

The index committees conduct an annual review every September, but changes to the indexes can take place at any time during the year, especially if the change is greater than a 5% move. Usually, a change takes place on the third Friday of March, June, September and December if the change is less than 5%.

Currently, there are no ETFs based on the S&P Global 1200 Index. However, investors can create this index by purchasing ETFs based

Table 18.9 Global Industry Classification System

Consumer staples	Consumer discretionary
Energy	Financials
Healthcare	Industrials
Information technology	Materials
Telecommunications	Utilities

on the seven S&P subsets, which are available through Barclay's iShares product.

Morgan Stanley Capital International

The Morgan Stanley Capital International (MSCI) family of indexes is robust. Currently, MSCI has crafted more than 20,000 indexes focused on various factors such as size, style, sector, region and country. Like FTSE and S&P, the MSCI indexes are market-cap-weighted and float-adjusted. MSCI develops its indexes based on the following process (see Figure 18.7):

- define the equity universe;
- determine the market-investable equity universe for each market;
- apply index rules to each potential security;
- create style segments within each size segment for each market; and
- create sector classifications based on the GICS.

Defining the equity universe requires examining all the listed securities in the 48 countries that comprise the MSCI indexes (23 developed markets and 25 emerging markets). The market-investable equity universe is created by taking the largest 99% of the equity universe for each country and applying a rules-based selection process.

The rules are similar to those of the other market-cap-weighted indexes. They focus on free-float-adjusted market capitalisation (minimum market cap greater than US$172 million), availability of foreign investment (MSCI calls this the foreign inclusion factor),

Figure 18.7 MSCI

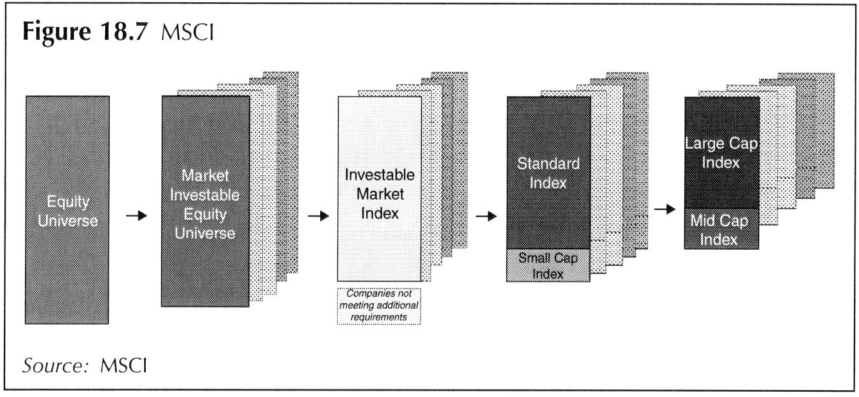

Source: MSCI

liquidity and trading length (must have more than three months of trading).

Once a security passes these thresholds, it is categorised by market cap. MSCI has a slightly different capitalisation rating process for developed and emerging markets, but the system has a buffer zone to minimise turnover. The zones are:

- large-cap index: 70% plus or minus 5%;
- standard index: 85% plus or minus 5%; and
- investable-market index: 99% plus or minus 1%.

The mid-cap coverage is the standard index minus the large-cap coverage, while the small-cap component is the investable market index minus the standard index.

After each security is categorised according to its market capitalisation, MSCI defines the holdings by style. Many index providers simply examine a company's price-to-book ratio (P/B) to determine whether its style is value or growth. MSCI is unique in this calculation in that it uses more than one factor to determine a company's style categorisation. For value, MSCI looks at P/B, 12-month forward earnings-to-price ratio and dividend-to-price ratio. The growth factors are long-term forward earnings per share growth rate, short-term forward earnings per share growth rate, current internal growth rate, long-term historical earnings per share growth trend and long-term sales per share growth trend. With MSCI's style criteria, a stock could fall into one category, both categories or neither category.

Finally, MSCI categorises securities under the GICS, similar to S&P. This allows a security to be classified into an appropriate sector.

Dow Jones Indexes and Wilshire Associates Incorporated

While few ETF products are currently based on the Dow Jones Wilshire Global indexes, they do offer great depth and coverage. Similar to the previous index families, the Dow Jones Wilshire Global indexes are weighted by float-adjusted market capitalisation. Dow Jones Wilshire strives to cover 98% of a country's market capitalisation for developed markets and 95% for emerging economies. The indexes are determined by a rules-based methodology similar to FTSE and MSCI. Currently, the indexes cover more than 60 countries and more than 12,000 securities – the highest for any of the index providers.

Dow Jones Wilshire uses International Monetary Fund criteria to determine whether a country is suitable for investment and categorise the country as developed or emerging. At present, 28 of the countries are considered developed and 33 are emerging. Whereas the FTSE and S&P indexes are broken down into seven regions, the Dow Jones Wilshire Global indexes use four regions: Americas, Asia/Pacific, Europe and Middle East/Africa.

The rules for inclusion include accessibility for non-residents, availability of real-time and historical market data, reliable data sources and readily available pricing. Any security that does not trade for 10 days in any quarter is excluded from the indexes.

Dow Jones Wilshire organises the companies by market capitalisation much like the other index providers. If a company falls within the 85th percentile, it is considered part of the large-cap index. All other stocks register in the small-cap index. The mid-cap index overlaps the large- and small-cap indexes with the companies in the 80% and 90% targets.

Similar to the S&P and MSCI, the Dow Jones Wilshire Global indexes are categorised into sector or industry groups. However, Dow Jones Wilshire uses a different classification system: the Industry Classification Benchmark (ICB). Both the GICS and ICB break companies into 10 industries, but the sub-sectors tend to differ.

The Dow Jones Wilshire indexes are monitored monthly to deal with initial public offerings and companies that fail to meet index membership requirements. All float factors are dealt with during quarterly reviews. Dow Jones Wilshire also continuously monitors for companies that are disqualified from inclusion due to delistings, bankruptcies, spin-offs, mergers, takeovers or any other factor that might cause disqualification.

FTSE RAFI

The FTSE RAFI indexes offer investors a considerably different vehicle from the market-cap-weighted index providers. The FTSE RAFI indexes are fundamentally weighted benchmarks. While FTSE offers the traditional market-cap-weighted indexes, it has teamed up with Rob Arnott's Research Affiliates group to offer these unique indexes. Rather than basing an index on price and available float, the FTSE RAFI creates indexes focused on sales, cashflow, book value and dividends. The argument FTSE RAFI makes for breaking from the traditional price-based market-cap-weighted design is that prices can be prone to speculation, and even bubbles, which leads to overweighting overpriced companies or sectors and underweighting undervalued holdings.

This index philosophy has struck a cord with the traditional market-cap-weighted advocates. They claim that the market is the most efficient vehicle for properly pricing securities. While the market may temporarily misprice stocks, it is difficult, if not impossible, to identify the mispriced securities any better than an efficient mechanism such as the free markets. This argument is beyond the scope of this chapter, but it is important to recognise the key difference in these approaches.

To create these fundamental indexes, the FTSE RAFI conducts five steps.

1. Select the company universe: For the international indexes, FTSE RAFI begins by using the companies from the market-cap-weighted FTSE Developed ex-US index.
2. Rank each company according to the fundamental measures: The ranking is based on the four key fundamental factors:
   - sales: company sales averaged over the past five years;
   - cashflow: operating income plus depreciation averaged over the prior five years;
   - book value: the company's book value at the review date; and
   - dividends: total dividend distributions, both regular and special, averaged over the past five years.
3. Create a composite fundamental value: The average of the company's scores based on the four factors are combined to get a composite fundamental value.
4. Rank the companies in descending order based on their composite fundamental value: The top 1,000 companies are assigned to the FTSE RAFI benchmark.
5. Weight the stocks: FTSE RAFI weights the stocks for the indexes by dividing the composite fundamental value by its free-float adjusted market capitalisation.

FTSE RAFI conducts an annual review of the indexes every March. Any changes to the indexes are conducted after the close of the index calculation on the third Friday of March.

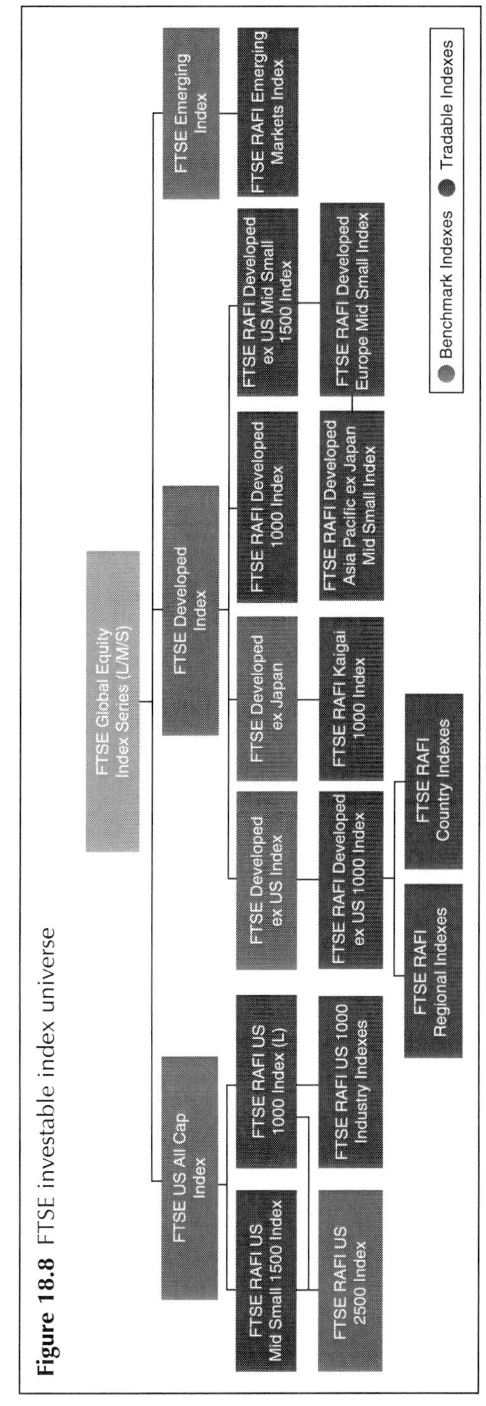

Figure 18.8 FTSE investable index universe

WisdomTree indexes

Unlike the other ETF providers, WisdomTree creates its own indexes, rather than licensing from an index provider. The WisdomTree indexes are fundamentally weighted like the FTSE RAFI products. However, considerable differences exist between the two methodologies. Instead of focusing on four fundamental measures, the WisdomTree indexes focus on earnings and dividends. Also, the FTSE RAFI products factor all four of its measurements into each of its indexes whereas WisdomTree created two "families" of indexes – one based on dividends and the other on earnings.

WisdomTree believes a fundamental approach based on dividends provides a superior risk/return for investors for five reasons:

- dividends provide a compelling basis for stock values;
- the reinvestment of dividends accounted for 96% of the stock market's return after inflation;
- dividends may provide a higher return during bear markets;
- dividends are a sign of profitability and protection from earnings manipulations; and
- the tax rate on qualified dividends makes them appealing to investors compared with other forms of interest, which is taxed at ordinary income tax rates.

For its earnings indexes, WisdomTree argues that weighing companies by core earnings reduces the price-to-earnings ratio (P/E) for the index. Core earnings come from S&P Core Earnings data, which eliminates one-time events such as business sales, write-downs, and other items. WisdomTree also discards any companies without actual earnings, which it feels improves returns, since the speculative, riskier companies will not be part of the index. WisdomTree claims this inefficiency for dividends and earnings exists across all market capitalisations, all geographic regions and all industry sectors.

GLOBAL ETFs

After understanding the index composition process, investors can then decide on which ETFs to use for their international equity allocation. This section examines some frequently used international equity ETFs by objective. It starts with global funds. Global ETFs cover the entire world's stock market. These instruments provide investors with the ability to capture the entire world's market – both

US and international – with one trade. The various global indexes differ dramatically on their holdings and operation.

Vanguard Total World Stock Index ETF

The Vanguard Total World Stock Index ETF (VT) is designed to track the performance of the FTSE All-World Index, a free-float-adjusted, market-cap-weighted index designed to capture 98% of the world's capitalisation. The index comprises approximately 2,900 large- and mid-cap stocks located in 47 countries from developed and emerging markets.

Like all Vanguard ETFs, the VT is a share class of the Vanguard Total World Stock Index fund. The VT was launched June 26, 2008. One of the primary benefits of the Vanguard offering is its low internal expense ratio, only 0.25%. Another benefit for this global fund is its diversification relative to the other global ETFs. The largest holding for all the Global ETFs is Exxon-Mobil. However, with the Vanguard Total World Stock Index, Exxon-Mobil makes up only 1.4% of the fund, whereas it comprises more than 5% of the other offerings. The VT also has the lowest allocation to the US at 41%. At the time of writing, it had just launched, and assets-under-management information was unavailable.

iShares S&P Global 100 Index Fund

Barclay's current global ETF product is based on the S&P Global 100, which is a subset of S&P's Global 1200 World index. The S&P Global 100 focuses on 100 large-cap companies that earn a large percentage of their revenues outside of their home countries. Each company must have a market capitalisation of at least US$5 billion and have fixed assets or production facilities in more than one country.

The country allocation in this index is heavily favoured to the US and the major developed countries in Europe. Pacific-based companies have a low allocation with only 7.04% allocated to companies from Japan, Korea and Australia. The fund has a very low allowance of emerging markets. Investors in this fund need to realise they are essentially purchasing a US and developed Europe fund with only 105 companies.

The fund, which began trading in December 2000, has the largest amount of assets under management for the global ETF offerings, with just over US$1 billion. It also has an expense ratio of 0.4%, which is considerably higher than its counterparts.

SPDR Dow Jones Global Titans (DGT)

Like the iShares S&P Global 100 Index Fund, the SPDR Dow Jones Global Titans ETF is for investors who want to own a large-cap fund focused on companies that do a great deal of their business outside the US. The Dow Jones Global Titans index contains the world's largest global companies. The index is created by ranking companies according to market capitalisation. A proprietary model then chooses the top 50 companies based on various factors such as market cap, assets, book value, sales and profits. Compared with the Vanguard and iShares global ETFs, the SPDR DJ Global Titans has the strongest value tilt. The P/E is just over 11, while its competitors are both over 14. Also, it has the lowest P/B at 2.21.

The SPDR DJ Global Titans is heavily weighted with companies from the US (almost 56%) and energy companies (practically 22%). As with the iShares global ETF, the vast majority of the holdings are US or developed European companies with very little allocated to the Pacific region corporations or emerging markets.

BROAD INTERNATIONAL ETFs

These ETFs mirror the structure and purpose of the global funds with one exception. Whereas the global funds include US corporations, the broad international funds do not. They still combine companies

Table 18.10 Global market ETF statistics

	Vanguard Total World Stock ETF	iShares S&P Global 100 Index Fund	SPDR DJ Global Titans ETF
Number of stocks	2,910	108	51
Expense ratio	0.25%	0.4	0.5
Median market capitalisation	32.7 billion	67 billion	170 billion
Price–earnings ratio	14.9	14.74	11.05
Price–book ratio	2.3	3.09	2.21
Foreign holdings (%)	59	54	45
Trading volume	17,552	243,642	15,787
Assets under management	N/A	1.36 billion	157 million
Inception date	Jun 26, 2008	Dec 5, 2000	Sep 25, 2000

Table 18.11 Percentage holdings by country

	Vanguard Total World Stock ETF (%)	iShares S&P Global 100 Index Fund (%)	SPDR DJ Global Titans ETF (%)
US	41	46.41	55.82
Japan	8.49	4.72	3.43
UK	8.84	13.91	14.75
France	5.14	9.11	3.68
Germany	3.85	8.03	4.49
Canada	3.47	0.04	0
Australia	2.97	1.29	1.88
Switzerland	2.88	5.71	6.65
Brazil	2.11	0	1.14
China	1.01	0	0
India	1.11	0	0
Russia	1.22	0	0
Italy	1.75	0.62	1.30
Korea	1.73	0.93	1.06

Table 18.12 Top 10 holdings

Vanguard Total World Stock ETF	(%)	iShares S&P Global 100	(%)	SPDR DJ Global Titans ETF	(%)
Exxon Mobil	1.40	Exxon Mobil	5.37	Exxon Mobil	6.79
GE	0.90	GE	4.37	GE	4.07
Microsoft	0.80	Microsoft	2.68	Microsoft	3.15
AT&T	0.70	Proctor & Gamble	2.54	BP PLC	3.03
BP PLC	0.70	Nestlé SA-Reg	2.33	Proctor & Gamble	2.94
Total SA	0.60	HSBC Holdings	2.31	Chevron Corp	2.92
Chevron Corp	0.60	BP PLC	2.26	AT&T	2.86
Proctor & Gamble	0.60	Johnson & Johnson	2.17	Johnson & Johnson	2.81
HSBC Holdings	0.60	Chevron	2.1	HSBC Holdings	2.71
Nestlé	0.60	Total SA	2.09	Nestlé	2.64

with various market caps from developed and emerging markets, and they provide investors with the ability to capture a large portion of the equity marketplace with one trade.

The broad international ETFs are ideal for investors looking to invest internationally, but they want to control the allocation between international and US assets. They also serve investors who are deploying a core-and-explore (or core/satellite) portfolio. Investors can allocate a portion of their portfolio to a well-diversified

Table 18.13 Percentage holdings by industry

	Vanguard Total World Stock ETF	iShares S&P Global 100 Index Fund	SPDR DJ Global Titans ETF
Financials	41	19.36	15.6
Energy	8.49	14.73	21.66
Consumer staples	8.84	13.59	12.59
Information technology	5.14	12.89	15.63
Healthcare	3.85	10.17	13.11
Industrials	3.47	8.34	5.49
Consumer discretionary	2.97	7.87	2.04
Telecommunications	2.88	4.69	8.53
Materials	2.11	4.62	3.44
Utilities	1.01	2.52	1.9

international fund and then attempt to capture alpha with other holdings.

SPDR MSCI ACWI ex-US ETF

This is the first of two broad international ex-US ETFs managed by State Street Global Advisors (SSGA). The MSCI ACWI ex-US index is a free-float-adjusted market-capitalisation index designed to measure equity market performance in all global developed and emerging markets outside the US. The underlying index contains 2,240 stocks with an average market capitalisation of US$47 billion. SSGA have attempted to replicate the index with 632 holdings with a market-capitalisation average of US$59 billion. At the time of writing, this ETF has been trading for only 18 months, but it has lagged the performance of its underlying index by a much wider margin than its expense ratio. The ETF has trailed its index by 1.16% since inception while the internal expense ratio is just 0.35%. As the ETF gathers more assets and adds positions, it will probably improve its tracking error, but this should be noted by potential investors.

SPDR S&P International Dividend ETF (DWX)

This is the second all-world ex-US offering by SSGA. Like its first offering, SSGA excludes countries listed in the US. This ETF differs from its SSGA brethren in that it does not attempt to replicate the returns of the entire market. It is much narrower in its focus. This ETF tracks the S&P International Dividend index, which invests in the 100 highest dividend-paying stocks listed in the S&P/Citigroup Broad Market index. This holding is appropriate for yield investors searching for international markets. The current yield is 8.5% compared with 2.92% for SSGA's other broad international ETF.

Vanguard FTSE All World ex-US ETF (VEU)

This ETF is similar to the SPDR MSCI ACWI ex-US in that it attempts to provide investors with a broad-based market-cap-weighted ETF that spans the entire developed and emerging markets outside the US. Contrary to the SPDR offering, Vanguard comes very close to

Table 18.14 Broad international ETF statistics

	Vanguard FTSE All World ex-US ETF	SPDR S&P International Dividend ETF	SPDR MSCI ACWI ex-US ETF
Number of stocks	2,207	102	632
Expense ratio (%)	0.25	0.45	0.35
Median market capitalisation	37.2 billion	11.7 billion	59 billion
Price–earnings ratio	13.5	9.9	12.51
Price–book ratio	2.1	1.7	2.01
Trading volume	285,000	2,500	208,000
Assets under management	1.9 billion	29.5 million	316 million
Inception date	Mar 2, 2007	Feb 12, 2008	Jan 1, 2007

Table 18.15 Percentage holdings by country

	Vanguard FTSE All World ex-US ETF (%)	SPDR S&P International Dividend ETF (%)	SPDR MSCI ACWI ex-US ETF (%)
Japan	14.50	0	15.29
UK	14.50	25.02	16.36
France	8.10	1.85	7.95
Germany	6.50	0	6.90
Canada	3.47	17.46	7.03
Australia	5.10	8.76	5.18
Switzerland	4.80	0	5.13
Brazil	2.11	0	2.40
China	2.30	0	2.44
India	1.90	0	1.61
Russia	2.10	0	1.74
Italy	3	7.78	2.89
Korea	2.90	0	2.79

Table 18.16 Top 10 holdings

Vanguard FTSE All World ex-US ETF	(%)	SPDR S&P International Dividend ETF	(%)	SPDR MSCI ACWI ex-US ETF	(%)
BP PLC	1.10	Kungsleden AB	3.93	BP PLC	1.39
Total SA	1.10	Frontline LTD	3.38	HSBC	1.11
HSBC Holdings PLC	1	Enerplus Resources Fund	3.29	Nestlé	1.09
Nestlé SA	0.90	Penn West Energy Trust	3.06	Total SA	1.02
Vodafone Group PLC	0.80	Barratt Developments	2.75	Vodafone Group	1.01
Royal Dutch Shell PLC	0.80	Outokumpu OYJ	2.73	Taiwan Semiconductor	0.87
Petroleo Brasileriro SA	0.80	Trygvesta A/S	2.65	Royal Dutch Shell	0.87
OAO Gazprom	0.70	Telfonica O2 Czech Republic	2.51	Toyota Motor	0.81
BHP Billiton LTD	0.70	IMI PLC	2.49	BHP Billiton	0.81
E.ON AG	0.70	Lloyds TSP Group	2.44	GlaxoSmithKline	0.75

Table 18.17 Percentage holdings by industry

	SPDR S&P International Dividend ETF	SPDR MSCI ACWI ex-US ETF
Financials	23.17	25.77
Energy	16.56	11.99
Consumer staples	4.05	6.65
Information technology	1.86	6.87
Healthcare	2.31	5.04
Industrials	9.87	12.14
Consumer discretionary	20.45	8.64
Telecommunications	6.55	6.68
Materials	11.46	11.48
Utilities	3.72	4.67

replicating its index. The Vanguard ETF has 2,207, stocks while the FTSE All World ex-US index tracks 2,307. Due to this tight replication, the Vanguard ETF has tracked its index closely since its inception in March 2007. The tracking error is just 5bp, which is well below its 0.25% expense ratio.

DEVELOPED-MARKETS INTERNATIONAL ETFs

After moving from global to broad international, the next step is parsing the international ETF world into developed markets. While the definition of a developed markets varies among index providers, some common traits exist. The international countries in the developed markets are large, established countries with liquid markets, stable governments, reliable legal systems and solid banking structures. Also, the GDP per capita is often a factor with US$20,000 as the benchmark. For example, MSCI lists 23 nations as developed markets, as we see in Table 18.18.

MSCI is also considering adding South Korea and Israel to the list of developed markets. Currently, both are categorised as emerging economies.

Since the developed markets are considered more stable, the largest percentage of foreign ETFs fall in this category. For this chapter, the broad developed international ETFs will be explored in depth. The other ETFs based on the developed markets will be discussed at the end, where the specialised, sector and country ETFs are discussed.

iShares MSCI EAFE Index Fund (EFA)

This is the largest developed-market ETF by assets under management with over US$41 billion. Like many ETFs, iShares benefited by being the first to market with its EFA product. It was launched in August 2001, which gives it five years of asset gathering and name recognition before its closest competitor arrived on the scene.

This ETF tracks the MSCI Europe, Australia and Far East (EAFE) index. This is a market-cap-weighted index composed to cover 85% of the total market capitalisation of the international developed markets. This fund has approximately 818 holdings and covers two-thirds of the underlying index holdings of 1,200. This has allowed Barclays to adequately track the MSCI EAFE index. The three-year, five-year and from-inception tracking error is below its annual

Table 18.18 MSCI developed market countries

Europe		Pacific	North America
UK	Italy	Japan	US
France	Netherlands	Hong Kong	Canada
Germany	Norway	Australia	
Austria	Portugal	New Zealand	
Belgium	Spain	Singapore	
Denmark	Sweden		
Finland	Switzerland		
Greece	Ireland		

expense ratio of 0.34%. The iShares EAFE also provides investors with adequate liquidity since more than 11 million shares are traded, on average, each day.

Vanguard Europe Pacific Index (VEA)

This ETF is Vanguard's answer to the iShares EAFE product. As with other Vanguard ETFs, this fund is actually a share class of one of its mutual funds. However, it is not based on the Developed Markets index fund, as many investors assume. The VEA is actually based on Vanguard's Tax Managed International mutual fund.

While both the iShares and Vanguard offerings track the same index, a couple key differences do exist. The Vanguard ETF offers a much lower internal expense ratio compared with the iShares product, 0.12% versus 0.34%, respectively. Also, the VEA holds 1,040 stocks compared with iShares' 808. This should help Vanguard track the underlying index better than the iShares EFA, in theory, although the iShares ETF has done a solid job of minimising tracking error to date.

Since this product was launched only on July 7, 2007, it is difficult to tell how well it will track the MSCI EAFE, but the VEA will probably closely track the index, since it holds 97% of the positions in the MSCI EAFE and has such a low expense ratio. Another reason to expect a small tracking error is that the underlying Vanguard fund of which the VEA is a share class has stayed within 10bp of the MSCI EAFE since its inception in 1999. In fact, it has outperformed the MSCI EAFE in many periods.

Despite its recent release, the VEA has garnered considerable assets in its initial year, almost US$1.4 billion at the time of writing. While still small compared with the iShares EFA, this number is especially impressive considering that the VEA's parent mutual fund has gathered only US$2.5 billion since its inception nine years ago.

SPDR S&P World ex-US ETF

The SPDR S&P World ex-US ETF (GWL) tracks the performance of the S&P/Citigroup BMI World ex-US index, which is a free-float, market-capitalisation-weighted index that measures the investable universe of companies in the developed markets outside the US. The underlying index holds 5,702 stocks, which is much broader than the MSCI EAFE's 1,200. The large percentage of the additional holdings fall in the mid- and small-cap universe. However, the GWL currently only holds 658 positions. This opens the ETF to a possible large tracking error. However, State Street has apparently deployed a solid replication process, since the tracking error is well under the internal expense ratio to date. Of course, the ETF has traded for only a year and a half. As this ETF gathers more assets, the holdings should increase, which should improve the tracking error further.

Another distinction between the SPDR and the MSCI EAFE-based ETFs is the presence of Canada. Canada comprises just over 8% of the S&P/Citigroup BMI World ex-US index. The MSCI EAFE does not hold companies from any North American countries. So, if investors are looking to capture the entire international developed markets outside the US, the SPDR products could be appropriate.

Powershares FTSE RAFI Developed Markets ex-US Portfolio

The Powershares FTSE RAFI Developed Markets ex-US Portfolio (PXF) is Powershares' answer to the broad-based, international, developed ETF. Rather than a market-cap-weighted ETF, Powershares is a fundamentally weighted product using the methodology described earlier. This particular product invests in the 1,000 equities with the highest fundamental strength based on book value, income, sales and dividends. Like the GWL, the PXF invests in all developed countries outside the US, which includes Canada. It holds a 4.4% weighting in Canadian corporations.

Compared with its market-cap-weighted competitors, the fundamentally weighted PXF has a heavy value tilt. Almost 60% of its holdings meet the standard definition of value, and its P/E and P/B is 20% below the market-cap-weighted offerings in the developed international space. Financial companies, which usually fall in the value camp, make up 32% of this Powershares ETF as compared with 24% for the other ETFs described so far.

Another glaring difference from the other internationally developed ETFs is its internal expense ratio of 0.75%. This is more than twice as high as the SPDR S&P World ex-US ETF, the costliest ETF of the market-cap-weighted ETFs, and six times higher than the Vanguard Europe Pacific ETF.

While value typically outperforms blended and growth funds over time, which bodes well for this Powershares product, investors need to determine whether the value premium is worth the additional cost.

WisdomTree DEFA Fund

The WisdomTree DEFA fund (DWM) is another fundamentally weighted ETF. The DWM tracks the performance of dividend-paying stocks in the industrialised world, excluding the US and Canada. The underlying index weighs the 2,443 stocks it follows by the dividend yield. While the DEFA index tracks 2,443 stocks, the actual ETF holds only 543, making it the least diversified of all the international developed ETFs. The DWM also holds companies from all market capitalisations. Currently, the fund contains 78% of large-cap, 15% mid-cap, and 7% small-cap stocks.

Like its fundamentally weighted competitor, the WisdomTree DEFA Fund has a heavy value bias with a low P/E, 11.4, and P/B value, 1.8. DEFA also has a high reliance on financial stocks, over 30%, like the Powershares FTSE RAFI ETF. Investors can acquire this value tilt with the DEFA holding at a much lower cost than the Powershares product. The WisdomTree DEFA fund has a 0.48% annual expense fee.

The WisdomTree DEFA fund does have some considerable differences from all the other international developed ETFs. It holds a much lower percentage in Japanese stocks and a much higher allocation to Italian, Spanish and Australian stocks. DEFA also contains twice the number of telecommunications and consumer staples stocks than its counterparts. Along with these features, DEFA sports the highest dividend yield, currently approaching 6%. Investors searching for value or higher dividend yields may do well with the WisdomTree DEFA Fund.

EMERGING-MARKETS INTERNATIONAL ETFs

iShares MSCI Emerging Markets Index Fund

Just like its international developed holding, Barclays benefited for being first to market with its iShares MSCI Emerging Markets Index Fund (EEM). EEM is the behemoth of the emerging-markets ETFs with almost US$21 billion under management. The iShares ETF is based on MSCI's Emerging Markets index, which aims to cover 85% of the total market capitalisation of the publicly traded securities in the emerging-markets economies. EEM holds 335 of the

Table 18.19 Developed-markets statistics

	Vanguard Europe Pacific Index	SPDR S&P World ex-US ETF	Powershares FTSE RAFI Developed Markets ex-US	iShares MSCI EAFE Index Fund	WisdomTree DEFA Fund
Number of stocks	1,040	658	1,016	818	543
Expense ratio (%)	0.12	0.35	0.75	0.34	0.48
Median market capitalisation	42.8 billion	48 billion	59 billion	58 billion	N/A
Price–earnings ratio	13.1	11.22	10.13	15.44	11.4
Price–book ratio	2	1.72	1.51	2.83	1.8
Trading volume	496,000	5,239	18,200	11,490,000	62,500
Assets under management	1.4 billion	22.5 million	78.1 million	41.7 billion	425 million
Inception date	July 7, 2007	Apr 20, 2007	Jun 25, 2007	Aug 14, 2001	Jun 16, 2006

Table 18.20 Percentage holdings by country

	Vanguard Europe Pacific Index (%)	SPDR S&P World ex-US ETF (%)	Powershares FTSE RAFI Developed Markets ex-US (%)	iShares MSCI EAFE Index Fund (%)	WisdomTree DEFA Fund (%)
Japan	21.10	18.81	18.19	19.93	8.60
UK	21.40	17.67	22.28	21.34	22.40
France	10.30	8.32	11.39	10.68	13.02
Germany	9.10	7.73	10.05	9.11	7.58
Canada	0	8.34	4.40	0	0
Australia	6.30	6.18	4.35	6.36	8.47
Switzerland	6.90	5.99	5.07	7.20	3.60
Italy	4	3.49	4.99	3.87	7.56
Spain	4.20	4.84	3.52	4.74	7.67
Netherlands	2.80	3.07	4.08	3.02	3.91
Hong Kong	2.20	2.08	3.10	2.16	4.74
Finland	1.70	1.99	2.89	1.85	1.79
Singapore	1.20	1.06	2.79	1.15	1.80

785 stocks that comprise the MSCI Emerging Markets index. This seems to be an adequate number as its five-year tracking error is only 23bp, well below the 74bp expense ratio.

Vanguard Emerging Market Stock Index (VWO)

Just as Vanguard created a mirroring ETF in the international developed markets, it has done so at the emerging-markets level as well. Vanguard's Emerging Market ETF is based on the MSCI Emerging

Table 18.21 Top 10 holdings

Vanguard Europe Pacific Index	(%)	SPDR S&P World ex-US ETF	(%)	Powershares FTSE RAFI Developed Markets ex-US	(%)	iShares MSCI EAFE Index Fund	(%)	WisdomTree DEFA Fund	(%)
BP PLC	1.60	BP	1.29	BP PLC	2.01	BP PLC	1.74	HSBC Holdings PLC	1.91
HSBC Holdings PLC	1.60	Total	1.14	HSBC	1.95	Total SA	1.51	Telefonica S.A.	1.90
Nestlé SA	1.50	Vodafone	1.04	ING Groep	1.72	HSBC Holdings PLC	1.45	Banco Santander Central	1.82
Total SA	1.30	Nestlé SA	1	Total SA	1.45	Nestlé SA	1.44	Eni Spa	1.82
Vodafone Group PLC	1.30	HSBC Holdings	0.97	Vodafone Group	1.41	Vodafone Group PLC	1.27	Total SA	1.71
BHP Billiton LTD	1.10	Novartis Ag	0.94	Daimler AG	1.14	Royal Dutch Shell	1.18	BP PLC	1.61
Toyota Motor	1.10	Samsung Electronics	0.92	Royal Dutch Shell	1.10	BHP Billiton LTD	1.13	Vodafone Group PLC	1.48
E.ON AG	1	Royal Dutch Shell	0.91	Toyota Motor	1	E.ON AG	1.03	China Mobile Ltd	1.40
Banco Santander Central	1	Roche Holdings	0.89	Royal Bank Scotland	0.99	Toyota Motor	1.01	Nestlé SA	1.16
Telefonica SA	1	E.ON Ag	0.85	BNP Paribas	0.91	Roche Holding AG	1.01	Deutsche Telekom	1.14

Table 18.22 Percentage holdings by industry

	Vanguard Europe Pacific Index	SPDR S&P World ex-US ETF	Powershares FTSE RAFI Developed Markets ex-US	iShares MSCI EAFE Index Fund	WisdomTree DEFA Fund
Financials	24.77	24.99	32.82	24.77	30.52
Energy	9.25	10.34	9.09	9.25	9.94
Consumer staples	7.96	6.32	6.87	7.96	14.31
Information technology	5.11	6.4	3.6	5.11	0.71
Healthcare	6.51	7.09	3.87	6.51	1.01
Industrials	11.97	13.66	10.3	11.97	7.31
Consumer discretionary	9.91	9.74	12.85	9.91	7.35
Telecommunications	5.6	5.22	6.99	5.6	13.23
Materials	11.8	10.7	7.62	11.8	6.39
Utilities	6.27	5.28	5.99	6.27	8.98

Market index just like the iShares emerging fund. And the competitive advantages that Vanguard maintains in the developed markets also apply to the emerging-markets holdings as well.

The most obvious difference between the two ETFs is the internal expense fee. Vanguard charges 25bp per year, the lowest of any emerging ETF, while the iShares offering costs 74bp annually. Additionally, the Vanguard offering holds 822 positions compared with EEM's 335. This has resulted in a tighter tracking error than with the iShares fund. Vanguard has managed to keep its tracking error to 16bp since the launch of VWO in March 2005. However, the EEM holds a distinct advantage in assets managed and trading volume – two critical factors that affect liquidity.

SPDR S&P Emerging Markets ETF (GMM)

With just over one year under its belt, the SPDR Emerging Markets ETF has garnered almost US$44 million in assets. Compared with the iShares and Vanguard offerings, this is a small amount, but it is solid for the first year. This fund has a stronger value tilt than its market-cap-weighted competitors. This could be due to the replication process by State Street more than the index. Again, the GMM has existed for only a year, but its tracking error should concern potential investors. To date, the fund varied from its bogey by 1.19%, which is well above its 60bp expense ratio. Another pertinent point is that the fund does not include South Korean stocks. State Street considers South Korea to be a developed country.

WisdomTree Emerging Markets High Yielding Equity Fund

The WisdomTree Emerging Markets High Yielding Equity Fund (DEM) is a fundamentally weighted index that invests in companies falling in the top 30% of dividend yield of the WisdomTree High Yielding Equity index. This methodology has allowed the DEM to yield an impressive 5.1%, which more than doubles any of its competitors.

Another interesting feature of this holding is its allocation differences relative to the other emerging-markets ETFs. The DEM holds a healthy allocation to companies in Poland, Turkey and Thailand. Contrary to the other emerging-markets ETFs, its allocation to the more popular emerging countries of Russia, China and India is very low, roughly 2.5%. Also, its largest country allocation is Taiwan, which comprises almost 29% of the fund.

One downside to this ETF is its expense ratio of 0.63%. This is substantially higher than the market-cap-weighted funds. WisdomTree's backtested data shows the fund makes up for its higher cost, but investors need to be wary of backtested data.

Powershares FTSE RAFI Emerging Markets (PHX)

Launched in September 2007, the Powershares Emerging Markets ETF has raked in a respectable US$95 million in assets. Like the other Powershares ETFs based on the RAFI methodology, this fund weights companies based on a four-factor model. This weighting method has resulted in a fund where the top 10 holdings comprise 44% of the fund's allocation. The PHX also has a much lower number of companies in its fund (163). Investors need to feel comfortable with lower diversification compared with the other emerging-markets ETFs. However, the founder of the RAFI methodology, Rob Arnott, believes that the fundamental approach yields more alpha for emerging-markets stocks than any other asset class. With an annual fee of 85bp, investors hope that Arnott is right.

INTERNATIONAL SMALL CAP ETFs

International small cap is the newest addition to the international ETF marketplace. These offerings entered the marketplace approximately

Table 18.23 Emerging-markets statistics

	Vanguard Emerging Markets Stock Index	SPDR S&P Emerging Markets ETF	Powershares FTSE RAFI Emerging Markets	iShares MSCI Emerging Markets Index Fund	WisdomTree Emerging Markets High Yielding Equity Fund
Number of stocks	822	477	163	335	312
Expense ratio (%)	0.25	0.60	0.85	0.74	0.63
Median market capitalisation	18.3 billion	40.8 billion	59 billion	15.64 billion	219 million
Price–earnings ratio	13.7	10.48	10.41	18.01	10.09
Price–book ratio	2.5	1.98	2.71	3.88	1.89
Trading volume	1,950,000	11,700	34,000	16,500,000	62,500
Assets under management	7.1 billion	43.6 million	98.5 million	20.9 billion	425 million
Inception date	Mar 4, 2005	Mar 17, 2007	Sep 27, 2007	April 17, 2003	Jul 7, 2007

Table 18.24 Percentage holdings by country

	Vanguard Emerging Markets Stock Index (%)	SPDR S&P Emerging Markets ETF (%)	Powershares FTSE RAFI Emerging Markets (%)	iShares MSCI Emerging Markets Index Fund (%)	WisdomTree Emerging Markets High Yielding Equity Fund (%)
Brazil	17.60	17.32	14.81	16.40	8.80
China	11.10	16.95	18.65	11.99	1.23
Korea	12.70	0	18.06	11.95	8.20
Russia	11.10	10.29	10.11	10.62	1.21
Taiwan	10.60	10.71	15.56	9.94	28.91
South Africa	6.70	8.87	6.29	7.45	9.26
India	5.80	7.52	3.22	5.56	0.05
Mexico	5	6.63	6.80	5.26	3.10
Israel	2.50	3.17	1.55	3.71	3.57

two years ago. However, the growth in offerings has been explosive. Before these ETFs joined the scene, US investors had little access to this asset class. There were very few mutual funds or separately managed accounts that offered access to international small-cap.

However, the International small cap ETFs require extra attention from potential investors. While many of the global, developed and emerging ETFs contain similar country and top holding profiles, the international small cap ETFs do not. These ETFs have the largest

Table 18.25 Top 10 holdings

Vanguard Emerging Markets Stock Index	(%)	SPDR S&P Emerging Markets ETF	(%)	Powershares FTSE RAFI Emerging Markets	(%)	iShares MSCI Emerging Market Index Fund	(%)	WisdomTree Emerging Markets High Yielding Equity Fund	(%)
OAO Gazprom-Reg	4.10	OAO Gazprom-Reg	4.51	Taiwan Semiconductor	8.59	OAO Gazprom-Reg	4.17	Taiwan Semiconductor	5.06
China Mobile	2.40	Petrol Brasileiros	2.25	PetroChina	8.35	Samsung	3.22	Bank Pekao	2.33
Petroleo Brasileiro	4.10	China Mobile	2.14	POSCO	4.53	Petroleo Brasileiro	3.12	Formosa Petrochemical	2.24
Samsung Electronics	1.60	Petrol Brasileiros Preferred	2.07	OAO Gazprom-Reg	4.38	Taiwan Semiconductor	2.97	Chunghwa Telecom	2.11
America Movil	1.40	America Movil Sab	1.90	Kookmin Bank	4.28	Posco	2.56	Nan Ya Plastic	2.06
LUKOIL Sponsored ADR	1.40	Cia Vale Rio Doce	1.63	Chunghwa Telecom	3.08	Chunghwa Telecom	2.26	CPFL Energia	2.03
Companhia Vale do Rio Doce Preferred	1.30	Taiwan Semicon	1.56	LUKOIL	3	China Mobile	2.15	Inco	1.97
Companhia Vale do Rio Doce	1.10	Cia Vale Rio Doce Preferred	1.43	Korea Electric	2.86	CIA Vale do Rio Doce	2.05	Telefonica O2 Czech Rep	1.92
Sasol Ltd	1.10	Teva Pharma	1.35	Petro Brasileiro	2.63			Grupo Mexico	1.91
		LUKOIL	1.32	Shinhan Financial	2.23			Telekomunikacja Polska	1.84

Table 18.26 Percentage holdings by industry

	Vanguard Emerging Markets Stock Index	SPDR S&P Emerging Markets ETF	Powershares FTSE RAFI Emerging Markets	iShares MSCI Emerging Markets Index Fund	WisdomTree Emerging Markets High Yielding Equity Fund
Financials	20.35	20.62	19	17.52	22.86
Energy	15.25	21.32	25.41	20.79	9.18
Consumer staples	3.45	5.19	2.92	3.11	3.68
Information technology	12.32	9.56	14.78	13.64	11.64
Healthcare	1.59	2.27	0.56	1.68	0.11
Industrials	5.95	6.96	2.36	5.71	6.61
Consumer discretionary	7.71	4.95	0.34	2.95	4.1
Telecommunications	11.12	11.48	16.25	11.89	17.99
Materials	19.85	14.47	13.03	18.15	16.56
Utilities	2.8	3.19	5.26	3.7	7.27

variance in structure, so investors must understand the product's construction before investing. Picking the appropriate international small-cap ETF is not as simple as picking the lowest expense ratio or highest volume. This asset class requires real diligence. But, as stated earlier, this asset class offers the largest diversification benefits to domestic equities, so it may be worth investors' time and effort.

WisdomTree International SmallCap Dividend Fund

The WisdomTree International SmallCap Dividend Fund (DLS) enjoyed the first-to-market advantage in the international small cap arena. Launched in June 2006, this ETF has more than US$470 million in assets under management, which is US$130 million more than its closest competitor.

Like the other WisdomTree funds, this ETF is a fundamentally weighted product. The stocks included in this fund comprise the bottom 25% of the market capitalisation for the WisdomTree DEFA index. The companies are then weighted by dividend yield. The focus on dividends creates a unique offering relative to its competitors. For instance, the DLS currently yields 2.83%, which is more than 100bp greater than the market-cap-weighted funds. This dividend tilt also resulted in a fund with double the exposure to Australian and Singapore corporations. The fund also has a much higher exposure to consumer discretionary stocks – almost 24%.

Its expense ratio of 58bp is competitive to the other international small-cap ETFs, especially considering that most fundamentally weighted ETFs usually carry higher expense ratios than market-cap-weighted funds. The DLS offers investors considerable diversification with over 800 holdings.

Powershares FTSE RAFI Developed Markets ex-US Small–Mid Portfolio

The Powershares FTSE RAFI Developed Markets ex-US Small–Mid Portfolio (PDN) utilises its four-factor fundamental scoring system to the 1,500 stocks that make up the FTSE RAFI Developed Markets ex-US Small–Mid index. Investors must realise that this ETF acts more like a mid-cap fund than a pure small-cap ETF. Sixty-one per cent of the PDN is invested in mid-cap holdings. This Powershares ETF provides exposure to Canadian stocks unlike most of the international small cap ETFs. The current allocation to Canada is just over 7%.

Like the WisdomTree ETF, the PDN offers investors broad diversification with almost 1,500 positions and a higher dividend yield of 2.52%. One area of concern for investors is the low asset base and average trading volume. This is partially due to its short-lived existence (September 2007 inception), but investors should take note before investing in this fund.

iShares EAFE Small Cap Index Fund (SCZ)

Based on the MSCI EAFE Small Cap Index, this iShares fund has gathered a considerable amount of assets in a short period of time – almost US$156 million since December 2007. The impressive beginning could be due to investors' comfort with the MSCI indexes, or investors may be focusing on the 40bp expense ratio, the lowest among the international Small Cap ETFs. Either way, the fund's growth is impressive.

However, it is only 40% of the size of its closest market-cap-weighted offering, the SPDR S&P International Small Cap ETF. The SPDR product had an eight-month head start, but large differences exist in the products, which should play out in the future. The SPDR ETF, which uses the S&P International Small Cap index, includes a healthy dose of Canadian companies as well as a heavier weighting of Japanese stocks. The SPDR fund also underweights firms from the largest European economies of Great Britain, Germany and France compared with the iShares ETF. The iShares Small Cap Fund has a distinct advantage with its expense ratio. It charges 20bp less than the SPDR fund.

iShares FTSE Developed Small Cap ex-North America Index Fund

The FTSE Developed Small Cap ex-North America Index Fund (IFSM) is iShares' second offering in the broad-based international small-cap asset class. Released one month before the EAFE Small Cap Fund, the IFSM has not fared as well as SCZ. It manages approximately US$23 million in assets compared with US$156 million for its iShares partner. While the exact reasons for the variance is unknown, it is probably due more to the marketing of the product than the actual product composition. The two indexes are quite similar as far as the countries and industries targeted are concerned. Certainly, differences exist, but the differences probably do not explain the asset size discrepancy. The IFSM product does have an expense ratio that is 10bp greater, which may contribute to the asset difference. The ETF marketplace has seen many funds close due to poor investor reception. If the asset base for IFSM does not increase, this ETF could face that fate.

SPDR S&P International Small Cap ETF

The SPDR S&P International Small Cap ETF (GWX) was the first market-cap-weighted ETF in the small international category, and its first-to-market advantage is apparent in its asset size. It manages an asset base of over US$343 million, despite an internal expense fee that is one-third higher than its market-cap-weighted competitors. The SPDR offering also holds the fewest positions of any broad-based international small-cap ETF with 492.

Despite these drawbacks, GWX offers investors some differences relative to the other available funds. The S&P index provides exposure to countries not found in its competitors. For instance, Canada comprises almost 12% of the SPDR fund while emerging economies such as China and South Korea hold a small representation.

Also, the managers at State Street seem to be replicating the index well. Since its April 2007 inception, the fund remained within 45bp of the index, which is well below the 60bp expense ratio. This period may be too short to be a meaningful data point, but, if GWX is typical of most ETFs, replication should be easier as assets grow, since the managers can purchase more of the holdings in the underlying index.

FOCUSED INTERNATIONAL EQUITY ETFs

The international equity ETF marketplace offers investors numerous choices beyond the core, broad-based ETFs. Currently, more than 120 international equity funds exist beyond the ETFs just

Table 18.27 International small-cap statistics

	iShares FTSE Developed Small Cap ex-North America Index Fund	SPDR S&P International Small Cap ETF	Powershares FTSE RAFI Developed Markets ex-US Small–Mid	iShares MSCI EAFE Small Cap Index Fund	WisdomTree Intl SmallCap Dividend Fund
Number of stocks	566	492	1,464	618	819
Expense ratio (%)	0.50	0.60	0.75	0.40	0.58
Price–earnings ratio	18.55	12.39	11.96	17.36	10.59
Price–book ratio	3.09	1.38	2.13	2.73	1.13
Trading volume	7,500	35,000	6,800	63,180	45,000
Assets under management	22.5 million	343.4 million	23.5 million	155.4 million	470 million
Inception date	Nov 12, 2007	Apr 20, 2007	Sep 27, 2007	Dec 10, 2007	Jun 6, 2006

Table 18.28 Percentage by country

	iShares FTSE Developed Small Cap ex-North America Index Fund (%)	SPDR S&P International Small Cap ETF (%)	Powershares FTSE RAFI Developed Markets ex-US Small–Mid (%)	iShares MSCI EAFE Small Cap Index Fund (%)	WisdomTree Intl SmallCap Dividend Fund (%)
Japan	16.53	31.20	34.39	25.20	22.63
UK	22.49	11.73	13.21	19.04	19.32
Australia	6.25	8.99	6.89	7.87	16.83
Germany	5.56	3.07	3.60	6.31	3.62
France	6.30	2.92	3.40	4.92	2.88
Switzerland	5.92	1.96	3.62	4.70	0.29
Italy	4.27	2.43	3.22	4.33	5.99
Hong Kong	2.64	2.66	6.80	2.05	2.32
Singapore	2.07	2.51	1.55	2.01	4.18

Table 18.29 Top 10 holdings

iShares FTSE Developed Small Cap ex-North America Index Fund		SPDR S&P International Small Cap ETF		Powershares FTSE RAFI Developed Markets ex-US Small–Mid		iShares MSCI EAFE Small Cap Index Fund		WisdomTree Intl SmallCap Dividend Fund	
PSP Swiss Property	0.56	Nippon Shinyaku Co	0.71	Sirns Group Ltd	0.4	Sagami Railway Co	0.56	Yell Group	0.59
Kureha Corp	0.52	Duvernay Oil Corp	0.68	Agrium Inc	0.29	Conwert Immobilien	0.51	Kungsleden	0.57
Grifols SA	0.47	Crescent Pt. Energy	0.66	Yamaguchi Financial	0.26	Cofinimmo	0.47	Electrocomponents PLC	0.57
Toho Bank	0.47	Haw Par Corp Ltd	0.63	SBM Offshore	0.24	Sparkassen Immobilien	0.44	Bradford & Bingley PLC	0.54
Macquarie Intl Infra Fund	0.44	Rangold Resources	0.58	Stagecoach Group	0.24	Café De Coral Holdings	0.42	David Jones LTD	0.54
Doutour Nichires Holdings	0.43	Hong Leong Finance	0.57	OneSteel Ltd	0.24	PSP Swiss Property	0.38	Orion OYJ	0.52
Amer PLC	0.43	Eldorado Gold Corp New	0.57	Norddeutsche	0.23	Chyoda Corp	0.38	Vector LTD	0.51
KAS Bank	0.43	Nankai Elec Rail	0.53	Kikkoman Corp	0.23	Drax Group PLC	0.36	Jardine Lloyd Thompson	0.46
FL Smidth & Co	0.42	Toyo Suisan Kaisha	0.53	Tullow Oil PLC	0.23	SGL Carbon AG	0.36	Nexity	0.46
Nokian Renkaat	0.42	Kas Bank	0.53	Cobharn PLC	0.22	Inmarsat PLC	0.35	Adelaide Brighton Ltd	0.43

Table 18.30 Percentage holdings by industry

	iShares FTSE Developed Small Cap ex-North America Index Fund	SPDR S&P International Small Cap ETF	Powershares FTSE RAFI Developed Markets ex-US Small–Mid	iShares MSCI EAFE Small Cap Index Fund	WisdomTree Intl SmallCap Dividend Fund
Financials	20.4	16.38	18.3	19.06	18.6
Energy	7.74	8.49	5.05	7.57	1.44
Consumer staples	8.71	4.8	9.24	4.36	6.49
Information technology	5.18	10.37	8.06	7.9	8.11
Healthcare	5.53	6.86	4.04	5.55	3.93
Industrials	27.96	24.44	24.49	24.63	24.4
Consumer discretionary	11.76	17.6	17.75	16.79	23.87
Telecommunications	0.68	0.43	0.78	0.58	0.78
Materials	8.61	9.73	10.73	9.85	9.25
Utilities	2.09	0.91	1.55	2.41	2.37

described. These ETFs are generally focused on specific industries, countries or speciality indexes.

Industry-based ETFs are ideal for investors hoping to add alpha to a portfolio by exploiting industry trends or undervalued sectors. Investors have a choice of more than 34 international ETFs focused on various industries. Many of these ETFs are based on the Global Industry Classification Standard (GICS) employed by S&P and MSCI. Others are specialised and focus on a small niche. Three popular providers of these boutique ETFs are Claymore, Market Vectors and HealthShares. Claymore offers investors unique offerings such as its SWM Canadian Energy Income Fund and S&P Global Water ETF. Market Vectors provides investors with the opportunity to invest in the alternative energy, nuclear energy, agribusiness, gold mining and environmental services industries, while HealthShares focuses on narrow segments of the medical field. Investors looking to access a particular sector in the international market need to carefully examine the fund holdings. Many of these industry ETFs are global funds and hold a large allocation to US companies.

For investors seeking exposure to a particular country or region, a plethora of options are available. At present, more than 65 ETFs exist that focus on individual countries or regions of the world. Barclays alone has created 22 iShares that concentrate on individual

Table 18.31 International industry ETF

Holding	Ticker symbol	Expense ratio (%)	Holding	Ticker symbol	Expense ratio (%)
HealthShares European Drugs	HRJ	0.75	PowerShares International Listed Private Equity	PFP	0.75
iShares S&P Global Consumer Discretionary	RXI	0.48	PowerShares Global Energy	PBD	0.75
iShares S&P Global Consumer Staples	KXI	0.48	PowerShares Global Water Portfolio	PIO	0.75
iShares S&P Global Energy	IXC	0.48	WisdomTree International Basic Materials	DBN	0.58
iShares S&P Global Financials	IXG	0.48	SPDR FTSE/Macquarie Global Infrastructure 100	GII	0.60
iShares S&P Global Healthcare	IXJ	0.48	WisdomTree International Communications	DGG	0.58
iShares S&P Global Industrials	EXI	0.48	WisdomTree International Consumer Cyclical	DPC	0.58
iShares S&P Global Materials	MXI	0.48	WisdomTree International Consumer Non-Cyclical	DPC	0.58
iShares S&P Global Technology	IXN	0.48	WisdomTree International Energy	DKA	0.58
iShares S&P Global Telecommunications	IXP	0.48	WisdomTree International Financial	DRF	0.58
iShares S&P Global Utilities	JXI	0.48	WisdomTree International Healthcare	DBR	0.58
Market Vectors Global Alternative Energy	GEX	0.65	WisdomTree International Industrial	DDI	0.58
Market Vectors Agribusiness	MOO	0.65	WisdomTree International Technology	DBT	0.58
Market Vectors Gold Miners	GDX	0.55	WisdomTree International Utilities	DBU	0.58
Market Vectors Environmental Services	EVX	0.55	Claymore Clear Global Exchanges, Brokers, Asset Managers	EXB	0.65
Market Vectors Nuclear Energy	NLR	0.65	Claymore SWM Canadian Energy Income	ENY	0.65
Market Vectors Steel	SLX	0.55	Claymore S&P Global Water	CGW	0.65

Table 18.32 Country/regional ETF

Holding	Ticker symbol	Expense ratio (%)	Holding	Ticker symbol	Expense ratio (%)
iShares MSCI EMU	EZU	0.54	PowerShares BLDRs Europe 100 ADR	ADRU	0.30
iShares MSCI Pacific ex-Japan	EPP	0.50	PowerShares BLDRs Asia 50 ADR	ADRA	0.30
iShares S&P Asia 50	AIA	0.50	PowerShares Dynamic Asia 50 ADR	PUA	0.80
iShares S&P Europe 350	IEV	0.60	PowerShares Dynamic Europe	PEH	0.75
iShares S&P Latin America 40	ILF	0.50	PowerShares FTSE RAFI Asia Pacific ex-Japan	PAF	0.80
iShares MSCI Australia	EWA	0.59	PowerShares FTSE RAFI Europe	PEH	0.75
iShares MSCI Austria	EWO	0.54	PowerShares FTSE RAFI Japan	PJO	0.75
iShares MSCI Belgium	EWK	0.54	PowerShares FTSE RAFI Asia Pacific ex-Japan Small–Mid	PDQ	0.75
iShares MSCI Canada	EWC	0.59	PowerShares FTSE RAFI Europe Small–Mid	PWD	0.75
iShares MSCI Chile	ECH	0.74	SPDR Russell/Nomura Prime Japan	JPP	0.50
iShares MSCI France	EWQ	0.54	SPDR Russell/Nomura Small Cap Japan	JSC	0.55
iShares MSCI Germany	EWG	0.54	SPDR S&P BRIC 40	BIK	0.40
iShares MSCI Hong Kong	EWH	0.59	SPDR S&P Emerging Latin America	GML	0.60
iShares MSCI Italy	EWI	0.54	SPDR S&P Emerging Middle East & Africa	GAF	0.60
iShares MSCI Japan	EWJ	0.59	SPDR S&P Emerging Europe	GUR	0.60
iShares MSCI Netherlands	EWN	0.54	SPDR S&P Emerging Asia Pacific	GMF	0.60
iShares MSCI Singapore	EWS	0.59	Vanguard MSCI European	VGK	0.18
iShares MSCI Spain	EWP	0.54	Vanguard MSCI Pacific	VPL	0.18
iShares MSCI Sweden	EWD	0.54	WisdomTree Europe Total Dividend	DEB	0.48
iShares MSCI Switzerland	EWL	0.54	WisdomTree Europe High Yielding Equity	DEW	0.58
iShares MSCI United Kingdom	EWU	0.54	WisdomTree Europe Small Cap Dividend	DFE	0.58
iShares FTSE/HINHUA China 25	FXI	0.74	WisdomTree Japan Total Dividend	DXJ	0.48
iShares MSCI BRIC	BKF	0.75	WisdomTree Japan High Yielding Equity	DNL	0.58
iShares MSCI Brazil	EWZ	0.74	WisdomTree Japan Small Cap Dividend	DFJ	0.58
iShares MSCI Malaysia	EWM	0.59	WisdomTree Pacific ex-Japan Total Dividend	DND	0.48
iShares MSCI Mexico	EWW	0.59	WisdomTree Pacific ex-Japan High Yielding	DNH	0.58
iShares MSCI South Africa	EZA	0.74	Claymore/AlphaShares China Small Cap Index	HAO	0.70
iShares MSCI South Korea	EWY	0.74	Claymore BNY BRIC	EEB	0.60
iShares MSCI Taiwan	EWT	0.74	First Trust ISE Chindia	FNI	0.60
Russia ETF	RSX	0.69			

countries in the developed and emerging markets. One regional tactic garnering considerable assets and ETF attention is investing in the BRIC nations – Brazil, Russia, India and China. Currently, 12 ETFs exist that focus on these four emerging economies. Claymore has even developed an ETF for investors who want a concentrated country position but are uncertain of which country to invest. The Claymore/Zacks Country Rotation ETF bases its fund on Zacks' proprietary country selection process.

Along with industry, country and regional access, investors have access to other speciality international ETFs. Through international ETFs, investors can access real estate, bonds, currency plays and narrower indexes.

Conducting extensive research on the international equity ETFs is essential for investors. Hopefully, this chapter provided ideas as to what vehicles to research as well as the benefits of incorporating international equity ETFs into a portfolio.

REFERENCES

Brandhorst, E., 2002, "International Diversification" State Street Global Advisors, July 15, URL: http://web.archive.org/web/20080214103922/http:/www.ssga.com/library/resh/ericbrandhorstinternationaldiversification71502/page.html.

Korn, Donald Jay, 2005, "Leaning Towards Lockstep", *Financial Planning Magazine*, November.

Philips, Christopher B., 2008, "International Equity: Considerations and Recommendations", Vanguard Investment Counseling and Research, p. 5.

19

Building Diversified Global Portfolios with Exchange-Traded Funds

Richard A. Ciuba, Lisa Meyer, John Prestbo

Dow Jones Indexes

In attempting to build an international investment portfolio many will seek help from professional advisers, while a few masochists will go it alone. Execution of a robust international strategy typically occurs through mutual funds, exchange traded funds (ETFs), individual securities or professionally managed separate accounts. Here we will focus on ways you can go about constructing uncomplicated, yet diversified, portfolios using ETFs.

Although we refer to several specific ETFs, we are not recommending any particular funds because we do not know enough about every reader's own finances, risk tolerances or long-term goals. We can, however, do two things for you. First, we will give you some background on how professionals go about building their portfolios. Do not expect hard and fast rules, because there are not any. No two money managers are going to see things the same way or make the same choices. But a familiarity with the basic process they use and the philosophies they espouse can help you build a portfolio that suits your own investment profile. If you are going it alone, knowing a little bit about how the pros think can perhaps help you better define what should and should not be in your portfolio.

Second, we will discuss ways you can set up a basic international asset-allocation plan based on your risk tolerance and your investment horizon. We will illustrate these plans with some strictly hypothetical ETF portfolios. They are not intended for you to copy. Instead, they suggest some ideas about what shape your own portfolio might take, depending on how much time and energy you want to devote to it. We move from a hands-off portfolio,[1] consisting of a few ETFs, to a more complicated portfolio that consists partly of ETFs and partly of exchange-traded notes (ETNs), which bring in some alternative assets classes that are not available in a traditional ETF format. We also will explain ways you can monitor your portfolio and periodically rebalance it, either to meet your changing circumstances or to take advantage of new investing opportunities as they come along.

HOW THE PROS DO IT

Professional money managers, whether domestic or international, invariably have a philosophy of investing and a system to implement it. They may be growth managers or value managers, market timers, momentum players, or money-flow investors. They may do their research from the top down or the bottom up. They may confine themselves to small capitalisation stocks or large caps, developed markets or emerging. They almost always use screens to identify stocks they may want to own, but they may hold a stock anywhere from a few hours to several years. They all have some method for determining when to sell.

The philosophies and systems that professionals use have two functions. The first and more obvious one is to organise what might otherwise become a chaotic process. We have watched amateur investors drive themselves bonkers chasing the latest rumour or hot stock or even the best-performing mutual fund of the past month, completely ignoring its lousy long-term performance or basic fundamentals. Another reason the pros set up elaborate guidelines and mechanisms is to have something to sell the novice investor looking for help. By explaining to you in sometimes arcane terminology how their systems work and how successful they have been (or are going to be!), money managers can persuade you into thinking that you just cannot manage all this financial stuff yourself. Never mind that many managers wind up using the same mumbo-jumbo to explain why they failed to meet the performance of an unmanaged, low-cost index. It is just a matter of time, they reassure you, until their system proves its worth.

We think that virtually anyone with some interest and who is willing to dedicate the time to pursue an investment programme on their own can use a mix of ETFs to set up a very respectable long-term international portfolio. You will not have the resources to devote to your portfolio that the professionals employ. But, if you know something about how they operate, you can adapt the techniques that work for you and leave behind much of the scrambling that comes from managing multimillion-dollar portfolios and having your performance measured against other managers every three months.

VALUE, GROWTH OR NEITHER?

Growth and value are probably the two most fundamental investing philosophies. Essentially, a value manager looks for stocks that are selling at less than the intrinsic value of the company. He or she buys in the hope that other investors will eventually discover this price discrepancy and bid up the stock to or even beyond that intrinsic value. Growth managers, on the other hand, look for companies that are growing considerably faster than the economy in which they operate. They are willing to pay a premium price to climb aboard that fast train and ride it until it begins to slow. In both cases, of course, the investor is assuming that they know something that other investors do not yet know, and that the stock is cheaper than it should be and will be. Each camp spends considerable time boasting about the success of its system and dissecting the flaws in the other's method.

International investors who pursue a value approach to investing operate at some disadvantages compared with their colleagues who stick only to domestic stocks. Value investing at the professional level requires that the investor have a very good feel for what a company is really worth, compared with what the stock price says it is worth. In the US, researchers have access to a substantial amount of very solid data because public companies must disclose tremendous amounts of information about themselves that conform to very detailed accounting standards, and the Securities and Exchange Commission watches over the whole process with a stern eye. But as soon as you leave the US borders those standards may not be as strong. It is surprisingly difficult to get timely information on big foreign companies and quite a bit harder to find out much about small companies in emerging markets, although the Internet has advanced this process in recent years. So, determining what a foreign company is really worth becomes a far more speculative undertaking for the international investor.

The international growth investor faces some of the same problems that confront the value investor. The "growth" that these managers are buying is growth in earnings. The manager must properly investigate foreign companies' earnings and also adequately analyse the overall growth in the market or region in which the firms operate – a tedious task for any international growth investor. Thus, building a properly diversified portfolio becomes daunting and not something a typical investor would want to attempt. Additionally, the ability to make quick sell decisions is highly prized due to the volatility of many foreign markets, especially emerging markets. Most growth investors who take their discipline seriously are quick on the trigger. As soon as a company – or even a country – shows signs that its quarter-to-quarter or year-to-year growth is flagging, the stock or market is sold.

ASSET ALLOCATION

Asset allocation is the process of dividing an investment portfolio among stocks, bonds, cash and perhaps real estate. It is not something that every money manager has to worry about. Many, for example, are mandated by their fund or firm to be only in stocks and a bit of cash.

Of those, some are required to be mostly in specific kinds of stocks, such as Asian growth stocks. Still others do nothing but invest in bonds. But, for broad-line money managers who are paid to make virtually all of their clients' investment decisions, the first question is how much of a portfolio should be in each of the various asset classes. Like stocks, both bonds and cash (short-term investments, such as 90-day Treasury bills) are available in various forms outside the US.[2] The most ambitious money managers consider them all as potential homes for the money in their care.

The asset allocation process usually begins with an assessment of a client's long-term goals. Older investors generally look foremost for preservation of capital, recognising that safety necessarily produces more moderate returns; a conservative portfolio would tend to have a large weighting of bonds. Younger or more adventurous investors are willing to sacrifice some of the safety to achieve higher returns; they prefer a high ratio of stocks in a portfolio. A moderate portfolio for middle-ground investors would typically be split about 65% in stocks and 35% in bonds. For those who are willing or eager to take advantage of foreign opportunities, the majority of their portfolio, say about 75%, would be in domestic stocks or bonds while the remainder would be in foreign issues. A more aggressive portfolio might be 80% in stocks and only 20% in bonds; fully half of the stock and bond choices could be outside the US.

Once a client's risk tolerance has been taken into account, the process begins to determine which regions of the world outside the US will be likeliest to offer the best choices. For stocks, the choices will depend heavily on whether the manager has a growth or value orientation to stock investing, as we have discussed. For bonds, though, things change dramatically. Since bonds are inherently a safety vehicle for many investors, the first criterion is to choose countries with low credit risk, which would tend to exclude most emerging markets. Indeed, the field for conservative bond investments generally is confined to Japan and the major nations of Europe. Most money managers tend to stick to sovereign or government debt issues, although some will use highly rated corporate bonds. Research can produce lists of which countries are experiencing slower growth and expect declining rates of inflation (and consequently rising bond prices) and which countries have accelerating economic growth and therefore can be expected to encounter rising inflation, higher interest and lower bond prices. Execution of any allocation decision containing foreign bonds, however, can be somewhat difficult; currently the field of ETFs that contain foreign fixed-income securities is somewhat limited.

For more aggressive accounts, money managers will sometimes take additional risks with the bond portions of portfolios as well as the stock portions. That typically involves buying government debt issued by nations that are less than AAA credit risks. While the yields on such bonds are higher, so is the price volatility. A correct bet can produce an admirable yield, coupled over time with a large capital gain. A wrong bet of course produces just the opposite.

Hovering over all these decisions are currency concerns. All other things being equal, higher interest rates tend to produce a stronger currency. But, since things are never equal, many money managers with conservative clients tend to hedge at least part of their currency exposures. Aggressive managers are more eclectic, some avoiding the additional costs of hedging as a drag on performance, while others hedge modestly.

TAKE IT FROM THE TOP

Once they have defined what kind of stock investor they are – growth or value – many money managers begin the process of assembling the stock portions of their portfolios by doing "top-down" research. For the international money manager, this means identifying the regions or countries of the world that have the macroeconomic environments suitable to the kinds of companies and stocks that dovetail with their particular investment philosophy. For the value manager, that means identifying countries where markets have fallen because the economy is weak, there are political problems, or something else is undermining investor confidence. Growth managers, on the other hand, are looking for countries or regions where economic growth is accelerating. That is where they expect to find companies profiting from that growth by increasing market share or providing new products or services.

FROM THE BOTTOM UP

After top-down research has identified the countries or regions in which a money manager wants to shop, the really hard part begins: "Bottom-up" research basically tries to identify the specific stocks that will go into the portfolio. This is the point at which many professionals use "screens" and "filters" to weed out companies that clearly do not fit the manager's philosophy. Various criteria are used. Value managers might, for instance, ask their computer to identify every company on a given stock exchange that has a price-to-earnings ratio of 10 or less. If they want to be sure the stocks they buy are liquid enough that they can get in and out of them easily, they might then ask the computer to eliminate those low P/E stocks that were not traded every day for the past year. Growth investors' criteria will obviously be different. They might seek out small companies that have posted 35% or better earnings gains for the past two years.

Once the screens have produced fairly narrow lists of possible investment candidates, the fundamental analysis begins. Each company is assessed individually, its performance compared with industry averages and other specific companies in the same or similar businesses. After all, a company's low P/E might be entirely justified because its management is poor, or it might be a market overreaction to a temporary setback.

Companies that once again survive the weeding-out process now receive close scrutiny. Analysts attempt to project earnings and dividend growth (when appropriate) out three to five years using forecasting models that range from the ultra-simplistic (simply graphing a line through the past two years' earnings and extending the line another three years) to complex statistical models that demand computer power. Once the earnings have been forecast, the manager turns to determining what investors are likely to pay to own the company that produces the earnings. The key to projecting stock prices is to remember that it is not what you would be willing to pay that matters: it is what somebody else is willing to pay. Companies that have been identified as selling at lower prices than they are worth now and will be worth in the future enter the final cut, where only the cheapest are added to portfolios. Understand, though, that "cheap" is a very relative concept. Aggressive growth managers will pay many times more than value managers for a stock that they like. Yet to these growth managers the stock is still "cheap" because they figure somebody else will pay them considerably more for it later than they are paying for it now. Under different circumstances – such as an ageing bull market in which investors have bid up stock prices far beyond what the companies or the whole economy can deliver – this would be the "greater fool" theory: it does not matter what I pay for a stock, because a bigger fool will come along and buy the shares at an even higher price. The spectacular run-up in Chinese shares, which ended in October 2007, provides a recent real-world example of this theory.

INCORPORATING MOMENTUM

Momentum is nothing more than a measure of how fast a market or stock is rising or falling, incorporating both price levels and trading volumes. While few money managers admit to using it exclusively, many at least give it a nod. At its best, momentum analysis helps an investor choose between two otherwise equally desirable markets. The one that is rising faster, by whatever measures the investor takes into account, will be chosen over the one where conditions are somewhat more sedate. It is tricky to incorporate momentum in an international strategy because there is often insufficient historical data, especially in emerging markets, to judge previous market trends in search of insight into current conditions. However, considering that most ETFs are passively based on published indexes, you will typically find that historical index data is easily obtained and can be substituted historically for trading data on ETFs that have recently been issued. At its worst, momentum investing is considered by some a lemming-like behaviour and thus is not recommended for any but the most agile speculators.

GETTING OUT OF WHAT YOU ARE INTO

Professional money managers like to talk about their sophisticated and very successful methods of choosing stocks to buy. You do not hear nearly as much about how they determine what and when to sell. Yet getting out of a stock or a market is almost as important to a manager's overall performance as getting in. Of course, knowing when to sell is more critical for a money manager whose performance is generally subjected to scrutiny every quarter, than it is to a long-term investor with a five- to ten-year horizon. Even though the sample ETF portfolios discussed below include rebalancing techniques, it is worthwhile for every investor to think about when it is time to sell.

One commonly cited rule is to sell a stock only when there is something better to buy. We think that is too simplistic. The most sensible money managers set targets that, once hit, trigger the decision to sell, or at least to re-evaluate whether the stock or fund still has the characteristics that made it attractive in the first place. Growth managers tend to do more buying and selling overall than do value managers. Growth portfolios often turn over entirely in the course of a year, while some value managers hold their stocks patiently for three or more years. The difference is that the growth managers are looking for spectacular rates of growth that, if they continued for long, would turn some tiny company into the equivalent of Google in a matter of a few years. Obviously, high rates of growth cannot continue for ever, or even for very long. At the first sign of a slowdown, the alert growth manager bails out of a stock.

Value managers, on the other hand, think they have identified a value that no one else has seen. They are willing to wait until that value becomes apparent to other investors. In the end, the stock is sold when some preordained event occurs: growth slows, or others recognise the value that you saw earlier. Just remember that every purchase or sale of a stock or ETF costs money. Transaction costs can become a substantial burden to any portfolio with high turnover.

BUILDING YOUR OWN INTERNATIONAL PORTFOLIO

Now it is your turn to do some work. Your own international investments should be a reflection of your risk tolerance, your time horizon and your ability and willingness to monitor and adjust your investments. Over time you will have to make occasional changes in your stock, bond, domestic and international allocations as your time horizon or risk profile changes.

There are some basic points to keep in mind as you decide how much of your money you want to invest internationally and where to put it. Especially important is the concept of risk. The risk you are willing to take with your investments has to be matched to an appropriate period of time. If you will need US$25,000 six months from now for a down payment on a new house or for your child's first year in college, do not invest that money in stocks. You want it somewhere safe, such as a bank savings account. You want to minimise the risk that you will not have that money when you need it.

On the other hand, if you are laying away US$25,000 as part of a retirement plan that you might not activate for 20 years, you most decidedly do not want that money in a bank savings account. Sure, the US$25,000 plus a little interest will be there when you need it 20 years from now. But during that period there will almost certainly be some years in which inflation runs higher than the interest you are earning on that money in a basic savings account. It is entirely possible that 20 years hence you will have US$35,000 in the savings account, but it will be worth only US$20,000 after adjusting for inflation. Your seemingly risk-free investment has wound up losing 20% of its value!

THE ASSET-ALLOCATION DECISION

You should treat an international investment portfolio as part of an overall plan, not as some separate facet of your investing life. You will almost certainly have established a domestic portfolio of some sort, whether something as simple as a savings account and a mutual fund or two, or a much more complex mixture of individual stocks and bonds you have picked after substantial research. Your international portfolio will become part of that existing investment programme. Again, we do not know enough about any individual's finances, existing security holdings, risk tolerances or long-term goals. If we did, we, like many other investment professionals, would most likely use modern portfolio theory (MPT) to create a portfolio blended with existing security holdings and new potential additions. The MPT method blends portfolios of non-correlated securities (using historical or projected risk and performance return data) in an attempt to maximise overall projected portfolio return while minimising overall portfolio risk. Various portfolio blends are plotted along an "efficient frontier" curve and an investor then selects a portfolio along the curve that best suits their individual tolerance for risk or desire for return. When adding or eliminating securities from a blended portfolio using the MPT method, the objective is to bring additional diversification benefits and projected return while reducing overall portfolio risk, with risk being the potential for loss in invested assets.

In any case, the first basic decision you must make is how much money to put to work abroad. Part of the answer will depend on whether you will be reallocating existing investments to your foreign portfolio or will be investing "new" money – that is, funds that were perhaps parked in a savings account or maybe inherited. If you are reallocating domestic investments to build your foreign portfolio, go slowly. Rather than do it all at once, set out to achieve that goal over a period of time, perhaps a number of years. You do not want to be selling things willy-nilly just to raise the money to get to that 40% level instantly. You might use the old technique of dollar-cost averaging to reach your goal. Dollar-cost averaging is a method of investing that requires you to invest a specified amount at specified periods, say US$1,000 every month. By doing this, you will buy more of any given asset when its price is lower and less of it when the price has risen. That is exactly what the ideal investing equation says you should be doing: buying low.

So, what are you selling to raise that cash? Well, the other part of the ideal investment equation dictates that you should sell high. Perhaps the domestic stocks, bonds or funds in your existing portfolio that have experienced the best price gains will be candidates for selling. But, before you sell off the crown jewels of your portfolio, review the entire portfolio carefully. You are almost certain to have made one or two mistakes in previous choices and you might as well admit it, swallow your pride and dump them to allocate the money abroad.

There are numerous ways to figure out how to divide your money between your domestic portfolio and your foreign portfolio. Some investors figure that the US represents some 40% of the world's total market capitalisation,[3] and they set up their portfolios to reflect that. There is at least some logic to that method. But keep in mind though that it might be best in the long run to keep a larger proportion of your portfolio in the currency you have to live with. The counter-argument to this is twofold. If you are in the US and own a house and car or have substantial insurance policies, you already have a very large proportion of your total assets in US dollars; thus, this argument goes, you should skew your investment portfolios more heavily towards non-US dollar assets. Second, once leaving the gold standard, it is viewed by many that the value of the US dollar has depreciated greatly as compared with a basket of foreign currencies.

Additionally, there are those who simply do not like the idea of having much money invested outside the confines of the US border. They are unwilling to put even 10% of their portfolios abroad. Ten percent seems to be the level that most people coming to foreign investing for the first time can be comfortable with, and that is important. If you are not comfortable with your investments, you are going to worry and lose sleep. Nothing is worth that.

STOCKS OR BONDS?

In the US a diversified portfolio often contains at least a smattering of bonds, and that smattering tends to grow to a larger proportion of a portfolio as an investor nears retirement. The objective in shifting money from stocks to bonds, of course, is to take a more conservative posture, relying more heavily on the sure income that flows from bonds and less on the variable returns available from stocks. Unless you have some compelling reason to seek out higher rates of interest income than can be generated through ownership of domestic US bonds – whether Treasury, municipal or corporate – an investor new to international markets generally should avoid foreign bonds and bond funds, at least initially. It is simply impossible to generate the kind of safe income you can earn through US bonds by going abroad, because something will always be slightly out of kilter. In most cases there will be currency risk that you do not have at home. In situations where you minimise currency risk by buying bonds issued by countries whose currencies are tied to the US dollar, there is a higher credit risk; there are no countries whose currency tied to the US dollar that are as creditworthy as the US.

ETFs VERSUS INDIVIDUAL STOCKS

For most of us, ETFs are going to be one of the best ways to begin building a portfolio of foreign securities. First, global and international ETFs offer one-stop, one-decision shopping. If you maintain a brokerage account, discount or full service, you can search any number of ETF-related websites to obtain ETF lists and prospectuses and then dial your broker or enter the ticker to place a trade once your decision has been made.

Second, it is a way for those of us with smaller amounts to invest to achieve the necessary diversification that will make this whole exercise worthwhile. ETFs can let you start with as little as a one-share purchase, although you are not advised to due to commission cost.

Third, owning an ETF, while not worry-free, requires far less time and effort than monitoring the performance of a dozen or more individual foreign stocks while at the same time studying research reports on another two or three dozen for likely replacement candidates. Of course, owning an ETF does require some oversight and thought on your part; it just demands less of you than a portfolio of individual stocks.

THE ROLE OF EMERGING MARKETS

What has transpired over the past few years demonstrates that many emerging markets have the potential, over the long haul, to provide superior growth rates and better market returns than the big industrialised nations. The spectacular returns that the Brazil, Russia, India and China (BRIC) markets had enjoyed in 2005, 2006 and 2007 attracted millions of investors.[4] We want to enjoy some of those gains and so should you. However, you must be prepared for the inevitable steep declines that occur in these markets. Those same BRIC markets that did so well produced a negative 56.85% return in the 10 months ended October 31, 2008.

A REBALANCING ACT

With this track record, some novice investors avoid emerging markets altogether. Others permit minimal exposure: typically 10% to 15% of an international portfolio. Some more aggressive investors allocate as much as 40% to 50% of their international portfolios to emerging markets. That percentage may be large enough to produce a healthy kicker in good years, but, in a bad year, it might negate more modest gains elsewhere in portfolio.

Once you have executed a well-diversified portfolio of domestic and foreign securities using ETFs, the work is not over. Various assets are going to perform better than others and that can lead, over a period of time, to a distortion in your carefully constructed asset-allocation plan. For example, let us assume that you want to be a little aggressive with the emerging markets portion of your overall portfolio, putting maybe 40% of your international funds in that category. If you experience two years of spectacular returns from emerging markets, that part of your portfolio could rise to represent 50% or more of your international allocation. That is getting a little dicey by anyone's measure. So you would want to sell enough of your emerging-market ETFs to rebalance that portion of your portfolio back at the 40% level you originally set. It can be psychologically difficult to take money out of such a winning category; but, if you had done so at the end of 2005, 2006 and 2007, for example, you would have saved at least some of your international portfolio from the ensuing correction (depending on where you put it).[5]

Equally difficult, perhaps, is rebalancing a portfolio to add more funds to a losing category. Again we will use emerging markets as our example, since they are likely to be more volatile than other categories. If, conservative soul that you are, you had pegged emerging markets as 10% of your international portfolio and two years of subpar performance brings that category down to the 5% level, it might be time to add some money in that sector. In this hypothetical situation, after two years of bad performance a rally is potentially nearer now than it was before. In any event if the reason for your initial asset allocation has not changed (other than that you have become either elated or frightened by the performance of some category), you may want to stick with your initial decision by periodically rebalancing your portfolio.

A LOOK AT THE PORTFOLIOS

Now we can start to assemble some hypothetical portfolios that will demonstrate the range of possibilities available to any investor. We do not recommend any of these portfolios. They are described here simply to give you an idea of how you can achieve international diversification given your own risk tolerance, skills, interest, time horizon and investable funds. We do not recommend any of the ETFs that we use to illustrate these hypothetical portfolios; they are just illustrations. Circumstances change constantly, and what looks like a perfectly reasonable ETF to own today may be something to be avoided six months from now.

The minimum-maintenance, minimum-cost portfolio

Here is a portfolio that should appeal to those who want to put the maximum amount of their money to work in an investment while paying the minimum amounts possible in fees, commissions and operating costs. The foundation of this low-maintenance, low-cost portfolio is index ETFs. Index funds and index-linked ETFs are designed to mimic the performance of some chosen stock or bond market index. By far the most popular US domestic index funds focus on the Standard & Poor's 500-stock index, a measure of the performance of 500 large-capitalisation stocks. One advantage of broad-based index funds is that they incur fewer trading transaction costs, among other things, and thus typically have much lower-than-average total fund expense ratios. The result: they are cheaper for long-term investors to hold.

For simplicity's sake, assume for planning purposes that your entire portfolio amounts to US$100,000. Knowing that you want a low-cost, low-maintenance portfolio, we will assume that the entire US$100,000 now sits in a Vanguard Total Stock Market ETF (VTI), placed there by your adviser. To diversify this portfolio internationally, you could move US$50,000 of your total account into international ETFs. For example, you might invest in two other Vanguard ETFs: the Europe ETF plus the Pacific ETF in equal parts, in an effort to duplicate the EAFE[6] index. Or, if you prefer a single-ETF option, then the FTSE All-World ex-US ETF could be used. Here is what your low-maintenance, low-cost, well-diversified foreign portfolio would look like:

Vanguard Total Stock Market ETF (VTI)	US$50,000
Vanguard European ETF (VGK)	US$25,000
Vanguard Pacific ETF (VPL)	US$25,000

If you want to be marginally active as an investor, you can take a look, say once a year, at your portfolio and do a basic rebalancing act, taking money out of the best-performing ETF or ETFs and putting it in the worst-performing, so that you always have half your money at work in the domestic ETF and half at work in foreign ETFs.

A slightly jazzier low-cost, low-maintenance approach

Now go back to your basic US$100,000 portfolio and assume that you have been looking for a little extra boost without any extra work or cost. We might construct a portfolio with some exposure to small stocks, such as adding an ETF linked to the Russell 2000 index of US small-cap stocks. This gives you a play on small stocks for those times when they are hot, but you still have the basic safety of a blue-chip index fund. Let us apply the same boost principle to building a low-cost, low-maintenance diversified portfolio that includes emerging-market stocks. Take half your portfolio value and put it to work just as we did in the previous example in international stocks, splitting most of it evenly between Vanguard's European and Pacific ETFs to replicate performance of the EAFE Index, and add a smaller allocation to emerging markets. Now you have most of your world-wide exposure to larger, very liquid stocks, with 20% of your portfolio in smaller (but far from tiny) US stocks and some riskier, but hopefully more rewarding (over the long term), emerging markets. Here is the result:

Vanguard Total Stock Market ETF (VTI)	US$40,000
iShares Russell 2000 ETF (IWM)	US$10,000
Vanguard European ETF (VGK)	US$20,000
Vanguard Pacific ETF (VPL)	US$20,000
Vanguard Emerging Markets ETF (VWO)	US$10,000

There are a number of other US ETF families out there from which you can choose such as SPDR's, WisdomTree, First Trust and Claymore, to name a few. When you go about selecting an ETF, make sure the underlying index to which the ETF is linked is one where you can find readily available data. Although the point of indexing is that you do not have to look every day at the portfolio (as well you should not), you will want to know where to find the index data when you are ready to rebalance.

UPPING THE ANTE: A GLOBAL PORTFOLIO WITH ALTERNATIVES

OK, you want more. To get it, you must do more and pay more. We are still assuming you do not have a lot of time to devote to your portfolio, but to get superior risk-adjusted performance you must study the records of various ETFs and their underlying asset classes and make some decisions about risk versus return. We move up to the next level, at which we begin to tap your own pain in certain areas. You start each day with a stop at the local filling station to spend US$50 to fill your car's petrol tank. From these and other real-world sessions – such as the doubling of the cost of a pizza – you have developed a strong sense about the movement of commodity prices and you want to take advantage of it with a portfolio allocation. Because you are a wise investor, your portfolio already looks like one of those we have constructed earlier: broadly diversified globally. What to do about this commodity play you have in mind?

First, do not cash in all your chips and buy platinum or Robustus coffee futures. That is market timing and in markets that you and most of us do not really know all that much about. Remember that in the long run you will probably do best by remaining well diversified around the globe in a number if asset classes. If you wanted to pull 10% to 20% of your total holdings out of both US and foreign-equity ETFs you could go with one of the broad-based commodity index exchange-traded notes (ETNs). Here is what the modified sample US$100,000 portfolio would like:

Vanguard Total Stock Market ETF (VTI)	US$36,000
iShares Russell 2000 ETF (IWM)	US$9,000
Vanguard European ETF (VGK)	US$18,000
Vanguard Pacific ETF (VPL)	US$18,000
Vanguard Emerging Markets ETF (VWO)	US$9,000
iPath DJAIG Commodity Index ETN (DJP)	US$10,000

You will note that each of the ETFs in the existing portfolio has been reduced by 10% to create a 10% allocation of your total US$100,000 to the iPath DJAIG Commodity ETN.

You do not have to limit yourself to one additional asset class, either. Pretend you have a fondness for international travel, staying in hotels and changing money. You are also smart and know the benefits of additional diversification. So, instead of putting only 10% into a commodity ETF and not making any changes on everything else, you take another 5% or 10% from your ETF portfolio and buy exposure to baskets of foreign currencies and global real estate.

A portfolio like this is not meant to frighten you but rather provide added diversification and superior risk-adjusted returns. Here is the result:

Vanguard Total Stock Market ETF (VTI)	US$34,200
iShares Russell 2000 ETF (IWM)	US$8,550
Vanguard European ETF (VGK)	US$17,100
Vanguard Pacific ETF (VPL)	US$17,100
Vanguard Emerging Markets ETF (VWO)	US$8,550
iPath DJAIG Commodity Index ETN (DJP)	US$9,500
SPDR DJW Global Real Estate (RWO)	US$2,500
DB G10 Currency Harvest Fund (DBV)	US$2,500

Here we have taken 5% from each ETF in the existing portfolio and reallocated 2.5% to each of the two portfolio additions.

Obviously we could go on and on adding allocations to asset classes such as TIPs, infrastructure or others in an attempt to increase portfolio diversification or seek better risk-adjusted returns. With the examples above we did not attempt to review the position weights of these various assets compared with index market weights, or look at historical performance of the combinations, or look at the risk/return profile of these portfolios in an efficient frontier setting. Our goal here was not to display our investing prowess but rather to show how easily you could go about creating an easy-to-implement, diversified, global ETF portfolio. Fortunately, there is currently a wide array of ETFs available in the market that cover most established asset classes, thus giving investors plenty of options to construct any number of portfolio variations. Indeed, the proliferation of products offering exposure to ever finer slices of the capital markets and the array of alternative asset classes now available in ETF form make it possible to create effective portfolios without much work and with complete transparency. We would expect any investor to test and research individual ETFs and portfolio combinations based on their individual circumstances, especially if they intend to be more hands-on or dive into alternative classes.

One last point: be sure to understand what you are paying for, for high management fees can take a bite out of your profits. ETFs are presumed to be low-cost investment vehicles, but the fees on some products linked to more niche and exotic asset classes can be higher than broad market equity ETFs. Also, keep in mind that, when you buy and sell ETF shares, you pay a commission to a broker for each trade. So, if you are purchasing many small US dollar amounts of ETFs, your brokerage commissions could offset any fee savings from investing in ETFs versus traditional index mutual funds.

A well-diversified portfolio is an important part of investing wisely. ETFs can save time and money because the evaluation and monitoring of the markets and components underlying the index is done by the index provider; thus, investors receive the expertise already embedded in the index to which the ETF is linked. In most cases, however, the index providers leave the decisions about the exact combination of the various ETFs or ETNs in a portfolio up to the money managers.

All information in this chapter is provided "as is". Dow Jones & Company Inc and the authors of this chapter do not make any representation regarding the accuracy or completeness of this chapter, the content of which may change without notice, and specifically disclaim liability related to this chapter. Dow Jones & Company Inc does not sponsor, endorse, market or promote investment products based on Dow Jones indexes, and Dow Jones & Company Inc makes no representation regarding the advisability of investing in such products. Dow Jones & Company Inc is not providing investment, tax or other professional advice through the publication of this chapter or through the publication of Dow Jones' indexes or in connection herewith.

The ETFs and ETNs referenced in this chapter are examples provided solely for informational purposes. No representation is being made that any stocks, portfolio, financial instrument, or investment will or is likely to achieve profits or losses similar to those shown or described in this chapter. Actual performance will vary based on many factors, including market conditions and applicable fees and expenses related to actual trading. Past performance is not necessarily indicative of future results and future accuracy and profitable results cannot be guaranteed.

The views expressed in this chapter are the personal opinions of Richard A. Ciuba, Lisa Meyer and John Prestbo, the authors of this chapter, and not the opinions of Dow Jones & Company Inc.

1 The simplest of all portfolios would be a single global market equity index ETF such as the iShares MSCI ACWI (ACWI) ETF or the Vanguard Total World Stock ETF (VT), or more concentrated blue-chip ETFs along the lines of the SPDR DJ Global Titans (DGT) or iShares S&P Global 100 (IOO).

2 SPDR offers a DB Int'l Government Inflation-Protected Bond ETF (WIP) and Barclays has an Int'l Treasury Bond ETF (BWX).

3 As of October 2008 the US market represented an average capitalisation weight of 48.2% within the global market as represented by the Dow Jones Wilshire Global Total Market Index during the period of January 1992 to October 2008.

4 Annual total returns of the Dow Jones BRIC 50 index over 2005, 2006 and 2007 of 58.19%, 62.91% and 55.39% respectively.

5 The Dow Jones World Developed Markets Ex-US Index declined 43.72% in 2008 through October 31, versus declines of 56.85% for the Dow Jones BRIC 50 Index, 49.98% for the DJ World Emerging Markets Index and 32.94% for the DJ Wilshire 5000 US Market Index.

6 EAFE is a market-capitalisation-based index published by MSCI Barra and used by many investors as a representation of foreign-market exposure.

20

Exchange-Traded Funds in the Middle East: Opportunities and Challenges in the GCC Countries

Sulaiman T. Al-Abduljader; Imad A. Moosa

Coast Investment and Development Co, KSC; Monash University

The Gulf Cooperation Council (GCC) region is on its way to becoming an internationally recognised economic bloc with flourishing financial markets.[1] During the period 2002–5, the GCC stock markets recorded the highest returns among stock markets worldwide. With the apparent growth in the region, interest in gaining exposure to the GCC untapped markets has surfaced. Yet unfamiliarity with these markets is a factor that can impede the tendency of foreigners to tap them. Global investors face several problems when investing in the GCC markets, most noticeable is the lack of transparency and barriers to information access. Nonetheless, investors are beginning to find it much easier to gain exposure to these markets via exchange-traded funds (ETFs) and index-related investments. A question then arises as to the current status of ETFs and index-related investment products in the GCC markets.

This chapter investigates the opportunities and challenges of investing in the GCC markets. The chapter starts with an overview of the GCC economy and discusses recent economic, monetary and financial developments. The current regulatory initiatives taken for the purpose of attracting foreign investors are discussed subsequently. The chapter will then discuss the opportunities of investing in the region passively and the potential of ETF growth in the region. Finally, some recommendations and challenges facing GCC countries with respect to ETF development are suggested.

THE GCC ECONOMY

In June 2008, oil prices hit a record high exceeding the US$140-per-barrel threshold. For the past several years, oil prices witnessed a substantial rise, driven by strong global demand (presumably to fuel Chinese and Indian economic growth). Given the limited supply of this precious commodity, the basic law of supply and demand seems to prevail in pushing the price to unprecedented levels. Holding 29% of the world's proven oil reserves and one-fifth of the world's proven gas reserves, it is not surprising that the GCC oil-exporting countries have benefited from the sustained rise in oil prices.

The combined nominal and real GDP of the six GCC countries witnessed growth rates of 16% and 6% in 2006 to reach US$716 billion and US$442 billion, respectively. This tremendous growth was fuelled by the five-fold rise in oil prices since 2002. The main worry for the Gulf economies, however, is resurgent and rising inflation, mainly due to US dollar-pegged exchange rates. GCC oil earnings are denominated in US dollars while the majority of their capital-goods imports are denominated in the euro and other currencies, resulting in higher domestic prices. The weakness of the US dollar is not the only source of inflation, as it has been fuelled by other factors such as rising food prices and wages and strong domestic demand. Figure 20.1 displays the levels of nominal GDP in the six GCC countries, whereas Figure 20.2 shows real GDPs and the corresponding growth rates.

The GCC states' external positions have also benefited from the oil boom, as the majority of their exports are hydrocarbons and related products. Current account surpluses have been substantial, particularly in the larger oil-producing countries. Foreign exchange receipts have been mainly channelled towards boosting foreign reserves, and oil revenue windfalls have provided a significant boost to fiscal performance in the GCC.

The increased robustness of the GCC countries' balance-sheet positions has led to a series of rating upgrades in the past few years. The Standard & Poor's ratings as of January 2007 are presented in Table 20.1. Despite improvement in ratings, there are still a number of challenges facing the GCC. Broadly, these challenges fall under the categories of diversification, inflation and geopolitical risk. In isolation, the effect of such challenges on credit ratings

Figure 20.1 Nominal GDP (US$000)

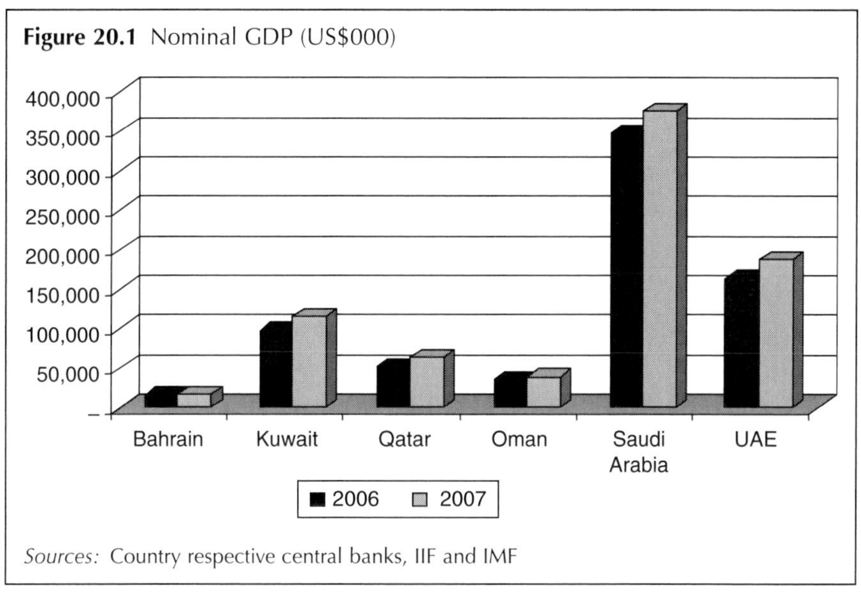

Sources: Country respective central banks, IIF and IMF

Figure 20.2 GCC real GDP (US$ million)

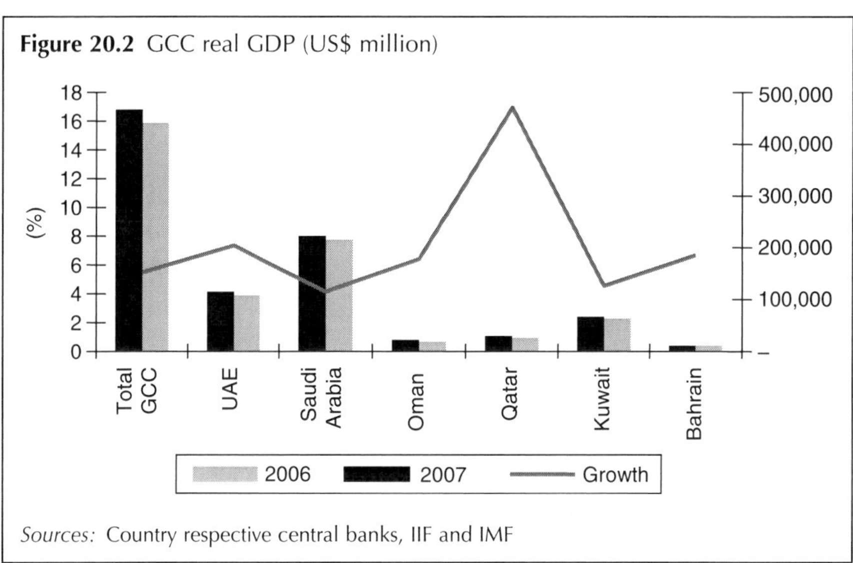

Sources: Country respective central banks, IIF and IMF

is currently dwarfed by the sheer balance-sheet strength of these countries. Taken together, however, these factors represent a potential constraint on further improvements in ratings.

High oil prices clearly have a positive effect on the economic and fiscal performance of the GCC states. Indeed, the current oil boom

Table 20.1 GCC economic snapshot (2008)

GCC countries	Rank by GDP	GDP growth 2006–7 (%)	Currency vs US$	Foreign currency rating
Saudi Arabia	1	8.1	3.75	AA–/Stable/A–1+
UAE	2	15.7	3.67	AA/Stable/A–1+
Kuwait	3	17.2	0.292	AA–/Stable/A–1+
Qatar	4	20.6	3.64	AA–/Stable/A–1+
Oman	5	9.5	0.385	A/Stable/A–1
Bahrain	6	5.5	0.376	A/Stable/A–1

Sources: S&P and national central banks

has strengthened all the key macroeconomic indicators in all six countries. The continuing flow of petrodollars (money earned through the sale of oil) will continue to remain in the limelight and improve the ratings of GCC countries even further.

After the formation of the GCC in 1981, the supreme council drafted an economic agreement that defines the road map for financial integration. The agreement became effective in March 1983. A grand plan was later ratified to establish a common GCC market by 2007, and a monetary union with a common currency by 2010. It is expected that the anticipated common market would give GCC nationals a broader flexibility in movement, residency and employment. In January 2008, the common market was announced and a GCC common electronic market was put in place.

Several initiatives were taken towards the introduction of a common currency. All states pegged their currencies against the US dollar, and as a result Kuwait switched from a basket to a US dollar peg. Then in May 2007, the Central Bank of Kuwait (CBK) announced its abandonment of the US dollar peg back to a basket peg.[2] Kuwait was the second GCC country, after Oman, to abandon the US dollar peg. Consequently, some doubts have surfaced over the success of the anticipated GCC common currency. However, the governor of the CBK announced on numerous occasions that Kuwait was firm in its intent and contribution towards a successful execution (Al-Abduljader 2008).

GCC STOCK MARKETS: AN OVERVIEW

The rise in oil prices since 2002 and efforts to diversify income streams have bestowed upon the GCC countries unprecedented growth. The same trend has been seen in the stock markets, which staged a full recovery after the correction of 2006. In 2007, the aggregate GCC market capitalisation bypassed US$1 trillion (Figure 20.3). The market depth of the GCC is evident. With the exception of Oman, the market capitalisation to GDP ratio of the GCC markets is in excess of 100% (Figure 20.4).

In 2007, the GCC witnessed 33 initial public offerings (IPOs) compared with 23 in 2006. As market sentiment improved in the second half of the year, IPO stocks emerged as the better deals,

Figure 20.3 GCC aggregate stock market data

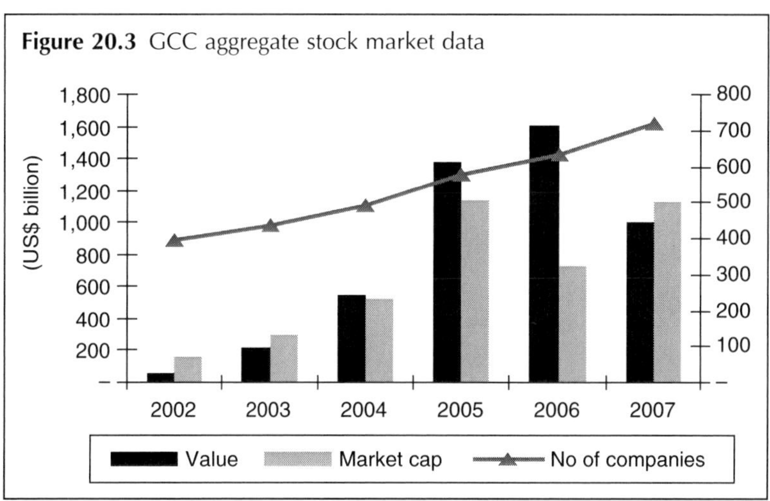

Figure 20.4 GCC market capitalisation/nominal GDP (2007)

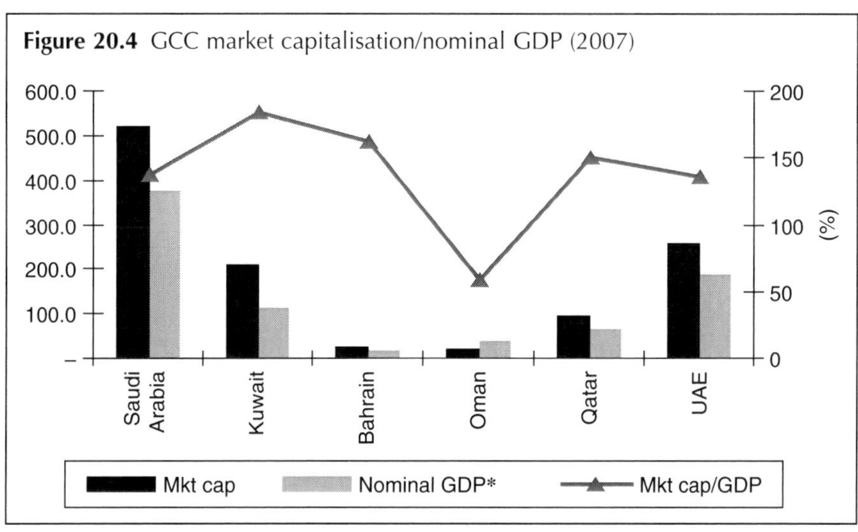

outperforming other stocks. The average IPO size was US$327 million in 2006 and US$319 million in 2007, whereas the total amount raised through IPOs increased 40% in 2007. Going forward, it is estimated that 116 public offerings are likely to be launched by 2010. However, to date, only 42 companies have assigned a share issue manager for the float, while others have announced their intention to carry out studies for further IPOs. Buoyed by rising corporate earnings, stock markets in the GCC countries are moving towards another strong growth in the years to come, despite the setbacks of 2008 amid the credit crunch.

A BRIEF HISTORY OF THE GCC STOCK MARKETS

The GCC markets are viewed as newly established markets. Nonetheless, the Kuwait stock market, which is the oldest in the region, represented the GCC stock market from the 1960s to the early 1990s. Essentially, GCC investors were active traders in the Kuwaiti over-the-counter (OTC) market (what was referred to as the Al-Manakh market). In the 1970s, shareholding companies were established in Kuwait and other Gulf states and were traded in Kuwait's Al-Manakh market. Throughout the past five decades, the GCC stock markets (proxied by Kuwait) have experienced their fair share of turbulence. The most evident is the Al-Manakh crash in 1982, which resulted in approximately US$90 billion in outstanding debt. This section discusses the reasons for the subsequent steps and policies taken by governments towards improving GCC financial markets and setting higher standards.

Kuwait

The government of Kuwait decreed Law No. 27 in October 1962, which aimed at supervising and administering securities trading in Kuwait. The law was positioned to organise the working of shareholding companies. The market picked up momentum in 1973 when the average stock price increased 200%. The growth of stock trading in the 1970s was due to an innovative trading tool (referred to as "forward trading"), which was executed by unregulated brokers and investors. In 1977, the number of traded shares rose 338% compared with the previous year. Interestingly, market capitalisation in 1977 made the Kuwait market one of the 10 largest markets in the world. Exaggerated forward transactions could not be sustained. Consequently, the market declined, triggering government intervention in the form of acquiring stakes in distressed shareholding companies and banning any further IPOs.

Following strict government regulation in the late 1970s, an unregulated OTC market was developed and the speculators moved their attention towards establishing shareholding companies in other GCC countries and trading their shares in the Al-Manakh market. Trading GCC-domiciled companies, combined with the postdated-cheque system, tempted investors to participate.

A postdated-cheque system is a form of payment that dominated the Al-Manakh trade settlement. An investor would write a cheque with a predetermined premium (say 20%) to purchase a set number of shares. The cheque, however, was to be cleared at a future date (say in $T + 1$ months). The acquirer of the shares would then sell the shares for a premium (say 40%) before the cheque was due. This extended web of transactions eventually led to the birth of an uncontrollable and unregulated credit market. Share transactions were executed by unregulated and untrained brokers, and the number of shares traded was estimated to be four times that of the volume of the official stock market.

By mid-1982, some investors started cashing in cheques prior to the agreed date, which led to there being numerous incidents of insufficient funds. The market was exposed, and there was an apparent void in the share settlement process. By August 1982, the market crash was evident and the outstanding debt amounted to KD26.7 billion. The market crash, which was later called the "Al-Manakh Crash", was considered by many to be one of history's most spectacular market crashes.[3]

After the market shock of Al-Manakh, the government took major steps in closing the market down and setting up the first regulated and organised stock exchange in the GCC region. First, the Kuwait Clearing Co (KCC) was established to circumvent a possible liquidity crisis. In 1983, the Ministry of Finance established the Corporation for Settlement of Company Forward Share Transactions to handle settlements and liquidation procedures of outstanding debt. The same year witnessed the establishment of the Kuwait Stock Exchange after an Amiri Decree was issued, aiming at setting a new trading system and an independent body to oversee all operational aspects of stock trading.

Ever since, a stream of ministerial resolutions have been issued, aiming to develop market regulations further, enhance trading transparency and ensure effective clearing and settlement. In the years that followed, the Kuwait Stock Exchange grew to become one of the most developed in the region. In the 1990s and through the beginning of the new millennium, neighbouring GCC stock exchanges were formed.

Saudi Arabia

The first shareholding company established in the Kingdom of Saudi Arabia was in the 1930s, and by 1975 the number of shareholding companies had grown to 14. It was not until 1984 that the market was recognised officially when the Saudi Arabian Monetary Agency (SAMA) was formed and given the authority to regulate and monitor financial securities transactions. In July 2003, the Capital Market Authority (CMA) was established to take over the regulatory and supervision responsibilities of the Kingdom's capital markets activities. Consequently, the Council of Ministers approved the formation of the Saudi Stock Exchange Co (TADAWUL) in accordance with Article 20 of the Capital Market Law of March 2007.

United Arab Emirates

The Abu Dhabi Securities Exchange (ADX) was formed in November 2000 as an independent legal entity. The stated mission of the ADX is "to lead the development of the capital market in the UAE". Since then, the ADX has opened branches across the UAE in Fujeirah, Ras Al-Khaimah, Sharjah and Zayed City.

The Dubai International Financial Exchange (DIFX), perhaps the most recognised regional exchange, was licensed in September 2005. From the outset, the DIFX began to take a pioneering approach towards providing unique trading features to the public. For instance, it is to date the only exchange to allow multi-currency listing as well as listing structured products.

In September 2007, Nasdaq-OMX and Borse Dubai (the parent company) entered into irrevocable undertakings whereby Borse Dubai would become a 19.99% shareholder of Nasdaq. Thus, Nasdaq would purchase all OMX shares owned by Borse Dubai and become a strategic shareholder and a commercial partner with the DIFX. The transaction also involved the DIFX acquiring the 28% stake in the London Stock Exchange from Nasdaq, while Nasdaq would hold 33% of DIFX. The pioneering merger and acquisition (M&A) transaction is expected to drive the DIFX technical capabilities and create value from the combined synergies.

Oman

The Muscat Securities Market was formed in accordance with the Royal Decree (53/88) of June 1988, which aimed towards organisation and supervision of the financial sector. In 1998, the new Capital Market Law, from the Royal Decree (80/98), led to the establishment of the Capital Market Authority (CMA) and an independent managed security monitoring (MSM) exchange. Consequently, various regulations were implemented for the development of the exchange's innovation and operational efficiency.

Bahrain

Following the Legislative Decree No 6/1982 concerning the governing of stockbroking activities, Decree 4/1987 was enacted to establish the Bahrain Stock Exchange in February 1987. Moreover, Resolution No 13/1988 was passed with respect to the internal regulation of the Bahrain Stock Exchange. The law aimed at setting the administrative and trading frameworks for the Exchange.

Qatar

The Doha Securities Market (DSM) started its operations in accordance with Decree (14)-1995 in May 1997. Subsequently, an automated clearing system was introduced in 1998, and the fully electronic trading capabilities became operational in 2002. In May 2005, the Qatar Financial Centre was formed. Later, the Qatar Financial Centre Regulatory Authority (QFCRA) was established as an independent body reporting to the Council of Ministers and aimed at regulating and supervising all aspects of the Qatar financial services industry.

In June 2008, the State of Qatar and NYSE Euronext announced a strategic partnership to transform the Doha Securities Market into an international player in the global stock exchange industry. The announcement stated that the transaction was expected to be finalised by the end of 2008. The transaction involves the acquisition by NYSE Euronext of a 25% stake for US$250 million in the

DSM, and the DSM would therefore capitalise on the technical capabilities of the NYSE Euronext.

DESCRIPTIVE ANALYSIS OF THE GCC STOCK MARKETS

The consensus is that the GCC markets are classified as "emerging" markets. However, various features and trading mechanisms in GCC stock markets differentiate them from other emerging markets and from developed markets. The aggregate market capitalisation in the GCC exceeds US$1 trillion, and the growth prospects remain strong. This section describes the GCC stock markets and provides summary statistics on GCC stock market performance.

Market depth

On July 28, 2008, market capitalisation amounted to US$1.08 trillion with an average price/earnings (P/E) multiple of 15.62 and a dividend yield of 2.5%. The aggregate GCC stock market reflects healthy economic conditions and further growth prospects. The market capitalisation composition shows that Saudi Arabia accounts for 41% while UAE and Kuwait represent 21% and 19%, respectively (Figure 20.5). The number of listed companies in the GCC totalled 626, representing a variety of sectors, mainly financial, telecommunications, real estate and construction materials.

For most stock exchanges, stock ownership was limited to GCC citizens until the beginning of the millennium. Today, foreign ownership is permitted in all GCC markets with the exception of Saudi Arabia. However, foreign ownership has some limitations. For instance,

Figure 20.5 GCC market capitalisation (allocation by country, July 28, 2008)

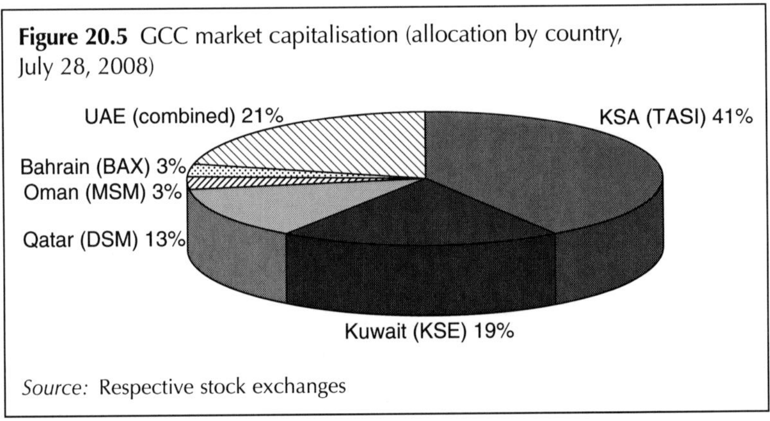

Source: Respective stock exchanges

foreign investors are limited to a 49% stake in listed commercial banks. Some limitations on bank ownership also exist in Qatar and the UAE. Table 20.2 provides an overview of the GCC stock markets.

Market liquidity

Market liquidity remained strong as 2007 recorded a 68% increase with 246 billion shares traded. In value terms, Saudi Arabia accounted for 63% of the trades, followed by Kuwait and the UAE. Table 20.3 provides a summary of statistics across the GCC markets.

Market performance

GCC stock markets have witnessed substantial growth over the past few years. This growth came at a time when global markets suffered unhealthy conditions and the spillover of the subprime crisis in the summer of 2007. Figure 20.6 displays the performance

Table 20.2 Overview of GCC stock markets (July 28, 2008)

Market	Market cap (US$ billion)	No of listed companies	Foreign ownership
Saudi Arabia (TASI)	455	96	No
Kuwait (KSE)	206	200	Yes (limited)
Qatar (DSM)	137	38	Yes (limited)
Oman (MSM)	28	146	Yes
Bahrain (BAX)	31	52	Yes
UAE (combined)	229	94	Yes (limited)
Dubai	104	30	
Abu Dhabi	125	64	

Source: Respective stock exchanges

Table 20.3 GCC trading volume (February 2008)

Market	Volume (million)	% of volume traded	Value traded (US$ million)	% of value traded
Saudi Arabia	5,290	20	57,911	63
Kuwait	7,399	28	12,752	14
UAE	12,873	49	17,117	19
Qatar	196	1	2,820	3
Oman	320	1	667	1
Bahrain	302	1	539	1

Source: Kuwait Financial Centre Research

Figure 20.6 Performance of selected GCC stock markets

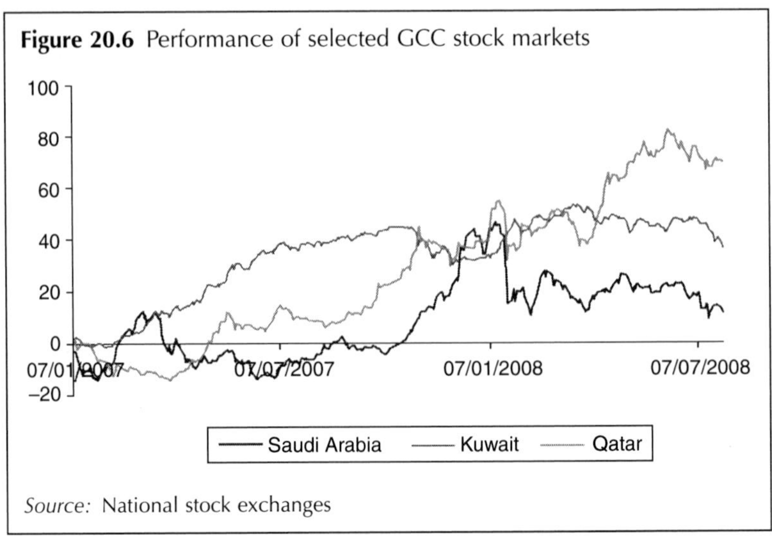

Source: National stock exchanges

of selected GCC markets. Favourable economic conditions seem to reflect positive stock market trends. With record high oil prices, government spending on infrastructure and services seems to enhance corporate profitability and, consequently, stock prices. It is estimated that more than US$1 trillion is expected to be spent on infrastructure projects over the next five–ten years.

GCC markets in optimal portfolios

While portfolio managers strive to achieve optimal portfolios, extensive research is typically directed towards assets with positive performance and a reasonable degree of risk. Emerging markets have been attracting attention in this respect. Indian and Chinese markets witnessed a downturn, while the GCC market continued to post positive returns. During the past two years, the GCC markets maintained their position as a strong candidate for an effective global portfolio diversification. Figure 20.7 shows a plot of stock prices in the GCC markets compared with the S&P 500 and the FTSE 100 indexes. The fact remains, however, that foreign ownership in the GCC markets is typically kept to a minimum. The UAE stock markets are the only ones that have a significant foreign participation.

As foreign investors seem tempted to invest in the GCC stock markets, several problems are encountered. First, most stock markets in the region are relatively new, which means that historical price data

Figure 20.7 US, Europe and GCC market performance

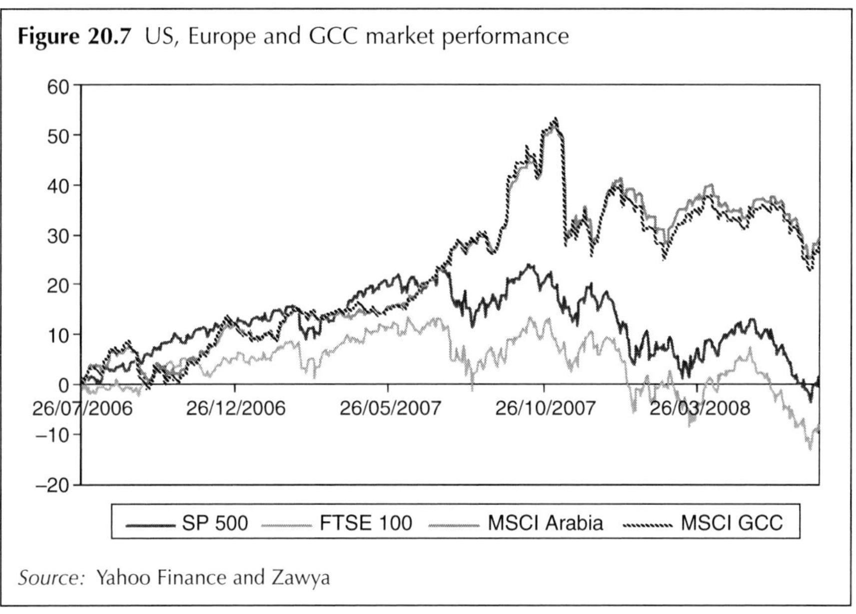

Source: Yahoo Finance and Zawya

is insufficient for proper analysis. Second, global investors could face the problems of the heterogeneity of trading procedures and instruments. Third, global investors are also concerned about market manipulation, lack of transparency, financial disclosure and simple market research. Major investment banks have only recently begun GCC coverage, and this is why global investors are relatively unfamiliar with these markets.

INDEXES AND INDEX-RELATED PRODUCTS IN THE GCC

Since 2006, GCC capital market participants recognised the benefits that indexing provides to the market. In addition to it being a mere benchmarking indicator, much attention has been drawn towards the identification of an adequate benchmark for fund performance analysis and respective compensation schemes. After witnessing the 2006 market decline, investors started to emphasise relative performance of portfolios and traditional mutual funds as opposed to absolute returns. Another aspect is the need for a transparent, independent and passive approach towards market exposure. Individual investors became victims of price manipulation and rumours on virtually non-operational listed companies. The Kuwait stock market was the least affected, given the experience of the 1980s. With the apparent lack of trading knowledge and insightful analysis in the GCC, it is inevitable to see investors in trouble.

The GCC indexes picked up in the early 1990s with limited transparency and almost no consistency across the region. Market indexes were either price-weighted or market-capitalisation-weighted. All official benchmarks did not derive liquid, investable indexes. The sectoral indexes do not follow a standardised set of rules, which makes sector differences evident across the region.

Consequently, two industry-classification benchmarks were developed by the four leading index companies. In 1999, the Global Industry Classification Standard (GICS) was developed by Morgan Stanley Capital International (MSCI) and Standard & Poor's (S&P) to satisfy the financial community's need for a standardised set of industry classification. In 2005, FTSE and Dow Jones joined a partnership to develop what is referred to as the Industry Classification Benchmarks (ICB). Although more than 70% of the world's market capitalisation applies either of the above-mentioned standards to its securities, the Middle East stock markets were left out. In 2006, Coast Investment and Development Co obtained the ICB licence from FTSE and Dow Jones and decomposed the sector indexes in the Kuwait stock market in accordance with the ICB. It is hoped that stock exchanges in other GCC countries will adopt either standard and unify its sector classification across the region.

In the late 1990s, regional investment banks began creating a set of benchmarks as effective trackers and better representatives of the markets. Consequently, open-ended index funds were developed and managed by regional banks to replicate the performance of these trackers. In 2002, momentum picked up and the methodologies used to calculate the indexes were examined in detail. Only recently did investors begin to appreciate the need for independent and transparent index calculations. Asset managers calculating and disseminating country and regional indexes while managing index funds (replicating the index created by the asset manager), provide a clear example of conflict of interest. Therefore, the market called for internationally recognised index companies to come to the rescue to ensure independence and transparency.

Currently, three stock exchanges in the GCC mandate one of the four leading index companies to develop a broad market benchmark. Dow Jones developed the DJ MSM and the DJ Bahrain Index for Oman and Bahrain, respectively. Moreover, FTSE developed the FTSE DIFX UAE20 Index for the Dubai Stock Exchange and FTSE Coast Kuwait 40 to replicate the Kuwait stock market performance. All four index companies have developed various country-based and region-based indexes. MSCI and S&P have also developed country and regional indexes, including Sharia-compliant indexes for the GCC and the Middle East.

It is anticipated that the next decade will witness substantial growth in index-related products. Various regional investment banks have introduced innovative investment products, such as capital-guaranteed funds and leveraged portfolios and certificates linked to regional and country indexes. The development of derivative markets and financial engineering in the region will boost the level of product innovation.

Table 20.4 presents the current stance of derivative markets in the GCC. It is evident that Kuwait is the only stock market with futures and options trading. Nevertheless, both contracts are long-only. In addition to inducing further speculation, the incomplete derivative markets in the GCC causes significant imbalances and limits the ability of hedge funds to indulge in synthetic shorting by applying various long–short strategies. However, opportunities arise as financial markets develop and investors' appetite picks up. The structural development of regional stock exchanges will have a positive impact on index-related products in the region.

ETFs IN THE GCC: OPPORTUNITIES AND CHALLENGES

ETFs are seen as the solution for foreign investors to gain exposure in the region. As the empirical evidence suggests, the value the GCC exposure provides to a global portfolio is an opportunity for

Table 20.4 Derivatives in the GCC

GCC	Futures	Forward	Options	Debt	Margin	Listed funds
KSA	No	No	No	No	Yes	No
UAE	No	No	No	Yes	Yes	Yes
Kuwait	Yes	Yes	Yes	Yes	Yes	Yes
Oman	No	No	No	No	No	No
Qatar	No	No	No	No	No	No
Bahrain	No	No	No	No	No	Yes

investors to enhance their risk/return profiles. Up to June 2008, there were no ETFs replicating the region. In the subsequent two months, four ETFs were launched, of which three were listed in the US markets and one in the London Stock Exchange. The underlying indexes were the Dow Jones, Nasdaq and FTSE. Table 20.5 provides a summary of the recently launched ETFs.

The above-mentioned ETFs were listed in three exchanges and, since the first launch, were able to attract US$85.8 million in assets. The stream of ETFs launched in a relatively short period of time reveals the growing interest of global investors in the GCC markets. Given that all ETFs were listed in the summer, the average volume traded is relatively low. The expense ratios ranged between 65 and 98 basis points. Table 20.6 presents expense ratios, closing prices and volume of the four ETFs.

Analysing the underlying indexes

A brief analysis of the underlying indexes of the recently launched ETFs shows that most of the indexes were recently created. The composition and methodology of the underlying indexes deserve some investigation. Table 20.7 provides a broad description of the underlying indexes of the recently launched ETFs.

It is apparent that three of the existing underlying indexes were launched either simultaneously with the ETF or seven days prior to launch. Only the FTSE-Coast Kuwait 40 had been launched and

Table 20.5 Descriptive statistics of regional ETFs (July 31, 2008)

Exchange-traded fund	Fund ticker	Date of listing	Exchange	ETF manager	AUM (US$)
WisdomTree Middle East Dividend Fund	GULF	30/06/2008	Nasdaq	Wisdom Tree	13,993,940
PowerShares MENA Frontier Countries	PMNA	09/07/2008	Nasdaq	Invesco PowerShares	32,525,000
Gulf States Index ETF	MES	22/07/2008	NYSE	Van Eck Global	7,608,000
Lyxor ETF FTSE Coast Kuwait 40	LKUU	28/07/2008	LSE	Lyxor AM	31,690,000

Source: Bloomberg

Table 20.6 Price, volume and cost of regional ETFs (as of August 15, 2008)

Fund	Total expense ratio (%)	Close price (US$)	Average volume
WisdomTree Middle East Dividend Fund	0.88	23.31	NA
PowerShares MENA Frontier Countries	0.95	23.23	41,140
Gulf States Index ETF	0.98	38.04	NA
Lyxor ETF FTSE Coast Kuwait 40	0.65	48.65	669

Source: Bloomberg/Reuters

Table 20.7 Description of ETF underlying indexes

Fund	Index	No of constituents	Index inception
WisdomTree Middle East Dividend Fund	WisdomTree Middle East Dividend	68	30/06/2008
PowerShares MENA Frontier Countries	Nasdaq OMX MENA Index	66	30/06/2008
Gulf States Index ETF	DJ GCC Titans 40 Index	40	14/07/2008
Lyxor ETF FTSE Coast Kuwait 40	FTSE Coast Kuwait 40 Index	40	26/02/2007

Source: Index providers

calculated for more than a year before the corresponding ETF was listed. This may cause concern for investors, particularly since the market sustains some unique characteristics that might require incorporating them in the index calculation. Perhaps it would be wise to allow indexes to disseminate for some time prior to licensing for ETFs. For one, the index would be able to build a live track record as opposed to statistical backtesting. It is common practice that hypothetical testing imposes the assumption that returns and dividends are reinvested as well as assuming a constant free-float adjustment.

Also, index providers are encouraged to allow pre-licence dissemination to accommodate the region's unique corporate action announcements. In many instances, corporate action announcements require verification of details and dates. An example might be an announcement of a rights offering with an undetermined date. Another concern is allowing index providers to build awareness on free-float adjustment procedures in the region. It is critical to distinguish between long-term holdings and defensive, short-term holdings. The latter have occurred numerously in 2007 when an interrelated group of companies interchanged blocks of shares to realise capital gains.

As for the index methodologies, WisdomTree Middle East is a fundamentally weighted index, whereas the Nasdaq, Dow Jones and FTSE indexes are market-capitalisation-weighted. All indexes take into account free-float, foreign-ownership restrictions and liquidity. The indexes also impose capping on single stocks exceeding a certain threshold. A key concern when defining the ground rules of the index is setting the procedures for liquidity screening. It must be noted that, during periodic constituent reviews, index committees should recognise the observation that newly listed companies tend to be highly traded for the first quarter but do not necessarily continue to be liquid. Another observation is that index committees ought to review the trends of the underlying group of companies to capture artificial or incidental active trades on a certain stock that should be treated as an outlier.

Indexes and ETFs: trading strategies in the GCC

In the world of indexing, much interest is currently drawn towards fundamental and quantitative-based approaches. Devising profitable trading strategies through fundamental indexing requires insightful analysis on the region's trading behaviour and liquidity drivers. First, it is important to test the price–volume asymmetry and investigate the causality effect. Second, examining the role of fundamentalists and technicians should help index providers in constructing profitable rules-driven underlying indexes.

We begin with the price–volume relation. Osbourne (1959) was one of the earlier studies to investigate the price–volume relation. Subsequently, Ying (1966) brought attention to the concept of asymmetry in the relation. Some economists – such as Al-Loughani (1999), Al-Saad (2004), Al-Muraikhi (2005) and Al-Saad and Moosa (2008) – estimated the price–volume relation in GCC stock markets. Al-Muraikhi backtested a trading rule based on the price–volume relation over 11 consecutive weeks and found it to be profitable.

Moosa and Al-Abduljader (2006) and Al-Abduljader (2008) tested asymmetry using cross-sectional data. Al-Abduljader (2008) augmented the price volume model to include company size and other fundamental variables. The augmented asymmetric model can be written as

$$v_{j,t} = \alpha + \beta_j^+ \Delta p_{j,t}^+ + \beta^- \Delta p_{j,t}^- + \gamma c_{j,t} + \delta ep_{j,t} + \phi pe_{j,t} + \lambda pb_{j,t} + \mu_{j,t} \quad \textbf{(20.1)}$$

which includes market capitalisation, earnings per share, price-over-earnings multiple and price-over-book-value multiple. The empirical results show that company size and profitability measures have significant explanatory power in determining trading volume.

Moving into the role of fundamentalists and technicians in the stock market, Frankel and Froot (1990) and Moosa and Korczak (2000) proposed models to differentiate between the roles of fundamentalists and technicians in exchange rate determination. Consequently, Al-Muraikhi (2005) and Al-Abduljader (2008) tested the model on Kuwaiti indexes. The model can be written as

$$\Delta p_t = \gamma_0 + \gamma_1(\overline{p}_{t-1} - p_{t-1}) + \gamma_2 \sum_{i=1}^{\infty} \beta^i \Delta p_{t-i} + \varepsilon_t \quad \textbf{(20.2)}$$

where $\gamma_0 = 0$, $\gamma_1 > 0$ and $\gamma_2 > 0$, $\gamma_1 + \gamma_2 = 1$. The model shows that fundamentalists buy/sell stocks on the basis of deviations from the equilibrium price, $\overline{p}$, whereas technicians trade on the basis of changes in price with respect to trading rules, charting and/or technical indicators. Technicians are represented by a geometrically declining distributed lag of past stock price changes, as proposed by Moosa and Korczak (2000). The empirical results show that both fundamentalists and technicians are, more or less, equally important. Index providers and their corresponding product development departments are urged to set dynamic modelling structures to capture the time-varying weights of both fundamentalists and technicians in the GCC stock price determination.

Benefits of ETFs in the Middle East

Examining the benefits of ETFs in the Middle East can take two approaches. We begin with the global perspective of the benefits of ETFs related to the GCC markets. Much of the interest of growing emerging markets comes in the form of gaining exposure. Therefore, region or country asset allocation is preferred over security selection.

Studies carried out by Solnik (1974), Lessard (1976) and Biger (1979) have demonstrated the benefits of international diversification. The benefits of ETF diversification from a global perspective can be investigated by analysing the effect of the risk/return profile of a global all-equity portfolio. The risk/return profile of a portfolio was originally recognised in the work of Markowitz (1952) on the modern portfolio theory (MPT). Consequently, the portfolio mean return, R_p, can be calculated as

$$R_p = \sum w_i R_i \tag{20.3}$$

where R_i is the return on asset i and w_i is the weight of asset i in the portfolio. The portfolio variance can be calculated as

$$\sigma_p^2 = \sum_i^n \sum_j^n w_i w_j \sigma_i \sigma_j \rho_{ij} \tag{20.4}$$

where σ_p^2 is the portfolio variance and σ_i and σ_j are the standard deviations of assets i and j while w_i and w_j are their respective weights in the portfolio. ρ_{ij} is the correlation coefficient between the two asset returns.

Subsequently, Black and Litterman (1992) extended the work on mean-variance optimisation by introducing a model of strategic asset allocation using reverse optimisation. The model enables portfolio managers to define practical expected returns as opposed to traditional CAPM expected return model that is a function of beta. The model can be written as

$$E[\mathbf{R}] = [(\tau\mathbf{\Sigma})^{-1} + \mathbf{P}'\mathbf{\Omega}^{-1}\mathbf{P}]^{-1}[(\tau\mathbf{\Sigma})^{-1}\mathbf{\Pi} + \mathbf{P}'\mathbf{\Omega}^{-1}\mathbf{Q}] \tag{20.5}$$

where $E[\mathbf{R}]$ is the combined return vector ($N \times 1$), τ is a scalar, $\mathbf{\Sigma}$ is the covariance matrix *($N \times N$)* matrix $\mathbf{P}$ is the view participation matrix *($K \times N$)* matrix that identifies the assets involved in the views, $\mathbf{\Pi}$ is the diagonal covariance matrix of error terms from the expressed views representing uncertainty in each ($K \times K$) matrix, $\mathbf{\Omega}$ is the implied excess returns over the risk-free rate ($N \times 1$ column vector), and $\mathbf{Q}$ is the view vector ($K \times 1$ column vector).

The GCC can be regarded as part of the "emerging markets" asset class along with the BRIC (Brazil, Russia, India and China) markets. To illustrate the benefit that GCC markets add to a global portfolio,

Al-Abduljader (2008) investigated the effect of the risk/return portfolio of a global all-equity portfolio when adding the GCC as a substitute for the Chinese or Indian markets. Over a period of six years, the GCC markets (proxied by Kuwait) are found to enhance the risk/return profile and push the efficient frontier northwest.[4] Figure 20.8 displays the two efficient frontiers.

Concerns about heterogeneity

Global investors are concerned about the heterogeneity of trading rules, different trading hours and time zones, intra-day liquidity of the underlying securities and foreign ownership restrictions. For instance, the Kuwait Stock Exchange imposes a "unit" bracket system in which a predefined number of shares for a given transaction is set for the listed securities traded in the cash market. Consequently, an "odd lot" market (sometimes referred to as a fractions market) is a relatively illiquid market used to trade shares not constituting a complete unit. Saudi Arabia is the only exchange in the GCC that trades on Saturdays and also implements a two-session trading day (the morning session is 10 am–12 pm and the evening session is 4:30 pm–6:30 pm). Almost all GCC markets tend to reduce official trading hours during the month of Ramadan, which varies in exact dates in calendar years.

Figure 20.8 Efficient frontier of global portfolios (January 2001–April 2006)

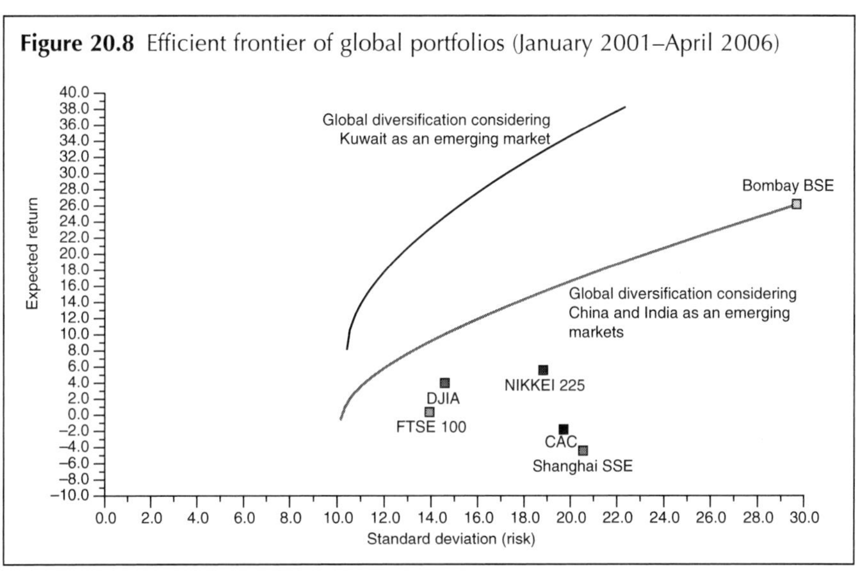

Despite the apparent concerns, ETFs have become an ideal vehicle for global investors who wish to gain exposure without diving into the particularities of trading mechanisms. For one, ETFs provide the performance of the index through full, sample or synthetic replication. Synthetic replication was recently introduced in Europe, demonstrating the lowest tracking error in emerging-market ETFs. Second, while most of the current open-ended mutual funds with GCC specialisation charge anywhere between 100 and 250bp per annum plus incentive fees, ETFs provide investors with a competitive cost structure (the four existing ETFs charge a total expense ratio (TER) between 65 and 95bp). Since the funds are passively managed, no incentive fees are applied. Third, the internationally recognised underlying indexes provide investors with complete transparency and frequent reporting. The constituents are rebalanced periodically and data is typically disseminated to major financial information terminals such as Reuters and Bloomberg. Financial engineers could now provide better pricing on structured products with GCC stocks. Furthermore, market makers and delta-one traders could quote baskets to investors in the secondary market by which intra-day trading would be available to investors in multiple currencies when listed in major stock markets.

Benefits of ETF local diversification

From a local perspective, almost all GCC exchanges expressed interest in importing the ETF trading platforms, allowing ETFs to be listed upon the completion of the regulatory and technical requirements. Interest in the implementation of ETFs in the region is attributable to several current concerns. To start with, the regional stock markets are dominated by retail investors, which create high volatility. Individual investors typically base their trading decisions on either shallow analysis or market rumours. Although market manipulation is usually directed to smaller companies, the trickle effect usually leads to unjustified market behaviour. Various studies, such as Moosa and Al-Abduljader (2006) and Al-Muraikhi (2005), confirmed the presence of asymmetry in some stock markets in the GCC. As a result, ETFs are seen as the solution for untrained individual investors to buy the market or certain sectors without being driven by company-specific news and/or expected stock reactions.

The effect of news on stock prices has been investigated by Moosa and Al-Abduljader (2006). Previously, Fama *et al* (1969) and Waud (1970) studied the effect of news on stock prices by testing the efficient market hypothesis to find out how fast stock prices respond to news. Since it is difficult to identify the news component in the GCC (due to lack of published data) it was extracted using autoregressive moving average (ARMA) models, value-at-risk (VaR) models and the Hodrick-Prescott (HP) filter to test for robustness. The estimated news model has the following specification

$$\begin{aligned} s_t - E_{t-1}s_t &= \alpha_0 + \alpha_1(g_t - E_{t-1}g_t) + \alpha_2(m_t - E_{t-1}m_t) \\ &\quad + \alpha_3(p_t - E_{t-1}p_t) + \alpha_4(r_t - E_{t-1}r_t) \\ &\quad + \alpha_5(i_t - E_{t-1}i_t) + \varepsilon_t \end{aligned} \tag{20.6}$$

where g is government spending, m is the money supply, p is the general price level, r is government revenue, and i is the interest rate. News pertaining to government revenue and the money supply turned out to be statistically significant.

ETFs can also act as the initial framework for other structures that could be provided to the retail market. Having liquid tradable indexes would allow investment managers to present various structures and products such as listed equity derivatives, capital-guarantee notes and quantitative index-linked notes. As the market appreciates the power and the transparency of index-linked products, ETFs will become the underlying basket for such products and act as the preferred vehicle for complex structures. With the current lack of diverse investment options, the ETF market provides flexibility further innovation.

Furthermore, ETFs allow local investors to invest in other regions and asset classes. As an alternative to existing global open-ended mutual funds, ETFs provide low cost, intra-day trading to other markets and asset classes. Investors can trade in local currencies and do not require much analysis on the underlying constituents but rather a view on the aggregate perspective of the market or asset class. Some studies examined diversification benefits within the GCC, as constructing a basket of GCC country indexes was found to reduce risk. Testing for the variance reduction as proposed by Moosa and Al-Deehani (2008), and studies such as Al-Abduljader (2008) found that diversification within the GCC can reduce the portfolio variance by 61%.

Finally, the ETF market in the region will evidently become the catalyst for the institutionalisation of capital markets. Although ETFs have become the tool for active management and seeking alpha, asset managers will be able (through ETFs) to facilitate liquidity and direct investors to internationally screened liquid assets.

Challenges for ETFs in the region

It is imperative that the region's regulatory bodies and stock exchanges comprehend the essence of ETFs and learn from the experience of developed and other emerging stock markets. It is advisable that stock exchanges customise the solution with respect to current market conditions and encourage participants to innovate and diversify the product base.

The ambitious plan for ETFs in the GCC requires some conditions to be modified. Markets such as Kuwait, Abu Dhabi, Bahrain and Oman should expedite the establishment of an independent capital-market authority (CMA). The foreseen entities should be responsible for the regulation and supervision of capital markets' maintenance and improvement. For instance, Kuwait and Bahrain currently delegate their respective central banks and/or stock exchanges to undertake CMA roles.

Moreover, precision in regulations ensures transparency and avoids various controversies that occurred on stock exchanges in the past. Another important aspect of a successful framework is maintaining an efficient process for the purpose of acknowledging and approving (or otherwise) fund applications and prospectuses. The current ambiguity of some regulators in the region makes it difficult for asset managers and investment banks to anticipate responses from regulators, which disrupts the administrative and marketing plans. Such delays could cause losses. The Central Bank of Bahrain, for instance, should be taken as an example of a prompt and transparent regulator with dynamic functions and internationally recognised legal standards. For ETF regulation, the Financial Services Authority (FSA) in the UK sets a good example in terms of efficient processing with defined maximum review periods and responses.

Concluding remarks

This chapter has presented an overview of the GCC stock markets and the potential benefits and challenges of ETFs in the region. As the recent growth of the GCC economies has been reflected in the performance of stock markets, global investors have started to realise the diversification benefits of investing in the region as part of the "emerging markets" allocation. ETFs with a GCC exposure that are listed in major US and European exchanges remove most of the global investors' current concerns and allow investors to tap into country-specific stock markets and various growing sectors within the region. From a local perspective, ETFs listed in the region's stock markets support retail investors and present transparent, broad market and sector products that many have been waiting for.

Despite the current challenges the regulators face, history will inevitably repeat itself as seen in other emerging markets. The fact that the region's investment players are viewed as proactive and innovative in many cases puts comfort in the anticipated growth of ETFs in the region. Strong market fundamentals and predicted economic indicators in the region provide general optimism on future performance. The overall market conditions will drive further innovation and stability in the region.

1 The GCC countries are Saudi Arabia, Kuwait , UAE, Qatar, Oman and Bahrain.

2 Ferreira (2007) estimated the basket to be made up of US dollars 70%, euro 20%, sterling 5% and yen 5%.

3 See, for instance, Al-Sultan (1989), Kindleberger (1996) and Ridesic (1998).

4 Kuwait is used as a proxy for the GCC for several reasons. Kuwait is the largest market after Saudi Arabia and permits foreign stock ownership. The rest of the GCC countries have been either recently established or that their markets are relatively small and illiquid. It is also proven that, historically, Kuwait has acted as the GCC market in the 1980s, when the official and parallel stock markets were trading GCC domiciled companies. Furthermore, it is realised that all recently launched ETFs place the largest weight on the Kuwaiti market. The Dow Jones GCC allocates 52.3%, Nasdaq MENA 17.29% (largest after Egypt), WisdomTree ME 26.52% and FTSE Kuwait is 100% allocation to the Kuwaiti market. The country allocation for Dow Jones, Nasdaq and WisdomTree are as of July 10, 2008; June 30, 2008 and August 15, 2008, respectively.

REFERENCES

Al-Abduljader, S., 2008, "An Empirical Investigation into the Workings of an Emerging Stock Market: The Case of Kuwait", PhD Thesis, La Trobe University.

Al-Loughani, N., 1999, "Analysis of Price–Volume Causal Relation in the Kuwait Stock Market", *Journal of Economic and Administrative Science* 15, pp. 25–47, in Arabic.

Al-Muraikhi, H., 2005, "Speculation in Emerging Financial Markets: The Case of Kuwait Stock and Foreign Exchange Markets", PhD thesis, La Trobe University.

Al-Saad, K., 2004, "Asymmetry in the Price-Volume Relationship: Evidence from the Kuwait Stock Market", *Journal of Accounting and Finance* 3, pp. 53–65.

Al-Saad, K. and Moosa, I., 2008, "Asymmetry in the Price-Volume Relationship: Evidence Based on Individual Company Stocks Traded in an Emerging Stock Market", *Applied Financial Economics Letters* 4, pp. 151–5.

Al-Sultan, F., 1989, "Averting Financial Crisis-Kuwait", United Nations.

Biger, N., 1997, "Exchange Risk Implications of International Portfolio Diversification", *Journal of International Business Studies* 10, pp. 64–74.

Black, F. and Litterman, R., 1992, "Global Portfolio Optimisation", *Financial Analysts Journal* 48, pp. 28–43.

Fama, E. F. *et al*, 1969, "The Adjustment of Stock Prices to New Information", *International Economic Review* 10, pp. 1–21.

Ferreira, P., 2007, "Kuwait", Emerging Markets Research, Société Générale.

Frankel, J. and Froot, K., 1990, "The Rationality of the Foreign Exchange Rate: Chartists, Fundamentalists and Trading in the Foreign Exchange Market", *American Economic Review* 80, pp. 181–5.

Kindleberger, C., 1996, *Manias, Panics and Crashes: A History of Financial Crises* (New York: John Wiley & Sons).

Lessard, D. R., 1976, "World, Country and Industry Relationships in Equity Returns: Implications for Risk Reduction Through International Diversification", *Financial Analysts Journal* 32, pp. 32–8.

Markowitz, H., 1952, "Portfolio Selection", *Journal of Finance* 7, pp. 77–91.

Moosa, I. and Al-Abduljader, S., 2006, "Is the Price-Volume Relationship Asymmetric? Cross Sectional Evidence from an Emerging Stock Market", *Journal of Investment Management and Financial Innovation* 3, pp. 80–90.

Moosa, I. and Al-Deehani, T., 2008, "The Myth of International Diversification", *Economia Internazionale*, forthcoming.

Moosa, I. and Korczak, M., 2000, "Is the Price-Volume Relationship Symmetric in the Futures Markets?", *Journal of Financial Studies* 7, pp. 1–15.

Osbourne, M., 1959, "Brownian Motion in the Stock Market", *Operations Research* 7, pp. 145–73.

Ridesic, S., 1998, "Kuwait's Al-Manakh Stock Market", INFORMS working paper, Ivey School of Business, University of Western Ontario.

Solnik, B. H., 1974, "Why Not Diversify Internationally rather than Domestically?", *Financial Analysts Journal* 30, July/August, pp. 48–54.

Waud, R., 1970, "Public Interpretation of Federal Reserve Discount Rate Changes: Evidence on the 'Announcement Effect' ", *Econometrica* 38, pp. 231–50.

Ying, C., 1966, "Stock Market Prices and Volume Sales", *Econometrica* 34, pp. 676–86.

21

401(k) Plans: The Unconquered Frontier for ETFs

Kevin D. Mahn

Hennion & Walsh Asset Management

Exchange-traded funds (ETFs) have been one of the fastest-growing product types on Wall Street in recent years. According to the Investment Company Institute (ICI), there were 680 ETFs with more than US$610 billion in assets as of May 2008. While this dwarfs in comparison with the US mutual fund marketplace, which has 8,067 mutual funds and more than US$12 trillion in assets as of the same date, it is still noteworthy. However, consider that, less than eight years ago, there were only 80 ETFs with just over US$65 billion in assets. That represents growth rates over that time period of 750% and 831% respectively. This growth rate compares very favourably with mutual fund growth rates of –1.08% and 76% over the same time period. Further, consider that it took ETFs less than 14 years to amass the asset total that it took mutual funds roughly 58 years to achieve. ETFs have clearly been accepted in the investment community and continue to gain market share.

The future growth projections for ETFs are equally impressive. Morgan Stanley is currently predicting that, by 2011, US ETF assets could exceed US$1.4 trillion with total global assets pushing the US$2 trillion level. Further, WisdomTree Investments has predicted that, three years from now, we could be looking at 2,000–3,000 total ETFs.

Not only has the number of ETFs and assets within ETFs grown at a staggering pace but the types and depth of ETFs have increased as well. ETFs now come in all different shapes and sizes. There are now exchange-traded products that cover the major asset and sub-asset

Figure 21.1 ETF assets (in US$ millions) – growth trend

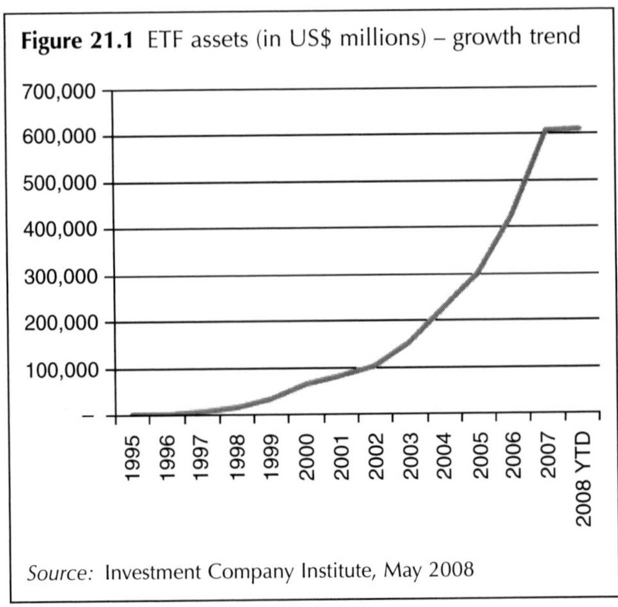

Source: Investment Company Institute, May 2008

Figure 21.2 Number of ETFs – growth trend

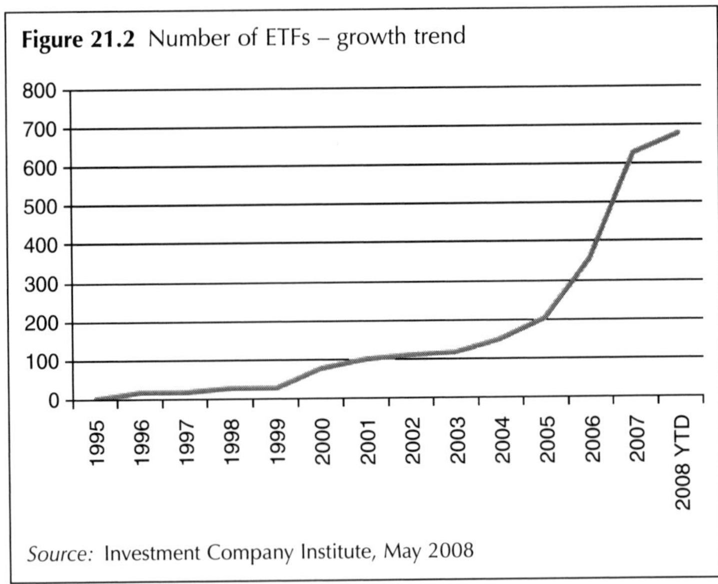

Source: Investment Company Institute, May 2008

classes. There are exchange-traded products that cover specific sectors and geographies. There are exchange-traded products that allow investors to access the commodity and foreign currency markets in a more convenient manner than through traditional means. There are even exchange-traded products that effectively short, on leveraged and non-leveraged bases, certain asset classes, sub-asset classes, sectors, alternative investment categories and geographies.

All of this product development has been accompanied by new, often complex product structures that need to be understood by investors before contemplating an investment in such a product. Some examples of these product structures include the following.

- Open-end index fund: This type of fund represents the vast majority of ETFs in the marketplace today. This type of fund is registered under the Investment Company Act of 1940. They typically will operate in a passive manner by tracking an underlying index. Dividends are reinvested in the funds on the day they are received and paid out to shareholders on a quarterly basis.
- Unit investment trusts: This type of fund is also registered under the Investment Company Act of 1940. They have a specified termination date and generally must fully replicate their underlying indexes. Dividends are not reinvested in the funds on the day they are received but are paid out to shareholders on a quarterly basis. The first, largest and most actively traded US ETF – the SPDR Trust, Series 1 ("the Spider") – is one example of this product structure.
- Grantor Trusts: This type of fund is not registered under the Investment Company Act of 1940 and the underlying composition of the fund is fixed outside of corporate actions that could alter its composition. In opposition to the open-end index fund and unit investment trust product structure, dividends are not reinvested in the funds on the day they are received but rather distributed directly to shareholders of grantor trusts. The Merrill Lynch HOLDR funds are examples of this type of product structure.
- Exchange-traded notes: This type of fund is not registered under the Investment Company Act of 1940 but rather is registered under the Securities Act of 1933. Exchange-traded Notes (ETNs) are basically a combination of an ETF and a bond. ETNs are unsecured debt securities that trade on an exchange and pay a return linked to the performance of a given index. Unlike ETFs, ETNs also introduce credit risk to the issuer of the ETN. Barclays' iPath products are examples of ETNs.
- Actively managed ETFs: This is the newest of the exchange-traded product structures and the product, and is causing the greatest

deal of concern to open-end mutual fund companies that employ active management styles. As opposed to the traditional passive mandate of ETFs, actively managed ETFs attempt to leverage the low-cost, tax-efficient nature of the ETF product structure while employing active portfolio management techniques. The first actively managed ETF was the Bear Stearns Current Yield ETF, which came to market on May 25, 2008.

These product enhancements have led many advisers and investors to start utilising exchange-traded products on a more widespread basis when constructing and managing diversified portfolios. Borrowing from the often-cited core-satellite portfolio strategy example, some advisers, when working with their clients, may use ETFs to access certain segments of the market on a satellite basis, while others are actually using ETFs as the core part of their portfolio strategies. In this regard, after advisers determine the appropriate asset-allocation strategy for their clients, they then utilise ETFs to implement that asset-allocation strategy in both taxable and tax-deferred accounts. When referring to the latter, ETF penetration to date has only really taken place in individual retirement accounts (IRAs) as opposed to qualified retirement plans such as 401(k)s. Why? The answer to the question is lengthy and somewhat complicated, so let us begin by providing a landscape of the current 401(k) marketplace in the US.

According to the ICI, as issued in its Research Fundamentals report in April 2008, as of September 30, 2007:

- total US retirement assets climbed to US$17.8 trillion;
- retirement savings account for almost 40% of all household financial assets in the US;
- IRAs held US$4.8 trillion in assets;
- mutual funds account for 47% of IRA assets;
- US citizens held US$4.5 trillion in all employer-based defined contribution plans – US$3.1 trillion of this total was held in 401(k) plans;
- mutual funds account for 53% of defined contribution plan assets (using the May 2008 ICI mutual fund assets of US$12 trillion, this would mean that approximately 20% of total mutual fund assets come from defined contribution plans);

- almost 90% of lifecycle mutual fund assets are held in retirement accounts; and
- almost 50% of lifestyle mutual fund assets are held in retirement accounts.

It can be concluded from the statistics above that the US retirement marketplace is large and continues to grow in terms of both size and level of importance to the US household. In this regard, McKinsey & Co has estimated that defined contribution plans will double in size by 2015 to somewhere between US$7.5 trillion and US$8.5 trillion in assets under management (Carpenter 2008). This can be attributed to several factors. First, companies have shifted from offering defined benefit pension plans to their employees to offering less costly defined contribution plans. Secondly, US citizens can no longer rely on social security or corporate pension plan benefits for a secure and comfortable retirement as they did in previous generations. US citizens now find themselves often trying to play catch-up with their retirement savings and have only 401(k) plans or IRAs to turn to as tax-deferred investment vehicles. According to the 2008 Employee Benefit Research Institute Retirement Confidence Survey, 49% of workers report total savings and investment (not including their primary residence or any defined benefit plans) of less than US$50,000. Even more concerning, this survey also showed that 22% of workers and 28% of retirees say they have no savings of any kind.

401(k) plans are generally the more preferred vehicle as they currently allow for higher tax-deferred annual contribution amounts than IRAs (ie, 2008 contribution limits are US$15,500 for individuals under the age of 50, US$20,500 for individuals over the age of 50 for 401(k) plans, while only US$5,000 for individuals under the age of 50, US$6,000 for individuals over the age of 50 for IRAs) and often have some employer incentives associated with them (eg, matches, profit sharing and so forth) to increase their annual retirement savings even further.

The National Retirement Risk Index (NRRI) has shown that even if households work to age 65 and annuitise all their financial assets, including the potential receipts from reverse mortgages on their homes, nearly 45% will be "at risk" of being unable to maintain their standard of living in retirement (NRRI 2007). As a result, US citizens are looking not only to save more but to invest more wisely. Hence, the growing trend toward lifecycle or lifestyle funds within 401(k) plans that offer built-in diversification and rebalancing. Lifecycle and lifestyle funds leverage the same asset-allocation-geared investment philosophies as have been employed by the largest pension plans and endowments in the country for years. Individual investors are now just catching on to this strategic investment approach by

Figure 21.3 Lifecycle funds

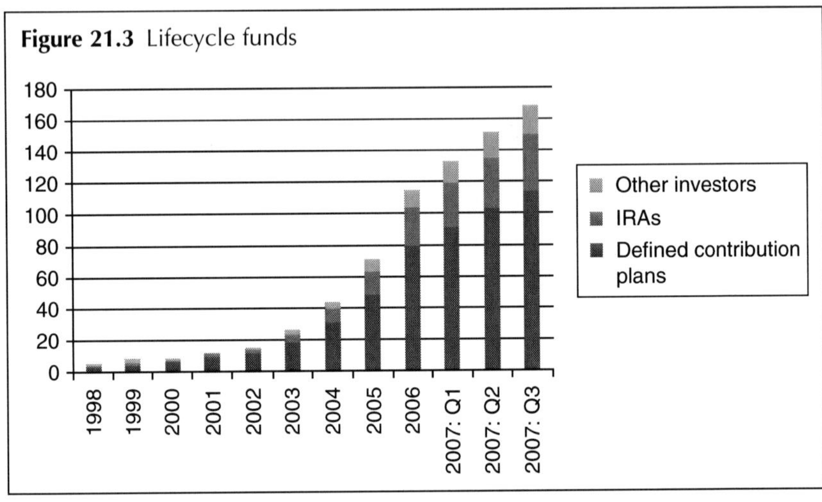

Figure 21.4 Lifestyle funds

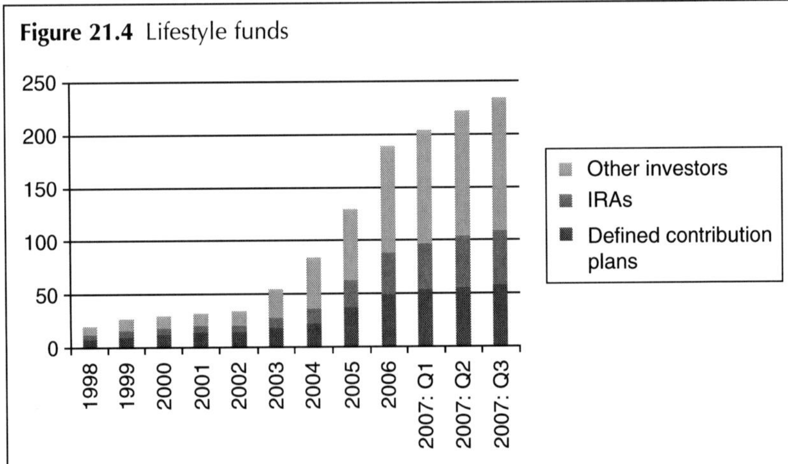

Source: Investment Company Institute, Research Fundamentals, April 2008
Notes: A lifestyle mutual fund maintains a predetermined risk level and generally contains "conservative", "aggressive" or "moderate" in the fund's name. A lifecycle mutual fund is a hybrid fund that typically rebalances to an increasingly conservative portfolio as the target date of the fund (mentioned in its name) approaches.

abandoning emotional decision making, buying high/selling low, timing the market and chasing the hot sector/stock tactics.

These types of product offerings further increase the dominance that mutual funds already have in 401(k) plans.

Mutual funds continue to maintain a high market share within IRAs as well.

It is within IRAs, however, that ETFs have started to gain some traction. As previously discussed in this chapter, investors have flocked to ETFs in recent years due to their often-cited advantages when compared with traditional mutual funds. These advantages include:

- liquidity – ETFs trade like stocks all throughout the trading day;
- lower annual expense ratios;
- transparency – an investor in an ETF does not have to wait until the end of the quarter to see the entire composition of the fund over the previous quarter as they would have to with a traditional mutual fund;
- ability to short or buy certain ETFs on margin;
- asset class/sector/geography coverage of ETFs;
- short/hedge strategies availability through ETFs; and
- greater tax efficiency – although the tax efficiencies of ETFs are lost within a tax-deferred account, that alone does not diminish

Table 21.1 401(k) assets in mutual funds

Year	Mutual fund assets (US$ billions) in 401(k) plans	Mutual fund % share of total 401(k) assets
1997	479	38
1998	616	40
1999	811	45
2000	820	48
2001	796	47
2002	707	45
2003	922	48
2004	1,092	50
2005	1,239	52
2006	1,476	53
2007	1,656	54

Source: Investment Company Institute, Research Fundamentals, April 2008

Table 21.2 IRA assets in mutual funds

Year	Mutual fund assets in IRAs (US$ billions)	Mutual fund % share of total IRA assets
1997	763	44
1998	961	45
1999	1,257	47
2000	1,231	47
2001	1,166	45
2002	1,043	41
2003	1,309	44
2004	1,491	45
2005	1,664	46
2006	1,977	47
2007	2,243	47

Source: Investment Company Institute, Research Fundamentals, April 2008

the potential value of a well-constructed ETF portfolio within a tax-deferred account; however, when you consider a Roth IRA (an IRA that is funded with after-tax contributions), the overall value of a well-constructed ETF portfolio within a tax-deferred account is even greater.

With all of these apparent advantages, the outpouring of demand from plan participants and the general push for less convoluted expense structures (eg, in early 2007, the Government Accountability Office (GAO) approached the US House of Representatives calling for more transparency in 401(k) fees), ETFs still have not found their way on to the majority of 401(k) platforms. Let us look at some of the main reasons for this lack of 401(k) market penetration.

1. Product knowledge: ETFs are still a relatively new investment product and are widely misunderstood by advisers and individual investors alike. Hence, from a fiduciary perspective, participant education is necessary for any products offered on a company 401(k) plan.
2. Costs: These can be one of the disadvantages of ETFs with respect to 401(k) plans when annual expense ratios are compared against certain open-end, index-tracking mutual funds. Although considerably lower than actively managed mutual funds and generally lower than most index-tracking mutual funds, ETF annual expense

ratios can be higher than, or comparable to, certain index-tracking mutual funds. See Table 21.3 for an asset-class-specific example using six randomly selected funds.

Further, an additional cost for ETFs – seeing that ETFs trade like stocks throughout the trading day at a market price, as opposed to mutual funds, which trade at net asset value (NAV) at the end of the trading day – is the bid–ask spread for each ETF. Finally, there are commissions associated with ETF trading – both purchases and sales – which could have a long-term impact on returns for frequent traders. Conversely, ETFs do not have 12b-1 fees, so they offer more fee transparency than traditional mutual funds and can help with enhanced requirements for complete fee disclosure.

3. Performance: Does the performance of ETFs justify their placement on a 401(k) plan in place of traditional mutual funds? Presumably out of fear of potential litigation, plan sponsors are debating this question themselves. Rather than looking at actively managed

Table 21.3 Sample ETF and index-tracking mutual fund expense ratio comparisons

Fund ticker	Fund name	Product type	Asset class	Annual expense ratio (%)
SPY	SPDR S&P 500 ETF	ETF	Large-cap blend	0.10
RSP	Rydex S&P Equal Weight	ETF	Large-cap blend	0.40
VFINX	Vanguard 500 Index	Index-tracking mutual fund	Large-cap blend	0.15
FUSEX	Fidelity Spartan US Equity Index Fund	Index-tracking mutual fund	Large cap blend	0.10
OAKVX	Oak Value	Actively managed mutual fund	Large cap blend	1.36
MDLRX	Blackrock Funds Large Cap Core Funds	Actively managed mutual fund	Large-cap blend	1.14

Source: Morningstar, July 29, 2008

mutual funds that would represent more of an apples-to-oranges comparison, it is more relevant to compare ETF performance to index tracking mutual fund performance after, of course, factoring in expense ratios, to answer this question. To help provide some insight, Table 21.4 looks at the same six randomly selected large-cap blend funds from Table 21.3 in terms of trailing total returns.

One conclusion that can be reached from this limited sampling of data is that passively managed fund strategies, whether they are ETFs or index tracking mutual funds, seem, fairly consistently, to beat actively managed mutual funds in certain asset classes. However, this is a notion that has been purported in the investment community for quite some time – most aggressively by John Bogle, the founder and retired CEO of the Vanguard Group. Some could even argue that offering actively managed mutual funds on

Table 21.4 Sample ETF and index-tracking mutual fund historical performance comparisons

Fund ticker	Fund name	Product type	YTD total return %	1-year total return %	3-year total return %	5-year total return %
SPY	SPDR S&P 500 ETF	ETF	−11.64	−11.44	3.02	7.17
RSP	Rydex S&P Equal Weight	ETF	−10.58	−14.06	2.00	9.08
VFINX	Vanguard 500 Index	Index-tracking mutual fund	−11.55	−11.15	3.18	7.24
FUSEX	Fidelity Spartan US Equity Index Fund	Index-tracking mutual fund	−11.53	−11.12	3.24	7.28
OAKVX	Oak Value	Actively managed mutual fund	−12.18	−13.76	0.78	4.45
MDLRX	Blackrock Funds Large Cap Core Funds	Actively managed mutual fund	−15.52	−16.03	1.49	8.59

Source: Morningstar (all performance data is as of July 29, 2008; market returns are displayed for ETF trailing total returns and NAVs are displayed for mutual fund trailing total returns; past performance is not an indication of future results)

a 401(k) platform could expose more risk from a fiduciary perspective than passively managed ETFs or index tracking mutual funds.

4. Tax efficiencies: The in-kind redemption feature associated with ETFs has made them more tax-efficient when compared with traditional mutual funds, but this advantage is lost within tax-deferred investment vehicles such as the 401(k) plan.
5. Fiduciary responsibilities: After overcoming any performance concerns, many plan sponsors are still likely to be uncomfortable with the concept of being one of the first to put a relatively new product such as the ETF, which, like a stock, trades with associated commissions, on their platform, especially without providing extensive education, as discussed in point 1 to their plan participants on the nuances of the different types of ETFs. However, once proper education is provided, offering ETFs in a 401(k), in the author's opinion, would not expose any more risk to a fiduciary than offering mutual funds and would certainly present less risk than offering their own company stock on the plan. Talk about risk! A Hewitt Associates study of 401(k) plan participants found that more than 27% of the nearly 1.5 million plan participants surveyed who could invest in their company stock had 50% or more of their 401(k) plan assets invested in those shares (Blanchett and Kirsten 2008).
6. Trading/fractional shares: ETFs can be purchased only in whole share amounts, whereas mutual funds can be purchased in fractional share amounts. This is a critical distinction for 401(k) plan participants, as they do not typically defer an exact US dollar amount out of each paycheque to coincide with the price of the ETF(s) that they are looking to purchase. Additionally, certain ETFs have round-lot trading restrictions (for example, HOLDR ETFs have 100-share round-lot trading restrictions), which can further complicate trading.
7. Record keeping: Most 401(k) custodial/record-keeping platforms, some of which still are not able to provide account valuations on a daily basis, are set up to handle mutual funds, which trade only once a day, as opposed to ETFs, which can trade throughout the trading day. Overhauling these platforms can be expensive.

Given these penetration difficulties – some valid, others are not so valid for the reasons provided – several software/platform solutions are now available that allow for direct ETF investments in 401(k) plans. Following are four of the solutions that are currently available, although there are sure to be more in development and potentially in place as you are reading this chapter.

1. Self-directed brokerage account: ETFs have long been available through 401(k) self-directed brokerage accounts just as individual securities such as stocks and bonds have been. Though only 16% of 401(k) plans offer self-directed brokerage accounts today,[1] they still can be a valuable and flexible tool for investors saving for their retirement. Self-directed brokerage accounts increase the investment options available to participants but, in so doing, can also result in more frequent trading and confusion among participants. As a result, fiduciary concerns arise with plan sponsors, which is why self-directed brokerage account utilisation has not increased further and, when utilised, is often implemented with limitations (eg, no commodities). Regardless, self-directed brokerage accounts still represent one way to invest in ETFs directly through a 401(k) plan.
2. Invest n Retire: Founded in 2000, the Invest n Retire 401(k) platform now allows employees to own whole and fractional shares of ETFs in their retirement portfolio without forcing them to shoulder the expense of setting up self-directed brokerage accounts. Platform ETFs presently include PowerShares, Morningstar, Select Sector SPDRs, Vanguard and Barclays and institutional index funds from Dimensional Fund Advisors. Custody services are provided by Fiserv ISS, a division of Fiserv Inc, and their stated minimum account size is US$5 million in plan assets.
3. Benefit Street: Founded in 1993, Benefit Street now offers the direct purchase of ETFs for 401(k) plans. Whereas some 401(k) plans offer ETFs as part of a separately managed brokerage account or as part of a collective trust (this will be discussed later), the Benefit Street offering is made up of direct ETFs. They believe that their state-of-the-art technology can greatly reduce trading costs and enhance participant education as it relates to building a portfolio of ETFs. Custody services are provided by Reliance Trust Co.
4. WisdomTree Investments: WisdomTree offers an open-architecture platform featuring Wisdom Tree's own ETFs – most of which are

based on dividend-weighted indexes, while some are earnings-weighted indexes. On their 401(k) ETF programme, ETFs are traded on an omnibus basis, which can substantially reduce, and potentially eliminate, trading commissions. Custody services are provided by the International Clearing Trust Co, a wholly owned subsidiary of TD Ameritrade. Optional third-party administration services are provided by Professional Capital Services.

For those looking for a quicker, and perhaps less costly, way to get ETFs into their 401(k) plans, other ETF solutions that are not specific to any particular software solution are available today. Some of these solutions, which can consist of funds of ETFs or collective investment funds, include the following.

1. Fiserv Trust Target Date Blueprint Funds: These represent another ETF investment approach through a pooled account vehicle called a collective investment fund (CIF). The Target Date Blueprint Funds may invest in Claymore ETFs, non-Claymore ETFs, and other mutual funds in order to fulfill their asset-allocation strategies. The funds pool together ETF purchases and sales help to reduce trading costs, and collective funds themselves eliminate many record-keeping issues because they look, act and trade like mutual funds and are available on virtually any record-keeping platform. Some of the Claymore ETFs included as underlying investments in the Target Date Blueprint Funds are:
   - Claymore/Ocean Tomo Patent ETF;
   - Claymore/Great Companies Large-Cap Growth Index ETF;
   - Claymore/Ocean Tomo Growth Index ETF;
   - Claymore/Zacks Yield Hog ETF;
   - Claymore/Zacks Mid Cap Core ETF;
   - Claymore/Sabrient Stealth ETF;
   - Claymore/Robeco Developed International Equity ETF; and
   - Claymore/BNY BRIC ETF.

   Collective fund structures do add another level of explicit and implicit costs though in order to get ETFs into the 401(k) plan structure.
2. SmartGrowth Mutual Funds: Launched in June of 2007, the SmartGrowth Mutual Funds, for which this chapter author is the portfolio manager, are target-risk, open-end mutual funds that

track the Lipper Optimal Target Risk Indices. The Lipper Optimal Target Risk Indices are a set of five, asset-allocation-oriented indexes that are rebalanced quarterly and designed to assess the trade-off between risk and return in diversified portfolios. Lipper's Optimal Target Risk Indices are objective, risk-based tools composed of carefully selected ETFs whose historical returns, correlations, liquidity and expenses are analysed in an effort to identify the appropriate mix for five levels of progressively increasing risk-and-return benchmarks. Due to their open-end mutual-fund structure, these funds of ETFs could be implemented on most 401(k) platforms today. A listing of the A-share classes (other shares classes may be available as well) of these funds is provided in Table 21.5.

3. Seligman TargetHorizon ETF Portfolios: Launched in October of 2005 and 2006, the Seligman TargetHorizon ETF Portfolios are target-date, open-end mutual funds comprising ETFs and designed for different retirement years. According to the Seligman Website, the TargetHorizon ETF Portfolios offer "a simple, easy way to get sophisticated risk-management strategies, the ease and convenience of target-date funds and cost-effective diversification through ETFs ... all in a mutual fund." Due to their open-end mutual-fund structure, these funds of ETFs could be

Table 21.5 SmartGrowth mutual funds

Fund ticker	Fund name	Net expense ratio* (%)	Inception date
LPCAX	SmartGrowth® Lipper Optimal Conservative Index Fund	1.50	01/06/07
LPMAX	SmartGrowth® Lipper Optimal Moderate Index Fund	1.50	01/06/07
LPGAX	SmartGrowth® Lipper Optimal Growth Index Fund	1.50	01/06/07

Source: Morningstar, June 30, 2008
*Gross expense ratios for the SmartGrowth Mutual Funds are: LPGAX: 14.53%; LPMAX: 16.72%; and LPCAX: 52.66%. Voluntary fee waivers are in effect. There can be no assurance that the adviser will continue to waive fees.

implemented on most 401(k) platforms today. A listing of the A share classes (other shares classes may be available as well) of these funds is provided in Table 21.6.

4. Federated Target ETF Funds: Launched in April of 2006, the Federated Target ETF Funds are similar to the Seligman Target Horizon ETF Portfolios in that they are also target-date, open-end mutual funds comprising ETFs and designed for different retirement years. Their investment objectives are to seek capital appreciation and current income consistent with its current asset allocation, which will emphasise a decreasing allocation to equity securities as the fund's target year approaches. Due to their open-end mutual-fund structure, these funds of ETFs could be implemented on most 401(k) platforms today. A listing of the A-share classes (other shares classes may be available as well) of these funds is provided in Table 21.7.
5. Wilmington ETF Allocation Fund: Launched in December 2005, the Wilmington ETF Allocation Fund seeks long-term capital appreciation. It invests primarily in ETFs. The fund is designed to provide cost-effective exposure to a broad range of US and non-US equity securities.

While these strategies will allow for a quicker and less complicated path towards getting ETFs on to 401(k) plans, they do contain some of the cost and fee transparency issues that typical mutual funds possess. However, as noted earlier, currently available direct ETF investment options come with their own set of costs and

Table 21.6 Seligman TargetFunds

Fund ticker	Fund name	Net expense ratio* (%)	Inception date
SHVAX	Seligman TargetFund Core	1.19	03/10/05
STJAX	Seligman TargetFund 2015	1.21	03/10/05
STKAX	Seligman TargetFund 2025	1.19	03/10/05
STZAX	Seligman TargetFund 2035	1.25	02/10/06
STQAX	Seligman TargetFund 2045	1.24	02/10/06

Source: Morningstar, June 30, 2008
*Gross expense ratios for the Seligman TargetHorizon ETF Portfolios are: SHVAX: 1.38%; STJAX: 1.52%; STKAX: 1.56%; STZAX: 6.75%; and STQAX: 11.30%. Voluntary fee waivers are in effect. There can be no assurance that the adviser will continue to waive fees.

Table 21.7 Federated Target ETF funds

Fund ticker	Fund name	Net expense ratio*	Inception date
FTQAX	Federated Target ETF 2015	0.71%	06/04/06
FTWAX	Federated Target ETF 2025	0.72%	06/04/06
FTHAX	Federated Target ETF 2035	0.70%	06/04/06

Source: Morningstar, June 30, 2008
*Gross expense ratios for the Federated Target ETF Funds are: FTQAX: 20.51%; FTWAX: 10.17%; and FTHAX: 16.30%. Voluntary fee waivers are in effect. There can be no assurance that the adviser will continue to waive fees.

Table 21.8 Wellington ETF Allocation Fund

Fund ticker	Fund name	Net expense ratio*	Inception date
WETFX	Wellington ETF Allocation Fund	1.23%	20/12/05

Source: Morningstar, June 30, 2008
*Gross expense ratio for the Wilmington ETF Allocation Fund is: FTQAX: 1.79%. Voluntary fee waivers are in effect. There can be no assurance that the Adviser will continue to waive fees.

complications as well. Notwithstanding these issues, ETFs remain a highly sought-after investment option for 401(k) plan sponsors and participants alike. Based on the growing trend towards asset-allocation-oriented portfolios (eg, target date, target risk, lifecycle), we would suggest that diversified portfolios of ETFs that are rebalanced regularly and oriented towards an investor's risk profile have the greatest potential of gaining significant market share in the 401(k) marketplace. Whether this is through the aforementioned funds of ETFs, a collective investment fund or an investment adviser who manages their own portfolios of ETFs, is irrelevant.

The time for ETFs in 401(k) plans is near, if not upon us already, and the rewards for ETF product sponsors will be significant. If ETFs can gain a 10% market share of 401(k) plans by the year 2015, the year that McKinsey & Co predicts that assets under management in defined contribution plans could grow to US$8.5 trillion, this would equate to an additional US$850 billion in ETF assets. This is precisely why 401(k) plans, and the sticky underlying assets that are associated with them, are considered the Holy Grail for packaged products such as ETFs. The penetration of ETFs into 401(k) plans is no longer a question of "if" but rather a question of "when" and "by how much". Our predication is that significant penetration will take place within the next two to three years. The product, if implemented properly, is just too good an option for 401(k) plans to justify taking any longer. This penetration will not necessarily be at the full expense of mutual funds, since we do believe that the two products can, and most likely, will coexist on 401(k) plans – at least initially.

1 See *Collected Wisdom™ on Self Directed Brokerage Account* at URL: http://www.401khelpcenter.com/cw/cw_self_directed.html.

REFERENCES

Blanchett, D. and G. Kirsten, 2008, "Why ETFs and 401(k)s will Never Match", *Journal of Portfolio Management*, July/August 2008.

Carpenter, D., 2008, Associated Press Newswires, June 26.

NRII, 2007, "Is There Really a Retirement Savings Crisis?", analysis.

22

Use of ETFs in Managed Accounts

Ron Pruitt

Placemark Investments

The flexibility and unique characteristics of exchange-traded funds (ETFs) has resulted in a proliferation of uses in the delivery of financial advice. One such example is in the managed-account industry. ETFs share many common marketing characteristics with managed accounts and as such both have experienced significantly higher growth rates than mutual funds. Developing a greater understanding of managed accounts and how ETFs are utilised in this industry will benefit ETF product creators, distributors, advisers and clients.

A PRIMER ON MANAGED ACCOUNTS

Managed accounts were originally created in the early 1970s by a group within E. F. Hutton with the intention of bringing institutional consulting discipline used to manage pension assets to the management of retail client assets. During the past decade there has been a tremendous amount of innovation in this industry to streamline the delivery of advice as well as to improve the ability to customise the advice for each individual client. This velocity of innovation has brought with it a proliferation of marketing and product terminology, thus making it more challenging for outsiders to understand the basics of managed accounts.

"Separately managed accounts" (SMAs) refers to the original structure used to deliver managed-account advice. When a client invests in an SMA, a brokerage account is opened up for the client. Money managers who would traditionally manage a mutual fund directly trade individual securities on behalf of the client. The client sees all trades in their own account and all fees are typically paid directly out of the account. Since the manager has full trading control over the client's account, this results in having multiple accounts with one account for each manager. Thus, in comparing a client who owns five mutual funds to a client who invests in SMAs, the client in SMAs would have five accounts, one utilised by each manager, whereas a client using funds could own all the funds in a single account.

Firms distributing SMAs to clients are typically referred to as sponsors and maintain the infrastructure necessary for the delivery of accounts. The internal groups that run SMA programmes are referred to as managed-account groups (MAGs). These groups handle marketing of the programme, research, selection and ongoing due diligence of manager strategies offered through the programme and operations (to include account opening/management, ownership of the accounting systems for tracking each account, calculation of performance results and delivery of performance reports).

Unified managed accounts (UMAs) are a newer form of managed account where multiple investment strategies are included in a single custodial account. Sub-accounting techniques are used by either a third party, typically referred to as an overlay portfolio manager (OPM), or a MAG to track the performance of each individual strategy within the account. There are both subtle benefits to the UMA (much easier to move assets between strategies, ability to custom tailor accounts more easily, ability to manage the tax consequences of all strategies collectively) and more obvious benefits to clients and advisers (less paperwork, fewer accounts, administrative simplification). It is a common belief within the managed-account industry that UMAs will be the catalyst that will make managed accounts as prolific as mutual funds (Rodier 2008). Due to their popularity, there have been a multitude of abbreviations that all refer to various product offerings that are all similar (at least from the perspective of a single account structure). Terms such as MDA (Multiple-Discipline Account), MSP (Multiple-Strategy Portfolio), CDP (Consults Diversified Portfolio), DMA (Diversified Managed Account) and MMA (Multi-Manager Account) all refer to various offerings that present multiple strategies (some, however, offer very few if any of the more subtle benefits and are purely a way to simplify the account structure). UMAs are not limited to offering SMA-type strategies, and many will utilise mutual funds and ETFs along with SMA-type strategies.

MANAGED-ACCOUNT SELLING POINTS

Now that we have defined what managed accounts are, readers may be asking themselves why they are needed. Put another way, you may ask what unique benefits are provided by managed accounts that cannot be fulfilled with ETFs and mutual funds. A study was conducted during 2001 by Merrill Lynch and Prince and Associates (*Financial Advisor* 2001) surveying clients who selected managed accounts to determine the primary reasons they chose this approach. Clients identified four key reasons why they preferred to utilise managed accounts; understanding the key selling points will also help the reader to appreciate the similarities to ETFs.

The four reasons were as follows.

- Access to unavailable managers: Clients identified this as their number-one reason for selecting managed accounts.
- Tax efficiency: A common issue with traditional funds (largely avoided by ETFs) are that capital gains are accumulated and paid only when the fund manager sells the asset. Thus, it is possible to buy a fund that has embedded gains from assets that have not been sold yet. The fund can have negative returns such that a client loses some of their initial investment and may be subjected to taxation. Since managed-account clients own the securities themselves, they have "their own" basis. The taxation of funds is one area with a significant number of additional nuances, which provide marketing differences to ETFs and SMAs. These will be explored in greater detail throughout the chapter.
- Fees: Clients cited an asset-based fee structure as their third reason and an all-inclusive fee structure as their fourth reason. Recognising that all-inclusive fees are important to clients has been an impediment to use of funds (which have embedded fees) in managed accounts.
- Transparency: While not identified in the 2002 survey, another reason that many sales professionals cite as a key factor in marketing managed accounts is the full transparency of fees and business practices. After the mutual-fund scandals that occurred with

short-term trading and late trading in funds in 2003, this became a stronger selling point.

ETFs AND MANAGED ACCOUNTS COMPARED

Similarity: taxation – control over capital gains

As mentioned earlier, managed accounts and ETFs are similar with respect to capital-gains realisation. By transferring lower-basis shares of an ETF to institutions (via in-kind transfers), ETFs are able to sell off lower-basis (higher-gain) tax lots and thus reduce or eliminate capital gains that have been accumulated in the fund. This combined with the lower turnover of most ETFs results in lower capital-gains distributions to taxable investors. Taxes are not avoided for ever: since investors in ETFs have their own basis, the capital gains will be realised when the individual investor sells the fund. Flows out of ETFs, however, can result in higher turnover and if those redemptions come from retail investors (where in-kind transfers are not feasible) the ETF may require capital-gains distributions similar to mutual funds.

Since managed-account investors own their own securities, their taxation is not impacted by redemptions of other investors. Accordingly, there is no such thing as capital-gains distributions and capital gains are limited to portfolio sales decisions by the manager as well as the client's decisions to take cash out of the investment. Managed-account investors can also request that managers keep turnover below a certain level (thus controlling the amount of gains realised) and can change managers and move the assets to another manager without selling if they feel the manager is not fulfilling their needs.

The reduction and/or elimination of capital-gains distribution is one of the most common characteristics between ETFs and managed accounts. This control and avoidance of unplanned capital gains is paramount to the attractiveness and success of both of these products.

Similarity: taxation – tax lot identification[1]

For readers familiar with mutual-fund investing, the idea of average cost basis may be familiar. There are several methods by which investors of mutual funds can track their cost basis, including averaging the basis of several tax lots, which, if utilised, reduces the gains realised per tax lot (but eliminates the opportunity to pick the most favourable lot, thus preventing picking the tax lots that would result in the lowest possible gains). Once a mutual-fund investor elects a specific method for managing their basis, they are required to utilise that method each year unless the Internal Revenue Service (or relevant tax collection agency in your country) permits the investor to revoke that election. This initial election thus has significant implications for the ability to manage taxation over the life of the investment.

Unlike mutual funds, the purchase of ETFs and the ownership of individual securities via managed accounts must use specific identification.[2] In the absence of an investor specifying which tax lot they are selling, it is assumed they are selling their oldest tax lots first (referred to as FIFO or first in, first out). Other methods used for picking tax lots include LIFO (last in, first out), HIFO (highest basis, first out), min tax (similar to HIFO but considers the tax rate of short-term versus long-term holdings), as well as more granular methods for managing taxes (considering previously realised gains and losses, time of the year, average holding period and so forth, so as to manage the lowest multi-year tax impact).

The requirement to identify lots places an additional burden on taxable investors, however, doing so can benefit clients. When investors and their advisers utilise specific methods, they have the opportunity to reduce gains realisation more so than can be achieved with mutual-fund average-cost methods.

Difference: active versus passive strategies

While ETFs and managed accounts share similar characteristics in avoiding capital-gains distributions and control of tax lot identification, the typical strategies implemented within each distribution vehicle vary. While some ETF providers are working towards changing this paradigm, the lion's share of ETF strategies offered today are passive strategies. A passive strategy seeks to match the performance of a specified benchmark and typically does so by holding all securities in the benchmark at the exact same weights as the benchmark (also referred to as full-name replication).

Alternatively, most managed accounts seek to outperform a target benchmark (exceptions will be noted later) net of the fees that are paid to the manager (also referred to as active investment management). Active management strategies vary from subtle strategies such as enhanced indexing to very aggressive strategies that take material risks in attempting to outperform their index. Active management risk is measured via tracking error, which measures the magnitude of the periodic differences in performance (tracking error is typically measured as the standard deviation of the monthly performance differences annualised by multiplying the result times the square root of 12). Tracking error for actively managed strategies can vary from about 1% to about 10%. A strategy with a tracking error of 1% would be expected to be plus or minus 1% of the benchmark return in a given year 68% of the time, within 2% of the benchmark return 95% of the time, and within 3% of the benchmark return 99.7% of the time. For a tracking error of 10%, the deviations would be 10%, 20% and 30% for 68%, 95% and 99.7%, respectively.

For pretax returns, it can be demonstrated that on average actively managed strategies will underperform passively managed strategies net of fees (Sharpe 1991). This does not mean that all strategies will underperform, simply that the group as a whole will on average underperform. Whether certain strategies can consistently outperform a benchmark on a pretax basis is a highly debated topic among academics and practitioners. However, substantial evidence exists to suggest that tax strategies that seek to improve after-tax returns can outperform with persistence when tracking error to a target benchmark is managed closely similar to enhanced indexing strategies (Berkin and Ye 2003). It is worth noting that the methods used to manage after-tax returns are available to ETFs, mutual funds (to a lesser extent when they use an average-cost basis) and managed accounts. However, the extent to which the strategies can be utilised varies based on direct ownership of individual securities.

Difference: ownership structure and the ability to sell individual constituents

The lion's share of ETFs are offered as open-end funds (similar to most mutual funds) or unit investment trusts (UITs) and as such are registered under the Investment Company Act of 1940. Exceptions to this include grantor trusts, exchange-traded notes and partnerships, which are not typically used for investments in equities of developed countries. When an individual buys shares of an investment company, they do not directly own the securities and instead own shares in an investment company that (per the investment company's prospectus) invests in securities.

Unlike typical corporations, who pay taxes on the profits from investments when they are sold, investment companies distribute the gains to shareholders (thus capital-gains distributions) and are not subject to double taxation (US corporations pay taxes on their profits and investors pay taxes on any dividends that are paid). These capital-gains distributions can be short-term or long-term and are distributed *pro rata* to all investors in the fund as a percentage of the fund that they own. Individuals are taxed on the gains that are distributed to them, with short-term gains being treated as income and long-term gains receiving preferential tax treatment. In the event that an investment company ends up selling securities at losses, they reduce gains of other securities sold. If the investment company has more losses than gains, then the losses are not distributed to clients and can be used to offset future gains within the fund for up to eight years.

Ownership of individual securities via managed accounts as compared with investment companies is very different in three respects. First, unlike with ownership in an investment company, which cannot distribute losses because the individual owns each security, the individual can sell any security at a loss and get the immediate benefit of those losses. Second, individuals own each security themselves so they can choose to sell that security. For example, a managed-account manager may have two investors, one that invested in a security six years ago and one that invested six months ago. It is much more likely that stocks purchased several years ago are at a gain and that at least some of the stocks purchased recently are at losses. The manager can choose (or be requested by their client) to sell a stock for the client who has losses, even though the manager may not be selling the security for the client who holds the security at a gain. Third, when short-term gains are sold by the manager they are short-term capital gains. While short-term capital gains are taxed at the same rate as income, short-term capital gains can be offset by other losses that the client may have, whereas short-term distributions from investment companies are taxed as income and cannot be offset by other losses.

INDIVIDUAL SECURITY OWNERSHIP AND VOLATILITY

As previously discussed, one method for managing after-tax returns, loss harvesting, can be performed with holdings of mutual funds,

ETFs and individual securities. If average cost methods are used, mutual funds have a reduced opportunity to pick specific lots that are at greater losses. There is, however, a much larger opportunity trade-off that applies to both mutual funds and ETFs, which is that an investor can realise losses only when the entire tax lot of a fund is at a loss. For example, let us assume that a fund manager buys 10 positions; half appreciate and the other half depreciate such that the performance of the group is zero. If an investor owned the fund, there would be no losses to realise, whereas an individual who owned the individual shares would be able to realise some amount of losses on half of the assets. The difference in performance of securities (the cross section of security returns) thus becomes an important factor in enabling effective loss harvesting and tax management.

The implications of cross-sectional volatility can be illustrated by conducting Monte Carlo simulations of portfolios held as funds and as individual securities. The advantage of running Monte Carlo simulations is that a large number of iterations can be run to simulate all likely market scenarios, thus better illustrating the impact under all realistic market conditions.[3] Each time the simulation is run, a portfolio is constructed as a fund and as individual securities. An investor in the fund can sell the fund only when it achieves a specific loss threshold, whereas an investor who purchased the individual securities can sell any security when it is at a specific loss threshold. For purposes of simplicity, wash sales are ignored and securities are immediately repurchased after they are sold at losses. The aforementioned simulation was repeated for 5,000 iterations and Table 22.1 shows the results. For example, if an investor were to invest US$100,000 in a fund for five years and sold the fund whenever it exceeded a 5% loss, the investor would be able to generate losses of 8.5% of their initial investment or US$8,500. The same investor who bought the exact same securities as made up the fund would be able to generate 31.8% of their initial investment in losses, or US$31,800.

Generally speaking, selling small losses is less beneficial, since the loss value is smaller and the transaction costs are larger. As an investor increases their loss threshold (such that only larger losses are sold), the losses generated from owning a fund versus the individual constituents of the fund decrease. Across the entirety of the simulation and loss thresholds, by owning individual securities an investor can

Table 22.1 Potential losses generated as a percentage of original investment via ownership of funds versus individual securities

Loss threshold (%)	Investment vehicle	% losses through X years (as % of original investment)					
		1 (%)	3 (%)	5 (%)	10 (%)	30 (%)	50 (%)
5	Fund	4.8	7.5	8.5	9.2	9.4	9.4
	Individual securities	15.3	26.0	31.8	39.9	51.3	55.3
10	Fund	2.7	5.3	6.6	7.8	8.1	8.1
	Individual securities	13.1	23.7	29.9	38.2	49.6	53.7
15	Fund	2.1	4.9	5.7	6.4	6.6	6.6
	Individual securities	12.1	23.2	28.9	37.1	48.6	52.7
20	Fund	0.8	2.6	4.0	4.9	5.0	5.0
	Individual securities	9.6	20.8	27.1	35.2	47.1	51.5

Source: Placemark Investments

realise 5.5 times as many losses as holding the exact same securities in a fund. Thus, when taxes are an important consideration for a client, they should seek either to own individual securities to create the greatest possible flexibility or to own a combination of less diversified funds that can be sold individually, thus creating more opportunities to harvest losses.

ETF FEATURES POPULAR WITH MANAGED-ACCOUNT GROUPS AND MANAGERS

While there are certainly nuances between ETFs and managed accounts, the usage of ETFs in managed-account programmes is on the rise, which clearly indicates that the similarities promote enough commonality to make them particularly interesting to managed-account groups and money managers. Two specific features of ETFs not previously discussed make ETFs much more managed-account-friendly, namely, low expense ratios and the lack of short-term redemption penalties.

Since managed accounts have full transparency of fees, the embedded fee structure of funds does create the potential for client concerns. Sponsors of managed accounts are sensitive to this and thus the low expense ratios of ETFs are attractive when funds are purchased. In essence, the low expense ratio provides for a low-cost means of maintaining market exposure in certain asset classes either on a temporary or permanent basis as more fully described in the next section.

Traditional mutual fund investors face the risk that short-term traders may buy in and sell funds in relatively short periods of time. This results in several negative consequences to long-term shareholders. First, clients buying or selling frequently may force the investment manager of the fund to sell or purchase securities at less than opportune times. Second, investment managers may need to maintain higher levels of cash because they choose neither to invest cash nor to make it available for redemptions. Finally, short-term trading could be used to exploit perceived stale fund valuations. Namely, when a fund values its assets, this is divided by the number of shares and thus produces a net asset value (NAV). When a fund holds assets in thinly traded securities, assets for funds where trading is frozen or assets in foreign securities whose closing prices are set based on the local market close, the NAV may not be representative of current market conditions. A trader could buy the fund and subsequently sell the fund the next day to exploit the "stale" NAV. In order to combat these risks, mutual funds subject investors who do not hold the assets for a specified period of time to a penalty. While these short-term redemption penalties are designed to protect individual shareholders, it makes it more difficult to buy funds for valid short-term investment purposes (to be discussed in the next section) without being subjected to these fees. Since ETFs are traded throughout the trading day, they rely on the market supply and demand and internal mechanisms (the ability to deliver in kind and create shares) to protect shareholders, thus they do not need to rely on short-term redemption penalties and can be used for valid short-term market exposure needs without additional cost to investors.

PRIMARY USES OF ETFs IN MANAGED ACCOUNTS

Fulfil exposure to specific asset classes

When a client is investing US$1 million or less, the use of managed accounts can introduce challenges in achieving the ideal asset allocation. More specifically, since traditional managed accounts have a US$100,000 investment minimum, any desired allocation to a strategy of less than 10% is not achievable. Additionally, it is typically desirable to provide a buffer from the account minimum and the target allocation so that, if the market declines, it is possible to rebalance back to the target allocation. In other words, if a client invests US$1,000,000 and has a 10% allocation to an emerging-markets strategy that has a US$100,000 investment minimum, if the market declines and the value of their account drops to US$950,000, it is not possible to maintain a 10% emerging-markets allocation.

The use of UMAs and an overlay manager reduces this challenge, since the individual managers typically provide the overlay manager with their target portfolio and the overlay manager implements all the trading for the client. In this framework, the minimums for each strategy can drop to US$25,000 or less, thus reducing the minimum assets from US$1 million to US$250,000 in the example above. The US$100,000 account minimums are typically a function of the overhead costs to set up and run an account, which are not an issue when all the assets are managed by a single manager. The minimums thus become a function of the theoretical minimum to successfully manage the strategy. For example, assume a money manager holds 49 securities plus cash, all equally weighted, thus 2% for each position. Additionally, this manager typically buys into any new stock equally in four tranches to reduce the risk that their buys will change the market price of the security. This would mean the typical trade for this manager would be 0.50% or 50 basis points (bp). If the highest price stock the manager would likely purchase is US$200, this strategy could not be implemented without altering the strategy with less than US$40,000 (US$200/0.50%). In addition to theoretical minimum issues, fixed-income investments present not only minimum issues but issues with liquidity of bonds, which makes it more difficult to invest in fixed-income strategies via a UMA. So, while the UMA reduces the challenge of account minimums and asset allocation, it does not entirely eliminate the issue.

Placemark Investments is a leading provider of UMAs and works with a large number of managed-account managers (more than 325 products from 160 managers as of November 2008) and works with a significant number of managed-account sponsors. Thus, Placemark's business is a reasonable snapshot of the managed-account business and should help to make the theoretical challenges more tangible. As of April 4, 2008, the average number of positions held in managed-account strategies was 49.5 securities; 25% of the accounts managed by Placemark were US$187,500 or less in size; and 25% of all accounts had a target allocation that was less than or equal to 10%. Given the number of firms and cross section of clients that Placemark works with, it is reasonable to expect that this is representative of the typical retail client and thus better quantifies the challenge with fulfilling an investor's allocation solely with managed accounts. The data above would suggest that at least 10% of existing UMA clients cannot fulfil their entire asset allocation using only managed accounts.

Many managed-account groups provide ongoing advice and recommendations in terms of target asset allocation; for purposes of diversification and providing a more optimal risk/return combination they will often recommend to diversify across a wider number of asset classes and styles. The smaller allocations in the asset allocation often include small-cap growth and value strategies, emerging-markets strategies, international strategies, REIT investments and convertible-bond strategies. Thus, the desire for smaller allocations, in particular with clients who have less to invest and where there are more individual securities to hold for each strategy, will drive the need to seek alternatives to managed accounts. The result of the desire for smaller allocations plus the use of fixed income is the largest driver of ETF and fund use in UMAs (Figure 22.1 shows a

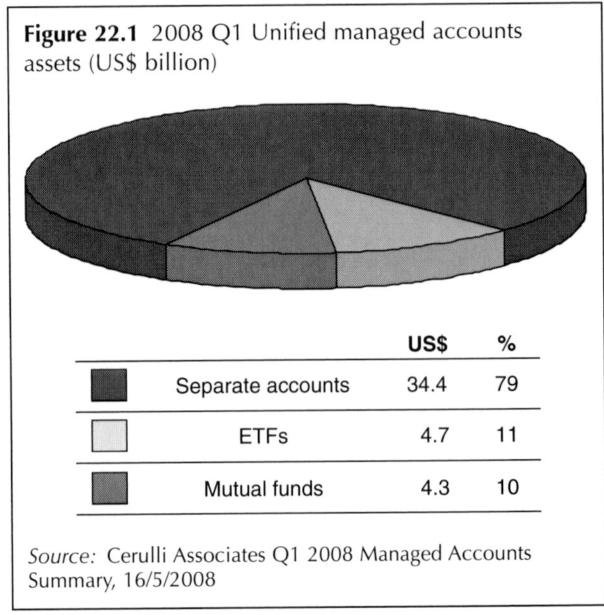

Figure 22.1 2008 Q1 Unified managed accounts assets (US$ billion)

		US$	%
■	Separate accounts	34.4	79
□	ETFs	4.7	11
■	Mutual funds	4.3	10

Source: Cerulli Associates Q1 2008 Managed Accounts Summary, 16/5/2008

recent snapshot of how often funds and ETFs are utilised). It is worth noting that, as of the fourth quarter of 2007, based on the same Cerulli data, ETF use in UMAs surpassed that of mutual funds.

ETFs as a substitute security

The first reason presented above for the use of ETFs within the managed-account industry, fulfilling an entire strategy or allocation for a client account, is one purpose that can also be fulfilled by mutual funds. It is expected that, since managed accounts are typically actively managed vehicles and ETFs are typically passive, mutual funds will continue to be utilised in this fashion. Unlike with the situation above, however, ETFs tend to be used almost exclusively (as opposed to mutual funds) for purposes of substitute securities. Substitute securities are utilised on a temporary to semi-permanent basis when an investor prefers not to or cannot own a specific security. In these situations, a managed-account manager or overlay manager has four specific choices: buying other individual securities in place of the securities that cannot be owned; buying additional amounts of individual securities they already own; leaving in cash; buying a fund.

Of the various options for substitute securities, cash is the least favourable choice as the client loses capital market exposure, and the lack of this exposure typically introduces higher levels of tracking-error risk. More sophisticated strategies will buy other individual securities, as they can more closely replicate the specific security attributes and investment philosophy; yet they also introduce additional stock-specific risk and an additional research burden for the manager. For these reasons, many managers will utilise funds; in these instances, ETFs are used in most circumstances over mutual funds, because of lower fees, passive management and lack of short-term redemption penalties in the event that the manager's process necessitates selling the substitute in a shorter than expected period of time.

The two most common reasons for requiring substitute securities are security restrictions and loss harvesting. Clients can utilise security restrictions as a mechanism to communicate securities or groups of securities (such as all stocks in an industry or sector or stocks that are not consistent with the investor's social preferences, such as stocks that are associated with adult entertainment) that they prefer or are prohibited from holding (such as securities of a competitor or where they are an insider). In most circumstances the client's preferences or limitations are semi-permanent and, as such, the substitute securities will typically be held as long as the manager would have otherwise purchased a security that was restricted.

Data from Placemark Investments serves as an indication of the extent to which restrictions are utilised in practice. Again using data from April 4, 2008, 10.5% of accounts managed by Placemark had at least a single security restriction. In most instances, the client security restrictions do not conflict with a manager's preferred holdings and only 3.8% of accounts Placemark manages (roughly 36% of accounts with restrictions) have securities that are restricted and that overlap with the preferred holdings from money managers. In the 3.8% of accounts that have restriction overlap, that overlap averages 8% of the desired weight of the manager's models ranging from less than 1% to extreme instances where approximately 50% of all securities on the client's restriction list overlap with the manager's recommended holdings.

The second typical reason that necessitates alternate securities is loss harvesting. Research demonstrates that a client with a 35% income tax rate can add 56bp annually to a single strategy's after-tax return (by reducing other capital gains and reinvesting the proceeds) (Berkin and Ye 2003). Loss harvesting involves selling securities that have declined in value in order to utilise the losses to offset other gains (as well as up to US$3,000 in ordinary income). In order to avoid a wash sale, the security cannot be repurchased for 31 days after the sale of the security. Therefore the client has a temporary need for a substitute security. In these instances, mutual-fund short-term redemption penalties become an impediment from utilising traditional funds and thus ETFs become a *de facto* choice for managers who prefer not to purchase other securities and/or leave the proceeds in cash.

ETF allocation strategies as separate accounts

As mentioned earlier with respect to fixed income, running separate account strategies with securities that have limited liquidity can be a significant challenge. Not only does it introduce problems executing trades, it can also create challenges when new clients enter a strategy and the securities may not be available. For these same reasons, money managers have developed all ETF strategies to execute strategies that would otherwise be challenging to implement with individual securities. These strategies are being implemented within UMA programmes as well as individual, separately managed accounts.

The proliferation of more concentrated ETFs that focus on sectors, countries, fixed-income segments and commodities has opened up the opportunities for a multitude of new strategies. Examples of strategies that comprise ETFs that have been introduced by money managers include international strategies that tactically rotate across countries; international strategies that rotate among developing and emerging markets; multi-cap investment strategies that allocate among various equity styles; and tactical-allocation strategies that shift allocations across asset classes. Without ETFs it would not be practical to implement many of these strategies cost-effectively and in a timely fashion. Furthermore, capturing a greater cross section of security returns can afford similar opportunities for loss harvesting, as discussed earlier.

ETFs for basket risk exposure

As previously alluded to, research demonstrates that loss harvesting can add significant value to after-tax returns and this value is maximised by owning individual securities and thus having the greatest exposure to the cross section of security returns. An important caveat with respect to loss harvesting is how loss harvesting is utilised with respect to gains the client may realise. In order to produce sufficient losses, it is fairly typical to offer strategies that are designed to be passive with respect to stock selection so that the portfolio closely matches the pretax performance of the intended benchmark and utilises the majority of turnover towards generating losses. One challenge for index managers is replicating the performance of a benchmark when it is not feasible to own every security in the benchmark. As illustrated in Figure 22.2, cap-weighted benchmarks can be dominated by the largest-capitalisation stocks in the index. Seventy-two securities from the Russell 1000[4] comprise only 28% of the holdings of the benchmark but make up 80% of the benchmark's weight, and so replicating the remaining 20% of the index requires investing in a significant number of positions that may not be practical, depending on the size of the investment by

Figure 22.2 Russell 1000 Index cap breakdown

Number of securities	% of the capitalisation (%)	% of the names (%)
5	10	1
18	25	2
72	50	7
282	80	28
999	100	100

the client. This is consistent with all capitalisation-weighted indexes and can introduce challenges for index managers.

The unique risk characteristics of the smaller-capitalisation securities further exacerbate the situation. As illustrated in Figure 22.3, the performance of the smallest 800 securities within the Russell 1000 (which comprise the Russell Midcap Index) has been significantly different from the performance of the largest securities. In fact, over the previous five years, mid-cap securities have outperformed the Russell 1000, of which they are a subset, by 445bp annually. This presents a challenge not only for an index fund manager but also for any manager who benchmarks their results against a large-cap index.

Unless managers are able and willing to hold a significant number of securities (which may not be practical based on the amount a client is investing), they will likely under weight of the unique risk of the smaller capitalisation securities that are in their target benchmark. Additionally, since this performance is not linearly related to capitalisation, it is likely that a manager who maintains the same average market capitalisation as their target benchmark may not fully protect themselves against this risk.

Placemark has developed an index replication strategy that utilises small allocations to ETFs to maintain exposure to smaller capitalisation securities. By purchasing a small target weight to a mid-cap ETF/ETFs a manager can effectively buy the equivalent of 800 additional securities in many cases each of these securities would only amount to a fraction of a single share if the same securities were purchased individually. While the use of ETFs in this fashion is not widespread in practice, it is our opinion that performance attribution

Figure 22.3 Trailing returns (April 2003 to March 2008)

	1 yr	3 yr	5 yr
Russell 1000 Index (%)	–5.4	6.2	11.9
Russell Midcap Index (%)	–8.9	7.4	16.3

Source: Russell Investments
Notes: The Russell Midcap Index is a subset of the Russell 1000 Index. It includes approximately 800 of the smallest securities based on a combination of their market cap and current index membership.

and analysis will drive more managers towards similar methods to help manage their tracking error.

SUMMARY

ETFs and managed accounts share similar characteristics such that ETFs have seen increased use within the managed account industry and in particular within unified managed accounts (UMAs). The low cost beta aspect of funds with the ability to freely trade them on the market without being subjected to short-term redemption penalties presents many opportunities that can be utilised by managed account sponsors, ETF providers and money managers to enable better solutions for clients. It is expected that these common characteristics will result in continued utilisation of ETFs in managed accounts and that they will see a growing share of assets within this industry segment.

1 As this chapter is written by a US-based author the examples used with regards to taxation are from a US investor point of view and therefore comments with regards to tax, capital gains, tax lots, wash sales etc may not be applicable outside the US.

2 Note that a more recent opinion by at least some practitioners is that average cost basis reporting may be available for ETFs structured as open-end index funds and/or Grantor Trusts. See http://www.kitces.com/blog/index.php?/archives/28-Using-average-cost-accounting-for-Exchange-Traded-Funds.html for details.

3 For the simulation, the average stock market return is assumed to be 10% over 50 years. Any given year (or combination of years) can be at a loss or gain, so it is possible to have bear markets, bull markets and relatively stable markets. The annual volatility of the market is assumed to be 15% with the average individual security risk assumed to be 37.5%. Using a CAPM construct, the average beta is assumed to be 1 and average correlation among securities is 0.40.

4 Russell Investment Group is the source and owner of the trademarks, service marks and copyrights related to the Russell Indexes. Russell® is a trademark of the Russell Investment Group.

REFERENCES

Berkin, Andrew L. and Ye, Jia, 2003, "Tax Management, Loss Harvesting, and HIFO Accounting", *Financial Analysts' Journal* 59(4), July/August, pp. 91–102.

Financial Advisor, 2001, "An Alternative for the Affluent", September.

Rodier, Melanie, 2008, "UMAs Continue to Grow in Turbulent Financial Markets", *Wall Street and Technology*, October 28.

Sharpe, William F., 1991, "The Arithmetic of Active Management", *Financial Analysts' Journal* 47(1), January/February, pp. 7–9.

23

Accident and Genius: What History Tells Us About the Future of ETFs

Albert S. Neubert

Information Management Network

BEFORE EXCHANGE-TRADED FUNDS

Exchange-traded funds (ETFs), as we know them today, have an interesting history and one that took some odd twists and turns to arrive at the well-conceived and well-designed product that is booming in popularity. There was some very original and creative thought put into the predecessors of ETFs and, through a major market disruption in 1987 and by virtue of a regulatory turf war, product designers never gave up and kept going back to the drawing board to come up with what was obviously an inherent demand for an index fund that traded like a stock.

INDEX OPTIONS AND FUTURES, AND PROGRAMME TRADING

The history of the ETF starts with the history of indexing, which started in 1971 with the first institutional index fund, managed by Wells Fargo. Vanguard pioneered the first indexed mutual fund in 1976 and indexed funds in total had around US$10 billion in assets tied to the strategy by 1980, the vast majority of that from public and corporate pension funds.

In February 1982, the first index futures contract was launched at the Kansas City Board of Trade, and it was based on the Value Line Composite index, but that was followed shortly thereafter by the S&P 500 futures contract, which was launched by the Chicago Mercantile Exchange in April 1982. This was really the first time that the indexing concept was converted from a portfolio of the securities

Table 23.1 A historical record of exchange-traded index portfolios

Product name/ description	Year introduced	Exchange	Tracking index	Cash-based	Security-based	Regulatory juristiction	Trading today
Index futures	1982	Kansas City Board of Trade	Value Line Composite	Yes	No	CFTC	Yes
Index options	1983	Chicago Board Options Exchange	CBOE 100	Yes	No	SEC	Yes
Equity Stock Portfolio	1988	New York Stock Exchange	S&P 500	No	Yes	SEC	No
Cash Index Participation Units	1989	Philadelphia Stock Exchange	S&P 500	Yes	No	SEC	No
Equity Index Participation Units	1989	American Stock Exchange	S&P 500	Yes	No	SEC	No
Value Index Participation Units	1989	Chicago Board Options Exchange	S&P 500	Yes	No	SEC	No
SuperShares	1989	American Stock Exchange and Chicago Board Options Exchange	S&P 500	No	Yes	SEC	No
Toronto Index Participation Shares	1990	Toronto Stock Exchange	Toronto 35 Index	No	Yes	Canadian securities regulation	Yes
Standard & Poor's Depositary Receipts	1993	American Stock Exchange	S&P 500	No	Yes	SEC	Yes

that comprised the index into a derivative vehicle that allowed investors either to hedge or to speculate on the underlying index in one convenient trade.

One of the main reasons for launching the index futures contracts was the need by index fund managers to hedge their cashflows and not suffer tracking error to their fund because of cash "drag". Other reasons included the ability to hedge actively managed funds in market downturns without liquidating positions in the portfolio, the ability to "synthetically" get exposure to an index without purchasing the underlying securities and the ability by portfolio managers to enhance their portfolios, or even "port" the market equity exposure to another asset class.

In March 1983 the Chicago Board Options Exchange (CBOE) launched index options based on the exchange's own index of 100 stocks, which was designed to replicate the performance of the S&P 500. Soon after, the CBOE launched S&P 500 index options and S&P took over the CBOE 100 and it became the S&P 100. Just as in the example of the futures contracts above, another derivative instrument, based on the underlying target index, was created to help investors utilise index strategies without directly owning the securities within the indexes.

In both cases, with index futures and options, there came another major force in the market, which, while anticipated, was never quite imagined by the "experts" to become as powerful as it did. It was index arbitrage, and it was caused by discrepancies between the futures pricing and the physical basket of securities that comprised the underlying indexes. Index arbitrageurs were doing their own basket trades, either long or short, against the futures contract in order to profit from the pricing discrepancies between the markets. Thus, this could be looked at as the first "off-exchange-traded funds" and it had a powerful effect on moving the US equity markets in short periods of time on any given trading day.

BIRTH OF THE CASH INDEX PARTICIPATION UNIT

The story now shifts to a stock exchange. It was in 1985 that the Philadelphia Stock Exchange (PHLX) began toying with the idea of creating an index fund that traded on the exchange. It would be called an index participation unit (IPU) and it would be strictly a cash-settled instrument, so the PHLX named the product Cash

Index Participation units, or CIPs, or IPs for short. However, it still would not be a physical basket of the securities that made up an index but, instead, would be a security that tracked the index without an underlying portfolio. Led by the PHLX president and CEO, Nicholas Giordano, and product developers Arnold Staloff and Joseph Rizzello, this effort took a number of years to hatch and was finally filed for trading approval with the SEC in February 1988.

This came after the great market crash on October 19, 1987, when the Dow Jones Industrial Average went into a free fall and closed down 508 points, a whopping loss of 22%. Fingers immediately pointed to two culprits: programme trading (index basket trading mainly by arbitrageurs) and portfolio insurance, which was another way of basket trading in the form of futures contracts designed to protect portfolios from losses. Technology was the great facilitator in that this off-exchange-traded-fund capability was now being executed effectively, but without an orderly open market process, and the results were disastrous.

The federal government undertook a review of the crash and produced a "Report of the Presidential Task Force on Market Mechanisms", commonly referred to as the Brady Commission report, and named after Treasury Secretary Nicholas Brady of the Reagan administration. The report produced a much broader economic picture of the collapse but, clearly, portfolio insurance and programme trading facilitated the sell-off over a compressed timeframe. One of the recommendations of the report was that off-exchange-traded fund trading, ie, programme trading, be moved on to the stock exchanges. Clearly, this was a signal to the exchanges to create a product to meet a market and regulatory need.

Thus, the idea of the index participation security was now more viable, although it did not directly address the solution because the product was designed without a physical basket of index securities behind it. But it certainly forced exchange product developers to start looking at ways to link the physical basket to a single security that could be traded like a stock.

EQUITY STOCK PORTFOLIO

In 1988, the New York Stock Exchange tried its hand at creating such a product with the Equity Stock Portfolio, or ESP, which was designed to be based on the S&P 500 and had a unit size of US$5 million.

The product was to be traded using the Exchange's Designated Order Turnaround, or "DOT", system. It was a step in the right direction but the inflexibility of the unit size and lack of a mechanism to keep the units in balance with the actual S&P index created a whole new set of headaches for potential users and the concept died a quick and uneventful death.

COMPETING FACTIONS ENTER THE FRAY

Returning to the PHLX's CIPs, the innovative concept of an index portfolio trading as a security on a stock exchange drew immediate attention from competitors in three forms. One was competing securities exchanges. The American Stock Exchange (AMEX) product development team, led by Nate Most and Steven Bloom, got hold of the PHLX's SEC filing and made some adjustments and filed their own version of the CIP, which was called Equity Participation Units, or EIPs, and they were based on the S&P 500 index. Simultaneously, the Chicago Board Options Exchange (CBOE) also added new wrinkles to the CIP version and called their product Value Index Participation units, or VIPs. Both AMEX and CBOE filed with the SEC for trading and, on April 11, 1989, they received approval for trading. CIPs, VIPs and EIPs were launched in May 1989 but under a cloud of legal proceedings, as we shall soon see.

The second competing faction that had an eagle eye on IPUs was the futures industry in the form of the Chicago Mercantile Exchange and Chicago Board Options Exchange (CBOT), which saw the new instruments as a direct threat to the index futures trading business (note that CBOT did not have an index futures trading operation at this time). A suit was filed by the CME and CBOT and it declared that IPUs were futures contracts and should be regulated by the Commodity Futures Trading Commission (CFTC) and not the SEC. Therefore, IPUs should be reviewed and approved, or not, for trading by the CFTC and only on registered futures exchanges, and not on securities exchanges.

A third competing interest also joined the fray. The Investment Company Institute (ICI), which is the trade and lobbying association for the mutual fund industry, saw IPs as a threat to its constituents. The ICI argued that IPUs, if found not to be futures and instead be classified as securities, should fall within the bounds of the Investment Company Act of 1940. Since the Options Clearing

Corp (OCC) would be the facilitator of IP transactions, it would have to become a registered investment adviser under the 1940 Act.

The products did start trading on the three exchanges and, while under a cloud of doubt because of the lawsuit, volumes on the AMEX product surged to as many as 5,000 contracts per day within a month of start-up, a faster growth rate than even the S&P 500 futures contract at the CME some seven years earlier. PHLX's CIPs never got the same traction or support, given the potential for an adverse legal outcome, and VIPs were similarly lacklustre when they were launched.

THE MISSING LINK TO THE MODERN ETF

It was also in 1988 that the Toronto Stock Exchange (TSE) took an interest in IPUs and representatives of the TSE met with the product development team at PHLX to learn more about the concept and hopefully make some modifications to the product. The TSE was witnessing a live experiment south of the border and, while Canadian securities and derivatives regulations were not as rigid as in the US, the TSE wanted to develop its ETF as a security tied to an actual basket of the index constituent securities. Thus, the TSE path turned out to be the real "missing" link to the current ETF as we know it today. TSE launched its first IPU, based on the Toronto 35 Index in March 1990.

THE MECHANICS OF AN IPU

With the IPU being the critical evolutionary development point on the way to the modern ETF, it is time to examine how these instruments really worked and to see why they drew so much attention. IPs were "contracts" and not securities, based on the value of a target index, such as the S&P 500, and had a life, in perpetuity, like a stock. IPs were bought and paid for in cash and were bought on margin at the same rate as for stock, or 50% of the purchase price. The IP unit value was determined by the exchange in a ratio to the index value such that the contract value had a total value that appealed to some number of investors being targeted. For example, the IP could have been set at the index value times 10, 50 or 100 and this value is what the buyer would receive on cash-out day.

Interestingly, as with a closed-end mutual fund, the buyer of an IP received dividends approximating the value of the actual dividend payouts of the stock in the underlying index portfolio on a quarterly basis. But, it is how the dividend was paid that was a unique feature of IPs. The "short" investor ponied up the dividend payment through the 150% margin that was put up when taking the position, and which comprised 100% of the long buyer's position plus a 50% cash payment. The short's view was strictly from the perspective of a speculator or hedger using a futures contract. The IP acted like the futures contract, terminating on cash-out day, plus an option held by the long investor to roll the contract to the next cash-out date. IP cash-out days were designed, not coincidently, to align with index futures and option expiration dates, generally the third Friday of March, June, September and December.

Long and short investors did not deal directly with each other: rather the exchanges used the Options Clearing Corp, or OCC, to facilitate the position process. The OCC would issue the IP to the long investor and took the long's cash payment and paid the short investor but acquired the short's obligation to pay at cash-out time. The OCC guaranteed the short's obligations to the long investor, secured with the short investor's 150% margin. During the quarter, the short investor was required to put up an amount that would equal the approximate value of the quarterly dividend payment of the underlying target index. The OCC randomly chose a short investor to match up with a cashing-out long investor in order to facilitate payment. Thus, longs and shorts only create the instrument and any matching thereafter went through the OCC. Either a long or short could effectively close its own position by making an offsetting transaction using the OCC clearing mechanism.

The AMEX and CBOE IPs differed slightly. The PHLX's CIPs allowed the long investor to cash out on any business day, but with a discount of 0.5% from the value of the index, but the long could cash out quarterly without the 0.5% penalty being applied. The AMEX EIPs permitted the long investor to cash out quarterly for money or shares of stock in a ratio matching the index, a step closer to the IP contract being linked to the index portfolio. The AMEX designed the EIPs such that holders of 500 or more EIP units based on the S&P index, each with a multiplier of 100, could exercise the right to receive securities, but they had to pay a "delivery charge" that would be established by the AMEX. Ironically, the mechanism used to facilitate this process was the failed Equity Stock Portfolio single-order transaction platform designed by the NYSE a year earlier. Writers of EIPs could volunteer to deliver stock but, if not enough did, a "physical delivery facilitator" at the AMEX would buy stock in the market, using proceeds from liquidated short positions.

The CBOE's VIPs were designed with a semiannual cash-out date. The CBOE differentiated its product by allowing both long and short investors to cash out by tendering the value of the index on the cash-out date. If there were too many shorts seeking to close their positions relative to the long investors, the OCC would step in and choose additional long positions at random to pay off the short investors.

THE DEATH KNELL OF THE CASH IPU

In the end, the futures exchanges won the argument that IPs were "futures-like". The quarterly cash-out feature created an element of "futurity", and, despite PHLX's daily cash-out feature, which came with a penalty, their CIPs product was really tied to the quarterly cash-out feature as well. Thus, ICI dropped its suit and IPs in the US were delisted and existing positions unwound. This branch of the evolutionary tree for the ETF became extinct.

ANOTHER EVOLUTIONARY BRANCH – SUPERSHARES

Following the crash of 1987, there was another forerunner to the modern ETF that deserves mention because it offered some of the features that the developers of the first ETF in the US took note of and incorporated into their thinking. They were called Supershares and they were created by Leland, O'Brien, Rubenstein Associates. That was the organisation that promoted the notion of portfolio insurance using index futures, a major flashpoint in the 1987 crash, so, right out of the gate, the product was launched in an atmosphere of suspicion and apprehension. Throw in the fact that the product was extraordinarily complicated and had high fees, it had little chance of success and indeed died a quick death following its launch in 1989.

The Supershares had three features: an Index SuperUnit, Priority SuperShares and Appreciation SuperShares. Index SuperUnits traded on the American Stock Exchange and were based on a fully collateralised basket of stocks tracking the S&P 500. The SuperUnits received all dividends on the index and were redeemable for cash or securities. They could also be separated into the component parts, Priority SuperShares and Appreciation SuperShares. Priority SuperShares were traded on the CBOE and served the equivalent of a buy-write strategy, and they received all the dividend income on the index. They traded at a discount to the SuperUnits and could be combined with Appreciation SuperShares and redeemed for cash or securities. The upside potential was capped at the termination or strike price equivalent. Appreciation SuperShares also traded as a single security on the CBOE and functioned like a long-dated call option. Upside potential was unlimited, they received no dividend income, and they could be combined with Priority SuperShares and redeemed for cash or securities.

EVOLUTION CONTINUES TO THIS DAY —THE EXCHANGE-TRADED NOTE

One lesson to be learned from this evolutionary path to the modern ETF is that it does not end with the ETF and in fact, the exchange-traded note, or ETN, is another branch in the ETF development process. Even the ETF and ETN are complex products and there will be efforts made to streamline the exchange-traded index portfolio, and now actively managed portfolios of securities, such that the costs to the investor are lower yet.

The ETN branch of development is a structured note, similar to a bond with the full faith and credit of the issuer standing by as the "guarantor" of the return being paid on the note. That payment is linked to either an index or a basket of securities. The primary reason for the structured note versus the traditional ETF structure is the fact that the target tracking portfolio tends to be either illiquid stocks or commodities (represented by derivative contracts). The traditional ETF structure is not well suited to facilitate the trades in the creation and redemption process, although the market turmoil of September and October 2008 have proved to have a severe impact on the ETN structure, with wide spreads and poor tracking of the underlying portfolio at times.

BACK TO THE FUTURE

The IPU and Toronto Index Participations structures offer clues as to the path future development might take. Looking back at the downfall of IPUs following the legal action from the futures industry, it was easy to understand why the futures industry viewed with great scepticism and apprehension the rise of the ETF. Clearly, the advent of the ETF threatened the futures industry in the same way as did the IPU. Ironically, the ETF provided more liquidity to the futures industry, as opposed to competing with it directly.

As a result, product developers revisiting the IPU structure and addressing the key features that were challenged by the futures industry nearly 20 years ago might find a more receptive environment for this simple and effective product. Those features that need to be addressed include the settlement timing, clearing mechanism and the dividend payment feature. While the IPU would not be a security such as the ETF, it could be structured to avoid being classified as a futures or options contract and fulfil another need to execute portfolio trades in a very efficient, low-cost manner.

In interviews with colleagues who were instrumental in the development of most of the popular index securities and derivatives traded today, they all agreed on one thing: ETFs and ETNs are not the last great index portfolio trading innovation – and that is a certainty.

24

Trends and Future of ETFs

Michael Jabara

Citigroup Investment Research

Presented in this chapter are the author's thoughts and opinions on the current and future state of the exchange-traded fund (ETF) market. The author has been analysing ETFs for six and a half years and has witnessed a rapidly evolving industry that is constantly innovating on both the product and structure side. Since 2005, as a member of the Citigroup ETF research team, the author has noticed that investor interest has grown exponentially and ETFs have become more mainstream. This chapter aims to describe the marketplace the way the author sees it, which may be different from the way it is portrayed by the media and other industry analysts.

Note that when the initialism ETF is used in this chapter, it refers to those that trade on US exchanges and are structured as open-end investment companies as well as unit investment trusts. Also included are Holding Company Depositary Receipts (HOLDRS) and other ETFs structured as grantor trusts. In addition, the author includes ETFs structured as limited partnerships and other types of trusts. Finally, exchange-traded notes (ETNs) are placed under the ETF umbrella.

ASSETS AND FUNDS

The growth of the ETF market has been remarkable. What was just US$34 billion in assets scattered among 30 ETFs at the end of 1999 has grown into a US$539 billion market with 845 ETFs as of December 31, 2008. Since the end of 2002, ETF assets have grown by more than 400% and the number of funds has grown by approximately 600%. ETFs have benefited from both a rise in financial market values (in some cases) and new money pouring into the space as the product has become more popular. In particular, ETF assets grew more than 40% in 2003, 2004 and 2007. While the ETF market has clearly made great strides in its relatively short existence, it still pales in comparison to the size of the US mutual fund industry (US$9 trillion as of November 30, 2008, according to ICI). In 2008 asset growth halted and assets actually declined from the end of 2007 as weak financial markets generated headwinds for the industry. Poor financial markets did not stall fund growth, however. In 2008, fund growth was 26%.

Despite weak financial markets, ETFs continued to come to market. The number of funds coming to market is growing at a much quicker pace than assets. New ETF sponsors have looked to capitalise on the boom in hopes of capturing market share while the larger, more well-known sponsors have sought to fill out their product lines. Table 24.1 shows the pace of new funds versus asset growth more clearly. This was especially noticeable in 2006 and

Figure 24.1 ETF assets and number of funds

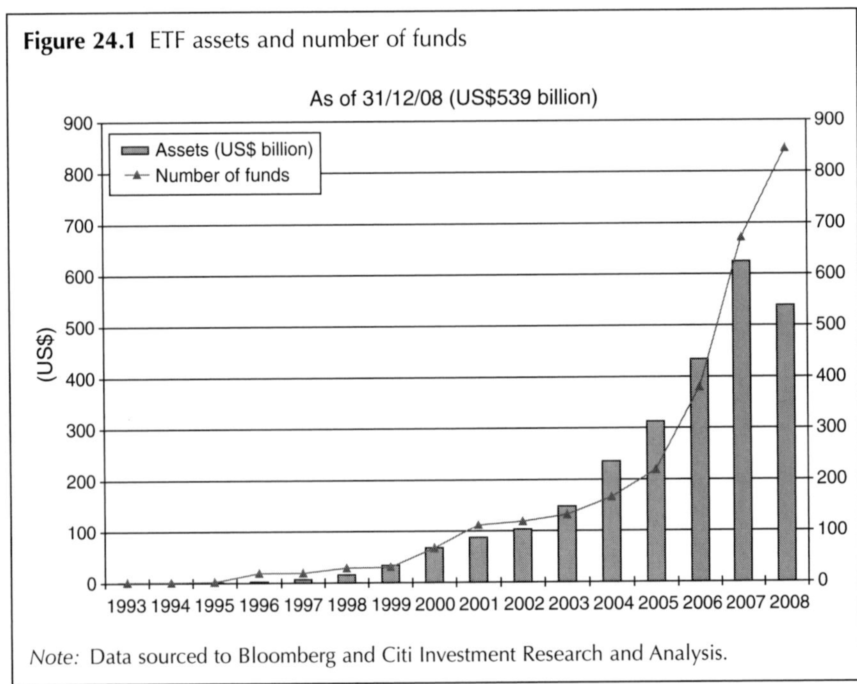

Note: Data sourced to Bloomberg and Citi Investment Research and Analysis.

Table 24.1 ETF growth

	Assets (%)	Funds (%)	Shares (%)
2001	28.8	67.2	60.5
2002	18.2	6.3	50.4
2003	43.8	10.9	21.5
2004	59.0	25.8	48.9
2005	32.7	31.9	34.5
2006	38.9	73.5	26.8
2007	43.9	76.8	29.9
2008	–13.8	25.7	53.5

Note: Data sourced to Bloomberg and Citi Investment Research and Analysis.

2007, when the number of ETFs grew at more than 70% each year. The rate of issuance as compared with asset growth is disturbing and may signify a lack of demand for many of the new products; however, assets can turn very quickly and are highly dependent on financial market performance. Another global bull market would undoubtedly get assets moving in the right direction again. The author believes issuance will remain strong going forward, as there are currently hundreds of ETFs in registration with the Securities and Exchange Commission (SEC) seeking approval. Although this number seems intimidating, many of the products in registration are inverse and leveraged products based on indexes that ETFs currently track.

Not every product filed with the SEC awaiting approval will make it to market; nevertheless, a significant percentage will. There is currently a proposal in front of the SEC known as Rule 6c-11, which could potentially increase the pace of ETF issuance. Proposed Rule 6c-11 states that ETFs would not be required to file for exemptive relief with the SEC provided they meet certain criteria, most notably that they be structured as open-end funds and that they provide complete transparency. This clearly would not apply to all ETF structures; however, if this proposal passes, it should expedite the ETF registration process for those funds that meet SEC criteria.

In addition to asset and fund growth, let us look at share count growth. A rising number of shares is a result of net creations and generally an indication of demand. As evidenced in Table 24.1, share counts have grown at healthy rates and in 2008 surged to levels not seen since 2004. The author believes we will see declining rates of growth in the ETF industry across numerous metrics in the years ahead. As any industry matures and its base gets wider, it is a lot more difficult to generate the growth numbers that were produced in its infancy. Over the long term, the author believes ETF assets, funds and share counts will grow, albeit at a slower pace, on average, than they have in the past eight years.

ACCESS TO MOST FINANCIAL MARKETS

Over the past few years investors have benefited from the wave of new ETFs coming to market. Investors have access to most financial markets including, but not limited to, industries and sub-industries, commodities, currencies, numerous fixed-income markets, more international markets, and inverse and leveraged funds, as well as ETFs that utilise strategies such as covered call writing, long/short strategies and lifecycle funds, to name a few.

The options and availability of so many different asset classes has enabled investors, especially smaller investors, to participate in areas of the market that are often operationally difficult for them to do in a cost-effective and sometimes tax-efficient manner. Not every area has been successful in taking in assets, but, as these products generate track records and more investors embrace the advantages of ETFs, we may see some of these products thrive. In addition to the trading flexibility and tax efficiency, the access to so many different types of markets is, the author believes, one of the most important advantages compared with traditional index funds. The options and access within the ETF marketplace dwarf traditional index fund options.

ETF ISSUANCE

ETF issuance was robust in 2008. In 2008, 231 ETFs came to market while 58 ETFs were closed. Of the 58 that closed most were liquidated while several were products that de-listed and are no longer taking creation units. For all purposes, those funds that de-listed are closed. Heavy issuance occurred in commodity-based, domestic and international equity ETFs. It is not surprising to see the heaviest issuance in commodities given their strong performance in 2007 and the first half of 2008 coupled with their ability to take in new money in the form of net inflows.

Figure 24.2 2008 new fund breakdown

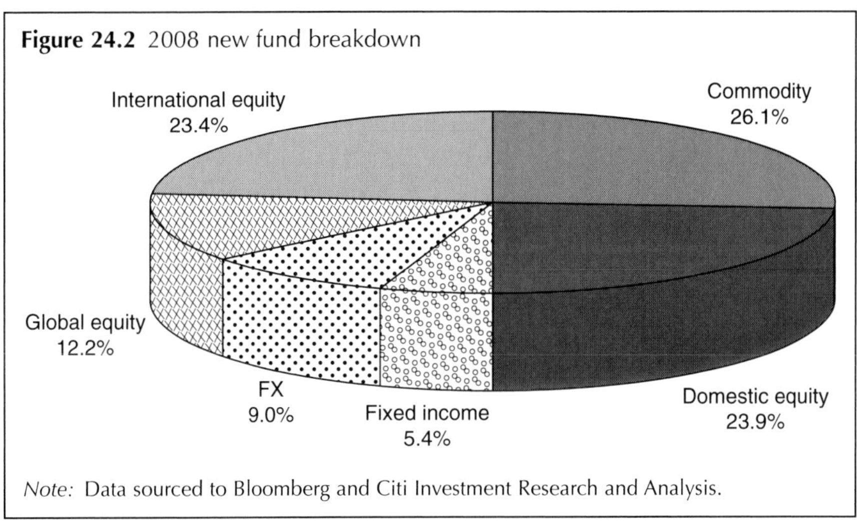

Note: Data sourced to Bloomberg and Citi Investment Research and Analysis.

Being first to market and supporting a product are key to attracting assets. In addition to being first to market and supporting a product, launching an ETF into a "hot" market can also really help attract assets. A prime example of being first to market lies in two very similar gold products. The SPDR Gold Shares (GLD) came to market just two months before the iShares COMEX Gold Trust (IAU), yet GLD has more than 10 times as much in assets. The differences in these ETFs as far as product design and marketing are concerned is negligible. Examples in 2008 of launching products into "hot" markets include the launch of a number of alternative energy and commodity ETFs such as the Claymore/MAC Global Solar Energy Index ETF (TAN). When these products came to market there were a lot of headlines pertaining to both of these areas of the marketplace.

While the sheer number of new products in 2008 was impressive, they have only about US$7.7 billion in assets or on average US$35 million apiece. Not much on a per fund basis and even worse if we strip out a few outliers. Like the industry as a whole, the US$7.7 billion is concentrated among a few ETFs. Granted, ETFs should be given some time to attract assets. The success of a product should not be decided in months and in fact could take years, especially if investors look at returns. ETFs need time to build track records, especially ETFs that track alpha-seeking indexes. Backtested data is not enough.

It is also worth pointing out that more and more ETFs are coming to market that are not structured under the Investment Company Act of 1940. In fact, of the new ETFs that survived 2008, 59 are structured as ETNs. In addition to ETNs, a couple of products are structured as limited partnerships, while a number of others are structured as types of trusts. Given the ability to access difficult financial markets via products that do not fall under the Investment Company Act of 1940, the author anticipates ETF issuance in some of these alternative structures to remain strong assuming the Internal Revenue Service (IRS) and SEC retain their status quo on the structures and their taxation.

MORE PRODUCT

The future of ETFs looks positive and a number of funds should continue to come to market. However, product development will be key for sponsors. Besides inverse and leveraged products, which we will see more of judging by the sheer number in registration with the SEC, most major, well-known indexes are already taken by ETF sponsors. Therefore, and something we have been seeing for about six years when PowerShares introduced their first ETFs, new indexes will be developed to generate alpha and designed in order for products to be based on.

As index providers search for new ideas it appears that we are getting further away from the traditional market-capitalisation or price-weighted indexes that we have grown accustomed to. These non-traditional types of indexes are not necessarily worse than long-established indexes, but rather different. Many are quantitatively driven and have subjective methodologies. Investors need to spend more time digging through index methodologies and understanding when one index may perform better than another and why. As an example, an equally weighted index may outperform a market-capitalisation-weighted index in an environment when small- or mid-cap stocks outperform large-cap stocks.

International ETF issuance may continue to remain strong in years to come as investors think globally and look to diversify away from the US and access faster growing economies. Commodity launches could also remain robust, yet may be dependent on the direction of underlying commodity markets. Theme-based niche products launched into hot markets will remain commonplace as ETF sponsors battle for market share and assets. The author believes much of the new product that comes to market, as has been the case recently, over the next couple of years will struggle to gather assets as the ETF market becomes saturated.

There is an overload of product that has come to the market very quickly the past few years and much of it is very similar. Most investors are not distinguishing the minor differences in ETFs within the same categories. There is a lack of ETF research and people who can perform due diligence on the products. ETFs now come in all shapes and sizes, with different structures, different indexes and different taxation ramifications. Do new products make sense from an investment perspective, or are sponsors launching as many products as possible and seeing what sticks? It seems that we are seeing more of the latter, which could come back to haunt the industry. In addition to indexed-based ETFs, more actively managed ETFs may also come out.

As a consequence of all the new ETFs and their structures, broker-dealers are beginning to block certain funds via a due-diligence process to protect themselves and their clients. Going forward, broker-dealers will become stricter in whom they do business with as it pertains to ETFs, as they seek to avoid problems that generally arise when something grows as quickly as ETFs have. Broker-dealers want to make sure that ETFs are sustainable and sponsors are viable, they want products that clients can understand, and also want to feel confident that funds can do what their backtested models claim they can do.

CONCENTRATION

There is no question that the ETF industry has grown; but this growth has not been evenly distributed. Ranking ETFs by asset size, the largest ETF, SPDR S&P 500 ETF (SPY), has nearly three times as many assets as the second largest fund (US$62 billion more in assets), iShares MSCI EAFE Index Fund (EFA), which has more than US$10 billion than the third-largest fund, SPDR Gold Shares (GLD). Coincidentally, these are also some of the older funds as well as the more liquid. They also have strong followings among both institutional and retail investors.

ETF industry assets are extraordinarily top-heavy, with the bulk of the assets residing in the top 50 ETFs. The top 50 ETFs (6% of the

Table 24.2 Top 50 ETFs ranked by assets at year-end 2008

Ticker	Name	Approximate expense ratio (%)	Inception date	Net assets (US$)	Six-month average daily trading volume (shares mln)
1 SPY	SPDR S&P 500	0.10	29/1/1993	93,922,161,982	368.0
2 EFA	iShares MSCI EAFE	0.35	14/8/2001	31,912,962,000	26.2
3 GLD	SPDR Gold Shares	0.40	18/11/2004	21,691,990,000	15.9
4 EEM	iShares MSCI Emerging Markets	0.75	11/4/2003	19,207,705,500	94.3
5 IVV	iShares S&P 500	0.09	19/5/2000	15,653,040,000	7.1
6 QQQQ	PowerShares QQQ	0.18	10/3/1999	12,537,380,000	204.0
7 IWM	iShares Russell 2000	0.20	26/5/2000	11,017,693,000	109.0
8 IWF	iShares Russell 1000 Growth	0.20	26/5/2000	10,678,200,000	5.7
9 AGG	iShares Barclays Aggregate Bond	0.24	26/9/2003	9,522,130,000	0.6
10 IWD	iShares Russell 1000 Value	0.20	26/5/2000	9,230,991,000	4.6
11 VTI	Vanguard Total Stock Market	0.07	31/5/2001	9,149,295,109	6.9
12 DIA	DIAMONDS Trust	0.18	14/1/1998	8,966,068,794	31.6
13 TIP	iShares Barclays TIPS Bond	0.20	5/12/2003	8,685,651,000	0.7
14 XLF	Financial Select Sector SPDR	0.23	22/12/1998	7,792,900,462	216.0
15 SHY	iShares Barclays 1–3 Year T-Bond	0.15	26/7/2002	7,691,320,000	1.3
16 LQD	iShares iBoxx $ Investment Grade Corporate Bond	0.15	26/7/2002	7,006,792,000	0.7
17 MDY	S&P 400 MidCap Depositary Receipts	0.25	4/5/1995	6,782,970,250	9.3
18 FXI	iShares FTSE/Xinhua China 25	0.74	8/10/2004	5,884,312,500	36.3
19 IWB	iShares Russell 1000	0.15	19/5/2000	5,788,498,500	4.9
20 EWJ	iShares MSCI Japan	0.54	18/3/1996	5,642,328,000	30.6
21 VWO	Vanguard Emerging Markets	0.25	10/3/2005	5,034,843,387	4.1
22 IVW	iShares S&P 500 Growth	0.18	26/5/2000	4,992,918,000	2.6
23 XLE	Energy Select Sector SPDR	0.23	16/12/1998	4,453,804,285	43.7

24	DVY	iShares DJ Select Dividend	0.40	7/11/2003	3,966,424,000	1.0
25	IWR	iShares Russell MidCap	0.20	20/7/2001	3,832,960,000	1.9
26	IJH	iShares S&P MidCap 400	0.20	26/5/2000	3,748,038,000	1.3
27	IJR	iShares S&P SmallCap 600	0.20	26/5/2000	3,745,242,000	2.8
28	SSO	ProShares Ultra S&P 500	0.95	21/6/2006	3,545,700,000	50.6
29	IWN	iShares Russell 2000 Value	0.25	28/7/2000	3,545,484,000	3.1
30	EWZ	iShares MSCI Brazil	0.70	14/7/2000	3,470,538,000	18.8
31	IWV	iShares Russell 3000	0.20	26/5/2000	3,195,256,000	1.2
32	IVE	iShares S&P 500 Value	0.18	26/5/2000	3,111,393,000	2.2
33	IEF	iShares Barclays 7–10 Year T-Bond	0.15	26/7/2002	3,010,122,000	0.4
34	BND	Vanguard Total Bond Market	0.11	10/4/2007	2,931,033,000	0.3
35	VUG	Vanguard Growth	0.10	30/1/2004	2,720,405,030	0.8
36	GDX	Market Vectors Gold Miners	0.55	22/5/2006	2,672,494,250	5.9
37	OEF	iShares S&P 100	0.20	27/10/2000	2,670,378,000	2.9
38	VEU	Vanguard FTSE All-World ex-US	0.25	8/3/2007	2,554,160,353	1.0
39	IWO	iShares Russell 2000 Growth	0.25	28/7/2000	2,492,216,000	3.3
40	UYG	ProShares Ultra Financials	0.95	1/2/2007	2,414,170,500	104.0
41	SLV	iShares Silver Trust	0.50	28/4/2006	2,356,312,500	7.0
42	IWS	iShares Russell MidCap Value	0.25	24/7/2001	2,355,975,000	2.1
43	SDS	ProShares UltraShort S&P 500	0.95	13/7/2006	2,251,331,250	43.5
44	VEA	Vanguard Europe Pacific	0.12	26/7/2007	2,237,474,995	1.4
45	XLP	Cons. Staples Select Sector SPDR	0.23	22/12/1998	2,232,702,248	5.6
46	USO	United States Oil	0.62	10/4/2006	2,179,452,000	15.4
47	VTV	Vanguard Value	0.10	30/1/2004	2,148,816,327	0.9
48	XLV	Health Care Select Sector SPDR	0.23	22/12/1998	2,060,032,378	5.9
49	IWP	iShares Russell MidCap Growth	0.25	1/8/2001	1,991,995,000	1.3
50	XLU	Utilities Select Sector SPDR	0.23	22/12/1998	1,958,556,454	7.6

Note: Data sourced to Bloomberg and Citi Investment Research and Analysis.

universe) comprise 74% of assets (US$399 billion) and the top five ETFs contain 34% of all ETF assets. An interesting point is that ETFs ranked 101–845 represent only 14% of all ETF assets and there are 376 ETFs with assets less than US$25 million. This is astonishing, and the author would have to assume, on a standalone basis, that ETFs with assets of US$25 million or less are money-losing propositions for their sponsors. Some of these ETFs are new and have not had much of a chance to gain traction; however, there are a number that have been in existence for more than a year that have struggled to take in money. Given these statistics, ETFs may not be quite as popular as they are perceived by the media. Making broad generalisations about strong growth and popularity of the funds across the board can be misleading. Assets and interest are concentrated within a small percentage of ETFs, which makes the movements of a select group of funds vital to the industry as a whole. As the industry grows, this may change; however, it is not likely to change dramatically in the foreseeable future. Figures 24.3 and 24.4 highlight the concentration.

Figure 24.3 ETF rankings by assets at year-end 2008

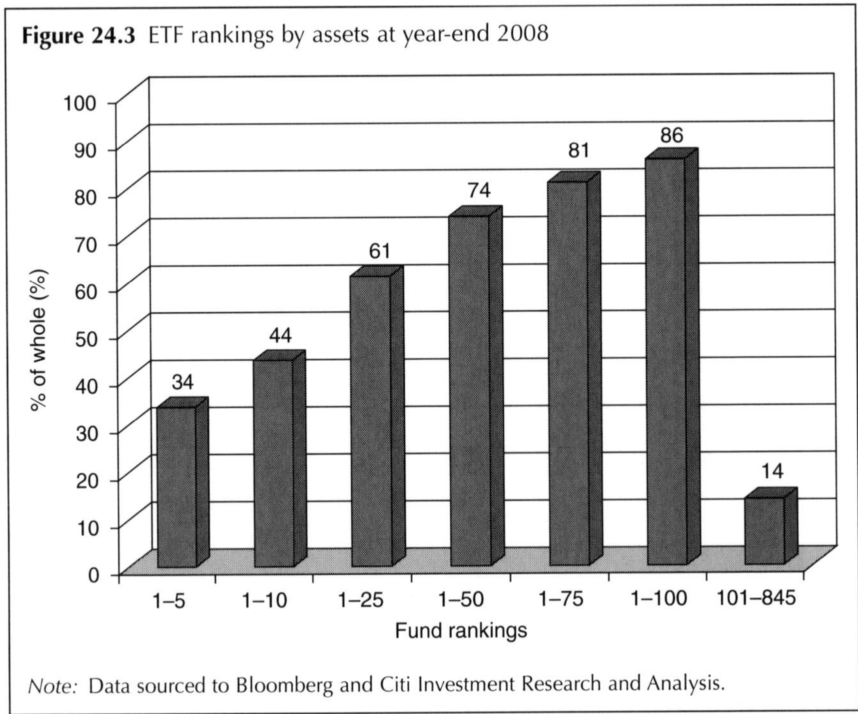

Note: Data sourced to Bloomberg and Citi Investment Research and Analysis.

Figure 24.4 ETF concentration at year-end 2008

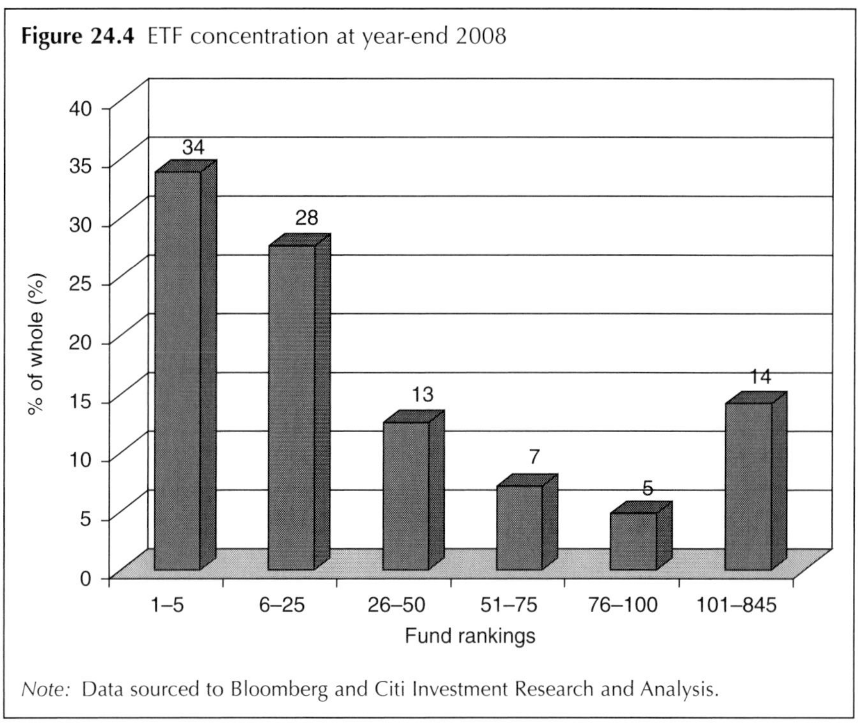

Note: Data sourced to Bloomberg and Citi Investment Research and Analysis.

ETF LANDSCAPE

As the ETF industry has evolved, so has its landscape. ETFs have always been dominated by equity funds. As of December 31, 2008, equity ETFs represent 78% of ETFs (by number of funds), of which 51% is allocated to domestic equities. While equity-based ETFs continue to dominate the landscape, their footprint has been shrinking. At December 31, 2005, equity ETFs made up 97% of the ETF marketplace and, as recently as December 31, 2007, equity ETFs made up 86% of all funds. In three years, equity-based ETFs have become less influential as investors can now get access to most financial markets via ETFs.

This trend is likely to continue as investors look to diversify outside of equities. Much of this seems to be driven by the constant desire to purchase non-correlating assets, or assets that investors believe to be non-correlated. In particular, commodities, fixed-income and foreign-currency ETFs have increased their market shares in a relatively short time period. Commodities have seen their market share

Table 24.3 Shifts in ETFs by type

Type	31/12/05 (%)	31/12/06 (%)	31/12/07 (%)	31/12/08 (%)
Domestic equity	73	72	63	51
International equity	20	19	19	21
Fixed income	3	2	8	7
Global equity	4	3	4	6
Commodity	1	3	5	11
FX	0	2	2	4

Note: Data sourced to Bloomberg and Citi Investment Research and Analysis.

jump to 11% from 1% while fixed-income has seen its market share jump to 7% from 3%. Foreign-currency ETFs have grown to 4% of total ETFs from not even having a presence at the end of 2005.

ETF FLOWS

ETF growth has come not only from financial market appreciation but also from new money, in the form of net creations, entering the space. At Citigroup we have been tracking ETF flow data since the end of 2005 and the data is quite impressive. Despite the ups and downs of the market and outflows in the open-end mutual fund space, ETFs have consistently posted net inflows since the end of 2005. In fact, over this time period, ETFs posted outflows only three months, two of which occurred in 2008. ETFs generally post strong inflows during the fourth quarter as investors look to position themselves for year end, active managers benchmark themselves to major indexes as well as tax-management strategies, and during the first quarter of the year they tend to unwind some of these positions, which results in lighter flows.

In 2006 ETFs had net inflows of US$70 billion, in 2007 net inflows of US$150 billion, and in 2008 net inflows of US$185 billion. Analysing and attempting to draw conclusions from mutual fund flow data has been commonplace for years. Given the relatively small size of the ETF market compared with the mutual fund industry, their much shorter history (bulk of ETFs have come out in the past eight years and growth rates were highest in 2006 and 2007) and asset concentration make it difficult to draw firm conclusions. The industry is simply too new and there remains an allure about investing in the product in general. In addition, attaining flow data for every ETF is difficult.

Also, flows tend to be concentrated, like assets, in a handful of funds. SPY often dictates flows for the industry as a whole. Generally, when SPY has significant net inflows, ETFs post strong flows and the opposite happens when SPY has a weak month. In 2008, SPY took in US$38 billion in new money, or more than 20% of total ETF flows and in 2007, SPY posted US$31 billion in net inflows which was also more than 20% of total net inflows.

SPONSORS

The number of ETF sponsors has been expanding for years and this growth continued in 2008. There are currently 28 ETF sponsors that range from large commercial banks all the way to start-ups. Given the growth in the ETF arena it seems enticing for new sponsors to enter the fray. That being said, the ETF business is a low-margin one that thrives on economies of scale. Despite not needing hoards of research analysts, there is a great deal of manpower and skill involved when creating and managing an ETF. ETF sponsors spend a great deal of time and money on product development; they also must have both risk- and tax-management policies in place from a portfolio-management standpoint; and, finally, sponsors must support their products in the secondary market both internally and externally through large sales forces.

Like assets, sponsor market share is also highly concentrated. As shown in Figure 24.5, the top four ETF sponsors (Barclays Global Investors-includes Barclays Bank, State Street Global Advisors, the Vanguard Group and Invesco PowerShares Capital Management) dominate the landscape with approximately 90% of market share. Digging deeper, Barclays and State Street comprise 77% of the industry. Barclays dominates the marketplace and is the clear leader with 48% of market share. Barclays has been the eight-hundred-pound gorilla for a number of years; however, it has seen its market share slide a bit. At the end of 2006, Barclays commanded 58% of the marketplace. As more sponsors enter the ETF marketplace it will be interesting to see whether or not the top players continue to dominate, though the indications are that they will. Given Barclays' advantage, it is difficult to imagine them losing their top spot in the foreseeable future. The top four sponsors have made large investments in their ETF businesses and have strong brand recognition, large sales forces, interactive tools on their websites and

Figure 24.5 ETF assets by fund sponsor at year-end 2008

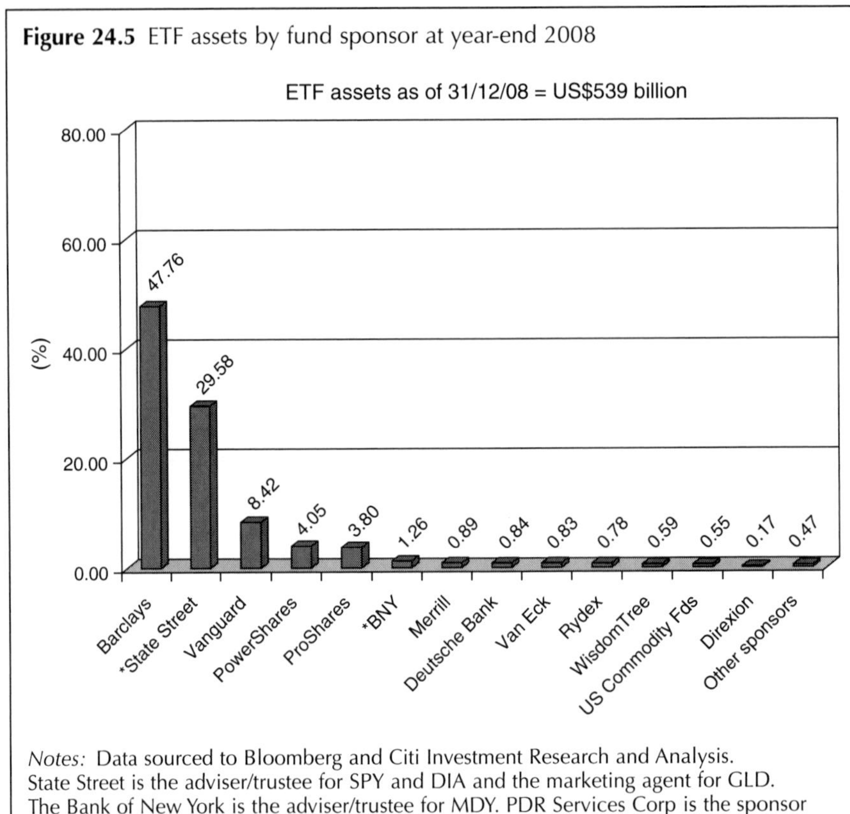

Notes: Data sourced to Bloomberg and Citi Investment Research and Analysis. State Street is the adviser/trustee for SPY and DIA and the marketing agent for GLD. The Bank of New York is the adviser/trustee for MDY. PDR Services Corp is the sponsor for SPY, DIA, and MDY. World Gold Trust Services, LLC is the sponsor for GLD.

a willingness to educate investors not only about their products but also about the benefits of ETFs in general. These common traits have undoubtedly contributed to their success.

In spite of the stranglehold that the top sponsors have on the industry, there have been some up-and-comers, especially of late. In particular, ProShare Advisors has more than doubled its market share from 1.5% at the end of 2007 to 3.8% at December 31, 2008. Given the area that the firm specialises in, it is not all that surprising to see such strong growth. ProShare Advisors offers inverse and leveraged ETFs, which have been extremely popular given volatile markets.

The specialities and types of products that sponsors bring to market vary and are constantly evolving. Barclays, State Street and Vanguard generally bring out ETFs that track beta indexes, while

PowerShares aims to bring out products that track alpha-seeking indexes and more recently have a suite of actively managed ETFs that do not track indexes at all. The top three asset gatherers track well-known indexes from providers such as Russell, S&P, MSCI and Dow Jones. Given the familiarity of these index providers, it is not all that surprising that the bulk of ETF assets are tied to them. These indexes are used as benchmarks by both institutional and retail investors, and the notion that most active managers do not outperform their benchmarks results in a mentality of "If you can't beat 'em, you might as well as join 'em".

When ranking sponsors based on the number of ETFs in their product line-up, Barclays, as indicated in Figure 24.6, is once again the leader with 209 funds. PowerShares comes in at a distant second with 124 ETFs, followed by State Street with 80 ETFs and ProShare Advisors with 76. Based on the number of ETFs it has in

Figure 24.6 Number of ETFs by fund sponsor as of year-end 2008

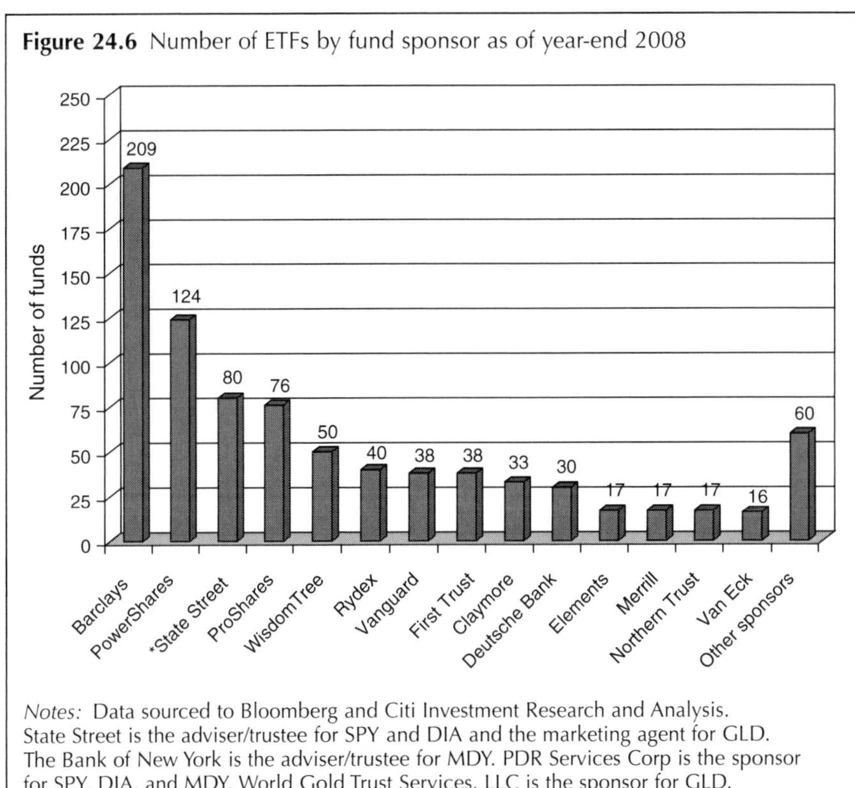

Notes: Data sourced to Bloomberg and Citi Investment Research and Analysis. State Street is the adviser/trustee for SPY and DIA and the marketing agent for GLD. The Bank of New York is the adviser/trustee for MDY. PDR Services Corp is the sponsor for SPY, DIA, and MDY. World Gold Trust Services, LLC is the sponsor for GLD.

registration with the SEC, ProShare Advisors could easily jump a spot or two in the rankings.

MORE PLAYERS

Strong industry growth over the years has not gone unnoticed by asset-management companies, banks and investors looking to capitalise on the boom. The industry is becoming crowded judging by the number of entrants just in 2008. As time goes on, we are likely to see more asset-management companies become involved in the space as ETFs become more of a threat to their mutual fund businesses. A catalyst for this could be the launch of non-transparent, actively managed ETFs whereby asset-management companies may launch versions of their open-end mutual funds in ETF format. This is a way down the road; however, with the amount of money at stake, it would not be all that surprising to see the big asset-management companies become more involved in bringing ETFs to market.

Commercial banks, are currently players in the ETF space and in fact the largest player, Barclays, is a commercial bank. They offer all types of ETFs, including traditional 1940 Act funds, ETNs and trusts, and they also act as index providers. Some commercial banks, such as UBS, recently got involved in the space launching ETNs, some even launching them off their structured-product desks. The author does not believe we will see a great deal of additional ETN issuance given the unsecured debt nature of the product and credit concerns among banks.

Given the well-publicised success of PowerShares and its subsequent purchase by Invesco Ltd, there have been a number of ETF startup companies that have launched products. There will undoubtedly be more startups, some self-funded, others funded by venture capitalists, looking to grow assets and eventually sell their stakes. The multiples that are placed on asset managers and the prospects of the ETF industry have to be enticing for those thinking about starting ETF companies. That being said, the landscape is extremely competitive, and as we have seen, assets are highly concentrated and many of the newer products have failed to take on assets.

Traditional mutual fund houses may also enter the ETF business the way Invesco did. They may purchase an ETF sponsor in the hope of gaining access to the growth of the ETF market based on the product suite the sponsor has available. Furthermore, looking down the road, this may be the perfect avenue to launch actively managed ETFs, based on their existing portfolio managers and strategies. This strategy may be something of a hedge for a traditional mutual fund house and ensure that they will participate in asset growth whether it comes from mutual funds or ETFs. Over the past few years rumblings have been heard that traditional mutual fund houses have shown interest in certain ETF sponsors. We may see more action on this front if ETF growth continues and/or if actively managed ETFs take off.

CONSOLIDATION

The ETF business flourishes on economies of scale given the low average expense ratio for the industry. Due to the current number of players, and the economies that can be drawn, it would not be that surprising to see consolidation in the space. Mergers and acquisitions could occur among and/or between both the larger and smaller sponsors. Big benefits can be achieved by sharing portfolio-management skills, back-office operations and sales forces. We may also see sponsors purchasing individual funds from one another rather than their complete suite. Based on the concentration of assets in the industry, certain ETFs are more valuable than others. In other words, there are a lot of ETFs that do not make sense to keep open from an economic standpoint.

We will also most likely continue to see partnerships develop. For instance, WisdomTree and Dreyfus commenced a partnership in early 2008 that will help in the distribution of WisdomTree's ETFs as well as seeing Dreyfus acting as a sub-adviser to specific products. Partnerships have been commonplace in the ETF marketplace for years; however, as sponsors battle for market share and distribution, these relationships will be crucial in order to grow assets. The author believes partnerships will become even more relevant if ETFs start to make their way into 401(k) plans. The 401(k) business thrives on relationships, which many new ETF sponsors simply do not have.

CLOSURES

In addition to the 58 ETFs that closed in 2008, there have already been announced ETF closures in 2009. We are bound to see more closures given that 376 funds have less than US$25 million in assets, many of which have been around for more than a year. You would think that, at some point, an ETF that fails to bring in assets becomes such a cost burden to its sponsor that the logical thing to do is close it. Given the size of the industry, up until 2008, there had been relatively few closures. However, the closures that have occurred have come from all types of sponsors. Even some of the heavyweights such as Barclays and State Street have shut down funds. ETFs are shuttered for numerous reasons, primarily due to a lack of assets and backing. They are also closed because they may not meet diversification requirements under the Investment Company Act of 1940, no longer make investment sense, or may even breach a threshold that triggers a termination event as stated by prospectus.

It is also important to point out that, just because an ETF lacks assets, it does not mean a sponsor will close it. Many sponsors look at their ETF suite as a whole and are willing to have their successful, profitable products carry the load while their smaller, less successful ETFs try to gain traction. This would be more feasible for the larger, more profitable sponsors that can afford to carry money-losing products for extended periods.

If ETF closures were to accelerate they might give the industry a black eye. No one wants to invest in a product only to find that it is closing six months after they placed money in it. Mass closures could make investors think twice before investing in certain products and, if the closures came strictly from the smaller sponsors, it would be very difficult for smaller players to attract assets. That being said, we must put closures in context. Traditional open-end mutual funds close up all the time; and, even if an ETF closes, an ETF investor receives their money back at net asset value (minus some minor closure costs). The major downside is that investors are forced to liquidate their position at potentially an inopportune time that could trigger a taxable event.

SEED CAPITAL

Prior to the commencement of trading, ETFs are seeded with money by "authorised participants", which are typically specialists or market makers. Seed capital allows ETFs to start off with some level of assets, helps get the product of the ground and provides inventory that can be sold to investors. Given the demise of specialists, the inability to borrow money and the sheer number of new products that need to be seeded, capital has become scarce. This could force, and is already forcing, sponsors to be more selective about the products they bring to market. Selectivity may slow product launches down and may result in more thoughtful launches. This might be viewed as a positive, because it makes sponsors think twice before asking for capital because there is only so much available.

On the cover, a lack of seed capital is a negative for the industry, but the author believes it favours the larger sponsors and will continue to drive assets their way. The larger sponsors with a number of successful products from a trading standpoint most likely have deeper relationships and more sway over specialists and market makers than smaller sponsors with fewer products that do not trade as much.

Good products should not have problems finding seed money. The issue here is that it is often difficult to predict how successful an ETF will be. Some of the most successful ETFs from an asset-gathering and trading standpoint come as a surprise to some analysts, and the author is sure also to sponsors. The marginal ETF sponsors that are looking to launch ETFs into crowded areas of the marketplace will suffer most. As the ranks of specialists continue to decline, ETF sponsors will need to look elsewhere for seed capital.

A few ideas have been mooted, but nothing concrete. One potential idea is to have ETF sponsors seed their own products. In order for this to come to fruition, ETF sponsors may be required to file for some type of exemptive relief. Seeding your own ETF may violate SEC affiliation rules and result in a conflict of interest. If this were possible, and sponsors could seed their own products, it would clearly favour the larger players with deeper pockets. Another idea is to figure out some way for ETF sponsors to compensate specialists/ market makers for seeding their products. Compensating specialists/ market makers may also violate regulatory issues; however, the industry does need to come up with some type of solution because the specialist system, as it has existed in the past, is going to look much different going forward, if it exists at all.

EXPENSES

ETFs are often seen as being low-cost investment vehicles that have expense ratios at a fraction of what actively managed open-end mutual funds charge. As ETFs and their structures have become more complex, their expense ratios have increased. At year-end 2005, the average ETF had an expense ratio of 0.40%. By year-end 2007, that number jumped to 0.53% and at the end of 2008 stood at 0.56%. While this 40% increase in fees is troubling, the increase is not as dramatic on a market-cap-weighted basis. At year-end 2005 the average fee for an ETF, on a market-cap-weighted basis, was 0.27%. By year-end 2007 the average market-cap-weighted fee had crept up to only 0.31% and at the end of 2008 remained at 0.31%. This reiterates prior points showing that assets have flowed towards some of the lower-priced, older ETFs, while many of the higher-priced, newer products have not been all that popular.

New and smaller ETF players also need to charge more because they do not have the economies of scale that some of the larger players have and cannot compete with heavyweights such as Vanguard, which is known throughout the industry as a low-cost provider, on price. In addition, expense ratios must be high enough in order to make it economical for not only the ETF sponsor, but also the index provider who licenses their index out to the sponsor. Part of the thinking may also be that, even if a product is priced above the average ETF, it may still look cheap compared with an open-end mutual fund. The recent increase on a market-cap-weighted basis is undoubtedly due to the surge in assets on a relative basis of the inverse and leveraged products as some of these ETFs have expense ratios approaching 1%.

Expense ratios on products that track beta indexes should come down, as competition is fairly tight. Beta indexes, except for minor differences, are commodities, and, as time goes on, pricing will be increasingly important given its impact on returns. We have already witnessed expense ratio reductions by some of the larger ETF sponsors as they hope to make their products more attractive to investors and pass along cost savings. This should help the weighted average expense ratio of the industry as a whole, given the number of assets tied to beta indexes.

While expense ratios on ETFs that track beta indexes should come down, it is anticipated that expense ratios on newer products as well as ETFs that track non-beta indexes will remain high. ETFs out of smaller sponsors, ETFs that track alpha-seeking indexes, ETFs that track areas of the market that are more difficult to get access to, leveraged and inverse ETFs, and actively managed ETFs will all drive the average expense ratio for the industry higher. On the cover, higher expense ratios are not a good thing for the end investor. However, in certain instances, access to challenging and unique markets justifies some of these higher fees, and ETFs are often priced attractively compared with competing products outside the ETF space.

USERS/LIQUIDITY

Who is using ETFs? ETFs are used by institutional, retail and individual investors and, judging by asset growth over the years, each one of these groups is using ETFs more. As the number of offerings and ETF education has increased, so, it seems, has investor participation. ETF usage varies depending on the investor. Hedge funds often use them as trading vehicles, mutual funds for cash equitisation and retail and individual investors as long-term buy-and-hold strategies. Options are also available on a significant amount of the ETF universe, which gives investors leveraged ways to participate in up, down and sideways markets.

As global wealth shifts, international investors looking to the US ETF market may become significant ETF players. While there are ETFs that trade on non-US exchanges, the US ETF market is by far the largest. What better way for international investors to gain access to financial markets without having to pick individual securities? This could give a boost to the industry and, judging by enquiries received, it appears that international investors are becoming more aware of the advantages of ETFs and want to invest in US-traded ETFs.

ETFs are natural fits in fee-based platforms that broker-dealers have been migrating to and registered investment advisers have embraced, while the tradability of the product has also been attractive for commission-based business. Given the volume on some of the larger ETFs and the flexibility that ETFs provide relative to open-end mutual funds (can be shorted, options available) it is safe to assume that institutional players have been and remain extraordinarily active in the space. Despite the ETF creation/redemption mechanism it is the author's experience that institutional investors have flocked to the most liquid ETFs, placing emphasis on daily volume and bid–ask spreads. Given light volume on certain ETFs, it can be difficult for them to gain traction, considering that, without institutional participation, liquidity and assets may never pick up. It can be tough to pinpoint and get accurate usage numbers; however, as liquidity picks up, we should see all levels of investors increase their usage.

Over the past 10 years, trading in most exchange-traded products has changed dramatically. A great deal of ETF trading is already occurring off the exchanges and through electronic markets. While having a specialist does help on some of the less liquid products, the notion that most volume is occurring via electronic trading platforms should help the end-investor from a cost standpoint. This should increase liquidity, which should drive down bid–ask spreads further and result in more of the returns going to the investor, although improvements in liquidity may be offset to some extent by some of the ETFs coming to market that do not gain interest and hardly trade. Naturally, those products that are less liquid will have wider bid–ask spreads.

ETFs IN 401(k)s

To date, ETF usage in 401(k) plans has been relatively limited. While ETF growth numbers have been spectacular, they would probably look even more impressive if they achieved widespread usage in 401(k) plans. A number of ETF sponsors are working on ways to incorporate ETFs in 401(k) plans; however, there have been many roadblocks and progress has been very slow. Companies and their employees have been participating in 401(k) plans for more than 25 years and have been successfully using mutual funds. It becomes a major task changing the way people think, especially given the success mutual funds have enjoyed in the plans. The author also thinks mutual fund houses that have large amounts of assets from 401(k) plans are going to do everything in their power to retain these assets.

The reason why ETFs are not widely used in 401(k) plans is twofold. First, some of the advantages that ETFs provide are nullified in retirement accounts; and, second, there are operational/cost issues that must be overcome. Given the tax-deferral status of 401(k) plans, the tax efficiency of ETFs is irrelevant. It does not matter whether a fund pays a capital gain because nothing is taxed until the investor withdraws money from the account. Intra-day trading is another advantage that ETFs offer. Intra-day trading is somewhat useless for the average 401(k) investor, given the long-term investment horizons – which should not be based on frequent trading – of retirement investors and the automatic contributions they make. Low expense ratios are also often touted as advantages for ETFs. However, there are a number of traditional index mutual funds that have expense ratios just as low as ETFs.

The second and bigger problem lies on the operational/cost side. Every time an ETF share is purchased, an investor must pay a commission and deal with a bid–ask spread. If, for an example, an investor is purchasing a small number of shares every two weeks, the costs would be prohibitive and eat into long-term returns. In addition to the costs, ETFs cannot be purchased in fractional shares, which makes dollar-cost averaging difficult. This is relevant in 401(k) plans because investors generally contribute US dollar amounts rather than specifying share amounts when they make their contributions. The way around the costs and fractional share amounts is to group or pool ETFs and have plan participants purchase ETFs from this pool. Grouping or pooling does not completely eliminate the costs of purchasing and selling ETFs; however, it does spread the costs out and makes them more manageable. This does, however, create more back-office work and more expenses due to the allocation work.

Where ETFs do have a major advantage in 401(k) plans is the combination of low expense ratios, passive management and the availability of so many different asset classes. Traditional index mutual funds do not offer anywhere near as many options or access to as many markets as ETFs currently do. Investors in 401(k)s could potentially build a more diversified asset-allocation model with low expenses by using ETFs. Actively managed mutual funds would not be able to compete on the cost front, while index mutual funds would lack the access to asset classes that some ETFs provide.

The amount of assets allocated to 401(k) plans (US$3 trillion as of December 31, 2007, according to ICI) leads the author to believe that someone will find a way to overcome the hurdles and incorporate ETFs into these plans. This, in the author's opinion, is one of the two things that could propel ETF assets to much higher levels (the other being actively managed ETFs). There are critics who do not think ETF options are necessary in 401(k) plans; however, the author thinks the plan participant should be the one to make that decision. It is their money and, if they want to invest in ETFs and get access to different asset classes in a cost-efficient manner, so be it. It is just as easy to make the argument that plan participants should not be investing in actively managed mutual funds because most underperform their benchmarks over periods of time.

ACTIVELY MANAGED ETFs

The long-awaited and highly anticipated launch of actively managed ETFs occurred in the first half of 2008. For years, industry experts and investors have anxiously awaited the arrival of these products which, like participation in 401(k) plans, could take ETF assets to the next level. Like participation in 401(k) plans, the outlook for actively managed ETFs really taking off is murky. Investors have been drawn to ETFs because of their index-based nature and the fact that most active managers do not outperform their benchmarks. Why would investors flock to actively managed ETFs that pose the same portfolio manager issues as actively managed mutual funds? Proponents of actively managed ETFs state they would be similar to actively managed mutual funds with all the bells and whistles of traditional ETFs; that is, an investor would receive professional management wrapped in a product that provides greater tax efficiency, intra-day trading flexibility and potentially slightly lower expense ratios.

Investors have to accept that there are greater risks associated with actively managed ETFs. In addition to market risk, investors now take on management risk. Greater due diligence is required. A manager's track record and experience must be analysed, on both an absolute and risk-adjusted basis. Furthermore, a manager's buy-and-sell disciplines must be taken into account as well as the depth and experience of management, number of assets under their belt and the size of their team. These are just a few of the areas that investors should analyse when determining whether or not to invest in a particular actively managed ETF.

Actively managed ETFs should be separated into two categories. There is the current suite of actively managed ETFs available that are transparent, in that they publish their holdings and creation baskets on a daily basis. These actively managed ETFs occupy two segments of the marketplace. There are actively managed, fixed-income ETFs that cover the short end of the yield curve and are sponsored by

WisdomTree and PowerShares, and there are equity-based, actively managed ETFs issued by PowerShares that are based on quantitative models. The common thread between these ETFs is their transparency. These products were able to make it to market and receive SEC approval because they were willing to disclose their holdings daily. The second group of actively managed ETFs, which are currently not available and a number of sponsors and participants are working on, will not reveal their complete creation basket and will not exhibit the transparency that the current ETFs provide.

Transparency has been the sticking point with actively managed ETFs from day one. Most active managers do not want investors front-running their trades or copying their intellectual capital. They have a problem revealing their holdings on, at minimum, a daily basis. The revelation of a creation basket keeps the market price of an ETF close to its net asset value and really is the structural key to ETFs. Without transparency, ETFs would probably trade at meaningful premiums and discounts to net asset value like a closed-end fund.

It can be argued that the first round of actively managed ETFs on the equity side are not all that different from many existing ETFs in the marketplace that track indexes based on quantitative models. Other than stating that they are not benchmarking themselves to an index and more frequent rebalancing, there is not a great deal of difference.

The author sees the greatest potential for actively managed ETFs in a product that looks similar to an actively managed mutual fund in that a portfolio manager is selecting stocks. An ETF of this nature would provide the investor with active investment, greater tax efficiency, intra-day trading and competitive pricing. We could see big-name portfolio managers or fund companies offering ETF versions of their existing mutual funds as either a share class of an existing mutual fund or a standalone product with similar traits as an existing mutual fund. Vanguard currently has a share class patent based on its existing mutual fund line-up; however, it does have active mutual funds and could therefore take advantage of its competitive position.

In order for actively managed ETFs to take off, we are going to need to see a major fund company get involved. It may be hesitant about revealing its holdings daily; however, if it can figure out a way to post a creation basket with similar traits to, but different holdings from, its underlying portfolio, it would be a boon for the industry. If actively managed ETFs take off, they pose a serious threat to the mutual fund industry. This is probably not going to happen any time in the near future; however, if sponsors can get around some of the hurdles, there is great upside potential.

One of the major drivers of ETF growth and liquidity has been institutional participation. The author does not envision institutional investors wanting exposure to another actively managed portfolio that does not exhibit a great deal of transparency. Without an ETF track record it also may take time for actively managed ETFs to gain assets. Generally, investors looking to buy into an active strategy want to see live performance for a number of years before they feel comfortable investing. In fact, rating services such as Morningstar, in many instances, require three-year returns prior to rating funds. This could therefore limit the growth of actively managed ETFs and make it difficult for them to get off the ground.

CONCLUSIONS

The biggest key to growth in the ETF marketplace has to do with the growth of underlying financial markets. Declining financial markets are major headwinds for the ETF industry. Net inflows can offset declining financial markets only so much. In addition to underlying markets, investors must continue to embrace the product. ETFs must be designed with the end user in mind and, as mentioned earlier, innovation and sponsor creativity will be key in bringing out successful products.

The author believes we will see all groups embrace ETFs more and see more investors building asset-allocation models strictly around ETFs. This push will probably come from the broker-dealers as they realise the advantages that ETFs provide to their clients. Broker-dealers have been slow in embracing ETFs as they have struggled to figure out ways to make money from them. The author believes many broker-dealers have now figured out that the true value-added will come from making the asset allocation call and simply using ETFs as tools to implement the strategy.

While the future looks bright for ETFs, it is often what we do not know that can hurt us most. Could some event slow or even reverse asset growth in the industry? Will there be some type of blow-up or will an ETF sponsor do something that places a black eye on the industry? Generally, increased success results in increased scrutiny. As the industry grows it is only logical for it to receive more attention.

Due to the run-up in commodity prices in early 2008 there has been a great deal of talk about the role of speculators in these markets. ETF investors that purchase commodity ETFs would fall under the speculator category, as they are not taking physical delivery of the goods and are not end-users of the commodities. If some type of legislation were to pass or if a regulatory body made a ruling limiting the role of speculators in the commodity markets, it could potentially have an effect on not only the underlying commodities markets, but also the ETFs themselves. It is too early to know what the ramifications would be; however, commodity ETFs currently have nearly US$36 billion in assets, making them legitimate players in commodity markets. Granted, more than half of that is in ETFs that physically purchase the commodity rather than use futures markets. This is something to continue to monitor.

Most ETFs are extraordinarily tax-efficient in that they rarely pay capital gains. One potential problem for the industry lies in the favourable tax treatment that in-kind transfers of shares receive. Most ETFs are created and redeemed in kind rather than in cash. In-kind transfers of shares are currently considered non-taxable events. If the IRS were to make a ruling that would consider this process a taxable event, it could have a negative impact on the industry, as capital gain payouts could occur more frequently. The author views this as a tax loophole that ETFs are able to exploit due to the way they are designed. If this loophole were to close, one of the major advantages, albeit not the only one, that ETFs provide would cease to exist.

Index

100-share contract, 252
401(k) marketplace, 524, 536
401(k) retirement plans, 2
500-stock index, 5

A

absolute-size parameters, 22
active approach, 315
active element, 442
active investment strategy, 58
active management risk, 544
active management strategies, 543
adequate market liquidity, 439
aggregate assets, 1
aggregate fixed-income ETF, 295
aggregate market capitalisation, 504
aggregate volatility, 227
aggressive bonds, 230
aggressive investors, 486
aggressive portfolio, 479
alpha, 14
  generators, 15
  index, 183
American option, 245
American Stock Exchange, 130, 193
Appreciation SuperShares, 564
asset-allocation approach, 372
asset-allocation model, 201, 202
asset-allocation plan, 487
asset-allocation strategy, 205, 206, 524
asset-allocation theory, 205
asset-class benchmarks, 49
asset diversification, 374
asset price, 252
asset-weighted average exotic beta, 317
augmented asymmetric model, 513
automotive transportation, 382
autoregressive moving average (ARMA) models, 517
average cost methods, 546

B

backwardated market, 389
backwardation, 393
basic allocation models, 46
basket approach, 183, 408
basket instrument, 2
basket peg, 498
bear market analysis, 319
bear spread call option, 264
benchmark index, 101, 115, 160, 168, 177
beta, 14
  index group, 16
  producers, 15
bid–ask spread, 236
Big Mac Index, 416
biotechnology, 9
blended portfolios, 299
blue-chip index fund, 489
Bogle-defined investment world, 8
bond funds, 285
bond indexes, 289
bond interest rate, 277
bond market, 275, 286
bond mutual funds, 271, 297
book-equity value, 31
book-value metric, 30
break-even point, 260
broad-based benchmarks, 161
broad-based index, 7
  fund, 16
broad-based investments, 200
broad-based market indexes, 304
broad domestic stock market, 334
broad indexes, 14
broad international funds, 450
broad market equity ETFs, 491
broad market indexes, 46
broad stock market, 339

brokerage firm, 367
bubble periods, 33
buffer zones, 440
bull call spread investment strategy, 263
bull spread option, 261
buy-and-hold approach, 218
buy-write strategy, 565

C
call bull spread, 265
call option, 376
call risk, 275
capital asset pricing model, 41, 215, 216
capital gain payouts, 593
capital-gains distributions, 542
capitalisation rating process, 444
capitalisation-weighted equity index, 67
capitalisation-weighted index funds, 25
capitalisation-weighted methodology, 69
cap-weighted benchmarks, 553
cap-weighted ETFs, 25
cap-weighted index, 18, 27, 35
cap-weighted portfolio, 27
cap-weighted S&P 500, 29
carry strategy, 411
cash-equivalent portfolio, 184
cash equitisation, 587
cashflows, 7, 27, 129, 285, 559
cash market, 385
cash-out date, 564
cash-settled instrument, 559
Cerulli data, 551
Chicago Board Options Exchange (CBOE), 559, 561
Chicago Mercantile Exchange, 557
classic index fund, 8
Claymore ETFs, 533
Clear Spin-Off Index, 65
closed-end mutual fund, 562
collar strategy, 267
collective investment fund, 536
commercial mortgage-backed bonds, 282
commodity-based ETF, 355, 365, 366
commodity-based funds, 364
commodity-based index, 359
commodity benchmark, 367
commodity ETF's benchmark, 398
commodity market, 390, 394
commodity price, 371
commodity trusts, 137
composite fundamental value, 446
composite index, 557
conservative bonds, 230
contango market, 389
conventional index mutual fund, 130
convertible bonds, 70, 285
core-satellite strategy, 176
corporate bond, 275
correlation levels, 428
correlation matrix, 334
cost-effective market, 403
covered call strategy, 256
creation and redemption process, 365, 565
credit bonds, 271, 282
credit risk, 176, 313, 421
cross-sectional volatility, 546
crude oil benchmark, 360
currency-based exchange products, 426
currency market, 401
  volatility, 419

D
DB G10 Currency Harvest Fund (DBV), 491
db x-trackers Euro STOXX 50 ETF, 171
db x-trackers MSCI World ETF, 161
delta-neutral, 259
Deutsche Bank Liquid Commodity Index, 357
directional approach, 369
diversification, 131, 188, 197, 234, 286, 333
  benefits, 519
  strategy, 197, 205
  tools, 197

diversified index, 78
diversified passive approach, 38
diversified portfolio, 274, 478
dividend indexes, 60
dividend-paying stocks, 458
dividend-weighted indexes, 533
dollar peg, 498
domestic equity, 273
domestic portfolio, 483
domestic stock benchmarks, 347
domestic US bonds, 485
dotcom stocks, 16
Dow Jones Global Titans index, 450
Dow Jones Industrial Average, 1, 4
Dow Jones stock index, 4
Dow Jones Wilshire 5000 Index, 301
due-diligence process, 146
dynamic functions, 518

E

EAFE benchmark, 428
earnings-weighted indexes, 533
economic-cycle-based tactical outlook approach, 233
efficient-market hypothesis, 405
emerging-markets allocation, 549
emerging-markets arena, 435
emerging-markets strategy, 549
energy-commodity ETFs, 353, 372
energy-related commodities, 356, 381
energy-related stocks, 371
equilibrium price, 513
equity-based exchange-traded index funds, 117
equity ETF market, 299
equity funds, 50, 577
equity index, 65
  funds, 134
equity market, 363, 452
  benchmark, 96
  cap, 371
equity premium puzzle, 410
equity stock portfolio, 560
European ETF market, 175
European index, 172
European option, 245
exchange-listed stocks, 6
exchange rate, 402
exchange-traded commodities (ETCs), 358
exchange-traded funds
  arena, 579
  assets, 576
  bandwagon, 2, 8
  based portfolio, 212
  classifications methods, 43
  development process, 565
  explosion, 143
  index exposure, 37
  investors trade, 152
  issuance, 570
  liquidity, 153
  marketplace, 299, 394, 467, 583, 592
  portfolio assets, 101
  price, 20
  registration process, 569
  limit taxable capital gains distributions, 196
  tax efficiency, 132
  transactions, 145
exchange-traded grantor trusts, 85
exchange-traded index portfolio, 565
exchange-traded notes (ETNs), 476, 523
exemptive relief, 2
exotic beta, 313
expected stock reactions, 516
explicit costs, 152
Ex-US applications, 34
Exxon's stock, 370

F

Fama–French approach, 23
financial integration, 498
First Trust S&P REIT Index Fund, 338
Fiserv Trust Target Date Blueprint Funds, 533
fixed-income allocation, 296
Fixed-income assets, 273
fixed-income benchmarks, 291
fixed-income ETF market, 300

fixed-income index, 291
fixed-income mutual funds, 50
fixed-income portfolio, 285
fixed-income space, 178
float-adjusted indexes, 69
float-adjusted market capitalisation, 441, 444
forecasting models, 481
foreign bonds, 70, 479
foreign-equity ETFs, 117
foreign equity market, 406
foreign portfolio, 484
forward market, 386
fractions market, 515
free-float-adjusted market capitalisation, 443
frequency, 419
front-month contract, 395
front-month-only approach, 393
fundamental approach, 448
Fundamental Index, 33, 41
  approach, 32
  ETF strategy, 39
  portfolio, 30, 34, 37
  strategies, 25, 26
fundamentals-based models, 414
fund diversification, 69
fund performance analysis, 507
fund's expense ratio, 153
fund's target benchmark, 134
fund's tax efficiency, 133

G
GCC stock markets, 495
geopolitical risk, 496
global all-equity portfolio, 514
global equity markets, 24
Global ex-US portfolio, 42
Global Industry Classification System (GICS), 442
global portfolio diversification, 506
gold fund, 56
Goldman Sachs Commodities Index, 70
grantor trust flow, 137
grantor trust product, 137
growth portfolios, 482
Growth stocks, 22, 149

H
hands-off portfolio, 476
hedge fund, 369
  strategies, 191, 329
heterogeneity, 515
high-dividend-paying stocks, 9
historic return data, 200
Hodrick-Prescott (HP) filter, 517
holistic approach, 53
hybrid fund, 526

I
ideal asset allocation, 548
ideal investment equation, 484
implementation plan, 199
implicit costs, 152
index arbitrageurs, 559
index-based investment products, 1
index-based mutual funds, 205
Index-based tracking, 205
index classification mythology, 43
index construction methods, 49
index ETFs track securities indexes, 43
index fund, 7, 557
  exposure, 37
index futures contracts, 559
index links, 1
index mutual funds, 13, 144, 433, 435
index options, 247, 559
index participation unit (IPU), 559
index portfolio, 13, 562, 563
  trading, 561
index replication strategy, 554
index strategy boxes (ISBs), 44
index strategy map, 43, 50
  analysis, 83
index swap, 171
index tracking error, 206
index-tracking mutual funds, 528
inefficient indexing, 41
inefficient market, 41
inflation-linked bonds, 271
Inflation-linked international bonds, 292
inflation-protected portfolio, 345
in-kind redemption process, 132

in-kind transaction process, 137
institutional-strength portfolios, 194
Intellidex index methodology, 64
intended asset-allocation
model, 209
inter-day liquidity, 195
interest rate risk, 284
international equity allocation, 448
international equity ETFs, 427, 473
international equity mutual
funds, 437
international investment
portfolio, 483
intra-day liquidity, 401, 515
intra-day trading, 516
investable-market index, 444
investment-grade bonds, 283
Investment-grade corporate
bonds, 283
investment policy statement
(IPS), 198
investment portfolio, 26, 239,
336, 478
investment process, 217
investment strategy, 2, 8, 43, 198,
210, 410, 416
investment structure, 193
investment tool, 205
investment vehicle, 199
IP transactions, 562
IP unit value, 562
IPU structure, 566
iShares emerging fund, 461
iShares KLD Select Social Index
ETF, 61
iShares MSCI EAFE Index
Fund, 573
iShares Small Cap Fund, 467
iShares S&P Global 100 Index
Fund, 449, 450

K
Kuwaiti over-the-counter (OTC)
market, 500

L
laddered portfolio strategies, 297
laddered strategy, 298
large-cap blend funds, 82, 530
LargeCap Dividend Index, 81
large-cap index, 445
large-cap stocks, 206
Lehman Aggregate Bond
Index, 201
Lehman Aggregate Bond
Market, 55
Lehman Multiverse Index, 301
lifecycle funds, 570
lifecycle mutual fund
assets, 525
life-strategy fund, 74
life-strategy index, 74
liquidity, 144
risk, 275, 313
seekers, 402
London Stock Exchange, 159
long-term capital gains, 378
long-term peer-group data, 40
long-term treasury bonds, 281
loss harvesting, 552
low-cost market index funds, 49

M
market benchmark, 48
market capitalisation, 5, 20, 25, 45,
46, 62, 67, 236, 431, 439, 445,
499, 500, 504
weighting, 13
market-cap-weighted
approach, 432
market-cap-weighted basis, 586
market-cap-weighted funds, 462
market-cap-weighted index,
18, 455
market index, 44, 139
funds, 44, 47
market liquidity, 505
market-neutral approach, 230
market-neutral base, 228
market-neutral investment, 148
market P/E ratio, 38
market portfolio, 8, 216
market price, 5, 249, 255
market risk, 276, 284
market vectors, 470
market volatility, 162

mean–variance-efficient portfolio, 45
mean variance optimisation, 411
mechanical trading strategy, 48
mid-cap fund, 466
mid-cap index, 445
moderate-risk investors, 348
modern portfolio theory (MPT), 484, 514
modern stock indexes, 13
momentum, 481
  analysis, 481
  investing strategies, 222
  strategy, 417
money-market ETFs, 178
Monte Carlo simulations, 546
mortgage-backed bonds, 282
MSCI Global Consumer Staples Index, 39
MSCI World ex-US Index, 36
multi-asset-allocation portfolio, 372
multi-cap investment strategies, 553
multi-currency, 502
multiple-asset approach, 369
multiple-asset-class portfolio, 217
multiple-investment strategy, 372
multiple-strategy portfolio, 540
municipal bond portfolios, 330
mutual-fund average-cost methods, 543
mutual fund flow data, 578
mutual-fund investor, 543
mutual-fund portfolio, 198

N
naked call option, 250
Nasdaq Composite Index, 60
National Retirement Risk Index (NRRI), 525
Neo asset allocation, 189
net asset value (NAV), 89, 423
neutral strategy, 258
New York Stock Exchange, 45, 361
non-beta indexes, 586
non-correlating assets, 577
non-fundamental currency, 416
non-industry investors, 382
non-taxable events, 593
non-traditional assets, 108
non-US dollar assets, 485

O
obsolete funds, 309
obsolete open-end funds, 310
OCC clearing mechanism, 563
odd lot market, 515
off-exchange-traded funds, 559
open-end fund structure, 156
Open-end index fund, 523
open-end mutual funds, 1, 308, 582
open-end real-estate funds, 312
open-end sector funds, 309
opportunistic hedging, 187
optimisation strategy, 128
option spread strategies, 261
option strategy, 265
option-related strategies, 371
order flow-based models, 406
out-of-the-money call option, 370
over-the-counter (OTC) market, 386

P
passive approach, 315
passive broad-market funds, 11
passive diversification, 37
passive growth index, 60
passive portfolio management, 10
passive strategic approach, 231
payoff, 267
Philadelphia Stock Exchange (PHLX), 559
portfolio, 473, 557
  allocation, 201, 490
  assets, 93, 99
  construction process, 217
  diversification, 334, 347
  investments, 102
  market, 208
  plan, 199
  process, 198
  risk, 215, 291, 427, 484
  strategy, 219
  variance, 514, 517
  weights, 25, 28, 32

postdated-cheque system, 501
potential gain, 370
potential taxable capital-gains distributions, 132
PowerShares Dynamic Market Portfolio, 64, 76
price momentum, 74
price-to-book ratios, 19
price-to-earnings ratio, 448, 480
price volatility, 479
price volume model, 513
price-weighted index, 37
pricing errors, 29
profitability, 513
programme trading, 560
proprietary methodology, 9
proprietary model, 450
pro rata interest, 157
protective put strategy, 254
prudent tax strategy, 248
public and corporate pension funds, 557
put bear spread, 265
put bull spread, 265
put option, 250

Q

quantitative selection methods, 63
quant models, 17

R

RAFI approach, 34
RAFI US Large Company Index, 31
range-bound markets, 412
rating funds, 592
real alpha, 313
  analysis, 316, 326
rebalancing strategy, 199, 208, 209
Regulation M, 119
REIT bear market, 351
Research Affiliates Fundamental Index (RAFI), 31
retirement portfolio, 532
revenue bonds, 283
reverse optimisation, 514
risk-and-return benchmarks, 534
risk-and-return parameters, 200
risk-aversion, 419
risk budget, 295
risk exposure, 172
risk-free assets, 410
risk-free rate, 514
risk-neutral, 405
  efficient-markets hypothesis, 412
  investor, 257
risk premium, 409
risk tolerance, 475
robber barons, 3
robust international strategy, 475
Rogers International Commodity Index, 357
roll mechanism, 404
rules-based selection process, 443
Russell Midcap Index, 554
Russell 1000 index, 206

S

sales index, 30
scale factor, 19
sector allocation analysis, 328
sector funds, 10
sector index ETF, 39
sector rotation strategies, 296
Securities and Exchange Commission (SEC), 1
security selection method, 44, 57
security selection process, 64
Security selection strategy, 80
security weighting method, 44
security weighting strategy, 80
Seed capital, 584
Seligman TargetHorizon ETF Portfolios, 534
semiannual cash-out date, 564
shallow analysis, 516
share settlement process, 501
Sharpe ratio, 32, 339, 428
short-term capital gains, 378
short-term distributions, 545
short-term treasury ETF, 298
single-country index portfolios, 130
SmartGrowth Mutual Funds, 533
social-awareness index, 58
social security funds, 2
solid replication process, 457

Standard & Poor's 500 Index, 354
standard statistics index, 5
standard statistics methodology, 5
static allocation, 438
statistical models, 17
stock basket, 96
stock capitalisation, 72, 76
stock exchange, 425, 559
stock indexes, 13
stock market, 2, 3, 6, 18, 26, 513
  investments, 342
stock pickers, 17
stock-price indexes, 4
stock-selection methods, 16
stock-selection process, 147
stock-selection strategies, 205
strategic-allocation strategies, 184
strategic asset allocation, 202, 204, 205, 215, 291, 514
strategic hedging, 187
strategic investment approach, 526
strategic portfolio, 216
strategy index, 44, 78
strike price, 255
substitute basket, 174
superior asset allocations, 333
synthetic replication-based approach, 166, 177
synthetic replication ETF, 168
synthetic replication method, 159

T
tactical asset allocation, 215, 320
tactical portfolio, 185
target-date funds, 299, 534
target index, 559, 562, 563
target-risk, 533
target tracking portfolio, 565
taxable bond, 283
taxable event, 593
taxable investors, 543
tax efficiency, 144, 541
tax-exempt bonds, 70
tax-exempt municipal bonds, 283
tax-loss harvesting, 146
tax-management strategies, 578
T-bills, 272
time horizon, 32, 418, 483
Tokyo stock exchange, 19
tolerance bands, 209
top-down valuation approach, 222
Toronto Stock Exchange (TSE), 562
tracking-error risk, 551
tracking strategy, 206
tradable index fund, 128
trade-offs, 158
traditional asset allocation, 189
traditional beta-based index, 16
traditional core indexed portfolio, 38
traditional equity ETFs, 159
traditional ETF structure, 565
traditional index funds, 27, 103
traditional market-capitalisation, 572
traditional market-cap-weighted indexes, 445
traditional mutual-fund-based portfolios, 194
traditional mutual fund, 582
  investors, 548
traditional replication method, 166
traditional stock ETF, 363
treasury bond, 275
trial-and-error attempts, 2
trickle effect, 516

U
uncorrelated assets, 6
unit bracket system, 515
unit-investment-trust (UIT) ETFs, 128
US stock exchange, 87
US Treasury bonds, 70

V
value-at-risk (VaR) models, 517
Vanguard Europe Pacific Index (VEA), 456
Vanguard fund, 456
Vanguard Index Funds, 95
Vanguard's investor share index fund, 435
virtual contagion, 1
volatile equity market, 273
volatility risk, 313

W
Wall Street Journal, 4, 5
wealth-eroding effect, 37
weeding-out process, 481
weighting approach, 19
weighting methods, 66
Wilmington ETF Allocation Fund, 535
Wilshire 5000 Index, 6
winning stocks, 212
WisdomTree DEFA Fund, 458
WisdomTree Dividend Index, 60
WisdomTree funds, 465
WisdomTree indexes, 448
WisdomTree Investments, 521, 532
World market cap, 431
world's equity market capitalisation, 236

Z
Zacks' proprietary country selection process, 473
Zacks Sector Rotation Index, 74
zero counterparty exposure, 174
zero coupon bond, 359
zero-sum game, 401
zero tracking error, 160